GEORG WILHELM FRIEDRICH HEGEL

THE
PHILOSOPHY OF
HISTORY

Prefaces by
CHARLES HEGEL
and the translator,
J. SIBREE

A new Introduction by
PROFESSOR C. J. FRIEDRICH,
Harvard University

DOVER PUBLICATIONS, INC.
NEW YORK

Published in Canada by General Publishing Company, Ltd., 30 Lesmill Road, Don Mills, Toronto, Ontario.
Published in the United Kingdom by Constable and Company, Ltd., 10 Orange Street, London WC 2.

This Dover edition, first published in 1956, is an unabridged and unaltered republication of the last revision of the translation by J. Sibree, published by The Colonial Press in 1899. This Dover edition contains a new introduction by Professor C. J. Friedrich.

Standard Book Number: 486-20112-0

Manufactured in the United States of America
Dover Publications, Inc.
180 Varick Street
New York, N. Y. 10014

INTRODUCTION TO DOVER EDITION

There has been a veritable Hegel Renaissance, especially in France and Germany. This renewed interest in Hegel is preoccupied with Hegel's metaphysical and religious ideas. The favorite work and the one having given rise to the most interesting discussions is the *Phenomenology of the Spirit*. The most remarkable book in this trend is Alexandre Kojève, *Introduction à la Lecture de Hegel—Leçons sur la Phenomenologie de l'Esprit*. It is an extraordinary reassessment in light of the Marxist sequel to Hegel's thought. The *Philosophy of History* has been pushed aside a bit by these writings.

And yet, the *Philosophy of History* remains the heart and center of Hegel's philosophy. What is more, it is the work that has exerted the most profound influence over the years. And rightly so. For Hegel's whole philosophy is historically conceived. As Karl Löwith put it: "His whole system is as fundamentally thought out in historical terms as no other philosophy before him." (Karl Löwith, *Von Hegel zu Nietzsche*, p. 44.) All his most basic notions, such as the world spirit, reason, freedom, receive their meaning and significance within a historical context.

There is at present a vastly increased interest in the "philosophy of history," that is to say in the broad meaning of the entirety of history. Spengler and Toynbee, Rosenstock-Hüssy and Rüstow testify to this broadening concern for an over-all view. Interestingly enough, not one of these striking contemporary writers argues his case in strictly philosophical terms. Nor does any one of them address himself to the philosopher as such. Toynbee and Rosenstock-Hüssy wish to speak as historians, and their work is informed by a large amount of historical scholarship, which gives it its flavor, even though professional historians may sneer at it. Spengler speaks essentially as the *homme de lettres*, while Rüstow casts his thought in sociological terms. But the fact is that the work of all of these and of quite a few others besides actually not only involves but also states a philosophy of history. Yet can it truly be said that, in strictly philosophical terms, they are superior to Hegel? Hegel not only did not pretend that his work was "history" or "sociology" but very explicitly rejected this notion, declaring very definitely that he was putting forward a philosophical framework for history, that he was not writing history, but philosophy.

What, then, is the bearing of the striking array of facts which he marshals? Their bearing is this: they make concrete, visible, indeed tangible, the abstractions of the Hegelian philosophy. And this "concretization" is a very important task from Hegel's viewpoint. He was bitterly opposed to the "abstractions" of eighteenth-century rationalism, which he believed to have led to the French Revolution. But abstractness is not only a fault of the *philosophes*: it is the fault of everyday speech. In an amusing little essay on "Who thinks abstractly?" he once tried to show how faulty is the reasoning of the man in the street, or rather the kitchen maid, because it uses terms "abstractly," that is to say without the richness of associations that only breadth and depth can provide.

It is for this Hegelian insistence upon concreteness that we must read the body of the work, rather than the "introduction" which is forever being reproduced and discussed. For in this celebrated introduction the broad terms of reference are stated abstractly; they gain their true meaning for the reader only when they are placed within the context of the panorama of world history as unfolded by Hegel in the body of the work. It is therefore a happy thought to make available this work in its entirety in the old translation of Sibree. I do not think that Sibree's translation is the last word. Moreover, it is based upon Karl Hegel's original edition of the *Philosophy of History*, built upon such lecture notes as were available to him. We know today that there exist numerous additional lecture notes, and the learned editor of the new edition of Hegel's works, Johannes Hoffmeister, will no doubt eventually provide us with a superior critical text.* But in the meantime, the student needs the text of Hegel's entire work, and the only available text is that of Karl Hegel and Sibree's translation thereof. Moreover, as Kuno Fischer observed many years ago, it is the *Philosophy of History* of Karl Hegel that has exerted the all-engulfing influence which it has had. The subtle points of divergence, interesting to the specialist, may well be neglected by him who wishes to get the vision that was Hegel's.

That vision was most extraordinary. History is seen as the march of freedom through the world. This march of freedom is interpreted as what the World Spirit wants, as it seeks to realize itself. And in its effort to realize itself, it employs peoples, world-historical peoples to do its work.

---

* Georg Lasson, who edited the Introduction anew (2nd ed. 1920), was able to show, on the basis of a manuscript he discovered, which parts of the Introduction were unquestionably Hegel's, and these are now available to the English reader in my *The Philosophy of Hegel*, pp. 1–43.

Hegel at times speaks of the peoples as if they were nations, and this has given rise to a good deal of misunderstanding. Hegel has even been called the philosopher of the modern nation-state, who provided a spiritual apotheosis for the nation and its role in world history. But all we need to do is to look at his basic pattern, his broad conception to see the error of this common view of the Hegelian philosophy of history. "The Orient knew and knows only that one is free, the Greek and Roman world that some are free; the Germanic world knows that all are free." In these terms: Orient, Greek and Roman, Germanic, we are actually confronted with entities much larger than the modern nations. What Hegel is manifestly talking about is the great cultures or civilizations.

There is one further crucial thought that this pattern does not contain nor allow for, but which is decisive for Hegel. This is the coming of Christ. If we read the extraordinary pages in which Hegel testifies to the complete change that came into the world with the coming of Christ we cannot but realize that these great cultures, put to work by the world spirit in its effort to realize itself, are radically affected by the *action of one being*, which revolutionized history so that it never was the same afterward. "The nature of God of being pure spirit is *revealed to man in the Christian religion*. And what is the spirit? He is the One, the infinite consistent within Himself, the pure identity. . . . It is part of the appearance of the Christian God that it is unique . . . ; it can happen only once. . . ." And Hegel is emphatic in setting this coming of Christ within its historical context: "Here we see the world-historical importance and significance of the Jewish people; for from it has sprung the higher development by which the spirit arrived at absolute self-consciousness. . . ." And what of the Germanic peoples?† These Germanic peoples, i.e. Western civilization, were assigned the task of realizing the full implications of the Christian message.

Hegel was and wanted to be a Christian philosopher. To the end of his life he maintained that he considered himself a Lutheran. He rejected, in other words, those interpretations of his thought which put them into a pantheistic framework. He believed in a personal God whose spirit, the Holy Ghost of Christian doctrine, was at work shaping the destiny of man. What then of the future? Unlike Marx, Spengler and Toynbee, Hegel refused to speak of the future. His was a deep sense of the contingent in history. This was in keeping with his strong emphasis on freedom. The range of mean-

---

† These, *nota bene*, include the French, the English and the rest of Western culture, as well as the Germans, and Sibree is very wrong in translating Germanic (*Germanisch*) as German (*Deutsch*).

ings of this crucial term is complex in Hegel's philosophy, but it is fairly clear that freedom in Hegel's sense is predominantly "the idea." He defines it thus in his *Philosophy of Law and Right*, §21:

The truth, however, of this formal universality which is by itself indeterminate and receives its determination from each material to which it is applied consists in a universality which *determines itself, which is the will, is freedom.* Since this will has the universality, has it itself as the infinite form, as its content, its object and its end, it is not only the will which is free in itself, but also the will which is free for itself—the true idea.‡

As contrasted with this difficult concept, Hegel considered the notion that freedom (of the will) is merely "that one can do what one wants" to be the result of a complete lack of philosophical education. In such a notion there is as yet no inkling of "what the will which is free in itself, is, namely law, right, ethics." In short, freedom for Hegel consists in a conscious recognition and acceptance of the good which systems of values, and more especially the Christian system of values, contain.

Yet he steadfastly refused to engage in speculations as to how this freedom, as the priceless bond between man and the world spirit, might evolve in the future. America and Russia, two worlds with a spiritual content as yet undefined, may in Hegel's view well be destined to realize a new configuration of the world spirit. If so, philosophers will be able to fathom it when it has occurred, but not Hegel. For "to understand what exists is the task of philosophy, for what exists, is reason." But this proud claim did not seduce Hegel into overlooking the time-conditioned relativity of all thought, the dependence of the thinker upon his own period, people and culture—what is nowadays referred to by that ugly naturalistic phrase "climate of opinion." Hegel says, "As to the individual, everyone is the son of his own time, and therefore philosophy is *its time comprehended in thought.*"§ And he saw his own time as one that marked the end of a world-historical epoch, the end of Christian and Germanic (i.e. Western) culture. In his own famous phrase: "When philosophy paints gray in gray, a form of life has become old, and this gray in gray cannot rejuvenate it, only understand it. The owl of Minerva begins its flight when dusk is falling." Shall we

§ Both of these quotations are from the Introduction to the *Philosophy of Law and Right*, cf. my edition, p. 226.

‡ See p. 234 of my *The Philosophy of Hegel*; cf. also the new edition of *Grundlinien der Philosophie des Rechts* (1955) by J. Hoffmeister, who gives Hegel's own marginal notes to the book.

say he was wrong? Was not the world of the liberal, bourgeois, monarchical, constitutional nation state entering its last phase in the earlier nineteenth century?

It was this melancholy, this profound resignation in Hegel which inspired both admiration and protest. The admiration led some of his followers into conservatism and reaction, the protest led others into progressivism and revolution. It is my belief that both essentially misunderstood Hegel. In so misunderstanding him they may well have been right, but this rightness would be outside the scope of philosophy. It would be politics. Hegel was neither reactionary nor revolutionary, nor indeed any politician at all. But for all that, he revolutionized the sciences of man, of culture and society, and neither the humanities nor the social sciences have ever since been able to think and talk again in the naive and simple terms that characterized them before Hegel wrote. This is true not only in spite of, but more particularly because of, the fact that they rejected Hegel's metaphysics, no less than his religion. Marx, who prided himself on having turned Hegel down side up, was scornful about the detractors of Hegel who did not grasp the real depth of his mind and thought. But did he himself? His famous observation that "the ideal is nothing but the material world reflected by the human mind, and translated into forms of thought," makes one doubt it. Certainly the Dialectical Materialism (*Diamat*) cultivated by the Communist Party in the USSR, China and the Satellites is a travesty of Hegelian dialectics.

An extended discussion of the influence of Hegel, and more especially of his philosophy of history, would amount to a history of most learning and scholarship, excepting the natural sciences, for the last 125 years. To become acquainted with Hegel is therefore to become acquainted with oneself and one's intellectual background You may reject Hegel in the end, as I do, but you will have gained perspective by knowing why. In any case, the reading of the *Philosophy of History* is an exciting and at times a strenuous journey.

C. J. Friedrich

"*The History of the World is not intelligible apart from a Government of the World.*"—*W. V.* HUMBOLDT

TRANSLATOR'S INTRODUCTION

HEGEL'S Lectures on the Philosophy of History are recognized in Germany as a popular introduction to his system; their form is less rigid than the generality of metaphysical treatises, and the illustrations, which occupy a large proportion of the work, are drawn from a field of observation more familiar perhaps, than any other, to those who have not devoted much time to metaphysical studies. One great value of the work is that it presents the leading facts of history from an altogether novel point of view. And when it is considered that the writings of Hegel have exercised a marked influence on the political movements of Germany, it will be admitted that his theory of the universe, especially that part which bears directly upon politics, deserves attention even from those who are the most exclusive advocates of the " practical."

A writer who has established his claim to be regarded as an authority, by the life which he has infused into metaphysical abstractions, has pronounced the work before us, " one of the pleasantest books on the subject he ever read." *

And compared with that of most German writers, even the style may claim to be called vigorous and pointed. If therefore in its English dress the " Philosophy of History " should be found deficient in this respect, the fault must not be attributed to the original.

It has been the aim of the translator to present his author to the public in a really English form, even at the cost of a circumlocution which must sometimes do injustice to the merits of the original. A few words however have necessarily been used in a rather unusual sense; and one of them is of very frequent occurrence. The German " Geist," in Hegel's nomenclature, includes both intelligence and will, the latter even more expressly than the former. It embraces in fact man's

* Mr. G. H. Lewes, in his Biographical History of Philosophy, Vol. IV., Ed. 1841.

entire mental and moral being, and a little reflection will make
it obvious that no term in our metaphysical vocabulary could
have been well substituted for the more theological one,
" Spirit," as a fair equivalent. It is indeed only the impersonal
and abstract use of the term that is open to objection; an objection which can be met by an appeal to the best classical usage;
viz. the rendering of the Hebrew רוּחַ and Greek πνεῦμα in the
authorized version of the Scriptures. One indisputable instance may suffice in confirmation: " Their horses (*i.e.* of the
Egyptians) are flesh and not *spirit.*" (Isaiah xxxi. 3.) It is
pertinent to remark here, that the comparative disuse of this
term in English metaphysical literature, is one result of that
alienation of theology from philosophy with which continental
writers of the most opposite schools agree in taxing the speculative genius of Britain—an alienation which mainly accounts
for the gulf separating English from German speculation, and
which will, it is feared, on other accounts also be the occasion
of communicating a somewhat uninviting aspect to the following pages.

    The distinction which the Germans make between " Sittlich-
keit " and " Moralität," has presented another difficulty. The
former denotes conventional morality, the latter that of the
heart or conscience. Where no ambiguity was likely to arise,
both terms have been translated " morality." In other cases
a stricter rendering has been given, modified by the requirements of the context. The word " moment " is, as readers of
German philosophy are aware, a veritable crux to the translator.
In Mr. J. R. Morell's very valuable edition of Johnson's Translation of Tennemann's " Manual of the History of Philosophy,"
the following explanation is given: " This term was bor-
rowed from mechanics by Hegel (see his " Wissenschaft der
Logik," Vol. 3, P. 104, Ed. 1841). He employs it to denote the contending forces which are mutually dependent,
and whose contradiction forms an equation. Hence his
formula, *Esse* = Nothing. Here *Esse* and Nothing are mo-
mentums, giving birth to *Werden, i.e.* Existence. Thus the
momentum contributes to the same oneness of operation in contradictory forces that we see in mechanics, amidst contrast and
diversity, in weight and distance, in the case of the balance."
But in several parts of the work before us this definition is not
strictly adhered to, and the translator believes he has done

justice to the original in rendering the word by " successive " or " organic phase." In the chapter on the Crusades another term occurs which could not be simply rendered into English. The definite, positive, and present embodiment of essential being is there spoken of as " ein *Dieses*," " das *Dieses*," etc., literally " a *This*," " the *This*," for which repulsive combination a periphrasis has been substituted, which, it is believed, is not only accurate but expository. Paraphrastic *additions*, however, have been, in fairness to the reader, enclosed in brackets [ ]; and the philosophical appropriation of ordinary terms is generally indicated by capitals, *e.g.* " Spirit," " Freedom," " State," " Nature," etc.

The limits of a brief preface preclude an attempt to explain the Hegelian method in its wider applications; and such an undertaking is rendered altogether unnecessary by the facilities which are afforded by works so very accessible as the translation of Tennemann above mentioned, Chälybæus's " Historical Development of Speculative Philosophy, from Kant to Hegel," Blakey's " History of the Philosophy of Mind," Mr. Lewes's " Biographical History of Philosophy," besides treatises devoted more particularly to the Hegelian philosophy. Among these latter may be fairly mentioned the work of a French professor, M. Vera, " Introduction à la Philosophie de Hegel," a lucid and earnest exposition of the system at large; and the very able summary of Hegel's " Philosophy of Right," by T. C. Sandars, late fellow of Oriel College, which forms one of the series of " Oxford Essays " for 1855, and which bears directly on the subject of the present volume.

It may, nevertheless, be of some service to the reader to indicate the point of view from which this " Philosophy of History " is composed, and to explain the leading idea.

The aim and scope of that civilizing process which all hopeful thinkers recognize in history, is the attainment of Rational Freedom. But the very term freedom supposes a previous bondage; and the question naturally arises: " Bondage to what? "—A superficial inquirer may be satisfied with an answer referring it to the *physical power* of the ruling body. Such a response was deemed satisfactory by a large number of political speculators in the last century, and even at the beginning of the present; and it is one of the great merits of an influential thinker of our days to have expelled this *idolum fori*, which

had also become an *idolum theatri*, from its undue position;
and to have revived the simple truth that all stable organizations
of men, all religious and political communities, are based upon
principles which are far beyond the control of the One or the
Many. And in these principles or some phase of them every
man in every clime and age is born, lives and moves. The
only question is: Whence are those principles derived? Whence
spring those primary beliefs or superstitions, religious and political, that hold society together? They are no inventions of
" priestcraft " or " kingcraft," for to them priestcraft and kingcraft owe their power. They are no results of a *Contrat Social*,
for with them society originates. Nor are they the mere sug-
gestions of man's weakness, prompting him to propitiate the
powers of nature, in furtherance of his finite, earthborn desires.
Some of the phenomena of the religious systems that have prevailed in the world might seem thus explicable; but the Nihil-
ism of more than one Oriental creed, the suicidal strivings of
the Hindoo devotee to become absorbed in a divinity recognized
as a pure negation, cannot be reduced to so gross a formula;
while the political superstition that ascribes a divine right to
the feebleness of a woman or an infant is altogether untouched
by it. Nothing is left therefore but to recognize them as " fancies," " delusions," " dreams," the results of man's vain imagination—to class them with the other absurdities with which the
abortive past of humanity is by some thought to be only too
replete; or, on the other hand, to regard them as the rudimen-
tary teachings of that essential intelligence in which man's
intellectual and moral life originates. With Hegel they are the
objective manifestation of infinite reason—the first promptings
of Him who having " made of one blood all nations of men for
to dwell on the face of the earth, hath determined *the times before appointed*, and the bounds of their habitation, if haply they
might feel after and find him "—τοῦ γὰρ καὶ γένος ἐσμέν. And
it is these καιροὶ προτεταγμένοι, these determined and organic
epochs in the history of the world that Hegel proposes to distinguish and develop in the following treatise.

Whatever view may be entertained as to the origin or importance of those elementary principles, and by whatever general
name they may be called—Spontaneous, Primary, or Objective
Intelligence—it seems demonstrable that it is in some sense or
other to its *own* belief, its *own* reason or essential being, that

imperfect humanity is in bondage; while the perfection of social existence is commonly regarded as a deliverance from that bondage. In the Hegelian system, this paradoxical condition is regarded as one phase of that antithesis which is presented in all spheres of existence, between the subjective and the objective, but which it is the result of the natural and intellectual processes that constitute the life of the universe, to annul by merging into one absolute existence. And however startling this theory may be as applied to other departments of nature and intelligence, it appears to be no unreasonable formula for the course of civilization, and which is substantially as follows: In less cultivated nations, political and moral restrictions are looked upon as objectively posited; the constitution of society, like the world of natural objects, is regarded as something into which a man is inevitably born; and the individual feels himself bound to comply with requirements of whose justice or propriety he is not allowed to judge, though they often severely test his endurance, and even demand the sacrifice of his life. In a state of high civilization, on the contrary, though an equal self-sacrifice be called for, it is in respect of laws and institutions which are felt to be just and desirable. This change of relation may, without any very extraordinary use of terms, or extravagance of speculative conceit, be designated the harmonization or réconciliation of objective and subjective intelligence. The successive phases which humanity has assumed in passing from that primitive state of bondage to this condition of rational freedom form the chief subject of the following lectures.

The mental and moral condition of individuals and their social and religious conditions (the subjective and objective manifestations of reason) exhibit a strict correspondence with each other in every grade of progress. " They that make them are like unto them," is as true of religious and political ideas as of religious and political idols. Where man sets no value on that part of his mental and moral life which makes him superior to the brutes, brute life will be an object of worship and bestial sensuality will be the genius of the ritual. Where mere inaction is the *finis bonorum*, absorption in nothingness will be the aim of the devotee. Where, on the contrary, active and vigorous virtue is recognized as constituting the real value of man— where subjective spirit has learned to assert its own freedom, both against irrational and unjust requirements from without, and caprice, passion, and sensuality, from within, it will demand a living, acting, just, and holy, embodiment of Deity as the only possible object of its adoration. In the same degree, political principles also will be affected. Where mere nature predominates, no legal relations will be acknowledged but those based on natural distinction; rights will be inexorably associated with " caste." Where, on the other hand, spirit has attained its freedom, it will require a code of laws and political constitution, in which the rational subordination of nature to reason that prevails in its own being, and the strength it feels to resist sensual seductions shall be distinctly mirrored.

Between the lowest and highest grades of intelligence and will, there are several intervening stages, around which a complex of derivative ideas, and of institutions, arts, and sciences, in harmony with them, are aggregated. Each of these aggregates has acquired a name in history as a distinct nationality. Where the distinctive principle is losing its vigor, as the result of the expansive force of mind of which it was only the temporary embodiment, the national life declines, and we have the transition to a higher grade, in which a comparatively abstract and limited phase of subjective intelligence and will—to which corresponds an equally imperfect phase of objective reason—is exchanged for one more concrete, and vigorous—one which develops human capabilities more freely and fully, and in which right is more adequately comprehended.

The goal of this contention is, as already indicated, the self-realization, the complete development of spirit, whose proper nature is freedom—freedom in both senses of the term, *i.e.* liberation from *outward* control—inasmuch as the law to which it submits has its own explicit sanction—and emancipation from the *inward* slavery of lust and passion.

The above remarks are not designed to afford anything like a complete or systematic analysis of Hegel's " Philosophy of History," but simply to indicate its leading conception, and if possible to contribute something towards removing a prejudice against it on the score of its resolving facts into mystical paradoxes, or attempting to construe them *à priori*. In applying the theory, some facts may not improbably have been distorted, some brought into undue prominence, and others altogether neglected. In the most cautious and limited analysis of the past, failures and perversions of this kind are inevitable: and a comprehensive view of history is proportionately open to mistake. But it is another question whether the principles applied in this work to explain the course which civilization has followed, are a correct inference from historical facts, and afford a reliable clue to the explanation of their leading aspects.

The translator would remark, in conclusion, that the " Introduction " will probably be found the most tedious and difficult part of the treatise; he would therefore suggest a cursory reading of it in the first instance, and a second perusal as a *résumé* of principles which are more completely illustrated in the body of the work.

J. SIBREE.

CHARLES HEGEL'S PREFACE

THE changed form in which Hegel's lectures on the Philosophy of History are re-issued, suggests the necessity of some explanation respecting the relation of this second edition both to the original materials from which the work was compiled, and to their first publication.

The lamented Professor Gans, the editor of the " Philosophy of History," displayed a talented ingenuity in transforming lectures into a book; in doing so he followed for the most part Hegel's latest deliveries of the course, because they were the most popular, and appeared most adapted to his object.

He succeeded in presenting the lectures much as they were delivered in the winter of 1830–31; and this result might be regarded as perfectly satisfactory, if Hegel's various readings of the course had been more uniform and concordant, if indeed they had not rather been of such a nature as to supplement each other. For however great may have been Hegel's power of condensing the wide extent of the phenomenal world by thought, it was impossible for him entirely to master and to present in a uniform shape the immeasurable material of history in the course of one semester. In the first delivery in the winter of 1822–23, he was chiefly occupied with unfolding the philosophical idea, and showing how this constitutes the real kernel of history, and the impelling soul of world-historical peoples. In proceeding to treat of China and India, he wished, as he said himself, only to show by example how philosophy ought to comprehend the character of a nation; and this could be done more easily in the case of the stationary nations of the East, than in that of peoples which have a *bonâ fide* history and a historical development of character. A warm predilection made him linger long with the Greeks, for whom he always felt a youthful enthusiasm; and after a brief consideration of the Roman World he endeavored finally to condense the Mediæval Period and the Modern Time into a few lectures; for time pressed, and when, as in the Christian World, the thought no longer lies concealed among the multitude of phenomena, but announces itself and is obviously present in history, the philosopher is at liberty to abridge his discussion of it; in fact, nothing more is needed than to indicate the impelling idea. In the later readings, on the other hand, China, India, and the East generally were more speedily despatched, and more time and attention devoted to the German World. By degrees the philosophical and abstract occupied less space, the historical matter was expanded, and the whole became more popular.

It is easy to see how the different readings of the course supplement each other, and how the entire substance cannot be gathered without uniting the philosophical element which predominates in the earlier, and which must constitute the basis of the work, with the historical expansion which characterizes the latest deliveries.

Had Hegel pursued the plan which most professors adopt, in adapting notes for use in the lecture room, of merely appending emendations and additions to the original draught, it would be correct to suppose that his latest readings would be also the most matured. But as, on the contrary, every delivery was with him a new act of thought, each gives only the expression of that degree of philosophical energy which animates his mind at the time; thus, in fact, the two first deliveries of 1822–23 and 1824–25, exhibit a far more comprehensive vigor of idea and expression, a far richer store of striking thoughts and appropriate images, than those of later date; for that first inspiration which accompanied the thoughts when they first sprang into existence, could only lose its living freshness by repetition.

From what has been said, the nature of the task which a new edition involved is sufficiently manifest. A treasury of thought of no trifling value had to be recovered from the first readings, and the tone of originality restored to the whole. The printed text therefore was made the basis, and the work of inserting, supplementing, substituting, and transforming (as the case seemed to require), was undertaken with the greatest possible respect for the original. No scope was left for the individual views of the editor, since in all such alterations Hegel's manuscripts were the sole guide. For while the first publication of these lectures—a part of the introduction excepted—followed the notes of the hearers only, the second edition has endeavored to supplement it by making Hegel's own manuscripts the basis throughout, and using the notes only for the purpose of rectification and arrangement. The editor has striven after uniformity of tone through the whole work simply by allowing the author to speak everywhere in his own words; so that not only are the new insertions taken verbatim from the manuscripts, but even where the printed text was retained in the main, peculiar expressions which the hearer had lost in transcription, were restored.

For the benefit of those who place vigor of thought in a formal schematism, and with polemical zeal assert its exclusive claim against other styles of philosophizing, the remark may be added that Hegel adhered so little to the subdivisions which he had adopted, that he made some alterations in them on occasion of every reading of the course—treated Buddhism and Lamaism, *e.g.*, sometimes before, sometimes after India, sometimes reduced the Christian World more closely to the German nations, sometimes took in the Byzantine Empire, and so on. The new edition has had but few alterations to make in this respect.

When the association for publishing Hegel's works did me the honor to intrust me with the re-editing of my father's "Philosophy of History," it also named as advocates of the claims of the first edition, and as representatives of Professor Gans, who had been removed from its circle by death, three of its members, Geh. Ober-Regierungs Rath Dr. Schulze, Professor von Henning, and Professor Hotho, to whose revision the work in its new shape was to be submitted. In this revision, I not only enjoyed the acquiescence of those most estimable men and valued friends in the alterations I had made, but also owe them a debt of thanks for many new emendations, which I take the opportunity of thus publicly discharging.

In conclusion, I feel constrained to acknowledge that my gratitude to that highly respected association for the praiseworthy deed of love to science, friendship, and disinterestedness, whose prosecution originated it and still holds it together, could be increased only by the fact of its having granted me also a share in editing the works of my beloved father.

CHARLES HEGEL.

CONTENTS

INTRODUCTION

	PAGE
I. Original History	I
II. Reflective History	4
III. Philosophical History	8
Geographical Basis of History	79
CLASSIFICATION OF HISTORIC DATA	103

PART I.—THE ORIENTAL WORLD

Principle of the Oriental World	111
SECTION I. China	116
SECTION II. India	139
SECTION II. Continued. India—Buddhism	167
SECTION III. Persia	173
Chapter I. The Zend People	176
Chapter II. The Assyrians, Babylonians, Medes, and Persians	182
Chapter III. The Persian Empire and its Constituent Parts	187
Persia	188
Syria and Semitic Western Asia	191
Judæa	195
Egypt	198
Transition to the Greek World	219

PART II.—THE GREEK WORLD

The Region of Spirit	223
SECTION I. The Elements of the Greek Spirit	225
SECTION II. Phases of Individuality Æsthetically Conditioned	241
Chapter I. The Subjective Work of Art	241
Chapter II. The Objective Work of Art	244
Chapter III. The Political Work of Art	250
The War with the Persians	256
Athens	258
Sparta	262
The Peloponnesian War	265
The Macedonian Empire	271
SECTION III. Fall of the Greek Spirit	275

PART III.—THE ROMAN WORLD

PAGE
Distinction between the Roman, Persian, and Greek Principle..... 278
  SECTION I. Rome to the Time of the Second Punic War........ 283
    Chapter I. The Elements of the Roman Spirit.............. 283
    Chapter II. History of Rome to the Second Punic War...... 296
  SECTION II. Rome from the Second Punic War to the Emperors. 306
  SECTION III. Chapter I. Rome under the Emperors............. 314
    Chapter II. Christianity 318
    Chapter III. The Byzantine Empire........................... 336

PART IV.—THE GERMAN WORLD

The Principle of Spiritual Freedom............................. 341
  SECTION I. The Elements of the Christian German World...... 347
    Chapter   I. The Barbarian Migrations 347
    Chapter II. Mahometanism 355
    Chapter III. The Empire of Charlemagne.................... 360
  SECTION II. The Middle Ages................................. 366
    Chapter   I. The Feudality and the Hierarchy................ 366
    Chapter II. The Crusade................................... 389
    Chapter III. The Transition from Feudalism to Monarchy.... 398
  SECTION III. The Modern Time............................... 412
    Chapter   I. The Reformation.............................. 412
    Chapter II. Influence of the Reformation on Political Develop-
              ment... 427
    Chapter III. The Éclaircissement and Revolution............ 438

PHILOSOPHY OF HISTORY

INTRODUCTION

THE subject of this course of Lectures is the Philosophical History of the World. And by this must be understood, not a collection of general observations respecting it, suggested by the study of its records, and proposed to be illustrated by its facts, but Universal History itself.* To gain a clear idea, at the outset, of the nature of our task, it seems necessary to begin with an examination of the other methods of treating History. The various methods may be ranged under three heads:

I. Original History.
II. Reflective History.
III. Philosophical History.

I. Of the first kind, the mention of one or two distinguished names will furnish a definite type. To this category belong *Herodotus, Thucydides,* and other historians of the same order, whose descriptions are for the most part limited to deeds, events, and states of society, which they had before their eyes, and whose spirit they shared. They simply transferred what was passing in the world around them, to the realm of re-presentative intellect. An external phenomenon is thus translated into an internal conception. In the same way the *poet* operates upon the material supplied him by his emotions; projecting it into an image for the conceptive faculty. These original historians did, it is true, find statements and narratives of other men ready to hand. One person cannot be an eye or ear witness of everything. But they make use of such aids only as the poet does of that heritage of an already-formed language, to which he owes so much; merely as an ingredient. Historiographers

---

* I cannot mention any work that will serve as a compendium of the course, but I may remark that in my " Outlines of the Philosophy of Law," §§ 341-360, I have already given a definition of such a Universal History as it is proposed to develop, and a syllabus of the chief elements or periods into which it naturally divides itself.

bind together the fleeting elements of story, and treasure them up for immortality in the Temple of Mnemosyne. Legends, Ballad-stories, Traditions, must be excluded from such original history. These are but dim and hazy forms of historical apprehension, and therefore belong to nations whose intelligence is but half awakened. Here, on the contrary, we have to do with people fully conscious of what they were and what they were about. The domain of reality—actually seen, or capable of being so—affords a very different basis in point of firmness from that fugitive and shadowy element, in which were engendered those legends and poetic dreams whose historical prestige vanishes, as soon as nations have attained a mature individuality.

Such original historians, then, change the events, the deeds, and the states of society with which they are conversant, into an object for the conceptive faculty. The narratives they leave us cannot, therefore, be very comprehensive in their range. Herodotus, Thucydides, Guicciardini, may be taken as fair samples of the class in this respect. What is present and living in their environment is their proper material. The influences that have formed the writer are identical with those which have moulded the events that constitute the matter of his story. The author's spirit, and that of the actions he narrates, is one and the same. He describes scenes in which he himself has been an actor, or at any rate an interested spectator. It is short periods of time, individual shapes of persons and occurrences, single, unreflected traits, of which he makes his picture. And his aim is nothing more than the presentation to posterity of an image of events as clear as that which he himself possessed in virtue of personal observation, or life-like descriptions. Reflections are none of his business, for he lives in the spirit of his subject; he has not attained an elevation above it. If, as in Cæsar's case, he belongs to the exalted rank of generals or statesmen, it is the prosecution of *his own aims* that constitutes the history.

Such speeches as we find in Thucydides (for example) of which we can positively assert that they are not *bonâ fide* reports, would seem to make against out statement that a historian of his class presents us no reflected picture; that persons and people appear in his works in *propriâ personâ*. Speeches, it must be allowed, are veritable transactions in the human commonwealth; in fact, very gravely influential transactions. It is, indeed, often said, " Such and such things are only talk ; " by way of demonstrating their harmlessness. That for which this excuse is brought may be mere " talk " ; and talk enjoys the important privilege of being harmless. But addresses of peoples to peoples, or orations directed to nations and to princes, are integrant constituents of history. Granted that such orations as those of Pericles—that most profoundly accomplished, genuine, noble statesman—were elaborated by Thucydides, it must yet be maintained that they were not foreign to the character of the speaker. In the orations in question, these men proclaim the maxims adopted by their countrymen, and which formed their own character ; they record their views of their political relations, and of their moral and spiritual nature ; and the principles of their designs and conduct. What the historian puts into their mouths is no supposititious system of ideas, but an uncorrupted transcript of their intellectual and moral habitudes.

Of these historians, whom we must make thoroughly our own, with whom we must linger long, if we would live with their respective nations, and enter deeply into their spirit : of these historians, to whose pages we may turn not for the purposes of erudition merely, but with a view to deep and genuine enjoyment, there are fewer than might be imagined. Herodotus the *Father,* i.e., the *Founder* of History, and Thucydides have been already mentioned. Xenophon's *Retreat of the Ten Thousand,* is a work equally original. Cæsar's *Commentaries* are the simple masterpiece of a mighty spirit. Among the ancients, these annalists were necessarily great captains and statesmen. In the Middle Ages, if we except the Bishops, who were placed in the very centre of the political world, the Monks monopolize this category as näive chroniclers who were as decidedly *isolated* from active life as those elder annalists had been connected with it. In modern times the relations are entirely altered. Our culture is essentially comprehensive, and immediately changes all events into historical representations. Belonging to the class in question, we have vivid, simple, clear narrations—especially of military transactions—which might fairly take their place with those of Cæsar. In richness of matter and fulness of detail as regards strategic appliances, and attendant circumstances, they are even more instructive. The French " Memoires," also, fall under this category. In

many cases these are written by men of mark, though relating
to affairs of little note. They not unfrequently contain a large
proportion of anecdotal matter, so that the ground they occupy is narrow and trivial. Yet they are often veritable masterpieces in history; as those of Cardinal Retz, which in fact
trench on a larger historical field. In Germany such masters
are rare. Frederick the Great ("Histoire de Mon Temps") is
an illustrious exception. Writers of this order must occupy
an elevated position. Only from such a position is it possible
to take an extensive view of affairs—to see everything. This
is out of the question for him, who from below merely gets
a glimpse of the great world through a miserable cranny.

II. The second kind of history we may call the *reflective.*
It is history whose mode of representation is not really confined by the limits of the time to which it relates, but whose
spirit transcends the present. In this second order a strongly
marked variety of species may be distinguished.

1. It is the aim of the investigator to gain a view of the
entire history of a people or a country, or of the world, in
short, what we call *Universal History.* In this case the working up of the historical material is the main point. The workman approaches his task with *his own* spirit; a spirit distinct
from that of the element he is to manipulate. Here a very
important consideration will be the principles to which the author refers the bearing and motives of the actions and events
which he describes, and those which determine the form of his
narrative. Among us Germans this reflective treatment and
the display of ingenuity which it occasions assume a manifold
variety of phases. Every writer of history proposes to himself
an original method. The English and French confess to general principles of historical composition. Their standpoint is
more that of cosmopolitan or of national culture. Among us
each labors to invent a purely individual point of view. Instead
of writing history, we are always beating our brains to discover
how history ought to be written. This first kind of Reflective
History is most nearly akin to the preceding, when it has no
farther aim than to present the annals of a country complete.
Such compilations (among which may be reckoned the works
of Livy, Diodorus Siculus, Johannes von Müller's History of
Switzerland) are, if well performed, highly meritorious.
Among the best of the kind may be reckoned such annalists

as approach those of the first class; who give so vivid a transcript of events that the reader may well fancy himself listening to contemporaries and eye-witnesses. But it often happens that the individuality of tone which must characterize a
writer belonging to a different culture, is not modified in
accordance with the periods such a record must traverse. The
spirit of the writer is quite other than that of the times of
which he treats. Thus Livy puts into the mouths of the old
Roman kings, consuls, and generals, such orations as would
be delivered by an accomplished advocate of the Livian era,
and which strikingly contrast with the genuine traditions of
Roman antiquity (*e. g.* the fable of Menenius Agrippa). In
the same way he gives us descriptions of battles, as if he had
been an actual spectator; but whose features would serve
well enough for battles in any period, and whose distinctness
contrasts on the other hand with the want of connection and
the inconsistency that prevail elsewhere, even in his treatment
of chief points of interest. The difference between such a
compiler and an original historian may be best seen by comparing Polybius himself with the style in which Livy uses,
expands, and abridges his annals in those periods of which
Polybius's account has been preserved. Johannes von Müller
has given a stiff, formal, pedantic aspect to his history, in the
endeavor to remain faithful in his portraiture to the times
he describes. We much prefer the narratives we find in old
Tschudy. All is more näive and natural than it appears in
the garb of a fictitious and affected archaism.

A history which aspires to traverse long periods of time,
or to be universal, must indeed forego the attempt to give individual representations of the past as it actually existed. It
must foreshorten its pictures by abstractions; and this includes
not merely the omission of events and deeds, but whatever is
involved in the fact that Thought is, after all, the most tren-
chant epitomist. A battle, a great victory, a siege, no longer
maintains its original proportions, but is put off with a bare
mention. When Livy *e. g.* tells us of the wars with the Volsci,
we sometimes have the brief announcement: "This year war
was carried on with the Volsci."

2. A second species of Reflective History is what we may
call the *Pragmatical*. When we have to deal with the Past,
and occupy ourselves with a remote world, a Present rises

into being for the mind—produced by its own activity, as the reward of its labor. The occurrences are, indeed, various; but the idea which pervades them—their deeper import and connection—is *one*. This takes the occurrence out of the category of the Past and makes it virtually Present. Pragmatical (didactic) reflections, though in their nature decidedly abstract, are truly and indefeasibly of the Present, and quicken the annals of the dead Past with the life of to-day. Whether, indeed, such reflections are truly interesting and enlivening, depends on the writer's own spirit. Moral reflections must here be specially noticed—the moral teaching expected from history; which latter has not infrequently been treated with a direct view to the former. It may be allowed that examples of virtue elevate the soul, and are applicable in the moral instruction of children for impressing excellence upon their minds. But the destinies of peoples and states, their interests, relations, and the complicated tissue of their affairs, present quite another field. Rulers, Statesmen, Nations, are wont to be emphatically commended to the teaching which experience offers in history. But what experience and history teach is this—that peoples and governments never have learned anything from history, or acted on principles deduced from it. Each period is involved in such peculiar circumstances, exhibits a condition of things so strictly idiosyncratic, that its conduct must be regulated by considerations connected with itself, and itself alone. Amid the pressure of great events, a general principle gives no help. It is useless to revert to similar circumstances in the Past. The pallid shades of memory struggle in vain with the life and freedom of the Present. Looked at in this light, nothing can be shallower than the oft-repeated appeal to Greek and Roman examples during the French Revolution. Nothing is more diverse than the genius of those nations and that of our times. Johannes v. Müller, in his " Universal History " as also in his " History of Switzerland," had such moral aims in view. He designed to prepare a body of political doctrines for the instruction of princes, governments, and peoples (he formed a special collection of doctrines and reflections—frequently giving us in his correspondence the exact number of apophthegms which he had compiled in a week) ; but he cannot reckon this part of his labor as among the best that he accomplished. It is only a thorough, liberal, comprehensive view of historical relations (such *e. g.* as we find in Montesquieu's "Esprit des Loix"), that can give truth and interest to reflections of this order. One Reflective History, therefore, supersedes another. The materials are patent to every writer: each is likely enough to believe himself capable of arranging and manipulating them; and we may expect that each will insist upon his own spirit as that of the age in question. Disgusted by such reflective histories, readers have often returned with pleasure to a narrative adopting no particular point of view. These certainly have their value; but for the most part they offer only material for history. We Germans are content with such. The French, on the other hand, display great genius in reanimating bygone times, and in bringing the past to bear upon the present condition of things.

3. The third form of Reflective History is the *Critical.* This deserves mention as pre-eminently the mode of treating history, now current in Germany. It is not history itself that is here presented. We might more properly designate it as a History of History; a criticism of historical narratives and an investigation of their truth and credibility. Its peculiarity in point of fact and of intention, consists in the acuteness with which the writer extorts something from the records which was not in the matters recorded. The French have given us much that is profound and judicious in this class of composition. But they have not endeavored to pass a merely critical procedure for substantial history. They have duly presented their judgments in the form of critical treatises. Among us, the so-called "higher criticism," which reigns supreme in the domain of philology, has also taken possession of our historical literature. This "higher criticism" has been the pretext for introducing all the anti-historical monstrosities that a vain imagination could suggest. Here we have the other method of making the past a living reality; putting subjective fancies in the place of historical data; fancies whose merit is measured by their boldness, that is, the scantiness of the particulars on which they are based, and the peremptoriness with which they contravene the best established facts of history.

4. The last species of Reflective History announces its fragmentary character on the very face of it. It adopts an abstract position; yet, since it takes general points of view (*e.g.* as the

History of Art, of Law, of Religion), it forms a transition to the Philosophical History of the World. In our time this form of the history of ideas has been more developed and brought into notice. Such branches of national life stand in close relation to the entire complex of a people's annals; and the question of chief importance in relation to our subject is, whether the connection of the whole is exhibited in its truth and reality, or referred to merely external relations. In the latter case, these important phenomena (Art, Law, Religion, etc.) appear as purely accidental national peculiarities. It must be remarked that, when Reflective History has advanced to the adoption of general points of view, if the position taken is a true one, these are found to constitute—not a merely external thread, a superficial series—but are the inward guiding soul of the occurrences and actions that occupy a nation's annals. For, like the soul-conductor Mercury, the Idea is in truth, the leader of peoples and of the World; and Spirit, the rational and necessitated will of that conductor, is and has been the director of the events of the World's History. To become acquainted with Spirit in this its office of guidance, is the object of our present undertaking. This brings us to

III. The third kind of history—the *Philosophical*. No explanation was needed of the two previous classes; their nature was self-evident. It is otherwise with this last, which certainly seems to require an exposition or justification. The most general definition that can be given, is, that the Philosophy of History means nothing but the *thoughtful consideration of it*. Thought is, indeed, essential to humanity. It is this that distinguishes us from the brutes. In sensation, cognition, and intellection; in our instincts and volitions, as far as they are truly human, Thought is an invariable element. To insist upon Thought in this connection with history may, however, appear unsatisfactory. In this science it would seem as if Thought must be subordinate to what is given, to the realities of fact; that this is its basis and guide: while Philosophy dwells in the region of self-produced ideas, without reference to actuality. Approaching history thus prepossessed, Speculation might be expected to treat it as a mere passive material; and, so far from leaving it in its native truth, to force it into conformity with a tyrannous idea, and to construe it, as the phrase is, " *à priori.*" But as it is the business of history simply to adopt into its records what is and has been, actual occurrences and transactions; and since it remains true to its character in proportion as it strictly adheres to its data, we seem to have in Philosophy, a process diametrically opposed to that of the historiographer. This contradiction, and the charge consequently brought against speculation, shall be explained and confuted. We do not, however, propose to correct the innumerable special misrepresentations, trite or novel, that are current respecting the aims, the interests, and the modes of treating history, and its relation to Philosophy.

The only Thought which Philosophy brings with it to the contemplation of History, is the simple conception of *Reason;* that Reason is the Sovereign of the World; that the history of the world, therefore, presents us with a rational process. This conviction and intuition is a hypothesis in the domain of history as such. In that of Philosophy it is no hypothesis. It is there proved by speculative cognition, that Reason—and this term may here suffice us, without investigating the relation sustained by the Universe to the Divine Being—is *Substance,* as well as *Infinite Power;* its own *Infinite Material* underlying all the natural and spiritual life which it originates, as also the *Infinite Form*—that which sets this Material in motion. On the one hand, Reason is the *substance* of the Universe; viz., that by which and in which all reality has its being and subsistence. On the other hand, it is the *Infinite Energy* of the Universe; since Reason is not so powerless as to be incapable of producing anything but a mere ideal, a mere intention—having its place outside reality, nobody knows where; something separate and abstract, in the heads of certain human beings. It is *the infinite complex of things,* their entire Essence and Truth. It is its own material which it commits to its own Active Energy to work up; not needing, as finite action does, the conditions of an external material of given means from which it may obtain its support, and the objects of its activity. It supplies its own nourishment, and is the object of its own operations. While it is exclusively its own basis of existence, and absolute final aim, it is also the energizing power realizing this aim; developing it not only in the phenomena of the Natural, but also of the Spiritual Universe—the History of the World. That this " Idea " or " Reason " is the *True,* the *Eternal,* the absolutely *powerful* essence; that it reveals itself in the World, and that in that World nothing else is revealed but this and its honor and glory—is the thesis which, as we have said, has been proved in Philosophy, and is here regarded as demonstrated.

In those of my hearers who are not acquainted with Philosophy, I may fairly presume, at least, the existence of a *belief* in Reason, a desire, a thirst for acquaintance with it, in entering upon this course of Lectures. It is, in fact, the wish for rational insight, not the ambition to amass a mere heap of acquirements, that should be presupposed in every case as possessing the mind of the learner in the study of science. If the clear idea of Reason is not already developed in our minds, in beginning the study of Universal History, we should at least have the firm, unconquerable faith that Reason *does* exist there; and that the World of intelligence and conscious volition is not abandoned to chance, but must show itself in the light of the self-cognizant Idea. Yet I am not obliged to make any such preliminary demand upon your faith. What I have said thus provisionally, and what I shall have further to say, is, even in reference to *our* branch of science, not to be regarded as hypothetical, but as a summary view of the whole; the *result of the investigation* we are about to pursue; a result which happens to be known to *me*, because I have traversed the entire field. It is only an inference from the history of the World, that its development has been a rational process; that the history in question has constituted the rational necessary course of the World-Spirit—that Spirit whose nature is always one and the same, but which unfolds this its one nature in the phenomena of the World's existence. This must, as before stated, present itself as the ultimate *result* of History. But we have to take the latter as it is. We must proceed historically—empirically. Among other precautions we must take care not to be misled by professed historians who (especially among the Germans, and enjoying a considerable authority), are chargeable with the very procedure of which they accuse the Philosopher—introducing *à priori* inventions of their own into the records of the Past. It is, for example, a widely current fiction, that there was an original primeval people, taught immediately by God, endowed with perfect insight and wisdom, possessing a thorough knowledge of all natural laws and spiritual truth; that there have been such or such sacerdotal peoples; or, to mention a more specific averment, that there was a Roman Epos, from which the Roman historians derived the early annals of their city, etc. Authorities of this kind we leave to those talented historians by profession, among whom (in Germany at least) their use is not uncommon.—We might then announce it as the first condition to be observed, that we should faithfully adopt all that is historical. But in such general expressions themselves, as " faithfully " and " adopt," lies the ambiguity. Even the ordinary, the " impartial " historiographer, who believes and professes that he maintains a simply receptive attitude; surrendering himself only to the data supplied him—is by no means passive as regards the exercise of his thinking powers. He brings his categories with him, and sees the phenomena presented to his mental vision, exclusively through these media. And, especially in all that pretends to the name of science, it is indispensable that Reason should not sleep—that reflection should be in full play. To him who looks upon the world rationally, the world in its turn presents a rational aspect. The relation is mutual. But the various exercises of reflection—the different points of view—the modes of deciding the simple question of the relative importance of events (the first category that occupies the attention of the historian), do not belong to this place.

I will only mention two phases and points of view that concern the generally diffused conviction that Reason has ruled, and is still ruling in the world, and consequently in the world's history; because they give us, at the same time, an opportunity for more closely investigating the question that presents the greatest difficulty, and for indicating a branch of the subject, which will have to be enlarged on in the sequel.

I. One of these points is, that passage in history, which informs us that the Greek Anaxagoras was the first to enunciate the doctrine that νοῦς, Understanding generally, or Reason, governs the world. It is not intelligence as self-conscious Reason—not a Spirit as such that is meant; and we must clearly distinguish these from each other. The movement of the solar system takes place according to unchangeable laws. These laws are Reason, implicit in the phenomena in question. But neither the sun nor the planets, which revolve around it according to these laws, can be said to have any consciousness of them.

A thought of this kind—that Nature is an embodiment of Reason; that it is unchangeably subordinate to universal laws, appears nowise striking or strange to us. We are accustomed to such conceptions, and find nothing extraordinary in them. And I have mentioned this extraordinary occurrence, partly to show how history teaches, that ideas of this kind, which may seem trivial to us, have not always been in the world; that, on the contrary, such a thought makes an epoch in the annals of human intelligence. Aristotle says of Anaxagoras, as the originator of the thought in question, that he appeared as a sober man among the drunken. Socrates adopted the doctrine from Anaxagoras, and it forthwith became the ruling idea in Philosophy—except in the school of Epicurus, who ascribed all events to chance. " I was delighted with the sentiment "—Plato makes Socrates say—" and hoped I had found a teacher who would show me Nature in harmony with Reason, who would demonstrate in each particular phenomenon its specific aim, and in the whole, the grand object of the Universe. I would not have surrendered this hope for a great deal. But how very much was I disappointed, when, having zealously applied myself to the writings of Anaxagoras, I found that he adduces only external causes, such as Atmosphere, Ether, Water, and the like." It is evident that the defect which Socrates complains of respecting Anaxagoras's doctrine, does not concern the principle itself, but the shortcoming of the propounder in applying it to Nature in the concrete. Nature is not deduced from that principle: the latter remains in fact a mere abstraction, inasmuch as the former is not comprehended and exhibited as a development of it—an organization produced by and from Reason. I wish, at the very outset, to call your attention to the important difference between a conception, a principle, a truth limited to an *abstract* form and its determinate application, and concrete development. This distinction affects the whole fabric of philosophy; and among other bearings of it there is one to which we shall have to revert at the close of our view of Universal History, in investigating the aspect of political affairs in the most recent period.

We have next to notice the rise of this idea—that Reason directs the World—in connection with a further application of it, well known to us—in the form, viz., of the *religious truth*, that the world is not abandoned to chance and external contingent causes, but that a *Providence* controls it. I stated above, that I would not make a demand on your faith, in regard to the principle announced. Yet I might appeal to your belief in it, *in this religious aspect,* if, as a general rule, the nature of philo-sophical science allowed it to attach authority to presupposi-tions. To put it in another shape—this appeal is forbidden, because the science of which we have to treat, proposes itself to furnish the proof (not indeed of the abstract *Truth* of the doctrine, but) of its correctness as compared with facts. The truth, then, that a Providence (that of God) presides over the events of the World—consorts with the proposition in question; for *Divine* Providence is Wisdom, endowed with an infinite Power, which realizes its aim, viz., the absolute rational design of the World. Reason is Thought conditioning itself with perfect freedom. But a difference—rather a contradiction—will manifest itself, between this belief and our principle, just as was the case in reference to the demand made by Socrates in the case of Anaxagoras's dictum. For that belief is simi-larly indefinite; it is what is called a belief in a general Provi-dence, and is not followed out into definite application, or dis-played in its bearing on the grand total—the entire course of human history. But to *explain* History is to depict the pas-sions of mankind, the genius, the active powers, that play their part on the great stage; and the providentially determined process which these exhibit, constitutes what is generally called the "plan" of Providence. Yet it is this very plan which is supposed to be concealed from our view: which it is deemed presumption, even to wish to recognize. The ignorance of Anaxagoras, as to how intelligence reveals itself in actual existence, was ingenuous. Neither in his consciousness, nor in that of Greece at large, had that thought been farther ex-panded. He had not attained the power to apply his general principle to the concrete, so as to deduce the latter from the former. It was Socrates who took the first step in compre-hending the union of the Concrete with the Universal. Anax-agoras, then, did not take up a *hostile* position toward such an application. The common belief in Providence *does;* at least it opposes the use of the principle on the large scale, and denies the possibility of discerning the plan of Providence. In isolated cases this plan is supposed to be manifest. Pious persons are encouraged to recognize in particular circumstances, something more than mere chance; to acknowledge the guiding hand of God; *e.g.,* when help has unexpectedly come to an individual in great perplexity and need. But these instances of providential design are of a limited kind, and concern the accomplishment of nothing more than the desires of the individual in question. But in the history of the World, the *Individuals* we have to do with are *Peoples;* Totalities that are States. We cannot, therefore, be satisfied with what we may call this " peddling " view of Providence, to which the belief alluded to limits itself. Equally unsatisfactory is the merely abstract, undefined belief in a Providence, when that belief is not brought to bear upon the details of the process which it conducts. On the contrary our earnest endeavor must be directed to the recognition of the ways of Providence, the means it uses, and the historical phenomena in which it manifests itself; and we must show their connection with the general principle above mentioned. But in noticing the recognition of the plan of Divine Providence generally, I have implicitly touched upon a prominent question of the day; viz., that of the possibility of knowing God: or rather—since public opinion has ceased to allow it to be a matter of *question*—the *doctrine* that it is impossible to know God. In direct contravention of what is commanded in holy Scripture as the highest duty—that we should not merely love, but *know* God—the prevalent dogma involves the denial of what is there said; viz., that it is the Spirit (der Geist) that leads into Truth, knows all things, penetrates even into the deep things of the Godhead. While the Divine Being is thus placed beyond our knowledge, and outside the limit of all human things, we have the convenient license of wandering as far as we list, in the direction of our own fancies. We are freed from the obligation to refer our knowledge to the Divine and True. On the other hand, the vanity and egotism which characterize it, find, in this false position, ample justification; and the pious modesty which puts far from it the knowledge of God, can well estimate how much furtherance thereby accrues to its own wayward and vain strivings. I have been unwilling to leave out of sight the connection between our thesis—that Reason governs and has governed the World— and the question of the possibility of a knowledge of God, chiefly that I might not lose the opportunity of mentioning the imputation against Philosophy of being shy of noticing re-

ligious truths, or of having occasion to be so; in which is
insinuated the suspicion that it has anything but a clear conscience in the presence of these truths. So far from this being
the case, the fact is, that in recent times Philosophy has been
obliged to defend the domain of religion against the attacks
of several theological systems. In the Christian religion God
has revealed Himself—that is, he has given us to understand
what He is; so that He is no longer a concealed or secret
existence. And this possibility of knowing Him, thus afforded
us, renders such knowledge a duty. God wishes no narrow-
hearted souls or empty heads for his children; but those whose
spirit is of itself indeed, poor, but rich in the knowledge of
Him; and who regard this knowledge of God as the only valuable possession. That development of the thinking spirit,
which has resulted from the revelation of the Divine Being as
its original basis, must ultimately advance to the *intellectual*
comprehension of what was presented in the first instance, to
feeling and *imagination*. The time must eventually come for
understanding that rich product of active Reason, which the
History of the World offers to us. It was for awhile the fashion to profess admiration for the wisdom of God, as displayed
in animals, plants, and isolated occurrences. But, if it be allowed that Providence manifests itself in such objects and
forms of existence, why not also in Universal History? This
is deemed too great a matter to be thus regarded. But Divine
Wisdom, *i.e.*, Reason, is one and the same in the great as in the
little; and we must not imagine God to be too weak to exercise
his wisdom on the grand scale. Our intellectual striving aims
at realizing the conviction that what was *intended* by eternal
wisdom, is actually *accomplished* in the domain of existent,
active Spirit, as well as in that of mere Nature. Our mode
of treating the subject is, in this aspect, a Theodicæa—a justification of the ways of God—which Leibnitz attempted meta-
physically, in his method, *i.e.*, in indefinite abstract categories—
so that the ill that is found in the World may be comprehended,
and the thinking Spirit reconciled with the fact of the existence
of evil. Indeed, nowhere is such a harmonizing view more
pressingly demanded than in Universal History; and it can
be attained only by recognizing the *positive* existence, in which
that negative element is a subordinate, and vanquished nullity.
On the one hand, the ultimate design of the World must be

perceived; and, on the other hand, the fact that this design has been actually realized in it, and that evil has not been able permanently to assert a competing position. But this conviction involves much more than the mere belief in a superintending νοῦς, or in "Providence." "Reason," whose sovereignty over the World has been maintained, is as indefinite a term as "Providence," supposing the term to be used by those who are unable to characterize it distinctly—to show wherein it consists, so as to enable us to decide whether a thing is rational or irrational. An adequate definition of Reason is the first desideratum; and whatever boast may be made of strict adherence to it in explaining phenomena—without such a definition we get no farther than mere words. With these observations we may proceed to the second point of view that has to be considered in this Introduction.

II. The inquiry into the *essential destiny* of Reason—as far as it is considered in reference to the World—is identical with the question, *what is the ultimate design of the World?* And the expression implies that that design is destined to be realized. Two points of consideration suggest themselves; first, the *import* of this design—its abstract definition; and secondly, its *realization.*

It must be observed at the outset, that the phenomenon we investigate—Universal History—belongs to the realm of *Spirit.* The term *"World,"* includes both physical and psychical Nature. Physical Nature also plays its part in the World's History, and attention will have to be paid to the fundamental natural relations thus involved. But Spirit, and the course of its development, is our substantial object. Our task does not require us to contemplate Nature as a Rational System in itself —though in its own proper domain it proves itself such—but simply in its relation to *Spirit.* On the stage on which we are observing it—Universal History—Spirit displays itself in its most concrete reality. Notwithstanding this (or rather for the very purpose of comprehending the *general* principles which this, its form of *concrete reality,* embodies) we must premise some abstract characteristics of the *nature of Spirit.* Such an explanation, however, cannot be given here under any other form than that of bare assertion. The present is not the occasion for unfolding the idea of Spirit speculatively; for whatever has a place in an Introduction, must, as already observed, be taken as simply historical; something assumed as having been explained and proved elsewhere; or whose demonstration awaits the sequel of the Science of History itself.

We have therefore to mention here:

(1) The abstract characteristics of the nature of Spirit.

(2) What means Spirit uses in order to realize its Idea.

(3) Lastly, we must consider the shape which the perfect embodiment of Spirit assumes—the State.

(1) The nature of Spirit may be understood by a glance at its direct opposite—*Matter*. As the essence of Matter is Gravity, so, on the other hand, we may affirm that the substance, the essence of Spirit is Freedom. All will readily assent to the doctrine that Spirit, among other properties, is also endowed with Freedom; but philosophy teaches that all the qualities of Spirit exist only through Freedom; that all are but means for attaining Freedom; that all seek and produce this and this alone. It is a result of speculative Philosophy, that Freedom is the sole truth of Spirit. Matter possesses gravity in virtue of its tendency toward a central point. It is essentially composite; consisting of parts that *exclude* each other. It seeks its Unity; and therefore exhibits itself as self-destructive, as verging toward its opposite [an indivisible point]. If it could attain this, it would be Matter no longer, it would have perished. It strives after the realization of its Idea; for in Unity it exists *ideally*. Spirit, on the contrary, may be defined as that which has its centre in itself. It has not a unity outside itself, but has already found it; it exists *in* and *with itself*. Matter has its essence out of itself; Spirit is *self-contained existence* (Bei-sich-selbst-seyn). Now this is Freedom, exactly. For if I am dependent, my being is referred to something else which I am not; I cannot exist independently of something external. I am free, on the contrary, when my existence depends upon myself. This self-contained existence of Spirit is none other than self-consciousness—consciousness of one's own being. Two things must be distinguished in consciousness; first, the fact *that I know;* secondly, *what I know.* In *self* consciousness these are merged in one; for Spirit *knows itself*. It involves an appreciation of its own nature, as also an energy enabling it to realize itself; to make itself *actually* that which it is *potentially*. According to this abstract definition it may be said of Universal History, that it is the exhibition of Spirit in the process of working out the knowledge of

that which it is potentially. And as the germ bears in itself
the whole nature of the tree, and the taste and form of its
fruits, so do the first traces of Spirit virtually contain the whole
of that History. The Orientals have not attained the knowledge that Spirit—Man *as such*—is free; and because they
do not know this, they are not free. They only know that
one is free. But on this very account, the freedom of that one
is only caprice; ferocity—brutal recklessness of passion, or
a mildness and tameness of the desires, which is itself only
an accident of Nature—mere caprice like the former.—That
one is therefore only a Despot; not a *free man.* The consciousness of Freedom first arose among the Greeks, and therefore
they were free; but they, and the Romans likewise, knew only
that *some* are free—not man as such. Even Plato and Aristotle did not know this. The Greeks, therefore, had slaves;
and their whole life and the maintenance of their splendid liberty, was implicated with the institution of slavery: a fact
moreover, which made that liberty on the one hand only an
accidental, transient and limited growth; on the other hand,
constituted it a rigorous thraldom of our common nature—of
the Human. The German nations, under the influence of Christianity, were the first to attain the consciousness, that man, as
man, is free: that it is the *freedom* of Spirit which constitutes
its essence. This consciousness arose first in religion, the inmost region of Spirit; but to introduce the principle into the
various relations of the actual world, involves a more extensive
problem than its simple implantation; a problem whose solution and application require a severe and lengthened process
of culture. In proof of this, we may note that slavery did not
cease immediately on the reception of Christianity. Still less
did liberty predominate in States; or Governments and Constitutions adopt a rational organization, or recognize freedom
as their basis. That application of the principle to political relations; the thorough moulding and interpenetration of the
constitution of society by it, is a process identical with history
itself. I have already directed attention to the distinction here
involved, between a principle as such, and its *application; i.e.,*
its introduction and carrying out in the actual phenomena of
Spirit and Life. This is a point of fundamental importance
in our science, and one which must be constantly respected as
essential. And in the same way as this distinction has at-

tracted attention in view of the *Christian* principle of self-consciousness—Freedom; it also shows itself as an essential one,
in view of the principle of Freedom *generally.* The History of
the world is none other than the progress of the consciousness
of Freedom; a progress whose development according to the
necessity of its nature, it is our business to investigate.

The general statement given above, of the various grades in
the consciousness of Freedom—and which we applied in the
first instance to the fact that the Eastern nations knew only
that *one* is free; the Greek and Roman world only that *some*
are free; while *we* know that all men absolutely (man *as man*)
are free—supplies us with the natural division of Universal
History, and suggests the mode of its discussion. This is
remarked, however, only incidentally and anticipatively; some
other ideas must be first explained.

The destiny of the spiritual World, and—since this is the
substantial World, while the physical remains subordinate to
it, or, in the language of speculation, has no truth *as against*
the spiritual—*the final cause of the World at large,* we allege
to be the *consciousness* of its own freedom on the part of Spirit,
and *ipso facto,* the *reality* of that freedom. But that this term
" Freedom," without further qualification, is an indefinite, and
incalculable ambiguous term; and that while that which it
represents is the *ne plus ultra* of attainment, it is liable to an
infinity of misunderstandings, confusions and errors, and to
become the occasion for all imaginable excesses—has never
been more clearly known and felt than in modern times. Yet,
for the present, we must content ourselves with the term itself
without farther definition. Attention was also directed to the
importance of the infinite difference between a principle in the
abstract, and its realization in the concrete. In the process
before us, the essential nature of freedom—which involves in
it absolute necessity—is to be displayed as coming to a consciousness of itself (for it is in its very nature, self-consciousness) and thereby realizing its existence. Itself is its own
object of attainment, and the sole aim of Spirit. This result
it is, at which the process of the World's History has been continually aiming; and to which the sacrifices that have ever and
anon been laid on the vast altar of the earth, through the long
lapse of ages, have been offered. This is the only aim that sees
itself realized and fulfilled; the only pole of repose amid the

ceaseless change of events and conditions, and the sole efficient
principle that pervades them. This final aim is God's purpose
with the world; but God is the absolutely perfect Being, and
can, therefore, will nothing other than himself—his own Will.
The Nature of His Will—that is, His Nature itself—is what
we here call the Idea of Freedom; translating the language of
Religion into that of Thought. The question, then, which we
may next put, is: What means does this principle of Freedom
use for its realization? This is the second point we have to
consider.

(2) The question of the *means* by which Freedom develops
itself to a World, conducts us to the phenomenon of History
itself. Although Freedom is, primarily, an undeveloped idea,
the means it uses are external and phenomenal; presenting
themselves in History to our sensuous vision. The first glance
at History convinces us that the actions of men proceed from
their needs, their passions, their characters and talents; and
impresses us with the belief that such needs, passions and interests are the sole springs of action—the efficient agents in
this scene of activity. Among these may, perhaps, be found
aims of a liberal or universal kind—benevolence it may be, or
noble patriotism; but such virtues and general views are but
insignificant as compared with the World and its doings. We
may perhaps see the Ideal of Reason actualized in those who
adopt such aims, and within the sphere of their influence; but
they bear only a trifling proportion to the mass of the human
race; and the extent of that influence is limited accordingly.
Passions, private aims, and the satisfaction of selfish desires,
are on the other hand, most effective springs of action. Their
power lies in the fact that they respect none of the limitations
which justice and morality would impose on them; and that
these natural impulses have a more direct influence over man
than the artificial and tedious discipline that tends to order and
self-restraint, law and morality. When we look at this display
of passions, and the consequences of their violence; the Un-
reason which is associated not only with them, but even (rather
we might say *especially*) with *good* designs and righteous aims;
when we see the evil, the vice, the ruin that has befallen the
most flourishing kingdoms which the mind of man ever created;
we can scarce avoid being filled with sorrow at this universal
taint of corruption: and, since this decay is not the work of

mere Nature, but of the Human Will—a moral embitterment—
a revolt of the Good Spirit (if it have a place within us) may
well be the result of our reflections. Without rhetorical exaggeration, a simply truthful combination of the miseries that
have overwhelmed the noblest of nations and polities, and the
finest exemplars of private virtue—forms a picture of most
fearful aspect, and excites emotions of the profoundest and
most hopeless sadness, counterbalanced by no consolatory result. We endure in beholding it a mental torture, allowing
no defence or escape but the consideration that what has happened could not be otherwise; that it is a fatality which no
intervention could alter. And at last we draw back from the
intolerable disgust with which these sorrowful reflections
threaten us, into the more agreeable environment of our individual life—the Present formed by our private aims and interests. In short we retreat into the selfishness that stands on
the quiet shore, and thence enjoys in safety the distant spectacle
of "wrecks confusedly hurled." But even regarding History
as the slaughter-bench at which the happiness of peoples, the
wisdom of States, and the virtue of individuals have been vic-
timized—the question involuntarily arises—to what principle,
to what final aim these enormous sacrifices have been offered.
From this point the investigation usually proceeds to that
which we have made the general commencement of our inquiry. Starting from this we pointed out those phenomena
which made up a picture so suggestive of gloomy emotions
and thoughtful reflections—as *the very field* which we, for our
part, regard as exhibiting only the means for realizing what
we assert to be the essential destiny—the absolute aim, or—
which comes to the same thing—the true *result* of the World's
History. We have all along purposely eschewed "moral reflections" as a method of rising from the scene of historical
specialties to the general principles which they embody. Besides, it is not the interest of such sentimentalities, really to
rise above those depressing emotions; and to solve the enigmas
of Providence which the considerations that occasioned them,
present. It is essential to their character to find a gloomy satisfaction in the empty and fruitless sublimities of that negative
result. We return them to the point of view which we have
adopted; observing that the successive steps (Momente) of
the analysis to which it will lead us, will also evolve the con-

ditions requisite for answering the inquiries suggested by the panorama of sin and suffering that history unfolds.

The *first* remark we have to make, and which—though already presented more than once—cannot be too often repeated when the occasion seems to call for it—is that what we call *principle, aim, destiny,* or the nature and idea of Spirit, is something merely general and abstract. Principle—Plan of Existence—Law—is a hidden, undeveloped essence, which *as such* —however true in itself—is not completely real. Aims, principles, etc., have a place in our thoughts, in our subjective design only; but not yet in the sphere of reality. That which exists for itself only, is a possibility, a potentiality; but has not yet emerged into Existence. A *second* element must be introduced in order to produce actuality—viz., actuation, realization; and whose motive power is the Will—the activity of man in the widest sense. It is only by this activity that that Idea as well as abstract characteristics generally, are realized, actualized; for of themselves they are powerless. The motive power that puts them in operation, and gives them determinate existence, is the need, instinct, inclination, and passion of man. That some conception of mine should be developed into act and existence, is my earnest desire: I wish to assert my personality in connection with it: I wish to be satisfied by its execution. If I am to exert myself for any object, it must in some way or other be *my* object. In the accomplishment of such or such designs I must at the same time find *my* satisfaction; although the purpose for which I exert myself includes a complication of results, many of which have no interest for me. This is the absolute right of personal existence—to find *itself* satisfied in its activity and labor. If men are to interest themselves for anything, they must (so to speak) have part of their existence involved in it; find their individuality gratified by its attainment. Here a mistake must be avoided. We intend blame, and justly impute it as a fault, when we say of an individual, that he is " interested " (in taking part in such or such transactions), that is, seeks only his private advantage. In reprehending this we find fault with him for furthering his personal aims without any regard to a more comprehensive design; of which he takes advantage to promote his own interest, or which he even sacrifices with this view. But he who is active in *promoting an object,* is not simply " interested," but interested in that object itself. Language faithfully expresses this distinction.—Nothing therefore happens, nothing is accomplished, unless the individuals concerned, seek their own satisfaction in the issue. They are particular units of society; *i.e.*, they have special needs, instincts, and interests generally, peculiar to themselves. Among these needs are not only such as we usually call necessities—the stimuli of individual desire and volition—but also those connected with individual views and convictions; or—to use a term expressing less decision—leanings of opinion; supposing the impulses of reflection, understanding, and reason, to have been awakened. In these cases people demand, if they are to exert themselves in any direction, that the object should commend itself to them; that in point of opinion—whether as to its goodness, justice, advantage, profit—they should be able to " enter into it " (dabei seyn). This is a consideration of especial importance in our age, when people are less than formerly influenced by reliance on others, and by authority; when, on the contrary, they devote their activities to a cause on the ground of their own understanding, their independent conviction and opinion.

We assert then that nothing has been accomplished without interest on the part of the actors; and—if interest be called passion, inasmuch as the whole individuality, to the neglect of all other actual or possible interests and claims, is devoted to an object with every fibre of volition, concentrating all its desires and powers upon it—we may affirm absolutely that *nothing great in the World* has been accomplished without *passion*. Two elements, therefore, enter into the object of our investigation; the first the Idea, the second the complex of human passions; the one the warp, the other the woof of the vast arras-web of Universal History. The concrete mean and union of the two is Liberty, under the conditions of morality in a State. We have spoken of the Idea of Freedom as the nature of Spirit, and the absolute goal of History. Passion is regarded as a thing of sinister aspect, as more or less immoral. Man is required to have no passions. Passion, it is true, is not quite the suitable word for what I wish to express. I mean here nothing more than the human activity as resulting from private interests—special, or if you will, self-seeking designs—with this qualification, that the whole energy of will and character is devoted to their attainment; that other interests (which would in themselves constitute attractive aims) or rather all things else, are sacrificed to them. The object in question is so bound up with the man's will, that it entirely and alone determines the " hue of resolution," and is inseparable from it. It has become the very essence of his volition. For a person is a specific existence; not man in general (a term to which no real existence corresponds) but a particular human being. The term " character " likewise expresses this idiosyncrasy of Will and Intelligence. But *Character* comprehends all peculiarities whatever; the way in which a person conducts himself in private relations, etc., and is not limited to his idiosyncrasy in its practical and active phase. I shall, therefore, use the term " passions "; understanding thereby the particular bent of character, as far as the peculiarities of volition are not limited to private interest, but supply the impelling and actuating force for accomplishing deeds shared in by the community at large. Passion is in the first instance the *subjective,* and therefore the *formal* side of energy, will, and activity—leaving the object or aim still undetermined. And there is a similar relation of formality to reality in merely individual conviction, individual views, individual conscience. It is always a question of essential importance, what is the purport of my conviction, what the object of my passion, in deciding whether the one or the other is of a true and substantial nature. Conversely, if it is so, it will inevitably attain actual existence—be realized.

From this comment on the second essential element in the historical embodiment of an aim, we infer—glancing at the institution of the State in passing—that a State is then well constituted and internally powerful, when the private interest of its citizens is one with the common interest of the State; when the one finds its gratification and realization in the other —a proposition in itself very important. But in a State many institutions must be adopted, much political machinery invented, accompanied by appropriate political arrangements—necessitating long struggles of the understanding before what is really appropriate can be discovered—involving, moreover, contentions with private interest and passions, and a tedious discipline of these latter, in order to bring about the desired harmony. The epoch when a State attains this harmonious conditon, marks the period of its bloom, its virtue, its vigor, and its prosperity. But the history of mankind does not begin with a *conscious* aim of any kind, as it is the case with the particular circles into which men form themselves of set purpose. The mere social instinct implies a conscious purpose of security for life and property; and when society has been constituted, this purpose becomes more comprehensive. The History of the World begins with its general aim—the realization of the Idea of Spirit—only in an *implicit* form (*an sich*) that is, as Nature; a hidden, most profoundly hidden, unconscious instinct; and the whole process of History (as already observed), is directed to rendering this unconscious impulse a conscious one. Thus appearing in the form of merely natural existence, natural will —that which has been called the subjective side—physical craving, instinct, passion, private interest, as also opinion and subjective conception—spontaneously present themselves at the very commencement. This vast congeries of volitions, interests and activities, constitute the instruments and means of the World-Spirit for attaining its object; bringing it to consciousness, and realizing it. And this aim is none other than finding itself—coming to itself—and contemplating itself in concrete actuality. But that those manifestations of vitality on the part of individuals and peoples, in which they seek and satisfy their own purposes, are, at the same time, the means and instruments of a higher and broader purpose of which they know nothing—which they realize unconsciously—might be made a matter of question; rather has been questioned, and in every variety of form negatived, decried and contemned as mere dreaming and " Philosophy." But on this point I announced my view at the very outset, and asserted our hypothesis—which, however, will appear in the sequel, in the form of a legitimate inference—and our belief, that Reason governs the world, and has consequently governed its history. In relation to this independently universal and substantial existence—all else is subordinate, subservient to it, and the means for its development. —The Union of Universal Abstract Existence generally with the Individual—the Subjective—that this alone is Truth, belongs to the department of speculation, and is treated in this general form in Logic.—But in the process of the World's History itself—as still incomplete—the abstract final aim of history is not yet made the distinct object of desire and interest. While these limited sentiments are still unconscious of the purpose they are fulfilling, the universal principle is implicit in them, and is realizing itself through them. The question also assumes the form of the union of *Freedom* and *Necessity;* the latent abstract process of Spirit being regarded as *Necessity,* while that which exhibits itself in the conscious will of men, as their interest, belongs to the domain of *Freedom.* As the metaphysical connection (*i.e.,* the connection in the Idea) of these forms of thought, belongs to Logic, it would be out of place to analyze it here. The chief and cardinal points only shall be mentioned.

Philosophy shows that the Idea advances to an infinite antithesis; that, viz., between the Idea in its free, universal form —in which it exists for itself—and the contrasted form of abstract introversion, reflection on itself, which is formal existence-for-self, personality, formal freedom, such as belongs to Spirit only. The universal Idea exists thus as the substantial totality of things on the one side, and as the abstract essence of free volition on the other side. This reflection of the mind on itself is individual self-consciousness—the polar opposite of the Idea in its general form, and therefore existing in absolute Limitation. This polar opposite is consequently limitation, particularization, for the universal absolute being; it is the side of its *definite existence;* the sphere of its formal reality, the sphere of the reverence paid to God.—To comprehend the absolute connection of this antithesis, is the profound task of metaphysics. This Limitation originates all forms of particularity of whatever kind. The formal volition [of which we have spoken] wills itself; desires to make its own personality valid in all that it purposes and does: even the pious individual wishes to be saved and happy. This pole of the antithesis, existing for itself, is—in contrast with the Absolute Universal Being—a special separate existence, taking cognizance of specialty only, and willing that alone. In short it plays its part in the region of mere phenomena. This is the sphere of particular purposes, in effecting which individuals exert themselves on behalf of their individuality—give it full play and objective realization. This is also the sphere of happiness and its opposite. He is happy who finds his condition suited to his special character, will, and fancy, and so enjoys himself in that condition. The History of the World is not the theatre of happiness. Periods of happiness are blank pages in it, for they are periods of harmony—periods when the antithesis is in abeyance. Reflection on self—the Freedom above described—is abstractly defined as the formal element of the activity of the absolute Idea. The realizing *activity* of which we have spoken is the middle term of the Syllogism, one of whose extremes is the Universal essence, the *Idea,* which reposes in the penetralia of Spirit; and the other, the complex of external things—objective matter. That activity is the medium by which the universal latent principle is translated into the domain of objectivity.

I will endeavor to make what has been said more vivid and clear by examples.

The building of a house is, in the first instance, a subjective aim and design. On the other hand we have, as means, the several substances required for the work—Iron, Wood, Stones. The elements are made use of in working up this material: fire to melt the iron, wind to blow the fire, water to set wheels in motion, in order to cut the wood, etc. The result is, that the wind, which has helped to build the house, is shut out by the house; so also are the violence of rains and floods, and the destructive powers of fire, so far as the house is made fireproof. The stones and beams obey the law of gravity—press downward—and so high walls are carried up. Thus the elements are made use of in accordance with their nature, and yet to co-operate for a product, by which their operation is limited. Thus the passions of men are gratified; they develop themselves and their aims in accordance with their natural tendencies, and build up the edifice of human society; thus fortifying a position for Right and Order *against themselves.*

The connection of events above indicated, involves also the fact, that in history an additional result is commonly produced by human actions beyond that which they aim at and obtain—that which they immediately recognize and desire. They gratify their own interest; but something further is thereby accomplished, latent in the actions in question, though not present to their consciousness, and not included in their design. An analogous example is offered in the case of a man who, from a feeling of revenge—perhaps not an unjust one, but produced by injury on the other's part—burns that other man's house. A connection is immediately established between the deed itself and a train of circumstances not directly included in it, taken abstractedly. In itself it consisted in merely presenting a small flame to a small portion of a beam. Events not involved in that simple act follow of themselves. The part of the beam which was set fire to is connected with its remote portions; the beam itself is united with the woodwork of the house generally, and this with other houses; so that a wide conflagration ensues, which destroys the goods and chattels of many other persons besides his against whom the act of revenge was first directed; perhaps even costs not a few men their lives. This lay neither in the deed abstractedly, nor in the design of the man who committed it. But the action has a further general bearing. In the design of the doer it was only revenge executed against an individual in the destruction of his property, but it is moreover a crime, and that involves punishment also. This may not have been present to the mind of the perpetrator, still less in his intention; but his deed itself, the general principles it calls into play, its substantial content entails it. By this example I wish only to impress on you the consideration, that in a simple act, something further may be implicated than lies in the intention and consciousness of the agent. The example before us involves, however, this additional consideration, that the substance of the act, consequently we may say the act itself, recoils upon the perpetrator—reacts upon him with destructive tendency. This union of the two extremes—the embodiment of a general idea in the form of direct reality, and the elevation of a speciality into connection with universal truth—is brought to pass, at first sight, under the conditions of an utter diversity of nature between the two, and an indifference of the one extreme towards the other. The aims which the agents set before them are limited and special; but it must be remarked that the agents themselves are intelligent thinking beings. The purport of their desires is interwoven with *general, essential* considerations of justice, good, duty, etc.; for mere desire—volition in its rough and savage forms—falls not within the scene and sphere of Universal History. Those general considerations, which form at the same time a norm for directing aims and actions, have a determinate purport; for such an abstraction as " good for its own sake," has no place in living reality. If men are to act, they must not only intend the Good, but must have decided for themselves whether this or that particular thing is a Good. What special course of action, however, is good or not, is determined, as regards the ordinary contingencies of private life, by the laws and customs of a State; and here no great difficulty is presented. Each individual has his position; he knows on the whole what a just, honorable course of conduct is. As to ordinary, private relations, the assertion that it is difficult to choose the right and good—the regarding it as the mark of an exalted morality to find difficulties and raise scruples on that score—may be set down to an evil or perverse will, which seeks to evade duties not in themselves of a perplexing nature; or, at any rate, to an idly reflective habit of mind—where a feeble will affords no sufficient exercise to the faculties—leaving them therefore to find occupation within themselves, and to expend themselves on moral self-adulation.

It is quite otherwise with the comprehensive relations that History has to do with. In this sphere are presented those momentous collisions between existing, acknowledged duties, laws, and rights, and those contingencies which are adverse to this fixed system; which assail and even destroy its foundations and existence; whose tenor may nevertheless seem good—on the large scale advantageous—yes, even indispensable and necessary. These contingencies realize themselves in History: they involve a general principle of a different order from that on which depends the *permanence* of a people or a State. This principle is an essential phase in the development of the *creating* Idea, of Truth striving and urging towards [consciousness of] itself. Historical men—*World-Historical Individuals*—are those in whose aims such a general principle lies.

Cæsar, in danger of losing a position, not perhaps at that time of superiority, yet at least of equality with the others who were at the head of the State, and of succumbing to those who were just on the point of becoming his enemies—belongs essentially to this category. These enemies—who were at the same time pursuing *their* personal aims—had the form of the constitution, and the power conferred by an appearance of justice, on their side. Cæsar was contending for the maintenance of his position, honor, and safety; and, since the power of his opponents included the sovereignty over the provinces of the Roman Empire, his victory secured for him the conquest of that entire Empire; and he thus became—though leaving the form of the constitution—the Autocrat of the State. That which secured for him the execution of a design, which in the first instance was of negative import—the Autocracy of Rome —was, however, at the same time an independently necessary feature in the history of Rome and of the world. It was not, then, his private gain merely, but an unconscious impulse that occasioned the accomplishment of that for which the time was ripe. Such are all great historical men—whose own particular aims involve those large issues which are the will of the World-Spirit. They may be called Heroes, inasmuch as they have derived their purposes and their vocation, not from the calm, regular course of things, sanctioned by the existing order; but from a concealed fount—one which has not attained to phenomenal, present existence—from that inner Spirit, still hidden beneath the surface, which, impinging on the outer world as on a shell, bursts it in pieces, because it is another kernel than that which belonged to the shell in question. They are men, therefore, who appear to draw the impulse of their life from themselves; and whose deeds have produced a condition of things and a complex of historical relations which appear to be only *their* interest, and *their* work.

Such individuals had no consciousness of the general Idea they were unfolding, while prosecuting those aims of theirs; on the contrary, they were practical, political men. But at the same time they were thinking men, who had an insight into the requirements of the time—*what was ripe for development.* This was the very Truth for their age, for their world; the species next in order, so to speak, and which was already formed in the womb of time. It was theirs to know this nascent principle; the necessary, directly sequent step in progress, which their world was to take; to make this their aim, and to expend their energy in promoting it. World-historical men— the Heroes of an epoch—must, therefore, be recognized as its clear-sighted ones; *their* deeds, *their* words are the best of that time. Great men have formed purposes to satisfy themselves, not others. Whatever prudent designs and counsels they might have learned from others, would be the more limited and inconsistent features in their career; for it was they who best understood affairs; from whom *others* learned, and approved, or at least acquiesced in—their policy. For that Spirit which had taken this fresh step in history is the inmost soul of all individuals; but in a state of unconsciousness which the great men in question aroused. Their fellows, therefore, follow these soul-leaders; for they feel the irresistible power of their own inner Spirit thus embodied. If we go on to cast a look at the fate of these World-Historical persons, whose vocation it was to be the agents of the World-Spirit—we shall find it to have been no happy one. They attained no calm enjoyment; their whole life was labor and trouble; their whole nature was nought else but their master-passion. When their object is attained they fall off like empty hulls from the kernel. They die early, like Alexander; they are murdered, like Cæsar; transported to St. Helena, like Napoleon. This fearful consolation—that historical men have not enjoyed what is called happiness, and of which only private life (and this may be passed under very various external circumstances) is capable —this consolation those may draw from history, who stand in need of it; and it is craved by Envy—vexed at what is great and transcendant—striving, therefore, to depreciate it, and to find some flaw in it. Thus in modern times it has been demonstrated *ad nauseam* that princes are generally unhappy on their thrones; in consideration of which the possession of a throne is tolerated, and men acquiesce in the fact that not themselves but the personages in question are its occupants. The Free Man, we may observe, is not envious, but gladly recognizes what is great and exalted, and rejoices that it exists.

It is in the light of those common elements which constitute the interest and therefore the passions of individuals, that these historical men are to be regarded. They are *great* men, because they willed and accomplished something great; not a mere fancy, a mere intention, but that which met the case and fell in with the needs of the age. This mode of considering them also excludes the so-called " psychological " view, which —serving the purpose of envy most effectually—contrives so to refer all actions to the heart—to bring them under such a subjective aspect—as that their authors appear to have done everything under the impulse of some passion, mean or grand —some *morbid craving*—and on account of these passions and cravings to have been not moral men. Alexander of Macedon partly subdued Greece, and then Asia; therefore he was possessed by a *morbid craving* for conquest. He is alleged to have acted from a craving for fame, for conquest; and the proof that these were the impelling motives is that he did that which resulted in fame. What pedagogue has not demonstrated of Alexander the Great—of Julius Cæsar—that they were instigated by such passions, and were consequently immoral men?—whence the conclusion immediately follows that he, the pedagogue, is a better man than they, because he has not such passions; a proof of which lies in the fact that he does not conquer Asia—vanquish Darius and Porus—but while he enjoys life himself, lets others enjoy it too. These psychologists are particularly fond of contemplating those peculiarities of great historical figures which appertain to them as private persons. Man must eat and drink; he sustains relations to friends and acquaintances; he has passing impulses and ebullitions of temper. " No man is a hero to his *valet-de-chambre*," is a well-known proverb; I have added—and Goethe repeated it ten years later—" but not because the former is no hero, but because the latter is a valet." He takes off the hero's boots, assists him to bed, knows that he prefers champagne, etc. Historical personages waited upon in historical literature by such psychological valets, come poorly off; they are brought down by these their attendants to a level with—or rather a few degrees below the level of—the morality of such exquisite discerners of spirits. The Thersites of Homer who abuses the kings is a standing figure for all times. Blows—that is beating with a solid cudgel—he does not get in every age, as in the Homeric one; but his envy, his egotism, is the thorn which he has to carry in his flesh; and the undying worm that gnaws him is the tormenting consideration that his excellent views and vituperations remain absolutely without result in the world. But our satisfaction at the fate of Thersitism also, may have its sinister side.

A World-historical individual is not so unwise as to indulge a variety of wishes to divide his regards. He is devoted to the One Aim, regardless of all else. It is even possible that such men may treat other great, even sacred interests, inconsiderately; conduct which is indeed obnoxious to moral reprehension. But so mighty a form must trample down many an innocent flower—crush to pieces many an object in its path.

The special interest of passion is thus inseparable from the active development of a general principle: for it is from the special and determinate and from its negation, that the Universal results. Particularity contends with its like, and some loss is involved in the issue. *It* is not the general idea that is implicated in opposition and combat, and that is exposed to danger. It remains in the background, untouched and uninjured. This may be called the *cunning of reason*—that it sets the passions to work for itself, while that which develops its existence through such impulsion pays the penalty, and suffers loss. For it is *phenomenal* being that is so treated, and of this, part is of no value, part is positive and real. The particular is for the most part of too trifling value as compared with the general: individuals are sacrificed and abandoned. The Idea pays the penalty of determinate existence and of corruptibility, not from itself, but from the passions of individuals.

But though we might tolerate the idea that individuals, their desires and the gratification of them, are thus sacrificed, and their happiness given up to the empire of chance, to which it belongs; and that as a general rule, individuals come under the category of means to an ulterior end—there is one aspect of human individuality which we should hesitate to regard in that subordinate light, even in relation to the highest; since it is absolutely no subordinate element, but exists in those individuals as inherently eternal and divine. I mean *morality, ethics, religion.* Even when speaking of the realization of the great ideal aim by means of individuals, the *subjective* element in them—their interest and that of their cravings and impulses, their views and judgments, though exhibited as the merely formal side of their existence—was spoken of as having an infinite right to be consulted. The first idea that presents itself in speaking of *means* is that of something external to the object, and having no share in the object itself. But merely natural things—even the commonest lifeless objects—used as means, must be of such a kind as adapts them to their purpose; they must possess something in common with it. Human beings least of all, sustain the bare external relation of mere means to the great ideal aim. Not only do they in the very act of realizing it, make it the occasion of satisfying personal desires, whose purport is diverse from that aim—but they share in that ideal aim itself; and are for that very reason objects of their own existence; not *formally* merely, as the world of living beings generally is—whose individual life is essentially subordinate to that of man, and is properly used *up* as an instrument. Men, on the contrary, are objects of existence to them-

selves, as regards the intrinsic import of the aim in question.
To this order belongs that in them which we would exclude
from the category of mere means—Morality, Ethics, Religion. That is to say, man is an object of existence in himself only in virtue of the Divine that is in him—that which
was designated at the outset as *Reason;* which, in view of its
activity and power of self-determination, was called *Freedom.*
And we affirm—without entering at present on the proof of
the assertion—that Religion, Morality, etc., have their foundation and source in that principle, and so are essentially elevated
above all alien necessity and chance. And here we must remark that individuals, to the extent of their freedom, are responsible for the depravation and enfeeblement of morals and
religion. This is the seal of the absolute and sublime destiny
of man—that he knows what is good and what is evil; that
his Destiny *is* his very ability to will either good or evil—in
one word, that he is the subject of moral imputation, imputation not only of evil, but of good; and not only concerning
this or that particular matter, and all that happens *ab extrâ*,
but *also* the good and evil attaching to his individual freedom.
The brute alone is simply innocent. It would, however, demand an extensive explanation—as extensive as the analysis
of moral freedom itself—to preclude or obviate all the misunderstandings which the statement that what is called innocence
imports the entire unconsciousness of evil—is wont to occasion.

In contemplating the fate which virtue, morality, even piety
experience in history, we must not fall into the Litany of
Lamentations, that the good and pious often—or for the most
part—fare ill in the world, while the evil-disposed and wicked
prosper. The term *prosperity* is used in a variety of meanings
—riches, outward honor, and the like. But in speaking of
something which in and for itself constitutes an aim of existence, that so-called well or ill-faring of these or those isolated
individuals cannot be regarded as an essential element in the
rational order of the universe. With more justice than happiness—or a fortunate environment for individuals—it is demanded of the grand aim of the world's existence, that it should
foster, nay involve the execution and ratification of good,
moral, righteous purposes. What makes men morally discontented (a discontent, by the bye, on which they somewhat pride

themselves), is that they do not find the present adapted to the realization of aims which they hold to be right and just (more especially in modern times, ideals of political constitutions); they contrast unfavorably things as they *are*, with their idea of things as they *ought* to be. In this case it is not private interest nor passion that desires gratification, but Reason, Justice, Liberty; and equipped with this title, the demand in question assumes a lofty bearing, and readily adopts a position not merely of discontent, but of open revolt against the actual condition of the world. To estimate such a feeling and such views aright, the demands insisted upon, and the very dogmatic opinions asserted, must be examined. At no time so much as in our own, have such general principles and notions been advanced, or with greater assurance. If in days gone by, history seems to present itself as a struggle of passions; in our time—though displays of passion are not wanting—it exhibits partly a predominance of the struggle of notions assuming the authority of principles; partly that of passions and interests essentially subjective, but under the mask of such higher sanctions. The pretensions thus contended for as legitimate in the name of that which has been stated as the ultimate aim of Reason, pass accordingly, for absolute aims—to the same extent as Religion, Morals, Ethics. Nothing, as before remarked, is now more common than the complaint that the *ideals* which imagination sets up are not realized—that these glorious dreams are destroyed by cold actuality. These Ideals—which in the voyage of life founder on the rocks of hard reality—may be in the first instance only subjective, and belong to the idiosyncrasy of the individual, imagining himself the highest and wisest. Such do not properly belong to this category. For the fancies which the individual in his isolation indulges, cannot be the model for universal reality; just as *universal* law is not designed for the units of the mass. These as such may, in fact, find their interests decidedly thrust into the background. But by the term " Ideal," we also understand the ideal of Reason, of the Good, of the True. Poets, as *e.g.* Schiller, have painted such ideals touchingly and with strong emotion, and with the deeply melancholy conviction that they could not be realized. In affirming, on the contrary, that the Universal Reason *does* realize itself, we have indeed nothing to do with the individual empirically regarded. That admits of degrees of better and worse, since here chance and speciality have received authority from the Idea to exercise their monstrous power. Much, therefore, in particular aspects of the grand phenomenon might be found fault with. This subjective fault-finding —which, however, only keeps in view the individual and its deficiency, without taking notice of Reason pervading the whole—is easy; and inasmuch as it asserts an excellent intention with regard to the good of the whole, and seems to result from a kindly heart, it feels authorized to give itself airs and assume great consequence. It is easier to discover a deficiency in individuals, in states, and in Providence, than to see their real import and value. For in this merely negative fault-finding a proud position is taken—one which overlooks the object, without having entered into it—without having comprehended its positive aspect. Age generally makes men more tolerant; youth is always discontented. The tolerance of age is the result of the ripeness of a judgment which, not merely as the result of indifference, is satisfied even with what is inferior; but, more deeply taught by the grave experience of life, has been led to perceive the substantial, solid worth of the object in question. The insight then to which—in contradistinction from those ideals—philosophy is to lead us, is, that the real world is as it ought to be—that the truly good—the universal divine reason—is not a mere abstraction, but a vital principle capable of realizing itself. This *Good*, this *Reason*, in its most concrete form, is God. God governs the world; the actual working of his government—the carrying out of his plan—is the History of the World. This plan philosophy strives to comprehend; for only that which has been developed as the result of it, possesses *bonâ fide* reality. That which does not accord with it, is negative, worthless existence. Before the pure light of this divine Idea—which is no mere Ideal— the phantom of a world whose events are an incoherent concourse of fortuitous circumstances, utterly vanishes. Philosophy wishes to discover the substantial purport, the real side of the divine idea, and to justify the so much despised Reality of things; for Reason is the comprehension of the Divine work. But as to what concerns the perversion, corruption, and ruin of religious, ethical, and moral purposes, and states of society generally, it must be affirmed, that in their *essence* these are in-

finite and eternal; but that the forms they assume may be of a
limited order, and consequently belong to the domain of mere
nature, and be subject to the sway of chance. They are therefore perishable, and exposed to decay and corruption. Religion
and morality—in the same way as inherently universal essences
—have the peculiarity of being present in the individual soul,
in the full extent of their Idea, and therefore truly and really;
although, they may not manifest themselves in it *in extenso*,
and are not applied to fully developed relations. The religion,
the morality of a limited sphere of life—that of a shepherd or
a peasant, *e.g.*—in its intensive concentration and limitation to
a few perfectly simple relations of life—has infinite worth; the
same worth as the religion and morality of extensive knowledge, and of an existence rich in the compass of its relations and
actions. This inner focus—this simple region of the claims of
subjective freedom—the home of volition, resolution, and action—the abstract sphere of conscience—that which comprises
the responsibility and moral value of the individual, remains
untouched; and is quite shut out from the noisy din of the
World's History—including not merely external and temporal
changes, but also those entailed by the absolute necessity inseparable from the realization of the Idea of Freedom itself.
But as a general truth this must be regarded as settled, that
whatever in the world possesses claims as noble and glorious,
has nevertheless a higher existence above it. The claim of the
World-Spirit rises above all special claims.

These observations may suffice in reference to the means
which the World-Spirit uses for realizing its Idea. Stated simply and abstractly, this mediation involves the activity of personal existences in whom Reason is present as their absolute,
substantial being; but a basis, in the first instance, still obscure
and unknown to them. But the subject becomes more complicated and difficult when we regard individuals not merely in
their aspect of activity, but more concretely, in conjunction
with a particular manifestation of that activity in their religion
and morality—forms of existence which are intimately connected with Reason, and share in its absolute claims. Here
the relation of mere means to an end disappears, and the chief
bearings of this seeming difficulty in reference to the absolute
aim of Spirit, have been briefly considered.

(3) The third point to be analyzed is, therefore—what is

the object to be realized by these means; *i.e.* what is the form it
assumes in the realm of reality. We have spoken of *means;*
but in the carrying out of a subjective, limited aim, we have
also to take into consideration the element of a *material,* either
already present or which has to be procured. Thus the question
would arise: What is the material in which the Ideal of Reason is wrought out? The primary answer would be—Personality itself—human desires—Subjectivity generally. In human
knowledge and volition, as its material element, Reason attains
positive existence. We have considered subjective volition
where it has an object which is the truth and essence of a reality, viz., where it constitutes a great world-historical passion.
As a subjective will, occupied with limited passions, it is dependent, and can gratify its desires only within the limits of this
dependence. But the subjective will has also a substantial life
—a reality—in which it moves in the region of *essential* being,
and has the essential itself as the object of its existence. This
essential being is the union of the *subjective* with the *rational*
Will: it is the moral Whole, the *State,* which is that form of reality in which the individual has and enjoys his freedom; but on
the condition of his recognizing, believing in, and willing that
which is common to the Whole. And this must not be understood as if the subjective will of the social unit attained its gratification and enjoyment through that common Will; as if this
were a means provided for its benefit; as if the individual, in
his relations to other individuals, thus limited his freedom, in
order that this universal limitation—the mutual constraint of
all—might secure a small space of liberty for each. Rather, we
affirm, are Law, Morality, Government, and they alone, the
positive reality and completion of Freedom. Freedom of a low
and limited order, is mere caprice; which finds its exercise in
the sphere of particular and limited desires.

Subjective volition—Passion—is that which sets men in activity, that which effects " practical " realization. The Idea is
the inner spring of action; the State is the actually existing,
realized moral life. For it is the Unity of the universal, essential Will, with that of the individual; and this is " Morality."
The Individual living in this unity has a moral life; possesses
a value that consists in this substantiality alone. Sophocles in
his Antigone, says, " The divine commands are not of yester-
day, nor of to-day; no, they have an infinite existence, and no

one could say whence they came." The laws of morality are
not accidental, but are the essentially Rational. It is the very
object of the State that what is essential in the practical activity
of men, and in their dispositions, should be duly recognized;
that it should have a manifest existence, and maintain its position. It is the absolute interest of Reason that this moral Whole
should exist; and herein lies the justification and merit of
heroes who have founded states—however rude these may have
been. In the history of the World, only those peoples can come
under our notice which form a state. For it must be understood
that this latter is the realization of Freedom, *i.e.* of the absolute
final aim, and that it exists for its own sake. It must further be
understood that all the worth which the human being possesses
—all spiritual reality, he possesses only through the State. For
his spiritual reality consists in this, that his own essence—Reason—is objectively present to him, that it possesses objective
immediate existence for him. Thus only is he fully conscious;
thus only is he a partaker of morality—of a just and moral social
and political life. For Truth is the Unity of the universal and
subjective Will; and the Universal is to be found in the State,
in its laws, its universal and rational arrangements. The State
is the Divine Idea as it exists on Earth. We have in it, therefore, the object of History in a more definite shape than before;
that in which Freedom obtains objectivity, and lives in the enjoyment of this objectivity. For Law is the objectivity of
Spirit; volition in its true form. Only that will which obeys
law, is free; for it obeys itself—it is independent and so free.
When the State or our country constitutes a community of existence; when the subjective will of man submits to laws—the
contradiction between Liberty and Necessity vanishes. The
Rational has necessary existence, as being the reality and substance of things, and we are free in recognizing it as law, and
following it as the substance of our own being. The objective
and the subjective will are then reconciled, and present one
identical homogeneous whole. For the morality (*Sittlichkeit*)
of the State is not of that ethical (*moralische*) reflective kind, in
which one's own conviction bears sway; this latter is rather the
peculiarity of the modern time, while the true antique morality
is based on the principle of abiding by one's duty [to the state
at large]. An Athenian citizen did what was required of him,
as it were from instinct: but if I reflect on the object of my

activity, I must have the consciousness that my will has been called into exercise. But morality is Duty—substantial Right —a " *second* nature " as it has been justly called; for the *first* nature of man is his primary merely animal existence.

The development *in extenso* of the Idea of the State belongs to the Philosophy of Jurisprudence; but it must be observed that in the theories of our time various errors are current respecting it, which pass for established truths, and have become fixed prejudices. We will mention only a few of them, giving prominence to such as have a reference to the object of our history.

The error which first meets us is the direct contradictory of our principle that the state presents the realization of Freedom; the opinion, viz., that man is free by *nature*, but that in *society*, in the State—to which nevertheless he is irresistibly impelled —he must limit this natural freedom. That man is free by Nature is quite correct in one sense; viz., that he is so according to the Idea of Humanity; but we imply thereby that he is such only in virtue of his destiny—that he has an undeveloped power to become such; for the " Nature " of an object is exactly synonymous with its " Idea." But the view in question imports more than this. When man is spoken of as " free by Nature," the mode of his existence as well as his destiny is implied. His merely natural and primary condition is intended. In this sense a " state of Nature " is assumed in which mankind at large are in the possession of their natural rights with the unconstrained exercise and enjoyment of their freedom. This assumption is not indeed raised to the dignity of the historical fact; it would indeed be difficult, were the attempt seriously made, to point out any such condition as actually existing, or as having ever occurred. Examples of a savage state of life can be pointed out, but they are marked by brutal passions and deeds of violence; while, however rude and simple their conditions, they involve social arrangements which (to use the common phrase) *restrain* freedom. That assumption is one of those nebulous images which theory produces; an idea which it cannot avoid originating, but which it fathers upon real existence, without sufficient historical justification.

What we find such a state of Nature to be in actual experience, answers exactly to the Idea of a *merely* natural condition. Freedom as the *ideal* of that which is original and natural, does not exist *as original and natural*. Rather must it be first sought out and won; and that by an incalculable medial discipline of the intellectual and moral powers. The state of Nature is, therefore, predominantly that of injustice and violence, of untamed natural impulses, of inhuman deeds and feelings. Limitation is certainly produced by Society and the State, but it is a limitation of the mere brute emotions and rude instincts; as also, in a more advanced stage of culture, of the premeditated self-will of caprice and passion. This kind of constraint is part of the instrumentality by which only, the consciousness of Freedom and the desire for its attainment, in its true—that is Rational and Ideal form—can be obtained. To the Ideal of Freedom, Law and Morality are indispensably requisite; and they are in and for themselves, universal existences, objects and aims; which are discovered only by the activity of thought, separating itself from the merely sensuous, and developing itself, in opposition thereto; and which must on the other hand, be introduced into and incorporated with the originally sensuous will, and that contrarily to its natural inclination. The perpetually recurring misapprehension of Freedom consists in regarding that term only in its *formal*, subjective sense, abstracted from its essential objects and aims; thus a constraint put upon impulse, desire, passion—pertaining to the particular individual as such—a limitation of caprice and self-will is regarded as a fettering of Freedom. We should on the contrary look upon such limitation as the indispensable proviso of emancipation. Society and the State are the very conditions in which Freedom is realized.

We must notice a second view, contravening the principle of the development of moral relations into a legal form. The *patriarchal* condition is regarded—either in reference to the entire race of man, or to some branches of it—as exclusively that condition of things, in which the legal element is combined with a due recognition of the moral and emotional parts of our nature; and in which justice as united with these, truly and really influences the intercourse of the social units. The basis of the patriarchal condition is the family relation; which develops the *primary* form of conscious morality, succeeded by that of the State as its *second* phase. The patriarchal condition is one of transition, in which the family has already advanced to the position of a race or people; where the union, therefore, has already ceased to be simply a bond of love and confidence,

and has become one of plighted service. We must first examine
the ethical principle of the Family. The Family may be reckoned as virtually a single person; since its members have either
mutually surrendered their individual personality, (and consequently their legal position towards each other, with the rest of
their particular interests and desires) as in the case of the
Parents; or have not yet attained such an independent personality—(the Children—who are primarily in that merely
natural condition already mentioned). They live, therefore, in
a unity of feeling, love, confidence, and faith in each other. And
in a relation of natural love, the one individual has the consciousness of himself in the consciousness of the other; he lives
out of self; and in this mutual self-renunciation each regains
the life that had been virtually transferred to the other; gains,
in fact, that other's existence and his own, as involved with that
other. The farther interests connected with the necessities and
external concerns of life, as well as the development that has
to take place within their circle, *i.e.* of the children, constitute
a common object for the members of the Family. The Spirit
of the Family—the Penates—form one substantial being, as
much as the Spirit of a People in the State; and morality in
both cases consists in a feeling, a consciousness, and a will, not
limited to individual personality and interest, but embracing
the common interests of the members generally. But this
unity is in the case of the Family essentially one of *feeling;* not
advancing beyond the limits of the merely *natural.* The piety
of the Family relation should be respected in the highest degree
by the State; by its means the State obtains as its members
individuals who are already moral (for as mere *persons* they are
not) and who in uniting to form a state bring with them that
sound basis of a political edifice—the capacity of feeling one
with a Whole. But the expansion of the Family to a patriarchal
unity carries us beyond the ties of blood-relationship—the simply natural elements of that basis; and outside of these limits
the members of the community must enter upon the position
of independent personality. A review of the patriarchal condition, *in extenso*, would lead us to give special attention to the
Theocratical Constitution. The head of the patriarchal clan
is also its priest. If the Family in its general relations, is not
yet separated from civic society and the state, the separation of
religion from it has also not yet taken place; and so much the

less since the piety of the hearth is itself a profoundly subjective state of feeling.

We have considered two aspects of Freedom,—the objective and the subjective; if, therefore, Freedom is asserted to consist in the individuals of a State all agreeing in its arrangements, it is evident that only the subjective aspect is regarded. The natural inference from this principle is, that no law can be valid without the approval of all. This difficulty is attempted to be obviated by the decision that the minority must yield to the majority; the majority therefore bear the sway. But long ago J. J. Rousseau remarked, that in that case there would be no longer freedom, for the will of the *minority* would cease to be respected. At the Polish Diet each single member had to give his consent before any political step could be taken; and this kind of freedom it was that ruined the State. Besides, it is a dangerous and false prejudice, that the People *alone* have reason and insight, and know what justice is; for each popular faction may represent itself as the People, and the question as to what constitutes the State is one of advanced science, and not of popular decision.

If the principle of regard for the individual will is recognized as the only basis of political liberty, viz., that nothing should be done by or for the State to which all the members of the body politic have not given their sanction, we have, properly speaking, no *Constitution*. The only arrangement that would be necessary, would be, first, a centre having no *will* of its own, but which should take into consideration what appeared to be the necessities of the State; and, secondly, a contrivance for calling the members of the State together, for taking the votes, and for performing the arithmetical operations of reckoning and comparing the number of votes for the different propositions, and thereby deciding upon them. The State is an *abstraction*, having even its generic existence in its citizens; but it is an actuality, and its simply generic existence must embody itself in individual will and activity. The want of government and political administration in general is felt; this necessitates the selection and separation from the rest of those who have to take the helm in political affairs, to decide concerning them, and to give orders to other citizens, with a view to the execution of their plans. If *e.g.* even the people in a Democracy resolve on a war, a general must head the army. It is only by a Constitution that the *abstraction*—the State—attains life and reality; but this involves the distinction between those who command and those who obey.—Yet obedience seems inconsistent with liberty, and those who command appear to do the very opposite of that which the fundamental idea of the State, viz. that of Freedom, requires. It is, however, urged that—though the distinction between commanding and obeying is absolutely necessary, because affairs could not go on without it—and indeed this seems only a compulsory limitation, external to and even contravening freedom in the abstract—the constitution should be at least so framed, that the citizens may obey as little as possible, and the smallest modicum of free volition be left to the commands of the superiors;—that the substance of that for which subordination is necessary, even in its most important bearings, should be decided and resolved on by the People—by the will of many or of all the citizens; though it is supposed to be thereby provided that the State should be possessed of vigor and strength as a reality—an individual unity.—The primary consideration is, then, the distinction between the governing and the governed, and the political constitutions in the abstract have been rightly divided into Monarchy, Aristocracy, and Democracy; which gives occasion, however, to the remark that Monarchy itself must be further divided into Despotism and Monarchy proper; that in all the divisions to which the leading Idea gives rise, only the generic character is to be made prominent—it being not intended thereby that the particular category under review should be exhausted as a Form, Order, or Kind in its *concrete* development. But especially it must be observed, that the above-mentioned divisions admit of a multitude of particular modifications—not only such as lie within the limits of those classes themselves—but also such as are mixtures of several of these essentially distinct classes, and which are consequently misshapen, unstable, and inconsistent forms. In such a collision, the concerning question is, what is the *best constitution;* that is, by what arrangement, organization, or mechanism of the power of the State its object can be most surely attained. This object may indeed be variously understood; for instance, as the calm enjoyment of life on the part of the citizens, or as Universal Happiness. Such aims have suggested the so-called Ideals of Constitutions, and—as a particular branch of the subject—Ideals of the Education of Princes (Fenelon), or of the governing body—the aristocracy at large (Plato); for the chief point they treat of is the condition of those subjects who stand at the head of affairs: and in these Ideals the concrete details of political organization are not at all considered. The inquiry into the best constitution is frequently treated as if not only the theory were an affair of subjective independent conviction, but as if the introduction of a constitution recognized as the best—or as superior to others—could be the result of a resolve adopted in this theoretical manner; as if the form of a constitution were a matter of free choice, determined by nothing else but reflection. Of this artless fashion was that deliberation—not indeed of the Persian *people*, but of the Persian *grandees*, who had conspired to overthrow the pseudo-Smerdis and the Magi, after their undertaking had succeeded, and when there was no scion of the royal family living—as to what constitution they should introduce into Persia; and Herodotus gives an equally naïve account of this deliberation.

In the present day, the Constitution of a country and people is not represented as so entirely dependent on free and deliberate choice. The fundamental but abstractly (and therefore imperfectly) entertained conception of Freedom, has resulted in the Republic being very generally regarded—in *theory*—as the only just and true political constitution. Many even, who occupy elevated official positions under monarchical constitutions—so far from being opposed to this idea—are actually its supporters; only they see that such a constitution, though the best, cannot be realized under all circumstances; and that —while men are what they are—we must be satisfied with less freedom; the monarchical constitution—under the given circumstances, and the present moral condition of the people— being even regarded as the most advantageous. In this view also, the necessity of a particular constitution is made to depend on the condition of the people in such a way as if the latter were non-essential and accidental. This representation is founded on the distinction which the reflective understanding makes between an idea and the corresponding reality; holding to an abstract and consequently untrue idea; not grasping it in its completeness, or—which is virtually, though not in point of form, the same—not taking a concrete view of a people and a state. We shall have to show further on, that the constitution

adopted by a people makes one substance—one spirit—with its
religion, its art and philosophy, or, at least, with its conceptions and thoughts—its culture generally; not to expatiate
upon the additional influences, *ab extrâ*, of climate, of neighbors, of its place in the World. A State is an individual totality,
of which you cannot select any particular side, although a
supremely important one, such as its political constitution;
and deliberate and decide respecting it in that isolated form.
Not only is that constitution most intimately connected with
and dependent on those other spiritual forces; but the form
of the entire moral and intellectual individuality—comprising
all the forces it embodies—is only a step in the development of
the grand Whole—with its place preappointed in the process;
a fact which gives the highest sanction to the constitution in
question, and establishes its absolute necessity.—The origin
of a state involves imperious lordship on the one hand, instinctive submission on the other. But even obedience—lordly
power, and the fear inspired by a ruler—in itself implies some
degree of voluntary connection. Even in barbarous states this
is the case; it is not the isolated will of individuals that prevails; individual pretensions are relinquished, and the general
will is the essential bond of political union. This unity of the
general and the particular is the Idea itself, manifesting itself
as a *state*, and which subsequently undergoes further development within itself. The abstract yet necessitated process in the
development of truly independent states is as follows:—They
begin with regal power, whether of patriarchal or military origin. In the next phase, particularity and individuality assert
themselves in the form of Aristocracy and Democracy. Lastly,
we have the subjection of these separate interests to a single
power; but which can be absolutely none other than one outside of which those spheres have an independent position, viz.,
the Monarchical. Two phases of royalty, therefore, must be
distinguished—a primary and a secondary one. This process
is necessitated, so that the form of government assigned to
a particular stage of development *must* present itself: it is
therefore no matter of choice, but is that form which is adapted
to the spirit of the people.

In a Constitution the main feature of interest is the self-
development of the *rational,* that is, the *political* condition of
a people; the setting free of the successive elements of the

Idea: so that the several powers in the State manifest themselves as separate—attain their appropriate and special perfection—and yet in this independent condition, work together for
one object, and are held together by it—*i.e.,* form an organic
whole. The State is thus the embodiment of rational freedom,
realizing and recognizing itself in an objective form. For its
objectivity consists in this—that its successive stages are not
merely ideal, but are present in an appropriate reality; and
that in their separate and several working, they are absolutely
merged in that agency by which the totality—the soul—the
individuate unity—is produced, and of which it is the result.

The State is the Idea of Spirit in the external manifestation
of human Will and its Freedom. It is to the State, therefore,
that change in the aspect of History indissolubly attaches itself;
and the successive phases of the Idea manifest themselves in it
as distinct political *principles.* The Constitutions under which
World-Historical peoples have reached their culmination, are
peculiar to them; and therefore do not present a generally applicable political basis. Were it otherwise, the differences of
similar constitutions would consist only in a peculiar method
of expanding and developing that generic basis; whereas they
really originate in diversity of principle. From the comparison
therefore of the political institutions of the ancient World-Historical peoples, it so happens, that for the most recent principle
of a Constitution—for the principle of our own times—nothing
(so to speak) can be learned. In science and art it is quite
otherwise; *e.g.,* the ancient philosophy is so decidedly the basis
of the modern, that it is inevitably contained in the latter, and
constitutes its basis. In this case the relation is that of a continuous development of the same structure, whose foundation-
stone, walls, and roof have remained what they were. In Art,
the Greek itself, in its original form, furnishes us the best
models. But in regard to political constitution, it is quite otherwise: here the Ancient and the Modern have not their essential
principle in common. Abstract definitions and dogmas respecting just government—importing that intelligence and virtue
ought to bear sway—are, indeed, common to both. But nothing is so absurd as to look to Greeks, Romans, or Orientals,
for models for the political arrangements of our time. From
the East may be derived beautiful pictures of a patriarchal
condition, of paternal government, and of devotion to it on

the part of peoples; from Greeks and Romans, descriptions of popular liberty. Among the latter we find the idea of a Free Constitution admitting all the citizens to a share in deliberations and resolves respecting the affairs and laws of the Commonwealth. In our times, too, this is its general acceptation; only with this modification, that—since our states are so large, and there are so many of "the Many," the latter—direct action being impossible—should by the indirect method of elective substitution express their concurrence with resolves affecting the common weal; that is, that for legislative purposes generally, the people should be represented by deputies. The so-called Representative Constitution is that form of government with which we connect the idea of a free constitution; and this notion has become a rooted prejudice. On this theory People and Government are separated. But there is a perversity in this antithesis; an ill-intentioned *ruse* designed to insinuate that the People are the totality of the State. Besides, the basis of this view is the principle of isolated individuality—the absolute validity of the subjective will—a dogma which we have already investigated. The great point is, that Freedom in its Ideal conception has not subjective will and caprice for its principle, but the recognition of the universal will; and that the process by which Freedom is realized is the free development of its successive stages. The subjective will is a merely formal determination—a *carte blanche*—not including what it is that is willed. Only the *rational* will is that universal principle which independently determines and unfolds its own being, and develops its successive elemental phases as organic members. Of this Gothic-cathedral architecture the ancients knew nothing.

At an earlier stage of the discussion we established the two elemental considerations: first, the *idea* of freedom as the absolute and final aim; secondly, the *means* for realizing it, *i.e.*, the subjective side of knowledge and will, with its life, movement, and activity. We then recognized the State as the moral Whole and the Reality of Freedom, and consequently as the objective unity of these two elements. For although we make this distinction into two aspects for our consideration, it must be remarked that they are intimately connected; and that their connection is involved in the idea of each when examined separately. We have, on the one hand, recognized the Idea in

the definite form of Freedom conscious of and willing itself—
having itself alone as its object: involving at the same time,
the pure and simple Idea of Reason, and likewise, that which
we have called subject—self-consciousness—Spirit actually existing in the World. If, on the other hand, we consider Subjectivity, we find that subjective knowledge and will is Thought.
But by the very act of thoughtful cognition and volition, I will
the universal object—the substance of absolute Reason. We
observe, therefore, an essential union between the objective side
—the Idea—and the subjective side—the personality that conceives and wills it.—The *objective* existence of this union is the
State, which is therefore the basis and centre of the other concrete elements of the life of a people—of Art, of Law, of Morals, of Religion, of Science. All the activity of Spirit has only
this object—the becoming conscious of this union, *i.e.*, of its
own Freedom. Among the forms of this conscious union *Religion* occupies the highest position. In it, Spirit—rising above
the limitations of temporal and secular existence—becomes
conscious of the Absolute Spirit, and in this consciousness of
the self-existent Being, renounces its individual interest; it
lays this aside in Devotion—a state of mind in which it refuses
to occupy itself any longer with the limited and particular.
By Sacrifice man expresses his renunciation of his property,
his will, his individual feelings. The religious concentration
of the soul appears in the form of feeling; it nevertheless
passes also into reflection; a form of worship (*cultus*) is a
result of reflection. The second form of the union of the objective and subjective in the human spirit is *Art*. This advances farther into the realm of the actual and sensuous than
Religion. In its noblest walk it is occupied with representing,
not indeed, the Spirit of God, but certainly the Form of God;
and in its secondary aims, that which is divine and spiritual
generally. Its office is to render visible the Divine; presenting
it to the imaginative and intuitive faculty. But the True is the
object not only of conception and feeling, as in Religion—and
of intuition, as in Art—but also of the thinking faculty; and
this gives us the third form of the union in question—*Philosophy*. This is consequently the highest, freest, and wisest
phase. Of course we are not intending to investigate these
three phases here; they have only suggested themselves in

virtue of their occupying the same general ground as the object here considered—the *State*.

The general principle which manifests itself and becomes an object of consciousness in the State—the form under which all that the State includes is brought—is the whole of that cycle of phenomena which constitutes the *culture* of a nation. But the definite *substance* that receives the form of universality, and exists in that concrete reality which is the State—is the Spirit of the People itself. The actual State is animated by this spirit, in all its particular affairs—its Wars, Institutions, etc. But man must also attain a conscious realization of this his Spirit and essential nature, and of his original identity with it. For we said that morality is the identity of the *subjective* or *personal* with the *universal* will. Now the mind must give itself an express consciousness of this; and the focus of this knowledge is *Religion*. Art and Science are only various aspects and forms of the same substantial being.—In considering Religion, the chief point of inquiry is, whether it recognizes the True—the Idea—only in its separate, abstract form, or in its true unity; in *separation*—God being represented in an abstract form as the Highest Being, Lord of Heaven and Earth, living in a remote region far from human actualities—or in its *unity*—God, as Unity of the Universal and Individual; the Individual itself assuming the aspect of positive and real existence in the idea of the Incarnation. Religion is the sphere in which a nation gives itself the definition of that which it regards as the True. A definition contains everything that belongs to the essence of an object; reducing its nature to its simple characteristic predicate, as a mirror for every predicate —the generic soul pervading all its details. The conception of God, therefore, constitutes the general basis of a people's character.

In this aspect, religion stands in the closest connection with the political principle. Freedom can exist only where Individuality is recognized as having its positive and real existence in the Divine Being. The connection may be further explained thus:—Secular existence, as merely temporal—occupied with particular interests—is consequently only relative and unauthorized; and receives its validity only in as far as the universal soul that pervades it—its principle—receives absolute validity; which it cannot have unless it is recognized as the definite manifestation, the phenomenal existence of the Divine Essence. On this account it is that the State rests on Religion. We hear this often repeated in our times, though for the most part nothing further is meant than that individual subjects as God-fearing men would be more disposed and ready to perform their duty; since obedience to King and Law so naturally follows in the train of reverence for God. This reverence, indeed, since it exalts the general over the special, may even turn upon the latter—become fanatical—and work with incendiary and destructive violence against the State, its institutions, and arrangements. Religious feeling, therefore, it is thought, should be sober—kept in a certain degree of coolness—that it may not storm against and bear down that which should be defended and preserved by it. The possibility of such a catastrophe is at least latent in it.

While, however, the correct sentiment is adopted, that the State is based on Religion, the position thus assigned to Religion supposes the State already to exist; and that subsequently, in order to maintain it, Religion must be brought into it—in buckets and bushels as it were—and impressed upon people's hearts. It is quite true that men must be trained to religion, but not as to something whose existence has yet to begin. For in affirming that the State is based on Religion —that it has its roots in it—we virtually assert that the former has proceeded from the latter; and that this derivation is going on now and will always continue; *i.e.,* the principles of the State must be regarded as valid in and for themselves, which can only be in so far as they are recognized as determinate manifestations of the Divine Nature. The form of Religion, therefore, decides that of the State and its constitution. The latter actually originated in the particular religion adopted by the nation; so that, in fact, the Athenian or the Roman State was possible only in connection with the specific form of Heathenism existing among the respective peoples; just as a Catholic State has a spirit and constitution different from that of a Protestant one.

If that outcry—that urging and striving for the implantation of Religion in the community—were an utterance of anguish and a call for help, as it often seems to be, expressing the danger of religion having vanished, or being about to vanish entirely from the State—that would be fearful indeed—

worse, in fact, than this outcry supposes; for it implies the belief in a resource against the evil, viz., the implantation and inculcation of religion; whereas religion is by no means a thing to be so produced; its *self-production* (and there can be no other) lies much deeper.

Another and opposite folly which we meet with in our time, is that of pretending to invent and carry out political constitutions independently of religion. The Catholic confession, although sharing the Christian name with the Protestant, does not concede to the State an inherent Justice and Morality—a concession which in the Protestant principle is fundamental. This tearing away of the political morality of the Constitution from its natural connection, is necessary to the genius of that religion, inasmuch as it does not recognize Justice and Morality as independent and substantial. But thus excluded from intrinsic worth—torn away from their last refuge—the sanctuary of conscience—the calm retreat where religion has its abode—the principles and institutions of political legislation are destitute of a real centre, to the same degree as they are compelled to remain abstract and indefinite.

Summing up what has been said of the State, we find that we have been led to call its vital principle, as actuating the individuals who compose it—Morality. The State, its laws, its arrangements, constitute the rights of its members; its natural features, its mountains, air, and waters, are *their* country, their fatherland, their outward material property; the history of this State, *their* deeds; what their ancestors have produced, belongs to them and lives in their memory. All is their possession, just as they are possessed by it; for it constitutes their existence, their being.

Their imagination is occupied with the ideas thus presented, while the adoption of these laws, and of a fatherland so conditioned is the expression of their will. It is this matured totality which thus constitutes *one* Being, the spirit of *one* People. To it the individual members belong; each unit is the Son of his Nation, and at the same time—in as far as the State to which he belongs is undergoing development—the Son of his Age. None remains behind it, still less advances beyond it. This spiritual Being (the Spirit of his Time) is his; he is a representative of it; it is that in which he originated, and in which he lives. Among the Athenians the word Athens had a double import; suggesting primarily, a complex of political institutions, but no less, in the second place, that Goddess who represented the Spirit of the People and its unity.

This Spirit of a People is a *determinate* and particular Spirit, and is, as just stated, further modified by the degree of its historical development. This Spirit, then, constitutes the basis and substance of those other forms of a nation's consciousness, which have been noticed. For Spirit in its self-consciousness must become an object of contemplation to itself, and objectivity involves, in the first instance, the rise of differences which make up a total of distinct spheres of objective spirit; in the same way as the Soul exists only as the complex of its faculties, which in their form of concentration in a simple unity produce that Soul. It is thus *One Individuality* which, presented in its essence as God, is honored and enjoyed in *Religion;* which is exhibited as an object of sensuous contemplation in *Art;* and is apprehended as an intellectual conception, in *Philosophy.* In virtue of the original identity of their essence, purport, and object, these various forms are inseparably united with the Spirit of the State. Only in connection with this particular religion, can this particular political constitution exist; just as in such or such a State, such or such a Philosophy or order of Art.

The remark next in order is, that each particular National genius is to be treated as only One Individual in the process of Universal History. For that history is the exhibition of the divine, absolute development of Spirit in its highest forms— that gradation by which it attains its truth and consciousness of itself. The forms which these grades of progress assume are the characteristic " National Spirits " of History; the peculiar tenor of their moral life, of their Government, their Art, Religion, and Science. To realize these grades is the boundless impulse of the World-Spirit—the goal of its irresistible urging; for this division into organic members, and the full development of each, is its Idea.—Universal History is exclusively occupied with showing how Spirit comes to a recognition and adoption of the Truth: the dawn of knowledge appears; it begins to discover salient principles, and at last it arrives at full consciousness.

Having, therefore, learned the abstract characteristics of the nature of Spirit, the means which it uses to realize its

Idea, and the shape assumed by it in its complete realization in phenomenal existence—namely, the State—nothing further remains for this introductory section to contemplate but

III. *The course of the World's History.*—The mutations which history presents have been long characterized in the general, as an advance to something better, more perfect. The changes that take place in Nature—how infinitely manifold soever they may be—exhibit only a perpetually self-repeating cycle; in Nature there happens "nothing new under the sun," and the multiform play of its phenomena so far induces a feeling of *ennui;* only in those changes which take place in the region of Spirit does anything new arise. This peculiarity in the world of mind has indicated in the case of man an altogether different destiny from that of merely natural objects—in which we find always one and the same stable character, to which all change reverts;—namely, a *real* capacity for change, and that for the better—an impulse of *perfectibility.* This principle, which reduces change itself under a law, has met with an unfavorable reception from religions—such as the Catholic—and from States claiming as their just right a stereotyped, or at least a stable position. If the mutability of worldly things in general—political constitutions, for instance—is conceded, either Religion (as the Religion of *Truth*) is absolutely excepted, or the difficulty escaped by ascribing changes, revolutions, and abrogations of immaculate theories and institutions, to accidents or imprudence—but principally to the levity and evil passions of man. The principle of Perfectibility indeed is almost as indefinite a term as mutability in general; it is without scope or goal, and has no standard by which to estimate the changes in question: the improved, more perfect, state of things towards which it professedly tends is altogether undetermined.

The principle of *Development* involves also the existence of a latent germ of being—a capacity or potentiality striving to realize itself. This formal conception finds actual existence in Spirit; which has the History of the World for its theatre, its possession, and the sphere of its realization. It is not of such a nature as to be tossed to and fro amid the superficial play of accidents, but is rather the absolute arbiter of things; entirely unmoved by contingencies, which, indeed, it applies and manages for its own purposes. Development, however, is also a property of organized natural objects. Their existence presents itself, not as an exclusively dependent one, subjected to external changes, but as one which expands itself in virtue of an internal unchangeable principle; a simple essence—whose existence, *i.e.*, as a germ, is primarily simple—but which subsequently develops a variety of parts, that become involved with other objects, and consequently live through a continuous process of changes;—a process nevertheless, that results in the very contrary of change, and is even transformed into a *vis conservatrix* of the organic principle, and the form embodying it. Thus the organized *individuum* produces itself; it expands itself *actually* to what it was always *potentially.*—So Spirit is only that which it attains by its own efforts; it makes itself *actually* what it always was *potentially.*—That development (of *natural organisms*) takes place in a direct, unopposed, unhindered manner. Between the Idea and its realization—the essential constitution of the original germ and the conformity to it of the existence derived from it—no disturbing influence can intrude. But in relation to Spirit it is quite otherwise. The realization of *its* Idea is mediated by consciousness and will; these very faculties are, in the first instance, sunk in their primary *merely* natural life; the first object and goal of their striving is the realization of their merely natural destiny—but which, since it is Spirit that animates it, is possessed of vast attractions and displays great power and [moral] richness. Thus Spirit is at war with itself; it has to overcome itself as its most formidable obstacle. That development which in the sphere of Nature is a peaceful growth, is in that of spirit, a severe, a mighty conflict with itself. What Spirit really strives for is the realization of its Ideal being; but in doing so, it hides that goal from its own vision, and is proud and well satisfied in this alienation from it.

Its expansion, therefore, does not present the harmless tranquillity of mere growth, as does that of organic life, but a stern reluctant working against itself. It exhibits, moreover, not the mere formal conception of development, but the attainment of a definite result. The goal of attainment we determined at the outset: it is Spirit in its *Completeness,* in its essential nature. *i.e.*, Freedom. This is the fundamental object, and therefore also the leading principle of the development—that whereby it receives meaning and importance (as in the Roman history, Rome is the object—consequently that which directs our consideration of the facts related) ; as, conversely, the phenomena of the process have resulted from this principle alone, and only as referred to it, possess a sense of value. There are many considerable periods in History in which this development seems to have been intermitted; in which, we might rather say, the whole enormous gain of previous culture appears to have been entirely lost; after which, unhappily, a new commencement has been necessary, made in the hope of recovering—by the assistance of some remains saved from the wreck of a former civilization, and by dint of a renewed incalculable expenditure of strength and time—one of the regions which had been an ancient possession of that civilization. We behold also *continued* processes of growth; structures and systems of culture in particular spheres, rich in kind, and well developed in every direction. The merely formal and indeterminate view of development in general can neither assign to one form of expansion superiority over the other, nor render comprehensible the object of that decay of older periods of growth; but must regard such occurrences—or, to speak more particularly, the retrocessions they exhibit—as external contingencies; and can only judge of particular modes of development from indeterminate points of view; which—since the development, as such, is all in all—are relative and not absolute goals of attainment.

Universal History exhibits the *gradation* in the development of that principle whose substantial *purport* is the consciousness of Freedom. The analysis of the successive grades, in their abstract form, belongs to Logic; in their concrete aspect to the Philosophy of Spirit. Here it is sufficient to state that the first step in the process presents that immersion of Spirit in Nature which has been already referred to; the second shows it as advancing to the consciousness of its freedom. But this initial separation from Nature is imperfect and partial, since it is derived immediately from the merely natural state, is consequently related to it, and is still encumbered with it as an essentially connected element. The third step is the elevation of the soul from this still limited and special form of freedom to its pure universal form; that state in which the spiritual essence attains the consciousness and feeling of itself. These grades are the ground-principles of the general process; but how each of them on the other hand involves within *itself* a process of formation—constituting the links in a dialectic of transition—to particularize this must be reserved for the sequel.

Here we have only to indicate that Spirit begins with a germ of infinite possibility, but *only* possibility—containing its substantial existence in an undeveloped form, as the object and goal which it reaches only in its resultant—full reality. In actual existence Progress appears as an advancing from the imperfect to the more perfect; but the former must not be understood abstractly as *only* the imperfect, but as something which involves the very opposite of itself—the so-called perfect —as a *germ* or impulse. So—reflectively, at least—*possibility* points to something destined to become actual; the Aristotelian δύναμις is also *potentia,* power and might. Thus the Imperfect, as involving its opposite, is a contradiction, which certainly exists, but which is continually annulled and solved; the instinctive movement—the inherent impulse in the life of the soul—to break through the rind of mere nature, sensuousness, and that which is alien to it, and to attain to the light of consciousness, *i.e.* to itself.

We have already made the remark how the commencement of the history of Spirit must be conceived so as to be in harmony with its Idea—in its bearing on the representations that have been made of a primitive " *natural* condition," in which freedom and justice are supposed to exist, or to have existed. This was, however, nothing more than an assumption of historical existence, conceived in the twilight of theorizing reflection. A pretension of quite another order—not a mere inference of reasoning, but making the claim of historical fact, and that supernaturally confirmed—is put forth in connection with a different view that is now widely promulgated by a certain class of speculatists. This view takes up the idea of the primitive paradisiacal conditon of man, which had been previously expanded by the Theologians, after their fashion —involving, *e.g.,* the supposition that God spoke with Adam in Hebrew—but remodelled to suit other requirements. The high authority appealed to in the first instance is the biblical narrative. But this depicts the primitive condition, partly only in the few well-known traits, but partly either as in man generically—human nature at large—or, so far as Adam is to be taken as an individual, and consequently one person—as existing and completed in *this one,* or *only in one* human pair. The

biblical account by no means justifies us in imagining a *people*,
and a historical condition of such people, existing in that primitive form; still less does it warrant us in attributing to them
the possession of a perfectly developed knowledge of God and
Nature. " Nature," so the fiction runs, " like a clear mirror of
God's creation, had originally lain revealed and transparent to
the unclouded eye of man." * Divine Truth is imagined to
have been equally manifest. It is even hinted, though left in
some degree of obscurity, that in this primary condition men
were in possession of an indefinitely extended and already expanded body of religious truths immediately revealed by God.
This theory affirms that all religions had their historical commencement in this primitive knowledge, and that they polluted
and obscured the original Truth by the monstrous creations of
error and depravity; though in all the mythologies invented
by Error, traces of that origin and of those primitive true
dogmas are supposed to be present and cognizable. An important interest, therefore, accrues to the investigation of the
history of ancient peoples, that, viz., of the endeavor to trace
their annals up to the point where such fragments of the primary revelation are to be met with in greater purity than lower
down.†

We owe to the interest which has occasioned these investigations, very much that is valuable; but this investigation bears
direct testimony against itself, for it would seem to be awaiting
the issue of an historical demonstration of that which is pre-

* Fr. von Schlegel, " Philosophy of
History," p. 91, Bohn's Standard Library.

† We have to thank this interest for
many valuable discoveries in Oriental
literature, and for a renewed study of
treasures previously known, in the department of ancient Asiatic Culture,
Mythology, Religions, and History. In
Catholic countries, where a refined literary taste prevails, Governments have
yielded to the requirements of speculative inquiry, and have felt the necessity
of allying themselves with learning and
philosophy. Eloquently and impressive-
ly has the Abbé Lamennais reckoned it
among the criteria of the true religion,
that it must be the universal—that is,
catholic—and the oldest in date; and the
Congregation has labored zealously and
diligently in France towards rendering
such assertions no longer mere pulpit
tirades and authoritative dicta, such as
were deemed sufficient formerly. The
religion of Buddha—a god-man—which
has prevailed to such an enormous extent. has especially attracted attention.
The Indian Timûrtis, as also the Chinese
abstraction of the Trinity, has furnished

clearer evidence in point of subject matter. The savans, M. Abel Remusat and
M. Saint Martin, on the one hand, have
undertaken the most meritorious investigations in the Chinese literature, with a
view to make this also a base of operations for researches in the Mongolian
and, if such were possible, in the Thibe-
tian; on the other hand, Baron von
Eckstein, in his way (*i.e.*, adopting
from Germany superficial physical conceptions and mannerisms, in the style of
Fr. v. Schlegel, though with more geniality than the latter) in his periodical, " Le
Catholique "—has furthered the cause of
that primitive Catholicism generally, and
in particular has gained for the savans
of the Congregation the support of the
Government; so that it has even set on
foot expeditions to the East, in order to
discover there treasures still concealed;
(from which further disclosures have
been anticipated, respecting profound
theological questions. particularly on the
higher antiquity and sources of Buddhism), and with a view to promote the interests of Catholicism by this circuitous
but scientifically interesting method.

supposed by it as historically established. That advanced condition of the knowledge of God, and of other scientific, *e.g.*
astronomical knowledge (such as has been falsely attributed to
the Hindoos); and the assertion that such a condition occurred
at the very beginning of History—or that the religions of
various nations were traditionally derived from it, and have
developed themselves in degeneracy and depravation (as is represented in the rudely-conceived so-called " Emanation System ");—all these are suppositions which neither have, nor—
if we may contrast with their arbitrary subjective origin, the
true conception of History—can attain historical confirmation.

The only consistent and worthy method which philosophical
investigation can adopt, is to take up History where Rationality
begins to manifest itself in the actual conduct of the World's
affairs (not where it is merely an undeveloped potentiality)—
where a condition of things is present in which it realizes itself
in consciousness, will and action. The inorganic existence of
Spirit—that of abstract Freedom—unconscious *torpidity* in respect to good and evil (and consequently to laws), or, if we
please to term it so, " blessed ignorance "—is itself not a subject
of History. *Natural,* and at the same time *religious* morality, is
the piety of the *family.* In this social relation, morality consists
in the members behaving towards each other *not as individuals*
—possessing an independent will; not as persons. The Family
therefore, is excluded from that process of development in which
History takes its rise. But when this self-involved spiritual
Unity steps beyond this circle of feeling and natural love, and
first attains the consciousness of personality, we have that dark,
dull centre of indifference, in which neither Nature nor Spirit
is open and transparent; and for which Nature and Spirit can
become open and transparent only by means of a further process—a very lengthened culture of that Will at length become
self-conscious. Consciousness alone is clearness; and is that
alone for which God (or any other existence) can be revealed.
In its true form—in absolute universality—nothing can be
manifested except to consciousness made percipient of it.
Freedom is nothing but the recognition and adoption of such
universal substantial objects as Right and Law, and the production of a reality that is accordant with them—the State. Nations may have passed a long life before arriving at this their
destination, and during this period, they may have attained

considerable culture in some directions. This ante-historical period—consistently with what has been said—lies out of our plan; whether a real history followed it, or the peoples in question never attained a political constitution.—It is a great discovery in history—as of a new world—which has been made within rather more than the last twenty years, respecting the Sanscrit and the connection of the European languages with it. In particular, the connection of the German and Indian peoples has been demonstrated, with as much certainty as such subjects allow of. Even at the present time we know of peoples which scarcely form a society, much less a State, but that have been long known as existing; while with regard to others, which in their advanced condition excite our especial interest, tradition reaches beyond the record of the founding of the State, and they experienced many changes prior to that epoch. In the connection just referred to, between the languages of nations so widely separated, we have a result before us, which proves the diffusion of those nations from Asia as a centre, and the so dissimilar development of what had been originally related, as an incontestable fact; not *as* an inference deduced by that favorite method of combining, and reasoning from, circumstances grave and trivial, which has already enriched and will continue to enrich history with so many fictions given out as facts. But that apparently so extensive range of events lies beyond the pale of history; in fact preceded it.

In our language the term *History* * unites the objective with the subjective side, and denotes quite as much the *historia rerum gestarum,* as the *res gestæ* themselves; on the other hand it comprehends not less what has *happened,* than the *narration* of what has happened. This union of the two meanings we must regard as of a higher order than mere outward accident; we must suppose historical narrations to have appeared contemporaneously with historical deeds and events. It is an internal vital principle common to both that produces them synchronously. Family memorials, patriarchal traditions, have an interest confined to the family and the clan. The uniform course of events which such a condition implies, is no subject of serious remembrance; though distinct transactions or turns of fortune, may rouse Mnemosyne to form conceptions of them—in the same way as love and the religious emotions provoke imagina-

* German, " Geschichte " from " Geschehen," to happen.—Ed.

tion to give shape to a previously formless impulse. But it is the State which first presents subject-matter that is not only *adapted* to the prose of History, but involves the production of such history in the very progress of its own being. Instead of merely subjective mandates on the part of government—sufficing for the needs of the moment—a community that is acquiring a stable existence, and exalting itself into a State, requires formal commands and laws—comprehensive and universally binding prescriptions; and thus produces a record as well as an interest concerned with intelligent, definite—and, in their results—lasting transactions and occurrences; on which Mnemosyne, for the behoof of the perennial object of the formation and constitution of the State, is impelled to confer perpetuity. Profound sentiments generally, such as that of love, as also religious intuition and its conceptions, are in themselves complete—constantly present and satisfying; but that outward existence of a political constitution which is enshrined in its rational laws and customs, is an *imperfect* Present; and cannot be thoroughly understood without a knowledge of the past.

The periods—whether we suppose them to be centuries or millennia—that were passed by nations before history was written among them—and which may have been filled with revolutions, nomadic wanderings, and the strangest mutations—are on that very account destitute of *objective* history, because they present no *subjective* history, no annals. We need not suppose that the records of such periods have accidentally perished; rather, because they were not possible, do we find them wanting. Only in a State cognizant of Laws, can distinct transactions take place, accompanied by such a clear consciousness of them as supplies the ability and suggests the necessity of an enduring record. It strikes every one, in beginning to form an acquaintance with the treasures of Indian literature, that a land so rich in intellectual products, and those of the profoundest order of thought, has no History; and in this respect contrasts most strongly with China—an empire possessing one so remarkable, one going back to the most ancient times. India has not only ancient books relating to religion, and splendid poetical productions, but also ancient codes; the existence of which latter kind of literature has been mentioned as a condition necessary to the origination of History—and yet History

itself is not found. But in that country the impulse of organization, in beginning to develop social distinctions, was immediately petrified in the merely natural classification according
to *castes;* so that although the laws concern themselves with
civil rights, they make even these dependent on natural distinctions; and are especially occupied with determining the
relations (Wrongs rather than Rights) of those classes towards
each other, *i.e.* the privileges of the higher over the lower. Consequently, the element of morality is banished from the pomp
of Indian life and from its political institutions. Where that
iron bondage of distinctions derived from nature prevails, the
connection of society is nothing but wild arbitrariness—transient activity—or rather the play of violent emotion without
any goal of advancement or development. Therefore no intelligent reminiscence, no object for Mnemosyne presents itself;
and imagination—confused though profound—expatiates in a
region, which, to be capable of History, must have had an aim
within the domain of Reality, and, at the same time, of substantial Freedom.

Since such are the conditions indispensable to a history, it
has happened that the growth of Families to Clans, of Clans to
Peoples, and their local diffusion consequent upon this numer-
ical increase—a series of facts which itself suggests so many
instances of social complication, war, revolution, and ruin—a
process which is so rich in interest, and so comprehensive in
extent—has occurred without giving rise to History; moreover, that the extension and organic growth of the empire of
articulate sounds has itself remained voiceless and dumb—a
stealthy, unnoticed advance. It is a fact revealed by philological monuments, that languages, during a rude condition of
the nations that have spoken them, have been very highly developed; that the human understanding occupied this theoretical region with great ingenuity and completeness. For Grammar, in its extended and consistent form, is the work of thought,
which makes its categories distinctly visible therein. It is,
moreover, a fact, that with advancing social and political civilization, this systematic completeness of intelligence suffers
attrition, and language thereupon becomes poorer and ruder:
a singular phenomenon—that the progress towards a more
highly intellectual condition, while expanding and cultivating
rationality, should disregard that intelligent amplitude and ex-

pressiveness—should find it an obstruction and contrive to do without it. Speech is the act of theoretic intelligence in a special sense; it is its *external* manifestation. Exercises of memory and imagination without language, are direct, [non-speculative] manifestations. But this act of theoretic intelligence itself, as also its subsequent development, and the more concrete class of facts connected with it—viz. the spreading of peoples over the earth, their separation from each other, their comminglings and wanderings—remain involved in the obscurity of a voiceless past. They are not acts of Will becoming self-conscious—of Freedom, mirroring itself in a phenomenal form, and creating for itself a proper reality. Not partaking of this element of substantial, veritable existence, those nations—notwithstanding the development of language among them—never advanced to the possession of a *history*. The rapid growth of language, and the progress and dispersion of Nations, assume importance and interest for concrete Reason, only when they have come in contact with States, or begin to form political constitutions themselves.

After these remarks, relating to the form of the *commencement* of the World's History, and to that ante-historical period which must be excluded from it, we have to state the direction of its course: though here only formally. The further definition of the subject in the concrete, comes under the head of arrangement.

Universal history—as already demonstrated—shows the development of the consciousness of Freedom on the part of Spirit, and of the consequent realization of that Freedom. This development implies a gradation—a series of increasingly adequate expressions or manifestations of Freedom, which result from its Idea. The logical, and—as still more prominent —the *dialectical* nature of the Idea in general, viz. that it is self-determined—that it assumes successive forms which it successively transcends; and by this very process of transcending its earlier stages, gains an affirmative, and, in fact, a richer and more concrete shape;—this necessity of its nature, and the necessary series of pure abstract forms which the Idea successively assumes—is exhibited in the department of *Logic*. Here we need adopt only one of its results, viz. that every step in the process, as differing from any other, has its determinate peculiar principle. In history this principle is idiosyncrasy of Spirit—

peculiar National Genius. It is within the limitations of this idiosyncrasy that the spirit of the nation, concretely manifested, expresses every aspect of its consciousness and will—the whole cycle of its realization. Its religion, its polity, its ethics, its legislation, and even its science, art, and mechanical skill, all bear its stamp. These special peculiarities find their key in that common peculiarity—the particular principle that characterizes a people; as, on the other hand, in the facts which History presents in detail, that common characteristic principle may be detected. That such or such a specific quality constitutes the peculiar genius of a people, is the element of our inquiry which must be derived from experience, and historically proved. To accomplish this, pre-supposes not only a disciplined faculty of abstraction, but an intimate acquaintance with the Idea. The investigator must be familiar *à priori* (if we like to call it so), with the whole circle of conceptions to which the principles in question belong—just as Keppler (to name the most illustrious example in this mode of philosophizing) must have been familiar *à priori* with ellipses, with cubes and squares, and with ideas of their relations, before he could discover, from the empirical data, those immortal " Laws " of his, which are none other than forms of thought pertaining to those classes of conceptions. He who is unfamiliar with the science that embraces these abstract elementary conceptions, is as little capable —though he may have gazed on the firmament and the motions of the celestial bodies for a lifetime—of *understanding* those Laws, as of *discovering* them. From this want of acquaintance with the ideas that relate to the development of Freedom, proceed a part of those objections which are brought against the philosophical consideration of a science usually regarded as one of mere experience; the so-called *à priori* method, and the attempt to insinuate ideas into the empirical data of history, being the chief points in the indictment. Where this deficiency exists, such conceptions appear alien—not lying within the object of investigation. To minds whose training has been narrow and merely subjective—which have not an acquaintance and familiarity with ideas—they are something strange—not embraced in the notion and conception of the subject which their limited intellect forms. Hence the statement that Philosophy does not understand such sciences. It must, indeed, allow that it has not that kind of Understanding which is the prevailing one in the domain of those sciences, that it does not proceed according to the categories of such Understanding, but according to the categories of *Reason*— though at the same time recognizing that Understanding, and its true value and position. It must be observed that in this very process of scientific *Understanding*, it is of importance that the essential should be distinguished and brought into relief in contrast with the so-called non-essential. But in order to render this possible, we must know what *is essential;* and that is —in view of the History of the World in general—the Consciousness of Freedom, and the phases which this consciousness assumes in developing itself. The bearing of historical facts on this category, is their bearing on the truly Essential. Of the difficulties stated, and the opposition exhibited to comprehensive conceptions in science, part must be referred to the inability to grasp and understand Ideas. If in Natural History some monstrous hybrid growth is alleged as an objection to the recognition of clear and indubitable classes or species, a sufficient reply is furnished by a sentiment often vaguely urged —that " the exception confirms the rule "; *i.e.* that is the part of a well-defined rule, to show the conditions in which it applies, or the deficiency or hybridism of cases that are abnormal. Mere Nature is too weak to keep its genera and species pure, when conflicting with alien elementary influences. If, *e.g.* on considering the human organization in its concrete aspect, we assert that brain, heart, and so forth are essential to its organic life, some miserable abortion may be adduced, which has on the whole the human form, or parts of it—which has been conceived in a human body and has breathed after birth therefrom—in which nevertheless no brain and no heart is found. If such an instance is quoted against the general conception of a human being—the objector persisting in using the name, coupled with a superficial idea respecting it—it can be proved that a real, concrete human being is a truly different object; that such a being must have a brain in its head, and a heart in its breast.

A similar process of reasoning is adopted, in reference to the correct assertion that genius, talent, moral virtues, and sentiments, and piety, may be found in every zone, under all political constitutions and conditions; in confirmation of which examples are forthcoming in abundance. If in this assertion, the accompanying distinctions are intended to be repudiated as unimportant or non-essential, reflection evidently limits itself to abstract categories; and ignores the specialities of the object in question, which certainly fall under no principle recognized by such categories. That intellectual position which adopts such merely formal points of view, presents a vast field for ingenious questions, erudite views, and striking comparisons; for profound seeming reflections and declamations, which may be rendered so much the more brilliant in proportion as the subject they refer to is indefinite, and are susceptible of new and varied forms in inverse proportion to the importance of the results that can be gained from them, and the certainty and rationality of their issues. Under such an aspect the well-known Indian Epopees may be compared with the Homeric; perhaps—since it is the vastness of the imagination by which poetical genius proves itself—preferred to them; as, on account of the similarity of single strokes of imagination in the attributes of the divinities, it has been contended that Greek mythological forms may be recognized in those of India. Similarly the Chinese philosophy, as adopting the One [τὸ ἕν] as its basis, has been alleged to be the same as at a later period appeared as Eleatic philosophy and as the Spinozistic System; while in virtue of its expressing itself also in abstract numbers and lines, Pythagorean and Christian principles have been supposed to be detected in it. Instances of bravery and indomitable courage—traits of magnanimity, of self-denial, and self-sacrifice, which are found among the most savage and the most pusillanimous nations—are regarded as sufficient to support the view that in these nations as much of social virtue and morality may be found as in the most civilized Christian states, or even more. And on this ground a doubt has been suggested whether in the progress of history and of general culture mankind have become better; whether their morality has been increased—morality being regarded in a subjective aspect and view, as founded on what the agent holds to be right and wrong, good and evil; not on a principle which is considered to be in and for itself right and good, or a crime and evil, or on a particular religion believed to be the true one.

We may fairly decline on this occasion the task of tracing the formalism and error of such a view, and establishing the true principles of morality, or rather of social virtue in opposition to false morality. For the History of the World occupies a higher ground than that on which morality has properly its position; which is personal character—the conscience of individuals—their particular will and mode of action; *these* have a value, imputation, reward or punishment proper to themselves. What the absolute aim of Spirit requires and accomplishes—what Providence does—transcends the obligations, and the liability to imputation and the ascription of good or bad motives, which attach to individuality in virtue of its social relations. They who on moral grounds, and consequently with noble intention, have resisted that which the advance of the Spiritual Idea makes necessary, stand higher in moral worth than those whose crimes have been turned into the means—under the direction of a superior principle—of realizing the purposes of that principle. But in such revolutions both parties generally stand within the limits of the same circle of transient and corruptible existence. Consequently it is only a formal rectitude—deserted by the living Spirit and by God—which those who stand upon ancient right and order maintain. The deeds of great men, who are the Individuals of the World's History, thus appear not only justified in view of that intrinsic result of which they were not conscious, but also from the point of view occupied by the secular moralist. But looked at from this point, moral claims that are irrelevant, must not be brought into collision with world-historical deeds and their accomplishment. The Litany of private virtues—modesty, humility, philanthropy and forbearance—must not be raised against them. The History of the World might, on principle, entirely ignore the circle within which morality and the so much talked of distinction between the moral and the politic lies—not only in abstaining from judgments, for the principles involved, and the necessary reference of the deeds in question to those principles, are a sufficient judgment of them—but in leaving Individuals quite out of view and unmentioned. What it has to record is the activity of the Spirit of Peoples, so that the individual forms which that spirit has assumed in the sphere of outward reality, might be left to the delineation of special histories.

The same kind of formalism avails itself in its peculiar manner of the indefiniteness attaching to genius, poetry, and even philosophy; thinks equally that it finds these everywhere. We have here products of reflective thought; and it is familiarity with those general conceptions which single out and name real

distinctions without fathoming the true depth of the matter—
that we call Culture. It is something merely formal, inasmuch
as it aims at nothing more than the analysis of the subject, whatever it be, into its constituent parts, and the comprehension of
these in their logical definitions and forms. It is not the free
universality of conception necessary for making an abstract
principle the object of consciousness. Such a consciousness of
Thought itself, and of its forms isolated from a particular object, is Philosophy. This has, indeed, the condition of its existence in culture; that condition being the taking up of the object of thought, and at the same time clothing it with the form
of universality, in such a way that the material content and the
form given by the intellect are held in an inseparable state;—
inseparable to such a degree that the object in question—which,
by the analysis of one conception into a multitude of conceptions, is enlarged to an incalculable treasure of thought—is regarded as a merely empirical datum in whose formation thought
has had no share.

But it is quite as much an act of Thought—of the Understanding in particular—to embrace in one simple conception
object which of itself comprehends a concrete and large significance (as Earth, Man—Alexander or Cæsar) and to designate it by one word—as to *resolve* such a conception—duly to
isolate in idea the conceptions which it contains, and to give
them particular names. And in reference to the view which
gave occasion to what has just been said, thus much will be
clear—that as reflection produces what we include under the
general terms Genius, Talent, Art, Science—formal culture
on every grade of intellectual development, not only can, but
must grow, and attain a mature bloom, while the grade in
question is developing itself to a State, and on this basis of
civilization is advancing to intelligent reflection and to general forms of thought—as in laws, so in regard to all else. In
the very association of men in a state, lies the necessity of
formal culture—consequently of the rise of the sciences and of
a cultivated poetry and art generally. The arts designated
" plastic," require besides, even in their technical aspect, the
civilized association of men. The poetic art—which has less
need of external requirements and means, and which has the
element of immediate existence, the voice, as its material—steps
forth with great boldness and with matured expression, even

under the conditions presented by a people not yet united in a political combination; since, as remarked above, language attains on its own particular ground a high intellectual development, prior to the commencement of civilization.

Philosophy also must make its appearance where political life exists; since that in virtue of which any series of phenomena is reduced within the sphere of culture, as above stated, is the Form strictly proper to Thought; and thus for philosophy, which is nothing other than the consciousness of this form itself—the Thinking of Thinking—the material of which its edifice is to be constructed, is already prepared by *general* culture. If in the development of the State itself, periods are necessitated which impel the soul of nobler natures to seek refuge from the Present in ideal regions—in order to find in them that harmony with itself which it can no longer enjoy in the discordant real world, where the reflective intelligence attacks all that is holy and deep, which had been spontaneously inwrought into the religion, laws and manners of nations, and brings them down and attenuates them to abstract godless generalities—Thought will be compelled to become Thinking Reason, with the view of effecting in its own element, the restoration of its principles from the ruin to which they had been brought.

We find then, it is true, among all world-historical peoples, poetry, plastic art, science, even philosophy; but not only is there a diversity in style and bearing generally, but still more remarkably in subject-matter; and this is a diversity of the most important kind, affecting the rationality of that subject-matter. It is useless for a pretentious æsthetic criticism to demand that our good pleasure should not be made the rule for the matter—the substantial part of their contents—and to maintain that it is the beautiful form as such, the grandeur of the fancy, and so forth, which fine art aims at, and which must be considered and enjoyed by a liberal taste and cultivated mind. A healthy intellect does not tolerate such abstractions, and cannot assimilate productions of the kind above referred to. Granted that the Indian Epopees might be placed on a level with the Homeric, on account of a number of those qualities of form—grandeur of invention and imaginative power, liveliness of images and emotions, and beauty of diction; yet the infinite difference of matter remains; consequently one of substantial importance and involving the interest of Reason, which is immediately concerned with the consciousness of the Idea of Freedom, and its expression in individuals. There is not only a classical *form*, but a classical order of *subject-matter;* and in a work of art form and subject-matter are so closely united that the former can only be classical to the extent to which the latter is so. With a fantastical, indeterminate material—and *Rule* is the essence of *Reason*—the form becomes measureless and formless, or mean and contracted. In the same way, in that comparison of the various systems of philosophy of which we have already spoken, the only point of importance is overlooked, namely, the character of that Unity which is found alike in the Chinese, the Eleatic, and the Spinozistic philosophy—the distinction between the recognition of that Unity as abstract and as concrete—concrete to the extent of being a unity in and by itself—a unity synonymous with Spirit. But that co-ordination proves that it recognizes only such an abstract unity; so that while it gives judgment respecting philosophy, it is ignorant of that very point which constitutes the interest of philosophy.

But there are also spheres which, amid all the variety that is presented in the substantial content of a particular form of culture, remain the same. The difference above-mentioned in art, science, philosophy, concerns the thinking Reason and Freedom, which is the self-consciousness of the former, and which has the same one root with Thought. As it is not the brute, but only the man that thinks, he only—and only because he is a thinking being—has Freedom. *His* consciousness imports this, that the individual comprehends itself as a *person*, that is, recognizes itself in its single existence as possessing universality—as capable of abstraction from, and of surrendering all speciality; and, therefore, as inherently infinite. Consequently those spheres of intelligence which lie beyond the limits of this consciousness are a common ground among those substantial distinctions. Even morality, which is so intimately connected with the consciousness of freedom, can be very pure while that consciousness is still wanting; as far, that is to say, as it expresses duties and rights only as *objective* commands; or even as far as it remains satisfied with the merely formal elevation of the soul—the surrender of the sensual, and of all sensual motives—in a purely negative, self-denying fashion. The *Chinese* morality—since Europeans have become acquainted with it and with the writings of Confucius—has obtained the greatest praise and proportionate attention from those who are familiar with the Christian morality. There is a similar acknowledgment of the sublimity with which the *Indian* religion and poetry, (a statement that must, however, be limited to the higher kind), but especially the Indian philosophy, expatiate upon and demand the removal and sacrifice of sensuality. Yet both these nations are, it must be confessed, *entirely* wanting in the essential consciousness of the Idea of Freedom. To the Chinese their moral laws are just like natural laws— external, positive commands—claims established by force— compulsory duties or rules of courtesy towards each other. Freedom, through which alone the essential determinations of Reason become moral sentiments, is wanting. Morality is a political affair, and its laws are administered by officers of government and legal tribunals. Their treatises upon it, (which are not law books, but are certainly addressed to the subjective will and individual disposition) read—as do the moral writings of the Stoics—like a string of commands stated as necessary for realizing the goal of happiness; so that it seems to be left free to men, on their part, to adopt such commands—to observe them or not; while the conception of an abstract subject, " a wise man " [*Sapiens*] forms the culminating point among the Chinese, as also among the Stoic moralists. Also in the Indian doctrine of the renunciation of the sensuality of desires and earthly interests, positive moral freedom is not the object and end, but the annihilation of consciousness—spiritual and even physical privation of life.

It is the concrete spirit of a people which we have distinctly to recognize, and since it is Spirit it can only be comprehended spiritually, that is, by thought. It is this alone which takes the lead in all the deeds and tendencies of that people, and which is occupied in realizing itself—in satisfying its ideal and becoming self-conscious—for its great business is self-production. But for spirit, the highest attainment is self-knowledge; an advance not only to the *intuition*, but to the *thought*—the clear conception of itself. This it must and is also destined to accomplish; but the accomplishment is at the same time its dissolution, and the rise of another spirit, another world-historical people, another epoch of Universal History. This transition and connection lead us to the connection of the whole—the idea of the World's History as such—which we have now to consider more closely, and of which we have to give a representation.

History in general is therefore the development of Spirit in *Time*, as Nature is the development of the Idea in *Space*.

If then we cast a glance over the World's-History generally, we see a vast picture of changes and transactions; of infinitely manifold forms of peoples, states, individuals, in unresting succession. Everything that can enter into and interest the soul of man—all our sensibility to *goodness, beauty, and greatness*—is called into play. On every hand aims are adopted and pursued, which we recognize, whose accomplishment we desire —we hope and fear for them. In all these occurrences and changes we behold human action and suffering predominant; everywhere something akin to ourselves, and therefore everywhere something that excites our interest for or against. Sometimes it attracts us by beauty, freedom, and rich variety, sometimes by energy such as enables even vice to make itself interesting. Sometimes we see the more comprehensive mass of some general interest advancing with comparative slowness, and subsequently sacrificed to an infinite complication of trifling circumstances, and so dissipated into atoms. Then, again, with a vast expenditure of power a trivial result is produced; while from what appears unimportant a tremendous issue proceeds. On every hand there is the motliest throng of events drawing us within the circle of its interest, and when one combination vanishes another immediately appears in its place.

The general thought—the category which first presents itself in this restless mutation of individuals and peoples, existing for a time and then vanishing—is that of *change* at large. The sight of the ruins of some ancient sovereignty directly leads us to contemplate this thought of change in its negative aspect. What traveller among the ruins of Carthage, of Palmyra, Persepolis, or Rome, has not been stimulated to reflections on the transiency of kingdoms and men, and to sadness at the thought of a vigorous and rich life now departed—a sadness which does not expend itself on personal losses and the uncertainty of one's own undertakings, but is a disinterested sorrow at the decay of a splendid and highly cultured national life! But the next consideration which allies itself with that of change, is, that change while it imports dissolution, involves at the same time the rise of a *new life*—that while death is the issue of life, life is also the issue of death. This is a grand conception; one which the Oriental thinkers attained, and which is perhaps the highest in their metaphysics. In the idea of *Metempsychosis* we find it evolved in its relation to individual existence; but a myth more generally known, is that of the *Phœnix* as a type of the Life of *Nature;* eternally preparing for itself its funeral pile, and consuming itself upon it; but so that from its ashes is produced the new, renovated, fresh life. But this image is only Asiatic; oriental not occidental. Spirit—consuming the envelope of its existence—does not merely pass into another envelope, nor rise rejuvenescent from the ashes of its previous form; it comes forth exalted, glorified, a purer spirit. It certainly makes war upon itself—consumes its own existence; but in this very destruction it works up that existence into a new form, and each successive phase becomes in its turn a material, working on which it exalts itself to a new grade.

If we consider Spirit in this aspect—regarding its changes not merely as rejuvenescent transitions, *i.e.,* returns to the same form, but rather as manipulations of itself, by which it multiplies the material for future endeavors—we see it exerting itself in a variety of modes and directions; developing its powers and gratifying its desires in a variety which is inexhaustible; because every one of its creations, in which it has already found gratification, meets it anew as material, and is a new stimulus to plastic activity. The abstract conception of mere change gives place to the thought of Spirit manifesting, developing, and perfecting its powers in every direction which its manifold nature can follow. What powers it inherently possesses we learn from the variety of products and formations which it originates. In this pleasurable activity, it has to do only with itself. As involved with the conditions of mere nature—internal and external—it will indeed meet in these not only opposition and hindrance, but will often see its endeavors thereby fail; often sink under the complications in which it is entangled either by Nature or by itself. But in such case it perishes in fulfilling its own destiny and proper function, and even thus exhibits the spectacle of self-demonstration as spiritual activity.

The very essence of Spirit is activity; it realizes its potentiality—makes itself its own deed, its own work—and thus it becomes an object to itself; contemplates itself as an objective existence. Thus is it with the Spirit of a people: it is a Spirit having strictly defined characteristics, which erects itself into an objective world, that exists and persists in a particular religious form of worship, customs, constitution, and political laws—in the whole complex of its institutions—in the events and transactions that make up its history. That is its work—that is what this particular Nation *is*. Nations are what their deeds are. Every Englishman will say: We are the men who navigate the ocean, and have the commerce of the world; to whom the East Indies belong and their riches; who have a parliament, juries, etc.—The relation of the individual to that Spirit is that he appropriates to himself this substantial existence; that it becomes his character and capability, enabling him to have a definite place in the world—to be *something*. For he finds the being of the people to which he belongs an already established, firm world—objectively present to him—with which he has to incorporate himself. In this its work, therefore—its world—the Spirit of the people enjoys its existence and finds its satisfaction.—A Nation is moral—virtuous—vigorous—while it is engaged in realizing its grand objects, and defends its work against external violence during the process of giving to its purposes an objective existence. The contradiction between its potential, subjective being—its inner aim and life—and its *actual* being is removed; it has attained full reality, has itself objectively present to it. But this having been attained, the activity displayed by the Spirit of the people in question is no longer needed; it has its desire. The Nation can still accomplish much in war and peace at home and abroad; but the living substantial soul itself may be said to have ceased its activity. The essential, supreme interest has consequently vanished from its life, for interest is present only where there is opposition. The nation lives the same kind of life as the individual when passing from maturity to old age—in the enjoyment of itself—in the satisfaction of being exactly what it desired and was able to attain. Although its imagination might have transcended that limit, it nevertheless abandoned any such aspirations as objects of *actual endeavor*, if the real world was less than favorable to their attainment—and restricted its aim by the conditions thus imposed. This mere *customary life* (the watch wound up and going on of itself) is that which brings on natural death. Custom is activity without opposition, for which there remains only a formal duration; in which the fulness and zest that originally characterized the aim of life are out of the question—a merely external sensuous existence which has ceased to throw itself enthusiastically into its object. Thus perish individuals, thus perish peoples by a natural death; and though the latter may continue in being, it is an existence without intellect or vitality; having no need of its institutions, because the need for them is satisfied—a political nullity and tedium. In order that a truly universal interest may arise, the Spirit of a People must advance to the adoption of some new purpose; but whence can this new purpose originate? It would be a higher, more comprehensive conception of itself—a transcending of its principle—but this very act would involve a principle of a new order, a new National Spirit.

Such a new principle does in fact enter into the Spirit of a people that has arrived at full development and self-realization; it dies not a simply natural death—for it is not a mere single individual, but a spiritual, generic life; in its case natural death appears to imply destruction through its own agency. The reason of this difference from the single natural individual, is that the Spirit of a people exists as a *genus,* and consequently carries within it its own negation, in the very generality which characterizes it. A people can only die a violent death when it has become naturally dead in itself, as, *e.g.,* the German Imperial Cities, the German Imperial Constitution.

It is not of the nature of the all-pervading Spirit to die this merely natural death; it does not simply sink into the senile life of mere custom, but—as being a National Spirit belonging to Universal History—attains to the consciousness of what its work is; it attains to a conception of itself. In fact it is world-historical only in so far as a *universal principle* has lain in its fundamental element—in its grand aim: only so far is the work which such a spirit produces, a moral, political organization. If it be mere desires that impel nations to activity, such deeds pass over without leaving a trace; or their traces are only ruin and destruction. Thus, it was first Chronos—Time—that ruled; the Golden Age, without moral products; and what was produced—the offspring of that Chronos—was devoured by it. It was Jupiter—from whose head Minerva sprang, and to whose circle of divinities belong Apollo and the Muses—that first put a constraint upon Time, and set a bound to its principle of decadence. He is the Political god, who produced a moral work—the State.

In the very element of an achievement the quality of generality, of thought, is contained; without thought it has no objectivity; that is its basis. The highest point in the development of a people is this—to have gained a conception of its life and condition—to have reduced its laws, its ideas of justice and morality to a science; for in this unity [of the objective and subjective] lies the most intimate unity that Spirit can attain to in and with itself. In its work it is employed in rendering itself an object of its own contemplation; but it cannot develop itself objectively in its essential nature, except in *thinking* itself.

At this point, then, Spirit is acquainted with its principles— the general character of its acts. But at the same time, in virtue of its very generality, this work of thought is different in point of form from the actual achievements of the national genius, and from the vital agency by which those achievements have been performed. We have then before us a *real* and an *ideal* existence of the Spirit of the Nation. If we wish to gain the general idea and conception of what the Greeks were, we find it in Sophocles and Aristophanes, in Thucydides and Plato. In these individuals the Greek spirit conceived and thought itself. This is the profounder kind of satisfaction which the Spirit of a people attains; but it is " ideal," and distinct from its " real " activity.

At such a time, therefore, we are sure to see a people finding satisfaction in the *idea* of virtue; putting *talk* about virtue partly side by side with actual virtue, but partly in the place of it. On the other hand pure, universal thought, since its nature is universality, is apt to bring the Special and Spontaneous—Belief, Trust, Customary Morality—to reflect upon itself, and its primitive simplicity; to show up the limitation with which it is fettered—partly suggesting reasons for renouncing duties, partly itself *demanding reasons,* and the connection of such requirements with Universal Thought; and not finding that connection, seeking to impeach the authority of duty generally, as destitute of a sound foundation.

At the same time the isolation of individuals from each other and from the Whole makes its appearance: their aggressive selfishness and vanity; their seeking personal advantage and consulting this at the expense of the State at large. That inward principle in transcending its outward manifestations is subjective also in *form*—viz., selfishness and corruption in the unbound passions and egotistic interests of men.

Zeus, therefore, who is represented as having put a limit to the devouring agency of Time, and stayed this transiency by having established something inherently and independently durable—Zeus and his race are themselves swallowed up, and that by the very power that produced them—the principle of thought, perception, reasoning, insight derived from rational grounds, and the requirement of such grounds.

Time is the negative element in the sensuous world. Thought is the same negativity, but it is the deepest, the infinite form of it, in which therefore all existence generally is dissolved; first *finite* existence—*determinate,* limited form: but existence *generally*, in its objective character, is limited; it appears therefore as a mere datum—something immediate—authority;— and is either intrinsically finite and limited, or presents itself as a limit for the thinking subject, and its infinite reflection on itself [unlimited abstraction].

But first we must observe how the life which proceeds from death, is itself, on the other hand, only individual life; so that, regarding the species as the real and substantial in this vicissitude, the perishing of the individual is a regress of the species into individuality. The perpetuation of the race is, therefore, none other than the monotonous repetition of the same kind of existence. Further, we must remark how perception—the comprehension of being by thought—is the source and birthplace of a new, and in fact higher form, in a principle which while it preserves, dignifies its material. For Thought is that *Universal*—that *Species* which is immortal, which preserves identity with itself. The particular form of Spirit not merely passes away in the world by natural causes in Time, but is annulled in the automatic self-mirroring activity of consciousness. Because this annulling is an activity of Thought, it is at the same time conservative and elevating in its operation. While then, on the one side, Spirit annuls the reality, the permanence of that which it *is,* it gains on the other side, the essence, the Thought, the Universal element of that which *it only was* [its transient conditions]. Its principle is no longer that immediate import and aim which it was previously, but the *essence* of that import and aim.

The result of this process is then that Spirit, in rendering itself objective and making this its being an object of thought, on the one hand destroys the determinate form of its being, on the other hand gains a comprehension of the universal element which it involves, and thereby gives a new form to its inherent principle. In virtue of this, the substantial character of the National Spirit has been altered—that is, its principle has risen into another, and in fact a higher principle.

It is of the highest importance in apprehending and comprehending History to have and to understand the thought involved in this transition. The individual traverses as a unity various grades of development, and remains the same individual; in like manner also does a people, till the Spirit which it embodies reaches the grade of universality. In this point lies the fundamental, the Ideal necessity of transition. This is the soul—the essential consideration—of the philosophical comprehension of History.

Spirit is essentially the result of its own activity: its activity is the transcending of immediate, simple, unreflected existence —the negation of that existence, and the returning into itself. We may compare it with the seed; for with this the plant begins, yet it is also the result of the plant's entire life. But the weak side of life is exhibited in the fact that the commencement and the result are disjoined from each other. Thus also is it in the life of individuals and peoples. The life of a people ripens a certain fruit; its activity aims at the complete manifestation of the principle which it embodies. But this fruit does not fall back into the bosom of the people that produced and matured it; on the contrary, it becomes a poison-draught to it. That poison-draught it cannot let alone, for it has an insatiable thirst for it: the taste of the draught is its annihilation, though at the same time the rise of a new principle.

We have already discussed the final aim of this progression. The principles of the successive phases of Spirit that animate the Nations in a necessitated gradation, are themselves only steps in the development of the one universal Spirit, which through them elevates and completes itself to a self-comprehending *totality*.

While we are thus concerned exclusively with the Idea of

Spirit, and in the History of the World regard everything as only its manifestation, we have, in traversing the past—however extensive its periods—only to do with what is *present;* for philosophy, as occupying itself with the True, has to do with the *eternally present.* Nothing in the past is lost for it, for the Idea is ever present; Spirit is immortal; with it there is no past, no future, but an essential *now.* This necessarily implies that the present form of Spirit comprehends within it all earlier steps. These have indeed unfolded themselves in succession independently; but what Spirit is it has always been essentially; distinctions are only the development of this essential nature. The life of the ever present Spirit is a circle of progressive embodiments, which looked at in one aspect still exist beside each other, and only as looked at from another point of view appear as past. The grades which Spirit seems to have left beh'nd it, it still possesses in the depths of its present.

GEOGRAPHICAL BASIS OF HISTORY

Contrasted with the universality of the moral Whole and with the unity of that individuality which is its active principle, the *natural* connection that helps to produce the Spirit of a People, appears an extrinsic element; but inasmuch as we must regard it as the ground on which that Spirit plays its part, it is an *essential* and *necessary* basis. We began with the assertion that, in the History of the World, the Idea of Spirit appears in its actual embodiment as a series of external forms, each one of which declares itself as an actually existing people. This existence falls under the category of Time as well as Space, in the way of natural existence; and the special principle, which every world-historical people embodies, has this principle at the same time as a *natural* characteristic. Spirit, clothing itself in this form of nature, suffers its particular phases to assume separate existence; for mutual exclusion is the mode of existence proper to mere nature. These natural distinctions must be first of all regarded as special possibilities, from which the Spirit of the people in question germinates, and among them is the Geographical Basis. It is not our concern to become acquainted with the land occupied by nations as an external locale, but with the natural type of the locality, as intimately connected with the type and character of the people which is the offspring of such a soil. This character is nothing more nor less than the mode and form in which nations make their appearance in History, and take place and position in it. Nature should not be rated too high nor too low: the mild Ionic sky certainly contributed much to the charm of the Homeric poems, yet this alone can produce no Homers. Nor in fact does it continue to produce them; under Turkish government no bards have arisen. We must first take notice of those natural conditions which have to be excluded once for all from the drama of the World's History. In the Frigid and in the Torrid zone the locality of World-historical peoples cannot be found. For awakening consciousness takes its rise surrounded by natural influences alone, and every development of it is the reflection of Spirit back upon itself in opposition to the immediate, unreflected character of mere nature. Nature is therefore one element in this antithetic abstracting process; Nature is the first standpoint from which man can gain freedom within himself, and this liberation must not be rendered difficult by natural obstructions. Nature, as contrasted with Spirit, is a quantitative mass, whose power must not be so great as to make its single force omnipotent. In the extreme zones man cannot come to free movement; cold and heat are here too powerful to allow Spirit to build up a world for *itself*. Aristotle said long ago, " When pressing needs are satisfied, man turns to the general and more elevated." But in the extreme zones such pressure may be said never to cease, never to be warded off; men are constantly impelled to direct attention to nature, to the glowing rays of the sun, and the icy frost. The true theatre of History is therefore the temperate zone; or, rather, its northern half, because the earth there presents itself in a continental form, and has a broad breast, as the Greeks say. In the south, on the contrary, it divides itself, and runs out into many points. The same peculiarity shows itself in natural products. The north has many kinds of animals and plants with common characteristics; in the south, where the land divides itself into points, natural forms also present individual features contrasted with each other.

The World is divided into *Old* and *New;* the name of *New* having originated in the fact that America and Australia have only lately become known to us. But these parts of the world are not only relatively new, but intrinsically so in respect of their entire physical and psychical constitution. Their geological antiquity we have nothing to do with. I will not deny the New World the honor of having emerged from the sea at the world's formation contemporaneously with the old: yet the Archipelago between South America and Asia shows a physical immaturity. The greater part of the islands are so constituted, that they are, as it were, only a superficial deposit of earth over rocks, which shoot up from the fathomless deep, and bear the character of novel origination. New Holland shows a not less immature geographical character; for in penetrating from the settlements of the English farther into the country, we discover immense streams, which have not yet developed themselves to such a degree as to dig a channel for themselves, but lose themselves in marshes. Of America and its grade of civilization, especially in Mexico and Peru, we have information, but it imports nothing more than that this culture was an entirely national one, which must expire as soon as Spirit approached it. America has always shown itself physically and psychically powerless, and still shows itself so. For the aborigines, after the landing of the Europeans in America, gradually vanished at the breath of European activity. In the United States of North America all the citizens are of European descent, with whom the old inhabitants could not amalgamate, but were driven back. The aborigines have certainly adopted some arts and usages from the Europeans, among others that of brandy-drinking, which has operated with deadly effect. In the South the natives were treated with much greater violence, and employed in hard labors to which their strength was by no means competent. A mild and passionless disposition, want of spirit, and a crouching submissiveness towards a Creole, and still more towards a European, are the chief characteristics of the native Americans; and it will be long before the Europeans succeed in producing any independence of feeling in them. The inferiority of these individuals in all respects, even in regard to size, is very manifest; only the quite southern races in Patagonia are more vigorous natures, but still abiding in their natural condition of rudeness and barbarism. When the Jesuits and the Catholic clergy proposed to accustom the Indians to European culture and manners (they have, as is well known, founded a state in Paraguay and convents in Mexico and California), they commenced a close intimacy with them, and prescribed for them the duties of the day, which, slothful though their disposition was, they complied with under the authority of the Friars. These prescripts (at midnight a bell had to remind them even of their matrimonial duties), were first, and very wisely, directed to the creation of wants—the springs of human activity generally. The weakness of the American physique was a chief reason for bringing the negroes to America, to employ their labor in the work that had to be done in the New World; for the negroes are far more susceptible of European culture than the Indians, and an English traveller has adduced instances of negroes having become competent clergymen, medical men, etc. (a negro first discovered the use of the Peruvian bark), while only a single native was known to him whose intellect was sufficiently developed to enable him to study, but who had died soon after beginning, through excessive brandy-drinking. The weakness of the human physique of America has been aggravated by a deficiency in the mere tools and appliances of progress—the want of *horses* and *iron,* the chief instruments by which they were subdued.

The original nation having vanished or nearly so, the effective population comes for the most part from Europe; and what takes place in America, is but an emanation from Europe. Europe has sent its surplus population to America in much the same way as from the old Imperial Cities, where trade-guilds were dominant and trade was stereotyped, many persons escaped to other towns which were not under such a yoke, and where the burden of imposts was not so heavy. Thus arose, by the side of Hamburg, Altona—by Frankfort, Offenbach—by Nürnburg, Fürth—and Carouge by Geneva. The relation between North America and Europe is similar. Many Englishmen have settled there, where burdens and imposts do not exist, and where the combination of European appliances and European ingenuity has availed to realize some produce from the extensive and still virgin soil. Indeed the emigration in question offers many advantages. The emigrants have got rid of much that might be obstructive to their interests at home, while they take with them the advantages of European independence of spirit, and acquired skill; while for those who are willing to work vigorously, but who have not found in Europe opportunities for doing so, a sphere of action is certainly presented in America.

America, as is well known, is divided into two parts, connected indeed by an isthmus, but which has not been the means of establishing intercourse between them. Rather, these two divisions are most decidedly distinct from each other. North America shows us on approaching it, along its eastern shore a wide border of level coast, behind which is stretched a chain of mountains—the blue mountains or Appalachians; further north the Alleghanies. Streams issuing from them water the country towards the coast, which affords advantages of the most desirable kind to the United States, whose origin belongs to this region. Behind that mountain-chain the St. Lawrence river flows (in connection with huge lakes), from south to north, and on this river lie the northern colonies of Canada. Farther west we meet the basin of the vast Mississippi, and the basins of the Missouri and Ohio, which it receives, and then debouches into the Gulf of Mexico. On the western side of this region we have in like manner a long mountain chain, running through Mexico and the Isthmus of Panama, and under the names of the Andes or Cordillera, cutting off an edge of coast along the whole west side of South America. The border formed by this is narrower and offers fewer advantages than that of North America. There lie Peru and Chili. On the east side flow eastward the monstrous streams of the Orinoco and Amazons; they form great valleys, not adapted however for cultivation, since they are only wide desert steppes. Towards the south flows the Rio de la Plata, whose tributaries have their origin partly in the Cordilleras, partly in the northern chain of mountains which separates the basin of the Amazon from its own. To the district of the Rio de la Plata belong Brazil, and the Spanish Republics. Colombia is the northern coast-land of South America, at the west of which, flowing along the Andes, the Magdalena debouches into the Caribbean Sea.

With the exception of Brazil, republics have come to occupy South as well as North America. In comparing South America (reckoning Mexico as part of it) with North America, we observe an astonishing contrast.

In North America we witness a prosperous state of things; an increase of industry and population civil order and firm freedom; the whole federation constitutes but a single state and has its political centres.   In South America, on the contrary, the republics depend only on military force; their whole history is a continued revolution; federated states become disunited; others previously separated become united; and all these changes originate in military revolutions.   The more special differences between the two parts of America show us two opposite directions, the one in political respects, the other in regard to religion.   South America, where the Spaniards settled and asserted supremacy, is Catholic; North America, although a land of sects of every name, is yet fundamentally, Protestant.   A wider distinction is presented in the fact, that South America was conquered, but North America colonized. The Spaniards took possession of South America to govern it, and to become rich through occupying political offices, and by exactions.   Depending on a very distant mother country, their desires found a larger scope, and by force, address and confidence they gained a great predominance over the Indians.   The North American States were, on the other hand, entirely *colonized*, by Europeans.   Since in England Puritans, Episcopalians, and Catholics were engaged in perpetual conflict, and now one party, now the other, had the upper hand, many emigrated to seek religious freedom on a foreign shore.   These were industrious Europeans, who betook themselves to agriculture, tobacco and cotton planting, etc.   Soon the whole attention of the inhabitants was given to labor, and the basis of their existence as a united body lay in the necessities that bind man to man, the desire of repose, the establishment of civil rights, security and freedom, and a community arising from the aggregation of individuals as atomic constituents; so that the state was merely something external for the protection of property. From the Protestant religion sprang the principle of the mutual confidence of individuals—trust in the honorable dispositions of other men; for in the Protestant Church the entire life—its activity generally—is the field for what it deems religious works.   Among Catholics, on the contrary, the basis of such a confidence cannot exist; for in secular matters only force and voluntary subservience are the principles of action; and the forms which are called Constitutions are in this case only a resort of necessity, and are no protection against mistrust.

If we compare North America further with Europe, we shall

find in the former the permanent example of a republican constitution. A subjective unity presents itself; for there is a President at the head of the State, who, for the sake of security against any monarchical ambition, is chosen only for four years. Universal protection for property, and a something approaching entire immunity from public burdens, are facts which are constantly held up to commendation. We have in these facts the fundamental character of the community—the endeavor of the individual after acquisition, commercial profit, and gain; the preponderance of *private* interest, devoting itself to that of the community only for its own advantage. We find, certainly, legal relations—a formal code of laws; but respect for law exists apart from genuine probity, and the American merchants commonly lie under the imputation of dishonest dealings under legal protection. If, on the one side, the Protestant Church develops the essential principle of confidence, as already stated, it thereby involves on the other hand the recognition of the validity of the element of feeling to such a degree as gives encouragement to unseemly varieties of caprice. Those who adopt this standpoint maintain, that, as everyone may have his peculiar way of viewing things *generally,* so he may have also a *religion* peculiar to himself. Thence the splitting up into so many sects, which reach the very acme of absurdity; many of which have a form of worship consisting in convulsive movements, and sometimes in the most sensuous extravagances. This complete freedom of worship is developed to such a degree, that the various congregations choose ministers and dismiss them according to their absolute pleasure; for the Church is no independent existence—having a substantial spiritual being, and correspondingly permanent external arrangement— but the affairs of religion are regulated by the good pleasure for the time being of the members of the community. In North America the most unbounded license of imagination in religious matters prevails, and that religious unity is wanting which has been maintained in European States, where deviations are limited to a few confessions. As to the political condition of North America, the general object of the existence of this State is not yet fixed and determined, and the necessity for a firm combination does not yet exist; for a real State and a real Government arise only after a distinction of classes has arisen, when wealth and poverty become extreme, and when such a

condition of things presents itself that a large portion of the
people can no longer satisfy its necessities in the way in which
it has been accustomed so to do. But America is hitherto
exempt from this pressure, for it has the outlet of colonization
constantly and widely open, and multitudes are continually
streaming into the plains of the Mississippi. By this means
the chief source of discontent is removed, and the continuation
of the existing civil condition is guaranteed. A comparison
of the United States of North America with European lands
is therefore impossible; for in Europe, such a natural outlet
for population, notwithstanding all the emigrations that take
place, does not exist. Had the woods of Germany been in
existence, the French Revolution would not have occurred.
North America will be comparable with Europe only after the
immeasurable space which that country presents to its inhabitants shall have been occupied, and the members of the political
body shall have begun to be pressed back on each other. North
America is still in the condition of having land to begin to cultivate. Only when, as in Europe, the direct increase of agriculturists is checked, will the inhabitants, instead of pressing outwards to occupy the fields, press inwards upon each other—
pursuing town occupations, and trading with their fellow-
citizens; and so form a compact system of civil society, and
require an organized state. The North American Federation
have no neighboring State (towards which they occupy a relation similar to that of European States to each other) one
which they regard with mistrust, and against which they must
keep up a standing army. Canada and Mexico are not objects
of fear, and England has had fifty years' experience, that *free*
America is more profitable to her than it was in a state of
dependence. The militia of the North American Republic
proved themselves quite as brave in the War of Independence,
as the Dutch under Philip II; but generally, where Independence is not at stake, less power is displayed, and in the
year 1814 the militia held out but indifferently against the
English.

America is therefore the land of the future, where, in the
ages that lie before us, the burden of the World's History shall
reveal itself—perhaps in a contest between North and South
America. It is a land of desire for all those who are weary of
the historical lumber-room of old Europe. Napoleon is re-

ported to have said: "*Cette vieille Europe m'ennuie.*" It is
for America to abandon the ground on which hitherto the History of the World has developed itself. What *has* taken place
in the New World up to the present time is only an echo of
the Old World—the expression of a foreign Life; and as a
Land of the Future, it has no interest for us here, for, as regards *History,* our concern must be with that which has been
and that which is. In regard to *Philosophy,* on the other hand,
we have to do with that which (strictly speaking) is neither
past nor future, but with that which *is,* which has an eternal
existence—with Reason; and this is quite sufficient to occupy us.

Dismissing, then, the New World, and the dreams to which
it may give rise, we pass over to the Old World—the scene of
the World's History; and must first direct attention to the
natural elements and conditions of existence which it presents.
America is divided into two parts, which are indeed connected
by an Isthmus, but which forms only an external, material
bond of union. The Old World, on the contrary, which lies
opposite to America, and is separated from it by the Atlantic
Ocean, has its continuity interrupted by a deep inlet—the
Mediterranean Sea. The three Continents that compose it
have an essential relation to each other, and constitute a totality.
Their peculiar feature is that they lie round this Sea, and therefore have an easy means of communication; for rivers and
seas are not to be regarded as disjoining, but as uniting. England and Brittany, Norway and Denmark, Sweden and Livonia,
have been united. For the three quarters of the globe the Mediterranean Sea is similarly the uniting element, and the centre
of World-History. Greece lies here, the focus of light in History. Then in Syria we have Jerusalem, the centre of Judaism
and of Christianity; southeast of it lie Mecca and Medina, the
cradle of the Mussulman faith; towards the west Delphi and
Athens; farther west still, Rome: on the Mediterranean Sea
we have also Alexandria and Carthage. The Mediterranean
is thus the heart of the Old World, for it is that which conditioned and vitalized it. Without it the History of the World
could not be conceived: it would be like ancient Rome or
Athens without the forum, where all the life of the city came
together. The extensive tract of eastern Asia is severed from
the process of general historical development, and has no share

in it; so also Northern Europe, which took part in the World's History only at a later date, and had no part in it while the Old World lasted; for this was exclusively limited to the countries lying round the Mediterranean Sea. Julius Cæsar's crossing the Alps—the conquest of Gaul and the relation into which the Germans thereby entered with the Roman Empire—makes consequently an epoch in History; for in virtue of this it begins to extend its boundaries beyond the Alps. Eastern Asia and that trans-Alpine country are the extremes of this agitated focus of human life around the Mediterranean—the beginning and end of History—its rise and decline.

The more special geographical distinctions must now be established, and they are to be regarded as essential, rational distinctions, in contrast with the variety of merely accidental circumstances. Of these characteristic differences there are three:—

(1) The arid elevated land with its extensive steppes and plains.

(2) The valley plains—the Land of Transition permeated and watered by great Streams.

(3) The coast region in immediate connection with the sea.

These three geographical elements are the essential ones, and we shall see each quarter of the globe triply divided accordingly. The first is the substantial, unvarying, metallic, elevated region, intractably shut up within itself, but perhaps adapted to send forth impulses over the rest of the world; the second forms centres of civilization, and is the yet undeveloped independence [of humanity]; the third offers the means of connecting the world together, and of maintaining the connection.

(1) *The elevated land.*—We see such a description of country in middle Asia inhabited by Mongolians (using the word in a general sense): from the Caspian Sea these Steppes stretch in a northerly direction towards the Black Sea. As similar tracts may be cited the deserts of Arabia and of Barbary in Africa; in South America the country round the Orinoco, and in Paraguay. The peculiarity of the inhabitants of this elevated region, which is watered sometimes only by rain, or by the overflowing of a river (as are the plains of the Orinoco) —is the patriarchal life, the division into single families. The region which these families occupy is unfruitful or productive

only temporarily: the inhabitants have their property not in the land—from which they derive only a trifling profit—but in the animals that wander with them. For a long time these find pasture in the plains, and when they are depastured, the tribe moves to other parts of the country. They are careless and provide nothing for the winter, on which account therefore, half of the herd is frequently cut off. Among these inhabitants of the upland there exist no legal relations, and consequently there are exhibited among them the extremes of hospitality and rapine; the last more especially when they are surrounded by civilized nations, as the Arabians, who are assisted in their depredations by their horses and camels. The Mongolians feed on mare's milk, and thus the horse supplies them at the same time with appliances for nourishment and for war. Although this is the form of their patriarchal life, it often happens that they cohere together in great masses, and by an impulse of one kind or another, are excited to external movement. Though previously of peaceful disposition, they then rush as a devastating inundation over civilized lands, and the revolution which ensues has no other result than destruction and desolation. Such an agitation was excited among those tribes under Genghis Khan and Tamerlane: they destroyed all before them; then vanished again, as does an overwhelming Forest-torrent—possessing no inherent principle of vitality. From the uplands they rush down into the dells: there dwell peaceful mountaineers—herdsmen who also occupy themselves with agriculture, as do the Swiss. Asia has also such a people: they are however on the whole a less important element.

(2) *The valley plains.*—These are plains, permeated by rivers, and which owe the whole of their fertility to the streams by which they are formed. Such a Valley-Plain is China—India, traversed by the Indus and the Ganges—Babylonia, where the Euphrates and the Tigris flow—Egypt, watered by the Nile. In these regions extensive Kingdoms arise, and the foundation of great States begins. For agriculture, which prevails here as the primary principle of subsistence for individuals, is assisted by the regularity of seasons, which require corresponding agricultural operations; property in land commences, and the consequent legal relations;—that is to say, the basis and foundation of the State, which becomes possible only in connection with such relations.

(3) *The coast land.*—A River divides districts of country from each other, but still more does the sea; and we are accustomed to regard water as the separating element. Especially in recent times has it been insisted upon that States must necessarily have been separated by natural features. Yet on the contrary, it may be asserted as a fundamental principle that nothing *unites* so much as water, for countries are nothing else than districts occupied by streams. Silesia, for instance, is the valley of the Oder; Bohemia and Saxony are the valley of the Elbe; Egypt is the valley of the Nile. With the sea this is not less the case, as has been already pointed out. Only Mountains separate. Thus the Pyrenees decidedly separate Spain from France. The Europeans have been in constant connection with America and the East Indies ever since they were discovered; but they have scarcely penetrated into the interior of Africa and Asia, because intercourse by land is much more difficult than by water. Only through the fact of being a sea, has the Mediterranean become a focus of national life. Let us now look at the character of the nations that are conditioned by this third element.

The sea gives us the idea of the indefinite, the unlimited, and infinite; and in *feeling his own infinite* in that Infinite, man is stimulated and emboldened to stretch beyond the limited: the sea invites man to conquest, and to piratical plunder, but also to honest gain and to commerce. The land, the mere Valley-plain attaches him to the soil; it involves him in an infinite multitude of dependencies, but the sea carries him out beyond these limited circles of thought and action. Those who navigate the sea, have indeed gain for their object, but the means are in this respect paradoxical, inasmuch as they hazard both property and life to attain it. The means therefore are the very opposite to that which they aim at. This is what exalts their gain and occupation above itself, and makes it something brave and noble. Courage is necessarily introduced into trade, daring is joined with wisdom. For the daring which encounters the sea must at the same time embrace wariness—cunning —since it has to do with the treacherous, the most unreliable and deceitful element. This boundless plain is absolutely yielding—withstanding no pressure, not even a breath of wind. It looks boundlessly innocent, submissive, friendly, and insinuating; and it is exactly this submissiveness which changes the sea into the most dangerous and violent element. To this deceitfulness and violence man opposes merely a simple piece of wood; confides entirely in his courage and presence of mind; and thus passes from a firm ground to an unstable support, taking his artificial ground with him. The Ship—that swan of the sea, which cuts the watery plain in agile and arching movements or describes circles upon it—is a machine whose invention does the greatest honor to the boldness of man as well as to his understanding. This stretching out of the sea beyond the limitations of the land, is wanting to the splendid political edifices of Asiatic States, although they themselves border on the sea—as for example, China. For them the sea is only the limit, the ceasing of the land; they have no positive relation to it. The activity to which the sea invites, is a quite peculiar one: thence arises the fact that the coast-lands almost always separate themselves from the states of the interior although they are connected with these by a river. Thus Holland has severed itself from Germany, Portugal from Spain.

In accordance with these data we may now consider the three portions of the globe with which History is concerned, and here the three characteristic principles manifest themselves in a more or less striking manner: Africa has for its leading classical feature the Upland, Asia the contrast of river regions with the Upland, Europe the mingling of these several elements.

Africa must be divided into three parts: one is that which lies south of the desert of Sahara—Africa proper—the Upland almost entirely unknown to us, with narrow coast-tracts along the sea; the second is that to the north of the desert—European Africa (if we may so call it)—a coastland; the third is the river region of the Nile, the only valley-land of Africa, and which is in connection with Asia.

Africa proper, as far as History goes back, has remained—for all purposes of connection with the rest of the World—shut up; it is the Gold-land compressed within itself—the land of childhood, which lying beyond the day of self-conscious history, is enveloped in the dark mantle of Night. Its isolated character originates, not merely in its tropical nature, but essentially in its geographical condition. The triangle which it forms (if we take the West Coast—which in the Gulf of Guinea makes a strongly indented angle—for one side, and in the same way the East Coast to Cape Gardafu for another) is on two sides so constituted for the most part, as to have a very narrow Coast Tract, habitable only in a few isolated spots. Next to this towards the interior, follows to almost the same extent, a girdle of marsh land with the most luxuriant vegetation, the especial home of ravenous beasts, snakes of all kinds—a border tract whose atmosphere is poisonous to Europeans. This border constitutes the base of a cincture of high mountains, which are only at distant intervals traversed by streams, and where they are so, in such a way as to form no means of union with the interior; for the interruption occurs but seldom below the upper part of the mountain ranges, and only in individual narrow channels, where are frequently found innavigable waterfalls and torrents crossing each other in wild confusion. During the three or three and a half centuries that the Europeans have known this border-land and have taken places in it into their possession, they have only here and there (and that but for a short time) passed these mountains, and have nowhere settled down beyond them. The land surrounded by these mountains is an unknown Upland, from which on the other hand the Negroes have seldom made their way through. In the sixteenth century occurred at many very distant points, outbreaks of terrible hordes which rushed down upon the more peaceful inhabitants of the declivities. Whether any internal movement had taken place, or if so, of what character, we do not know. What we do know of these hordes, is the contrast between their conduct in their wars and forays themselves— which exhibited the most reckless inhumanity and disgusting barbarism—and the fact that afterwards, when their rage was spent, in the calm time of peace, they showed themselves mild and well disposed towards the Europeans, when they became acquainted with them. This holds good of the Fullahs and of the Mandingo tribes, who inhabit the mountain terraces of the Senegal and Gambia. The second portion of Africa is the river district of the Nile—Egypt; which was adapted to become a mighty centre of independent civilization, and therefore is as isolated and singular in Africa as Africa itself appears in relation to the other parts of the world. The northern part of Africa, which may be specially called that of the *coast-territory* (for Egypt has been frequently driven back on itself, by the Mediterranean) lies on the Mediterranean and the Atlantic;

a magnificent territory, on which Carthage once lay—the site of the modern Morocco, Algiers, Tunis, and Tripoli. This part was to be—*must* be attached to Europe: the French have lately made a successful effort in this direction: like Hither-Asia, it looks Europe-wards. Here in their turn have Carthaginians, Romans, and Byzantines, Mussulmans, Arabians, had their abode, and the interests of Europe have always striven to get a footing in it.

The peculiarly African character is difficult to comprehend, for the very reason that in reference to it, we must quite give up the principle which naturally accompanies all *our* ideas— the category of Universality. In Negro life the characteristic point is the fact that consciousness has not yet attained to the realization of any substantial objective existence—as for example, God, or Law—in which the interest of man's volition is involved and in which he realizes his own being. This distinction between himself as an individual and the universality of his essential being, the African in the uniform, undeveloped oneness of his existence has not yet attained; sc that the Knowledge of an absolute Being, an Other and a Higher than his individual self, is entirely wanting. The Negro, as already observed, exhibits the natural man in his completely wild and untamed state. We must lay aside all thought of reverence and morality—all that we call feeling—if we would rightly comprehend him; there is nothing harmonious with humanity to be found in this type of character. The copious and circumstantial accounts of Missionaries completely confirm this, and Mahommedanism appears to be the only thing which in any way brings the Negroes within the range of culture. The Mahommedans too understand better than the Europeans, how to penetrate into the interior of the country. The grade of culture which the Negroes occupy may be more nearly appreciated by considering the aspect which *Religion* presents among them. That which forms the basis of religious conceptions is the consciousness on the part of man of a Higher Power—even though this is conceived only as a *vis naturæ*—in relation to which he feels himself a weaker, humbler being. Religion begins with the consciousness that there is something higher than man. But even Herodotus called the Negroes sorcerers:—now in *Sorcery* we have not the idea of a God, of a moral faith; it exhibits man as the highest power, regarding him as alone occupying a position of command over the power of Nature. We have here therefore nothing to do with a spiritual adoration of God, nor with an empire of Right. God thunders, but is not on that account recognized as God. For the soul of man, God must be more than a thunderer, whereas among the Negroes this is not the case. Although they are necessarily conscious of dependence upon nature—for they need the beneficial influence of storm, rain, cessation of the rainy period, and so on—yet this does not conduct them to the consciousness of a Higher Power: it is they who command the elements, and this they call " magic." The Kings have a class of ministers through whom they command elemental changes, and every place possesses such magicians, who perform special ceremonies, with all sorts of gesticulations, dances, uproar, and shouting, and in the midst of this confusion commence their incantations. The second element in their religion, consists in their giving an outward form to this supernatural power—projecting their hidden might into the world of phenomena by means of images. What they conceive of as the power in question, is therefore nothing really objective, having a substantial being and different from themselves, but the first thing that comes in their way. This, taken quite indiscriminately, they exalt to the dignity of a " Genius "; it may be an animal, a tree, a stone, or a wooden figure. This is their *Fetich*—a word to which the Portuguese first gave currency, and which is derived from *feitizo,* magic. Here, in the Fetich, a kind of objective independence as contrasted with the arbitrary fancy of the individual seems to manifest itself; but as the objectivity is nothing other than the fancy of the individual projecting itself into space, the human individuality remains master of the image it has adopted. If any mischance occurs which the Fetich has not averted, if rain is suspended, if there is a failure in the crops, they bind and beat or destroy the Fetich and so get rid of it, making another immediately, and thus holding it in their own power. Such a Fetich has no independence as an object of religious worship; still less has it æsthetic independence as a work of art; it is merely a creation that expresses the arbitrary choice of its maker, and which always remains in his hands. In short there is no relation of dependence in this religion. There is however one feature that points to something beyond;—the *Worship of the Dead*—in which their deceased forefathers and ancestors are regarded by them as a power influencing the living. Their idea in the matter is that these ancestors exercise vengeance and inflict upon man various injuries—exactly in the sense in which this was supposed of witches in the Middle Ages. Yet the power of the dead is not held superior to that of the living, for the Negroes command the dead and lay spells upon them. Thus the power in question remains substantially always in bondage to the living subject. Death itself is looked upon by the Negroes as no universal natural law; even this, they think, proceeds from evil-disposed magicians. In this doctrine is certainly involved the elevation of man over Nature; to such a degree that the chance volition of man is superior to the merely natural—that he looks upon this as an instrument to which he does not pay the compliment of treating it in a way conditioned by itself, but which he commands.*

But from the fact that man is regarded as the Highest, it follows that he has no respect for himself; for only with the consciousness of a Higher Being does he reach a point of view which inspires him with real reverence. For if arbitrary choice is the absolute, the only substantial objectivity that is realized, the mind cannot in such be conscious of any Universality. The Negroes indulge, therefore, that perfect *contempt* for humanity, which in its bearing on Justice and Morality is the fundamental characteristic of the race. They have moreover no knowledge of the immortality of the soul, although spectres are supposed to appear. The undervaluing of humanity among them reaches an incredible degree of intensity. Tyranny is regarded as no wrong, and cannibalism is looked upon as quite customary and proper. Among us instinct deters from it, if we can speak of instinct at all as appertaining to man. But with the Negro this is not the case, and the devouring of human flesh is altogether consonant with the general principles of the African race; to the sensual Negro, human flesh is but an object of sense—mere flesh. At the death of a King hundreds are killed and eaten; prisoners are butchered and their flesh sold in the markets; the victor is accustomed to eat the heart of his slain foe. When magical rites are performed, it frequently happens that the sorcerer kills the first that comes in his way and divides his body

* *Vide* Hegel's " Vorlesungen über die Philosophie der Religion," I. 284 and 289. 2d Ed.

among the bystanders. Another characteristic fact in reference to the Negroes is Slavery. Negroes are enslaved by Europeans and sold to America. Bad as this may be, their lot in
their own land is even worse, since there a slavery quite as absolute exists; for it is the essential principle of slavery, that
man has not yet attained a consciousness of his freedom, and
consequently sinks down to a mere Thing—an object of no
value. Among the Negroes moral sentiments are quite weak,
or more strictly speaking, non-existent. Parents sell their
children, and conversely children their parents, as either has the
opportunity. Through the pervading influence of slavery all
those bonds of moral regard which we cherish towards each
other disappear, and it does not occur to the Negro mind to expect from others what we are enabled to claim. The polygamy
of the Negroes has frequently for its object the having many
children, to be sold, every one of them, into slavery; and very
often naïve complaints on this score are heard, as for instance
in the case of a Negro in London, who lamented that he was
now quite a poor man because he had already sold all his relations. In the contempt of humanity displayed by the Negroes,
it is not so much a despising of death as a want of regard for
life that forms the characteristic feature. To this want of regard for life must be ascribed the great courage, supported by
enormous bodily strength, exhibited by the Negroes, who allow
themselves to be shot down by thousands in war with Europeans. Life has a value only when it has something valuable as
its object.

Turning our attention in the next place to the category of
political constitution, we shall see that the entire nature of this
race is such as to preclude the existence of any such arrangement. The standpoint of humanity at this grade is mere sensuous volition with energy of will; since universal spiritual
laws (for example, that of the morality of the Family) cannot
be recognized here. Universality exists only as arbitrary subjective choice. The political bond can therefore not possess
such a character as that free laws should unite the community.
There is absolutely no bond, no restraint upon that arbitrary
volition. Nothing but external force can hold the State together for a moment. A ruler stands at the head, for sensuous
barbarism can only be restrained by despotic power. But since
the subjects are of equally violent temper with their master,

they keep him on the other hand within limits. Under the chief there are many other chiefs with whom the former, whom we will call the King, takes counsel, and whose consent he must seek to gain, if he wishes to undertake a war or impose a tax. In this relation he can exercise more or less authority, and by fraud or force can on occasion put this or that chieftain out of the way. Besides this the Kings have other specified prerogatives. Among the Ashantees the King inherits all the property left by his subjects at their death. In other places all unmarried women belong to the King, and whoever wishes a wife, must buy her from him. If the Negroes are discontented with their King they depose and kill him. In Dahomey, when they are thus displeased, the custom is to send parrots' eggs to the King, as a sign of dissatisfaction with his government. Sometimes also a deputation is sent, which intimates to him, that the burden of government must have been very troublesome to him, and that he had better rest a little. The King then thanks his subjects, goes into his apartments, and has himself strangled by the women. Tradition alleges that in former times a state composed of women made itself famous by its conquests: it was a state at whose head was a woman. She is said to have pounded her own son in a mortar, to have besmeared herself with the blood, and to have had the blood of pounded children constantly at hand. She is said to have driven away or put to death all the males, and commanded the death of all male children. These furies destroyed everything in the neighborhood, and were driven to constant plunderings, because they did not cultivate the land. Captives in war were taken as husbands: pregnant women had to betake themselves outside the encampment; and if they had born a son, put him out of the way. This infamous state, the report goes on to say, subsequently disappeared. Accompanying the King we constantly find in Negro States, the executioner, whose office is regarded as of the highest consideration, and by whose hands, the King, though he makes use of him for putting suspected persons to death, may himself suffer death, if the grandees desire it. Fanaticism, which, notwithstanding the yielding disposition of the Negro in other respects, can be excited, surpasses, when roused, all belief. An English traveller states that when a war is determined on in Ashantee, solemn ceremonies precede it: among other things the bones of the King's mother are laved with human blood. As a prelude to the war, the King ordains an onslaught upon his own metropolis, as if to excite the due degree of frenzy. The King sent word to the English Hutchinson: ' Christian, take care, and watch well over your family. The messenger of death has drawn his sword and will strike the neck of many Ashantees; when the drum sounds it is the death signal for multitudes. Come to the King, if you can, and fear nothing for yourself." The drum beat, and a terrible carnage was begun; all who came in the way of the frenzied Negroes in the streets were stabbed. On such occasions the King has all whom he suspects killed, and the deed then assumes the character of a sacred act. Every idea thrown into the mind of the Negro is caught up and realized with the whole energy of his will; but this realization involves a wholesale destruction. These people continue long at rest, but suddenly their passions ferment, and then they are quite beside themselves. The destruction which is the consequence of their excitement, is caused by the fact that it is no positive idea, no thought which produces these commotions;—a physical rather than a spiritual enthusiasm. In Dahomey, when the King dies, the bonds of society are loosed; in his palace begins indiscriminate havoc and disorganization. All the wives of the King (in Dahomey their number is exactly 3,333) are massacred, and through the whole town plunder and carnage run riot. The wives of the King regard this their death as a necessity; they go richly attired to meet it. The authorities have to hasten to proclaim the new governor, simply to put a stop to massacre.

From these various traits it is manifest that want of self-control distinguishes the character of the Negroes. This condition is capable of no development or culture, and as we see them at this day, such have they always been. The only essential connection that has existed and continued between the Negroes and the Europeans is that of slavery. In this the Negroes see nothing unbecoming them, and the English who have done most for abolishing the slave-trade and slavery, are treated by the Negroes themselves as enemies. For it is a point of first importance with the Kings to sell their captured enemies, or even their own subjects; and viewed in the light of such facts, we may conclude *slavery* to have been the occasion of the increase of human feeling among the Negroes. The doctrine which we deduce from this condition of slavery among the

Negroes, and which constitutes the only side of the question that has an interest for our inquiry, is that which we deduce from the Idea: viz. that the " Natural condition " itself is one of absolute and thorough injustice—contravention of the Right and Just. Every intermediate grade between this and the realization of a rational State retains—as might be expected— elements and aspects of injustice; therefore we find slavery even in the Greek and Roman States, as we do serfdom down to the latest times. But thus existing in a State, slavery is itself a phase of advance from the merely isolated sensual existence— a phase of education—a mode of becoming participant in a higher morality and the culture connected with it. Slavery is in and for itself *injustice,* for the essence of humanity is *Freedom;* but for this man must be matured. The gradual abolition of slavery is therefore wiser and more equitable than its sudden removal.

At this point we leave Africa, not to mention it again. For it is no historical part of the World; it has no movement or development to exhibit. Historical movements in it—that is in its northern part—belong to the Asiatic or European World. Carthage displayed there an important transitionary phase of civilization; but, as a Phœnician colony, it belongs to Asia. Egypt will be considered in reference to the passage of the human mind from its Eastern to its Western phase, but it does not belong to the African Spirit. What we properly understand by Africa, is the Unhistorical, Undeveloped Spirit, still involved in the conditions of mere nature, and which had to be presented here only as on the threshold of the World's History.

Having eliminated this introductory element, we find ourselves for the first time on the real theatre of History. It now only remains for us to give a prefatory sketch of the Geographical basis of the Asiatic and European world. *Asia* is, characteristically, the *Orient* quarter of the globe—the region of origination. It is indeed a Western world for America; but as Europe presents on the whole, the centre and end of the old world, and is absolutely the *West*—so Asia is absolutely the *East.*

In Asia arose the Light of Spirit, and therefore the history of the World.

We must now consider the various localities of Asia. Its physical constitution presents direct antitheses, and the essential relation of these antitheses. Its various geographical principles are formations in themselves developed and perfected.

First, the northern slope, Siberia, must be eliminated. This slope, from the Altai chain, with its fine streams, that pour their waters into the northern Ocean, does not at all concern us here; because the Northern Zone, as already stated, lies out of the pale of History. But the remainder includes three very interesting localities. The first is, as in Africa, a massive Upland, with a mountain girdle which contains the highest summits in the World. This Upland is bounded on the South and Southeast, by the Mus-Tag or Imaus, parallel to which, farther south, runs the Himalaya chain. Towards the East, a mountain chain running from South to North, parts off the basin of the Amur. On the North lie the Altai and Songarian mountains; in connection with the latter, in the Northwest the Musart and in the West the Belur Tag, which by the Hindoo Coosh chain are again united with the Mus-Tag.

This high mountain-girdle is broken through by streams, which are dammed up and form great valley plains. These, more or less inundated, present centres of excessive luxuriance and fertility, and are distinguished from the European river districts in their not forming, as those do, proper valleys with valleys branching out from them, but river-plains. Of this kind are—the Chinese Valley Plain, formed by the Hoang-Ho and Yang-tse-Kiang (the yellow and blue streams)—next that of India, formed by the Ganges;—less important is the Indus, which in the north, gives character to the Punjaub, and in the south flows through plains of sand. Farther on, the lands of the Tigris and Euphrates, which rise in Armenia and hold their course along the Persian mountains. The Caspian sea has similar river valleys; in the East those formed by the Oxus and Jaxartes (Gihon and Sihon) which pour their waters into the Sea of Aral; on the West those of the Cyrus and Araxes (Kur and Aras).—The Upland and the Plains must be distinguished from each other; the third element is their intermixture, which occurs in Hither [Anterior] Asia. To this belongs Arabia, the land of the Desert, the upland of plains, the empire of fanaticism. To this belong Syria and Asia Minor, connected with the sea, and having constant intercourse with Europe.

In regard to Asia the remark above offered respecting geographical differences is especially true; viz. that the rearing of cattle is the business of the Upland—agriculture and industrial pursuits that of the valley-plains—while commerce and naviga-

tion form the third and last item. Patriarchal independence is
strictly bound up with the first condition of society; property
and the relation of lord and serf with the second; civil freedom
with the third. In the Upland, where the various kinds of cattle breeding, the rearing of horses, camels, and sheep, (not so
much of oxen) deserve attention, we must also distinguish the
calm *habitual* life of nomad tribes from the wild and restless
character they display in their conquests. These people, without developing themselves in a really historical form, are swayed
by a powerful impulse leading them to change their aspect as
nations; and although *they* have not attained an historical character, the beginning of History may be traced to them. It must
however be allowed that the peoples of the plains are more interesting. In agriculture itself is involved, *ipse facto,* the cessation of a roving life. It demands foresight and solicitude for
the future: reflection on a general idea is thus awakened; and
herein lies the principle of property and productive industry.
China, India, Babylonia, have risen to the position of cultivated
lands of this kind. But as the peoples that have occupied these
lands have been shut up within themselves, and have not appropriated that element of civilization which the sea supplies,
(or at any rate only at the commencement of their civilization)
and as their navigation of it—to whatever extent it may have
taken place—remained without influence on their culture—a relation to the rest of History could only exist in their case,
through their being sought out, and their character investigated
by others. The mountain-girdle of the upland, the upland itself,
and the river-plains, characterize Asia physically and spiritually: but they themselves are not concretely, really, historical
elements. The opposition between the extremes is simply recognized, not harmonized; a firm settlement in the fertile plains
is for the mobile, restless, roving, condition of the mountain
and Upland races, nothing more than a constant object of endeavor. Physical features distinct in the sphere of nature, assume an essential historical relation.—Anterior Asia has both
elements in one, and has, consequently, a relation to Europe;
for what is most remarkable in it, this land has not kept for
itself, but sent over to Europe. It presents the origination of all
religious and political principles, but Europe has been the scene
of their development.

Europe, to which we now come, has not the physical **varie-**

ties which we noticed in Asia and Africa. The European character involves the disappearance of the contrast exhibited by
earlier varieties, or at least a modification of it; so that we have
the milder qualities of a transition state. We have in Europe no
uplands immediately contrasted with plains. The three sections of Europe require therefore a different basis of classification.

The first part is Southern Europe—looking towards the
Mediterranean. North of the Pyrenees, mountain-chains run
through France, connected with the Alps that separate and cut
off Italy from France and Germany. Greece also belongs to
this part of Europe. Greece and Italy long presented the theatre of the World's History; and while the middle and north of
Europe were uncultivated, the World-Spirit found its home
here.

The second portion is the heart of Europe, which Cæsar
opened when conquering Gaul. This achievement was one of
manhood on the part of the *Roman* General, and more productive than that youthful one of Alexander, who undertook to
exalt the East to a participation in Greek life; and whose work,
though in its purport the noblest and fairest for the imagination,
soon vanished, as a mere Ideal, in the sequel.—In this centre
of Europe, France, Germany, and England are the principal
countries.

Lastly, the third part consists of the north-eastern States of
Europe—Poland, Russia, and the Slavonic Kingdoms. They
come only late into the series of historical States, and form and
perpetuate the connection with Asia. In contrast with the
physical peculiarities of the earlier divisions, these are, as already noticed, not present in a remarkable degree, but counterbalance each other.

THE PHILOSOPHY OF HISTORY

CLASSIFICATION OF HISTORIC DATA

IN the geographical survey, the course of the World's History has been marked out in its general features. The
Sun—the Light—rises in the East. Light is a simply self-
involved existence; but though possessing thus in itself universality, it exists at the same time as an individuality in the
Sun. Imagination has often pictured to itself the emotions
of a blind man suddenly becoming possessed of sight, beholding the bright glimmering of the dawn, the growing light, and
the flaming glory of the ascending Sun. The boundless forgetfulness of his individuality in this pure splendor, is his first
feeling—utter astonishment. But when the Sun is risen, this
astonishment is diminished; objects around are perceived, and
from them the individual proceeds to the contemplation of his
own inner being, and thereby the advance is made to the perception of the relation between the two. Then inactive contemplation is quitted for activity; by the close of day man has
erected a building constructed from his own inner Sun; and
when in the evening he contemplates this, he esteems it more
highly than the original external Sun. For now he stands in a
conscious relation to his Spirit, and therefore a *free* relation.
If we hold this image fast in mind, we shall find it symbolizing
the course of History, the great Day's work of Spirit.

The History of the World travels from East to West, for
Europe is absolutely the end of History, Asia the beginning.
The History of the World has an East κατ᾽ ἐξοχήν; (the term
East in itself is entirely relative), for although the Earth forms
a sphere, History performs no circle round it, but has on the
contrary a determinate East, viz., Asia. Here rises the outward
physical Sun, and in the West it sinks down: here consentaneously rises the Sun of self-consciousness, which diffuses a

103

nobler brilliance. The History of the World is the discipline of the uncontrolled natural will, bringing it into obedience to a Universal principle and conferring subjective freedom. The East knew and to the present day knows only that *One* is Free; the Greek and Roman world, that *some* are free; the German World knows that *All* are free. The first political form therefore which we observe in History, is *Despotism,* the second *Democracy* and *Aristocracy,* the third *Monarchy.*

To understand this division we must remark that as the State is the universal spiritual life, to which individuals by birth sustain a relation of confidence and habit, and in which they have their existence and reality—the first question is, whether their actual life is an unreflecting use and habit combining them in this unity, or whether its constituent individuals are reflective and personal beings having a properly subjective and independent existence. In view of this, *substantial* [objective] freedom must be distinguished from *subjective* freedom. Substantial freedom is the abstract undeveloped Reason implicit in volition, proceeding to develop itself in the State. But in this phase of Reason there is still wanting personal insight and will, that is, subjective freedom; which is realized only in the Individual, and which constitutes the reflection of the Individual in his own conscience.* Where there is merely substantial freedom, commands and laws are regarded as some-thing fixed and abstract, to which the subject holds himself in absolute servitude. These laws need not concur with the desire of the individual, and the subjects are consequently like children, who obey their parents without will or insight of their own. But as subjective freedom arises, and man descends from the contemplation of external reality into his own soul, the contrast suggested by reflection arises, involving the Negation of Reality. The drawing back from the actual world forms *ipso facto* an antithesis, of which one side is the absolute Being —the Divine—the other the human subject as an individual. In that immediate, unreflected consciousness which character-

---

* The essence of Spirit is self-determination or " Freedom." Where Spirit has attained mature growth, as in the man who acknowledges the absolute validity of the dictates of Conscience, the Individual is "a law to himself," and this Freedom is "realized." But in lower stages of morality and civilization, he *unconsciously projects* this legislative principle into some " governing power " (one or several), and obeys it as if it were an alien, extraneous force, not the voice of that Spirit of which he himself (though at this stage imperfectly) is an embodiment. The Philosophy of History exhibits the successive stages by which he reaches the consciousness, that it is *his own inmost being* that thus governs him —*i.e.* a consciousness of self-determination or " Freedom."—Ed.

izes the East, these two are not yet distinguished. The substantial world is distinct from the individual, but the antithesis has not yet created a schism between [absolute and subjective] Spirit.

The first phase—that with which we have to begin—is the *East*. Unreflected consciousness—substantial, objective, spiritual existence—forms the basis; to which the subjective will first sustains a relation in the form of faith, confidence, obedience. In the political life of the East we find a realized rational freedom, developing itself without advancing to *subjective* freedom. It is the childhood of History. Substantial forms constitute the gorgeous edifices of Oriental *Empires* in which we find all rational ordinances and arrangements, but in such a way, that individuals remain as mere accidents. These revolve round a centre, round the sovereign, who, as patriarch—not as despot in the sense of the *Roman* Imperial Constitution—stands at the head. For he has to enforce the moral and substantial: he has to uphold those essential ordinances which are already established; so that what among us belongs entirely to subjective freedom, here proceeds from the entire and general body of the State. The glory of Oriental conception is the One Individual as that substantial being to which all belongs, so that no other individual has a separate existence, or mirrors himself in his subjective freedom. All the riches of imagination and Nature are appropriated to that dominant existence in which subjective freedom is essentially merged; the latter looks for its dignity *not* in itself, but in that absolute object. All the elements of a complete State—even subjectivity—may be found there, but not yet harmonized with the grand substantial being. For outside the One Power—before which nothing can maintain an independent existence—there is only revolting caprice, which, beyond the limits of the central power, roves at will without purpose or result. Accordingly we find the wild hordes breaking out from the Upland—falling upon the countries in question, and laying them waste, or settling down in them, and giving up their wild life; but in all cases resultlessly lost in the central substance. This phase of Substantiality, since it has not taken up its antithesis into itself and overcome it, directly divides itself into two elements. On the one side we see duration, stability—Empires belonging to mere space, as it were [as distinguished from Time]—unhistorical History;—as for

example, in China, the State based on the Family relation;—
a paternal Government, which holds together the constitution
by its provident care, its admonitions, retributive or rather
disciplinary inflictions;—a prosaic Empire, because the antithesis of Form, viz., Infinity, Ideality, has not yet asserted itself.
On the other side, the Form of Time stands contrasted with
this spatial stability. The States in question, without undergoing any change in themselves, or in the principle of their
existence, are constantly changing their position towards each
other. They are in ceaseless conflict, which brings on rapid
destruction. The opposing principle of individuality enters into
these conflicting relations; but it is itself as yet only unconscious, merely natural Universality—Light, which is not yet
the light of the personal soul. This History, too (*i.e.,* of the
struggles before-mentioned) is, for the most part, really *unhistorical,* for it is only the repetition of the same majestic ruin.
The new element, which in the shape of bravery, prowess, magnanimity, occupies the place of the previous despotic pomp,
goes through the same circle of decline and subsidence. This
subsidence is therefore not really such, for through all this restless change no advance is made. History passes at this point—
and only outwardly, *i.e.,* without connection with the previous
phase—to Central Asia. Continuing the comparison with the
ages of the individual man, this would be the boyhood of History, no longer manifesting the repose and trustingness of the
child, but boisterous and turbulent. The Greek World may then
be compared with the period of adolescence, for here we have
individualities forming themselves. This is the *second* main
principle in human History. Morality is, as in Asia, a principle; but it is morality impressed on individuality, and consequently denoting the free volition of Individuals. Here, then,
is the Union of the Moral with the subjective Will, or the
Kingdom of *Beautiful Freedom,* for the Idea is united with
a plastic form. It is not yet regarded abstractedly, but immediately bound up with the Real, as in a beautiful work of Art;
the Sensuous bears the stamp and expression of the Spiritual.
This Kingdom is consequently true Harmony; the world of
the most charming, but perishable or quickly passing bloom:
it is the natural, unreflecting observance of what is *becoming*—
not yet true *Morality*. The individual will of the Subject
adopts unreflectingly the conduct and habit prescribed by Jus-

tice and the Laws. The Individual is therefore in unconscious unity with the Idea—the social weal. That which in the East is divided into two extremes—the substantial as such, and the individuality absorbed in it—meets here. But these distinct principles are only *immediately* in unity, and consequently involve the highest degree of contradiction; for this æsthetic Morality has not yet passed through the struggle of subjective freedom, in its second birth, its *palingenesis;* it is not yet purified to the standard of the free subjectivity that is the essence of true morality.

The third phase is the realm of abstract Universality (in which the Social aim absorbs all individual aims): it is the *Roman State,* the severe labors of the *Manhood* of History. For true manhood acts neither in accordance with the caprice of a despot, nor in obedience to a graceful caprice of its own; but works for a general aim, one in which the individual perishes and realizes his own private object only in that general aim. The State begins to have an abstract existence, and to develop itself for a definite object, in accomplishing which its members have indeed a share, but not a complete and concrete one [calling their whole being into play]. Free *individuals* are sacrificed to the severe demands of the *National* objects, to which they must surrender themselves in this service of abstract generalization. The Roman State is not a repetition of such a State of Individuals as the Athenian Polis was. The geniality and joy of soul that existed there have given place to harsh and rigorous toil. The interest of History is detached from individuals, but these gain for themselves abstract, formal Universality. The Universal subjugates the individuals; they have to merge their own interests in it; but in return the abstraction which they themselves embody—that is to say, their personality—is recognized: in their individual capacity they become persons with definite rights as such. In the same sense as individuals may be said to be incorporated in the abstract idea of Person, *National Individualities* (those of the Roman Provinces) have also to experience this fate: in this form of Universality their concrete forms are crushed, and incorporated with it as a homogeneous and indifferent mass. Rome becomes a Pantheon of all deities, and of all Spiritual existence, but these divinities and this Spirit do not retain their proper vitality.—The development of the State in question proceeds in two directions. On the one hand, as based on reflection—abstract Universality—it has the express outspoken antithesis in itself: it therefore essentially involves in itself the struggle which that antithesis supposes; with the necessary issue, that individual caprice—the purely contingent and thoroughly worldly power of *one despot*—gets the better of that abstract universal principle. At the very outset we have the antithesis between the Aim of the State as the abstract universal principle on the one hand, and the abstract personality of the individual on the other hand. But when subsequently, in the historical development, individuality gains the ascendant, and the breaking up of the community into its component atoms can only be restrained by external compulsion, then the subjective might of *individual despotism* comes forward to play its part, as if summoned to fulfil this task. For the mere abstract compliance with Law implies on the part of the subject of law the supposition that he has not attained to self-organization and self-control; and this principle of obedience, instead of being hearty and voluntary, has for its motive and ruling power only the arbitrary and contingent disposition of the individual; so that the latter is led to seek consolation for the loss of his freedom in exercising and developing his private right. This is the purely *worldly* harmonization of the antithesis. But in the next place, the pain inflicted by Despotism begins to be felt, and Spirit driven back into its utmost depths, leaves the godless world, seeks for a harmony in itself, and begins now an inner life—a complete concrete subjectivity, which possesses at the same time a substantiality that is not grounded in mere external existence. Within the soul therefore arises the *Spiritual* pacification of the struggle, in the fact that the individual personality, instead of following its own capricious choice, is purified and elevated into universality;—a subjectivity that of its own free will adopts principles tending to the good of all—reaches, in fact, a divine personality. To that worldly empire, this Spiritual one wears a predominant aspect of opposition, as the empire of a subjectivity that has attained to the knowledge of itself—itself in its essential nature—the Empire of Spirit in its full sense.

The *German* world appears at this point of development—the fourth phase of World-History. This would answer in the comparison with the periods of human life to its *Old Age*. The

Old Age of *Nature* is weakness; but that of *Spirit* is its perfect maturity and *strength,* in which it returns to unity with itself, but in its fully developed character as *Spirit*.—This fourth phase begins with the Reconciliation presented in Christianity; but only in the germ, without national or political development. We must therefore regard it as commencing rather with the enormous contrast between the spiritual, religious principle, and the barbarian Real World. For Spirit as the consciousness of an inner World is, at the commencement, itself still in an abstract form. All that is *secular* is consequently given over to rudeness and capricious violence. The *Mohammedan* principle—the enlightenment of the Oriental World—is the first to contravene this barbarism and caprice. We find it developing itself later and more rapidly than Christianity; for the latter needed eight centuries to grow up into a political form. But that principle of the German World which we are now discussing, attained concrete reality only in the history of the German Nations. The contrast of the Spiritual principle animating the *Ecclesiastical* State, with the rough and wild barbarism of the *Secular* State, is here likewise present. The Secular *ought* to be in harmony with the Spiritual principle, but we find nothing more than the *recognition* of that obligation. The Secular power forsaken by the Spirit, must in the first instance vanish in presence of the Ecclesiastical [as representative of Spirit]; but while this latter degrades itself to mere secularity, it loses its influence with the loss of its proper character and vocation. From this corruption of the Ecclesiastical element—that is, of the Church—results the higher form of rational thought. Spirit once more driven back upon itself, produces its work in an intellectual shape, and becomes capable of realizing the Ideal of Reason from the Secular principle alone. Thus it happens, that in virtue of elements of Universality, which have the principle of Spirit as their basis, the empire of Thought is established actually and concretely. The antithesis of Church and State vanishes. The Spiritual becomes reconnected with the Secular, and develops this latter as an independently organic existence. The State no longer occupies a position of real inferiority to the Church, and is no longer subordinate to it. The latter asserts no prerogative, and the Spiritual is no longer an element foreign to the State. Freedom has found the means of realizing its Ideal

—its true existence. This is the ultimate result which the process of History is intended to accomplish, and we have to traverse in detail the long track which has been thus cursorily traced out. Yet length of Time is something entirely relative, and the element of Spirit is Eternity. Duration, properly speaking, cannot be said to belong to it.

PART I

THE ORIENTAL WORLD

W E have to begin with the Oriental World, but not before the period in which we discover States in it. The diffusion of Language and the formation of races lie beyond the limits of History. History is prose, and myths fall short of History. The consciousness of external definite existence only arises in connection with the power to form abstract distinctions and assign abstract predicates; and in proportion as a capacity for expressing Laws [of natural or social life] is acquired, in the same proportion does the ability manifest itself, to comprehend objects in an unpoetical form. While the ante-historical is that which precedes political life, it also lies beyond self-cognizant life; though surmises and suppositions may be entertained respecting that period, these do not amount to facts. The Oriental World has as its inherent and distinctive principle the Substantial [the Prescriptive], in Morality. We have the first example of a subjugation of the mere arbitrary will, which is merged in this substantiality. Moral distinctions and requirements are expressed as Laws, but so that the subjective will is governed by these Laws as by an external force. Nothing subjective in the shape of disposition, Conscience, formal Freedom, is recognized. Justice is administered only on the basis of external morality, and Government exists only as the prerogative of compulsion. Our civil law contains indeed some purely compulsory ordinances. I can be compelled to give up another man's property, or to keep an agreement which I have made; but the Moral is not placed by *us* in the mere compulsion, but in the disposition of the subjects—their sympathy with the requirements of law. Morality is in the East likewise a subject of positive legislation, and although the moral prescriptions (the *substance* of their

Ethics) may be perfect, what should be internal subjective sentiment is made a matter of external arrangement. There is no want of a will to command moral actions, but of a will to perform them because commanded from *within*. Since Spirit has not yet attained subjectivity, it wears the appearance of spirituality still involved in the conditions of Nature. Since the external and the internal, Law and Moral Sense, are not yet distinguished—still form an undivided unity—so also do Religion and the State. The Constitution generally is a Theocracy, and the Kingdom of God is to the same extent also a secular Kingdom as the secular Kingdom is also divine. What we call God has not yet in the East been realized in consciousness, for our idea of God involves an elevation of the soul to the supersensual. While *we* obey, because what we are required to do is confirmed by an *internal* sanction, there the Law is regarded as inherently and absolutely valid without a sense of the want of this subjective confirmation. In the law men recognize not their own will, but one entirely foreign.

Of the several parts of Asia we have already eliminated as unhistorical, Upper Asia (so far and so long as its Nomad population do not appear on the scene of history), and Siberia. The rest of the Asiatic World is divided into four districts: first, the River-Plains, formed by the Yellow and Blue Stream, and the Upland of farther Asia—China and the Mongols. Secondly, the valley of the Ganges and that of the Indus. The third theatre of History comprises the river-plains of the Oxus and Jaxartes, the Upland of Persia, and the other valley-plains of the Euphrates and Tigris, to which Hither-Asia attaches itself. Fourthly, the River-plain of the Nile.

With *China* and the *Mongols*—the realm of theocratic despotism—History begins. Both have the patriarchal constitution for their principle—so modified in China, as to admit the development of an organized system of secular polity; while among the Mongols it limits itself to the simple form of a spiritual, religious sovereignty. In China the Monarch is Chief as Patriarch. The laws of the state are partly civil ordinances, partly moral requirements; so that the internal law—the knowledge on the part of the individual of the nature of his volition, as his own inmost self—even this is the subject of external statutory enactment. The sphere of subjectivity does not then, attain to maturity here, since moral laws are treated as legisla-

tive enactments, and law on its part has an ethical aspect. All
that we call subjectivity is concentrated in the supreme head of
the State, who, in all his legislation has an eye to the health,
wealth, and benefit of the whole. Contrasted with this secular
Empire is the spiritual sovereignty of the Mongols, at the head
of which stands the Lama, who is honored as God. In this
Spiritual Empire no secular political life can be developed.

In the second phase—the *Indian* realm—we see the unity
of political organization—a perfect civil machinery, such as
exists in China—in the first instance, broken up. The several
powers of society appear as dissevered and free in relation to
each other. The different castes are indeed, fixed; but in view
of the religious doctrine that established them, they wear the
aspect of *natural* distinctions. Individuals are thereby still
further stripped of proper personality—although it might appear as if they derived gain from the development of the distinctions in question. For though we find the organization
of the State no longer, as in China, determined and arranged
by the one all-absorbing personality [the head of the State]
the distinctions that exist are attributed to Nature, and so become differences of Caste. The unity in which these divisions
must finally meet, is a religious one; and thus arises Theocratic Aristocracy and its despotism. Here begins, therefore,
the distinction between the spiritual consciousness and secular
conditions; but as the *separation* implied in the above mentioned distinctions is the cardinal consideration, so also we find
in the religion the principle of the isolation of the constituent
elements of the Idea;—a principle which posits the harshest
antithesis—the conception of the purely abstract unity of God,
and of the purely sensual Powers of Nature. The connection
of the two is only a constant change—a restless hurrying from
one extreme to the other—a wild chaos of fruitless variation,
which must appear as madness to a duly regulated, intelligent
consciousness.

The third important form—presenting a contrast to the immovable unity of China and to the wild and turbulent unrest
of India—is the *Persian* Realm. China is quite peculiarly Oriental; India we might compare with Greece; Persia on the
other hand with Rome. In Persia namely, the Theocratic
power appears as a *Monarchy*. Now Monarchy is that kind
of constitution which does indeed unite the members of the

body politic in the head of the government as in a point; but regards that head neither as the absolute director nor the arbitrary ruler, but as a power whose will is regulated by the same principle of law as the obedience of the subject. We have thus a general principle, a Law, lying at the basis of the whole, but which, still regarded as a dictum of mere Nature [not as free and absolute Truth] is clogged by an antithesis [that of formal freedom on the part of man as commanded to obey positive alien requirements]. The representation, therefore, which Spirit makes of itself is, at this grade of progress, of a purely natural kind—Light. This Universal principle is as much a regulative one for the monarch as for each of his subjects, and the Persian Spirit is accordingly clear, illuminated—the idea of a people living in pure morality, as in a sacred community. But this has on the one hand as a merely natural Ecclesia, the above antithesis still unreconciled; and its sanctity displays the characteristics of a compulsory, external one. On the other hand this antithesis is exhibited in Persia in its being the Empire of hostile peoples, and the union of the most widely differing nations. The Persian Unity is not that abstract one of the Chinese Empire; it is adapted to rule over many and various nationalities, which it unites under the mild power of Universality as a beneficial Sun shining over all— waking them into life and cherishing their growth. This Universal principle—occupying the position of a root only—allows the several members a free growth for unrestrained expansion and ramification. In the organization of these several peoples, the various principles and forms of life have full play and continue to exist together. We find in this multitude of nations, roving Nomades; then we see in Babylonia and Syria commerce and industrial pursuits in full vigor, the wildest sensuality, the most uncontrolled turbulence. The coasts mediate a connection with foreign lands. In the midst of this confusion the spiritual God of the Jews arrests our attention—like Brahm, existing only for Thought, yet jealous and excluding from his being and abolishing all distinct speciality of manifestations [avatars], such as are freely allowed in other religions. This Persian Empire, then—since it can tolerate these several principles, exhibits the Antithesis in a lively active form, and is not shut up within itself, abstract and calm, as are China and India—makes a real transition in the History of the World.

If Persia forms the *external* transition to Greek life, the internal, *mental* transition is mediated by *Egypt*. Here the antitheses in their abstract form are broken through; a breaking through which effects their nullification. This undeveloped reconciliation exhibits the struggle of the most contradictory principles, which are not yet capable of harmonizing themselves, but, setting up the birth of this harmony as the problem to be solved, make themselves a riddle for themselves and for others, the solution of which is only to be found in the *Greek* World.

If we compare these kingdoms in the light of their various fates, we find the empire of the two Chinese rivers the only durable kingdom in the World. Conquests cannot affect such an empire. The world of the Ganges and the Indus has also been preserved. A state of things so destitute of [distinct] thought is likewise imperishable, but it is in its very nature destined to be mixed with other races—to be conquered and subjugated. While these two realms have remained to the present day, of the empires of the Tigris and Euphrates on the contrary nothing remains, except, at most, a heap of bricks; for the Persian Kingdom, as that of Transition, is by nature perishable, and the Kingdoms of the Caspian Sea are given up to the ancient struggle of Iran and Turan. The Empire of the solitary Nile is only present *beneath* the ground, in its speechless Dead, ever and anon stolen away to all quarters of the globe, and in their majestic habitations;—for what remains above ground is nothing else but such splendid tombs.

SECTION I

CHINA

W ITH the Empire of China History has to begin, for it is the oldest, as far as history gives us any information; and its *principle* has such substantiality, that for the empire in question it is at once the oldest and the newest. Early do we see China advancing to the condition in which it is found at this day; for as the contrast between objective existence and subjective freedom of movement in it, is still wanting, every change is excluded, and the fixedness of a character which recurs perpetually, takes the place of what we should call the truly historical. China and India lie, as it were, still outside the World's History, as the mere presupposition of elements whose combination must be waited for to constitute their vital progress. The unity of substantiality and subjective freedom so entirely excludes the distinction and contrast of the two elements, that by this very fact, substance cannot arrive at reflection on itself—at subjectivity. The Substantial [Positive] in its moral aspect, rules therefore, not as the moral disposition of the *Subject*, but as the despotism of the *Sovereign*.

No People has a so strictly continuous series of Writers of History as the Chinese. Other Asiatic peoples also have ancient traditions, but no History. The Vedas of the Indians are not such. The traditions of the Arabs are very old, but are not attached to a political constitution and its development. But such a constitution exists in China, and that in a distinct and prominent form. The Chinese traditions ascend to 3000 years before Christ; and the *Shu-King*, their canonical document, beginning with the government of Yao, places this 2357 years before Christ. It may here be incidentally remarked, that the other Asiatic kingdoms also reach a high antiquity. According to the calculation of an English writer, the Egyptian history (*e.g.*) reaches to 2207 years before Christ, the Assyrian to 2221, the Indian to 2204. Thus the traditions respecting the

principal kingdoms of the East reach to about 2300 years before the birth of Christ. Comparing this with the history of the
Old Testament, a space of 2400 years, according to the common
acceptation, intervened between the Noachian Deluge and the
Christian era. But Johannes von Müller has adduced weighty
objections to this number. He places the Deluge in the year
3473 before Christ—thus about 1000 years earlier—supporting
his view by the Septuagint. I remark this only with the view
of obviating a difficulty that may appear to arise when we meet
with dates of a higher age than 2400 years before Christ, and yet
find nothing about the Flood.—The Chinese have certain ancient canonical documents, from which their history, constitution, and religion can be gathered. The Vedas and the Mosaic records are similar books; as also the Homeric poems.
Among the Chinese these books are called *Kings*, and constitute the foundation of all their studies. The *Shu-King* contains
their history, treats of the government of the ancient kings, and
gives the statutes enacted by this or that monarch. The *Y-King*
consists of figures, which have been regarded as the bases of the
Chinese written character, and this book is also considered the
groundwork of the Chinese Meditation. For it begins with the
abstractions of Unity and Duality, and then treats of the concrete existences pertaining to these abstract forms of thought.
Lastly, the *Shi-King* is the book of the oldest poems in a great
variety of styles. The high officers of the kingdom were an-
ciently commissioned to bring with them to the annual festival
all the poems composed in their province within the year. The
Emperor in full court was the judge of these poems, and those
recognized as good received public approbation. Besides these
three books of archives which are specially honored and studied,
there are besides two others, less important, viz. the *Li-Ki* (or
Li-King) which records the customs and ceremonial observances pertaining to the Imperial dignity, and that of the State
functionaries (with an appendix, *Yo-King*, treating of music);
and the *Tshun-tsin*, the chronicle of the kingdom Lu, where
Confucius appeared. These books are the groundwork of the
history, the manners and the laws of China.

This empire early attracted the attention of Europeans, although only vague stories about it had reached them. It was
always marvelled at as a country which, self-originated, appeared to have no connection with the outer world.

In the thirteenth century a Venetian (Marco Polo) explored
it for the first time, but his reports were deemed fabulous.   In
later times, everything that he had said respecting its extent
and greatness was entirely confirmed.   By the lowest calculation, China has 150,000,000 of inhabitants; another makes the
number 200,000,000, and the highest raises it even to 300,000,-
000.   From the far north it stretches towards the south to India;
on the east it is bounded by the vast Pacific, and on the west it
extends towards Persia and the Caspian.   China Proper is over-
populated.   On both rivers, the Hoang-ho and the Yang-tse-
Kiang, dwell many millions of human beings, living on rafts
adapted to all the requirements of their mode of life.   The population and the thoroughly organized State-arrangements, de-
scending even to the minutest details, have astonished Europeans; and a matter of especial astonishment is the accuracy
with which their historical works are executed.   For in China
the Historians are some of the highest functionaries.   Two
ministers constantly in attendance on the Emperor, are commissioned to keep a journal of everything the Emperor does,
commands, and says, and their notes are then worked up and
made use of by the Historians.   We cannot go further into the
minutiæ of their annals, which, as they themselves exhibit no
development, would only hinder us in ours.   Their History
ascends to very ancient times, in which Fohi is named as the
Diffuser of culture, he having been the original civilizer of
China.   He is said to have lived in the twenty-ninth century before Christ—before the time, therefore, at which the Shu-King
begins; but the mythical and prehistorical is treated by Chinese Historians as perfectly historical.   The first region of
Chinese history is the north-western corner—China Proper—
towards that point where the Hoang-ho descends from the
mountains; for only at a later period did the Chinese empire
extend itself towards the south, to the Yang-tse-Kiang.   The
narrative begins with the period in which men lived in a wild
state, i.e. in the woods, when they fed on the fruits of the earth,
and clothed themselves with the skins of wild beasts.   There
was no recognition of definite laws among them.   To Fohi (who
must be duly distinguished from Fo, the founder of a new
religion) is ascribed the instruction of men in building themselves huts and making dwellings.   He is said to have directed
their attention to the change and return of seasons, to barter

and trade; to have established marriage; to have taught that
Reason came from Heaven, and to have given instructions for
rearing silkworms, building bridges, and making use of beasts
of burden. The Chinese historians are very diffuse on the subject of these various origins. The progress of the history is the
extension of the culture thus originated, to the south, and the
beginning of a state and a government. The great Empire
which had thus gradually been formed, was soon broken up
into many provinces, which carried on long wars with each
other, and were then re-united into a Whole. The dynasties
in China have often been changed, and the one now dominant
is generally marked as the twenty-second. In connection with
the rise and fall of these dynasties arose the different capital
cities that are found in this empire. For a long time Nankin
was the capital; now it is Pekin; at an earlier period other
cities. China has been compelled to wage many wars with the
Tartars, who penetrated far into the country. The long wall
built by Shi-hoang-ti—and which has always been regarded as
a most astounding achievement—was raised as a barrier against
the inroads of the northern Nomades. This prince divided the
whole empire into thirty-six provinces, and made himself especially remarkable by his attacks on the old literature, especially on the historical books and historical studies generally.
He did this with the design of strengthening his own dynasty,
by destroying the remembrance of the earlier one. After the
historical books had been collected and burned, many hundreds of the literati fled to the mountains, in order to save what
remained. Every one that fell into the Emperor's hands experienced the same fate as the books. This Book-burning is a
very important circumstance, for in spite of it the strictly canonical books were saved, as is generally the case. The first connection of China with the West occurred about 64 A.D. At that
epoch a Chinese emperor despatched ambassadors (it is said) to
visit the wise sages of the West. Twenty years later a Chinese
general is reported to have penetrated as far as Judea. At the
beginning of the eighth century after Christ, the first Christians
are reputed to have gone to China, of which visit later visitors
assert that they found traces and monuments. A Tartar kingdom, *Lyau-Tong*, existing in the north of China, is said to have
been reduced and taken possession of by the Chinese with the
help of the Western Tartars, about 1100 A.D. This, neverthe-

less, gave these very Tartars an opportunity of securing a footing in China. Similarly they admitted the Manchus with whom
they engaged in war in the sixteenth and seventeenth centuries,
which resulted in the present dynasty's obtaining possession of
the throne. Yet this new dynasty has not effected further
change in the country, any more than did the earlier conquest
of the Mongols in the year 1281. The Manchus that live in
China have to conform to Chinese laws, and study Chinese sciences.

We pass now from these few dates in Chinese history to the
contemplation of the *Spirit* of the constitution, which has always remained the same. We can deduce it from the general
principle, which is, the immediate unity of the substantial Spirit
and the Individual; but this is equivalent to the Spirit of the
Family, which is here extended over the most populous of
countries. The element of Subjectivity—that is to say, the reflection upon itself of the individual will in antithesis to the
Substantial (as the power in which it is absorbed) or the recognition of this power as *one with its own essential being*, in which
it knows itself *free*—is not found on this grade of development.
The universal Will displays its activity immediately through
that of the individual: the latter has no self-cognizance at all in
antithesis to Substantial, positive being, which it does not yet
regard as a power standing over against it—as, (*e.g.*) in Judaism,
the " Jealous God " is known as the negation of the Individual.
In China the Universal Will immediately commands what the
Individual is to do, and the latter complies and obeys with proportionate renunciation of reflection and personal independence.
If he does not obey, if he thus virtually separates himself from
the Substance of his being, inasmuch as this separation is not
mediated by a retreat within a personality of his own, the punishment he undergoes does not affect his subjective and internal, but simply his outward existence. The element of subjectivity is therefore as much wanting to this political totality
as the latter is on its side altogether destitute of a foundation
in the moral disposition of the subject. For the Substance is
simply an individual—the Emperor—whose law constitutes all
the disposition. Nevertheless, this ignoring of inclination does
not imply caprice, which would itself indicate inclination—
that is, subjectivity and mobility. Here we have the One Being of the State supremely dominant—the Substance, which,

still hard and inflexible, resembles nothing but itself—includes no other element.

This relation, then, expressed more definitely and more conformably with its conception, is that of the *Family*. On this form of moral union alone rests the Chinese State, and it is objective Family Piety that characterizes it. The Chinese regard themselves as belonging to their family, and at the same time as children of the State. In the Family itself they are not personalities, for the consolidated unity in which they exist as members of it is consanguinity and natural obligation. In the State they have as little independent personality; for there the patriarchal relation is predominant, and the government is based on the paternal management of the Emperor, who keeps all departments of the State in order. Five duties are stated in the *Shu-King* as involving grave and unchangeable fundamental relations. 1. The mutual one of the Emperor and people. 2. Of the Fathers and Children. 3. Of an elder and younger brother. 4. Of Husband and Wife. 5. Of Friend and Friend. It may be here incidentally remarked, that the number Five is regarded as fundamental among the Chinese, and presents itself as often as the number Three among us. They have five Elements of Nature—Air, Water, Earth, Metal, and Wood. They recognize *four* quarters of Heaven and a centre. Holy places, where altars are erected, consist of four elevations, and one in the centre.

The duties of the Family are absolutely binding, and established and regulated by law. The son may not accost the father, when he comes into the room; he must seem to contract himself to nothing at the side of the door, and may not leave the room without his father's permission. When the father dies, the son must mourn for three years—abstaining from meat and wine. The business in which he was engaged, even that of the State, must be suspended, for he is obliged to quit it. Even the Emperor, who has just commenced his government, does not devote himself to his duties during this time. No marriage may be contracted in the family within the period of mourning. Only the having reached his fiftieth year exempts the bereaved from the excessive strictness of the regulations, which are then relaxed that he may not be reduced in person by them. The sixtieth year relaxes them still further, and the seventieth limits mourning to the color of the dress.

A mother is honored equally with a father. When Lord Macartney saw the Emperor, the latter was sixty-eight years old,
(sixty years is among the Chinese a fundamental round number, as one hundred is among us), notwithstanding which he
visited his mother every morning on foot, to demonstrate his
respect for her. The New Year's congratulations are offered
even to the mother of the Emperor; and the Emperor himself
cannot receive the homage of the grandees of the court until
he has paid his to his mother. The latter is the first and constant counsellor of her son, and all announcements concerning
his family are made in her name.—The merits of a son are ascribed not to him, but to his father. When on one occasion the
prime minister asked the Emperor to confer titles of honor on
his father, the Emperor issued an edict in which it was said:
" Famine was desolating the Empire: Thy father gave rice to
the starving. What beneficence! The Empire was on the edge
of ruin: Thy father defended it at the hazard of his life. What
fidelity! The government of the kingdom was intrusted to thy
father: he made excellent laws, maintained peace and concord
with the neighboring princes, and asserted the rights of my
crown. What wisdom! The title therefore which I award to
him is: Beneficent, Faithful and Wise."—The Son had done
all that is here ascribed to the Father. In this way ancestors—
a fashion the reverse of ours—obtain titles of honor through
their posterity. But in return, every Father of a Family is
responsible for the transgressions of his descendants; duties
ascend, but none can be properly said to descend.

It is a great object with the Chinese, to have children who
may give them the due honors of burial, pay respect to their
memory after death, and decorate their grave. Although a
Chinese may have many wives, one only is the mistress of the
house, and the children of the subordinate wives have to honor
her absolutely as a mother. If a Chinese husband has no children by any of his wives, he may proceed to adoption with a
view to this posthumous honor. For it is an indispensable
requirement that the grave of parents be annually visited. Here
lamentations are annually renewed, and many, to give full vent
to their grief, remain there sometimes one or two months. The
body of a deceased father is often kept three or four months
in the house, and during this time no one may sit down on a
chair or sleep in a bed. Every family in China has a Hall of

Ancestors where all the members annually assemble; theie are placed representations of those who have filled exalted posts, while the names of those men and women who have been of less importance in the family are inscribed on tablets; the whole family then partake of a meal together, and the poor members are entertained by the more wealthy. It is said that a Mandarin who had become a Christian, having ceased to honor his ancestors in this way, exposed himself to great persecutions on the part of his relatives. The same minuteness of regulation which prevails in the relation between father and children, characterizes also that between the elder brother and the younger ones. The former has, though in a less degree than parents, claims to reverence.

This family basis is also the basis of the Constitution, if we can speak of such. For although the Emperor has the right of a Monarch, standing at the summit of a political edifice, he exercises it paternally. He is the Patriarch, and everything in the State that can make any claim to reverence is attached to him. For the Emperor is chief both in religious affairs and in science—a subject which will be treated of in detail further on.— This paternal care on the part of the Emperor, and the spirit of his subjects—who like children do not advance beyond the ethical principle of the family circle, and can gain for themselves no independent and civil freedom—makes the whole an empire, administration, and social code, which is at the same time moral and thoroughly prosaic—that is, a product of the Understanding without free Reason and Imagination.

The Emperor claims the deepest reverence. In virtue of his position he is obliged personally to manage the government, and must himself be acquainted with and direct the legislative business of the Empire, although the Tribunals give their assistance. Notwithstanding this, there is little room for the exercise of his individual will; for the whole government is conducted on the basis of certain ancient maxims of the Empire, while his constant oversight is not the less necessary. The imperial princes are therefore educated on the strictest plan. Their physical frames are hardened by discipline, and the sciences are their occupation from their earliest years. Their education is conducted under the Emperor's superintendence, and they are early taught that the Emperor is the head of the State and therefore must appear as the first and best in everything. An ex-

amination of the princes takes place every year, and a circumstantial report of the affair is published through the whole Empire, which feels the deepest interest in these matters. China
has therefore succeeded in getting the greatest and best governors, to whom the expression " Solomonian Wisdom " might
be applied; and the present Manchu dynasty has especially
distinguished itself by abilities of mind and body. All the
ideals of princes and of princely education which have been so
numerous and varied since the appearance of Fenelon's " Tele-
maque " are realized here. In Europe there can be no Solo-
mons. But here are the place and the necessity for such government; since the rectitude, the prosperity, the security of all,
depend on the one impulse given to the first link in the entire
chain of this hierarchy. The deportment of the Emperor is
represented to us as in the highest degree simple, natural, noble
and intelligent. Free from a proud taciturnity or repelling *hau-
teur* in speech or manners, he lives in the consciousness of his
own dignity and in the exercise of imperial duties to whose
observance he has been disciplined from his earliest youth. Besides the imperial dignity there is properly no elevated rank,
no nobility among the Chinese; only the princes of the imperial house, and the sons of the ministers enjoy any precedence
of the kind, and they rather by their position than by their
birth. Otherwise all are equal, and only those have a share in
the administration of affairs who have ability for it. Official
stations are therefore occupied by men of the greatest intellect
and education. The Chinese State has consequently been often
set up as an Ideal which may serve even us for a model.

The next thing to be considered is the *administration* of the
Empire. We cannot speak, in reference to China, of a *Constitution;* for this would imply that individuals and corporations
have independent rights—partly in respect of their particular
interests, partly in respect of the entire State. This element
must be wanting here, and we can only speak of an administration of the Empire. In China, we have the reality of absolute
equality, and all the differences that exist are possible only in
connection with that administration, and in virtue of the worth
which a person may acquire, enabling him to fill a high post
in the Government. Since equality prevails in China, but without any freedom, despotism is necessarily the mode of government. Among us, men are equal only before the law, and in

the respect paid to the property of each; but they have also many interests and peculiar privileges, which must be guaranteed, if we are to have what we call freedom. But in the Chinese Empire these special interests enjoy no consideration on their own account, and the government proceeds from the Emperor alone, who sets it in movement as a hierarchy of officials or Mandarins. Of these, there are two kinds—learned and military Mandarins—the latter corresponding to our Officers. The Learned Mandarins constitute the higher rank, for, in China, civilians take precedence of the military. Government officials are educated at the schools; elementary schools are instituted for obtaining elementary knowledge. Institutions for higher cultivation, such as our Universities, may, perhaps, be said not to exist. Those who wish to attain high official posts must undergo several examinations—usually three in number. To the third and last examination—at which the Emperor himself is present—only those can be admitted who have passed the first and second with credit; and the reward for having succeeded in this, is the immediate introduction into the highest Council of the Empire. The sciences, an acquaintance with which is especially required, are the History of the Empire, Jurisprudence, and the science of customs and usages, and of the organization and administration of government. Besides this, the Mandarins are said to have a talent for poetry of the most refined order. We have the means of judging of this, particularly from the Romance, *Ju-kiao-li*, or, " The Two Cousins," translated by Abel Remusat: in this, a youth is introduced who having finished his studies, is endeavoring to attain high dignities. The officers of the army, also, must have some mental acquirements; they too are examined; but civil functionaries enjoy, at stated above, far greater respect. At the great festivals the Emperor appears with a retinue of two thousand Doctors, *i.e.* Mandarins in Civil Offices, and the same number of military Mandarins. (In the whole Chinese State, there are about 15,000 civil, and 20,000 military Mandarins.) The Mandarins who have not yet obtained an office, nevertheless belong to the Court, and are obliged to appear at the great festivals in the Spring and Autumn, when the Emperor himself guides the plough. These functionaries are divided into eight classes. The first are those that attend the Emperor, then follow the viceroys, and so on. The Emperor governs by means of administrative bodies, for the most part composed of Mandarins. The Council of the Empire is the highest body of the kind: it consists of the most learned and talented men. From these are chosen the presidents of the other colleges. The greatest publicity prevails in the business of government. The subordinate officials report to the Council of the Empire, and the latter lay the matter before the Emperor, whose decision is made known in the Court Journal. The Emperor often accuses himself of faults; and should his princes have been unsuccessful in their examination, he blames them severely. In every Ministry, and in various parts of the Empire, there is a Censor (*Ko-tao*), who has to give the Emperor an account of everything. These Censors enjoy a permanent office, and are very much feared. They exercise a strict surveillance over everything that concerns the government, and the public and private conduct of the Mandarins, and make their report immediately to the Emperor. They have also the right of remonstrating with and blaming *him*. The Chinese History gives many examples of the noblemindedness and courage of these Ko-taos. For example: A Censor had remonstrated with a tyrannical sovereign, but had been severely repulsed. Nevertheless, he was not turned away from his purpose, but betook himself once more to the Emperor to renew his remonstrances. Foreseeing his death, he had the coffin brought in with him, in which he was to be buried. It is related of the Censors, that—cruelly lacerated by the torturers and unable to utter a sound—they have even written their animadversions with their own blood in the sand. These Censors themselves form yet another Tribunal which has the oversight of the whole Empire. The Mandarins are responsible also for performing duties arising from unforeseen exigencies in the State. If famine, disease, conspiracy, religious disturbances occur, they have to report the facts; not, however, to wait for further orders from government, but immediately to act as the case requires. The whole of the administration is thus covered by a network of officials. Functionaries are appointed to superintend the roads, the rivers, and the coasts. Everything is arranged with the greatest minuteness. In particular, great attention is paid to the rivers; in the Shu-King are to be found many edicts of the Emperor, designed to secure the land from inundations. The gates of every town are guarded by a watch, and the streets are barred all night. Government officers are always answerable to the higher Council. Every Mandarin is also bound to make known the faults he has committed, every five years; and the trustworthiness of his statement is attested by a Board of Control—the Censorship. In the case of any grave crime not confessed, the Mandarins and their families are punished most severely. From all this it is clear that the Emperor is the centre, around which everything turns; consequently the well-being of the country and people depends on him. The whole hierarchy of the administration works more or less according to a settled routine, which in a peaceful condition of things becomes a convenient habit. Uniform and regular, like the course of nature, it goes its own way, at one time as at another time; but the Emperor is required to be the moving, ever wakeful, spontaneously active Soul. If then the personal character of the Emperor is not of the order described— namely, thoroughly *moral*, laborious, and while maintaining dignity, full of energy—everything is relaxed, and the government is paralyzed from head to foot, and given over to carelessness and caprice. For there is no other legal power or institution extant, but this superintendence and oversight of the Emperor. It is not their own conscience, their own honor, which keeps the offices of government up to their duty, but an external mandate and the severe sanctions by which it is supported. In the instance of the revolution that occurred in the middle of the seventeenth century, the last Emperor of the dynasty was very amiable and honorable; but through the mildness of his character, the reins of government were relaxed, and disturbances naturally ensued. The rebels called the Manchus into the country. The Emperor killed himself to avoid falling into the hands of his enemies, and with his blood wrote on the border of his daughter's robe a few words, in which he complained bitterly of the injustice of his subjects. A Mandarin, who was with him, buried him, and then killed himself on his grave. The Empress and her attendants followed the example. The last prince of the imperial house, who was besieged in a distant province, fell into the hands of the enemy and was put to death. All the other attendant Mandarins died a voluntary death.

Passing from the administration to the *Jurisprudence* of China, we find the subjects regarded as in a state of nonage, in virtue of the principle of patriarchal government. No independent classes or orders, as in India, have interests of their own to defend. All is directed and superintended from above. All legal relations are definitely settled by rules; free sentiment —the moral standpoint generally—is thereby thoroughly obliterated.* It is formally determined by the laws in what way the members of the family should be disposed towards each other, and the transgression of these laws entails in some cases severe punishment. The second point to be noticed here, is the legal externality of the Family relations, which becomes almost slavery. Every one has the power of selling himself and his children; every Chinese buys his wife. Only the chief wife is a free woman. The concubines are slaves, and—like the children and every other chattel—may be seized upon in case of confiscation.

A third point is, that punishments are generally corporal chastisements. Among us, this would be an insult to honor; not so in China, where the feeling of honor has not yet developed itself. A dose of cudgelling is the most easily forgotten; yet it is the severest punishment for a man of honor, who desires not to be esteemed physically assailable, but who is vulnerable in directions implying a more refined sensibility. But the Chinese do not recognize a subjectivity in honor; they are the subjects rather of corrective than retributive punishment—as are children among us; for *corrective* punishment aims at improvement, that which is *retributive* implies veritable imputation of guilt. In the *corrective,* the deterring principle is only the fear of punishment, not any consciousness of wrong; for here we cannot presume upon any reflection upon the nature of the action itself. Among the Chinese all crimes—those committed against the laws of the Family relation, as well as against the State—are punished externally. Sons who fail in paying due honor to their Father or Mother, younger brothers who are not sufficiently respectful to elder ones, are bastinadoed. If a son complains of injustice done to him by his father, or a younger brother by an elder, he receives a hundred blows with a bamboo, and is banished for three years, *if he is in the right;*

* It is evident that the term " *moral standpoint* " is used here in the strict sense in which Hegel has defined it, in his " Philosophy of Law," as that of the self-determination of subjectivity, *free conviction* of the Good. The reader, therefore, should not misunderstand the use that continues to be made of the terms, morality, moral government, etc., in reference to the Chinese; as they denote morality only in the loose and ordinary meaning of the word—precepts or commands given with a view to producing good behavior—without bringing into relief the element of internal conviction.—ED.

if not, he is strangled. If a son should raise his hand against his father, he is condemned to have his flesh torn from his body with red-hot pincers. The relation between husband and wife is, like all other family relations, very highly esteemed, and unfaithfulness—which, however, on account of the seclusion in which the women are kept, can very seldom present itself—meets with severe animadversion. Similar penalties await the exhibition on the part of a Chinese of greater affection to one of his inferior wives than to the matron who heads his establishment, should the latter complain of such disparagement. In China, every Mandarin is authorized to inflict blows with the bamboo; even the highest and most illustrious—Ministers, Viceroys, and even the favorites of the Emperor himself—are punished in this fashion. The friendship of the Emperor is not withdrawn on account of such chastisement, and they themselves appear not sensibly touched by it. When, on one occasion, the last English embassy to China was conducted home from the palace by the princes and their retinue, the Master of the Ceremonies, in order to make room, without any ceremony cleared the way among the princes and nobles with a whip.

As regards responsibility, the distinction between *malice prepense* and blameless or accidental commission of an act is not regarded; for accident among the Chinese is as much charged with blame, as intention. Death is the penalty of accidental homicide. This ignoring of the distinction between accident and intention occasions most of the disputes between the English and the Chinese; for should the former be attacked by the latter—should a ship of war, believing itself attacked, defend itself, and a Chinese be killed as the consequence—the Chinese are accustomed to require that the Englishman who fired the fatal shot should lose his life. Everyone who is in any way connected with the transgressor, shares—especially in the case of crimes against the Emperor—the ruin of the actual offender: all his near kinsmen are tortured to death. The printers of an objectionable book and those who read it, are similarly exposed to the vengeance of the law. The direction which this state of things gives to private revenge is singular. It may be said of the Chinese that they are extremely sensitive to injuries and of a vindictive nature. To satisfy his revenge the offended person does not venture to kill his opponent, because the whole

family of the assassin would be put to death; he therefore
inflicts an injury on himself, to ruin his adversary. In many
towns it has been deemed necessary to contract the openings of
wells, to put a stop to suicides by drowning. For when anyone
has committed suicide, the laws ordain that the strictest investigation shall be made into the cause. All the enemies of the
suicide are arrested and put to the torture, and if the person
who has committed the insult which led to the act, can be discovered, he and his whole family are executed. In case of
insult therefore, a Chinese prefers killing himself rather than
his opponent; since in either case he must die, but in the former contingency will have the due honors of burial, and may
cherish the hope that his family will acquire the property of
his adversary. Such is the fearful state of things in regard to
responsibility and non-responsibility; all subjective freedom
and moral concernment with an action are ignored. In the
Mosaic Laws, where the distinction between *dolus, culpa,* and
casus, is also not yet clearly recognized, there is nevertheless
an asylum opened for the innocent homicide, to which he may
betake himself.—There is in China no distinction in the penal
code between higher and lower classes. A field-marshal of the
Empire, who had very much distinguished himself, was tra-
duced on some account, to the Emperor; and the punishment
for the alleged crime, was that he should be a spy upon those
who did not fulfil their duty in clearing away the snow from
the streets.—Among the legal relations of the Chinese we have
also to notice changes in the rights of possession and the introduction of slavery, which is connected there with it. The soil
of China, in which the chief possessions of the Chinese consist,
was regarded only at a late epoch as essentially the property
of the State. At that time the Ninth of all moneys from estates
was allotted by law to the Emperor. At a still later epoch serfdom was established, and its enactment has been ascribed to
the Emperor Shi-hoang-ti, who in the year 213 B.C., built the
Great Wall; who had all the writings that recorded the ancient
rights of the Chinese, burned; and who brought many independent principalities of China under his dominion. His wars
caused the conquered lands to become private property, and
the dwellers on these lands, serfs. In China, however, the distinction between Slavery and freedom is necessarily, not great,
since all are equal before the Emperor—that is, all are alike

degraded. As no honor exists, and no one has an individual right in respect of others, the consciousness of debasement predominates, and this easily passes into that of utter abandonment. With this abandonment is connected the great immorality of the Chinese. They are notorious for deceiving wherever they can. Friend deceives friend, and no one resents the attempt at deception on the part of another, if the deceit has not succeeded in its object, or comes to the knowledge of the person sought to be defrauded. Their frauds are most astutely and craftily performed, so that Europeans have to be painfully cautious in dealing with them. Their consciousness of moral abandonment shows itself also in the fact that the religion of Fo is so widely diffused; a religion which regards as the Highest and Absolute—as God—*pure Nothing;* which sets up contempt for individuality, for personal existence, as the highest perfection.

We come, then, to the consideration of the *religious* side of the Chinese Polity. In the patriarchal condition the religious exaltation of man has merely a human reference—simple morality and right-doing. The Absolute itself, is regarded partly as the abstract, simple rule of this right-doing—eternal rectitude; partly as the *power* which is its sanction. Except in these simple aspects, all the relations of the natural world, the postulates of subjectivity—of heart and soul—are entirely ignored. The Chinese in their patriarchal despotism need no such connection or mediation with the Highest Being; for education, the laws of morality and courtesy, and the commands and government of the Emperor embody all such connection and mediation as far as they feel the need of it. The Emperor, as he is the Supreme Head of the State, is also the Chief of its religion. Consequently, religion is in China essentially State-Religion. The distinction between it and Lamaism must be observed, since *the latter* is not developed to a State, but contains religion as a free, spiritual, disinterested consciousness. That *Chinese* religion, therefore, cannot be what *we* call religion. For to us religion means the retirement of the Spirit within itself, in contemplating its essential nature, its inmost Being. In these spheres, then, man is withdrawn from his relation to the State, and betaking himself to this retirement, is able to release himself from the power of secular government. But in China religion has not risen to this grade, for true

faith is possible only where individuals can seclude themselves
—can exist for themselves independently of any external compulsory power. In China the individual has no such life;—does
not enjoy this independence: in any direction he is therefore
dependent; in religion as well as in other things; that is, dependent on objects of nature, of which the most exalted is the
material heaven. On this depend harvest, the seasons of the
year, the abundance and sterility of crops. The Emperor, as
crown of all—the embodiment of power—alone approaches
heaven; individuals, as such, enjoy no such privilege. He it
is, who presents the offerings at the four feasts; gives thanks
at the head of his court, for the harvest, and invokes blessings
on the sowing of the seed. This " heaven " might be taken in
the sense of our term " God," as the Lord of Nature (we say,
for example, " Heaven protect us! ") ; but such a relation is
beyond the scope of Chinese thought, for here the one isolated
self-consciousness is substantial being, the Emperor himself,
the Supreme Power. Heaven has therefore no higher meaning
than Nature. The Jesuits indeed, yielded to Chinese notions
so far as to call the Christian God, " Heaven "—" Tien " ; but
they were on that account accused to the Pope by other Christian Orders. The Pope consequently sent a Cardinal to China,
who died there. A bishop who was subsequently despatched,
enacted that instead of " Heaven," the term " Lord of Heaven '
should be adopted. The relation to *Tien* is supposed to be such,
that the good conduct of individuals and of the Emperor brings
blessing; their transgressions on the other hand cause want
and evil of all kinds. The Chinese religion involves that primitive element of magical influence over nature, inasmuch as
human conduct absolutely determines the course of events. If
the Emperor behaves well, prosperity cannot but ensue; Heaven
must ordain prosperity. A second side of this religion is, that
as the general aspect of the relation to Heaven is bound up with
the person of the Emperor, he has also its more special bearings
in his hands; viz. the particular well-being of individuals and
provinces. These have each an appropriate *Genius* (Chen),
which is subject to the Emperor, who pays adoration only to
the general Power of Heaven, while the several Spirits of the
natural world follow his laws. He is thus made the proper
legislator for Heaven as well as for earth. To these Genii,
each of which enjoys a worship peculiar to itself, certain sculp-

tured forms are assigned. These are disgusting idols, which have not yet attained the dignity of art, because nothing spiritual is represented in them. They are therefore only terrific, frightful and negative; they keep watch—as among the Greeks do the River-Gods, the Nymphs, and Dryads—over single elements and natural objects. Each of the five Elements has its genius, distinguished by a particular color. The sovereignty of the dynasty that occupies the throne of China also depends on a Genius, and this one has a yellow color. Not less does every province and town, every mountain and river possess an appropriate Genius. All these Spirits are subordinate to the Emperor, and in the Annual Directory of the Empire are registered the functionaries and genii to whom such or such a brook, river, etc., has been intrusted. If a mischance occurs in any part, the Genius is deposed as a Mandarin would be. The Genii have innumerable temples (in Pekin nearly 10,000) to which a multitude of priests and convents are attached. These "Bonzes" live unmarried, and in all cases of distress are applied to by the Chinese for counsel. In other respects, however, neither they nor the temples are much venerated. Lord Macartney's Embassy was even quartered in a temple—such buildings beings used as inns. The Emperor has sometimes thought fit to secularize many thousands of these convents; to compel the Bonzes to return to civil life; and to impose taxes on the estates appertaining to the foundations. The Bonzes are soothsayers and exorcists: for the Chinese are given up to boundless superstitions. This arises from the want of subjective independence, and presupposes the very opposite of freedom of Spirit. In every undertaking—*e.g.* if the site of a house, or of a grave, etc., is to be determined—the advice of the Soothsayers as asked. In the Y-King certain lines are given, which supply fundamental forms and categories—on account of which this book is called the "Book of Fates." A certain meaning is ascribed to the combination of such lines, and prophetic announcements are deduced from this groundwork. Or a number of little sticks are thrown into the air, and the fate in question is prognosticated from the way in which they fall. What we regard as chance, as natural connection, the Chinese seek to deduce or attain by magical arts; and in this particular also, their want of spiritual religion is manifested.

With this deficiency of genuine subjectivity is connected

moreover, the form which Chinese *Science* assumes. In mentioning Chinese sciences we encounter a considerable clamor about their perfection and antiquity. Approaching the subject more closely, we see that the sciences enjoy very great respect, and that they are even publicly extolled and promoted by the Government. The Emperor himself stands at the apex of literature. A college exists whose special business it is to edit the decrees of the Emperor, with a view to their being composed in the best style; and this redaction assumes the character of an important affair of State. The Mandarins in their notifications have to study the same perfection of style, for the form is expected to correspond with the excellence of the matter. One of the highest Governmental Boards is the Academy of Sciences. The Emperor himself examines its members; they live in the palace, and perform the functions of Secretaries, Historians of the Empire, Natural Philosophers, and Geographers. Should a new law be proposed, the Academy must report upon it. By way of introduction to such report it must give the history of existing enactments; or if the law in question affects foreign countries, a description of them is required. The Emperor himself writes the prefaces to the works thus composed. Among recent Emperors *Kien-long* especially distinguished himself by his scientific acquirements. He himself wrote much, but became far more remarkable by publishing the principal works that China has produced. At the head of the commission appointed to correct the press, was a Prince of the Empire; and after the work had passed through the hands of all, it came once more back to the Emperor, who severely punished every error that had been committed.

Though in one aspect the sciences appear thus pre-eminently honored and fostered, there are wanting to them on the other side that free ground of subjectivity, and that properly scientific interest, which make them a truly theoretical occupation of the mind. A free, ideal, spiritual kingdom has here no place. What may be called scientific is of a merely empirical nature, and is made absolutely subservient to the Useful on behalf of the State—its requirements and those of individuals. The nature of their Written Language is at the outset a great hindrance to the development of the sciences. Rather, conversely, because a true scientific interest does not exist, the Chinese have acquired no better instrument for representing and imparting thought. They have, as is well known, beside a Spoken Language, a *Written Language;* which does not express, as our does, individual sounds—does not present the spoken words to the eye, but represents the ideas themselves by signs. This appears at first sight a great advantage, and has gained the suffrages of many great men—among others, of Leibnitz. In reality, it is anything but such. For if we consider in the first place, the effect of such a mode of writing on the Spoken Language, we shall find this among the Chinese very imperfect, on account of that separation. For our Spoken Language is matured to distinctness chiefly through the necessity of finding signs for each single sound, which latter, by reading, we learn to express distinctly. The Chinese, to whom such a means of orthoepic development is wanting, do not mature the modifications of sounds in their language to distinct articulations capable of being represented by letters and syllables. Their Spoken Language consists of an inconsiderable number of monosyllabic words, which are used with more than one signification. The sole methods of denoting distinctions of meaning are the connection, the accent, and the pronunciation—quicker or slower, softer or louder. The ears of the Chinese have become very sensible to such distinctions. Thus I find that the word *Po* has eleven different meanings according to the tone: denoting " glass "—" to boil "—" to winnow wheat "—" to cleave asunder "—" to water "—" to prepare "—" an old woman "— " a slave "—" a liberal man "—" a wise person "—" a little."— As to their Written Language, I will specify only the obstacles which it presents to the advance of the sciences. Our Written Language is very simple for a learner, as we analyze our Spoken Language into about twenty-five articulations, by which analysis, speech is rendered definite, the multitude of possible sounds is limited, and obscure intermediate sounds are banished: we have to learn only these signs and their combinations. Instead of twenty-five signs of this sort, the Chinese have many thousands to learn. The number necessary for use is reckoned at 9,353, or even 10,516, if we add those recently introduced; and the number of characters generally, for ideas and their combinations as they are presented in books, amounts to from 80,000 to 90,000. As to the sciences themselves, *History* among the Chinese comprehends the bare and definite facts, without any opinion or reasoning upon them. In the same way their *Jurisprudence* gives only fixed laws, and their *Ethics* only determinate duties, without raising the question of a subjective foundation for them. The Chinese have, however, in addition to other sciences, a *Philosophy*, whose elementary principles are of great antiquity, since the *Y-King*—the *Book of Fates*—treats of Origination and Destruction. In this book are found the purely abstract ideas of Unity and Duality; the Philosophy of the Chinese appears therefore to proceed from the same fundamental ideas as that of Pythagoras.* The fundamental principle recognized is *Reason—Tao;* that essence lying at the basis of the whole, which effects everything. To become acquainted with its forms is regarded among the Chinese also as the highest science; yet this has no connection with the educational pursuits which more nearly concern the State. The works of Lao-tse, and especially his work " Tao-te-King," are celebrated. Confucius visited this philosopher in the sixth century before Christ, to testify his reverence for him. Although every Chinaman is at liberty to study these philosophical works, a particular sect, calling itself *Tao-tse,* " Honorers of Reason," makes this study its special business. Those who compose it are isolated from civil life; and there is much that is enthusiastic and mystic intermingled with their views. They believe, for instance, that he who is acquainted with Reason, possesses an instrument of universal power, which may be regarded as all-powerful, and which communicates a supernatural might; so that the possessor is enabled by it to exalt himself to Heaven, and is not subject to death (much the same as the universal Elixir of Life once talked of among us). With the works of Confucius we have become more intimately acquainted. To him, China owes the publication of the *Kings,* and many original works on Morality besides, which form the basis of the customs and conduct of the Chinese. In the principal work of Confucius, which has been translated into English, are found correct moral apophthegms; but there is a circumlocution, a reflex character, and circuitousness in the thought, which prevents it from rising above mediocrity. As to the other sciences, they are not regarded as such, but rather as branches of knowledge for the behoof of practical ends. The Chinese are far behind in Mathematics, Physics, and Astronomy, notwithstand-

* *Vide* Hegel's " Vorlesungen über die Geschichte der Philosophie," vol. i. p. 138, etc.

ing their quondam reputation in regard to them. They knew many things at a time when Europeans had not discovered them, but they have not understood how to apply their knowledge: as *e.g.* the Magnet, and the Art of Printing. But they have made no advance in the application of these discoveries. In the latter, for instance, they continue to engrave the letters in wooden blocks and then print them off: they know nothing of movable types. Gunpowder, too, they pretended to have invented before the Europeans; but the Jesuits were obliged to found their first cannon. As to Mathematics, they understand well enough how to reckon, but the higher aspect of the science is unknown. The Chinese also have long passed as great astronomers. *Laplace* has investigated their acquisitions in this department, and discovered that they possess some ancient accounts and notices of Lunar and Solar Eclipses; but these certainly do not constitute a *science*. The notices in question are, moreover, so indefinite, that they cannot properly be put in the category of knowledge. In the Shu-King, *e.g.* we have two eclipses of the sun mentioned in the space of 1,500 years. The best evidence of the state of Astronomy among the Chinese, is the fact that for many hundred years the Chinese calendars have been made by Europeans. In earlier times, when Chinese astronomers continued to compose the calendar, false announcements of lunar and solar eclipses often occurred, entailing the execution of the authors. The telescopes which the Chinese have received as presents from the Europeans, are set up for ornament; but they have not an idea how to make further use of them. Medicine, too, is studied by the Chinese, but only empirically; and the grossest superstition is connected with its practice. The Chinese have as a general characteristic, a remarkable skill in imitation, which is exercised not merely in daily life, but also in art. They have not yet succeeded in representing the beautiful, as beautiful; for in their painting, perspective and shadow are wanting. And although a Chinese painter copies European pictures (as the Chinese do everything else) *correctly;* although he observes accurately how many scales a carp has; how many indentations there are in the leaves of a tree; what is the form of various trees, and how the branches bend;—the Exalted, the Ideal and Beautiful is not the domain of his art and skill. The Chinese are, on the other hand, too proud to learn anything from Europeans, although they must often recognize their superiority. A merchant in Canton had a European ship built, but at the command of the Governor it was immediately destroyed. The Europeans are treated as beggars, because they are compelled to leave their home, and seek for support elsewhere than in their own country. Besides, the Europeans, just because of their intelligence, have not yet been able to imitate the superficial and perfectly natural cleverness of the Chinese. Their preparation of varnishes—their working of metals, and especially their art of casting them extremely thin—their porcelain manufacture and many other things, have not yet been completely mastered by Europeans.

This is the character of the Chinese people in its various aspects. Its distinguishing feature is, that everything which belongs to Spirit—unconstrained morality, in practice and theory, Heart, inward Religion, Science and Art properly socalled—is alien to it. The Emperor always speaks with majesty and paternal kindness and tenderness to the people; who, however, cherish the meanest opinion of themselves, and believe that they are born only to drag the car of Imperial Power. The burden which presses them to the ground, seems to them to be their inevitable destiny; and it appears nothing terrible to them to sell themselves as slaves, and to eat the bitter bread of slavery. Suicide, the result of revenge, and the exposure of children, as a common, even daily occurrence, show the little respect in which they hold themselves individually, and humanity in general. And though there is no distinction conferred by birth, and everyone can attain the highest dignity, this very equality testifies to no triumphant assertion of the worth of the inner man, but a servile consciousness—one which has not yet matured itself so far as to recognize distinctions.

SECTION II

INDIA

INDIA, like China, is a phenomenon antique as well as modern; one which has remained stationary and fixed, and has received a most perfect home-sprung development. It has always been the land of imaginative aspiration, and appears to us still as a Fairy region, an enchanted World. In contrast with the Chinese State, which presents only the most prosaic Understanding, India is the region of phantasy and sensibility. The point of advance in principle which it exhibits to us may be generally stated as follows:—In China the patriarchal principle rules a people in a condition of nonage, the part of whose moral resolution is occupied by the regulating law, and the moral oversight of the Emperor. Now it is the interest of Spirit that *external* conditions should become *internal* ones; that the natural and the spiritual world should be recognized in the subjective aspect belonging to intelligence; by which process the unity of subjectivity and [positive] Being generally —or the Idealism of Existence—is established. This Idealism, then, is found in India, but only as an Idealism of imagination, without distinct conceptions;—one which does indeed free existence from Beginning and Matter [liberates it from temporal limitations and gross materiality], but changes everything into the merely Imaginative; for although the latter appears interwoven with definite conceptions and Thought presents itself as an occasional concomitant, this happens only through accidental combination. Since, however, it is the abstract and absolute Thought itself that enters into these dreams as their material, we may say that Absolute Being is presented here as in the ecstatic state of a dreaming condition. For we have not the dreaming of an actual Individual, possessing distinct personality, and simply unfettering the latter from limitation, but we have the dreaming of the unlimited absolute Spirit.

There is a beauty of a peculiar kind in women, in which their countenance presents a transparency of skin, a light and lovely roseate hue, which is unlike the complexion of mere health and vital vigor—a more refined bloom, breathed, as it were, by the soul within—and in which the features, the light of the eye, the position of the mouth, appear soft, yielding, and relaxed. This almost unearthly beauty is perceived in women in those days which immediately succeed child-birth; when freedom from the burden of pregnancy and the pains of travail is added to the joy of soul that welcomes the gift of a beloved infant. A similar tone of beauty is seen also in women during the magical somnambulic sleep, connecting them with a world of superterrestrial beauty. A great artist (Schoreel) has moreover given this tone to the dying Mary, whose spirit is already rising to the régions of the blessed, but once more, as it were, lights up her dying countenance for a farewell kiss. Such a beauty we find also in its loveliest form in the Indian World; a beauty of enervation in which all that is rough, rigid, and contradictory is dissolved, and we have only the soul in a state of emotion—a soul, however, in which the death of free self-reliant Spirit is perceptible. For should we approach the charm of this Flower-life—a charm rich in imagination and genius—in which its whole environment and all its relations are permeated by the rose-breath of the Soul, and the World is transformed into a Garden of Love—should we look at it more closely, and examine it in the light of Human Dignity and Freedom—the more attractive the first sight of it had been, so much the more unworthy shall we ultimately find it in every respect.

The character of Spirit in a state of Dream, as the generic principle of the Hindoo Nature, must be further defined. In a dream, the individual ceases to be conscious of self *as such,* in contradistinction from objective existences. When awake, I exist for myself, and the rest of creation is an external, fixed objectivity, as I myself am for it. As external, the rest of existence expands itself to a rationally connected whole; a system of relations, in which my individual being is itself a member—an individual being united with that totality. This is the sphere of *Understanding.* In the state of dreaming, on the contrary, this separation is suspended. Spirit has ceased to exist for itself in contrast with alien existence, and thus the separation of the external and individual dissolves before its universality—its *essence*. The dreaming Indian is therefore all that we call finite and individual; and, at the same time—as infinitely universal and unlimited—a something intrinsically divine. The Indian view of things is a Universal Pantheism, a Pantheism, however, of Imagination, not of Thought. One substance pervades the Whole of things, and all individualizations are directly vitalized and animated into particular Powers. The sensuous matter and content are in each case simply and in the rough taken up, and carried over into the sphere of the Universal and Immeasurable. It is not liberated by the free power of Spirit into a beautiful form, and idealized in the Spirit, so that the sensuous might be a merely subservient and compliant expression of the spiritual; but [the sensuous object itself] is expanded into the immeasurable and undefined, and the Divine is thereby made bizarré, confused, and ridiculous. These dreams are not mere fables—a play of the imagination, in which the soul only revelled in fantastic gambols: it is lost in them; hurried to and fro by these reveries, as by something that exists really and seriously for it. It is delivered over to these limited objects as to its Lords and Gods. Everything, therefore—Sun, Moon, Stars, the Ganges, the Indus, Beasts, Flowers—everything is a God to it. And while, in this deification, the finite loses its consistency and substantiality, intelligent conception of it is impossible. Conversely the Divine, regarded as essentially changeable and unfixed, is also by the base form which it assumes, defiled and made absurd. In this universal deification of all finite existence, and consequent degradation of the Divine, the idea of Theanthropy, the incarnation of God, is not a particularly important conception. The parrot, the cow, the ape, etc., are likewise incarnations of God, yet are not therefore elevated above their nature. The Divine is not individualized to a subject, to concrete Spirit, but degraded to vulgarity and senselessness. This gives us a general idea of the Indian view of the Universe. *Things* are as much stripped of rationality, of finite consistent stability of cause and effect, as *man* is of the steadfastness of free individuality, of personality, and freedom.

Externally, India sustains manifold relations to the History of the World. In recent times the discovery has been made, that the Sanscrit lies at the foundation of all those further developments which form the languages of Europe; *e.g.* the Greek, Latin, German. India, moreover, was the centre of emigration for all the western world; but this external historical relation is to be regarded rather as a merely physical diffusion of peoples from this point. Although in India the elements of further developments might be discovered, and although we could find traces of their being transmitted to the West, this transmission has been nevertheless so abstract [so superficial], that that which among later peoples attracts our interest, is not anything derived from India, but rather something concrete, which they themselves have formed, and in regard to which they have done their best to forget Indian elements of culture. The spread of Indian culture is prehistorical, for History is limited to that which makes an essential epoch in the development of Spirit. On the whole, the diffusion of Indian culture is only a dumb, deedless expansion; that is, it presents no political action. The people of India have achieved no foreign conquests, but have been on every occasion vanquished themselves. And as in this silent way, Northern India has been a centre of emigration, productive of merely physical diffusion, India as a *Land of Desire* forms an essential element in General History. From the most ancient times downwards, all nations have directed their wishes and longings to gaining access to the treasures of this land of marvels, the most costly which the Earth presents; treasures of Nature—pearls, diamonds, perfumes, rose-essences, elephants, lions, etc.—as also treasures of wisdom. The way by which these treasures have passed to the West, has at all times been a matter of World-historical importance, bound up with the fate of nations. Those wishes have been realized; this Land of Desire has been attained; there is scarcely any great nation of the East, nor of the Modern European West, that has not gained for itself a smaller or larger portion of it. In the old world, Alexander the Great was the first to penetrate by land to India, but even he only just touched it. The Europeans of the modern world have been able to enter into direct connection with this land of marvels only circuitously from the other side; and by way of the sea, which, as has been said, is the general uniter of countries. The English, or rather the East India Company, are the lords of the land; for it is the necessary fate of Asiatic Empires to be subjected to Europeans; and China will, some day or other, be obliged to submit to this fate. The number of inhabitants is near 200,000,000, of whom from 100,000,000 to 112,000,000 are directly subject to the English. The Princes who are not immediately subject to them have English Agents at their Courts, and English troops in their pay. Since the country of the Mahrattas was conquered by the English, no part of India has asserted its independence of their sway. They have already gained a footing in the Burman Empire, and passed the Brahmaputra, which bounds India on the east.

India Proper is the country which the English divide into two large sections: the *Deccan*—the great peninsula which has the Bay of Bengal on the east, and the Indian Sea on the west— and *Hindostan*, formed by the valley of the Ganges, and extending in the direction of Persia. To the northeast, Hindostan is bordered by the Himalaya, which has been ascertained by Europeans to be the highest mountain range in the world, for its summits are about 26,000 feet above the level of the sea. On the other side of the mountains the level again declines; the dominion of the Chinese extends to that point, and when the English wished to go to Lassa to the Dalai-Lama, they were prevented by the Chinese. Towards the west of India flows the Indus, in which the five rivers are united, which are called the *Pentjâb* (Punjab), into which Alexander the Great penetrated. The dominion of the English does not extend to the Indus; the sect of the Sikhs inhabits that district, whose constitution is thoroughly democratic, and who have broken off from the Indian as well as from the Mohammedan religion, and occupy an intermediate ground—acknowledging only one Supreme Being. They are a powerful nation, and have reduced to subjection Cabul and Cashmere. Besides these there dwell along the Indus genuine Indian tribes of the Warrior-Caste. Between the Indus and its twin-brother, the Ganges, are great plains. The Ganges, on the other hand, forms large Kingdoms around it, in which the sciences have been so highly developed, that the countries around the Ganges enjoy a still greater reputation than those around the Indus. The Kingdom of Bengal is especially flourishing. The Nerbuddah forms the boundary between the Deccan and Hindostan. The peninsula of the Deccan presents a far greater variety than Hindostan, and its rivers possess almost as great a sanctity as the Indus and the Ganges—which latter has become a general name for all the rivers in India, as the River κατ' ἐξοχήν. We call the inhabitants of the great country which we have now to consider *Indians,* from the river *Indus* (the English call them *Hindoos*). They themselves have never given a name to the whole, for it has never become one Empire, and yet we consider it as such.

With regard to the *political* life of the Indians, we must first consider the advance it presents in contrast with China. In China there prevailed an equality among all the individuals composing the empire; consequently all government was absorbed in its centre, the Emperor, so that individual members could not attain to independence and subjective freedom. The next degree in advance of this Unity is Difference, maintaining its independence against the all-subduing power of Unity. An organic life requires in the first place One Soul, and in the second place, a divergence into differences, which become organic members, and in their several offices develop themselves to a complete system; in such a way, however, that their activity reconstitutes that one soul. This freedom of separation is wanting in China. The deficiency is that diversities cannot attain to independent existence. In this respect, the essential advance is made in India, viz.: that independent members ramify from the unity of despotic power. Yet the distinctions which these imply are referred to Nature. Instead of stimulating the activity of a soul as their centre of union, and spontaneously realizing that soul—as is the case in organic life —they petrify and become rigid, and by their stereotyped character condemn the Indian people to the most degrading spiritual serfdom. The distinctions in question are the *Castes.* In every rational State there are distinctions which must manifest themselves. Individuals must arrive at subjective freedom, and in doing so, give an objective form to these diversities. But Indian culture has not attained to a recognition of freedom and inward morality; the distinctions which prevail are only those of occupations, and civil conditions. In a free state also, such diversities give rise to particular classes, so combined, however, that their members can maintain their individuality. In India we have only a division in masses—a division, however, that influences the whole political life and the religious consciousness. The distinctions of class, like that [rigid] Unity in China, remain consequently on the same original grade of *substantiality, i.e.* they are not the result of the free subjectivity of individuals. Examining the idea of a State and its various functions, we recognize the first essential function as that whose scope is the absolutely Universal; of which man becomes conscious first in Religion, then in Science. God, the Divine [το Θεῖον] is the absolutely Universal. The highest class therefore will be the one by which the Divine is presented and brought to bear on the community—the class of *Brahmins*. The second element or class, will represent subjective power and valor. Such power must assert itself, in order that the whole may stand its ground, and retain its integrity against other such totalities or states. This class is that of the Warriors and Governors—the *Cshatriyas;* although Brahmins often become governors. The third order of occupation recognized is that which is concerned with the specialities of life—the satisfying of its necessities—and comprehends agriculture, crafts and trade; the class of the *Vaisyas*. Lastly, the fourth element is the class of service, the mere instrument for the comfort of others, whose business it is to work for others for wages affording a scanty subsistence—the caste of *Sudras*. This servile class—properly speaking—constitutes no special organic class in the state, because its members only serve individuals: their occupations are therefore dispersed among them and are consequently attached to that of the previously mentioned castes.— Against the existence of " classes " generally, an objection has been brought—especially in modern times—drawn from the consideration of the State in its " aspect " of abstract equity. But equality in civil life is something absolutely impossible; for individual distinctions of sex and age will always assert themselves; and even if an equal share in the government is accorded to all citizens, women and children are immediately passed by, and remain excluded. The distinction between poverty and riches, the influence of skill and talent, can be as little ignored—utterly refuting those abstract assertions. But while this principle leads us to put up with variety of occupations, and distinction of the classes to which they are intrusted, we are met here in India by the peculiar circumstance that the individual belongs to such a class essentially by *birth,* and is bound to it for life. All the concrete vitality that makes its appearance sinks back into death. A chain binds down the life that was just upon the point of breaking forth. The promise of

freedom which these distinctions hold out is therewith completely nullified. What birth has separated mere arbitrary
choice has no right to join together again: therefore, the castes
preserving distinctness from their very origin, are presumed
not to be mixed or united by marriage. Yet even Arrian (Ind.
11) reckoned seven castes, and in later times more than thirty
have been made out; which, notwithstanding all obstacles, have
arisen from the union of the various classes. Polygamy necessarily tends to this. A Brahmin, *e.g.* is allowed three wives
from the three other castes, provided he has first taken one
from his own. The offspring of such mixtures originally belonged to no caste, but one of the kings invented a method of
classifying these casteless persons, which involved also the commencement of arts and manufactures. The children in question
were assigned to particular employments; one section became
weavers, another wrought in iron, and thus different classes
arose from these different occupations. The highest of these
mixed castes consists of those who are born from the marriage
of a Brahmin with a wife of the Warrior caste; the lowest
is that of the *Chandâlas,* who have to remove corpses, to execute criminals, and to perform impure offices generally. The
members of this caste are excommunicated and detested; and
are obliged to live separate and far from association with others.
The Chandâlas are obliged to move out of the way for their
superiors, and a Brahmin may knock down any that neglect
to do so. If a Chandâla drinks out of a pond it is defiled, and
requires to be consecrated afresh.

We must next consider the relative position of these castes.
Their origin is referred to a myth, which tells us that the
Brahmin caste proceeded from Brahma's mouth; the Warrior
caste from his arms; the industrial classes from his loins; the
servile caste from his foot. Many historians have set up the
hypothesis that the Brahmins originally formed a separate
sacerdotal nation, and this fable is especially countenanced by
the Brahmins themselves. A people consisting of priests alone
is, assuredly, the greatest absurdity, for we know *à priori,* that
a distinction of classes can exist only within a people; in every
nation the various occupations of life must present themselves,
for they belong to the objectivity of Spirit. *One* class necessarily
supposes another, and the rise of castes generally, is only a result of the united life of a nation. A nation of priests cannot

exist without agriculturists and soldiers. Classes cannot be brought together from without; they are developed only from within. They come forth from the interior of national life, and not conversely. But that these distinctions are here attributed to Nature, is a necessary result of the Idea which the East embodies. For while the individual ought properly to be empowered to choose his occupation, in the East, on the contrary, internal subjectivity is not yet recognized as independent; and if distinction obtrude themselves, their recognition is accompanied by the belief that the individual does not choose his particular position for himself, but receives it from Nature. In China the people are dependent—without distinction of classes —on the laws and moral decision of the Emperor; consequently on a human will. Plato, in his Republic, assigns the arrangement in different classes with a view to various occupations, to the choice of the governing body. Here, therefore, a moral, a spiritual power is the arbiter. In India, Nature is this governing power. But this natural destiny need not have led to that degree of degradation which we observe here, if the distinctions had been limited to occupation with what is earthly— to forms of objective Spirit. In the feudalism of mediæval times, individuals were also confined to a certain station in life; but for all there was a Higher Being, superior to the most exalted earthly dignity, and admission to holy orders was open to all. This is the grand distinction, that here Religion holds the same position towards *all;* that, although the son of a mechanic becomes a mechanic, the son of a peasant a peasant, and free choice is often limited by many restrictive circumstances, the *religious element* stands in the same relation to all, and all are invested with an absolute value by religion. In India the direct contrary is the case. Another distinction between the classes of society as they exist in the Christian world and those in Hindostan is the moral dignity which exists among us in every class, constituting that which man must possess in and through himself. In this respect the higher classes are equal to the lower; and while religion is the higher sphere in which all sun themselves, equality before the law—rights of person and of property—are gained for every class. But by the fact that in India, as already observed, differences extend not only to the objectivity of Spirit, but also to its absolute subjectivity, and thus exhaust all its relations—neither morality, nor justice, nor religiosity is to be found.

Every caste has its especial duties and rights. Duties and rights, therefore, are not recognized as pertaining to mankind generally, but as those of a particular caste. While we say, " Bravery is a virtue," the Hindoos say, on the contrary, " Bravery is the virtue of the *Cshatryas*." Humanity generally, human duty and human feeling do not manifest themselves; we find only duties assigned to the several castes. Everything is petrified into these distinctions, and over this petrifaction a capricious destiny holds sway. Morality and human dignity are unknown; evil passions have their full swing; the Spirit wanders into the Dream-World, and the highest state is Annihilation.

To gain a more accurate idea of what the *Brahmins* are, and in what the Brahminical dignity consists, we must investigate the Hindoo religion and the conceptions it involves, to which we shall have to return further on; for the respective rights of castes have their basis in a religious relation. *Brahmă* (neuter) is the Supreme in Religion, but there are besides chief divinities *Brahmâ* (masc.) *Vishnu* or *Krishna*—incarnate in infinitely diverse forms—and *Siva*. These form a connected Trinity. Brahmâ is the highest; but Vishnu or Krishna, Siva, the Sun moreover, the Air, etc., are also Brahm, *i.e.* Substantial Unity. To Brahm itself no sacrifices are offered; it is not honored; but prayers are presented to all other idols. Brahm itself is the Substantial Unity of All. The highest religious position of man, therefore is, being exalted to Brahm. If a Brahmin is asked what Brahm is, he answers: When I fall back within myself, and close all external senses, and say *ôm* to myself, that is Brahm. Abstract unity with God is realized in this abstraction from humanity. An abstraction of this kind may in some cases leave everything else unchanged, as does devotional feeling, momentarily excited. But among the Hindoos it holds a negative position towards all that is concrete; and the highest state is supposed to be this exaltation, by which the Hindoo raises himself to deity. The Brahmins, in virtue of their birth, are already in possession of the Divine. The distinction of castes involves, therefore, a distinction between present deities and mere limited mortals. The other castes may likewise become partakers in a *Regeneration;* but they must subject themselves to immense self-denial, torture and penance. Contempt of life, and of living humanity, is the chief feature

in this ascesis. A large number of the non-Brahminical population strive to attain *Regeneration*. They are called Yogis.
An Englishman who, on a journey to Thibet to visit the Dalai-
Lama, met such a Yogi, gives the following account: The Yogi
was already on the second grade in his ascent to Brahminical
dignity. He had passed the first grade by remaining for twelve
years on his legs, without ever sitting or lying down. At first
he had bound himself fast to a tree with a rope, until he had
accustomed himself to sleep standing. The second grade required him to keep his hands clasped together over his head
for twelve years in succession. Already his nails had almost
grown into his hands. The third grade is not always passed
through in the same way; generally the Yogi has to spend a
day between *five fires,* that is, between four fires occupying the
four quarters of heaven, and the Sun. He must then swing
backwards and forwards over the fire, a ceremony occupying
three hours and three-quarters. Englishmen present at an act
of this kind, say that in half an hour the blood streamed forth
from every part of the devotee's body; he was taken down and
presently died. If this trial is also surmounted, the aspirant
is finally buried alive, that is put into the ground in an upright
position and quite covered over with soil; after three hours
and three-quarters he is drawn out, and if he lives, he is supposed to have at last attained the spiritual power of a Brahmin.

Thus only by such negation of his existence does anyone
attain Brahminical power. In its highest degree this negation
consists in a sort of hazy consciousness of having attained perfect mental immobility—the annihilation of all emotion and all
volition;—a condition which is regarded as the highest among
the Buddhists also. However pusillanimous and effeminate
the Hindoos may be in other respects, it is evident how little
they hesitate to sacrifice themselves to the Highest—to Annihilation. Another instance of the same is the fact of wives burning themselves after the death of their husbands. Should a
woman contravene this traditional usage, she would be severed
from society, and perish in solitude. An Englishman states
that he also saw a woman burn herself because she had lost her
child. He did all that he could to divert her away from her
purpose; at last he applied to her husband who was standing
by, but he showed himself perfectly indifferent, as *he had more
wives at home.* Sometimes twenty women are seen throwing

themselves at once into the Ganges, and on the Himalaya range an English traveller found three women seeking the source of the Ganges, in order to put an end to their life in this holy river.   At a religious festival in the celebrated temple of Juggernaut in Orissa, on the Bay of Bengal, where millions of Hindoos assemble, the image of the god Vishnu is drawn in procession on a car: about five hundred men set it in motion, and many fling themselves down before its wheels to be crushed to pieces.   The whole seashore is already strewed with the bodies of persons who have thus immolated themselves.   Infanticide is also very common in India.   Mothers throw their children into the Ganges, or let them pine away under the rays of the sun.   The morality which is involved in respect for human life, is not found among the Hindoos.   There are besides those already mentioned, infinite modifications of the same principle of conduct, all pointing to annihilation.   This, *e.g.,* is the leading principle of the Gymnosophists, as the Greeks called them.   Naked Fakirs wander about without any occupation, like the mendicant friars of the Catholic church; live on the alms of others, and make it their aim to reach the highest degree of abstraction—the perfect deadening of consciousness; a point from which the transition to physical death is no great step.

This elevation which others can only attain by toilsome labor is, as already stated, the birthright of the Brahmins.   The Hindoo of another caste, must, therefore, reverence the Brahmin as a divinity; fall down before him, and say to him: "Thou art God."   And this elevation cannot have anything to do with moral conduct, but—inasmuch as all internal morality is absent—is rather dependent on a farrago of observances relating to the merest externalities and trivialities of existence.   Human life, it is said, ought to be a perpetual Worship of God.   It is evident how hollow such general aphorisms are, when we consider the concrete forms which they may assume.   They require another, a further qualification, if they are to have a meaning. The Brahmins are a present deity, but their spirituality has not yet been reflected inwards in contrast with Nature; and thus that which is purely indifferent is treated as of absolute importance.   The employment of the Brahmins consists principally in the reading of the Vêdas: they only have a right to read them.   Were a Sudra to read the Vêdas, or to hear them read, he would be severely punished, and burning oil must be poured into his ears. The external observances binding on the Brahmins are prodigiously numerous, and the Laws of Manu treat of them as the most essential part of duty. The Brahmin must rest on one particular foot in rising, then wash in a river; his hair and nails must be cut in neat curves, his whole body purified, his garments white; in his hand must be a staff of a specified kind; in his ears a golden earring. If the Brahmin meets a man of an inferior caste, he must turn back and purify himself. He has also to read in the Vêdas, in various ways: each word separately, or doubling them alternately, or backwards. He may not look to the sun when rising or setting, or when overcast by clouds or reflected in the water. He is forbidden to step over a rope to which a calf is fastened, or to go out when it rains. He may not look at his wife when she eats, sneezes, gapes, or is quietly seated. At the midday meal he may only have one garment on, in bathing never be quite naked. How minute these directions are, may be especially judged of from the observances binding on the Brahmins in regard to satisfying the calls of nature. This is forbidden to them in a great thoroughfare, on ashes, on ploughed land, on a hill, a nest of white ants, on wood destined for fuel, in a ditch, walking or standing, on the bank of a river, etc. At such a time they may not look at the sun, at water, or at animals. By day they should keep their face generally directed to the north, but by night to the south; only in the shade are they allowed to turn to which quarter they like. It is forbidden to everyone who desires a long life, to step on potsherds, cotton seeds, ashes, or sheaves of corn, or his urine. In the episode Nala, in the poem of Mahabharata, we have a story of a virgin who in her 21st year—the age in which the maidens themselves have a right to choose a husband—makes a selection from among her wooers. There are five of them; but the maiden remarks that four of them do not stand firmly on their feet, and thence infers correctly that they are Gods. She therefore chooses the fifth, who is a veritable man. But besides the four despised divinities there are two malevolent ones, whom her choice had not favored, and who on that account wish for revenge. They therefore keep a strict watch on the husband of their beloved in every step and act of life, with the design of inflicting injury upon him if he commits a misdemeanor.

The persecuted husband does nothing that can be brought against him, until at last he is so incautious as to step on his urine. The Genius has now an advantage over him; he afflicts him with a passion for gambling, and so plunges him into the abyss.

While, on the one hand, the Brahmins are subject to these strict limitations and rules, on the other hand their life is sacred; it cannot answer for crimes of any kind; and their property is equally secure from being attacked. The severest penalty which the ruler can inflict upon them amounts to nothing more than banishment. The English wished to introduce trial by jury into India—the jury to consist half of Europeans, half of Hindoos—and submitted to the natives, whose wishes on the subject were consulted, the powers with which the panel would be intrusted. The Hindoos were for making a number of exceptions and limitations. They said, among other things, that they could not consent that a Brahmin should be condemned to death; not to mention other objections, *e.g.* that looking at and examining a corpse was out of the question. Although in the case of a Warrior the rate of interest may be as high as three per cent., in that of a Vaisya four per cent., a Brahmin is never required to pay more than two per cent. The Brahmin possesses such a power, that Heaven's lightning would strike the King who ventured to lay hands on him or his property. For the meanest Brahmin is so far exalted above the King, that he would be polluted by conversing with him, and would be dishonored by his daughters choosing a prince in marriage. In Manu's Code it is said: "If anyone presumes to teach a Brahmin his duty, the King must order that hot oil be poured into the ears and mouth of such an instructor. If one who is only once-born, loads one who is twice-born with reproaches, a red hot iron bar ten inches long shall be thrust into his mouth." On the other hand a Sudra is condemned to have a red hot iron thrust into him from behind if he rest himself in the chair of a Brahmin, and to have his foot or his hand hewed off if he pushes against a Brahmin with hands or feet. It is even permitted to give false testimony, and to lie before a Court of Justice, if a Brahmin can be thereby freed from condemnation.

As the Brahmins enjoy advantages over the other Castes, the latter in their turn have privileges according to precedence, over their inferiors. If a Sudra is defiled by contact with a

Pariah, he has the right to knock him down on the spot. Humanity on the part of a higher Caste towards an inferior one is entirely forbidden, and a Brahmin would never think of assisting a member of another Caste, even when in danger. The other Castes deem it a great honor when a Brahmin takes their daughters as his wives—a thing however, which is permitted him, as already stated, only when he has already taken one from his own Caste. Thence arises the freedom the Brahmins enjoy in getting wives. At the great religious festivals they go among the people and choose those that please them best; but they also repudiate them at pleasure.

If a Brahmin or a member of any other Caste transgresses the above cited laws and precepts, he is himself excluded from his caste, and in order to be received back again, he must have a hook bored through the hips, and be swung repeatedly backwards and forwards in the air. There are also other forms of restoration. A Rajah who thought himself injured by an English Governor, sent two Brahmins to England to detail his grievances. But the Hindoos are forbidden to cross the sea, and these envoys on their return were declared excommunicated from their caste, and in order to be restored to it, they had to be born again from a golden cow. The imposition was so far lightened, that only those parts of the cow out of which they had to creep were obliged to be golden; the rest might consist of wood. These various usages and religious observances to which every Caste is subject, have occasioned great perplexity to the English, especially in enlisting soldiers. At first these were taken from the Sudra-Caste, which is not bound to observe so many ceremonies; but nothing could be done with them, they therefore betook themselves to the Cshatriya class. These however have an immense number of regulations to observe—they may not eat meat, touch a dead body, drink out of a pool in which cattle or Europeans have drunk, not eat what others have cooked, etc. Each Hindoo assumes one definite occupation, and that only, so that one must have an infinity of servants;—a Lieutenant has *thirty*, a Major *sixty*. Thus every Caste has its own duties; the lower the Caste, the less it has to observe; and as each individual has his position assigned by birth, beyond this fixed arrangement everything is governed by caprice and force. In the Code of Manu punishments increase in proportion to the inferiority of Castes, and there is a

distinction in other respects. If a man of a higher Caste brings
an accusation against an inferior without proof, the former is
not punished; if the converse occurs, the punishment is very
severe. Cases of theft are exceptional; in this case the higher
the Caste the heavier is the penalty.

In respect to property the Brahmins have a great advantage,
for they pay no taxes. The prince receives half the income from
the lands of others; the remainder has to suffice for the cost
of cultivation and the support of the laborers. It is an extremely important question, whether the cultivated land in India is recognized as belonging to the cultivator, or belongs to a
so-called manorial proprietor. The English themselves have
had great difficulty in establishing a clear understanding about
it. For when they conquered Bengal, it was of great importance
to them, to determine the mode in which taxes were to be raised
on property, and they had to ascertain whether these should be
imposed on the tenant cultivators or the lord of the soil. They
imposed the tribute on the latter; but the result was that the
proprietors acted in the most arbitrary manner: drove away
the tenant cultivators, and declaring that such or such an
amount of land was not under cultivation, gained an abatement
of tribute. They then took back the expelled cultivators as day-
laborers, at a low rate of wages, and had the land cultivated
on their own behalf. The whole income belonging to every
village is, as already stated, divided into two parts, of which one
belongs to the Rajah, the other to the cultivators; but proportionate shares are also received by the Provost of the place, the
Judge, the Water-Surveyor, the Brahmin who superintends
religious worship, the Astrologer (who is also a Brahmin, and
announces the days of good and ill omen), the Smith, the Carpenter, the Potter, the Washerman, the Barber, the Physician,
the Dancing Girls, the Musician, the Poet. This arrangement
is fixed and immutable, and subject to no one's will. *All political
revolutions*, therefore, are matters of indifference to the common Hindoo, for his lot is unchanged.

The view given of the relation of castes leads directly to the
subject of Religion. For the claims of caste are, as already
remarked, not merely secular, but essentially religious, and the
Brahmins in their exalted dignity are the very gods bodily
present. In the laws of Manu it is said: " Let the King, even
in extreme necessity, beware of exciting the Brahmins against

him; for they can destroy him with their power—they who create Fire, Sun, Moon, etc." They are servants neither of God nor of his People, but are God himself to the other Castes —a position of things which constitutes the perverted character of the Hindoo mind. The dreaming Unity of Spirit and nature, which involves a monstrous bewilderment in regard to all phenomena and relations, we have already recognized as the principle of the Hindoo Spirit. The Hindoo Mythology is therefore only a wild extravagance of Fancy, in which nothing has a settled form; which takes us abruptly from the Meanest to the Highest, from the most sublime to the most disgusting and trivial. Thus it is also difficult to discover what the Hindoos understand by Brahm. We are apt to take our conception of Supreme Divinity—the One—the Creator of Heaven and Earth—and apply it to the Indian Brahm. Brahma is distinct from Brahm—the former constituting one personality in contrasted relation to Vishnu and Siva. Many therefore call the Supreme Existence who is over the first mentioned deity, *Parabrahma*. The English have taken a good deal of trouble to find out what Brahm properly is. Wilford has asserted that Hindoo conceptions recognize two Heavens: the first, the earthly paradise, the second, Heaven in a spiritual sense. To attain them, two different modes of worship are supposed to be required. The one involves external ceremonies, Idol-Worship; the other requires that the Supreme Being should be honored in spirit. Sacrifices, purifications, pilgrimages are not needed in the latter. This authority states moreover that there are few Hindoos ready to pursue the second way, because they cannot understand in what the pleasure of the second heaven consists, and that if one asks a Hindoo whether he worships Idols, every one says " Yes! " but to the question, " Do you worship the Supreme Being? " every one answers " No." If the further question is put, " What is the meaning of that practice of yours, that silent meditation which some of your learned men speak of? " they respond, " When I pray to the honor of one of the Gods, I sit down—the foot of either leg on the thigh of the other—look towards Heaven, and calmly elevate my thoughts with my hands folded in silence; then I say, I am Brahm the Supreme Being. We are not conscious to ourselves of being Brahm, by reason of Maya (the delusion occasioned by the outward world). It is forbidden to pray to him, and to offer sacrifices to him in his own nature; for this would be to adore ourselves. In every case therefore, it is only emanations of Brahm that we address." Translating these ideas then into our own process of thought, we should call Brahm the pure unity of thought in itself—God in the incomplexity of his existence. No temples are consecrated to him, and he receives no worship. Similarly, in the Catholic religion, the churches are not dedicated to God, but to the saints. Other Englishmen, who have devoted themselves to investigating the conception of Brahm, have thought Brahm to be an unmeaning epithet, applied to all gods: so that Vishnu says, " I am Brahm "; and the Sun, the Air, the Seas are called Brahm. Brahm would on this supposition be substance in its simplicity, which by its very nature expands itself into the limitless variety of phenomenal diversities. For this abstraction, this pure unity, is that which lies at the foundation of All—the root of all definite existence. In the intellection of this unity, all objectivity falls away; for the purely Abstract is intellection itself in its greatest vacuity. To attain this Death of Life during life itself—to constitute this abstraction—requires the disappearance of all moral activity and volition, and of all intellection too, as in the Religion of Fo; and this is the object of the penances already spoken of.

The complement to the abstraction Brahm must then be looked for in the concrete complex of things; for the principle of the Hindoo religion is the Manifestation of Diversity [in " Avatars "]. These then, fall outside that abstract Unity of Thought, and as that which deviates from it, constitute the variety found in the world of sense, the variety of intellectual conceptions in an unreflected sensuous form. In this way the concrete complex of material things is isolated from Spirit, and, presented in wild distraction, except as re-absorbed in the pure ideality of Brahm. The other deities are therefore things of sense: Mountains, Streams, Beasts, the Sun, the Moon, the Ganges. The next stage is the concentration of this wild variety into substantial distinctions, and the comprehension of them as a series of divine persons. Vishnu, Siva, Mahâdeva are thus distinguished from Brahma. In the embodiment Vishnu, are presented those incarnations in which God has appeared as man, and which are always historical personages, who effected important changes and new epochs. The power of procreation is likewise a substantial embodiment; and in the excavations, grottos and pagodas of the Hindoos, the Lingam is always found as symbolizing the male, and the Lotus the female *vis procreandi*.

With this Duality—abstract unity on the one side and the abstract isolation of the world of sense on the other side—exactly corresponds the double form of *Worship*, in the relation of the human subjectivity to God. The one side of this duality of worship, consists in the abstraction of pure self-elevation—the abrogation of real self-consiousness; a negativity which is consequently manifested, on the one hand, in the attainment of torpid unconsciousness—on the other hand in suicide and the extinction of all that is worth calling life, by self-inflicted tortures. The other side of worship consists in a wild tumult of excess; when all sense of individuality has vanished from consciousness by immersion in the merely natural; with which individuality thus makes itself identical—destroying its consciousness of distinction from Nature. In all the pagodas, therefore, prostitutes and dancing girls are kept, whom the Brahmins instruct most carefully in dancing, in beautiful postures and attractive gestures, and who have to comply with the wishes of all comers at a fixed price. Theological doctrine—relation of religion to morality—is here altogether out of the question. On the one hand Love—Heaven—in short everything spiritual—is conceived by the fancy of the Hindoo; but on the other hand his conceptions have an actual sensuous embodiment, and he immerses himself by a voluptuous intoxication in the merely natural. Objects of religious worship are thus either disgusting forms produced by art, or those presented by Nature. Every bird, every monkey is a present god, an absolutely universal existence. The Hindoo is incapable of holding fast an object in his mind by means of rational predicates assigned to it, for this requires reflection. While a universal essence is wrongly transmuted into sensuous objectivity, the latter is also driven from its definite character into universality—a process whereby it loses its footing and is expanded to indefiniteness.

If we proceed to ask how far their religion exhibits the *Morality* of the Hindoos, the answer must be that the former is as distinct from the latter, as Brahm from the concrete existence of which he is the essence. To *us*, religion is the knowledge of that Being who is emphatically *our* Being, and therefore the substance of our knowledge and volition; the proper office of which latter is to be the mirror of this fundamental substance. But that requires this [Highest] Being to be *in se* a personality, pursuing divine aims, such as can become the purport of human action. Such an idea of a relation of the Being of God as constituting the universal basis or substance of human action—such a morality cannot be found among the Hindoos; for they have not the Spiritual as the import of their consciousness. On the one hand their virtue consists in the abstraction from all activity—the condition they call "Brahm." On the other hand every action with them is a prescribed external usage; not free activity, the result of inward personality. Thus the moral condition of the Hindoos, (as already observed) shows itself most abandoned. In this all Englishmen agree. Our judgment of the morality of the Hindoos is apt to be warped by representations of their mildness, tenderness, beautiful and sentimental fancy. But we must reflect that in nations utterly corrupt, there are sides of character which may be called tender and noble. We have Chinese poems in which the tenderest relations of love are depicted; in which delineations of deep emotion, humility, modesty, propriety are to be found; and which may be compared with the best that European literature contains. The same characteristics meet us in many Hindoo poems; but rectitude, morality, freedom of soul, consciousness of individual right are quite another thing. The annihilating of spiritual and physical existence has nothing concrete in it; and absorption in the abstractly Universal has no connection with the real. Deceit and cunning are the fundamental characteristics of the Hindoo. Cheating, stealing, robbing, murdering are with him habitual. Humbly crouching and abject before a victor and lord, he is recklessly barbarous to the vanquished and subject. Characteristic of the Hindoo's humanity is the fact that he kills no brute animal, founds and supports rich hospitals for brutes, especially for old cows and monkeys—but that through the whole land, no single institution can be found for human beings who are diseased or infirm from age. The Hindoos will not tread upon ants, but they are perfectly indifferent when poor wanderers pine away with hunger. The Brahmins are especially immoral. According to English reports, they do nothing but eat and sleep. In what is not forbidden them by the rules of their order they follow natural impulses entirely. When they take any part in public life they show themselves avaricious, deceitful, voluptuous. With those whom they have reason to fear, they are humble enough; for which they avenge themselves on their dependents. " I do not know an honest man among them," says an English authority. Children have no respect for their parents: sons maltreat their mothers.

It would lead us too far to give a detailed notice of Hindoo *Art* and *Science*. But we may make the general remark, that a more accurate acquaintance with its real value has not a little diminished the widely bruited fame of Indian Wisdom. According to the Hindoo principle of pure self-renouncing Ideality, and that [phenomenal] variety which goes to the opposite extreme of sensuousness, it is evident that nothing but abstract thought and imagination can be developed. Thus, *e.g.*, their grammar has advanced to a high degree of consistent regularity; but when substantial matter in sciences and works of art is in question, it is useless to look for it here. When the English had become masters of the country, the work of restoring to light the records of Indian culture was commenced, and William Jones first disinterred the poems of the Golden Age. The English exhibited plays at Calcutta: this led to a representation of dramas on the part of the Brahmins, *e.g.* the Sacontala of Calidasa, etc. In the enthusiasm of discovery the Hindoo culture was very highly rated; and as, when new beauties are discovered, the old ones are commonly looked down upon with contempt, Hindoo poetry and philosophy were extolled as far superior to the Greek. For our purpose the most important documents are the ancient and canonical books of the Hindoos, especially the *Vêdas*. They comprise many divisions, of which the fourth is of more recent origin. They consist partly of religious prayers, partly of precepts to be observed. Some manuscripts of these Vêdas have come to Europe, though in a complete form they are exceedingly rare. The writing is on palm leaves, scratched in with a needle. The Vêdas are very difficult to understand, since they date from the most remote antiquity, and the language is a much older Sanscrit. *Colebrooke* has indeed translated a part, but this itself is perhaps taken from a commentary, of which there are very many.* Two

* Only recently has Professor Rosen, residing in London, gone thoroughly into the matter and given a specimen of the text with a translation, " Rig-Vedæ Specimen, ed. Fr. Rosen. Lond. 1830." (More recently, since Rosen's death, the whole Rig-Veda, London, 1839, has been published from MSS. left by him.)

great epic poems, Ramayana and Mahabharata, have also reached Europe. Three quarto volumes of the former have been printed, the second volume is extremely rare.† Besides these works, the Puranas must be particularly noticed. The *Puranas* contain the history of a god or of a temple. They are entirely fanciful. Another Hindoo classical book is the Code of *Manu*. This Hindoo lawgiver has been compared with the Cretan Minos—a name which also occurs among the Egyptians; and certainly this extensive occurrence of the same name is noteworthy and cannot be ascribed to chance. Manu's code of morals, (published at Calcutta with an English translation by Sir W. Jones) forms the basis of Hindoo legislation. It begins with a Theogony, which is not only entirely different from the mythological conceptions of other peoples, (as might be expected) but also deviates essentially from the Hindoo traditions themselves. For in these also there are only some leading features that pervade the whole. In other respects everything is abandoned to chance, caprice and fancy; the result of which is that the most multiform traditions, shapes and names, appear in never ending procession. The time when Manu's code was composed, is also entirely unknown and undetermined. The traditions reach beyond twenty-three centuries before the birth of Christ: a dynasty of the Children of the Sun is mentioned, on which followed one of the Children of the Moon. Thus much, however, is certain, that the code in question is of high antiquity; and an acquaintance with it is of the greatest importance to the English, as their knowledge of Hindoo Law is derived from it.

After pointing out the Hindoo principle in the distinctions of caste, in religion and literature, we must also mention the mode and form of their *political* existence—the polity of the Hindoo *State*.—A State is a realization of Spirit, such that in it the self-conscious being of Spirit—the freedom of the Will— is realized as Law. Such an institution then, necessarily presupposes the consciousness of free will. In the Chinese State the moral will of the Emperor is the law: but so that subjective, inward freedom is thereby repressed, and the Law of Freedom governs individuals only as from without. In India the pri-

† "A. W. v. Schlegel has published the first and second Volume; the most important Episodes of the Mahabharata have been introduced to public notice by F. Bopp, and a complete Edition has appeared at Calcutta."—German Editor.

mary aspect of subjectivity—viz., that of the imagination—presents a union of the Natural and Spiritual, in which Nature
on the one hand, does not present itself as a world embodying
Reason, nor the Spiritual on the other hand, as consciousness
in contrast with Nature.   Here the antithesis in the [above-
stated] principle is wanting.   Freedom both as *abstract* will and
as *subjective* freedom is absent.   The proper basis of the State,
the principle of freedom is altogether absent: there cannot
therefore be any State in the true sense of the term.   This is the
first point to be observed: if China may be regarded as nothing
else but a State, Hindoo political existence presents us with a
people, but *no State.*   Secondly, while we found a moral despotism in *China,* whatever may be called a relic of political life
in *India,* is a despotism *without a principle,* without any rule of
morality and religion: for morality and religion (as far as the
latter has a reference to human action) have as their indispensable condition and basis the freedom of the Will.   In India,
therefore, the most arbitrary, wicked, degrading despotism has
its full swing.   China, Persia, Turkey—in fact Asia generally,
is the scene of despotism, and, in a bad sense, of tyranny; but
it is regarded as contrary to the due order of things, and is
disapproved by religion and the moral consciousness of individuals.   In those countries, tyranny rouses men to resentment;
they detest it and groan under it as a burden.   To them it is
an accident and an irregularity, not a necessity: it *ought* not to
exist.   But in India it is normal: for here there is no sense of
personal independence with which a state of despotism could
be compared, and which would raise revolt in the soul; nothing
approaching even a resentful protest against it, is left, except
the corporeal smart, and the pain of being deprived of absolute
necessaries and of pleasure.

In the case of such a people, therefore, that which we call
in its double sense, *History,* is not to be looked for; and here
the distinction between China and India is most clearly and
strongly manifest.   The Chinese possess a most minute history
of their country, and it has been already remarked, what arrangements are made in China, for having everything accurately noted down in their annals.   The contrary is the case in
India.   Though the recent discoveries of the treasures of
Indian Literature, have shown us what a reputation the Hindoos have acquired in Geometry, Astronomy, and Algebra—

that they have made great advances in Philosophy, and that among them, Grammar has been so far cultivated that no language can be regarded as more fully developed than the Sanscrit—we find the department of *History* altogether neglected, or rather non-existent. For History requires Understanding—the power of looking at an object in an independent objective light, and comprehending it in its rational connection with other objects. Those peoples therefore are alone capable of History, and of prose generally, who have arrived at that period of development (and can make that their starting point) at which individuals comprehend their own existence as independent, *i.e.* possess self-consciousness.

The Chinese are to be rated at what they have made of themselves, looking at them in the entirety of their State. While they have thus attained an existence independent of Nature, they can also regard objects as distinct from themselves—as they are actually presented—in a definite form and in their real connection. The Hindoos on the contrary are by birth given over to an unyielding destiny, while at the same time their Spirit is exalted to Ideality; so that their minds exhibit the contradictory processes of a dissolution of fixed rational and definite conceptions in their Ideality, and on the other side, a degradation of this ideality to a multiformity of sensuous objects. This makes them incapable of writing History. All that happens is dissipated in their minds into confused dreams. What we call historical truth and veracity—intelligent, thoughtful comprehension of events, and fidelity in representing them—nothing of this sort can be looked for among the Hindoos. We may explain this deficiency partly from that excitement and debility of the nerves, which prevent them from retaining an object in their minds, and firmly comprehending it, for in their mode of apprehension, a sensitive and imaginative temperament changes it into a feverish dream;—partly from the fact, that veracity is the direct contrary to their nature. They even lie knowingly and designedly where misapprehension is out of the question. As the Hindoo Spirit is a state of dreaming and mental transiency—a self-oblivious dissolution—objects also dissolve for it into unreal images and indefinitude. This feature is absolutely characteristic; and this alone would furnish us with a clear idea of the Spirit of the Hindoos, from which all that has been said might be deduced.

But History is always of great importance for a people; since by means of that it becomes conscious of the path of development taken by its own Spirit, which expresses itself in Laws, Manners, Customs, and Deeds. Laws, comprising morals and judicial institutions, are by nature the permanent element in a people's existence. But History presents a people with their own image in a condition which thereby becomes objective to them. Without History their existence in time is blindly self-involved—the recurring play of arbitrary volition in manifold forms. History fixes and imparts consistency to this fortuitous current—gives it the form of Universality, and by so doing posits a directive and restrictive rule for it. It is an essential instrument in developing and determining the Constitution—that is, a rational political condition; for it is the empirical method of producing the Universal, inasmuch as it sets up a permanent object for the conceptive powers.—It is because the Hindoos have no History in the form of annals (historia) that they have no History in the form of transactions (res gestæ); that is, no growth expanding into a veritable political condition.

Periods of time are mentioned in the Hindoo Writings, and large numbers which have often an astronomical meaning, but which have still oftener a quite arbitrary origin. Thus it is related of certain Kings that they had reigned 70,000 years, or more. Brahma, the first figure in the Cosmogony, and self-produced, is said to have lived 20,000 years, etc. Innumerable names of Kings are cited—among them the incarnations of Vishnu. It would be ridiculous to regard passages of this kind as anything historical. In their poems Kings are often talked of: these may have been historical personages, but they completely vanish in fable; e.g. they retire from the world, and then appear again, after they have passed ten thousand years in solitude. The numbers in question, therefore, have not the value and rational meaning which we attach to them.

Consequently the oldest and most reliable sources of Indian History are the notices of Greek Authors, after Alexander the Great had opened the way to India. From them we learn that their institutions were the same at that early period as they are now: Santaracottus (Chandragupta) is marked out as a distinguished ruler in the northern part of India, to which the Bactrian kingdom extended. The Mahometan historians sup-

ply another source of information; for the Mahometans began
their invasions as early as the tenth century. A Turkish slave
was the ancestor of the Ghiznian race. His son Mahmoud
made an inroad into Hindostan and conquered almost the whole
country. He fixed his royal residence west of Cabul, and at
his court lived the poet Ferdusi. The Ghiznian dynasty was
soon entirely exterminated by the sweeping attacks of the
Afghans and Moguls. In later times nearly the whole of India
has been subjected to the Europeans. What therefore is known
of Indian history, has for the most part been communicated
through foreign channels: the native literature gives only indistinct data. Europeans assure us of the impossibility of wad-
ing through the morasses of Indian statements. More definite
information may be obtained from inscriptions and documents,
especially from the deeds of gifts of land to pagodas and divinities; but this kind of evidence supplies names only. Another
source of information is the astronomical literature, which is
of high antiquity. Colebrooke thoroughly studied these writings; though it is very difficult to procure manuscripts, since
the Brahmins keep them very close; they are moreover disfigured by the grossest interpolations. It is found that the statements with regard to constellations are often contradictory, and
that the Brahmins interpolate these ancient works with events
belonging to their own time. The Hindoos do indeed possess
lists and enumerations of their Kings, but these also are of the
most capricious character; for we often find twenty Kings
more in one list than in another; and should these lists even
be correct, they could not constitute a history. The Brahmins
have no conscience in respect to truth. Captain Wilford had
procured manuscripts from all quarters with great trouble and
expense; he assembled a considerable number of Brahmins,
and commissioned them to make extracts from these works, and
to institute inquiries respecting certain remarkable events—
about Adam and Eve, the Deluge, etc. The Brahmins, to please
their employer, produced statements of the kind required; but
there was nothing of the sort in the manuscripts. Wilford
wrote many treatises on the subject, till at last he detected the
deception, and saw that he had labored in vain. The Hindoos
have, it is true, a fixed Era: they reckon from *Vicramâditya,* at
whose splendid court lived Calidasa, the author of the Sacontala. The most illustrious poets flourished about the same

time. " There were nine pearls at the court of Vicramâditya," say the Brahmins: but we cannot discover the date of this brilliant epoch. From various statements, the year 1491 B.C. has been contended for; others adopt the year 50 B.C., and this is the commonly received opinion. Bentley's researches at length placed Vicramâditya in the twelfth century B.C. But still more recently it has been discovered that there were five, or even eight or nine kings of that name in India; so that on this point also we are thrown back into utter uncertainty.

When the Europeans became acquainted with India, they found a multitude of petty Kingdoms, at whose head were Mahometan and Indian princes. There was an order of things very nearly approaching feudal organization; and the Kingdoms in question were divided into districts, having as governors Mahometans, or people of the Warrior Caste of Hindoos. The business of these governors consisted in collecting taxes and carrying on wars; and they thus formed a kind of aristocracy, the Prince's Council of State. But only as far as their princes are feared and excite fear, have they any power; and no obedience is rendered to them but by force. As long as the prince does not want money, he has troops; and neighboring princes, if they are inferior to him in force, are often obliged to pay taxes, but which are yielded only on compulsion. The whole state of things, therefore, is not that of repose, but of continual struggle; while moreover nothing is developed or furthered. It is the struggle of an energetic will on the part of this or that prince against a feebler one; the history of reigning dynasties, but not of peoples; a series of perpetually varying intrigues and revolts—not indeed of subjects against their rulers, but of a prince's son, for instance, against his father; of brothers, uncles and nephews in contest with each other; and of functionaries against their master. It might be believed that, though the Europeans found such a state of things, this was the result of the dissolution of earlier superior organizations. It might, for instance, be supposed that the period of the Mogul supremacy was of one of prosperity and splendor, and of a political condition in which India was not distracted religiously and politically by foreign conquerors. But the historical traces and lineaments that accidentally present themselves in poetical descriptions and legends, bearing upon the period in question, always point to the same divided condition—the result of war and of the instability of political relations; while contrary representations may be easily recognized as a dream, a mere fancy. This state of things is the natural result of that conception of Hindoo life which has been exhibited, and the conditions which it necessitates. The wars of the sects of the Brahmins and Buddhists, of the devotees of Vishnu and of Siva, also contributed their quota to this confusion.—There is indeed, a common character pervading the whole of India; but its several states present at the same time the greatest variety; so that in one Indian State we meet with the greatest effeminacy—in another, on the contrary, we find prodigious vigor and savage barbarity.

If then, in conclusion, we once more take a general view of the comparative condition of India and China, we shall see that China was characterized by a thoroughly unimaginative Understanding; a prosaic life amid firm and definite reality: while in the Indian world there is, so to speak, no object that can be regarded as real, and firmly defined—none that was not at its first apprehension perverted by the imagination to the very opposite of what it presents to an intelligent consciousness. In China it is the Moral which constitutes the substance of the laws, and which is embodied in external strictly determinate relations; while over all hovers the patriarchal providence of the Emperor, who like a Father, cares impartially for the interest of his subjects. Among the Hindoos, on the contrary—instead of this Unity—Diversity is the fundamental characteristic. Religion, War, Handicraft, Trade, yes, even the most trivial occupations are parcelled out with rigid separation—constituting as they do the import of the one will which they involve, and whose various requirements they exhaust. With this is bound up a monstrous, irrational imagination, which attaches the moral value and character of men to an infinity of outward actions as empty in point of intellect as of feeling; sets aside all respect for the welfare of man, and even makes a duty of the cruellest and severest contravention of it. Those distinctions being rigidly maintained, nothing remains for the one universal will of the State but pure caprice, against whose omnipotence only the fixed caste-distinctions avail for protection. The Chinese in their prosaic rationality, reverence as the Highest, only the abstract supreme lord; and they exhibit a contemptibly superstitious respect for the fixed and definite

Among the Hindoos there is no such superstition so far as it presents an antithesis to Understanding; rather their whole life and ideas are one unbroken superstition, because among them all is revery and consequent enslavement. Annihilation—the abandonment of all reason, morality and subjectivity—can only come to a positive feeling and consciousness of itself, by extravagating in a boundlessly wild imagination; in which, like a desolate spirit, it finds no rest, no settled composure, though it can content itself in no other way; as a man who is quite reduced in body and spirit finds his existence altogether stupid and intolerable, and is driven to the creation of a dream-world and a delirious bliss in Opium.

Section II.—(Continued).—India—Buddhism *

It is time to quit the Dream-State characterizing the Hindoo Spirit revelling in the most extravagant maze through all natural and spiritual forms; comprising at the same time the coarsest sensuality and anticipations of the profoundest thought, and on that very account—as far as free and rational reality is concerned—sunk in the most self-abandoned, helpless slavery; —a slavery, in which the abstract forms into which concrete human life is divided, have become stereotyped, and human rights and culture have been made absolutely dependent upon these distinctions. In contrast with this inebriate Dream-life, which in the sphere of reality is bound fast in chains, we have the *unconstrained* Dream-life; which on the one hand is ruder than the former—as not having advanced so far as to make this distinction of modes of life—but for the same reason, has not sunk into the slavery which this entails. It keeps itself more free, more independently firm in itself: its world of ideas is consequently compressed into simpler conceptions.

The Spirit of the Phase just indicated, is involved in the same fundamental principle as that assigned to Hindoo conceptions: but it is more concentrated in itself; its religion is simpler, and the accompanying political condition more calm and settled. This phase comprehends peoples and countries of the most varied complexion. We regard it as embracing

* As in Hegel's original plan and in the first lecture the transition from Indian Brahminism to Buddhism occupies the place assigned it here, and as this position of the chapter on Buddhism agrees better with recent investigations, its detachment from the place which it previously occupied and mention here will appear sufficiently justified.—Ed.

Ceylon, Farther India with the Burman Empire, Siam, Anam—
north of that Thibet, and further on the Chinese Upland with
its various populations of Mongols and Tartars. We shall not
examine the special individualities of these peoples, but merely
characterize their Religion, which constitutes the most interesting side of their existence. The Religion of these peoples is
Buddhism, which is the most widely extended religion on our
globe. In China Buddha is reverenced as *Fo;* in Ceylon as
Gautama; in Thibet and among the Mongols this religion has
assumed the phase of Lamaism. In China—where the religion
of Fo early received a great extension, and introduced a monastic life—it occupies the position of an integrant element of
the Chinese principle. As the Substantial form of Spirit which
characterizes China, develops itself only to a unity of *secular*
national life, which degrades individuals to a position of constant dependence, religion also remains in a state of dependence.
The element of freedom is wanting to it; for its object is the
principle of Nature in general—Heaven—Universal Matter.
But the [compensating] truth of this alienated form of Spirit
[Nature occupying the place of the Absolute Spirit] is *ideal*
Unity, the elevation above the limitation of Nature and of
existence at large;—the return of consciousness into the soul.
This element, which is contained in Buddhism, has made its
way in China, to that extent to which the Chinese have become
aware of the unspirituality of their condition, and the limitation
that hampers their consciousness.—In this religion—which may
be generally described as the religion of self-involvement [un-
developed Unity] *—the elevation of that unspiritual condition
to subjectivity, takes place in two ways; one of which is of
a negative, the other of an affirmative kind.

The *negative* form of this elevation is the concentration of
Spirit to the Infinite, and must first present itself under theological conditions. It is contained in the fundamental dogma,
that Nothingness is the principle of all things—that all proceeded from and returns to Nothingness. The various forms
found in the World are only modifications of procession
[thence]. If an analysis of these various forms were attempted,
they would lose their quality; for in themselves all things are
one and the same inseparable essence, and this essence is Noth-

* Compare Hegel's "Vorlesungen über die Philosophie der Religion," 2d Edition, Pt. I. p. 384.

ingness. The connection of this with the Metempsychosis can be thus explained: All [that we see] is but a change of Form. The inherent infinity of Spirit—infinite concrete self-dependence—is entirely separate from this Universe of phenomena. Abstract Nothingness is properly that which lies beyond Finite Existence—what we may call the Supreme Being. This real principle of the Universe is, it is said, in eternal repose, and in itself unchangeable. Its essence consists in the absence of activity and volition. For Nothingness is abstract Unity with itself. To obtain happiness, therefore, man must seek to assimilate himself to this principle by continual victories over himself; and for the sake of this, do nothing, wish nothing, desire nothing. In this condition of happiness, therefore, Vice or Virtue is out of the question; for the true blessedness is Union with Nothingness. The more man frees himself from all speciality of existence, the nearer does he approach perfection; and in the annihilation of all activity—in pure passivity—he attains complete resemblance to Fo. The abstract Unity in question is not a mere Futurity—a Spiritual sphere existing beyond our own; it has to do with the present; it is truth for man [as he is], and ought to be realized in him. In Ceylon and the Burman Empire—where this Buddhistic Faith has its roots—there prevails an idea, that man can attain by meditation, to exemption from sickness, old age and death.

But while this is the *negative* form of the elevation of Spirit from immersion in the Objective to a subjective realization of itself, this Religion also advances to the consciousness of an *affirmative* form. Spirit is the Absolute. Yet in comprehending Spirit it is a point of essential importance in what determinate form Spirit is conceived. When we speak of Spirit as universal, we know that for us it exists only in an inward conception; but to attain this point of view—to appreciate Spirit in the pure subjectivity of Thought and conception—is the result of a longer process of culture. At that point in history at which we have now arrived, the form of Spirit is not advanced beyond Immediateness [the idea of it is not yet refined by reflection and abstraction]. God is conceived in an immediate, unreflected form; not in the form of Thought—objectively. But this immediate Form is that of humanity. The Sun, the Stars do not come up to the idea of Spirit; but Man seems to realize it; and he, as *Buddha, Gaütama, Fo*—in the form of a departed teacher, and in the living form of the **Grand Lama**—receives divine worship. The Abstract Understanding generally objects to this idea of a Godman; alleging as a defect that the form here assigned to Spirit is an immediate [unreflected, unrefined] one—that in fact it is none other than Man in the concrete. Here the character of a whole people is bound up with the theological view just indicated. The *Mongols*— a race extending through the whole of central Asia as far as Siberia, where they are subject to the Russians—worship the Lama; and with this form of worship a simple political condition, a patriarchal life is closely united; for they are properly a Nomad people, and only occasionally are commotions excited among them, when they seem to be beside themselves, and eruptions and inundations of vast hordes are occasioned. Of the Lamas there are three: the best known is the Dalai-Lama, who has his seat at Lassa in the kingdom of Thibet. A second is the Teshoo-Lama, who under the title of Bantshen Rinbotshee resides at Teshoo-Lomboo; there is also a third in Southern Siberia. The first two Lamas preside over two distinct sects, of which the priests of one wear yellow caps, those of the other, red. The wearers of the yellow caps—at whose head is the Dalai-Lama, and among whose adherents is the Emperor of China—have introduced celibacy among the priests, while the red sect allow their marriage. The English have become considerably acquainted with the Teshoo-Lama and have given us descriptions of him.

The general form which the spirit of the Lamaistic development of Buddhism assumes, is that of a living human being; while in the original Buddhism it is a deceased person. The two hold in common the relationship to a man. The idea of a man being worshipped as God—especially a living man—has in it something paradoxical and revolting; but the following considerations must be examined before we pronounce judgment respecting it. The conception of Spirit involves its being regarded as inherently, intrinsically, universal. This condition must be particularly observed, and it must be discovered how in the systems adopted by various peoples this universality is kept in view. It is not the individuality of the subject that is revered, but that which is universal in him; and which among the Thibetians, Hindoos, and Asiatics generally, is regarded as the essence pervading all things. This substantial

Unity of Spirit is realized in the Lama, who is nothing but the form in which Spirit manifests itself; and who does not hold this Spiritual Essence as his peculiar property, but is regarded as partaking in it only in order to exhibit it to others, that they may attain a conception of Spirituality and be led to piety and blessedness. The Lama's personality as such—his particular individuality—is therefore subordinate to that substantial essence which it embodies. The second point which constitutes an essential feature in the conception of the Lama is the disconnection from Nature. The Imperial dignity of China involved [as we saw] a supremacy over the powers of Nature; while here spiritual power is directly separated from the *vis Naturæ*. The idea never crosses the minds of the Lama-worshippers to desire of the Lama to show himself Lord of Nature —to exercise magical and miraculous power; for from the being they call God, they look only for spiritual activity and the bestowal of spiritual benefits. Buddha has moreover the express names " Saviour of Souls "—" Sea of Virtue "—" the Great Teacher." Those who have become acquainted with the Teshoo-Lama depict him as a most excellent person, of the calmest temper and most devoted to meditation. Thus also do the Lama-worshippers regard him. They see in him a man constantly occupied with religion, and who when he directs his attention to what is human, does so only to impart consolation and encouragement by his blessing, and by the exercise of mercy and the bestowal of forgiveness. These Lamas lead a thoroughly isolated life and have a feminine rather than masculine training. Early torn from the arms of his parents the Lama is generally a well-formed and beautiful child. He is brought up amid perfect quiet and solitude, in a kind of prison: he is well catered for, and remains without exercise or childish play, so that it is not surprising that a feminine susceptible tendency prevails in his character. The Grand Lamas have under them inferior Lamas as presidents of the great fraternities. In Thibet every father who has four sons is obliged to dedicate one to a conventual life. The Mongols, who are especially devoted to Lamaism—this modification of Buddhism—have great respect for all that possesses life. They live chiefly on vegetables, and revolt from killing any animal, even a louse. This worship of the Lamas has supplanted Shamanism, that is, the religion of Sorcery. The Shamans—

priests of this religion—intoxicate themselves with strong drinks and dancing, and while in this state perform their incantations, fall exhausted on the ground, and utter words which pass for oracular. Since Buddhism and Lamaism have taken the place of the Shaman Religion, the life of the Mongols has been simple, prescriptive and patriarchal. Where they take any part in History, we find them occasioning impulses that have only been the groundwork of historical development. There is therefore little to be said about the political administration of the Lamas. A Vizier has charge of the secular dominion and reports everything to the Lama: the government is simple and lenient; and the veneration which the Mongols pay to the Lama, expresses itself chiefly in their asking counsel of him in political affairs.

SECTION III

PERSIA

A SIA separates itself into two parts—Hither and Farther Asia; which are essentially different from each other. While the Chinese and Hindoos—the two great nations of Farther Asia, already considered—belong to the strictly Asiatic, namely the Mongolian Race, and consequently possess a quite peculiar character, discrepant from ours; the nations of Hither Asia belong to the Caucasian, *i.e.* the European Stock. They are related to the West, while the Farther-Asiatic peoples are perfectly isolated. The European who goes from Persia to India, observes, therefore, a prodigious contrast. Whereas in the former country he finds himself still somewhat at home, and meets with European dispositions, human virtues and human passions—as soon as he crosses the Indus (*i.e.* in the *latter* region), he encounters the most repellent characteristics, pervading every single feature of society.

With the Persian Empire we first enter on continuous History. The Persians are the first Historical People; Persia was the first Empire that passed away. While China and India remain stationary, and perpetuate a natural vegetative existence even to the present time, this land has been subject to those developments and revolutions, which alone manifest a historical condition. The Chinese and the Indian Empire assert a place in the historical series only on their own account and for us [not for neighbors and successors]. But here in Persia first arises that light which shines itself, and illuminates what is around; for *Zoroaster's* " Light " belongs to the World of Consciousness—to Spirit as a relation to something distinct from itself. We see in the Persian World a pure exalted Unity, as the essence which leaves the special existences that inhere in it, free;—as the Light, which only manifests what bodies are in themselves;—a Unity which governs individuals only to excite them to become powerful for themselves—to develop and assert their individuality. Light makes no distinctions: the Sun shines on the righteous and the unrighteous, on high and low, and confers on all the same benefit and prosperity. Light is vitalizing only in so far as it is brought to bear on something distinct from itself, operating upon and developing that. It holds a position of antithesis to Darkness, and this antithetical relation opens out to us the principle of activity and life. The principle of development begins with the history of Persia. This therefore constitutes strictly the beginning of World-History; for the grand interest of Spirit in History, is to attain an unlimited immanence of subjectivity —by an absolute antithesis to attain complete harmony.*

Thus the transition which we have to make, is only in the sphere of the Idea, not in the external historical connection. The principle of this transition is that the Universal Essence, which we recognized in Brahm, now becomes perceptible to consciousness—becomes an object and acquires a positive import for man. Brahm is not worshipped by the Hindoos: he is nothing more than a condition of the Individual, a religious feeling, a non-objective existence—a relation, which for concrete vitality is that of annihilation. But in becoming objective, this Universal Essence acquires a positive nature: man becomes free, and thus occupies a position face to face as it were with the Highest Being, the latter being made objective for him. This form of Universality we see exhibited in Persia, involving a separation of man from the Universal essence; while at the same time the individual recognizes himself as identical with [a partaker in], that essence. In the Chinese and Indian principle, this distinction was not made. We found only a unit of the Spiritual and the Natural. But Spirit still involved in Nature has to solve the problem of freeing itself from the latter. Rights and Duties in India are intimately connected with special classes, and are therefore only peculiarities attaching to man by the arrangement of Nature. In China this unity presents itself under the conditions of *paternal* government. Man is not free there; he possesses no moral element, since he is identical with the external command [obedi-

---

* In earlier stages of progress, the mandates of Spirit (social and political law), are given as by a power alien to itself—as by some compulsion of mere Nature. Gradually it sees the untruth of this alien form of validity—recognizes these mandates as its own, and adopts them freely as a law of liberty. It then stands in clear opposition to its logical contrary—Nature.—ED.

ence is purely *natural,* as in the filial relation—not the result of reflection and principle]. In the Persian principle, Unity first elevates itself to the distinction from the merely natural; we have the negation of that unreflecting relation which allowed no exercise of mind to intervene between the mandate and its adoption by the will. In the Persian principle this unity is manifested as Light, which in this case is not simply light as such, the most universal physical element, but at the same time also *spiritual* purity—the Good. Speciality—the involvement with *limited* Nature—is consequently abolished. Light, in a physical and spiritual sense, imports, therefore, elevation—freedom from the merely natural. Man sustains a relation to Light—to the Abstract Good—as to something objective, which is acknowledged, reverenced, and evoked to activity by his Will. If we look back once more—and we cannot do so too frequently—on the phases which we have traversed in arriving at this point, we perceive in China the totality of a moral Whole, but excluding subjectivity;—this totality divided into members, but without independence in its various portions. We found only an external arrangement of this political Unity. In India, on the contrary, distinctions made themselves prominent; but the *principle* of separation was unspiritual. We found incipient subjectivity, but hampered with the condition, that the separation in question is insurmountable; and that Spirit remains involved in the limitations of Nature, and is therefore a self-contradiction. Above this purity of Castes is that purity of Light which we observe in Persia; that Abstract Good, to which all are equally able to approach, and in which all equally may be hallowed. The Unity recognized therefore, now first becomes a principle, not an external bond of soulless order. The fact that everyone has a share in that principle, secures to him personal dignity.

First as to *Geographical position,* we see China and India, exhibiting as it were the dull half-conscious brooding of Spirit, in fruitful plains—distinct from which is the lofty girdle of mountains with the wandering hordes that occupy them. The inhabitants of the heights, in their conquest, did not change the spirit of the plains, but imbibed it themselves. But in Persia the two principles—retaining their diversity—became united, and the mountain peoples with their principle became the predominant element. The two chief divisions which we have to mention are:—the Persian Upland itself, and the Valley Plains, which are reduced under the dominion of the inhabitants of the Uplands. That elevated territory is bounded on the east by the Soliman mountains, which are continued in a northerly direction by the Hindoo Koosh and Belur Tag. The latter separate the anterior region—Bactriana and Sogdiana, occupying the plains of the Oxus—from the Chinese Upland, which extends as far as Cashgar. That plain of the Oxus itself lies to the north of the Persian Upland, which declines on the south towards the Persian Gulf. This is the geographical position of Iran. On its western declivity lies Persia (Farsistan); higher to the north, Kourdistan—beyond this Armenia. Thence extend in a southwesterly direction the river districts of the Tigris and the Euphrates.—The elements of the Persian Empire are the Zend race—the old Parsees; next the Assyrian, Median and Babylonian Empire in the region mentioned; but the Persian Empire also includes Asia Minor, Egypt, and Syria, with its line of coast; and thus combines the Upland, the Valley Plains and the Coast region.

Chapter I.—The Zend People

The Zend People derived their name from the language in which the *Zend Books* are written, *i.e.* the canonical books on which the religion of the ancient Parsees is founded. Of this religion of the Parsees or Fire-worshippers, there are still traces extant. There is a colony of them in Bombay; and on the Caspian Sea there are some scattered families that have retained this form of worship. Their national existence was put an end to by the Mahometans. The great *Zerdusht*—called Zoroaster by the Greeks—wrote his religious books in the Zend language. Until nearly the last third of the eighteenth century,· this language and all the writings composed in it, were entirely unknown to Europeans; when at length the celebrated Frenchman, *Anquetil-Duperron,* disclosed to us these rich treasures. Filled with an enthusiasm for the Oriental World, which his poverty did not allow him to gratify, he enlisted in a French corps that was about to sail for India. He thus reached Bombay, where he met with the Parsees, and entered on the study of their religious ideas. With indescribable difficulty he succeeded in obtaining their religious books; making his way into their literature, and thus opening an entirely new and wide field of research, but which, owing to his imperfect acquaintance with the language, still awaits thorough investigation.

Where the Zend people, mentioned in the religious books of Zoroaster, lived, is difficult to determine. In Media and Persia the religion of Zoroaster prevailed, and Xenophon relates that Cyrus adopted it: but none of these countries was the proper habitat of the Zend people. Zoroaster himself calls it the pure Aryan: we find a similar name in Herodotus, for he says that the Medes were formerly called Arii—a name with which the designation Iran is connected. South of the Oxus runs a mountain chain in the ancient Bactriana—with which the elevated plains commence, that were inhabited by the Medes, the Parthians, and the Hyrcanians. In the district watered by the Oxus at the commencement of its course, Bactra—probably the modern Balk—is said to have been situated; from which Cabul and Cashmere are distant only about eight days' journey. Here in Bactriana appears to have been the seat of the Zend people. In the time of Cyrus we find the pure and original faith, and the ancient political and social relations such as they are described in the Zend books, no longer perfect. Thus much appears certain, that the Zend language, which is connected with the Sanscrit, was the language of the Persians, Medes, and Bactrians. The laws and institutions of the people bear an evident stamp of great simplicity. Four classes are mentioned: Priests, Warriors, Agriculturists, and Craftsmen. Trade only is not noticed; from which it would appear that the people still remained in an isolated condition. Governors of Districts, Towns, and Roads, are mentioned; so that all points to the social phase of society—the political not being yet developed; and nothing indicates a connection with other states. It is essential to note, that we find here no Castes, but only Classes, and that there are no restrictions on marriage between these different Classes; though the Zend writings announce civil laws and penalties, together with religious enactments.

The chief point—that which especially concerns us here—is the *doctrine* of Zoroaster. In contrast with the wretched hebetude of Spirit which we find among the Hindoos, a pure ether—an exhalation of Spirit—meets us in the Persian conception. In it, Spirit emerges from that substantial Unity of

Nature, that substantial destitution of import, in which a separation has not yet taken place—in which Spirit has not yet an independent existence in contraposition to its object. This people, namely, attained to the consciousness, that absolute Truth must have the form of Universality—of Unity. This Universal, Eternal, Infinite Essence is not recognized at first, as conditioned in any way; it is Unlimited Identity. This is properly (and we have already frequently repeated it) also the character of Brahm. But this Universal Being became objective, and their Spirit became the consciousness of this its Essence; while on the contrary among the Hindoos this objectivity is only the *natural* one of the Brahmins, and is recognized as pure Universality only in the destruction of consciousness. Among the Persians this negative assertion has become a positive one; and man has a relation to Universal Being of such a kind that he remains positive in sustaining it. This One, Universal Being, is indeed not yet recognized as the free Unity of Thought; not yet " worshipped in Spirit and in Truth "; but is still clothed with a form—that of Light. But Light is not a Lama, a Brahmin, a Mountain, a brute—this or that particular existence—but sensuous Universality itself; simple manifestation. The Persian Religion is therefore no idol-worship; it does not adore individual natural objects, but the Universal itself. Light admits, moreover, the signification of the Spiritual; it is the form of the Good and True—the substantiality of knowledge and volition as well as of all natural things. Light puts man in a position to be able to exercise choice; and he can only choose when he has emerged from that which had absorbed him. But Light directly involves an Opposite, namely, Darkness; just as Evil is the antithesis of Good. As man could not appreciate Good, if Evil were not; and as he can be really good only when he has become acquainted with the contrary, so the Light does not exist without Darkness. Among the Persians, *Ormuzd* and *Ahriman* present the antithesis in question. Ormuzd is the Lord of the kingdom of Light—of Good; Ahriman that of Darkness—of Evil. But there is a still higher being from whom both proceeded—a Universal Being not affected by this antithesis, called *Zeruane-Akerene*—the Unlimited All. The All, *i.e.* is something abstract; it does not exist for itself, and Ormuzd and Ahriman have arisen from it. This Dualism is commonly brought as a reproach against Oriental thought; and, as far as the contradiction is regarded as absolute, that is certainly an irreligious understanding which remains satisfied with it. But the very nature of Spirit demands antithesis; the principle of Dualism belongs therefore to the idea of Spirit, which, in its concrete form, essentially involves distinction. Among the Persians, Purity and Impurity have both become subjects of consciousness; and Spirit, in order to comprehend itself, must of necessity place the Special and Negative existence in contrast with the Universal and Positive. Only by overcoming this antithesis is Spirit twice-born —regenerated. The deficiency in the Persian principle is only that the Unity of the antithesis is not completely recognized; for in that indefinite conception of the Uncreated All, whence Ormuzd and Ahriman proceeded, the Unity is only the absolutely *Primal* existence, and does not reduce the contradictory elements to harmony in itself. Ormuzd creates of his own free will; but also according to the decree of Zeruane-Akerene (the representation wavers); and the harmonizing of the contradiction is only to be found in the contest which Ormuzd carries on with Ahriman, and in which he will at last conquer. Ormuzd is the Lord of Light, and he creates all that is beautiful and noble in the World, which is a Kingdom of the Sun. He is the excellent, the good, the positive in all natural and spiritual existence. Light is the *body of Ormuzd;* thence the worship of Fire, because Ormuzd is present in all Light; but he is not the Sun or Moon itself. In these the Persians venerate only the Light, which is Ormuzd. Zoroaster asks Ormuzd who he is? He answers: " My Name is the ground and centre of all existence—Highest Wisdom and Science—Destroyer of the Ills of the World, and maintainer of the Universe—Fulness of Blessedness—Pure Will," etc. That which comes from Ormuzd is living, independent, and lasting. Language testifies to his power; prayers are his productions. Darkness is on the contrary the body of Ahriman; but a perpetual fire banishes him from the temples. The chief end of every man's existence is to keep himself pure, and to spread this purity around him. The precepts that have this in view are very diffuse; the moral requirements are however characterized by mildness. It is said: if a man loads you with revilings, and insults, but subsequently humbles himself, call him your friend. We read in the Vendidad, that sacrifices consist chiefly of the flesh of clean animals, flowers and fruits, milk and perfumes. It is said there, " As man was created pure and worthy of Heaven, he becomes pure again through the law of the servants of Ormuzd, which is purity itself; if he purifies himself by sanctity of thought, word, and deed. What is ' Pure Thought '? That which ascends to the beginning of things. What is ' Pure Word '? The Word of Ormuzd (the Word is thus personified and imports the living Spirit of the whole revelation of Ormuzd). What is ' Pure Deed '? The humble adoration of the Heavenly Hosts, created at the beginning of things." It is implied in this that man should be virtuous: his own will, his subjective freedom is presupposed. Ormuzd is not limited to particular forms of existence. Sun, Moon, and five other stars, which seem to indicate the planets—those illuminating and illuminated bodies—are the primary symbols of Ormuzd; the *Amshaspand,* his first sons. Among these, Mitra is also named: but we are at a loss to fix upon the star which this name denotes, as we are also in reference to the others. The *Mitra* is placed in the Zend Books among the other stars; yet in the penal code moral transgressions are called " Mitrasins "—*e.g.* breach of promise, entailing 300 lashes; to which in the case of theft, 300 years of punishment in Hell are to be added. Mitra appears here as the presiding genius of man's inward higher life. Later on, great importance is assigned to Mitra as the mediator between Ormuzd and men. Even Herodotus mentions the adoration of Mitra. In Rome, at a later date, it became very prevalent as a secret worship; and we find traces of it even far into the middle ages. Besides those noticed there are other protecting genii, which rank under the Amshaspand, their superiors; and are the governors and preservers of the world. The council of the seven great men whom the Persian Monarch had about him was likewise instituted in imitation of the court of Ormuzd. The *Fervers*—a kind of Spirit-World —are distinguished from the creatures of the mundane sphere. The Fervers are not Spirits according to our idea, for they exist in every natural object, whether fire, water, or earth. Their existence is coeval with the origin of things; they are in all places, in highroads, towns, etc., and are prepared to give help to supplicants. Their abode is in Gorodman, the dwelling of the " Blessed," above the solid vault of heaven. As Son of Ormuzd we find the name Dshemshid: apparently the same as he whom the Greeks call Achæmenes, whose descendants are called Pishdadians—a race to which Cyrus was reported to belong. Even at a later period the Persians seem to have had the designation Achæmenians among the Romans. (Horace, Odes III. i. 44.) Dshemshid, it is said, pierced the earth with a golden dagger; which means nothing more than that he introduced agriculture. He is said then to have traversed the various countries, originated springs and rivers, and thereby fertilized certain tracts of land, and made the valleys teem with living beings, etc. In the Zendavesta, the name Gustasp is also frequently mentioned, which many recent investigators have been inclined to connect with Darius Hystaspes; an idea however that cannot be entertained for a moment, for this Gustasp doubtless belongs to the ancient Zend Race—to a period therefore antecedent to Cyrus. Mention is made in the Zend books of the Turanians also, *i.e.* the Nomade tribes of the north; though nothing historical can be thence deduced.

The *ritual observances* of the religion of Ormuzd import that men should conduct themselves in harmony with the Kingdom of Light. The great general commandment is therefore, as already said, spiritual and corporeal purity, consisting in many prayers to Ormuzd. It was made specially obligatory upon the Persians, to maintain living existences—to plant trees—to dig wells—to fertilize deserts; in order that Life, the Positive, the Pure might be furthered, and the dominion of Ormuzd be universally extended. External purity is contravened by touching a dead animal, and there are many directions for being purified from such pollution. Herodotus relates of Cyrus, that when he went against Babylon, and the river Gyndes engulfed one of the horses of the Chariot of the Sun, he was occupied for a year in punishing it, by diverting its stream into small canals, to deprive it of its power. Thus Xerxes, when the sea broke in pieces his bridges, had chains laid upon it as the wicked and pernicious being—Ahriman.

Chapter II.—The Assyrians, Babylonians, Medes, and Persians

As the Zend Race was the higher spiritual element of the Persian Empire, so in Assyria and Babylonia we have the element of external wealth, luxury and commerce. Traditions respecting them ascend to the remotest periods of History; but in themselves they are obscure, and partly contradictory; and this contradiction is the less easy to be cleared up, as they have no canonical books or indigenous works. The Greek historian Ctesias is said to have had direct access to the archives of the Persian Kings; yet we have only a few fragments remaining. Herodotus gives us much information; the accounts in the Bible are also valuable and remarkable in the highest degree, for the Hebrews were immediately connected with the Babylonians. In regard to the Persians, special mention must be made of the Epic, " Shah-nameh," by Ferdusi—a heroic poem in 60,000 strophes, from which Görres has given a copious extract. Ferdusi lived at the beginning of the eleventh century A.D. at the court of Mahmoud the Great, at Ghasna, east of Cabul and Candahar. The celebrated Epic just mentioned has the old heroic traditions of Iran (that is of West Persia proper) for its subject; but it has not the value of a historical authority, since its contents are poetical and its author a Mahometan. The contest of Iran and Turan is described in this heroic poem. Iran is Persia Proper—the Mountain Land on the south of the Oxus; Turan denotes the plains of the Oxus and those lying between it and the ancient Jaxartes. A hero, Rustan, plays the principal part in the poem; but its narrations are either altogether fabulous, or quite distorted. Mention is made of Alexander, and he is called Ishkander or Skander of Roum. Roum means the Turkish Empire (even now one of its provinces is called Roumelia), but it denotes also the *Roman;* and in the poem Alexander's Empire has equally the appellation Roum. Confusions of this kind are quite of a piece with the Mahometan views. It is related in the poem, that the King of Iran made war on Philip, and that this latter was beaten. The King then demanded Philip's daughter as a wife; but after he had lived a long time with her, he sent her away because her breath was disagreeable. On returning to her father, she gave birth to a son—Skander, who hastened to Iran to take possession of the throne after the death of his father.

Add to the above that in the whole of the poem no personage or narrative occurs that can be connected with Cyrus, and we have sufficient data for estimating its historical value. It has a value for us, however, so far as Ferdusi therein exhibits the spirit of his time, and the character and interest of Modern Persian views.

As regards *Assyria,* we must observe, that it is a rather indeterminate designation. Assyria Proper is a part of Mesopotamia, to the north of Babylon. As chief towns of this Empire are mentioned, Atur or Assur on the Tigris, and of later origin Nineveh, said to have been founded and built by Ninus, the Founder of the Assyrian Empire. In those times one City constituted the whole Empire—Nineveh for example: so also Ecbatana in Media, which is said to have had seven walls, between whose inclosures agriculture was carried on; and within whose innermost wall was the palace of the ruler. Thus too, Nineveh, according to Diodorus, was 480 Stadia (about 12 German miles—[55 English]) in circumference. On the walls, which were 100 feet high, were fifteen hundred towers, within which a vast mass of people resided. Babylon included an equally immense population. These cities arose in consequence of a twofold necessity—on the one hand that of giving up the nomad life and pursuing agriculture, handicrafts and trade in a fixed abode; and on the other hand of gaining protection against the roving mountain peoples, and the predatory Arabs. Older traditions indicate that this entire valley district was traversed by Nomads, and that this mode of life gave way before that of the cities. Thus Abraham wandered forth with his family from Mesopotamia westwards, into mountainous Palestine. Even at this day the country round Bagdad is thus infested by roving Nomads. Nineveh is said to have been built 2050 years before Christ; consequently the founding of the Assyrian Kingdom is of no later date. Ninus reduced under his sway also Babylonia, Media and Bactriana; the conquest of which latter country is particularly extolled as having displayed the greatest energy; for Ctesias reckons the number of troops that accompanied Ninus, at 1,700,000 infantry and a proportionate number of cavalry. Bactra was besieged for a very considerable time, and its conquest is ascribed to Semiramis; who with a valiant host is said to have ascended the steep acclivity of a mountain. The personality of Semiramis wavers between mythological and historical representations.   To her is ascribed the building of the Tower of Babel, respecting which we have in the Bible one of the oldest of traditions.—*Babylon* lay to the south, on the Euphrates, in a plain of great fertility and well adapted for agriculture.   On the Euphrates and the Tigris there was considerable navigation.   Vessels came partly from Armenia, partly from the South, to Babylon, and conveyed thither an immense amount of material wealth.   The land round Babylon was intersected by innumerable canals; more for purposes of agriculture—to irrigate the soil and to obviate inundations—than for navigation.   The magnificent buildings of Semiramis in Babylon itself are celebrated; though how much of the city is to be ascribed to the more ancient period, is undetermined and uncertain.   It is said that Babylon formed a square, bisected by the Euphrates.   On one side of the stream was the temple of Bel, on the other the great palaces of the monarchs.   The city is reputed to have had a hundred brazen (*i.e.* copper) gates, its walls being a hundred feet high, and thick in proportion, defended by two hundred and fifty towers. The thoroughfares in the city which led towards the river were closed every night by brazen doors.   *Ker Porter,* an Englishman, about twelve years ago (his whole tour occupied from 1817 to 1820) traversed the countries where ancient Babylon lay: on an elevation he thought he could discover remains still existing of the old tower of Babel; and supposed that he had found traces of the numerous roads that wound around the tower, and in whose loftiest story the image of Bel was set up. There are besides many hills with remains of ancient structures.   The bricks correspond with the description in the Biblical record of the building of the tower.   A vast plain is covered by an innumerable multitude of such bricks, although for many thousand years the practice of removing them has been continued; and the entire town of Hila, which lies in the vicinity of the ancient Babylon, has been built with them.   Herodotus relates some remarkable facts in the customs of the Babylonians, which appear to show that they were people living peaceably and neighborly with each other.   When anyone in Babylon fell ill, he was brought to some open place, that every passerby might have the opportunity of giving him his advice.   Marriageable daughters were disposed of by auction, and the high price offered for a belle was allotted as a dowry for her plainer neighbor. Such an arrangement was not deemed inconsistent with the obligation under which every woman lay of prostituting herself once in her life in the temple of Mylitta. It is difficult to discover what connection this had with their religious ideas. This excepted, according to Herodotus's account, immorality invaded Babylon only at a later period, when the people became poorer. The fact that the fairer portion of the sex furnished dowries for their less attractive sisters, seems to confirm his testimony so far as it shows a provident care for all; while that bringing of the sick into the public places indicates a certain neighborly feeling.

We must here mention the *Medes* also. They were, like the Persians, a mountain-people, whose habitations were south and southwest of the Caspian Sea and stretched as far as Armenia. Among these Medes the Magi are also noticed as one of the six tribes that formed the Median people, whose chief characteristics were fierceness, barbarism, and warlike courage. The capital Ecbatana was built by Dejoces, not earlier. He is said to have united under his kingly rule the tribes of the Medes, after they had made themselves free a second time from Assyrian supremacy, and to have induced them to build and to fortify for him a palace befitting his dignity. As to the religion of the Medes, the Greeks call all the oriental Priests, Magi, which is therefore a perfectly indefinite name. But all the data point to the fact that among the Magi we may look for a comparatively close connection with the Zend religion; but that, although the Magi preserved and extended it, it experienced great modifications in transmission to the various peoples who adopted it. Xenophon says, that Cyrus was the first that sacrificed to God according to the fashion of the Magi. The Medes therefore acted as a medium for propagating the Zend Religion.

The Assyrian-Babylonian Empire, which held so many peoples in subjection, is said to have existed for one thousand or fifteen hundred years. The last ruler was Sardanapalus—a great voluptuary, according to the descriptions we have of him. Arbaces, the Satrap of Media, excited the other satraps against him; and in combination with them, led the troops which assembled every year at Nineveh to pay the tribute, against Sardanapalus. The latter, although he had gained many victories, was at last compelled to yield before overwhelming force, and to shut himself up in Nineveh; and, when he could not longer offer resistance, to burn himself there with all his treasure. According to some chronologists, this took place 888 years B.C.; according to others, at the end of the seventh century. After this catastrophe the empire was entirely broken up: it was divided into an Assyrian, a Median, and a Babylonian Empire, to which also belonged the Chaldeans—a mountain people from the north which had united with the Babylonians. These several Empires had in their turn various fortunes; though here we meet with a confusion in the accounts which has never been cleared up. Within this period of their existence begins their connection with the Jews and Egyptians. The Jewish people succumbed to superior force; the Jews were carried captive to Babylon, and from them we have accurate information respecting the condition of this Empire. According to Daniel's statements there existed in Babylon a carefully appointed organization for government business. He speaks of Magians— from whom the expounders of sacred writings, the soothsayers, astrologers, Wise Men and Chaldeans who interpreted dreams, are distinguished. The Prophets generally say much of the great commerce of Babylon; but they also draw a terrible picture of the prevailing depravity of manners.

The real culmination of the Persian Empire is to be looked for in connection with the *Persian* people properly so called, which, embracing in its rule all Anterior Asia, came into contact with the Greeks. The Persians are found in extremely close and early connection with the Medes; and the transmission of the sovereignty to the Persians makes no essential difference; for Cyrus was himself a relation of the Median King, and the names of Persia and Media melt into one. At the head of the Persians and Medes, Cyrus made war upon Lydia and its king Crœsus. Herodotus relates that there had been wars before that time between Lydia and Media, but which had been settled by the intervention of the King of Babylon. We recognize here a system of States, consisting of Lydia, Media, and Babylon. The latter had become predominant and had extended its dominion to the Mediterranean Sea. Lydia stretched eastward as far as the Halys; and the border of the western coast of Asia Minor, the fair Greek colonies, were subject to it; a high degree of culture was thus already present in the Lydian Empire. Art and poetry were blooming there as cultivated by the Greeks. These colonies also were subjected to

Persia. Wise men, such as Bias, and still earlier, Thales, advised them to unite themselves in a firm league, or to quit their cities and possessions, and to seek out for themselves other habitations; (Bias meant Sardinia). But such a union could not be realized among cities which were animated by the bitterest jealousy of each other, and who lived in continual quarrel: while in the intoxication of affluence they were not capable of forming the heroic resolve to leave their homes for the sake of freedom. Only when they were on the very point of being subjugated by the Persians, did some cities give up certain for prospective possessions, in their aspiration after the highest good—Liberty. Herodotus says of the war against the Lydians, that it made the Persians who were previously poor and barbarous, acquainted for the first time with the luxuries of life and civilization. After the Lydian conquest Cyrus subjugated Babylon. With it he came into possession of Syria and Palestine; freed the Jews from captivity, and allowed them to rebuild their temple. Lastly, he led an expedition against the Massagetæ; engaged with them in the steppes between the Oxus and the Jaxartes, but sustained a defeat, and died the death of a warrior and conqueror. The death of heroes who have formed an epoch in the History of the World, is stamped with the character of their mission. Cyrus thus died in his mission, which was the union of Anterior Asia into one sover·eignty without an ulterior object.

Chapter III.—The Persian Empire and its Constituent Parts

The Persian Empire is an Empire in the *modern* sense— like that which existed in Germany, and the great imperial realm under the sway of Napoleon; for we find it consisting of a number of states, which are indeed dependent, but which have retained their own individuality, their manners, and laws. The general enactments, binding upon all, did not infringe upon their political and social idiosyncrasies, but even protected and maintained them; so that each of the nations that constitute the whole, had its own form of Constitution. As Light illuminates everything—imparting to each object a peculiar vitality —so the Persian Empire extends over a multitude of nations, and leaves to each one its particular character. Some have even kings of their own; each one its distinct language, arms, way of life, and customs. All this diversity coexists harmoniously under the impartial dominion of Light. The Persian Empire comprehends all the three geographical elements, which we classified as distinct. First, the Uplands of Persia and Media; next, the Valley-plains of the Euphrates and Tigris, whose inhabitants are found united in a developed form of civilization, with Egypt—the Valley-plain of the Nile—where agriculture, industrial arts and sciences flourished; and lastly a third element, viz. the nations who encounter the perils of the sea—the Syrians, the Phœnicians, the inhabitants of the Greek colonies and Greek Maritime States in Asia Minor. Persia thus united in itself the three natural principles, while China and India remained foreign to the sea. We find here neither that consolidated totality which China presents, nor that Hindoo life, in which an anarchy of caprice is prevalent everywhere. In Persia, the government, though joining all in a central unity, is but a combination of peoples—leaving each of them free. Thereby a stop is put to that barbarism and ferocity with which the nations had been wont to carry on their destructive feuds, and which the Book of Kings and the Book of Samuel sufficiently attest. The lamentations of the Prophets and their imprecations upon the state of things before the conquest, show the misery, wickedness and disorder that prevailed among them, and the happiness which Cyrus diffused over the region of Anterior Asia. It was not given to the Asiatics to unite self-dependence, freedom and substantial vigor of mind, with culture, *i.e.* an interest for diverse pursuits and an acquaintance with the conveniences of life. Military valor among them is consistent only with barbarity of manners. It is not the calm courage of order; and when their mind opens to a sympathy with various interests, it immediately passes into effeminacy; allows its energies to sink, and makes men the slaves of an enervated sensuality.

Persia

The Persians—a free mountain and nomad people—though ruling over richer, more civilized and fertile lands—retained on the whole the fundamental characteristics of their ancient mode of life. They stood with one foot on their ancestral territory, with the other on their foreign conquests. In his ancestral land the King was a friend among friends, and as if surrounded by equals. Outside of it, he was the lord to whom all were subject, and bound to acknowledge their dependence by the payment of tribute. Faithful to the Zend religion, the Persians give themselves to the pursuit of piety and the pure worship of Ormuzd. The tombs of the Kings were in Persia Proper; and there the King sometimes visited his countrymen, with whom he lived in relations of the greatest simplicity. He brought with him presents for them, while all other nations were obliged to make presents to him. At the court of the monarch there was a division of Persian cavalry which constituted the *élite* of the whole army, ate at a common table, and were subject to a most perfect discipline in every respect. They made themselves illustrious by their bravery, and even the Greeks awarded a tribute of respect to their valor in the Median wars. When the entire Persian host, to which this division belonged, was to engage in an expedition, a summons was first issued to all the Asiatic populations. When the warriors were assembled, the expedition was undertaken with that character of restlessness, that nomadic disposition which formed the idiosyncrasy of the Persians. Thus they invaded Egypt, Scythia, Thrace, and at last Greece; where their vast power was destined to be shattered. A march of this kind looked almost like an emigration: their families accompanied them. Each people exhibited its national features and warlike accoutrements, and poured forth *en masse*. Each had its own order of march and mode of warfare. Herodotus sketches for us a brilliant picture of this variety of aspect as it presented itself in the vast march of nations under Xerxes (two millions of human beings are said to have accompanied him). Yet, as these peoples were so unequally disciplined—so diverse in strength and bravery—it is easy to understand how the small but well-trained armies of the Greeks, animated by the same spirit, and under matchless leadership, could withstand those innumerable but disorderly hosts of the Persians. The provinces had to provide for the support of the Persian cavalry, which were quartered in the centre of the kingdom. Babylon had to contribute the third part of the supplies in question, and consequently appears to have been by far the richest district. As regards other branches of revenue, each people was obliged to supply the choicest of the peculiar produce which the district afforded. Thus Arabia gave frankincense, Syria purple, etc.

The education of the princes—but especially that of the heir to the throne—was conducted with extreme care. Till their seventh year the sons of the King remained among the women, and did not come into the royal presence. From their seventh year forward they were instructed in hunting, riding, shooting with the bow, and also in speaking the truth. There is one statement to the effect that the prince received instruction in the Magian lore of Zoroaster. Four of the noblest Persians conducted the prince's education. The magnates of the land, at large, constituted a kind of Diet. Among them Magi were also found. They are depicted as free men, animated by a noble fidelity and patriotism. Of such character seem the seven nobles—the counterpart of the Amshaspand who stand around Ormuzd—when after the unmasking of the false Smerdis, who on the death of King Cambyses gave himself out as his brother, they assembled to deliberate on the most desirable form of government. Quite free from passion, and without exhibiting any ambition, they agree that monarchy is the only form of government adapted to the Persian Empire. The Sun, and the horse which first salutes them with a neigh, decide the succession in favor of Darius. The magnitude of the Persian dominion occasioned the government of the provinces by viceroys—Satraps; and these often acted very arbitrarily to the provinces subjected to their rule, and displayed hatred and envy towards each other; a source of much evil. These satraps were only superior presidents of the provinces, and generally left the subject kings of the countries in possession of regal privileges. All the land and all the water belonged to the Great King of the Persians. " Land and Water " were the demands of Darius Hystaspes and Xerxes from the Greeks. But the King was only the abstract sovereign: the enjoyment of the country remained to the nations themselves; whose obligations were comprised in the maintenance of the court and the satraps, and the contribution of the choicest part of their property. Uniform taxes first make their appearance under the government of Darius Hystaspes. On the occasion of a royal progress the districts of the empire visited had to give presents to the King; and from the amount of these gifts we may infer the wealth of the unexhausted provinces. Thus the dominion of the Persians was by no means oppressive, either in secular or religious respects. The Persians, according to Herodotus, had no idols—in fact ridiculed anthropomorphic representations of the gods; but they tolerated every religion, although there may be found expressions of wrath against idolatry. Greek temples were destroyed, and the images of the gods broken in pieces.

Syria and the Semitic Western Asia

One element—the coast territory—which also belonged to the Persian Empire, is especially represented by Syria. It was peculiarly important to the Persian Empire; for when Continental Persia set out on one of its great expeditions, it was accompanied by Phœnician as well as by Greek navies. The Phœnician coast is but a very narrow border—often only two leagues broad—which has the high mountains of Lebanon on the East. On the seacoast lay a series of noble and rich cities, as Tyre, Sidon, Byblus, Berytus, carrying on great trade and commerce; which last, however, was too isolated and confined to that particular country, to allow it to affect the whole Persian state. Their commerce lay chiefly in the direction of the Mediterranean sea, and it reached thence far into the West. Through its intercourse with so many nations, Syria soon attained a high degree of culture. There the most beautiful fabrications in metals and precious stones were prepared, and there the most important discoveries, e.g. of Glass and of Purple, were made. Written language there received its first development, for in their intercourse with various nations, the need of it was soon felt. (So, to quote another example, Lord Macartney observes that in Canton itself, the Chinese had felt and expressed the need of a more pliable written language.) The Phœnicians discovered and first navigated the Atlantic Ocean. They had settlements in Cyprus and Crete. In the remote island of Thasos, they worked gold mines. In the south and southwest of Spain they opened silver mines. In Africa they founded the colonies of Utica and Carthage. From Gades they sailed far down the African coast, and according to some, even circumnavigated Africa. From Britain they brought tin, and from the Baltic, Prussian amber. This opens to us an entirely new principle. Inactivity ceases, as also mere rude valor; in their place appears the activity of Industry, and that considerate courage which, while it dares the perils of the deep, rationally bethinks itself of the means of safety. Here everything depends on Man's activity, his courage, his intelligence; while the objects aimed at are also pursued in the interest of Man. Human will and activity here occupy the foreground, not Nature and its bounty. Babylonia had its determinate share of territory, and human subsistence was there dependent on the course of the sun and the process of Nature generally. But the sailor relies upon himself amid the fluctuations of the waves, and eye and heart must be always open. In like manner the principle of Industry involves the very opposite of what is received from Nature; for natural objects are worked up for use and ornament. In Industry Man is an object to himself, and treats Nature as something subject to him, on which he impresses the seal of his activity. Intelligence is the valor needed here, and ingenuity is better than mere natural courage. At this point we see the nations freed from the fear of Nature and its slavish bondage.

If we compare their *religious* ideas with the above, we shall see in *Babylon,* in the *Syrian* tribes, and in *Phrygia,* first a rude, vulgar, sensual idolatry—a description of which in its principal features is given in the Prophets. Nothing indeed more specific than idolatry is mentioned; and this is an indefinite term. The Chinese, the Hindoos, the Greeks, practise idolatry; the Catholics, too, adore the images of saints; but in the sphere of thought with which we are at present occupied, it is the powers of Nature and of production generally that constitute the object of veneration; and the worship is luxury and pleasure. The Prophets give the most terrible pictures of this—though their repulsive character must be partly laid to the account of the hatred of Jews against neighboring peoples. Such representations are particularly ample in the Book of Wisdom. Not only was there a worship of natural objects, but also of the Universal Power of Nature—Astarte, Cybele, Diana of Ephesus. The worship paid was a sensuous intoxication, excess, and revelry: sensuality and cruelty are its two characteristic traits. "When they keep their holy days they act as if mad," ["they are mad when they be merry"—English Version] says the Book of Wisdom (xiv. 28). With a merely sensuous life—this being a form of consciousness which does not attain to general conceptions—cruelty is connected; because Nature itself is the Highest, so that Man has no value, or only the most trifling. Moreover, the genius of such a polytheism involves the de-

struction of its consciousness on the part of Spirit in striving
to identify itself with Nature, and the annihilation of the Spiritual generally.   Thus we see children sacrificed—priests of
Cybele subjecting themselves to mutilation—men making themselves eunuchs—women prostituting themselves in the temple.
As a feature of the court of Babylon it deserves to be remarked,
that when Daniel was brought up there, it was not required
of him to take part in the religious observances; and moreover
that food ceremonially pure was allowed him; that he was in
requisition especially for interpreting the dreams of the King,
because he had " the spirit of the holy gods."   The King proposes to elevate himself above sensuous life by dreams, as indications from a superior power.   It is thus generally evident,
that the bond of religion was lax, and that here no unity is to be
found.   For we observe also adorations offered to images of
kings; the power of Nature and the *King* as a spiritual Power,
are the Highest; so that in this form of idolatry there is manifested a perfect contrast to the Persian purity.

We find on the other hand something quite different among
the *Phœnicians,* that bold seafaring people.   Herodotus tells
us, that at Tyre Hercules was worshipped.   If the divinity in
question is not absolutely identical with the Greek demigod,
there must be understood by that name one whose attributes
nearly agree with his.   This worship is particularly indicative
of the character of the people; for it is Hercules of whom the
Greeks say, that he raised himself to Olympus by dint of human
courage and daring.   The idea of the Sun perhaps originated
that of Hercules as engaged in his twelve labors; but this basis
does not give us the chief feature of the myth, which is, that
Hercules is that scion of the gods who, by his virtue and exertion, made himself a god by human spirit and valor; and who,
instead of passing his life in idleness, spends it in hardship and
toil.   A *second* religious element is the worship of *Adonis,*
which takes place in the towns of the coast (it was celebrated
in Egypt also by the Ptolemies) ; and respecting which we find
a notable passage in the Book of Wisdom (xiv. 13, etc.), where
it is said : " The idols were not from the beginning—but were
invented through the vain ambition of men, because the latter
are short-lived.   For a father afflicted with untimely mourning,
when he had made an image of his child (Adonis) early taken
away, honored him as a god, who was a dead man, and deliv-

ered to those that were under him ceremonies and sacrifices "
(E. V. nearly). The feast of Adonis was very similar to the
worship of Osiris—the commemoration of his death—a funeral
festival, at which the women broke out into the most extravagant lamentations over the departed god. In India lamentation
is suppressed in the heroism of insensibility; uncomplaining,
the women there plunge into the river, and the men, ingenious
in inventing penances, impose upon themselves the direst tortures; for they give themselves up to the loss of vitality, in
order to destroy consciousness in empty abstract contemplation.
Here, on the contrary, human pain becomes an element of
worship; in pain man realizes his subjectivity: it is expected
of him—he may here indulge self-consciousness and the feeling
of actual existence. Life here regains its value. A universality
of pain is established: for death becomes immanent in the Divine, and the deity dies. Among the Persians we saw Light
and Darkness struggling with each other, but here both principles are united in one—the Absolute. The Negative is here,
too, the merely Natural; but as the death of a *god,* it is not
a limitation attaching to an individual object, but is pure Negativity itself. And this point is important, because the generic
conception that has to be formed of Deity is Spirit; which
involves its being concrete, and having in it the element of
negativity. The qualities of wisdom and power are also concrete qualities, but only as predicates; so that God remains
abstract substantial unity, in which differences themselves vanish, and do not become *organic* elements (Momente) of this
unity. But here the Negative itself is a *phase* of Deity—the
Natural—Death;—the worship appropriate to which is grief.
It is in the celebration of the death of Adonis, and of his resurrection, that the concrete is made conscious. Adonis is a youth,
who is torn from his parents by a too early death. In China;
in the worship of ancestors, these latter enjoy divine honor.
But parents in their decease only pay the debt of Nature. When
a *youth* is snatched away by death, the occurrence is regarded
as contrary to the proper order of things; and while affliction
at the death of parents is no *just* affliction, in the case of youth
death is a paradox. And this is the deeper element in the conception—that in the Divinity, Negativity—Antithesis—is manifested; and that the worship rendered to him involves both
elements—the pain felt for the divinity snatched away, and
the joy occasioned by his being found again.

Judæa

The next people belonging to the Persian empire, in that wide circle of nationalities which it comprises, is the *Jewish.* We find here, too, a canonical book—the *Old Testament;* in which the views of this people—whose principle is the exact opposite of the one just described—are exhibited. While among the Phœnician people the Spiritual was still limited by Nature, in the case of the Jews we find it entirely purified;— the pure product of Thought. Self-conception appears in the field of consciousness, and the Spiritual develops itself in sharp contrast to Nature and to union with it. It is true that we observed at an earlier stage the pure conception " Brahm "; but only as the universal being of Nature; and with this lim- itation, that Brahm is not himself an object of consciousness. Among the Persians we saw this abstract being become an object for consciousness, but it was that of sensuous intuition— as Light. But the idea of Light has at this stage advanced to that of " Jehovah "—the *purely One.* This forms the point of separation between the East and the West; Spirit descends into the depths of its own being, and recognizes the abstract fundamental principle as the Spiritual. Nature—which in the East is the primary and fundamental existence—is now de- pressed to the condition of a mere creature; and Spirit now occupies the first place. God is known as the creator of all men, as he is of all nature, and as absolute causality generally. But this great principle, as further conditioned, is *exclusive* Unity. This religion must necessarily possess the element of exclusiveness, which consists essentially in this—that only the One People which adopts it, recognizes the One God, and is acknowledged by him. The God of the Jewish People is the God only of Abraham and of his seed: National individuality and a special local worship are involved in such a conception of deity. Before him all other gods are false: moreover the distinction between " true " and " false " is quite abstract; for as regards the false gods, not a ray of the Divine is supposed to shine into them. But every form of spiritual force, and *à fortiori* every religion is of such a nature, that whatever be its peculiar character, an affirmative element is necessarily con- tained in it. However erroneous a religion may be, it possesses truth, although in a mutilated phase. In every religion there is a divine presence, a divine relation; and a philosophy of History has to seek out the spiritual element even in the most imperfect forms. But it does not follow that because it is a religion, it is therefore *good*. We must not fall into the lax conception, that the content is of no importance, but only the form. This latitudinarian tolerance the Jewish religion does not admit, being absolutely exclusive.

The Spiritual speaks itself here absolutely free of the Sensuous, and Nature is reduced to something merely external and undivine. This is the true and proper estimate of Nature at this stage; for only at a more advanced phase can the Idea attain a reconciliation [recognize itself] in this its alien form. Its first utterances will be in opposition to Nature; for Spirit, which had been hitherto dishonored, now first attains its due dignity, while Nature resumes its proper position. Nature is conceived as having the ground of its existence in another—as something posited, created; and this idea, that God is the lord and creator of Nature, leads men to regard God as the Exalted One, while the whole of Nature is only his robe of glory, and is expended in his service. In contrast with this kind of exaltation, that which the Hindoo religion presents is only that of indefinitude. In virtue of the prevailing spirituality the Sensuous and Immoral are no longer privileged, but disparaged as ungodliness. Only the One—Spirit—the Non-sensuous is the Truth; Thought exists free for itself, and true morality and righteousness can now make their appearance; for God is honored by righteousness, and right-doing is " walking in the way of the Lord." With this is conjoined happiness, life and temporal prosperity as its reward; for it is said: " that thou mayest live long in the land."—Here too also we have the possibility of a *historical* view; for the understanding has become prosaic; putting the limited and circumscribed in its proper place, and comprehending it as the form proper to finite existence: Men are regarded as individuals, not as incarnations of God; Sun as Sun, Mountains as Mountains—not as possessing Spirit and Will.

We observe among this people a severe religious ceremonial, expressing a relation to pure Thought. The individual as concrete does not become free, because the Absolute itself is not comprehended as *concrete* Spirit; since Spirit still appears posited as non-spiritual—destitute of its proper characteristics.

It is true that subjective feeling is manifest—the pure heart, repentance, devotion; but the particular concrete individuality has not become objective to itself in the Absolute. It therefore remains closely bound to the observance of ceremonies and of the Law, the basis of which latter is pure freedom in its abstract form. The Jews possess that which makes them what they are, through the *One:* consequently the individual has no freedom for itself. Spinoza regards the code of Moses as having been given by God to the Jews for a punishment—a rod of correction. The individual never comes to the consciousness of independence; on that account we do not find among the Jews any belief in the immortality of the soul; for individuality does not exist in and for itself. But though in Judaism the *Individual* is not respected, the *Family* has inherent value; for the worship of Jehovah is attached to the Family, and it is consequently viewed as a substantial existence. But the State is an institution not consonant with the Judaistic principle, and it is alien to the legislation of Moses. In the idea of the Jews, Jehovah is the God of Abraham, of Isaac, and Jacob; who commanded them to depart out of Egypt, and gave them the land of Canaan. The accounts of the Patriarchs attract our interest. We seen in this history the transition from the patriarchal nomade condition to agriculture. On the whole the Jewish history exhibits grand features of character; but it is disfigured by an exclusive bearing (sanctioned in its religion), towards the genius of other nations (the destruction of the inhabitants of Canaan being even commanded)—by want of culture generally, and by the superstition arising from the idea of the high value of their peculiar nationality. Miracles, too, form a disturbing feature in this history—*as history;* for as far as concrete consciousness is not free, concrete perception is also not free; Nature is undeified, but not yet understood.

The Family became a great nation; through the conquest of Canaan, it took a whole country into possession; and erected a Temple for the entire people, in Jerusalem. But properly speaking no *political* union existed. In case of national danger heroes arose, who placed themselves at the head of the armies; though the nation during this period was for the most part in subjection. Later on, kings were chosen, and it was they who first rendered the Jews independent. David even made conquests. Originally the legislation is adapted to a family only; yet in the books of Moses the wish for a king is anticipated. The priests are to choose him: he is not to be a foreigner— not to have horsemen in large numbers—and he is to have few wives. After a short period of glory the kingdom suffered internal disruption and was divided. As there was only one tribe of Levites and one Temple—*i.e.* in Jerusalem—idolatry was immediately introduced. The One God could not be honored in different Temples, and there could not be two kingdoms attached to one religion. However spiritual may be the conception of God as objective, the subjective side—the honor rendered to him—is still very limited and unspiritual in character. The two kingdoms, equally infelicitous in foreign and domestic warfare, were at last subjected to the Assyrians and Babylonians; through Cyrus the Israelites obtained permission to return home and live according to their own laws.

Egypt

The Persian Empire is one that has passed away, and we have nothing but melancholy relics of its glory. Its fairest and richest towns—such as Babylon, Susa, Persepolis—are razed to the ground; and only a few ruins mark their ancient site. Even in the more modern great cities of Persia—Ispahan and Shiraz—half of them has become a ruin; and they have not—as is the case with ancient Rome—developed a new life, but have lost their place almost entirely in the remembrance of the surrounding nations. Besides the other lands already enumerated as belonging to the Persian Empire, *Egypt* claims notice—characteristically the Land of Ruins; a land which from hoar antiquity has been regarded with wonder, and which in recent times also has attracted the greatest interest. Its ruins, the final result of immense labor, surpass in the gigantic and monstrous, all that antiquity has left us.

In Egypt we see united the elements which in the Persian monarchy appeared singly. We found among the Persians the adoration of Light—regarded as the Essence of universal Nature. This principle then develops itself in phases which hold a position of indifference towards each other. The one is the immersion in the sensuous—among the Babylonians and Syrians; the other is the Spiritual phase, which is twofold: first as the incipient consciousness of the concrete Spirit in the worship of Adonis, and then as pure and abstract thought among the Jews. In the former the concrete is deficient in unity; in the latter the concrete is altogether wanting. The next problem is then, to harmonize these contradictory elements; and this problem presents itself in Egypt. Of the representations which Egyptian Antiquity presents us with, one figure must be especially noticed, viz. *the Sphinx*—in itself a riddle—an ambiguous form, half brute, half human. The Sphinx may be regarded as a symbol of the Egyptian Spirit. The human head looking out from the brute body, exhibits Spirit as it begins to emerge from the merely Natural—to tear itself loose therefrom and already to look more freely around it; without, however, entirely freeing itself from the fetters Nature had imposed. The innumerable edifices of the Egyptians are half below the ground, and half rise above it into the air. The whole land is divided into a kingdom of life and a kingdom of death. The colossal statue of *Memnon* resounds at the first glance of the young morning Sun; though it is not yet the free light of Spirit with which it vibrates. Written language is still a hieroglyphic; and its basis is only the sensuous image, not the letter itself.

Thus the memorials of Egypt themselves give us a multitude of forms and images that express its character; we recognize a Spirit in them which feels itself compressed; which utters itself, but only in a sensuous mode.

Egypt was always the Land of Marvels, and has remained so to the present day. It is from the Greeks especially that we get information respecting it, and chiefly from Herodotus. This intelligent historiographer himself visited the country of which he wished to give an account, and at its chief towns made acquaintance with the Egyptian priests. Of all that he saw and heard, he gives an accurate record; but the deeper symbolism of the Egyptian mythology he has refrained from unfolding. This he regards as something sacred, and respecting which he cannot so freely speak as of merely external objects. Besides him Diodorus Siculus is an authority of great importance; and among the Jewish historians, Josephus.

In their architecture and hieroglyphics, the thoughts and conceptions of the Egyptians are expressed. A national work in the department of language is wanting: and that not only to us, but to the Egyptians themselves; they could not have any, because they had not advanced to an understanding of themselves. Nor was there any Egyptian history, until at last Ptolemy Philadelphus—he who had the sacred books of the Jews translated into Greek—prompted the High-Priest Manetho to write an Egyptian history. Of this we have only extracts —list of Kings; which however have occasioned the greatest perplexities and contradictory views. To become acquainted with Egypt, we must for the most part have recourse to the notices of the ancients, and the immense monuments that are left us. We find a number of granite walls on which hieroglyphics are graved, and the ancients have given us explanations of some of them, but which are quite insufficient. In recent times attention has especially been recalled to them, and after many efforts something at least of the hieroglyphic writing has been deciphered. The celebrated Englishman, *Thomas Young*, first suggested a method of discovery, and called attention to the fact, that there are small surfaces separated from the other hieroglyphics, and in which a Greek translation is perceptible. By comparison Young made out three names— Berenice, Cleopatra, and Ptolemy—and this was the first step in deciphering them. It was found at a later date, that a great part of the hieroglyphics are phonetic, that is, express sounds. Thus the figure of an eye denotes first the eye itself, but secondly the first letter of the Egyptian word that means " eye " (as in Hebrew the figure of a house, ב, denotes the letter *b*, with which the word בית, House, begins). The celebrated *Champollion* (the younger), first called attention to the fact that the phonetic hieroglyphs are intermingled with those which mark conceptions; and thus classified the hieroglyphs and established settled principles for deciphering them.

The *History* of Egypt, as we have it, is full of the greatest contradictions. The Mythical is blended with the Historical, and the statements are as diverse as can be imagined. European literati have eagerly investigated the lists given by Manetho and have relied upon them, and several names of kings have been confirmed by the recent discoveries. Herodotus says that according to the statements of the priests, gods had formerly reigned over Egypt, and that from the first human king down to the King Setho 341 generations, or 11,340 years, had passed away; but that the first human ruler was Menes (the resemblance of the name to the Greek Minos and the Hindoo Manu is striking). With the exception of the Thebaid—its most southern part—Egypt was said by them to have formed a lake; the Delta presents reliable evidence of having been produced by the silt of the Nile. As the Dutch have gained their territory from the sea, and have found means to sustain themselves upon it; so the Egyptians first acquired their country, and maintained its fertility by canals and lakes. An important feature in the history of Egypt is its descent from Upper to Lower Egypt—from the South to the North. With this is connected the consideration that Egypt probably received its culture from Ethiopia; principally from the island Meroe, which, according to recent hypotheses, was occupied by a sacerdotal people. Thebes in Upper Egypt was the most ancient residence of the Egyptian kings. Even in Herodotus's time it was in a state of dilapidation. The ruins of this city present the most enormous specimens of Egyptian architecture that we are acquainted with. Considering their antiquity they are remarkably well preserved: which is partly owing to the perpetually cloudless sky. The centre of the kingdom was then transferred to Memphis, not far from the modern Cairo; and lastly to Sais, in the Delta itself. The structures that occur in the locality of this city are of very late date and imperfectly preserved. Herodotus tells us that Memphis was referred to so remote a founder as Menes. Among the later kings must be especially noticed Sesostris, who, according to Champollion, is Ramses the Great. To him in particular are referred a number of monuments and pictures in which are depicted his triumphal processions, and the captives taken in battle. Herodotus speaks of his conquests in Syria, extending even to Colchis; and illustrates his statement by the great similarity between the manners of the Colchians and those of the Egyptians; these two nations and the Ethiopians were the only ones that had always practised circumcision. Herodotus says, moreover, that Sesostris had vast canals dug through the whole of Egypt, which served to convey the water of the Nile to every part. It may be generally remarked that the more provident the government in Egypt was, so much the more regard did it pay to the maintenance of the canals, while under negligent governments the desert got the upper hand; for Egypt was engaged in a constant struggle with the fierceness of the heat and with the water of the Nile. It appears from Herodotus, that the country had become impassable for cavalry in consequence of the canals; while, on the contrary, we see from the books of Moses, how celebrated Egypt once was in this respect. Moses says that if the Jews desired a king, he must not marry too many wives, nor send for horses from Egypt.

Next to Sesostris the Kings Cheops and Chephren deserve special mention. They are said to have built enormous pyramids and closed the temples of the priests. A son of Cheops —Mycerinus—is said to have reopened them; after him the Ethiopians invaded the country, and their king, Sabaco, made himself sovereign of Egypt. But Anysis, the successor of Mycerinus, fled into the marshes—to the mouth of the Nile; only after the departure of the Ethiopians did he make his appearance again. He was succeeded by Setho, who had been a priest of Phtha (supposed to be the same as Hephæstus): under his government, Sennacherib, King of the Assyrians, invaded the country. Setho had always treated the warrior-caste with great disrespect, and even robbed them of their lands; and when he invoked their assistance, they refused it. He was obliged therefore to issue a general summons to the Egyptians, and assembled a host composed of hucksters, artisans, and market people. In the Bible we are told that the enemies fled, and that it was the angels who routed them; but Herodotus relates that fieldmice came in the night and gnawed the quivers and bows of the enemy, so that the latter, deprived of their weapons, were compelled to flee. After the death of Setho, the Egyptians (Herodotus tells us) regarded themselves as free, and chose themselves twelve kings, who formed a federal union—as a symbol of which they built the Labyrinth, consisting of an immense number of rooms and halls above and below ground. In the year 650 B.C. one of these kings, Psammitichus, with the help of the Ionians and Carians (to whom he promised land in Lower Egypt), expelled the eleven other kings. Till that time Egypt had remained secluded from the rest of the world; and at sea it had established no connection with other nations. Psammitichus commenced such a connection, and thereby led the way to the ruin of Egypt. From this point the history becomes clearer, because it is based on Greek accounts. Psammitichus was followed by Necho, who began to dig a canal, which was to unite the Nile with the Red Sea, but which was not completed until the reign of Darius Nothus. The plan of uniting the Mediterranean Sea with the Arabian Gulf, and the wide ocean, is not so advantageous as might be supposed; since in the Red Sea—which on other accounts is very difficult to navigate—there prevails for about nine months in the year a constant north wind, so that it is only during three months that the passage from south to north is feasible. Necho was followed by Psammis, and the latter by Apries, who led an army against Sidon, and engaged with the Tyrians by sea: against Cyrene also he sent an army, which was almost annihilated by the Cyrenians. The Egyptians rebelled against him, accusing him of wishing to lead them to destruction; but this revolt was probably caused by the favor shown by him to the Carians and Ionians. Amasis placed himself at the head of the rebels, conquered the king, and possessed himself of the throne. By Herodotus he is depicted as a humorous monarch, who, however, did not always maintain the dignity of the throne. From a very humble station he had raised himself to royalty by ability, astuteness, and intelligence, and he exhibited in all other relations the same keen understanding. In the morning he held his court of judicature, and listened to the complaints of the people; but in the afternoon, feasted and surrendered himself to pleasure. To his friends, who blamed him on this account, and told him that he ought to give the whole day to business, he made answer: " If the bow is constantly on the stretch, it becomes useless or breaks." As the Egyptians thought less of him on account of his mean descent, he had a golden basin—used for washing the feet—made into the image of a god in high honor among the Egyptians; this he meant as a symbol of his own elevation. Herodotus relates, moreover, that he indulged in excesses as a private man, dissipated the whole of his property, and then betook himself to stealing. This contrast of a vulgar soul and a keen intellect is characteristic in an Egyptian king.

Amasis drew down upon him the ill-will of King Cambyses. Cyrus desired an oculist from the Egyptians; for at that time the Egyptian oculists were very famous, their skill having been called out by the numerous eye-diseases prevalent in Egypt. This oculist, to revenge himself for having been sent out of the country, advised Cambyses to ask for the daughter of Amasis in marriage; knowing well that Amasis would either be rendered unhappy by giving her to him, or on the other hand, incur the wrath of Cambyses by refusing. Amasis would not give his daughter to Cambyses, because the latter desired her as an inferior wife (for his lawful spouse must be a Persian) ; but sent him, under the name of his own daughter, that of Apries, who afterwards discovered her real name to Cambyses. The latter was so incensed at the deception, that he led an expedition against Egypt, conquered that country, and united it with the Persian Empire.

As to the Egyptian *Spirit,* it deserves mention here, that the Elians in Herodotus's narrative call the Egyptians the wisest of mankind. It also surprises us to find among them, in the vicinity of African stupidity, reflective intelligence, a thoroughly rational organization characterizing all institutions, and most astonishing works of art. The Egyptians were, like the Hindoos, divided into castes, and the children always continued the trade and business of their parents. On this account, also, the Mechanical and Technical in the arts was so much developed here; while the hereditary transmission of occupations did not produce the same disadvantageous results in the character of the Egyptians as in India. Herodotus mentions the seven following castes: the priests, the warriors, the neatherds, the swineherds, the merchants (or trading population generally), the interpreters—who seem only at a later date to have constituted a separate class—and, lastly, the seafaring class. Agriculturists are not named here, probably because agriculture was the occupation of several castes, as, *e.g.*, the warriors, to whom a portion of the land was given. Diodorus and Strabo give a different account of these caste-divisions. Only priests, warriors, herdsmen, agriculturists, and artificers are mentioned, to which latter, perhaps, tradesmen also belong. Herodotus says of the priests, that they in particular received arable land, and had it cultivated for rent; for the land generally was in the possession of the priests, warriors, and kings. Joseph was a minister of the king, according to Holy Scripture, and contrived to make him master of all landed property. But the several occupations did not remain so stereotyped as among the Hindoos; for we find the Israelites, who were originally herdsmen, employed also as manual laborers: and there was a king —as stated above—who formed an army of manual laborers alone. The castes are not rigidly fixed, but struggle with and come into contact with one another: we often find cases of their being broken up and in a state of rebellion. The warrior-caste, at one time discontented on account of their not being released from their abodes in the direction of Nubia, and desperate at not being able to make use of their lands, betake themselves to Meroë, and foreign mercenaries are introduced into the country.

Of the *mode of life* among the Egyptians, Herodotus supplies a very detailed account, giving prominence to everything which appears to him to deviate from Greek manners. Thus the Egyptians had physicians specially devoted to particular diseases; the women were engaged in outdoor occupations, while the men remained at home to weave. In one part of Egypt polygamy prevailed; in another, monogamy; the women had but one garment, the men two; they wash and bathe much, and undergo purification every month. All this points to a condition of settled peace. As to arrangements of police, the law required that every Egyptian should present himself, at a time appointed, before the superintendent under whom he lived, and state from what resources he obtained his livelihood. If he could not refer to any, he was punished with death. This law, however, was of no earlier date than Amasis. The greatest care, moreover, was observed in the division of the arable land, as also in planning canals and dikes; under Sabaco, the Ethiopian king, says Herodotus, many cities were elevated by dikes.

The business of *courts of justice* was administered with very great care. They consisted of thirty judges nominated by the district, and who chose their own president. Pleadings were conducted in writing, and proceeded as far as the " rejoinder." Diodorus thinks this plan very effectual, in obviating the perverting influence of forensic oratory, and of the sympathy of the judges. The latter pronounced sentence silently, and in a hieroglyphical manner. Herodotus says, that they had a symbol of truth on their breasts, and turned it towards that side in whose favor the cause was decided, or adorned the victorious party with it. The king himself had to take part in judicial business every day. Theft, we are told, was forbidden; but the law commanded that thieves should inform against themselves. If they did so, they were not punished, but, on the contrary, were allowed to keep a fourth part of what they had stolen. This perhaps was designed to excite and keep in exercise that cunning for which the Egyptians were so celebrated.

The *intelligence* displayed in their legislative economy, appears characteristic of the Egyptians. This intelligence, which manifests itself in the practical, we also recognize in the productions of art and science. The Egyptians are reported to have divided the year into twelve months, and each month into thirty days. At the end of the year they intercalated five additional days, and Herodotus says that their arrangement was better than that of the Greeks. The intelligence of the Egyptians especially strikes us in the department of mechanics. Their vast edifices—such as no other nation has to exhibit, and which excel all others in solidity and size—sufficiently prove their artistic skill; to whose cultivation they could largely devote themselves, because the inferior castes did not trouble themselves with political matters. Diodorus Siculus says, that Egypt was the only country in which the citizens did not trouble themselves about the state, but gave their whole attention to their private business. Greeks and Romans must have been especially astonished at such a state of things.

On account of its judicious economy, Egypt was regarded by the ancients as the pattern of a morally regulated condition of things—as an ideal such as Pythagoras realized in a limited select society, and Plato sketched on a larger scale. But in such ideals no account is taken of passion. A plan of society that is to be adopted and acted upon, as an absolutely complete one —in which everything has been considered, and especially the education and habituation to it, necessary to its becoming a second nature—is altogether opposed to the nature of Spirit, which makes contemporary life the object on which it acts; itself being the infinite impulse of activity to alter its forms. This impulse also expressed itself in Egypt in a peculiar way. It would appear at first as if a condition of things so regular, so determinate in every particular, contained nothing that had a peculiarity entirely its own. The introduction of a religious element would seem to be an affair of no critical moment, provided the higher necessities of men were satisfied; we should in fact rather expect that it would be introduced in a peaceful way and in accordance with the moral arrangement of things already mentioned. But in contemplating the *Religion* of the Egyptians, we are surprised by the strangest and most wonderful phenomena, and perceive that this calm order of things, bound fast by legislative enactment, is not like that of the

Chinese, but that we have here to do with a Spirit entirely
different—one full of stirring and urgent impulses. We have
here the African element, in combination with Oriental massiveness, transplanted to the Mediterranean Sea, that grand *locale*
of the display of nationalities; but in such a manner, that here
there is no connection with foreign nations—this mode of stimulating intellect appearing superfluous; for we have here a
prodigious urgent striving within the nationality itself, and
which within its own circle shoots out into an objective realization of itself in the most monstrous productions. It is that
African imprisonment of ideas combined with the infinite impulse of the spirit to realize itself objectively, which we find
here. But Spirit has still, as it were, an iron band around its
forehead; so that it cannot attain to the free consciousness
of its existence, but produces this only as the problem, the
enigma of its being.

The fundamental conception of that which the Egyptians
regard as the essence of being, rests on the determinate character of the natural world, in which they live; and more particularly on the determinate physical circle which the Nile and
the Sun mark out. These two are strictly connected—the position of the Sun and that of the Nile; and to the Egyptian this
is all in all. The Nile is that which essentially determines the
boundaries of the country; beyond the Nile-valley begins the
desert; on the north, Egypt is shut in by the sea, and on the
south by torrid heat. The first Arab leader that conquered
Egypt, writes to the Caliph Omar: " Egypt is first a vast sea
of dust; then a sea of fresh water; lastly, it is a great sea of
flowers. It never rains there; towards the end of July dew
falls, and then the Nile begins to overflow its banks, and Egypt
resembles a sea of islands." (Herodotus compares Egypt, during this period, with the islands in the Ægean.) The Nile
leaves behind it prodigious multitudes of living creatures: then
appear moving and creeping things innumerable; soon after,
man begins to sow the ground, and the harvest is very abundant. Thus the existence of the Egyptian does not depend
on the brightness of the sun, or the quantity of rain. For him,
on the contrary, there exist only those perfectly simple conditions, which form the basis of his mode of life and its occupations. There is a definite physical cycle, which the Nile pursues, and which is connected with the course of the Sun; the

latter advances, reaches its culmination, and then retrogrades. So also does the Nile.

This basis of the life of the Egyptians determines moreover the particular tenor of their religious views. A controversy has long been waged respecting the sense of meaning of the Egyptian religion. As early as the reign of Tiberius, the Stoic Chæremon, who had been in Egypt, explains it in a purely materialistic sense. The New Platonists take a directly opposite view, regarding all as symbols of a spiritual meaning, and thus making this religion a pure Idealism. Each of these representations is one-sided. Natural and spiritual powers are regarded as most intimately united—(the free spiritual import, however, has *not* been developed at this stage of thought)—but in such a way, that the extremes of the antithesis were united in the harshest contrast. We have spoken of the Nile, of the Sun, and of the vegetation depending upon them. This limited view of Nature gives the principle of the religion, and its subject-matter is primarily a history. The Nile and the Sun constitute the divinities, conceived under human forms; and the course of nature and the mythological history is the same. In the winter solstice the power of the sun has reached its minimum, and must be born anew. Thus also Osiris appears as born; but he is killed by Typhon—his brother and enemy—the burning wind of the desert. Isis, the Earth—from whom the aid of the Sun and of the Nile has been withdrawn—yearns after him: she gathers the scattered bones of Osiris, and raises her lamentation for him, and all Egypt bewails with her the death of Osiris, in a song which Herodotus calls Maneros. Maneros he reports to have been the only son of the first king of the Egyptians, and to have died prematurely; this song being also the Linus-Song of the Greeks, and the only song which the Egyptians have. Here again pain is regarded as something divine, and the same honor is assigned to it here as among the Phœnicians. Hermes then embalms Osiris; and his grave is shown in various places. Osiris is now judge of the dead, and lord of the kingdom of the Shades. These are the leading ideas. Osiris, the Sun, the Nile; this triplicity of being is united in one knot. The Sun is the symbol, in which Osiris and the history of that god are recognized, and the Nile is likewise such a symbol. The concrete Egyptian imagination also ascribes to Osiris and Isis the introduction of agriculture, the invention of the plough, the hoe, etc.; for Osiris gives not only the useful itself—the fertility of the earth —but, moreover, the means of making use of it. He also gives men laws, a civil order and a religious ritual; he thus places in men's hands the means of labor, and secures its result. Osiris is also the symbol of the seed which is placed in the earth, and then springs up—as also of the course of life. Thus we find this heterogeneous duality—the phenomena of Nature and the Spiritual—woven together into *one* knot.

The parallelism of the course of human life with the Nile, the Sun and Osiris, is not to be regarded as a mere allegory— as if the principle of birth, of increase in strength, of the culmination of vigor and fertility, of decline and weakness, exhibited itself in these different phenomena, in an equal or similar way; but in this variety imagination conceived only *one subject,* one vitality. This unity is, however, quite abstract: the heterogeneous element shows itself therein as pressing and urging, and in a confusion which sharply contrasts with Greek perspicuity. Osiris represents the Nile and the Sun: Sun and Nile are, on the other hand, symbols of human life—each one is signification and symbol at the same time; the symbol is changed into signification, and this latter becomes symbol of that symbol, which itself then becomes signification. None of these phases of existence is a Type without being at the same time a Signification; each is both; the one is explained by the other. Thus there arises one pregnant conception, composed of many conceptions, in which each fundamental nodus retains its individuality, so that they are not resolved into a general idea. The general idea—the thought itself, which forms the bond of analogy—does not present itself to the consciousness purely and freely as such, but remains concealed as an internal connection. We have a consolidated individuality, combining various phenomenal aspects; and which on the one hand is fanciful, on account of the combination of apparently disparate material, but on the other hand internally and essentially connected, because these various appearances are a particular prosaic matter of fact.

Besides this fundamental conception, we observe several special divinities, of whom Herodotus reckons three classes. Of the first he mentions eight gods; of the second twelve; of the third an indefinite number, who occupy the position towards the unity of Osiris of specific manifestations. In the first class, Fire and its use appears as Phtha, also as Knef, who is besides represented as the Good Genius; but the Nile itself is held to be that Genius, and thus abstractions are changed into concrete conceptions. *Ammon* is regarded as a great divinity, with whom is associated the determination of the equinox: it is he, moreover, who gives oracles. But Osiris is similarly represented as the founder of oracular manifestations. So the Procreative Power, banished by Osiris, is represented as a particular divinity. But Osiris is himself this Procreative Power. Isis is the Earth, the Moon, the receptive fertility of Nature. As an important element in the conception Osiris, *Anubis (Thoth)*—the Egyptian Hermes—must be specially noticed. In human activity and invention, and in the economy of legislation, the Spiritual, as such, is embodied; and becomes in this form—which is itself determinate and limited—an object of consciousness. Here we have the Spiritual, not as one infinite, independent sovereignty over nature, but as a particular existence, side by side with the powers of Nature—characterized also by intrinsic particularity. And thus the Egyptians had also specific divinities, conceived as spiritual activities and forces; but partly *intrinsically* limited—partly [so, as] contemplated under natural symbols.

The Egyptian Hermes is celebrated as exhibiting the spiritual side of their theism. According to Jamblichus, the Egyptian priests immemorially prefixed to all their inventions the name Hermes: Eratosthenes, therefore, called his book, which treated of the entire science of Egypt—" Hermes." Anubis is called the friend and companion of Osiris. To him is ascribed the invention of writing, and of science generally—of grammar, astronomy, mensuration, music, and medicine. It was he who first divided the day into twelve hours: he was moreover the first lawgiver, the first instructor in religious observances and objects, and in gymnastics and orchestics; and it was he who discovered the olive. But, notwithstanding all these spiritual attributes, this divinity is something quite other than the God of Thought. Only particular human arts and inventions are associated with him. Not only so; but he entirely falls back into involvement in existence, and is degraded under physical symbols. He is represented with a dog's head, as an imbruted god; and besides this mask, a particular natural object is bound up with the conception of this divinity; for he is at the same time Sirius, the Dog-Star. He is thus as limited in respect of what he embodies, as sensuous in the positive existence ascribed to him. It may be incidentally remarked, that as Ideas and Nature are not distin-guished from each other, in the same way the arts and appli-ances of human life are not developed and arranged so as to form a rational circle of aims and means. Thus medicine—deliberation respecting corporeal disease—as also the whole range of deliberation and resolve with regard to undertakings in life—was subjected to the most multifarious superstition in the way of reliance on oracles and magic arts. Astronomy was also essentially Astrology, and Medicine an affair of magic, but more particularly of Astrology. All astrological and sym-pathetic superstition may be traced to Egypt.

Egyptian *Worship* is chiefly Zoolatry. We have observed the union here presented between the Spiritual and the Natural: the more advanced and elevated side of this conception is the fact that the Egyptians, while they observed the Spiritual as manifested in the Nile, the Sun, and the sowing of seed, took the same view of the life of animals. To us Zoolatry is repul-sive. We may reconcile ourselves to the adoration of the material heaven, but the worship of brutes is alien to us; for the abstract natural element seems to us more generic, and therefore more worthy of veneration. Yet it is certain that the nations who worshipped the Sun and the Stars by no means occupy a higher grade than those who adore brutes, but con-trariwise; for in the brute world the Egyptians contemplate a hidden and incomprehensible principle. We also, when we contemplate the life and action of brutes, are astonished at their instinct—the adaptation of their movements to the object in-tended—their restlessness, excitability, and liveliness; for they are exceedingly quick and discerning in pursuing the ends of their existence, while they are at the same time silent and shut up within themselves. We cannot make out what it is that "possesses" these creatures, and cannot rely on them. A black tom-cat, with its glowing eyes and its now gliding, now quick and darting movement, has been deemed the presence of a malignant being—a mysterious reserved spectre: the dog, the canary-bird, on the contrary, appear friendly and sympathizing. The lower animals are the truly Incomprehensible. A *man* cannot by imagination or conception enter into the nature of a *dog*, whatever resemblance he himself might have to it; it remains something altogether alien to him. It is in two departments that the so-called Incomprehensible meets us—in living Nature and in Spirit. But in very deed it is only in Nature that we have to encounter the Incomprehensible; for the being manifest to itself is the essence [supplies the very definition of], Spirit: Spirit understands and comprehends Spirit. The obtuse self-consciousness of the Egyptians, therefore, to which the thought of human freedom is not yet revealed, worships the soul as still shut up within and dulled by the physical organization, and sympathizes with brute life. We find a veneration of mere vitality among other nations also: sometimes expressly, as among the Hindoos and all the Mongolians; sometimes in mere traces, as among the Jews: " Thou shalt not eat the blood of animals, for in it is the life of the animal." The Greeks and Romans also regarded birds as specially intelligent, believing that what in the human spirit was not revealed —the Incomprehensible and Higher—was to be found in them. But among the Egyptians this worship of beasts was carried to excess under the forms of a most stupid and non-human superstition. The worship of brutes was among them a matter of particular and detailed arrangement: each district had a brute deity of its own—a cat, an ibis, a crocodile, etc. Great establishments were provided for them; beautiful *mates* were assigned them; and, like human beings, they were embalmed after death. The bulls were buried, but with their horns protruding above their graves; the bulls embodying *Apis* had splendid monuments, and some of the pyramids must be looked upon as such. In one of those that have been opened, there was found in the most central apartment a beautiful alabaster coffin; and on closer examination it was found that the bones inclosed were those of the ox. This reverence for brutes was often carried to the most absurd excess of severity. If a man killed one designedly, he was punished with death; but even the undesigned killing of some animals might entail death. It is related, that once when a Roman in Alexandria killed a cat, an insurrection ensued, in which the Egyptians murdered the aggressor. They would let human beings perish by famine, rather than allow the sacred animals to be killed, or the provision made for them trenched upon. Still more than mere vital-

itv. the universal *vis vitæ* of productive nature was venerated
in a Phallus-worship; which the Greeks also adopted into the
rites paid by them to Dionysus. With this worship the greatest
excesses were connected.

The brute form is, on the other hand, turned into a symbol:
it is also partly degraded to a mere hieroglyphical sign. I refer
here to the innumerable figures on the Egyptian monuments,
of sparrow-hawks or falcons, dung-beetles, scarabæi, etc. It
is not known what ideas such figures symbolized, and we can
scarcely think that a satisfactory view of this very obscure subject is attainable. The dung-beetle is said to be the symbol
of generation—of the sun and its course; the Ibis, that of the
Nile's overflowing; birds of the hawk tribe, of prophecy—of
the year—of pity. The strangeness of these combinations results from the circumstance that we have not, as in our idea
of poetical invention, a general conception embodied in an image; but, conversely, we begin with a concept in the sphere
of sense, and imagination conducts us into the same sphere
again. But we observe the conception liberating itself from
the direct animal form, and the continued contemplation of it;
and that which was only surmised and aimed at in that form,
advancing to comprehensibility and conceivableness. The hidden meaning—the Spiritual—emerges as a human face from
the brute. The multiform sphinxes, with lions' bodies and
virgins' heads—or as male sphinxes ($\dot{\alpha}\nu\delta\rho\dot{o}\sigma\phi\iota\gamma\gamma\epsilon\varsigma$) with
beards—are evidence supporting the view, that the meaning
of the Spiritual is the problem which the Egyptians proposed
to themselves; as the enigma generally is not the utterance
of something unknown, but is the challenge to discover it—
implying a wish to be revealed. But conversely, the human
form is also disfigured by a brute face, with the view of giving
it a specific and definite expression. The refined art of Greece
is able to attain a specific expression through the spiritual character given to an image in the form of beauty, and does not need
to deform the human face in order to be understood. The
Egyptians appended an explanation to the human forms, even
of the gods, by means of heads and masks of brutes; Anubis
e.g. has a dog's head, Isis, a lion's head with bull's horns, etc.
The priests, also, in performing their functions, are masked
as falcons, jackals, bulls, etc.; in the same way the surgeon,
who has taken out the bowels of the dead (represented as flee-

ing, for he has laid sacrilegious hands on an object once hallowed by life) ; so also the embalmers and the scribes. The sparrow-hawk, with a human head and outspread wings, denotes the soul flying through material space, in order to animate a new body. The Egyptian imagination also created new forms —combinations of different animals: serpents with bulls' and rams' heads, bodies of lions with rams' heads, etc.

We thus see Egypt intellectually confined by a narrow, involved, close view of Nature, but breaking through this; impelling it to self-contradiction, and proposing to itself the problem which that contradiction implies. The [Egyptian] principle does not remain satisfied with its primary conditions, but points to that other meaning and spirit which lies concealed beneath the surface.

In the view just given, we saw the Egyptian Spirit working itself free from natural forms. This urging, powerful Spirit, however, was not able to rest in the subjective conception of that view of things which we have now been considering, but was impelled to present it to external consciousness and outward vision by means of Art.—For the religion of the Eternal One—the Formless—Art is not only unsatisfying, but—since its *object* essentially and exclusively occupies the thought— something sinful. But Spirit, occupied with the contemplation of particular natural forms—being at the same time a striving and plastic Spirit—changes the direct, natural view, *e.g.*, of the Nile, the Sun, etc., to images, in which Spirit has a share. It is, as we have seen, symbolizing Spirit; and as such, it endeavors to master these symbolizations, and to present them clearly before the mind. The more enigmatical and obscure it is to itself, so much the more does it feel the impulse to labor to deliver itself from its imprisonment, and to gain a clear objective view of itself.

It is the distinguishing feature of the Egyptian Spirit, that it stands before us as this mighty taskmaster. It is not splendor, amusement, pleasure, or the like that it seeks. The force which urges it is the impulse of self-comprehension; and it has no other material or ground to work on, in order to teach itself what it is—to realize itself for itself—than this working out its thoughts in stone; and what it engraves on the stone are its enigmas—these hieroglyphs. They are of two kinds— hieroglyphs *proper,* designed rather to express language, and

having reference to subjective conception; and a class of hieroglyphs of a different kind, viz. those enormous masses of architecture and sculpture, with which Egypt is covered.   While
among other nations history consists of a series of events—as,
e.g., that of the Romans, who century after century, lived only
with a view to conquest, and accomplished the subjugation of
the world—the Egyptians raised an empire equally mighty—
of achievements in works of art, whose ruins prove their inde-
structibility, and which are greater and more worthy of astonishment than all other works of ancient or modern time.

Of these works I will mention no others than those devoted
to the dead, and which especially attract our attention.   These
are, the enormous excavations in the hills along the Nile at
Thebes, whose passages and chambers are entirely filled with
mummies—subterranean abodes as large as the largest mining
works of our time: next, the great field of the dead in the plain
of Sais, with its walls and vaults: thirdly, those Wonders of
the World, the Pyramids, whose destination, though stated
long ago by Herodotus and Diodorus, has been only recently
expressly confirmed—to the effect, viz., that these prodigious
crystals, with their geometrical regularity, contain dead bodies:
and lastly, that most astonishing work, the Tombs of the Kings,
of which one has been opened by Belzoni in modern times.

It is of essential moment to observe, what importance this
realm of the dead had for the Egyptian: we may thence gather
what idea he had of man.   For in the Dead, man conceives of
man as stripped of all adventitious wrappages—as reduced to
his essential nature.   But that which a people regards as man
in his essential characteristics, that it is itself—such is its
character.

In the first place, we must here cite the remarkable fact which
Herodotus tells us, viz., that the Egyptians were the first to
express the thought that the soul of man is *immortal*.   But this
proposition that the soul is immortal, is intended to mean that
it is something other than Nature—that Spirit is inherently
independent.   The *ne plus ultra* of blessedness among the Hindoos, was the passing over into abstract unity—into Nothingness.   On the other hand, subjectivity, when free, is inherently
infinite: the Kingdom of free Spirit is therefore the Kingdom
of the Invisible—such as Hades was conceived by the Greeks.
This presents itself to men first as the empire of death—to the
Egyptians as the *Realm of the Dead*.

The idea that Spirit is immortal, involves this—that the human individual inherently possesses infinite value. The merely Natural appears limited—absolutely dependent upon something other than itself—and has its existence in that other; but Immortality involves the inherent infinitude of Spirit. This idea is first found among the Egyptians. But it must be added, that the soul was known to the Egyptians previously only as an atom—that is, as something concrete and particular. For with that view is immediately connected the notion of Metempsychosis—the idea that the soul of man may also become the tenant of the body of a brute. Aristotle too speaks of this idea, and despatches it in few words. Every subject, he says, has its particular organs, for its peculiar mode of action: so the smith, the carpenter, each for his own craft. In like manner the human soul has its peculiar organs, and the body of a brute cannot be its domicile. Pythagoras adopted the doctrine of Metempsychosis; but it could not find much support among the Greeks, who held rather to the concrete. The Hindoos have also an indistinct conception of this doctrine, inasmuch as with them the final attainment is absorption in the universal Substance. But with the Egyptians the Soul—the Spirit—is, at any rate, an affirmative being, although only abstractedly affirmative. The period occupied by the soul's migrations, was fixed at three thousand years; they affirmed, however, that a soul which had remained faithful to Osiris, was not subject to such a degradation—for such they deem it.

It is well known that the Egyptians embalmed their dead; and thus imparted such a degree of permanence, that they have been preserved even to the present day, and may continue as they are for many centuries to come. This indeed seems inconsistent with their idea of immortality; for if the soul has an independent existence, the permanence of the body seems a matter of indifference. But on the other hand it may be said, that if the soul is recognized as a permanent existence, honor should be shown to the body, as its former abode. The Parsees lay the bodies of the dead in exposed places to be devoured by birds; but among them the soul is regarded as passing forth into universal existence. Where the soul is supposed to enjoy continued existence, the body must also be considered to have some kind of connection with this continuance. Among us, indeed, the doctrine of the Immortality of the Soul assumes the higher form: Spirit is in and for itself eternal; its destiny is eternal blessedness.—The Egyptians made their dead into mummies; and did not occupy themselves further with them; no honor was paid them beyond this. Herodotus relates of the Egyptians, that when any person died, the women went about loudly lamenting; but the idea of Immortality is not regarded in the light of a consolation, as among us.

From what was said above, respecting the works for the Dead, it is evident that the Egyptians, and especially their kings, made it the business of their life to build their sepulchre, and to give their bodies a permanent abode. It is remarkable that what had been needed for the business of life, was buried with the dead. Thus the craftsman had his tools: designs on the coffin show the occupation to which the deceased had devoted himself; so that we are able to become acquainted with him in all the *minutiæ* of his condition and employment. Many mummies have been found with a roll of papyrus under their arm, and this was formerly regarded as a remarkable treasure. But these rolls contain only various representations of the pursuits of life—together with writings in the Demotic character. They have been deciphered, and the discovery has been made, that they are all deeds of purchase, relating to pieces of ground and the like; in which everything is most minutely recorded— even the duties that had to be paid to the royal chancery on the occasion. What, therefore, a person bought during his life, is made to accompany him—in the shape of a legal document— in death. In this monumental way we are made acquainted with the private life of the Egyptians, as with that of the Romans through the ruins of Pompeii and Herculaneum.

After the death of an Egyptian, judgment was passed upon him.—One of the principal representations on the sarcophagi is this judicial process in the realm of the dead. Osiris—with Isis behind him—appears, holding a balance, while before him stands the soul of the deceased. But judgment was passed on the dead by the living themselves; and that not merely in the case of private persons, but even of kings. The tomb of a certain king has been discovered—very large, and elaborate in its architecture—in whose hieroglyphs the name of the principal person is obliterated, while in the bas-reliefs and pictorial designs the chief figure is erased. This has been explained to import that the honor of being thus immortalized, was refused this king by the sentence of the Court of the Dead.

If Death thus haunted the minds of the Egyptians during life, it might be supposed that their disposition was melancholy. But the thought of death by no means occasioned depression. At banquets they had representations of the dead (as Herodotus relates), with the admonition: " Eat and drink—such a one wilt thou become, when thou art dead." Death was thus to them rather a call to enjoy Life. Osiris himself dies, and goes down into the realm of death, according to the above-mentioned Egyptian myth. In many places in Egypt, the sacred grave of Osiris was exhibited. But he was also represented as president of the Kingdom of the Invisible Sphere, and as judge of the dead in it; later on, Serapis exercised this function in his place. Of Anubis-Hermes the myth says, that he embalmed the body of Osiris: this Anubis sustained also the office of leader of the souls of the dead; and in the pictorial representations he stands, with a writing tablet in his hand, by the side of Osiris. The reception of the dead into the Kingdom of Osiris had also a profounder import, viz., that the individual was united with Osiris. On the lids of the sarcophagi, therefore, the defunct is represented as having himself become Osiris; and in deciphering the hieroglyphs, the idea has been suggested that the kings are called gods. The human and the divine are thus exhibited as united.

If, in conclusion, we combine what has been said here of the peculiarities of the Egyptian Spirit in all its aspects, its pervading principle is found to be, that the two elements of reality —Spirit sunk in Nature, and the impulse to liberate it—are here held together inharmoniously as contending elements. We behold the antithesis of Nature and Spirit—not the primary Immediate Unity [as in the less advanced nations], nor the Concrete Unity, where Nature is posited only as a basis for the manifestation of Spirit [as in the more advanced]; in contrast with the first and second of these Unities, the Egyptian Unity—combining contradictory elements—occupies a middle place. The two sides of this unity are held in abstract independence of each other, and their veritable union presented only as a problem. We have, therefore, on the *one* side, prodigious confusion and limitation to the particular; barbarous sensuality with African hardness, Zoolatry, and sensual enjoyment. It is stated that, in a public market-place, sodomy was committed by a woman with a goat. Juvenal relates, that human flesh was eaten and human blood drunk out of revenge. The *other* side is the struggle of Spirit for liberation—fancy displayed in the forms created by art, together with the abstract understanding shown in the mechanical labors connected with their production. The same intelligence—the power of altering the form of individual existences, and that steadfast thoughtfulness which can rise above mere phenomena—shows itself in their police and the mechanism of the State, in agricultural economy, etc.; and the contrast to this is the severity with which their customs bind them, and the superstition to which humanity among them is inexorably subject. With a clear understanding of the present, is connected the highest degree of impulsiveness, daring and turbulence. These features are combined in the stories which Herodotus relates to us of the Egyptians. They much resemble the tales of the Thousand and One Nights; and although these have Bagdad as the locality of their narration, their origin is no more limited to this luxurious court, than to the Arabian people, but must be partly traced to Egypt—as *Von Hammer* also thinks. The Arabian world is quite other than the fanciful and enchanted region there described; it has much more simple passions and interests. Love, Martial Daring, the Horse, the Sword, are the darling subjects of the poetry peculiar to the Arabians.

Transition to the Greek World

The Egyptian Spirit has shown itself to us as in all respects shut up within the limits of particular conceptions, and, as it were, imbruted in them; but likewise stirring itself within these limits—passing restlessly from one particular form into another. This Spirit never rises to the Universal and Higher, for it seems to be blind to that; nor does it ever withdraw into itself: yet it symbolizes freely and boldly with particular existence, and has already mastered it. All that is now required is to posit that particular existence—which contains the germ of ideality—as *ideal,* and to comprehend Universality itself, which is already potentially liberated from the particulars involving it.* It is the free, joyful Spirit of Greece that accomplishes this, and makes this its starting-point. An Egyptian

* Abstractions were to take the place of analogies. The power to connect particular conceptions as analogical, does but just fall short of the ability to comprehend the *general* idea which links them.—ED.

priest is reported to have said, that the Greeks remain eternally children. We may say, on the contrary, that the Egyptians are vigorous *boys,* eager for self-comprehension, who require nothing but clear understanding of themselves in an ideal form, in order to become *Young Men.* In the Oriental Spirit there remains as a basis the massive substantiality of Spirit immersed in Nature. To the Egyptian Spirit it has become impossible— though it is still involved in infinite embarrassment—to remain contented with *that.* The rugged African nature disintegrated that primitive Unity, and lighted upon the problem whose solution is Free Spirit.

That the Spirit of the Egyptians presented itself to their consciousness in the form of a *problem,* is evident from the celebrated inscription in the sanctuary of the Goddess Neith at Sais: *" I am that which is, that which was, and that which will be; no one has lifted my veil."* This inscription indicates the principle of the Egyptian Spirit; though the opinion has often been entertained, that its purport applies to all times. Proclus supplies the addition: *" The fruit which I have produced is Helios."* That which is clear to itself is, therefore, the result of, and the solution of, the problem in question. This lucidity is Spirit—the Son of Neith the concealed night-loving divinity. In the Egyptian Neith, Truth is still a problem. The Greek Apollo is its solution; his utterance is: *" Man, know thyself."* In this dictum is not intended a self-recognition that regards the specialities of one's own weaknesses and defects: it is not the individual that is admonished to become acquainted with his idiosyncrasy, but humanity *in general* is summoned to self-knowledge. This mandate was given for the Greeks, and in the Greek Spirit humanity exhibits itself in its clear and developed condition. Wonderfully, then, must the Greek legend surprise us, which relates, that the Sphinx—the great Egyptian symbol—appeared in Thebes, uttering the words: " What is that which in the morning goes on four legs, at midday on two, and in the evening on three? " Œdipus, giving the solution, *Man,* precipitated the Sphinx from the rock. The solution and liberation of that Oriental Spirit, which in Egypt had advanced so far as to propose the problem, is certainly this: that the Inner Being [the Essence] of Nature is Thought, which has its existence only in the human consciousness. But that time-honored antique solution given by Œdipus—who thus shows himself possessed of knowledge—is connected with a dire ignorance of the character of his own actions. The rise of spiritual illumination in the old royal house is disparaged by connection with abominations, the result of ignorance; and that primeval royalty must—in order to attain true knowledge and moral clearness—first be brought into shapely form, and be harmonized with the Spirit of the Beautiful, by civil laws and political freedom.

The *inward* or ideal transition, from Egypt to Greece is as just exhibited. But Egypt became a province of the great Persian kingdom, and the *historical* transition takes place when the Persian world comes in contact with the Greek. Here, for the first time, an historical transition meets us, viz. in the fall of an empire. China and India, as already mentioned, have remained—Persia has not. The transition to Greece is, indeed, internal; but here it shows itself also externally, as a transmission of sovereignty—an occurrence which from this time forward is ever and anon repeated. For the Greeks surrender the sceptre of dominion and of civilization to the Romans, and the Romans are subdued by the Germans. If we examine this fact of transition more closely, the question suggests itself—for example, in this first case of the kind, viz. Persia—why it sank, while China and India remain. In the first place we must here banish from our minds the prejudice in favor of duration, as if it had any advantage as compared with transience: the imperishable mountains are not superior to the quickly dismantled rose exhaling its life in fragrance. In Persia begins the principle of Free Spirit as contrasted with imprisonment in Nature; mere natural existence, therefore, loses its bloom, and fades away. The principle of separation from Nature is found in the Persian Empire, which, therefore, occupies a higher grade than those worlds immersed in the Natural. The necessity of advance has been thereby proclaimed. Spirit has disclosed its existence, and must complete its development. It is only when dead that the Chinese is held in reverence. The Hindoo kills himself—becomes absorbed in Brahm—undergoes a living death in the condition of perfect unconsciousness—or is a present god in virtue of his birth. Here we have no change; no advance is admissible, for progress is only possible through the recognition of the independence of Spirit. With the " Light " of the Persians begins a spiritual view of things, and here Spirit bids adieu to Nature. It is here, then, that we first find (as occasion called us to notice above) that the objective world remains free—that the nations are not enslaved, but are left in possession of their wealth, their political constitution, and their religion. And, indeed, this is the side on which Persia itself shows weakness as compared with Greece. For we see that the Persians could erect no empire possessing complete organization; that they could not " inform " the conquered lands with their principle, and were unable to make them into a harmonious Whole, but were obliged to be content with an aggregate of the most diverse individualities. Among these nations the Persians secured no inward recognition of the legitimacy of their rule; they could not establish their legal principles of enactments, and in organizing their dominion, they only considered themselves, not the whole extent of their empire. Thus, as Persia did not constitute, politically, *one* Spirit, it appeared weak in contrast with Greece. It was not the effeminacy of the Persians (although, perhaps, Babylon infused an enervating element) that ruined them, but the unwieldy, unorganized character of their host, as matched against Greek organization; *i.e.,* the superior principle overcame the inferior. The abstract principle of the Persians displayed its defectiveness as an unorganized, incompacted union of disparate contradictories; in which the Persian doctrine of Light stood side by side with Syrian voluptuousness and luxury, with the activity and courage of the sea-braving Phœnicians, the abstraction of pure Thought in the Jewish Religion, and the mental unrest of Egypt;—an aggregate of elements, which awaited their idealization, and could receive it only in *free Individuality*. The Greeks must be looked upon as the people in whom these elements interpenetrated each other: Spirit became introspective, triumphed over particularity, and thereby emancipated itself.

PART II

THE GREEK WORLD

AMONG the Greeks we feel ourselves immediately at home, for we are in the region of Spirit; and though the origin of the nation, as also its philological peculiarities, may be traced farther—even to India—the proper Emergence, the true Palingenesis of Spirit must be looked for in Greece first. At an earlier stage I compared the Greek world with the period of adolescence; not, indeed, in *that* sense, that youth bears within it a serious, anticipative destiny, and consequently by the very conditions of its culture urges towards an ulterior aim—presenting thus an inherently incomplete and immature form, and being then most defective when it would deem itself perfect—but in *that* sense, that youth does not yet present the activity of work, does not yet exert itself for a definite intelligent aim—but rather exhibits a concrete freshness of the soul's life. It appears in the sensuous, actual world, as Incarnate Spirit and Spiritualized Sense —in a Unity which owed its origin to Spirit. Greece presents to us the cheerful aspect of youthful freshness, of Spiritual vitality. It is here first that advancing Spirit makes *itself* the content of its volition and its knowledge; but in such a way that State, Family, Law, Religion, are at the same time objects aimed at by individuality, while the latter *is* individuality only in virtue of those aims. The [full-grown] man, on the other hand, devotes his life to labor for an objective aim; which he pursues consistently, even at the cost of his individuality.

The highest form that floated before Greek imagination was Achilles, the Son of the Poet, the Homeric Youth of the Trojan War. Homer is the element in which the Greek world lives, as man does in the air. The Greek life is a truly youthful achievement. Achilles, the ideal youth, of *poetry*, commenced it: Alexander the Great, the ideal youth of *reality*, concluded it. Both appear in contest with Asia. Achilles, as the principal figure in the national expedition of the Greeks against Troy, does not stand at its head, but is subject to the Chief of Chiefs; he cannot be made the leader without becoming a fantastic untenable conception. On the contrary, the second youth, Alexander—the freest and finest individuality that the real world has ever produced—advances to the head of this youthful life that has now perfected itself, and accomplishes the revenge against Asia.

We have, then, to distinguish three periods in Greek history: the first, that of the growth of real Individuality; the second, that of its independence and prosperity in external conquest (through contact with the previous World-historical people); and the third, the period of its decline and fall, in its encounter with the succeeding organ of World-History. The period from its origin to its internal completeness (that which enables a people to make head against its predecessor) includes its primary culture. If the nation has a basis—such as the Greek world has in the Oriental—a foreign culture enters as an element into its primary condition, and it has a double culture, one orignal, the other of foreign suggestion. The uniting of these two elements constitutes its training; and the first period ends with the combination of its forces to produce its real and proper vigor, which then turns against the very element that had been its basis. The second period is that of victory and prosperity. But while the nation directs its energies outwards, it becomes unfaithful to its principles at home, and internal dissension follows upon the ceasing of the external excitement. In Art and Science, too, this shows itself in the separation of the Ideal from the Real. Here is the point of decline. The third period is that of ruin, through contact with the nation that embodies a higher Spirit. The same process, it may be stated once for all, will meet us in the life of every world-historical people.

SECTION I

THE ELEMENTS OF THE GREEK SPIRIT

GREECE is [that form of] the Substantial [*i.e.* of Moral and Intellectual *Principle*], which is at the same time *individual*. The Universal [the Abstract], as such, is overcome; * the submersion in Nature no longer exists, and consentaneously the unwieldy character of *geographical* relations has also vanished. The country now under consideration is a section of territory spreading itself in various forms through the sea—a multitude of islands, and a continent which itself exhibits insular features. The Peloponnesus is connected with the continent only by a narrow isthmus: the whole of Greece is indented by bays in numberless shapes. The partition into small divisions of territory is the universal characteristic, while at the same time, the relationship and connection between them is facilitated by the sea. We find here mountains, plains, valleys, and streams of limited extent: no great river, no absolute Valley-Plain presents itself; but the ground is diversified by mountains and rivers in such a way as to allow no prominence to a single massive feature. We see no such display of physical grandeur as is exhibited in the East—no stream such as the Ganges, the Indus, etc., on whose plains a race delivered over to monotony is stimulated to no change, because its horizon always exhibits one unvarying form. On the contrary, that divided and multiform character everywhere prevails which perfectly corresponds with the varied life of Greek races and the versatility of the Greek Spirit.

This is the *elementary character* of the Spirit of the Greeks, implying the origination of their culture from independent individualities;—a condition in which individuals take their own ground, and are not, from the very beginning, patriarchally united by a bond of *Nature,* but realize a union through some

* That is, blind obedience to moral requirements—to principle abstracted from personal conviction or inclination, as among the Chinese.—ED.

other medium—through Law and Custom having the sanction
of Spirit. For beyond all other nations that of Greece attained
its form by *growth*. At the origin of their national unity, separation as a generic feature—inherent *distinctness* of character
—is the chief point that has to be considered. The first phase
in the subjugation of this, constitutes the primary period of
Greek culture; and only through such distinctness of character,
and such a subjugation of it, was the beautiful free Greek
Spirit produced. Of this principle we must have a clear conception. It is a superficial and absurd idea that such a beautiful
and truly free life can be produced by a process so incomplex
as the development of a race keeping within the limits of blood-
relationship and friendship. Even the plant, which supplies
the nearest analogy to such a calm, homogeneous unfolding,
lives and grows only by means of the antithetic activities of
light, air, and water. The only real antithesis that Spirit can
have, is itself spiritual: viz., its inherent heterogeneity, through
which alone it acquires the power of realizing itself as Spirit.
The history of Greece exhibits at its commencement this inter-
change and mixture of partly homesprung, partly quite foreign
stocks; and it was Attica itself—whose people was destined to
attain the acme of Hellenic bloom—that was the asylum of the
most various stocks and families. Every world-historical people, except the Asiatic kingdoms—which stands detached from
the grand historical catena—has been formed in this way. Thus
the Greeks, like the Romans, developed themselves from a
colluvies—a conflux of the most various nations. Of the multitude of tribes which we meet in Greece, we cannot say which
was the original Greek people, and which immigrated from foreign lands and distant parts of the globe; for the period of
which we speak belongs entirely to the unhistorical and obscure.
The *Pelasgi* were at that time a principal race in Greece. The
most various attempts have been made by the learned to harmonize the confused and contradictory account which we have
respecting them—a hazy and obscure period being a special
object and stimulus to erudition. Remarkable as the earliest
centres of incipient culture are Thrace, the native land of Or-
pheus—and Thessaly; countries which at a later date retreated
more or less into the background. From Phthiotis, the country
of Achilles, proceeds the common name *Hellenes*—a name
which, as Thucydides remarks, presents itself as little in Homer

in this comprehensive sense, as the term *Barbarians,* from whom the Greeks were not yet clearly distinguished. It must be left to special history to trace the several tribes, and their transformations. In general we may assume, that the tribes and individuals were prone to leave their country when too great a population occupied it, and that consequently these tribes were in a migratory condition, and practised mutual depredation. "Even now," says the discerning Thucydides, "the Ozolian Locrians, the Ætolians, and Acarnanians retain their ancient mode of life; the custom of carrying weapons, too, has maintained itself among them as a relic of their ancient predatory habits." Respecting the Athenians, he says, that they were the first who laid aside arms in time of peace. In such a state of things agriculture was not pursued; the inhabitants had not only to defend themselves against freebooters, but also to contend with wild beasts (even in Herodotus's time many lions infested the banks of the Nestus and Achelous); at a later time tame cattle became especially an object of plunder, and even after agriculture had become more general, men were still entrapped and sold for slaves. In depicting this original condition of Greece, Thucydides goes still further into detail.

Greece, then, was in this state of turbulence, insecurity, and rapine, and its tribes were continually migrating.

The other element in which the national life of the Hellenes was versed, was the *Sea.* The physique of their country led them to this amphibious existence, and allowed them to skim freely over the waves, as they spread themselves freely over the land—not roving about like the nomad populations, nor torpidly vegetating like those of the river districts. Piracy, not trade, was the chief object of maritime occupations; and, as we gather from Homer, it was not yet reckoned discreditable. The suppression of piracy is ascribed to Minos, and Crete is renowned as the land where security was first enjoyed; for there the state of things which we meet with again in Sparta was early realized, viz., the establishment in power of one party, and the subjugation of the other, which was compelled to obey and work for the former.

We have just spoken of heterogeneity as an element of the Greek Spirit, and it is well known that the rudiments of Greek civilization are connected with the advent of foreigners. This origin of their moral life the Greeks have preserved, with grateful recollection, in a form of recognition which we may call mythological.   In their mythology we have a definite record of the introduction of agriculture by Triptolemus, who was instructed by Ceres, and of the institution of marriage, etc. Prometheus, whose origin is referred to the distant Caucasus, is celebrated as having first taught men the production and the use of fire.   The introduction of iron was likewise of great importance to the Greeks; and while Homer speaks only of bronze, Æschylus calls iron " Scythian."   The introduction of the olive, of the art of spinning and weaving, and the creation of the horse by Poseidon, belong to the same category.

More historical than these rudiments of culture is the alleged arrival of *foreigners;* tradition tells us how the various states were founded by such foreigners.   Thus, Athens owes its origin to Cecrops, an Egyptian, whose history, however, is involved in obscurity.   The race of Deucalion, the son of Prometheus, is brought into connection with the various Greek tribes.   Pelops of Phrygia, the son of Tantalus, is also mentioned; next, Danaus, from Egypt: from him descend Acrisius, Danæ, and Perseus.   Pelops is said to have brought great wealth with him to the Peloponnesus, and to have acquired great respect and power there.   Danaus settled in Argos. Especially important is the arrival of Cadmus, of Phœnician origin, with whom phonetic writing is said to have been introduced into Greece; Herodotus refers it to Phœnicia, and ancient inscriptions then extant are cited to support the assertion. Cadmus, according to the legend, founded Thebes.

We thus observe a colonization by civilized peoples, who were in advance of the Greeks in point of culture: though we cannot compare this colonization with that of the English in North America, for the latter have not been blended with the aborigines, but have dispossessed them; whereas in the case of the settlers in Greece the adventitious and autochthonic elements were mixed together.   The date assigned to the arrival of these colonists is very remote—the fourteenth and fifteenth century before Christ.   Cadmus is said to have founded Thebes about 1490 B.C.—a date with which the Exodus of Moses from Egypt (1500 B.C.) nearly coincides.   Amphictyon is also mentioned among the Founders of Greek institutions; he is said to have established at Thermopylæ a union between many small tribes of Hellas proper and Thessaly—a combination with which the great Amphictyonic league is said to have originated.

These foreigners, then, are reputed to have established fixed *centres* in Greece by the erection of fortresses and the founding of royal houses. In Argolis, the walls of which the ancient fortresses consisted, were called Cyclopian; some of them have been discovered even in recent times, since, on account of their solidity, they are indestructible.

These walls consist partly of irregular blocks, whose interstices are filled up with small stones—partly of masses of stones carefully fitted into each other. Such walls are those of Tiryns and Mycenæ. Even now the gate with the lions, at Mycenæ, can be recognized by the description of Pausanias. It is stated of Prœtus, who ruled in Argos, that he brought with him from Lycia the Cyclopes who built these walls. It is, however, supposed that they were erected by the ancient Pelasgi. To the fortresses protected by such walls the princes of the heroic times generally attached their dwellings. Especially remarkable are the Treasure-houses built by them, such as the Treasure-house of Minyas at Orchomenus, and that of Atreus at Mycenæ. These fortresses, then, were the nuclei of small states; they gave a greater security to agriculture; they protected commercial intercourse against robbery. They were, however, as Thucydides informs us, not placed in the immediate vicinity of the sea, on account of piracy; maritime towns being of later date. Thus with those royal abodes originated the firm establishment of society. The relation of princes to subjects, and to each other, we learn best from Homer. It did not depend on a state of things established by law, but on superiority in riches, possessions, martial accoutrements, personal bravery, pre-eminence in insight and wisdom, and lastly, on descent and ancestry; for the princes, as heroes, were regarded as of a higher race. Their subjects obeyed them, not as distinguished from them by conditions of Caste, nor as in a state of serfdom, nor in the patriarchal relation—according to which the chief is only the head of the tribe or family to which all belong—nor yet as the result of the express necessity for a constitutional government; but only from the need, universally felt, of being held together, and of obeying a ruler accustomed to command—without envy and ill-will towards him. The Prince has just so much personal authority as he possesses the ability to acquire and to assert; but as this superiority is only the individually heroic, resting on personal merit, it does not continue long. Thus in Homer we see the suitors of Penelope taking possession of the property of the absent Ulysses, without showing the slightest respect to his son. Achilles, in his inquiries about his father, when Ulysses descends to Hades, indicates the supposition that, as he is old, he will be no longer honored. Manners are still very simple: princes prepare their own repasts; and Ulysses labors at the construction of his own house. In Homer's Iliad we find a King of Kings, a generalissimo in the great national undertaking—but the other magnates environ him as a freely deliberating council; the prince is honored, but he is obliged to arrange everything to the satisfaction of the others; he indulges in violent conduct towards Achilles, but, in revenge, the latter withdraws from the struggle. Equally lax is the relation of the several chiefs to the people at large, among whom there are always individuals who claim attention and respect. The various peoples do not fight as mercenaries of the prince in his battles, nor as a stupid serf-like herd driven to the contest, nor yet in their own interest; but as the companions of their honored chieftain—as witnesses of his exploits, and his defenders in peril. A perfect resemblance to these relations is also presented in the Greek Pantheon. Zeus is the Father of the Gods, but each one of them has his own will; Zeus respects them, and they him: he may sometimes scold and threaten them, and they then allow his will to prevail or retreat grumbling; but they do not permit matters to come to an extremity, and Zeus so arranges matters on the whole—by making this concession to one, that to another—as to produce satisfaction. In the terrestrial, as well as in the Olympian world, there is, therefore, only a lax bond of unity maintained; royalty has not yet become monarchy, for it is only in a more extensive society that the need of the latter is felt.

While this state of things prevailed, and social relations were such as have been described, that striking and great event took place—the union of the whole of Greece in a national undertaking, viz., the *Trojan War;* with which began that more extensive connection with Asia which had very important results for the Greeks. (The expedition of Jason to Colchis—also mentioned by the poets—and which bears an earlier date, was, as compared with the war of Troy, a very limited and isolated undertaking.) The occasion of that united expedition is said to have been the violation of the laws of hospitality by the son of an Asiatic prince, in carrying off the wife of his host. Agamemnon assembles the princes of Greece through the power and influence which he possesses. Thucydides ascribes his authority to his hereditary sovereignty, combined with naval power (Hom. Il. ii. 108), in which he was far superior to the rest. It appears, however, that the combination was effected without external compulsion, and that the whole armament was convened simply on the strength of individual consent. The Hellenes were then brought to act unitedly, to an extent of which there is no subsequent example. The result of their exertions was the conquest and destruction of Troy, though they had no design of making it a permanent possession. No external result, therefore, in the way of settlement ensued, any more than an enduring political union, as the effect of the uniting of the nation in the accomplishment of this single achievement. But the poet supplied an imperishable portraiture of their youth and of their national spirit, to the imagination of the Greek people; and the picture of this beautiful human heroism hovered as a directing ideal before their whole development and culture. So likewise, in the *Middle Ages,* we see the whole of Christendom united to attain one object—the conquest of the Holy Sepulchre; but, in spite of all the victories achieved, with just as little permanent result. The Crusades are the Trojan War of newly awakened Christendom, waged against the simple, homogeneous clearness of Mahometanism.

The royal houses perished, partly as the consequence of particular atrocities, partly through gradual extinction. There was no strictly moral bond connecting them with the tribes which they governed. The same relative position is occupied by the people and the royal houses in the Greek Tragedy also. The people is the Chorus—passive, deedless: the heroes perform the deeds, and incur the consequent responsibility. There is nothing in common between them; the people have no directing power, but only appeal to the gods. Such heroic personalities as those of the princes in question, are so remarkably suited for subjects of dramatic art on this very account—that they form their resolutions independently and individually, and are not guided by universal laws binding on every citizen; their conduct and their ruin are individual. The people appears separated from the royal houses, and these are regarded as an alien body—a higher race, fighting out the battles and undergoing the penalties of their fate, for themselves alone. Royalty having performed that which it had to perform, thereby rendered itself superfluous. The several dynasties are the agents of their own destruction, or perish not as the result of animosity, or of struggles on the side of the people: rather the families of the sovereigns are left in calm enjoyment of their power—a proof that the democratic government which followed is not regarded as something absolutely diverse. How sharply do the annals of other times contrast with this!

This fall of the royal houses occurs after the Trojan war, and many changes now present themselves. The Peloponnesus was conquered by the Heraclidæ, who introduced a calmer state of things, which was not again interrupted by the incessant migrations of races. The history now becomes more obscure; and though the several occurrences of the Trojan war are very circumstantially described to us, we are uncertain respecting the important transactions of the time immediately following, for a space of many centuries. No united undertaking distinguishes them, unless we regard as such that of which Thucydides speaks, viz., the war between the Chalcidians and Eretrians in Eubœa, in which many nations took part. The towns vegetate in isolation, or at most distinguish themselves by war with their neighbors. Yet, they enjoy prosperity in this isolated condition, by means of trade; a kind of progress to which their being rent by many party-struggles offers no opposition. In the same way, we observe in the Middle Ages the towns of Italy—which, both internally and externally, were engaged in continual struggle—attaining so high a degree of prosperity. The flourishing state of the Greek towns at that time is proved, according to Thucydides, also by the colonies sent out in every direction. Thus, Athens colonized Ionia and several islands; and colonies from the Peloponnesus settled in Italy and Sicily. Colonies, on the other hand, became relatively mother states; e.g. Miletus, which founded many cities on the Propontis and the Black Sea. This sending out of colonies—especially during the period between the Trojan war and Cyrus—presents us with a remarkable phenomenon. It can be thus explained. In the

several towns the people had the governmental power in their
hands, since they gave the final decision in political affairs. In
consequence of the long repose enjoyed by them, the population
and the development of the community advanced rapidly; and
the immediate result was the amassing of great riches, contemporaneously with which fact great want and poverty make their
appearance. Industry, in our sense, did not exist; and the
lands were soon occupied. Nevertheless a part of the poorer
classes would not submit to the degradations of poverty, for
everyone felt himself a free citizen. The only expedient, therefore, that remained, was colonization. In another country,
those who suffered distress in their own, might seek a free soil,
and gain a living as free citizens by its cultivation. Colonization
thus became a means of maintaining some degree of equality
among the citizens; but this means is only a palliative, and the
original inequality, founded on the difference of property, immediately reappears. The old passions were rekindled with
fresh violence, and riches were soon made use of for securing
power: thus " Tyrants " gained ascendancy in the cities of
Greece. Thucydides says, " When Greece increased in riches,
Tyrants arose in the cities, and the Greeks devoted themselves
more zealously to the sea." At the time of Cyrus, the History
of Greece acquires its peculiar interest; we see the various states
now displaying their particular character. This is the date,
too, of the formation of the distinct Greek Spirit. Religion and
political institutions are developed with it, and it is these important phases of national life which must now occupy our
attention.

In tracing up the rudiments of *Greek culture*, we first recall
attention to the fact, that the physical condition of the country
does not exhibit such a characteristic unity, such a uniform
mass, as to exercise a powerful influence over the inhabitants.
On the contrary, it is diversified, and produces no decided impression. Nor have we here the unwieldy unity of a family
or national combination; but, in the presence of scenery and
displays of elemental power broken up into fragmentary forms,
men's attention is more largely directed to themselves, and to
the extension of their immature capabilities. Thus we see the
Greeks—divided and separated from each other—thrown back
upon their inner spirit and personal energy, yet at the same
time most variously excited and cautiously circumspect. We

behold them quite undetermined and irresolute in the presence
of Nature, dependent on its contingencies, and listening anx-
iously to each signal from the external world; but, on the
other hand, intelligently taking cognizance of and appropriating that outward existence, and showing boldness and independent vigor in contending with it. These are the simple
elements of their culture and religion. In tracing up their mythological conceptions, we find natural objects forming the basis
—not *en masse*, however; only in dissevered forms. The Diana
of Ephesus (that is, Nature as the universal Mother), the Cybele and Astarte of Syria—such comprehensive conceptions remained Asiatic, and were not transmitted to Greece. For the
Greeks only *watch* the objects of Nature, and form *surmises*
respecting them; inquiring, in the depth of their souls, for the
hidden meaning. According to Aristotle's dictum, that Philosophy proceeds from Wonder, the Greek view of Nature also
proceeds from wonder of this kind. Not that in their experience, Spirit meets something extraordinary, which it compares
with the common order of things; for the intelligent view of a
regular course of Nature, and the reference of phenomena to
that standard, do not yet present themselves; but the Greek
Spirit was excited to wonder at the *Natural* in Nature. It does
not maintain the position of stupid indifference to it as something existing, and there an end of it; but regards it as something in the first instance foreign, in which, however, it has a
presentiment of confidence, and the belief that it bears something within it which is friendly to the human Spirit, and to
which it may be permitted to sustain a positive relation. This
Wonder, and this *Presentiment*, are here the fundamental categories; though the Hellenes did not content themselves with
these moods of feelings, but projected the hidden meaning,
which was the subject of the surmise, into a distinct conception
as an object of consciousness. The Natural holds its place in
their minds only after undergoing some transformation by
Spirit—not immediately. Man regards Nature only as an excitement to his faculties, and only the Spiritual which he has
evolved from it can have any influence over him. Nor is this
commencement of the Spiritual apprehension of Nature to be
regarded as an explanation suggested by *us;* it meets us in a
multitude of conceptions formed by the Greeks themselves.
The position of curious surmise, of attentive eagerness to catch

the meaning of Nature, is indicated to us in the comprehensive idea of *Pan*. To the Greeks Pan did not represent the *objective* Whole, but that indefinite neutral ground which involves the element of the *subjective;* he embodies that thrill which pervades us in the silence of the forests; he was, therefore, especially worshipped in sylvan Arcadia: (a " panic terror " is the common expression for a groundless fright). Pan, this thrill-exciting being, is also represented as playing on the flute; we have not the bare internal presentiment, for Pan makes himself audible on the seven-reeded pipe. In what has been stated we have, on the one hand, the Indefinite, which, however, holds communication with man; on the other hand the fact, that such communication is only a subjective imagining—an explanation furnished by the percipient himself. On the same principle the Greeks listened to the murmuring of the fountains, and asked what might be thereby signified; but the signification which they were led to attach to it was not the objective meaning of the fountain, but the subjective—that of the subject itself, which further exalts the Naiad to a Muse. The Naiads, or Fountains, are the external, objective origin of the Muses. Yet the immortal songs of the Muses are not that which is heard in the murmuring of the fountains; they are the productions of the thoughtfully listening Spirit—*creative* while *observant*. The interpretation and explanation of Nature and its transformations—the indication of their sense and import—is the act of the subjective Spirit; and to this the Greeks attached the name μαντεία. The general idea which this embodies, is the form in which man realizes his relationship to Nature. Μαντεία has reference both to the matter of the exposition and to the expounder who divines the weighty import in question. Plato speaks of it in reference to dreams, and to that delirium into which men fall during sickness; an interpreter, μάντις, is wanted to explain these dreams and this delirium. That Nature answered the questions which the Greek put to her, is in this converse sense true, that he obtained an answer to the questions of Nature from his own Spirit. The insight of the Seer becomes thereby purely poetical; Spirit supplies the signification which the natural image expresses. Everywhere the Greeks desired a clear presentation and interpretation of the Natural. Homer tells us, in the last book of the Odyssey, that while the Greeks were overwhelmed with sorrow for Achilles, a violent agitation came over the sea : the Greeks were on the point of dispersing in terror, when the experienced Nestor arose and interpreted the phenomenon to them. Thetis, he said, was coming, with her nymphs, to lament for the death of her son. When a pestilence broke out in the camp of the Greeks, the Priest Calchas explained that Apollo was incensed at their not having restored the daughter of his priest Chryses when a ransom had been offered. The Oracle was originally interpreted exactly in this way. The oldest Oracle was at Dodona (in the district of the modern Janina). Herodotus says that the first priestesses of the temple there, were from Egypt ; yet this temple is stated to be an ancient Greek one. The rustling of the leaves of the sacred oaks was the form of prognostication there. Bowls of metal were also suspended in the grove. But the sounds of the bowls dashing against each other were quite indefinite, and had no objective sense ; the sense—the signification—was imparted to the sounds only by the human beings who heard them. Thus also the Delphic priestesses, in a senseless, distracted state—in the intoxication of enthusiasm (μανία)—uttered unintelligible sounds ; and it was the μάντις who gave to these utterances a definite meaning. In the cave of Trophonius the noise of subterranean waters was heard, and apparitions were seen : but these indefinite phenomena acquired a meaning only through the interpreting, comprehending Spirit. It must also be observed, that these excitements of Spirit are in the first instance external, natural impulses. Succeeding them are internal changes taking place in the human being himself—such as dreams, or the delirium of the Delphic priestess—which require to be made intelligible by the μάντις. At the commencement of the Iliad, Achilles is excited against Agamemnon, and is on the point of drawing his sword ; but on a sudden he checks the movement of his arm, and recollects himself in his wrath, reflecting on his relation to Agamemnon. The Poet explains this by saying that it was Pallas-Athene (Wisdom or Consideration) that restrained him. When Ulysses among the Phæacians, has thrown his discus farther than the rest, and one of the Phæacians shows a friendly disposition towards him, the Poet recognizes in him Pallas-Athene. Such an explanation denotes the perception of the inner meaning, the sense, the underlying truth ; and the poets were in this way the teachers of the Greeks—especially Homer. *Μαντεία* in fact is Poesy—not a capricious indulgence of fancy, but an imagination which introduces the Spiritual into the Natural—in short a richly intelligent perception. The Greek Spirit, on the whole, therefore, is free from superstition, since it changes the *sensuous* into the *sensible*—the Intellectual—so that [oracular] decisions are derived from Spirit; although superstition comes in again from another quarter, as will be observed when impulsions from another source than the Spiritual, are allowed to tell upon opinion and action.

But the stimuli that operated on the Spirit of the Greeks are not to be limited to these objective and subjective excitements. The traditional element derived from foreign countries, the culture, the divinities and ritual observances transmitted to them *ab extra* must also be included. It has been long a much vexed question whether the arts and the religion of the Greeks were developed independently or through foreign suggestion. Under the conduct of a one-sided understanding the controversy is interminable; for it is no less a fact of history that the Greeks derived conceptions from India, Syria, and Egypt, than that the Greek conceptions are peculiar to themselves, and those others alien. Herodotus (II. 53) asserts, with equal decision, that " *Homer and Hesiod invented a Theogony for the Greeks,* and assigned to the gods their appropriate epithets " (a most weighty sentence, which has been the subject of deep investigation, especially by Creuzer)—and, in another place, that Greece took the names of its divinities from Egypt, and that the Greeks made inquiry at Dodona, whether they ought to adopt these names or not. This appears self-contradictory: it is, however, quite consistent; for the fact is that the Greeks evolved the Spiritual from the materials which they had received. The Natural, as *explained* by man—*i.e.* its internal essential element —is, as a universal principle, the beginning of the Divine. Just as in Art the Greeks may have acquired a mastery of technical matters from others—from the Egyptians especially—so in their religion the commencement might have been from without; but by their independent spirit they transformed the one as well as the other.

Traces of such foreign rudiments may be generally discovered (Creuzer, in his " Symbolik," dwells especially on this point). The amours of Zeus appear indeed as something isolated, extraneous, adventitious, but it may be shown that foreign theogonic representations form their basis. Hercules is, among the Hellenes, that Spiritual Humanity which by native energy attains Olympus through the twelve far-famed labors: but the foreign idea that lies at the basis is the Sun, completing its revolution through the twelve signs of the Zodiac. The Mysteries were only such ancient rudiments, and certainly contained no greater wisdom than already existed in the consciousness of the Greeks. All Athenians were initiated in the mysteries—Socrates excepted, who refused initiation, because he knew well that science and art are not the product of mysteries, and that Wisdom never lies among arcana. True science has its place much rather in the open field of consciousness.

In summing up the constituents of the *Greek Spirit*, we find its fundamental characteristic to be, that the freedom of Spirit is conditioned by and has an essential relation to some stimulus supplied by Nature. Greek freedom of thought is excited by an alien existence; but it is free because it transforms and virtually reproduces the stimulus by its own operation. This phase of Spirit is the medium between the loss of individuality on the part of man (such as we observe in the Asiatic principle, in which the Spiritual and Divine exists only under a Natural form), and Infinite Subjectivity as pure certainty of itself—the position that the Ego is the ground of all that can lay claim to substantial existence. The Greek Spirit as the medium between these two, begins with Nature, but transforms it into a mere objective form of its (Spirit's) own existence; Spirituality is therefore not yet absolutely free; not yet absolutely *self*-produced—is not self-stimulation. Setting out from surmise and wonder, the Greek Spirit advances to definite conceptions of the hidden meanings of Nature. In the subject itself too, the same harmony is produced. In Man, the side of his subjective existence which he owes to Nature, is the Heart, the Disposition, Passion, and Variety of Temperament: this side is then developed in a spiritual direction to free Individuality; so that the character is not placed in a relation to universally valid moral authorities, assuming the form of duties, but the Moral appears as a nature peculiar to the individual—an exertion of will, the result of disposition and individual constitution. This stamps the Greek character as that of *Individuality conditioned by Beauty*, which is produced by Spirit, transforming the merely Natural into an expression of its own being. The activity of Spirit does not yet possess in itself the material and organ of expression, but needs the excitement of Nature and the matter which Nature supplies: it is not free, self-determining Spirituality, but mere naturalness formed to Spirituality—Spiritual Individuality. The Greek Spirit is the plastic artist, forming the stone into a work of art. In this formative process the stone does not remain mere stone—the form being only superinduced from without; but it is made an expression of the Spiritual, even contrary to its nature, and thus *trans*formed. Conversely, the artist *needs* for his spiritual conceptions, stone, colors, sensuous forms to express his idea. Without such an element he can no more be conscious of the idea himself, than give it an objective form for the contemplation of others; since it cannot in Thought alone become an object to him. The Egyptian Spirit also was a similar laborer in Matter, but the Natural had not yet been subjected to the Spiritual. No advance was made beyond a struggle and contest with it; the Natural still took an independent position, and formed one side of the image, as in the body of the Sphinx. In Greek Beauty the Sensuous is only a sign, an expression, an envelope, in which Spirit manifests itself.

It must be added, that while the Greek Spirit is a transforming artist of this kind, it knows itself free in its productions; for it is their creator, and they are what is called the " work of man." They are, however, not merely this, but Eternal Truth —the energizing of Spirit in its innate essence, and quite as really not created as created by man. He has a respect and veneration for these conceptions and images—this Olympian Zeus—this Pallas of the Acropolis—and in the same way for the laws, political and ethical, that guide his actions. But He, the human being, is the womb that conceived them, he the breast that suckled them, he the Spiritual to which their grandeur and purity are owing. Thus he feels himself calm in contemplating them, and not only free in himself, but possessing the consciousness of his freedom; thus the honor of the Human is swallowed up in the worship of the Divine. Men honor the Divine in and for itself, but at the same time as their deed, their production, their phenomenal existence; thus the Divine receives its honor through the respect paid to the Human, and the Human in virtue of the honor paid to the Divine.

Such are the qualities of that *Beautiful Individuality*, which constitutes the centre of the Greek character. We must now consider the several radiations which this idea throws out in realizing itself. All issue in works of art, and we may arrange under three heads: the *subjective* work of art, that is, the culture of the man himself;—the *objective* work of art, *i.e.*, the shaping of the world of divinities;—lastly, the *political* work of art—the form of the Constitution, and the relations of the Individuals who compose it.

SECTION II

PHASES OF INDIVIDUALITY ÆSTHETICALLY
CONDITIONED

Chapter I.—The Subjective Work of Art

M AN with his necessities sustains a practical relation to
external Nature, and in making it satisfy his desires,
and thus using it up, has recourse to a system of *means*.
For natural objects are powerful, and offer resistance in various
ways. In order to subdue them, man introduces other natural
agents; thus turns Nature against itself, and invents *instruments*
for this purpose. These human inventions belong to Spirit,
and such an instrument is to be respected more than a mere
natural object. We see, too, that the Greeks are accustomed
to set an especial value upon them, for in Homer, man's delight
in them appears in a very striking way. In the notice of
Agamemnon's sceptre, its origin is given in detail: mention is
made of doors which turn on hinges, and of accoutrements and
furniture, in a way that expresses satisfaction. The honor of
human invention in subjugating Nature is ascribed to the gods.

But, on the other hand, man uses Nature for *ornament*, which
is intended only as a token of wealth and of that which man
has made of himself. We find Ornament, in this interest, already very much developed among the Homeric Greeks. It is
true that both barbarians and civilized nations ornament themselves; but barbarians content themselves with mere ornament;
—they intend their persons to please by an *external* addition.
But ornament by its very nature is destined only to beautify
something other than itself, viz. the human body, which is
man's immediate environment, and which, in common with
Nature at large, he has to transform. The spiritual interest of
primary importance is, therefore, the development of the body
to a perfect organ for the Will—an adaptation which may on
the one hand itself be the means for ulterior objects, and on the

other hand, appear as an object *per se*. Among the Greeks, then, we find this boundless impulse of individuals to *display themselves*, and to find their enjoyment in so doing. Sensuous enjoyment does not become the basis of their condition when a state of repose has been obtained, any more than the dependence and stupor of superstition which enjoyment entails. They are too powerfully excited, too much bent upon developing their individuality, absolutely to adore Nature, as it manifests itself in its aspects of power and beneficence. That peaceful condition which ensued when a predatory life had been relinquished, and liberal nature had afforded security and leisure, turned their energies in the direction of self-assertion—the effort to dignify themselves. But while on the one side they have too much independent personality to be subjugated by superstition, that sentiment has not gone to the extent of making them *vain;* on the contrary, essential conditions must be first satisfied, before this can become a matter of vanity with them. The exhilarating sense of personality, in contrast with sensuous subjection to nature, and the need, not of mere pleasure, but of the display of individual powers, in order thereby to gain special distinction and consequent enjoyment, constitute therefore the chief characteristic and principal occupation of the Greeks. Free as the bird singing in the sky, the individual only expresses what lies in his untrammelled human nature—[to give the world " assurance of a man "]—to have his importance recognized. This is the *subjective* beginning of Greek Art—in which the human being elaborates his physical being, in free, beautiful movement and agile vigor, to a work of art. The Greeks first trained their own persons to beautiful configurations before they attempted the expression of such in marble and in paintings. The innocuous contests of *games*, in which every one exhibits his powers, is of very ancient date. Homer gives a noble description of the games conducted by Achilles, in honor of Patroclus; but in all his poems there is no notice of statues of the gods, though he mentions the sanctuary at Dodona, and the treasure-house of Apollo at Delphi. The games in Homer consist in wrestling and boxing, running, horse and chariot races, throwing the discus or javelin, and archery. With these exercises are united dance and song, to express and form part of the enjoyment of social exhilaration, and which arts likewise blossomed into beauty. On the shield of Achilles,

Hephæstus represents, among other things, how beautiful youths and maidens move as quickly " with well-taught feet," as the potter turns his wheel. The multitude stand round enjoying the spectacle; the divine singer accompanies the song with the harp, and two chief dancers perform their evolutions in the centre of the circle.

These games and æsthetic displays, with the pleasures and honors that accompanied them, were at the outset only private, originating in particular occasions; but in the sequel they became an affair of the nation, and were fixed for certain times at appointed places. Besides the Olympic games in the sacred district of Elis, there were also held the Isthmian, the Pythian, and Nemean, at other places.

If we look at the inner nature of these sports, we shall first observe how Sport itself is opposed to serious business, to dependence and need. This wrestling, running, contending was no serious affair; bespoke no obligation of defence, no necessity of combat. Serious occupation is labor that has reference to some want. I or Nature must succumb; if the one is to continue, the other must fall. In contrast with this kind of seriousness, however, Sport presents the higher seriousness; for in it Nature is wrought into Spirit, and although in these contests the subject has not advanced to the highest grade of serious thought, yet in this exercise of his physical powers, man shows his Freedom, viz. that he has transformed his body to an organ of Spirit.

Man has immediately in one of his organs, the Voice, an element which admits and requires a more extensive purport than the mere sensuous Present. We have seen how *Song* is united with the Dance, and ministers to it: but, subsequently Song makes itself independent, and requires musical instruments to accompany it; it then ceases to be unmeaning, like the modulations of a bird, which may indeed express emotion, but which have no objective import; but it requires an import created by imagination and Spirit, and which is then further formed into an *objective work of art*.

Chapter II.—The Objective Work of Art

If the subject of Song as thus developed among the Greeks is made a question, we should say that its essential and absolute purport is *religious*. We have examined the Idea embodied in the Greek Spirit; and Religion is nothing else than this Idea made objective as the essence of being. According to that Idea, we shall observe also that the Divine involves the *vis naturæ* only as an element suffering a process of transformation to spiritual power. Of this Natural Element, as its origin, nothing more remains than the accord of analogy involved in the representation they formed of Spiritual power; for the Greeks worshipped God as Spiritual. We cannot, therefore, regard the Greek divinity as similar to the Indian—some Power of Nature for which the human shape supplies only an outward form. The essence is the Spiritual itself, and the Natural is only the point of departure. But on the other hand, it must be observed, that the divinity of the Greeks is not yet the *absolute,* free Spirit, but Spirit in a particular mode, fettered by the limitations of humanity—still dependent as a determinate individuality on external conditions. Individualities, objectively beautiful, are the gods of the Greeks. The divine Spirit is here so conditioned as to be not yet regarded as abstract Spirit, but has a *specialized existence*—continues to manifest itself in sense; but so that the sensuous is not its *substance*, but is only an *element* of its manifestation. This must be our leading idea in the consideration of the Greek mythology, and we must have our attention fixed upon it so much the more firmly, as—partly through the influence of erudition, which has whelmed essential principles beneath an infinite amount of details, and partly through that destructive analysis which is the work of the abstract Understanding—this mythology, together with the more ancient periods of Greek history, has become a region of the greatest intellectual confusion.

In the Idea of the Greek Spirit we found the two elements, Nature and Spirit, in such a relation to each other, that Nature forms merely the point of departure. This degradation of Nature is in the Greek mythology the turning point of the whole —expressed as the War of the Gods, the overthrow of the Titans by the race of Zeus. The transition from the Oriental to the Occidental Spirit is therein represented, for the Titans are the merely Physical—natural existences, from whose grasp sovereignty is wrested. It is true that they continue to be venerated, but not as governing powers; for they are relegated to the verge [the limbus] of the world. The Titans are powers of Nature, Uranus, Gæa, Oceanus, Selene, Helios, etc. Chronos expresses the dominion of abstract Time, which devours its children. The unlimited power of reproduction is restrained, and Zeus appears as the head of the new divinities, who embody a spiritual import, and are themselves Spirit.* It is not possible to express this transition more distinctly and naïvely than in this myth; the new dynasty of divinities proclaim their peculiar nature to be of a Spiritual order.

The second point is, that the new divinities retain natural elements, and consequently in themselves a determinate relation to the powers of Nature, as was previously shown. Zeus has his lightnings and clouds, and Hera is the creatress of the *Natural*, the producer of crescent vitality. Zeus is also the political god, the protector of morals and of hospitality. Oceanus, as such, is only the element of Nature which his name denotes. Poseidon has still the wildness of that element in his character; but he is also an ethical personage; to him is ascribed the building of walls and the production of the Horse. Helios is the sun as a natural element. This Light, according to the analogy of Spirit, has been transformed to self-consciousness, and Apollo has proceeded from Helios. The name Λύκειος points to the connection with light; Apollo was a herdsman in the employ of Admetus, but oxen not subjected to the yoke were sacred to Helios: his rays, represented as arrows, kill the Python. The idea of Light as the natural power constituting the basis of the representation, cannot be dissociated from this divinity; especially as the other predicates attached to it are easily united with it, and the explanations of Müller and others, who deny that basis, are much more arbitrary and far-fetched. For Apollo is the prophesying and discerning god—Light, that makes everything clear. He is, moreover, the healer and strengthener; as also the destroyer, for he kills men. He is the propitiating and purifying god, *e.g.*, in contravention of the Eumenides—the ancient subterrene divinities—who exact hard, stern justice. He himself is pure; he has no wife, but only a sister, and is not involved in various disgusting adventures, like

* See Hegel's "Vorles. über die Philos. der Religion," II. p. 102, sqq. (2d edition.)

Zeus; moreover, he is the discerner and declarer, the singer and leader of the dances—as the sun leads the harmonious dance of stars.—In like manner the Naiads became the Muses. The mother of the gods, Cybele—continuing to be worshipped at Ephesus as Artemis—is scarcely to be recognized as the Artemis of the Greeks—the chaste huntress and destroyer of wild beasts. Should it be said that this change of the Natural into the Spiritual is owing to our allegorizing, or that of the later Greeks, we may reply, that this transformation of the Natural to the Spiritual is the Greek Spirit itself. The epigrams of the Greeks exhibit such advances from the Sensuous to the Spiritual. But the abstract Understanding cannot comprehend this blending of the Natural with the Spiritual.

It must be further observed, that the Greek gods are to be regarded as individualities—not abstractions, like "Knowledge," "Unity," "Time," "Heaven," "Necessity." Such abstractions do not form the substance of these divinities; they are no allegories, no abstract beings, to which various attributes are attached, like the Horatian "*Necessitas clavis trabalibus.*" As little are the divinities symbols, for a symbol is only a sign, an adumbration of something else. The Greek gods express of themselves what they are. The eternal repose and clear intelligence that dignifies the head of Apollo, is not a symbol, but the expression in which Spirit manifests itself, and shows itself present. The gods are personalities, concrete individualities: an allegorical being has no qualities, but is itself one quality and no more. The gods are, moreover, special characters, since in each of them one peculiarity predominates as the characteristic one; but it would be vain to try to bring this circle of characters into a system. Zeus, perhaps, may be regarded as ruling the other gods, but not with substantial power; so that they are left free to their own idiosyncrasy. Since the whole range of spiritual and moral qualities was appropriated by the gods, the unity, which stood above them all, necessarily remained abstract; it was therefore formless and unmeaning Fact, [the absolute constitution of things]—Necessity, whose oppressive character arises from the absence of the Spiritual in it; whereas the gods hold a friendly relation to men, for they are Spiritual natures. That higher thought, the knowledge of Unity as God—the One Spirit—lay beyond that grade of thought which the Greeks had attained.

With regard to the *adventitious* and special that attaches to the Greek gods, the question arises, where the external origin of this adventitious element is to be looked for. It arises partly from local characteristics—the scattered condition of the Greeks at the commencement of their national life, fixing as this did on certain points, and consequently introducing local representations. The local divinities stand alone, and occupy a much greater extent than they do afterwards, when they enter into the circle of the divinities, and are reduced to a limited position; they are conditioned by the particular consciousness and circumstances of the countries in which they appear. There are a multitude of Herculeses and Zeuses, that have their local history like the Indian gods, who also at different places possess temples to which a peculiar legend attaches. A similar relation occurs in the case of the Catholic saints and their legends; though here, not the several localities, but the one " Mater Dei " supplies the point of departure, being afterwards localized in the most diversified modes. The Greeks relate the liveliest and most attractive stories of their gods—to which no limit can be assigned, since rich fancies were always gushing forth anew in the living Spirit of the Greeks. A second source from which adventitious specialities in the conception of the gods arose is that Worship of Nature, whose representations retain a place in the Greek myths, as certainly as they appear there also in a regenerated and transfigured condition. The preservation of the original myths, brings us to the famous chapter of the " *Mysteries*," already mentioned. These mysteries of the Greeks present something which, as unknown, has attracted the curiosity of all times, under the supposition of profound wisdom. It must first be remarked that their antique and primary character, in virtue of its very antiquity, shows their destitution of excellence—their inferiority;—that the more refined truths are not expressed in these mysteries, and that the view which many have entertained is incorrect, viz.—that the Unity of God, in opposition to polytheism, was taught in them. The mysteries were rather antique rituals; and it is as unhistorical as it is foolish, to assume that profound philosophical truths are to be found there; since, on the contrary, only natural ideas—ruder conceptions of the metamorphoses occurring everywhere in nature, and of the vital principle that pervades it—were the subjects of those mysteries. If we put together all the historical data pertinent to the question, the result we shall inevitably arrive at will be that the mysteries did not constitute a system of doctrines, but were sensuous ceremonies and exhibitions, consisting of symbols of the universal operations of Nature, as, *e.g.*, the relation of the earth to celestial phenomena. The chief basis of the representations of Ceres and Proserpine, Bacchus and his train, was the universal principle of Nature; and the accompanying details were obscure stories and representations, mainly bearing on the universal vital force and its metamorphoses. An analogous process to that of Nature, Spirit has also to undergo; for it must be twice-born, *i.e.* abnegate itself; and thus the representations given in the mysteries called attention, though only feebly, to the nature of Spirit. In the Greeks they produced an emotion of shuddering awe; for an instinctive dread comes over men, when a signification is perceived in a form, which as a sensuous phenomenon does not express that signification, and which therefore both repels and attracts—awakes surmises by the import that reverberates through the whole, but at the same time a thrill of dread at the repellent form. Æschylus was accused of having profaned the mysteries in his tragedies. The indefinite representations and symbols of the Mysteries, in which the profound import is only surmised, are an element alien to the clear pure forms, and threaten them with destruction; on which account the gods of Art remain separated from the gods of the Mysteries, and the two spheres must be strictly dissociated. Most of their gods the Greeks received from foreign lands—as Herodotus states expressly with regard to Egypt —but these exotic myths were transformed and spiritualized by the Greeks; and that part of the foreign theogonies which accompanied them, was, in the mouth of the Hellenes, worked up into a legendary narrative which often redounded to the disadvantage of the divinities. Thus also the brutes which continued to rank as gods among the Egyptians, were degraded to external signs, accompanying the Spiritual god. While they have each an individual character, the Greek gods are also represented as human, and this anthropomorphism is charged as a defect. On the contrary (we may immediately rejoin) man as the Spiritual constitutes the element of truth in the Greek gods, which rendered them superior to all elemental deities, and all mere abstractions of the One and Highest Being. On the other side it is alleged as an advantage of the Greek gods that they are represented as men—that being regarded as not the case with the Christian God. Schiller says:

" While the gods remained more human,
The men were more divine."

But the Greek gods must not be regarded as more human than the Christian God. Christ is much more a *Man:* he lives, dies —suffers death on the cross—which is infinitely more human than the humanity of the Greek Idea of the Beautiful. But in referring to this common element of the Greek and the Christian religions, it must be said of both, that if a manifestation of God is to be supposed at all, his natural form must be that of Spirit, which for sensuous conception is essentially the human; for no other form can lay claim to spirituality. God appears indeed in the sun, in the mountains, in the trees, in everything that has life; but a natural appearance of this kind, is not the form proper to Spirit: here God is cognizable only in the mind of the percipient. If God himself is to be manifested in a corresponding expression, that can only be the human form: for from this the Spiritual beams forth. But if it were asked: Does God *necessarily* manifest himself? the question must be answered in the affirmative; for there is no essential existence that does not manifest itself. The real defect of the Greek religion, as compared with the Christian, is, therefore, that in the former the *manifestation* constitutes the highest mode in which the Divine being is conceived to exist—the sum and substance of divinity; while in the Christian religion the manifestation is regarded only as a *temporary phase* of the Divine. Here the *manifested* God dies, and elevates himself to glory; only after death is Christ represented as sitting at the right hand of God. The Greek god, on the contrary, exists for his worshippers perennially *in the manifestation*—only in marble, in metal or wood, or as figured by the imagination. But why did God not appear to the Greeks in the flesh? Because man was not duly estimated, did not obtain honor and dignity, till he had more fully elaborated and developed himself in the attainment of the Freedom implicit in the æsthetic manifestation in question; the form and shaping of the divinity therefore continued to be the product of individual views, [not a general, impersonal one]. One element in Spirit is, that it produces itself— *makes* itself what it is: and the other is, that it is originally free

—that Freedom is its *nature* and its Idea.   But the Greeks, since they had not attained an intellectual conception of themselves, did not yet realize Spirit in its Universality—had not the idea of man and the essential unity of the divine and human nature according to the Christian view.   Only the self-reliant, truly subjective Spirit can bear to dispense with the phenomenal side, and can venture to assign the Divine Nature to Spirit alone. It then no longer needs to inweave the Natural into its idea of the Spiritual, in order to hold fast its conception of the Divine, and to have its unity with the Divine, externally visible; but while free Thought *thinks* the Phenomenal, it is content to leave it as it is;   for it also *thinks* that union of the Finite and the Infinite, and recognizes it not as a mere accidental union, but as the Absolute—the eternal Idea itself.   Since Subjectivity was not comprehended in all its depth by the Greek Spirit, the true reconciliation was not attained in it, and the human Spirit did not yet assert its true position.   This defect showed itself in the fact of Fate as pure subjectivity appearing superior to the gods; it also shows itself in the fact, that men derive their resolves not yet from themselves, but from their Oracles. Neither human nor divine subjectivity, recognized as infinite, has as yet, absolutely decisive authority.

Chapter III.—The Political Work of Art

The State unites the two phases just considered, viz., the Subjective and the Objective Work of Art.   In the State, Spirit is not a mere Object, like the deities, nor, on the other hand, is it merely subjectively developed to a beautiful physique.   It is here a living, universal Spirit, but which is at the same time the self-conscious Spirit of the individuals composing the community.

The *Democratical* Constitution alone was adapted to the Spirit and political condition in question.   In the East we recognized Despotism, developed in magnificent proportions, as a form of government strictly appropriate to the Dawn-Land of History. Not less adapted is the democratical form in Greece, to the part assigned to it in the same great drama.   In Greece, viz., we have the freedom of the Individual, but it has not yet advanced to such a degree of abstraction, that the subjective unit is conscious of direct dependence on the [general] substantial principle—

the State as such. In this grade of Freedom, the individual will is unfettered in the entire range of its vitality, and embodies that substantial principle [the bond of the political union], according to its particular idiosyncrasy. In Rome, on the other hand, we shall observe a harsh sovereignty dominating over the individual members of the State; as also in the German Empire, a monarchy, in which the Individual is connected with and has *devoirs* to perform not only in regard to the monarch, but to the whole monarchical organization.

The Democratical State is not Patriarchal—does not rest on a still unreflecting, undeveloped confidence—but implies laws, with the consciousness of their being founded on an equitable and moral basis, and the recognition of these laws as positive. At the time of the Kings, no political life had as yet made its appearance in Hellas; there are, therefore, only slight traces of Legislation. But in the interval from the Trojan War till near the time of Cyrus, its necessity was felt. The first Lawgivers are known under the name of The Seven Sages—a title which at that time did not imply any such character as that of the Sophists—teachers of wisdom, designedly [and systematically] proclaiming the Right and True—but merely thinking men, whose thinking stopped short of Science, properly so called. They were *practical* politicians; the good counsels which two of them—Thales of Miletus and Bias of Priene—gave to the Ionian cities, have been already mentioned. Thus Solon was commissioned by the Athenians to give them laws, as those then in operation no longer sufficed. Solon gave the Athenians a constitution by which all obtained equal rights, yet not so as to render the Democracy a quite abstract one. The main point in Democracy is moral disposition. *Virtue* is the basis of Democracy, remarks Montesquieu; and this sentiment is as important as it is true in reference to the idea of Democracy commonly entertained. The Substance, [the Principle] of Justice, the common weal, the general interest, is the main consideration; but it is so only as Custom, in the form of Objective Will, so that morality properly so called—subjective conviction and intention—has not yet manifested itself. Law exists, and is in point of substance, the Law of Freedom—rational [in its form and purport,] and valid *because it is Law, i.e.* without ulterior sanction. As in Beauty the Natural element—its sensuous coefficient—remains, so also in this customary morality,

laws assume the form of a necessity of Nature. The Greeks occupy the middle ground of *Beauty* and have not yet attained the
higher standpoint of Truth. While Custom and Wont is the
form in which the Right is willed and done, that form is a stable
one, and has not yet admitted into it the foe of [unreflected] immediacy—reflection and subjectivity of Will. The interests of
the community may, therefore, continue to be intrusted to the
will and resolve of the citizens—and this must be the basis of
the Greek constitution; for no principle has as yet manifested
itself, which can contravene such Choice conditioned by Custom, and hinder its realizing itself in action. The Democratic
Constitution is here the only possible one: the citizens are still
unconscious of particular interests, and therefore of a corrupting element: the Objective Will is in their case not disintegrated. Athene the goddess is Athens itself—*i.e.*, the real
and concrete spirit of the citizens. The divinity ceases to inspire their life and conduct, only when the Will has retreated
within itself—into the *adytum* of cognition and conscience—and
has posited the infinite schism between the Subjective and the
Objective. The above is the true position of the Democratic
polity; its justification and absolute necessity rest on this still
immanent Objective Morality. For the modern conceptions
of Democracy this justification cannot be pleaded. These provide that the interests of the community, the affairs of State,
shall be discussed and decided by the People; that the individual members of the community shall deliberate, urge their
respective opinions, and give their votes; and this on the
ground that the interests of the State and its concerns are the
interests of such individual members. All this is very well;
but the essential condition and distinction in regard to various
phases of Democracy is: *What is the character of* these individual members? They are absolutely authorized to assume their
position, only in as far as their will is still *Objective Will*—not
one that wishes this or that, not mere " good " will. For good
will is something particular—rests on the morality of individuals, on their conviction and subjective feeling. That very subjective Freedom which constitutes the principle and determines
the peculiar form of Freedom in *our* world—which forms the
absolute basis of our political and religious life, could not manifest itself in Greece otherwise than as a *destructive* element.
Subjectivity was a grade not greatly in advance of that occu-

pied by the Greek Spirit; that phase must of necessity soon
be attained: but it plunged the Greek world into ruin, for the
polity which that world embodied was not calculated for this
side of humanity—did not recognize this phase; since it had
not made its appearance when that polity began to exist. Of
the Greeks in the first and genuine form of their Freedom, we
may assert, that they had no conscience; the habit of living
for their country without further [analysis or] reflection, was
the principle dominant among them. The consideration of the
State in the abstract—which to our understanding is the essential point—was alien to them. Their grand object was their
country in its living and real aspect;—*this actual* Athens, this
Sparta, these Temples, these Altars, this form of social life, this
union of fellow-citizens, these manners and customs. To the
Greek his country was a necessary of life, without which existence was impossible. It was the Sophists—the " Teachers of
Wisdom "—who first introduced subjective reflection, and the
new doctrine that each man should act according to his own conviction. When reflection once comes into play, the inquiry is
started whether the Principles of Law (*das Recht*) cannot be
improved. Instead of holding by the existing state of things,
internal conviction is relied upon; and thus begins a subjective
independent Freedom, in which the individual finds himself in
a position to bring everything to the test of his own conscience,
even in defiance of the existing constitution. Each one has
his " principles," and that view which accords with his private
judgment he regards as *practically* the best, and as claiming
practical realization. This decay even Thucydides notices,
when he speaks of every one's thinking that things are going
on badly when he has not a hand in the management.

To this state of things—in which every one presumes to have
a judgment of his own—confidence in Great Men is antagonistic. When, in earlier times, the Athenians commission Solon to
legislate for them, or when Lycurgus appears at Sparta as lawgiver and regulator of the State, it is evidently not supposed
that the people in general think that they know best what is
politically right. At a later time also, it was distinguished personages of plastic genius in whom the people placed their confidence: Cleisthenes, *e.g.* who made the constitution still more
democratic than it had been—Miltiades, Themistocles, Aris-
tides, and Cimon, who in the Median wars stand at the head of

Athenian affairs—and Pericles, in whom Athenian glory centres as in its focus. But as soon as any of these great men had performed what was needed, envy intruded—*i.e.* the recoil of the sentiment of equality against conspicuous talent—and he was either imprisoned or exiled. Finally, the Sycophants arose among the people, aspersing all individual greatness, and reviling those who took the lead in public affairs.

But there are three other points in the condition of the Greek republics that must be particularly observed.

1. With Democracy in that form in which alone it existed in Greece, *Oracles* are intimately connected. To an independent resolve, a consolidated Subjectivity of the Will (in which the latter is determined by preponderating reasons) is absolutely indispensable; but the Greeks had not this element of strength and vigor in their volition. When a colony was to be founded, when it was proposed to adopt the worship of foreign deities, or when a general was about to give battle to the enemy, the oracles were consulted. Before the battle of Platæa, Pausanias took care that an augury should be taken from the animals offered in sacrifice, and was informed by the soothsayer Tisamenus that the sacrifices were favorable to the Greeks provided they remained on the hither side of the Asopus, but the contrary, if they crossed the stream and began the battle. Pausanias, therefore, awaited the attack. In their private affairs, too, the Greeks came to a determination not so much from subjective conviction as from some extraneous suggestion. With the advance of democracy we observe the oracles no longer consulted on the most important matters, but the particular views of popular orators influencing and deciding the policy of the State. As at this time Socrates relied upon his " Dæmon," so the popular leaders and the people relied on their individual convictions in forming their decisions. But contemporaneously with this were introduced corruption, disorder, and an unintermitted process of change in the constitution.

2. Another circumstance that demands special attention here, is the element of *Slavery*. This was a necessary condition of an æsthetic democracy, where it was the right and duty of every citizen to deliver or to listen to orations respecting the management of the State in the place of public assembly, to take part in the exercise of the Gymnasia, and to join in the celebration of festivals. It was a necessary condition of such occupations,

that the citizens should be freed from handicraft occupations; consequently, that what among us is performed by free citizens —the work of daily life—should be done by slaves. Slavery does not cease until the Will has been infinitely self-reflected * —until Right is conceived as appertaining to every freeman, and the term freeman is regarded as a synonym for man in his generic nature as endowed with Reason. But here we still occupy the standpoint of Morality as mere Wont and Custom, and therefore known only as a peculiarity attaching to a certain kind of existence [not as absolute and universal Law].

3. It must also be remarked, thirdly, that such democratic constitutions are possible only in small states—states which do not much exceed the compass of cities. The whole Polis of the Athenians is united in the one city of Athens. Tradition tells that Theseus united the scattered Demes into an integral totality. In the time of Pericles, at the beginning of the Peloponnesian War, when the Spartans were marching upon Attica, its entire population took refuge in the city. Only in such cities can the interests of all be similar; in large empires, on the contrary, diverse and conflicting interests are sure to present themselves. The living together in one city, the fact that the inhabitants see each other daily, render a common culture and a *living* democratic polity possible. In Democracy, the main point is that the character of the citizen be plastic, all " of a piece." He must be present at the critical stages of public business; he must take part in decisive crises with his entire personality—not with his vote merely; he must mingle in the heat of action—the passion and interest of the whole man being absorbed in the affair, and the warmth with which a resolve was made being equally ardent during its execution. That unity of opinion to which the whole community must be brought [when any political step is to be taken,] must be produced in the individual members of the state by *oratorical suasion.* If this were attempted by *writing*—in an abstract, lifeless way—no general fervor would be excited among the social units; and the greater the number, the less weight would each individual vote have. In a large empire a general inquiry might be made, votes might be gathered in the several communities, and the results reckoned up—as was done by the French Convention. But a political existence of this kind is destitute of life, and the World

* That is—the Objective and the Subjective Will must be harmonized.—Ed.

is *ipso facto* broken into fragments and dissipated into a mere Paper-world. In the French Revolution, therefore, the republican constitution never actually became a Democracy: Tyranny, Despotism, raised its voice under the mask of Freedom and Equality.

We come now to the Second Period of Greek History. The first period saw the Greek Spirit attain its æsthetic development and reach maturity—realize its *essential being*. The second shows it manifesting itself—exhibits it in its full glory as producing a work for the world, asserting its principle in the struggle with an antagonistic force, and triumphantly maintaining it against that attack.

The Wars with the Persians

The period of contact with the preceding World-Historical people, is generally to be regarded as the *second* in the history of any nation. The World-Historical contact of the Greeks was with the Persians; in that, Greece exhibited itself in its most glorious aspect. The occasion of the Median wars was the revolt of the Ionian cities against the Persians, in which the Athenians and Eretrians assisted them. That which, in particular, induced the Athenians to take their part, was the circumstance that the son of Pisistratus, after his attempts to regain sovereignty in Athens had failed in Greece, had betaken himself to the King of the Persians. The Father of History has given us a brilliant description of these Median wars, and for the object we are now pursuing we need not dwell long upon them.

At the beginning of the Median wars, Lacedæmon was in possession of the Hegemony, partly as the result of having subjugated and enslaved the free nation of the Messenians, partly because it had assisted many Greek states to expel their Tyrants. Provoked by the part the Greeks had taken in assisting the Ionians against him, the Persian King sent heralds to the Greek cities to require them to give Water and Earth, *i.e.* to acknowledge his supremacy. The Persian envoys were contemptuously sent back, and the Lacedæmonians went so far as to throw them into a well—a deed, however, of which they afterwards so deeply repented, as to send two Lacedæmonians to Susa in expiation. The Persian King then despatched an army to invade Greece. With its vastly superior force the

Athenians and Platæans, without aid from their compatriots, contended at Marathon under Miltiades, and gained the victory. Afterwards, Xerxes came down upon Greece with his enormous masses of nations (Herodotus gives a detailed description of this expedition); and with the terrible array of land-forces was associated the not less formidable fleet. Thrace, Macedon, and Thessaly were soon subjugated; but the entrance into Greece Proper—the Pass of Thermopylæ—was defended by three hundred Spartans and seven hundred Thespians, whose fate is well known. Athens, voluntarily deserted by its inhabitants, was ravaged; the images of the gods which it contained were " an abomination " to the Persians, who worshipped the Amorphous, the Unformed. In spite of the disunion of the Greeks, the Persian fleet was beaten at Salamis; and this glorious battle-day presents the three greatest tragedians of Greece in remarkable chronological association: for Æschylus was one of the combatants, and helped to gain the victory, Sophocles danced at the festival that celebrated it, and on the same day Euripides was born. The host that remained in Greece, under the command of Mardonius, was beaten at Platæa by Pausanias, and the Persian power was consequently broken at various points.

Thus was Greece freed from the pressure which threatened to overwhelm it. Greater battles, unquestionably, have been fought; but these live immortal not in the historical records of Nations only, but also of Science and of Art—of the Noble and the Moral generally. For these are World-Historical victories; they were the salvation of culture and Spiritual vigor, and they rendered the Asiatic principle powerless. How often, on other occasions, have not men sacrificed everything for one grand object! How often have not warriors fallen for Duty and Country! But here we are called to admire not only valor, genius and spirit, but the purport of the contest—the effect, the result, which are unique in their kind. In all other battles a particular interest is predominant; but the immortal fame of the Greeks is none other than their due, in consideration of the noble cause for which deliverance was achieved. In the history of the world it is not the formal [subjective and individual] valor that has been displayed, not the so-called merit of the combatants, but the importance of the cause itself, that must decide the fame of the achievement. In the case before us, the interest of the World's History hung trembling in the balance. Oriental des potism—a world united under one lord and sovereign—on the one side, and separate states—insignificant in extent and resources, but animated by free individuality—on the other side, stood front to front in array of battle. Never in History has the superiority of spiritual power over material bulk—and that of no contemptible amount—been made so gloriously manifest. This war, and the subsequent development of the states which took the lead in it, is the most brilliant period of Greece. Everything which the Greek principle involved, then reached its perfect bloom and came into the light of day.

The Athenians continued their wars of conquest for a considerable time, and thereby attained a high degree of prosperity; while the Lacedæmonians, who had no naval power, remained quiet. The antagonism of Athens and Sparta now commences —a favorite theme for historical treatment. It may be asserted that it is an idle inquiry, which of these two states justly claims the superiority, and that the endeavor should rather be, to exhibit each as in its own department a necessary and worthy phase of the Greek Spirit. On Sparta's behalf, *e.g.* many categories may be referred to in which she displays excellence; strictness in point of morals, subjection to discipline, etc., may be advantageously cited. But the leading principle that characterizes this state is Political Virtue, which Athens and Sparta have, indeed, in common, but which in the one state developed itself to a work of Art, viz., Free Individuality—in the other retained its substantial form. Before we speak of the Peloponnesian War, in which the jealousy of Sparta and Athens broke out into a flame, we must exhibit more specifically the fundamental character of the two states—their distinctions in a political and moral respect.

Athens

We have already become acquainted with Athens as an asylum for the inhabitants of the other districts of Greece, in which a very mixed population was congregated. The various branches of human industry—agriculture, handicraft, and trade (especially by sea)—were united in Athens, but gave occasion to much dissension. An antagonism had early arisen between ancient and wealthy families and such as were poorer. Three parties, whose distinction had been grounded on their local position and the mode of life which that position suggested, were then fully recognized. These were, the Pediæans—inhabitants of the plain, the rich and aristocratic; the Diacrians—mountaineers, cultivators of the vine and olive, and herdsmen, who were the most numerous class; and between the two [in political status and sentiment], the Paralians—inhabitants of the coast—the moderate party. The polity of the state was wavering between Aristocracy and Democracy. Solon effected, by his division into four property-classes, a medium between these opposites. All these together formed the popular assembly for deliberation and decision on public affairs; but the offices of government were reserved for the three superior classes. It is remarkable that even while Solon was still living and actually present, and in spite of his opposition, Pisistratus acquired supremacy. The constitution had, as it were, not yet entered into the blood and life of the community; it had not yet become the habit of moral and civil existence. But it is still more remarkable that Pisistratus introduced no legislative changes, and that he presented himself before the Areopagus to answer an accusation brought against him. The rule of Pisistratus and of his sons appears to have been needed for repressing the power of great families and factions—for accustoming them to order and peace, and the citizens generally, on the other hand, to the Solonian legislation. This being accomplished, that rule was necessarily regarded as superfluous, and the principles of a free code enter into conflict with the power of the Pisistratidæ. The Pisistratidæ were expelled, Hipparchus killed, and Hippias banished. Then factions were revived; the Alcmæonidæ, who took the lead in the insurrection, favored Democracy; on the other hand, the Spartans aided the adverse party of Isagoras, which followed the aristocratic direction. The Alcmæonidæ, with Cleisthenes at their head, kept the upper hand. This leader made the constitution still more democratic than it had been; the φυλαί, of which hitherto there had been only four, were increased to ten, and this had the effect of diminishing the influence of the clans. Lastly, Pericles rendered the constitution yet more democratic by diminishing the essential dignity of the Areopagus, and bringing causes that had hitherto belonged to it, before the Demos and the [ordinary] tribunals. Pericles was a statesman of plastic * antique character: when

* " Plastic," intimating his absolute devotion to statesmanship; the latter not being a mere mechanical addition, but diffused as a vitalizing and *formative* power through the whole man. The same term is used below to distinguish

he devoted himself to public life, he renounced private life, withdrew from all feasts and banquets, and pursued without intermission his aim of being useful to the state—a course of conduct by which he attained such an exalted position, that Aristophanes calls him the Zeus of Athens. We cannot but admire him in the highest degree: he stood at the head of a light-minded but highly refined and cultivated people; the only means by which he could obtain influence and authority over them, was his personal character and the impression he produced of his being a thoroughly noble man, exclusively intent upon the weal of the State, and of superiority to his fellow-citizens in native genius and acquired knowledge. In force of individual character no statesman can be compared with him.

As a general principle, the Democratic Constitution affords the widest scope for the development of great political characters; for it excels all others in virtue of the fact that it not only *allows of* the display of their powers on the part of individuals, but *summons* them to use those powers for the general weal. At the same time, no member of the community can obtain influence unless he has the power of satisfying the intellect and judgment, as well as the passions and volatility of a cultivated people.

In Athens a vital freedom existed, and a vital equality of manners and mental culture; and if inequality of property could not be avoided, it nevertheless did not reach an extreme. Together with this equality, and within the compass of this freedom, all diversities of character and talent, and all variety of idiosyncrasy could assert themselves in the most unrestrained manner, and find the most abundant stimulus to development in its environment; for the predominant elements of Athenian existence were the independence of the social units, and a culture animated by the Spirit of Beauty. It was Pericles who originated the production of those eternal monuments of sculpture, whose scanty remains astonish posterity; it was before this people that the dramas of Æschylus and Sophocles were performed; and later on those of Euripides—which, however, do not exhibit the same plastic moral character, and in which the principle of corruption is more manifest. To this people were addressed the orations of Pericles: from it sprung a band of men whose genius

the vitalizing morality that pervades the dramas of Æschylus and Sophocles, from the abstract sentimentalities of Euripides.—Ed.

has become classical for all centuries; for to this number belong, besides those already named, Thucydides, Socrates, Plato, and Aristophanes—the last of whom preserved entire the political seriousness of his people at the time when it was being corrupted; and who, imbued with this seriousness, wrote and dramatized with a view to his country's weal. We recognize in the Athenians great industry, susceptibility to excitement, and development of individuality within the sphere of Spirit conditioned by the morality of Custom. The blame with which we find them visited in Xenophon and Plato, attaches rather to that later period when misfortune and the corruption of the democracy had already supervened. But if we would have the verdict of the Ancients on the political life of Athens, we must turn, not to Xenophon, nor even to Plato, but to those who had a thorough acquaintance with the state in its full vigor—who managed its affairs and have been esteemed its greatest leaders —*i.e.*, to its Statesmen. Among these, Pericles is the Zeus of the human Pantheon of Athens. Thucydides puts into his mouth the most profound description of Athenian life, on the occasion of the funeral obsequies of the warriors who fell in the second year of the Peloponnesian War. He proposes to show for what a city and in support of what interests they had died; and' this leads the speaker directly to the essential elements of the Athenian community. He goes on to paint the character of Athens, and what he says is most profoundly thoughtful, as well as most just and true. " We love the beautiful," he says, " but without ostentation or extravagance; we philosophize without being seduced thereby into effeminacy and inactivity (for when men give themselves up to Thought, they get further and further from the Practical—from activity for the public, for the common weal). We are bold and daring; but this courageous energy in action does not prevent us from giving ourselves an account of what we undertake (we have a clear consciousness respecting it); among other nations, on the contrary, martial daring has its basis in deficiency of culture: we know best how to distinguish between the agreeable and the irksome; notwithstanding which, we do not shrink from perils." Thus Athens exhibited the spectacle of a state whose existence was essentially directed to realizing the Beautiful, which had a thoroughly cultivated consciousness respecting the serious side of public affairs and the interests of Man's Spirit and Life, and united with that consciousness, hardy courage and practical ability.

Sparta

Here we witness on the other hand rigid abstract virtue—a life devoted to the State, but in which the activity and freedom of individuality are put in the background. The polity of Sparta is based on institutions which do full justice to the interest of the State, but whose object is a lifeless equality—not free movement. The very first steps in Spartan History are very different from the early stages of Athenian development. The Spartans were Dorians—the Athenians Ionians; and this national distinction has an influence on their Constitution also. In reference to the mode in which the Spartan State originated, we observe that the Dorians invaded the Peloponnesus with the Heracleidæ, subdued the indigenous tribes, and condemned them to slavery; for the Helots were doubtless aborigines. The fate that had befallen the Helots, was suffered at a later epoch by the Messenians; for inhuman severity of this order was innate in Spartan character. While the Athenians had a family-life, and slaves among them were inmates of the house, the relation of the Spartans to the subjugated race was one of even greater harshness than that of the Turks to the Greeks; a state of warfare was constantly kept up in Lacedæmon. In entering upon office, the Ephors made an unreserved declaration of war against the Helots, and the latter were habitually given up to the younger Spartans to be practised upon in their martial exercises. The Helots were on some occasions set free, and fought against the enemy; moreover, they displayed extraordinary valor in the ranks of the Spartans; but on their return they were butchered in the most cowardly and insidious way. As in a slave-ship the crew are constantly armed, and the greatest care is taken to prevent an insurrection, so the Spartans exercised a constant vigilance over the Helots, and were always in a condition of war, as against enemies.

Property in land was divided, even according to the constitution of Lycurgus (as Plutarch relates) into equal parts, of which 9,000 only belonged to the Spartans—i.e., the inhabitants of the city—and 30,000 to the Lacedæmonians or Periæci. At the same time it was appointed, in order to maintain this equality, that the portions of ground should not be sold. But how little such an institution avails to effect its object, is proved by the fact, that in the sequel Lacedæmon owed its ruin chiefly to the inequality of possessions. As daughters were capable of inheriting, many estates had come by marriage into the possession of a few families, and at last all the landed property was in the hands of a limited number; as if to show how foolish it is to attempt a forced equality—an attempt which, while ineffective in realizing its professed object, is also destructive of a most essential point of liberty—the free disposition of property. Another remarkable feature in the legislation of Lycurgus, is his forbidding all money except that made of iron—an enactment which necessitated the abolition of all foreign business and traffic. The Spartans moreover had no naval force—a force indispensable to the support and furtherance of commerce; and on occasions when such a force was required, they had to apply to the Persians for it.

It was with an especial view to promote similarity of manners, and a more intimate acquaintance of the citizens with each other, that the Spartans had meals in common—a community, however, which disparaged family life; for eating and drinking is a private affair, and consequently belongs to domestic retirement. It was so regarded among the Athenians; with them association was not material but spiritual, and even their banquets, as we see from Xenophon and Plato, had an intellectual tone. Among the Spartans, on the other hand, the costs of the common meal were met by the contributions of the several members, and he who was too poor to offer such a contribution was consequently excluded.

As to the Political Constitution of Sparta, its basis may be called democratic, but with considerable modifications which rendered it almost an Aristocracy and Oligarchy. At the head of the State were two Kings, at whose side was a Senate (γερουσία), chosen from the best men of the State, and which also performed the functions of a court of justice—deciding rather in accordance with moral and legal customs, than with written laws.* The γερουσία was also the highest State-Council —the Council of the Kings, regulating the most important affairs. Lastly, one of the highest magistracies was that of the *Ephors*, respecting whose election we have no definite informa-

---

* Otfried Müller, in his " History of the Dorians," gives too dignified an aspect to this fact; he says that Justice was, as it were, imprinted on their minds. But such an imprinting is always something indefinite; laws must be *written*, that it may be distinctly known what is forbidden and what is allowed.

tion; Aristotle says that the mode of choice was exceedingly childish. We learn from Aristotle that even persons without nobility or property could attain this dignity. The Ephors had full authority to convoke popular assemblies, to put resolutions to the vote, and to propose laws, almost in the same way as the *tribuni plebis* in Rome. Their power became tyrannical, like that which Robespierre and his party exercised for a time in France.

While the Lacedæmonians directed their entire attention to the State, Intellectual Culture—Art and Science—was not domiciled among them. The Spartans appeared to the rest of the Greeks, stiff, coarse, awkward beings, who could not transact business involving any degree of intricacy, or at least performed it very clumsily. Thucydides makes the Athenians say to the Spartans: " You have laws and customs which have nothing in common with others; and besides this, you proceed, when you go into other countries, neither in accordance with these, nor with the traditionary usages of Hellas." In their intercourse at home, they were, on the whole, honorable; but as regarded their conduct towards other nations, they themselves plainly declared that they held their own good pleasure for the Commendable, and what was advantageous for the Right. It is well known that in Sparta (as was also the case in Egypt) the taking away of the necessaries of life, under certain conditions, was permitted; only the thief must not allow himself to be discovered. Thus the two States, Athens and Sparta, stand in contrast with each other. The morality of the latter is rigidly directed to the maintenance of the State; in the former we find a similar ethical relation, but with a cultivated consciousness, and boundless activity in the production of the Beautiful—subsequently, of the True also.

This Greek morality, though extremely beautiful, attractive and interesting in its manifestation, is not the highest point of view for Spiritual self-consciousness. It wants the form of Infinity, the reflection of thought within itself, the emancipation from the Natural element—(the Sensuous that lurks in the character of Beauty and Divinity [as comprehended by the Greeks])—and from that immediacy, [that undeveloped simplicity,] which attaches to their ethics. Self-Comprehension on the part of Thought is wanting—illimitable Self-Consciousness—demanding, that what is regarded by me as Right and Morality should have its confirmation in myself—from the testimony of my own Spirit; that the Beautiful (the Idea as manifested in sensuous contemplation or conception) may also become the True—an inner, supersensuous world. The standpoint occupied by the Æsthetic Spiritual Unity which we have just described, could not long be the resting-place of Spirit; and the element in which further advance and corruption originated, was that of Subjectivity—inward morality, individual reflection, and an inner life generally. The perfect bloom of Greek life lasted only about sixty years—from the Median wars, B.C. 492, to the Peloponnesian War, B.C. 431. The principle of subjective morality which was inevitably introduced, became the germ of corruption, which, however, showed itself in a different form in Athens from that which it assumed in Sparta: in Athens, as levity in public conduct, in Sparta, as private depravation of morals. In their fall, the Athenians showed themselves not only amiable, but great and noble—to such a degree that we cannot but lament it; among the Spartans, on the contrary, the principle of subjectivity develops itself in vulgar greed, and issues in vulgar ruin.

The Peloponnesian War

The principle of corruption displayed itself first in the external political development—in the contest of the states of Greece with each other, and the struggle of factions within the cities themselves. The Greek Morality had made Hellas unfit to form one common state; for the dissociation of small states from each other, and the concentration in cities, where the interest and the spiritual culture pervading the whole, could be identical, was the necessary condition of that grade of Freedom which the Greeks occupied. It was only a momentary combination that occurred in the Trojan War, and even in the Median wars a union could not be accomplished. Although the tendency towards such a union is discoverable, the bond was but weak, its permanence was always endangered by jealousy, and the contest for the Hegemony set the States at variance with each other. A general outbreak of hostilities in the Peloponnesian War was the consummation. Before it, and even at its commencement, Pericles was at the head of the Athenian nation—that people most jealous of its liberty; it was only his elevated personality and great genius that enabled him to maintain his position. After the wars with the Medes, Athens enjoyed

the Hegemony; a number of allies—partly islands, partly towns
—were obliged to contribute to the supplies required for continuing the war against the Persians; and instead of the contribution being made in the form of fleets or troops, the subsidy
was paid in money. Thereby an immense power was concentrated in Athens; a part of the money was expended in great
architectural works, in the enjoyment of which, since they were
products of Spirit, the allies had some share. But that Pericles
did not devote the whole of the money to works of Art, but also
made provision for the Demos in other ways, was evident after
his death, from the quantity of stores amassed in several maga-
zines, but especially in the naval arsenal. Xenophon says:
" Who does not stand in need of Athens? Is she not indispensable to all lands that are rich in corn and herds, in oil and wine
—to all who wish to traffic either in money or in mind?—to
craftsmen, sophists, philosophers, poets, and all who desire what
is worth seeing or hearing in sacred and public matters? "

In the Peloponnesian War, the struggle was essentially between Athens and Sparta. Thucydides has left us the history
of the greater part of it, and his immortal work is the absolute
gain which humanity has derived from that contest. Athens
allowed herself to be hurried into the extravagant projects of
Alcibiades; and when these had already much weakened her,
she was compelled to succumb to the Spartans, who were guilty
of the treachery of applying for aid to Persia, and who obtained
from the King supplies of money and a naval force. They were
also guilty of a still more extensive treason, in abolishing democracy in Athens and in the cities of Greece generally, and in
giving a preponderance to factions that desired oligarchy, but
were not strong enough to maintain themselves without foreign
assistance. Lastly, in the peace of Antalcidas, Sparta put the
finishing stroke to her treachery, by giving over the Greek
cities in Asia Minor to Persian dominion.

Lacedæmon had therefore, both by the oligarchies which it
had set up in various countries, and by the garrisons which it
maintained in some cities—as, e.g., Thebes—obtained a great
preponderance in Greece. But the Greek states were far more
incensed at Spartan oppression than they had previously been
at Athenian supremacy. With Thebes at their head, they cast
off the yoke, and the Thebans became for a moment the most
distinguished people in Hellas. But it was to two distinguished

men among its citizens that Thebes owed its entire power—
Pelopidas and Epaminondas; as for the most part in that state
we find the Subjective preponderant. In accordance with this
principle, Lyrical Poetry—that which is the expression of subjectivity—especially flourished there; a kind of subjective
amenity of nature shows itself also in the so-called Sacred
Legion which formed the kernel of the Theban host, and was
regarded as consisting of persons connected by amatory bonds
[*amantes* and *amati*] ; while the influence of subjectivity among
them was especially proved by the fact, that after the death of
Epaminondas, Thebes fell back into its former position. Weakened and distracted, Greece could no longer find safety in itself,
and needed an authoritative prop. In the towns there were
incessant contests; the citizens were divided into factions, as
in the Italian cities of the Middle Ages. The victory of one
party entailed the banishment of the other; the latter then
usually applied to the enemies of their native city, to obtain
their aid in subjugating it by force of arms. The various States
could no longer co-exist peaceably: they prepared ruin for
each other, as well as for themselves.

We have, then, now to investigate the *corruption* of the Greek
world in its profounder import, and may denote the principle of
that corruption as *subjectivity obtaining emancipation for itself.*
We see Subjectivity obtruding itself in various ways. Thought
—the subjectively Universal—menaces the beautiful religion of
Greece, while the passions of individuals and their caprice men-
ace its political constitution. In short, Subjectivity, comprehending and manifesting itself, threatens the existing state of
things in every department—characterized as that state of
things is by Immediacy [a primitive, unreflecting simplicity].
Thought, therefore, appears here as the principle of decay—
decay, viz. of Substantial [prescriptive] morality; for it introduces an antithesis, and asserts essentially rational principles.
In the Oriental states, in which there is no such antithesis,
moral freedom cannot be realized, since the highest principle is
[Pure] Abstraction. But when Thought recognizes its positive
character, as in Greece, it establishes principles; and these bear
to the real world the relation of Essence to Form. For the
concrete vitality found among the Greeks, is Customary Morality—a life for Religion, for the State, without further reflection,
and without analysis leading to abstract definitions, which must

lead away from the concrete embodiment of them, and occupy an antithetical position to that embodiment. Law is part of the existing state of things, with Spirit *implicit* in it. But as soon as Thought arises, it investigates the various political constitutions: as the result of its investigation it forms for itself an idea of an improved state of society, and demands that this ideal should take the place of things as they are.

In the principle of Greek Freedom, inasmuch as it is Freedom, is involved the self-emancipation of Thought. We observed the dawn of Thought in the circle of men mentioned above under their well-known appellation of the Seven Sages. It was they who first uttered general propositions; though at that time wisdom consisted rather in a concrete insight [into things, than in the power of abstract conception]. Parallel with the advance in the development of Religious Art and with political growth, we find a progressive strengthening of Thought, its enemy and destroyer; and at the time of the Peloponnesian War science was already developed. With the Sophists began the process of reflection on the existing state of things, and of ratiocination. That very diligence and activity which we observed among the Greeks in their practical life, and in the achievement of works of art, showed itself also in the turns and windings which these ideas took; so that, as material things are changed, worked up and used for other than their original purposes, similarly the essential being of Spirit—what is thought and known—is variously handled; it is made an object about which the mind can employ itself, and this occupation becomes an interest in and for itself. The movement of Thought—that which goes on within its sphere [without reference to an extrinsic object]—a process which had formerly no interest—acquires attractiveness on its own account. The cultivated Sophists, who were not erudite or scientific men, but masters of subtle turns of thought, excited the admiration of the Greeks. For all questions they had an answer; for all interests of a political or religious order they had general points of view; and in the ultimate development of their art, they claimed the ability to prove everything, to discover a justifiable side in every position. In a democracy it is a matter of the first importance, to be able to speak in popular assemblies—to urge one's opinions on public matters. Now this demands the power of duly presenting before them that point of view which we desire them to regard as essential. For such a purpose, intellectual culture is needed, and this discipline the Greeks acquired under their Sophists. This mental culture then became the means, in the hands of those who possessed it, of enforcing their views and interests on the Demos: the expert Sophist knew how to turn the subject of discussion this way or that way at pleasure, and thus the doors were thrown wide open to all human passions. A leading principle of the Sophists was, that " Man is the measure of all things "; but in this, as in all their apophthegms, lurks an ambiguity, since the term " Man " may denote Spirit in its depth and truth, or in the aspect of mere caprice and private interest. The Sophists meant Man simply as subjective, and intended in this dictum of theirs, that mere liking was the principle of Right, and that advantage to the individual was the ground of final appeal. This Sophistic principle appears again and again, though under different forms, in various periods of History; thus even in our own times subjective opinion of what is right —mere feeling—is made the ultimate ground of decision.

In Beauty, as the Greek principle, there was a concrete unity of Spirit, united with Reality, with Country and Family, etc. In this unity no fixed point of view had as yet been adopted within the Spirit itself, and Thought, as far as it transcended this unity, was still swayed by mere liking; [the Beautiful, the Becoming (τὸ πρέπον) conducted men in the path of moral propriety, but apart from this they had no firm abstract principle of Truth and Virtue]. But Anaxagoras himself had taught, that Thought itself was the absolute Essence of the World. And it was in *Socrates*, that at the beginning of the Peloponnesian War, the principle of subjectivity—of the absolute inherent independence of Thought—attained free expression. He taught that man has to discover and recognize in himself what is the Right and Good, and that this Right and Good is in its nature universal. Socrates is celebrated as a Teacher of Morality, but we should rather call him the *Inventor of Morality*. The Greeks had a *customary* morality; but Socrates undertook to teach them what moral virtues, duties, etc. were. The moral man is not he who merely wills and does that which is right—not the merely innocent man—but he who has the consciousness of what he is doing.

Socrates—in assigning to insight, to conviction, the determination of men's actions—posited the Individual as capable of a final moral decision, in contraposition to Country and to Customary Morality, and thus made himself an Oracle, in the Greek sense. He said that he had a δαιμόνιον within him, which counselled him what to do, and revealed to him what was advantageous to his friends. The rise of the inner world of Subjectivity was the rupture with the existing Reality. Though Socrates himself continued to perform his duties as a citizen, it was not the actual State and its religion, but the world of Thought that was his true home. Now the question of the existence and nature of the gods came to be discussed. The disciple of Socrates, Plato, banished from his ideal state, Homer and Hesiod, the originators of that mode of conceiving of religious objects which prevailed among the Greeks; for he desiderated a higher conception of what was to be reverenced as divine—one more in harmony with Thought. Many citizens now seceded from practical and political life, to live in the ideal world. The principle of Socrates manifests a revolutionary aspects towards the Athenian State; for the peculiarity of this State was, that Customary Morality was the form in which its existence was moulded, viz.—an inseparable connection of Thought with actual life. When Socrates wishes to induce his friends to reflection, the discourse has always a negative tone; he brings them to the consciousness that they do not know what the Right is. But when on account of the giving utterance to that principle which was advancing to recognition, Socrates is condemned to death, the sentence bears on the one hand the aspect of unimpeachable rectitude—inasmuch as the Athenian people condemns its deadliest foe—but on the other hand, that of a deeply tragical character, inasmuch as the Athenians had to make the discovery, that what they reprobated in Socrates had already struck firm root among themselves, and that they must be pronounced guilty or innocent with him. With this feeling they condemned the accusers of Socrates, and declared him guiltless. In Athens that higher principle which proved the ruin of the Athenian state, advanced in its development without intermission. Spirit had acquired the propensity to gain satisfaction for itself—to reflect. Even in decay the Spirit of Athens appears majestic, because it manifests itself as the free, the liberal—exhibiting its successive phases in their pure idiosyncrasy—in that form in which they really exist. Amiable and cheerful even in the midst of tragedy is the light-hearted-ness and nonchalance with which the Athenians accompany their [national] morality to its grave. We recognize the higher interest of the new culture in the fact that the people made themselves merry over their own follies, and found great entertainment in the comedies of Aristophanes, which have the severest satire for their contents, while they bear the stamp of the most unbridled mirth.

In Sparta the same corruption is introduced, since the social unit seeks to assert his individuality against the moral life of the community: but there we have merely the isolated side of particular subjectivity—corruption in its undisguised form, blank immorality, vulgar selfishness and venality. All these passions manifest themselves in Sparta, especially in the persons of its generals, who, for the most part living at a distance from their country, obtain an opportunity of securing advantages at the expense of their own state as well as of those to whose assistance they are sent.

The Macedonian Empire

After the fall of Athens, Sparta took upon herself the Hegemony; but misused it—as already mentioned—so selfishly, that she was universally hated. Thebes could not long sustain the part of humiliating Sparta, and was at last exhausted in the war with the Phocians. The Spartans and the Phocians—the former because they had surprised the citadel of Thebes, the latter because they had tilled a piece of land belonging to the Delphin Apollo—had been sentenced to pay considerable sums of money. Both states however refused payment; for the Amphictyonic Council had not much more authority than the old German Diet, which the German princes obeyed only so far as suited their inclination. The Phocians were then to be punished by the Thebans; but by an egregious piece of violence—by desecrating and plundering the temple at Delphi—the former attained momentary superiority. This deed completes the ruin of Greece; the sanctuary was desecrated, the god so to speak, killed; the last support of unity was thereby annihilated; reverence for that which in Greece had been as it were always the final arbiter—its monarchical principle—was displaced, insulted, and trodden under foot.

The next step in advance is then that quite simple one, that the place of the dethroned oracle should be taken by another deciding will—a *real* authoritative *royalty*. The foreign Macedonian King—Philip—undertook to avenge the violation of the oracle, and forthwith took its place, by making himself lord of Greece. Philip reduced under his dominion the Hellenic States, and convinced them that it was all over with their independence, and that they could no longer maintain their own footing. The charge of littleness, harshness, violence, and political treachery —all those hateful characteristics with which Philip has so often been reproached—did not extend to the young Alexander, when he placed himself at the head of the Greeks. He had no need to incur such reproaches; he had not to form a military force, for he found one already in existence. As he had only to mount Bucephalus, and take the rein in hand, to make him obsequious to his will, just so he found that Macedonian phalanx prepared for his purpose—that rigid well-trained iron mass, the power of which had been demonstrated under Philip, who copied it from Epaminondas.

Alexander had been educated by the deepest and also the most comprehensive thinker of antiquity—Aristotle; and the education was worthy of the man who had undertaken it. Alexander was initiated into the profoundest metaphysics: therefore his nature was thoroughly refined and liberated from the customary bonds of mere opinion, crudities and idle fancies. Aristotle left this grand nature as untrammelled as it was before his instructions commenced; but impressed upon it a deep perception of what the True is, and formed the spirit which nature had so richly endowed, to a plastic being, rolling freely like an orb through its circumambient ether.

Thus accomplished, Alexander placed himself at the head of the Hellenes, in order to lead Greece over into Asia. A youth of twenty, he commanded a thoroughly experienced army, whose generals were all veterans, well versed in the art of war. It was Alexander's aim to avenge Greece for all that Asia had inflicted upon it for so many years, and to fight out at last the ancient feud and contest between the East and the West. While in this struggle he retaliated upon the Oriental world what Greece had suffered from it, he also made a return for the rudiments of culture which had been derived thence, by spreading the maturity and culmination of that culture over the East; and, as it were, changed the stamp of subjugated Asia and assimilated it to a Hellenic land. The grandeur and the interest of this work were proportioned to his genius—to his peculiar youthful individuality—the like of which in so beautiful a form we have not seen a second time at the head of such an undertaking. For not only were the genius of a commander, the greatest spirit, and consummate bravery united in him, but all these qualities were dignified by the beauty of his character as a man and an individual. Though his generals are devoted to him, they had been the long tried servants of his father; and this made his position difficult: for his greatness and youth, is a humiliation to them, as inclined to regard themselves and the achievements of the past, as a complete work; so that while their envy, as in Clitus's case, arose to blind rage, Alexander also was excited to great violence.

Alexander's expedition to Asia was at the same time a journey of discovery; for it was he who first opened the Oriental World to the Europeans, and penetrated into countries—as *e.g.* Bactria, Sogdiana, northern India—which have since been hardly visited by Europeans. The arrangement of the march, and not less the military genius displayed in the disposition of battles, and in tactics generally, will always remain an object of admiration. He was great as a commander in battles, wise in conducting marches and marshalling troops, and the bravest soldier in the thick of the fight. Even the death of Alexander, which occurred at Babylon in the three and thirtieth year of his age, gives us a beautiful spectacle of his greatness, and shows in what relation he stood to his army: for he takes leave of it with the perfect consciousness of his dignity.

Alexander had the good fortune to die at the proper time; *i.e.* it may be called good fortune, but it is rather a necessity. That he may stand before the eyes of posterity as a youth, an early death must hurry him away. Achilles, as remarked above, *begins* the Greek World, and his antitype Alexander *concludes* it: and these youths not only supply a picture of the fairest kind in their own persons, but at the same time afford a complete and perfect type of Hellenic existence. Alexander finished his work and completed his ideal; and thus bequeathed to the world one of the noblest and most brilliant of visions, which our poor reflections only serve to obscure. For the great World-Historical form of Alexander, the modern standard applied by recent historical " Philistines "—that of virtue or morality—will by no means suffice. And if it be alleged in depreciation of his merit, that he had no successor, and left behind no dynasty, we may remark that the Greek kingdoms that arose in Asia after him, are his dynasty. For two years he was engaged in a campaign in Bactria, which brought him into contact with the Massagetæ and Scythians; and there arose the Græco-Bactrian kingdom which lasted for two centuries. Thence the Greeks came into connection with India, and even with China. The Greek dominion spread itself over northern India, and Sandrokottus (Chandraguptas) is mentioned as the first who emancipated himself from it. The same name presents itself indeed among the Hindoos, but for reasons already stated, we can place very little dependence upon such mention. Other Greek Kingdoms arose in Asia Minor, in Armenia, in Syria and Babylonia. But Egypt especially, among the kingdoms of the successors of Alexander, became a great centre of science and art; for a great number of its architectural works belong to the time of the Ptolemies, as has been made out from the deciphered inscriptions. Alexandria became the chief centre of commerce— the point of union for Eastern manners and tradition with Western civilization. Besides these, the Macedonian Kingdom, that of Thrace, stretching beyond the Danube, that of Illyria, and that of Epirus, flourished under the sway of Greek princes.

Alexander was also extraordinarily attached to the sciences, and he is celebrated as next to Pericles the most liberal patron of the arts. *Meier* says in his " History of Art," that his intelligent love of art would have secured him an immortality of fame not less than his conquests.

SECTION III

THE FALL OF THE GREEK SPIRIT

THIS third period in the history of the Hellenic World, which embraces the protracted development of the evil destiny of Greece, interests us less. Those who had been Alexander's Generals, now assuming an independent appearance on the stage of history as Kings, carried on long wars with each other, and experienced, almost all of them, the most romantic revolutions of fortune. Especially remarkable and prominent in this respect is the life of Demetrius Poliorcetes.

In Greece the States had preserved their existence: brought to a consciousness of their weakness by Philip and Alexander, they contrived to enjoy an apparent vitality, and boasted of an unreal independence. That self-consciousness which independence confers, they could not have; and diplomatic statesmen took the lead in the several States—orators who were not at the same time generals, as was the case formerly—*e.g.* in the person of Pericles. The countries of Greece now assume various relations to the different monarchs, who continued to contend for the sovereignty of the Greek States—partly also for their favor, especially for that of Athens: for Athens still presented an imposing figure—if not as a Power, yet certainly as the centre of the higher arts and sciences, especially of Philosophy and Rhetoric. Besides it kept itself more free from the gross excess, coarseness and passions which prevailed in the other States, and made them contemptible; and the Syrian and Egyptian kings deemed it an honor to make Athens large presents of corn and other useful supplies. To some extent too the kings of the period reckoned it their greatest glory to render and to keep the Greek cities and states independent. The *Emancipation of Greece* had as it were, become the general watch-word; and it passed for a high title of fame to be called the *Deliverer* of Greece. If we examine the hidden political bearing of this word, we shall find that it denotes the prevention of any indigenous Greek State from obtaining decided superiority, and keeping all in a state of weakness by separation and disorganization.

The special peculiarity by which each Greek State was distinguished from the others, consisted in a difference similar to that of their glorious divinities, each one of whom has his particular character and peculiar being, yet so that this peculiarity does not derogate from the divinity common to all. When therefore, this divinity has become weak and has vanished from the States, nothing but the bare particularity remains—the repulsive speciality which obstinately and waywardly asserts itself, and which on that very account assumes a position of absolute dependence and of conflict with others. Yet the feeling of weakness and misery led to combinations here and there. The *Ætolians* and their allies as a predatory people, set up injustice, violence, fraud, and insolence to others, as their charter of rights. Sparta was governed by infamous tyrants and odious passions, and in this condition was dependent on the Macedonian Kings. The Bœotian subjective character had, after the extinction of Theban glory, sunk down into indolence and the vulgar desire of coarse sensual enjoyment. The *Achæan* league distinguished itself by the aim of its union (the expulsion of Tyrants,) by rectitude and the sentiment of community. But this too was obliged to take refuge in the most complicated policy. What we see here on the whole, is a *diplomatic* condition—an infinite involvement with the most manifold foreign interests—a subtle intertexture and play of parties, whose threads are continually being combined anew.

In the internal condition of the states, which, enervated by selfishness and debauchery, were broken up into factions—each of which on the other hand directs its attention to foreign lands, and with treachery to its native country begs for the favors of the Kings—the point of interest is no longer the fate of these states, but the great *individuals*, who arise amid the general corruption, and honorably devote themselves to their country. They appear as great tragic characters, who with their genius, and the most intense exertion, are yet unable to extirpate the evils in question; and perish in the struggle, without having had the satisfaction of restoring to their fatherland, repose, order and freedom, nay, even without having secured a reputation with posterity free from all stain. Livy says in his prefatory remarks: " In our times we can neither endure our faults nor the means of correcting them." And this is quite as applicable to these Last of the Greeks, who began an undertaking which was as honorable and noble, as it was sure of being frustrated. Agis and Cleomenes, Aratus and Philopœmen, thus sunk under the struggle for the good of their nation. Plutarch sketches for us a highly characteristic picture of these times, in giving us a representation of the importance of individuals during their continuance.

The third period of the history of the Greeks brings us to their contact with that people which was to play the next part on the theatre of the World's History; and the chief excuse for this contact was—as pretexts had previously been—the liberation of Greece. After Perseus the last Macedonian King, in the year 168 B.C. had been conquered by the Romans and brought in triumph to Rome, the Achæan league was attacked and broken up, and at last in the year 146 B.C. Corinth was destroyed. Looking at Greece as Polybius describes it, we see how a noble nature such as his, has nothing left for it but to despair at the state of affairs and to retreat into Philosophy; or if it attempts to act, can only die in the struggle. In deadly contraposition to the multiform variety of passion which Greece presents—that distracted condition which whelms good and evil in one common ruin—stands a blind fate—an iron power ready to show up that degraded condition in all its weakness, and to dash it to pieces in miserable ruin; for cure, amendment, and consolation are impossible. And this crushing Destiny is the *Roman power.*

PART III

THE ROMAN WORLD

NAPOLEON, in a conversation which he once had with Goethe on the nature of Tragedy, expressed the opinion that its modern phase differed from the ancient, through our no longer recognizing a Destiny to which men are absolutely subject, and that Policy occupies the place of the ancient Fate [*La politique est la fatalité*]. This therefore he thought must be used as the modern form of Destiny in Tragedy—the irresistible power of circumstances to which individuality must bend. Such a power is the *Roman World*, chosen for the very purpose of casting the moral units into bonds, as also of collecting all Deities and all Spirits into the Pantheon of Universal dominion, in order to make out of them an abstract universality of power. The distinction between the Roman and the Persian principle is exactly this—that the former stifles all vitality, while the latter allowed of its existence in the fullest measure. Through its being the aim of the State, that the social units in their moral life should be sacrificed to it, the world is sunk in melancholy: its heart is broken, and it is all over with the Natural side of Spirit, which has sunk into a feeling of unhappiness. Yet only from this feeling could arise the supersensuous, the free Spirit in Christianity.

In the Greek principle we have seen spiritual existence in its exhilaration—its cheerfulness and enjoyment: Spirit had not yet drawn back into abstraction; it was still involved with the Natural element—the idiosyncrasy of individuals;—on which account the virtues of individuals themselves became moral works of art. Abstract universal Personality had not yet appeared, for Spirit must first develop itself to that form of abstract Universality which exercised the severe discipline over humanity now under consideration. Here, in Rome, then, we find that free universality, that abstract Freedom, which on the one hand sets an abstract state, a political constitution and power, over *concrete* individuality; on the other side creates a personality in opposition to that universality—the inherent freedom of the *abstract* Ego, which must be distinguished from individual idiosyncrasy. For Personality constitutes the fundamental condition of legal Right: it appears chiefly in the category of Property, but it is indifferent to the concrete characteristics of the living Spirit with which individuality is concerned. These two elements, which constitute Rome—political Universality on the one hand, and the abstract freedom of the individual on the other—appear, in the first instance, in the form of Subjectivity. This Subjectivity—this retreating into one's self which we observed as the corruption of the Greek Spirit—becomes here the ground on which a new side of the World's History arises. In considering the Roman World, we have not to do with a concretely spiritual life, rich in itself; but the world-historical element in it is the *abstractum* of Universality, and the object which is pursued with soulless and heartless severity, is mere *dominion*, in order to enforce that *abstractum*.

In Greece, *Democracy* was the fundamental condition of political life, as in the East, *Despotism;* here we have *Aristocracy* of a rigid order, in a state of opposition to the people. In Greece also the Democracy was rent asunder, but only in the way of factions; in Rome it is principles that keep the entire community in a divided state—they occupy a hostile position towards, and struggle with each other: first the Aristocracy with the Kings, then the Plebs with the Aristocracy, till Democracy gets the upper hand; then first arise factions in which originated that later aristocracy of commanding individuals which subjugated the world. It is this dualism that, properly speaking, marks Rome's inmost being.

Erudition has regarded the Roman History from various points of view, and has adopted very different and opposing opinions: this is especially the case with the more ancient part of the history, which has been taken up by three different classes of literati—Historians, Philologists, and Jurists. The Historians hold to the grand features, and show respect for the history as such; so that we may after all see our way best under their guidance, since they allow the validity of the records in the case of leading events. It is otherwise with the Philologists.

by whom generally received traditions are less regarded, and who devote more attention to small details which can be combined in various ways. These combinations gain a footing first as historical hypotheses, but soon after as established facts. To the same degree as the Philologists in their department, have the Jurists in that of Roman law, instituted the minutest examination and involved their inferences with hypothesis. The result is that the most ancient part of Roman History has been declared to be nothing but fable; so that this department of inquiry is brought entirely within the province of learned criticism, which always finds the most to do where the least is to be got for the labor. While on the one side the poetry and the myths of the Greeks are said to contain profound historical truths, and are thus transmuted into history, the Romans on the contrary have myths and poetical views affiliated upon them; and epopees are affirmed to be at the basis of what has been hitherto taken for prosaic and historical.

With these preliminary remarks we proceed to describe the *Locality*.

The Roman World has its centre in Italy; which is extremely similar to Greece, and, like it, forms a peninsula, only not so deeply indented. Within this country, the city of Rome itself formed the centre of the centre. Napoleon in his Memoirs takes up the question, which city—if Italy were independent and formed a totality—would be best adapted for its capital. Rome, Venice, and Milan may put forward claims to the honor; but it is immediately evident that none of these cities would supply a centre. Northern Italy constitutes a basin of the river Po, and is quite distinct from the body of the peninsula; Venice is connected only with Higher Italy, not with the south; Rome, on the other hand, would, perhaps, be naturally a centre for Middle and Lower Italy, but only artificially and violently for those lands which were subjected to it in Higher Italy. The Roman State rests geographically, as well as historically, on the element of force.

The locality of Italy, then, presents no natural unity—as the valley of the Nile; the unity was similar to that which Macedonia by its sovereignty gave to Greece; though Italy wanted that permeation by one spirit, which Greece possessed through equality of culture; for it was inhabited by very various races. Niebuhr has prefaced his Roman history by a profoundly erudite treatise on the peoples of Italy; but from which no connection between them and the Roman History is visible. In fact, Niebuhr's History can only be regarded as a *criticism* of Roman History, for it consists of a series of treatises which by no means possess the unity of history.

We observed subjective inwardness as the general principle of the Roman World. The course of Roman History, therefore, involves the expansion of undeveloped subjectivity—inward conviction of existence—to the visibility of the real world. The principle of subjective inwardness receives positive application in the first place only from without—through the particular volition of the sovereignty, the government, etc. The development consists in the purification of inwardness to abstract personality, which gives itself reality in the existence of private property; the mutually repellent social units can then be held together only by despotic power. The general course of the Roman World may be defined as this; the transition from the inner sanctum of subjectivity to its direct opposite. The development is here not of the same kind as that in Greece—the unfolding and expanding of its own substance on the part of the principle; but it is the transition to its opposite, which latter does not appear as an element of corruption, but is demanded and posited by the principle itself.—As to the particular sections of the Roman History, the common division is that into the Monarchy, the Republic, and the Empire—as if in these forms different principles made their appearance; but the same principle—that of the Roman Spirit—underlies their development. In our division, we must rather keep in view the course of History generally. The annals of every World-historical people were divided above into three periods, and this statement must prove itself true in this case also. *The first period* comprehends the rudiments of Rome, in which the elements which are essentially opposed, still repose in calm unity; until the contrarieties have acquired strength, and the unity of the State becomes a powerful one, through that antithetical condition having been produced and maintained within it. In this vigorous condition the State directs its forces outwards—*i.e.*, in the *second period*—and makes its *début* on the theatre of general history; this is the noblest period of Rome—the Punic Wars and the contact with the antecedent World-Historical people. A wider stage is opened, towards the East; the history at the epoch of this contact has been treated by the noble Polybius. The Roman Empire now acquired that world-conquering extension which paved the way for its fall. Internal distraction supervened, while the antithesis was developing itself to self-contradiction and utter incompatibility; it closes with Despotism, which marks the *third period*. The Roman power appears here in its pomp and splendor; but it is at the same time profoundly ruptured within itself, and the Christian Religion, which begins with the imperial dominion, receives a great extension. The third period comprises the contact of Rome with the North and the German peoples, whose turn is now come to play their part in History.

SECTION I

ROME TO THE TIME OF THE SECOND PUNIC WAR

Chapter I.—The Elements of the Roman Spirit

BEFORE we come to the Roman History, we have to consider the *Elements of the Roman Spirit* in general, and mention and investigate the origin of Rome with a reference to them. Rome arose *outside recognized countries,* viz., in an angle where three different districts met—those of the Latins, Sabines and Etruscans; it was not formed from some ancient stem, connected by natural patriarchal bonds, whose origin might be traced up to remote times (as seems to have been the case with the Persians, who, however, even then ruled a large empire); but Rome was from the very beginning, of artificial and violent, not spontaneous growth. It is related that the descendants of the Trojans, led by Æneas to Italy, founded Rome; for the connection with Asia was a much cherished tradition, and there are in Italy, France, and Germany itself (Xanten) many towns which refer their origin, or their names, to the fugitive Trojans. Livy speaks of the ancient tribes of Rome, the Ramnenses, Titienses, and Luceres. Now if we look upon these as distinct nations, and assert that they were really the elements from which Rome was formed—a view which in recent times has very often striven to obtain currency—we directly subvert the historical tradition. All historians agree that at an early period, shepherds, under the leadership of chieftains, roved about on the hills of Rome; that the first Roman community constituted itself as a predatory state; and that it was with difficulty that the scattered inhabitants of the vicinity were thus united. The details of these circumstances are also given Those predatory shepherds received every contribution to their community that chose to join them (Livy calls it a *colluvies*). The rabble of all the three districts between which Rome lay, was collected in the new city. The historians state that this point was very well chosen on a hill close to the river, and particularly adapted to make it an asylum for all delinquents. It is equally historical that in the newly formed state there were no women, and that the neighboring states would enter into no *connubia* with it: both circumstances characterize it as predatory union, with which the other states wished to have no connection. They also refused the invitation to their religious festivals; and only the Sabines—a simple agricultural people, among whom, as Livy says, prevailed a *tristis atque tetrica superstitio*—partly from superstition, partly from fear, presented themselves at them. The seizure of the Sabine women is also a universally received historical fact. This circumstance itself involves a very characteristic feature, *viz.*, that Religion is used as a means for furthering the purposes of the infant State. Another method of extension was the conveying to Rome of the inhabitants of neighboring and conquered towns. At a later date there was also a voluntary migration of foreigners to Rome; as in the case of the so celebrated family of the Claudii, bringing their whole clientela. The Corinthian Demaratus, belonging to a family of consideration, had settled in Etruria; but as being an exile and a foreigner, he was little respected there, and his son, Lucumo, could no longer endure this degradation. He betook himself to Rome, says Livy, because a *new* people and a *repentin a atque ex virtute nobilitas* were to be found there. Lucumo attained, we are told, such a degree of respect, that he afterwards became king.

It is this peculiarity in the founding of the State which must be regarded as the essential basis of the idiosyncrasy of Rome. For it directly involves the severest discipline, and self-sacrifice to the grand object of the union. A State which had first to form itself, and which is based on force, must be held together by force. It is not a moral, liberal connection, but a compulsory condition of subordination, that results from such an origin. The Roman *virtus* is valor; not, however, the merely personal, but that which is essentially connected with a union of associates; which union is regarded as the supreme interest, and may be combined with lawless violence of all kinds. While the Romans formed a union of this kind, they were not, indeed, like the Lacedæmonians, engaged in an internal contest with a conquered and subjugated people; but there arose a distinction and a struggle between *Patricians* and *Plebeians*. This distinction was mythically adumbrated in the hostile brothers, Romulus and Remus. Remus was buried on the Aventine mount; this is consecrated to the evil genii, and to it are directed the Secessions of the Plebs. The question comes, then, how this distinction originated? It has been already said, that Rome was formed by robber-herdsmen, and the concourse of rabble of all sorts. At a later date, the inhabitants of captured and destroyed towns were also conveyed thither. The weaker, the poorer, the later additions of population are naturally underrated by, and in a condition of dependence upon those who originally founded the state, and those who were distinguished by valor, and also by wealth. It is not necessary, therefore, to take refuge in a hypothesis which has recently been a favorite one—that the Patricians formed a particular race.

The dependence of the Plebeians on the Patricians is often represented as a perfectly legal relation—indeed, even a sacred one; since the patricians had the *sacra* in their hands, while the plebs would have been godless, as it were, without them. The plebeians left to the patricians their hypocritical stuff (*ad decipiendam plebem*, Cic.) and cared nothing for their sacra and auguries; but in disjoining political rights from these ritual observances, and making good their claim to those rights, they were no more guilty of a presumptuous sacrilege than the Protestants, when they emancipated the political power of the State, and asserted the freedom of conscience. The light in which, as previously stated, we must regard the relation of the Patricians and Plebeians is, that those who were poor, and consequently helpless, were compelled to attach themselves to the richer and more respectable, and to seek for their *patrocinium:* in this relation of protection on the part of the more wealthy, the protected are called *clientes*. But we find very soon a fresh distinction between the plebs and the clientes. In the contentions between the patricians and the plebeians, the clientes held to their patroni, though belonging to the plebs as decidedly as any class. That this relation of the clientes had not the stamp of right and law is evident from the fact, that with the introduction and knowledge of the laws among all classes, the cliental relation gradually vanished; for as soon as individuals found protection in the law, the temporary necessity for it could not but cease.

In the first predatory period of the state, every citizen was necessarily a soldier, for the state was based on war; this burden was oppressive, since every citizen was obliged to maintain himself in the field. This circumstance, therefore, gave rise to the contracting of enormous debts—the patricians becoming the creditors of the plebeians. With the introduction of laws, this arbitrary relation necessarily ceased; but only gradually, for the patricians were far from being immediately inclined to release the plebs from the cliental relation; they rather strove to render it permanent. The laws of the Twelve Tables still contained much that was undefined; very much was still left to the arbitrary will of the judge—the patricians alone being judges; the antithesis, therefore, between patricians and plebeians, continues till a much later period. Only by degrees do the plebeians scale all the heights of official station, and attain those privileges which formerly belonged to the patricians alone.

In the life of the Greeks, although it did not any more than that of the Romans originate in the patriarchal relation, *Family* love and the Family tie appeared at its very commencement, and the peaceful aim of their social existence had for its necessary condition the extirpation of freebooters both by sea and land. The founders of Rome, on the contrary—Romulus and Remus —are, according to the tradition, themselves freebooters—represented as from their earliest days thrust out from the Family, and as having grown up in a state of isolation from family affection. In like manner, the first Romans are said to have got their wives, not by free courtship and reciprocated inclination, but by force. This commencement of the Roman life in savage rudeness excluding the sensibilities of natural morality, brings with it one characteristic element—harshness in respect to the family relation; a selfish harshness, which constituted the fundamental condition of Roman manners and laws, as we observe them in the sequel. We thus find family relations among the Romans not as a beautiful, free relation of love and feeling; the place of confidence is usurped by the principle of severity, dependence, and subordination. Marriage, in its strict and formal shape, bore quite the aspect of a mere contract; the wife was part of the husband's property (*in manum conventio*), and the marriage ceremony was based on a *coemtio*, in a form such as might have been adopted on the occasion of any other purchase. The husband acquired a power over his wife, such as he had over his daughter; nor less over her property; so that everything which she gained, she gained for her husband. During the good times of the republic, the celebration of marriages included a religious ceremony—" confarreatio "—but which was omitted at a later period. The husband obtained not less power than by the *coemtio*, when he married according to the form called " usus " that is, when the wife remained in the house of her husband without having been absent a " trinoctium " in a year. If the husband had not married in one of the forms of the " in manum conventio," the wife remained either in the power of her father, or under the guardianship of her " agnates," and was free as regarded her husband. The Roman matron, therefore, obtained honor and dignity only through independence of her husband, instead of acquiring her honor through her husband and by marriage. If a husband who had married under the freer condition —that is, when the union was not consecrated by the " confarreatio "—wished to separate from his wife, he dismissed her without further ceremony. The relation of sons was perfectly similar: they were, on the one hand, about as dependent on the paternal power as the wife on the matrimonial; they could not possess property—it made no difference whether they filled a high office in the State or not (though the " *peculia castrensia*," and " *adventitia* " were differently regarded); but on the other hand, when they were emancipated, they had no connection with their father and their family. An evidence of the degree in which the position of children was regarded as analogous to that of slaves, is presented in the " *imaginaria servitus (mancipium)*," through which emancipated children had to pass. In reference to inheritance, morality would seem to demand that children should share equally. Among the Romans, on the contrary, testamentary caprice manifests itself in its harshest form.

Thus perverted and demoralized, do we here see the fundamental relations of ethics. The immoral active severity of the Romans in this private side of character, necessarily finds its counterpart in the passive severity of their political union. For the severity which the Roman experienced from the State he was compensated by a severity, identical in nature, which he was allowed to indulge towards his family—a servant on the one side, a despot on the other. This constitutes the Roman greatness, whose peculiar characteristic was stern inflexibility in the union of individuals with the State, and with its law and mandate. In order to obtain a nearer view of this Spirit, we must not merely keep in view the actions of Roman heroes, confronting the enemy as soldiers or generals, or appearing as ambassadors—since in these cases they belong, with their whole mind and thought, only to the state and its mandate, without hesitation or yielding—but pay particular attention also to the conduct of the plebs in times of revolt against the patricians. How often in insurrection and in anarchical disorder was the plebs brought back into a state of tranquillity by a mere form, and cheated of the fulfilment of its demands, righteous or unrighteous! How often was a Dictator, *e.g.*, chosen by the senate, when there was neither war nor danger from an enemy, in order to get the plebeians into the army, and to bind them to strict obedience by the military oath! It took Licinius ten years to carry laws favorable to the plebs; the latter allowed itself to be kept back by the mere formality of the veto on the part of other tribunes, and still more patiently did it wait for the long-delayed execution of these laws. It may be asked: By what were such a disposition and character produced? Produced it cannot be, but it is essentially latent in the origination of the State from that primal robber-community, as also in the idiosyncrasy of the people who composed it, and lastly, in that phase of the World-Spirit which was just ready for development. The elements of the Roman people were Etruscan, Latin and Sabine; these must have contained an inborn natural adaptation to produce the Roman Spirit. Of the spirit, the character, and the life of the ancient Italian peoples we know very little—thanks to the non-intelligent character of Roman historiography!—and that little, for the most part, from the Greek writers on Roman history. But of the general character of the Romans we may say that, in contrast with that primeval wild poetry and transmutation of the finite, which we observe in the East—in contrast with· the beautiful, harmonious poetry and well-balanced freedom of Spirit among the Greeks—here, among the Romans the *prose* of life makes its appearance—the self-consciousness of finiteness—the abstraction of the Understanding and a rigorous principle of personality, which even in the Family does not expand itself to natural morality, but remains the unfeeling non-spiritual unit, and recognizes the uniting bond of the several social units only in abstract universality.

This extreme prose of the Spirit we find in Etruscan art,

which though technically perfect and so far true to nature, has nothing of Greek Ideality and Beauty: we also observe it in the development of Roman Law and in the Roman religion.

To the constrained, non-spiritual, and unfeeling intelligence of the Roman world we owe the origin and the development of *positive law*. For we saw above, how in the East, relations in their very nature belonging to the sphere of outward or inward morality, were made legal mandates; even among the Greeks, morality was at the same time juristic right, and on that very account the constitution was entirely dependent on morals and disposition, and had not yet a fixity of principle within it, to counterbalance the mutability of men's inner life and individual subjectivity. The Romans then completed this important separation, and discovered a principle of right, which is external—*i.e.* one not dependent on disposition and sentiment. While they have thus bestowed upon us a valuable gift, in point of *form*, we can use and enjoy it without becoming victims to that sterile Understanding—without regarding it as the *ne plus ultra* of Wisdom and Reason. They were its victims, living beneath its sway; but they thereby secured for others Freedom of Spirit—viz., that inward Freedom which has consequently become emancipated from the sphere of the Limited and the External. Spirit, Soul, Disposition, Religion have now no longer to fear being involved with that abstract juristical Understanding. Art too has its external side; when in Art the mechanical side has been brought to perfection, Free Art can arise and display itself. But those must be pitied who knew of nothing but that mechanical side, and desired nothing further; as also those who, when Art has arisen, still regard the Mechanical as the highest.

We see the Romans thus bound up in that abstract understanding which pertains to finiteness. This is their highest characteristic, consequently also their highest consciousness, in Religion. In fact, constraint was the religion of the Romans; among the Greeks, on the contrary, it was the cheerfulness of free fantasy. We are accustomed to regard Greek and Roman religion as the same, and use the names Jupiter, Minerva, etc. as Roman deities, often without distinguishing them from those of Greeks. This is admissible inasmuch as the Greek divinities were more or less introduced among the Romans; but as the Egyptian religion is by no means to be regarded as identical with the Greek, merely because Herodotus and the Greeks form

to themselves an idea of the Egyptian divinities under the names
" Latona," " Pallas," etc., so neither must the Roman be con-
founded with the Greek. We have said that in the Greek religion the thrill of awe suggested by Nature was fully developed
to something Spiritual—to a free conception, a spiritual form of
fancy—that the Greek Spirit did not remain in the condition of
inward fear, but proceeded to make the relation borne to man by
Nature, a relation of freedom and cheerfulness. The Romans,
on the contrary, remained satisfied with a dull, stupid subjectivity; consequently, the external was only an Object—something
alien, something hidden. The Roman spirit which thus remained involved in subjectivity, came into a relation of constraint and dependence, to which the origin of the word " re-
ligio " (lig-are) points. The Roman had always to do with
something *secret;* in everything he believed in and sought for
something *concealed;* and while in the Greek religion everything is open and clear, present to sense and contemplation—
not pertaining to a future world, but something friendly, and of
this world—among the Romans everything exhibits itself as
mysterious, duplicate: they saw in the object first itself, and
then that which lies concealed in it: their history is pervaded
by this duplicate mode of viewing phenomena. The city of
Rome had besides its proper name another secret one, known
only to a few. It is believed by some to have been " Valentia,"
the Latin translation of " Roma "; others think it was " Amor "
(" Roma " read backwards). Romulus, the founder of the State,
had also another, a sacred name—" Quirinus "—by which title
he was worshipped: the Romans too were also called Quirites.
(This name is connected with the term " curia ": in tracing its
etymology the name of the Sabine town " Cures," has been had
recourse to.)

Among the Romans the religious thrill of awe remained undeveloped; it was shut up to the mere subjective certainty of its
own existence. Consciousness has therefore given itself no
spiritual objectivity—has not elevated itself to the theoretical
contemplation of the eternally divine nature, and to freedom in
that contemplation; it has gained no religious substantiality for
itself from Spirit. The bare subjectivity of conscience is characteristic of the Roman in all that he does and undertakes—in
his covenants, political relations, obligations, family relations,
etc.; and all these relations receive thereby not merely a legal

sanction, but as it were a solemnity analogous to that of an oath. The infinite number of ceremonies at the comitia, on assuming offices, etc., are expressions and declarations that concern this firm bond. Everywhere the sacra play a very important part. Transactions, naturally the most alien to constraint, became a *sacrum*, and were petrified, as it were, into that. To this category belongs, *e.g.*, in strict marriages, the *confarreatio*, and the auguries and auspices generally. The knowledge of these *sacra* is utterly uninteresting and wearisome, affording fresh material for learned research as to whether they are of Etruscan, Sabine, or other origin. On their account the Roman people have been regarded as extremely pious, both in positive and negative observances; though it is ridiculous to hear recent writers speak with unction and respect of these *sacra*. The Patricians were especially fond of them; they have therefore been elevated in the judgment of some, to the dignity of sacerdotal families, and regarded as the sacred gentes—the possessors and conservators of Roman religion: the plebeians then become the godless element. On this head what is pertinent has already been said. The ancient kings were at the same time also *reges sacrorum*. After the royal dignity had been done away with, there still remained a *Rex Sacrorum;* but he, like all the other priests, was subject to the *Pontifex Maximus*, who presided over all the " sacra," and gave them such a rigidity and fixity as enabled the patricians to maintain their religious power so long.

But the essential point in pious feeling is the subject matter with which it occupies itself—though it is often asserted, on the contrary, in modern times, that if pious feelings exist, it is a matter of indifference what object occupies them. It has been already remarked of the Romans, that their religious subjectivity did not expand into a free spiritual and moral comprehensiveness of being. It can be said that their piety did not develop itself into religion; for it remained essentially formal, and this formalism took its real side from another quarter. From the very definition given, it follows that it can only be of a finite, unhallowed order, since it arose outside the secret sanctum of religion. The chief characteristic of Roman Religion is therefore a hard and dry contemplation of certain voluntary aims, which they regard as existing absolutely in their divinities, and whose accomplishment they desire of them as embodying absolute power. These purposes constitute that for the sake of which they worship the gods, and by which, in a constrained, limited way, they are bound to their deities. The Roman religion is therefore the entirely *prosaic* one of narrow aspirations, expediency, profit. The divinities peculiar to them are entirely prosaic; they are conditions [of mind or body], sensations, or useful arts, to which their dry fancy, having elevated them to independent power, gave objectivity; they are partly abstractions, which could only become frigid allegories—partly conditions of being which appear as bringing advantage or injury, and which were presented as objects of worship in their original bare and limited form. We can but briefly notice a few examples. The Romans worshipped " Pax," " Tranquillitas," " Vacuna " (Repose), " Angeronia " (Sorrow and Grief), as divinities; they consecrated altars to the Plague, to Hunger, to Mildew (Robigo), to Fever, and to the Dea Cloacina. Juno appears among the Romans not merely as " Lucina," the obstetric goddess, but also as " Juno Ossipagina," the divinity who forms the bones of the child, and as " Juno Unxia," who anoints the hinges of the doors at marriages (a matter which was also reckoned among the " sacra "). How little have these prosaic conceptions in common with the beauty of the spiritual powers and deities of the Greeks! On the other hand, Jupiter as " Jupiter Capitolinus " represents the generic essence of the Roman Empire, which is also personified in the divinities " Roma " and " Fortuna Publica."

It was the Romans especially who introduced the practice of not merely supplicating the gods in time of need, and celebrating " lectisternia," but of also making solemn promises and vows to them. For help in difficulty they sent even into foreign countries, and imported foreign divinities and rites. The introduction of the gods and most of the Roman temples thus arose from necessity—from a vow of some kind, and an obligatory, not disinterested acknowledgment of favors. The Greeks on the contrary erected and instituted their beautiful temples, and statues, and rites, from love to beauty and divinity for their own sake.

Only one side of the Roman religion exhibits something attractive, and that is the festivals, which bear a relation to country life, and whose observance was transmitted from the earliest times. The idea of the *Saturnian* time is partly their basis—the conception of a state of things antecedent to and beyond the limits of civil society and political combination; but their import is partly taken from Nature generally—the Sun, the course of the year, the seasons, months, etc., (with astronomical intimations)—partly from the particular aspects of the course of Nature, as bearing upon pastoral and agricultural life. There were festivals of sowing and harvesting and of the seasons; the principal was that of the Saturnalia, etc. In this aspect there appears much that is naïve and ingenuous in the tradition. Yet this series of rites, on the whole, presents a very limited and prosaic appearance; deeper views of the great powers of nature and their generic processes are not deducible from them; for they are entirely directed to external vulgar advantage, and the merriment they occasioned, degenerated into a buffoonery unrelieved by intellect. While among the Greeks their tragic art developed itself from similar rudiments, it is on the other hand remarkable that among the Romans the scurrilous dances and songs connected with the rural festivals, were kept up till the latest periods without any advance from this naïve but rude form to anything really artistic.

It has already been said that the Romans adopted the *Greek* Gods, (the mythology of the Roman poets is entirely derived from the Greeks); but the worship of these beautiful gods of the imagination appears to have been among them of a very cold and superficial order. Their talk of Jupiter, Juno, Minerva, sounds like a mere theatrical mention of them. The Greeks made their Pantheon the embodiment of a rich intellectual material, and adorned it with bright fancies; it was to them an object calling forth continual invention and exciting thoughtful reflection; and an extensive, nay inexhaustible treasure, has thus been created for sentiment, feeling and thought, in their mythology. The Spirit of the Romans did not indulge and delight itself in that play of a thoughtful fancy; the Greek mythology appears lifeless and exotic in their hands. Among the Roman poets—especially Virgil—the introduction of the gods is the product of a frigid Understanding and of imitation. The gods are used in these poems as machinery, and in a merely superficial way; regarded much in the same way as in our didactic treatises on the belles-lettres, where among other directions we find one relating to the use of such machinery in epics—in order to produce astonishment.

The Romans were as essentially different from the Greeks in

respect to their public *games*. In these the Romans were, properly speaking, only spectators. The mimetic and theatrical representation, the dancing, foot-racing and wrestling, they left to manumitted slaves, gladiators, or criminals condemned to death. Nero's deepest degradation was his appearing on a public stage as a singer, lyrist and combatant. As the Romans were only spectators, these diversions were something foreign to them; they did not enter into them with their whole souls. With increasing luxury the taste for the baiting of beasts and men became particularly keen. Hundreds of bears, lions, tigers, elephants, crocodiles, and ostriches, were produced, and slaughtered for mere amusement. A body consisting of hundreds, nay thousands of gladiators, when entering the amphitheatre at a certain festival to engage in a sham sea-fight, addressed the Emperor with the words: " Those who are devoted to death salute thee," to excite some compassion. In vain! the whole were devoted to mutual slaughter. In place of human sufferings in the depths of the soul and spirit, occasioned by the contradictions of life, and which find their solution in Destiny, the Romans instituted a cruel reality of corporeal sufferings: blood in streams, the rattle in the throat which signals death, and the expiring gasp were the scenes that delighted them.—This cold negativity of naked murder exhibits at the same time that murder of all spiritual objective aim which had taken place in the soul. I need only mention in addition, the auguries, auspices, and Sibylline books, to remind you how fettered the Romans were by superstitions of all kinds, and that they pursued exclusively their own aims in all the observances in question. The entrails of beasts, flashes of lightning, the flight of birds, the Sibylline dicta determined the administration and projects of the State. All this was in the hands of the patricians, who consciously made use of it as a mere outward, [non-spiritual, secular] means of constraint to further their own ends and oppress the people.

The distinct elements of Roman religion are, according to what has been said, subjective religiosity and a ritualism having for its object purely superficial external aims. Secular aims are left entirely free, instead of being limited by religion—in fact they are rather justified by it. The Romans are invariably pious, whatever may be the substantial character of their actions. But as the sacred principle here is nothing but an empty form, it is exactly of such a kind that it can be an instrument in the power of the devotee; it is taken possession of by the individual, who seeks his private objects and interests; whereas the truly Divine possesses on the contrary a concrete power in itself. But where there is only a powerless form, the individual—the Will, possessing an independent concreteness able to make that form its own, and render it subservient to its views—stands above it. This happened in Rome on the part of the patricians. The possession of sovereignty by the patricians is thereby made firm, sacred, incommunicable, peculiar: the administration of government, and political privileges, receive the character of hallowed private property. There does not exist therefore a substantial national unity—not that beautiful and moral necessity of united life in the Polis; but every " gens " is itself firm, stern, having its own Penates and sacra; each has it own political character, which it always preserves: strict, aristocratic severity distinguished the Claudii; benevolence towards the people, the Valerii; nobleness of spirit, the Cornelii. Separation and limitation were extended even to marriage, for the *connubia* of patricians with plebeians were deemed profane. But in that very subjectivity of religion we find also the principle of arbitrariness: and while on the one hand we have arbitrary choice invoking religion to bolster up private possession, we have on the other hand the revolt of arbitrary choice against religion. For the same order of things can, on the one side, be regarded as privileged by its religious form, and on the other side wear the aspect of being merely a matter of choice—of arbitrary volition on the part of man. When the time was come for it to be degraded to the rank of a mere form, it was necessarily known and treated as a form—trodden under foot—represented as formalism.—The inequality which enters into the domain of sacred things forms the transition from religion to the bare reality of political life. The consecrated inequality of will and of private property constitutes the fundamental condition of the change. The Roman principle admits of *aristocracy* alone as the constitution proper to it, but which directly manifests itself only in an antithetical form—internal inequality. Only from necessity and the pressure of adverse circumstances is this contradiction momentarily smoothed over; for it involves a duplicate power, the sternness and malevolent isolation of whose components can only be mastered and bound together by a still greater sternness, into a unity maintained by force.

Chapter II.—The History of Rome to the Second Punic War

In the first period, several successive stages display their characteristic varieties. The Roman State here exhibits its first phase of growth, under Kings; then it receives a republican constitution, at whose head stand Consuls. The struggle between patricians and plebeians begins; and after this has been set at rest by the concession of the plebeian demands, there ensues a state of contentment in the internal affairs of Rome, and it acquires strength to combat victoriously with the nation that preceded it on the stage of general history. As regards the accounts of the first Roman kings, every datum has met with flat contradiction as the result of criticism; but it is going too far to deny them all credibility. Seven kings in all, are mentioned by tradition; and even the " Higher Criticism " is obliged to recognize the last links in the series as perfectly historical. Romulus is called the founder of this union of freebooters; he organized it into a military state. Although the traditions respecting him appear fabulous, they only contain what is in accordance with the Roman Spirit as above described. To the second king, Numa, is ascribed the introduction of the religious ceremonies. This trait is very remarkable from its implying that religion was introduced later than political union, while among other peoples religious traditions make their appearance in the remotest periods and before all civil institutions. The king was at the same time a priest (*rex* is referred by etymologists to ῥέζειν— to sacrifice. As is the case with states generally, the Political was at first united with the Sacerdotal, and a theocratical state of things prevailed. The King stood here at the head of those who enjoyed privileges in virtue of the *sacra*.

The separation of the distinguished and powerful citizens as senators and patricians took place as early as the first kings. Romulus is said to have appointed 100 *patres*, respecting which however the Higher Criticism is sceptical. In religion, arbitrary ceremonies—the *sacra*—became fixed marks of distinction, and peculiarities of the *gentes* and orders. The internal organization of the State was gradually realized. Livy says that as Numa established all divine matters, so Servius Tullius introduced the different Classes, and the Census, according to which the share of each citizen in the administration of public affairs was determined. The patricians were discontented with this scheme, especially because Servius Tullius abolished a part of the debts owed by the plebeians, and gave public lands to the poorer citizens, which made them possessors of landed property. He divided the people into six classes, of which the first together with the knights formed ninety-eight centuries, the inferior classes proportionately fewer. Thus, as they voted by centuries, the class first in rank had also the greatest weight in the State. It appears that previously the patricians had the power exclusively in their hands, but that after Servius's division they had merely a preponderance; which explains their discontent with his institutions. With Servius the history becomes more distinct; and under him and his predecessor, the elder Tarquinius, traces of prosperity are exhibited. Niebuhr is surprised that according to Dionysius and Livy, the most ancient constitution was democratic, inasmuch as the vote of every citizen had equal weight in the assembly of the people. But Livy only says that Servius abolished the *suffragium viritim*. Now in the *comitia curiata*—the cliental relation, which absorbed the plebs, extending to all—the patricians alone had a vote, and *populus* denoted at that time only the patricians. Dionysius therefore does not contradict himself, when he says that the constitution according to the laws of Romulus was strictly aristocratic.

Almost all the Kings were foreigners—a circumstance very characteristic of the origin of Rome. Numa, who succeeded the founder of Rome, was according to the tradition, one of the Sabines—a people which under the reign of Romulus, led by Tatius, is said to have settled on one of the Roman hills. At a later date however the Sabine country appears as a region entirely separated from the Roman State. *Numa* was followed by *Tullus Hostilius*, and the very name of this king points to his foreign origin. *Ancus Martius*, the fourth king, was the grandson of Numa. *Tarquinius Priscus* sprang from a Corinthian family, as we had occasion to observe above. *Servius Tullius* was from Corniculum, a conquered Latin town; *Tarquinius Superbus* was descended from the elder Tarquinius. Under this last king Rome reached a high degree of prosperity: even at so early a period as this, a commercial treaty is said to have been concluded with the Carthaginians; and to be disposed to reject this as mythical would imply forgetfulness of the connection which Rome had, even at that time, with the Etrurians and other bordering peoples whose prosperity depended on trade and maritime pursuits. The Romans were probably even then acquainted with the art of writing, and already possessed that clear-sighted comprehension which was their remarkable characteristic, and which led to that perspicuous historical composition for which they are famous.

In the growth of the inner life of the state, the power of the Patricians had been much reduced; and the kings often courted the support of the people—as we see was frequently the case in the mediæval history of Europe—in order to steal a march upon the Patricians. We have already observed this in Servius Tullius. The last king, Tarquinius Superbus, consulted the senate but little in state affairs; he also neglected to supply the place of its deceased members, and acted in every respect as if he aimed at its utter dissolution. Then ensued a state of political excitement which only needed an occasion to break out into open revolt. An insult to the honor of a matron—the invasion of that sanctum sanctorum—by the son of the king, supplied such an occasion. The kings were banished in the year 244 of the City and 510 of the Christian Era (that is, if the building of Rome is to be dated 753 B.C.) and the royal dignity abolished forever.

The Kings were expelled by the patricians, not by the plebeians; if therefore the patricians are to be regarded as possessed of " divine right " as being a sacred race, it is worthy of note that we find them here contravening such legitimation; for the King was their High Priest. We observe on this occasion with what dignity the sanctity of marriage was invested in the eyes of the Romans. The principle of subjectivity and piety (pudor) was with them the religious and guarded element; and its violation becomes the occasion of the expulsion of the Kings, and later on of the Decemvirs too. We find monogamy therefore also looked upon by the Romans as an understood thing. It was not introduced by an express law; we have nothing but an incidental testimony in the Institutes, where it is said that marriages under certain conditions of relationship are not allowable, because a man may not have two wives. It is not until the reign of Diocletian that we find a law expressly determining that no one belonging to the Roman empire may have two wives, " since according to a pretorian edict also, infamy attaches to such a condition " (*cum etiam in edicto prætoris hujusmodi viri infamia notati sunt*). Monogamy therefore is regarded as naturally valid, and is based on the principle of subjectivity.—Lastly, we must also observe that royalty was not abrogated here as in Greece by suicidal destruction on the part of the royal races, but was exterminated in hate. The King, himself the chief priest, had been guilty of the grossest profanation; the principle of subjectivity revolted against the deed, and the patricians, thereby elevated to a sense of independence, threw off the yoke of royalty. Possessed by the same feeling, the plebs at a later date rose against the patricians, and the Latins and the Allies against the Romans; until the equality of the social units was restored through the whole Roman dominion (a multitude of slaves, too, being emancipated) and they were held together by simple Despotism.

Livy remarks that Brutus hit upon the right epoch for the expulsion of the kings, for that if it had taken place earlier, the state would have suffered dissolution. What would have happened, he asks, if this homeless crowd had been liberated earlier, when living together had not yet produced a mutual conciliation of dispositions?—The constitution now became in *name* republican. If we look at the matter more closely it is evident (Livy ii. 1) that no other essential change took place than the transference of the power which was previously *permanent* in the King, to *two annual* Consuls. These two, equal in power, managed military and judicial as well as administrative business; for prætors, as supreme judges, do not appear till a later date.

At first all authority remained in the hands of the consuls; and at the beginning of the republic, externally and internally, the state was in evil plight. In the Roman history a period occurs as troubled as that in the Greek which followed the extinction of the dynasties. The Romans had first to sustain a severe conflict with their expelled King, who had sought and found help from the Etrurians. In the war against Porsena the Romans lost all their conquests, and even their independence: they were compelled to lay down their arms and to give hostages; according to an expression of Tacitus (Hist. 3, 72) it seems as if Porsena had even taken Rome. Soon after the expulsion of the Kings we have the contest between the patricians and plebeians; for the abolition of royalty had taken place exclusively to the advantage of the aristocracy, to which the royal power was transferred, while the plebs lost the protection which the Kings had afforded it. All magisterial and juridical power, and all property in land was at this time in the hands of the patricians; while the people, continually dragged out to war, could not employ themselves in peaceful occupations: handicrafts could not flourish, and the only acquisition the plebeians could make was their share in the booty. The patricians had their territory and soil cultivated by slaves, and assigned some of their land to their clients, who on condition of paying taxes and contributions—as tenant cultivators, therefore—had the usufruct of it. This relation, on account of the form in which the dues were paid by the Clientes, was very similar to vassalage: they were obliged to give contributions towards the marriage of the daughters of the Patronus, to ransom him or his sons when in captivity, to assist them in obtaining magisterial offices, and to make up the losses sustained in suits at law. The administration of justice was likewise in the hands of the patricians, and that without the limitations of definite and written laws; a desideratum which at a later period the Decemvirs were created to supply. All the power of government belonged moreover to the patricians, for they were in possession of all offices—first of the consulship, afterwards of the military tribuneship and censorship (instituted A.U.C. 311) —by which the actual administration of government as likewise the oversight of it, was left to them alone. Lastly, it was the patricians who constituted the Senate. The question as to how that body was recruited appears very important. But in this matter no systematic plan was followed. Romulus is said to have founded the senate, consisting then of one hundred members; the succeeding kings increased this number, and Tarquinius Priscus fixed it at three hundred. Junius Brutus restored the senate, which had very much fallen away, *de novo.* In after times it would appear that the censors and sometimes the dictators filled up the vacant places in the senate. In the second Punic War, A.U.C. 538, a dictator was chosen, who nominated one hundred and seventy-seven new senators: he selected those who had been invested with curule dignities, the plebeian Ædiles, Tribunes of the People and Quæstors, citizens who had gained *spolia opima* or the *corona civica.* Under Cæsar the number of the senators was raised to eight hundred; Augustus reduced it to six hundred. It has been regarded as great negligence on the

part of the Roman historians, that they give us so little information respecting the composition and redintegration of the
senate. But this point which appears to us to be invested
with infinite importance, was not of so much moment to the
Romans at large; they did not attach so much weight to formal
arrangements, for their principal concern was, *how* the government was conducted. How in fact can we suppose the constitutional rights of the ancient Romans to have been so well
defined, and that at a time which is even regarded as mythical,
and its traditionary history as epical?

The people were in some such oppressed condition as, *e.g.*
the Irish were a few years ago in the British Isles, while they
remained at the same time entirely excluded from the government. Often they revolted and made a secession from the city.
Sometimes they also refused military service; yet it always
remains a very striking fact that the senate could so long resist
superior numbers irritated by oppression and practised in war;
for the main struggle lasted for more than a hundred years.
In the fact that the people could so long be kept in check is
manifested its respect for legal order and the *sacra*. But of
necessity the plebeians at last secured their righteous demands,
and their debts were often remitted. The severity of the patricians their creditors, the debts due to whom they had to discharge by slave-work, drove the plebs to revolts. At first it
demanded and received only what it had already enjoyed under
the kings—landed property and protection against the powerful. It received assignments of land, and Tribunes of the
People—functionaries that is to say, who had the power to
put a veto on every decree of the senate. When this office
commenced, the number of tribunes was limited to two: later
there were ten of them; which however was rather injurious
to the plebs, since all that the senate had to do was to gain
over one of the tribunes, in order to thwart the purpose of all
the rest by his single opposition. The plebs obtained at the
same time the *provocatio ad populum:* that is, in every case of
magisterial oppression, the condemned person might appeal
to the decision of the people—a privilege of infinite importance
to the plebs, and which especially irritated the patricians. At
the repeated desire of the people the *Decemviri* were nominated
—the Tribunate of the People being suspended—to supply the
desideratum of a determinate legislation; they perverted, as

is well known, their unlimited power to tyranny; and were driven from power on an occasion entailing similar disgrace to that which led to the punishment of the Kings. The dependence of the clientela was in the meantime weakened; after the decemviral epoch the clientes are less and less prominent and are merged in the plebs, which adopts resolutions (*plebiscita*); the senate by itself could only issue *senatus consulta,* and the tribunes, as well as the senate, could now impede the comitia and elections. By degrees the plebeians effected their admissibility to all dignities and offices; but at first a plebeian consul, ædile, censor, etc., was not equal to the patrician one, on account of the sacra which the latter kept in his hands; and a long time intervened after this concession before a plebeian actually became a consul. It was the tribunis plebis, Licinius, who established the whole cycle of these political arrangements —in the second half of the fourth century, A.U.C. 387. It was he also who chiefly commenced the agitation for the *lex agraria,* respecting which so much has been written and debated among the learned of the day. The agitators for this law excited during every period very great commotions in Rome. The plebeians were practically excluded from almost all the landed property, and the object of the Agrarian Laws was to provide lands for them—partly in the neighborhood of Rome, partly in the conquered districts, to which colonies were to be then led out. In the time of the Republic we frequently see military leaders assigning lands to the people; but in every case they were accused of striving after royalty, because it was the kings who had exalted the plebs. The Agrarian Law required that no citizen should possess more than five hundred *jugera:* the patricians were consequently obliged to surrender a large part of their property. *Niebuhr* in particular has undertaken extensive researches respecting the agrarian laws, and has conceived himself to have made great and important discoveries: he says, *viz.* that an infringement of the sacred right of property was never thought of, but that the state had only assigned a portion of the public lands for the use of the plebs, having always had the right of disposing of them as its own property. I only remark in passing that Hegewisch had made this discovery before Niebuhr, and that Niebuhr derived the particular data on which his assertion rests from Appian and Plutarch; that is from Greek authors, respecting whom he himself allows that we should have recourse to them only in an extreme case. How often does Livy, as well as Cicero and others, speak of the Agrarian laws, while nothing definite can be inferred from their statements!—This is another proof of the inaccuracy of the Roman historians. The whole affair ends in nothing but a useless question of jurisprudence. The land which the patricians had taken into possession or in which colonies settled, was originally public land; but it also certainly belonged to those in possession, and our information is not at all promoted by the assertion that it always remained public land. This discovery of Niebuhr's turns upon a very immaterial distinction, existing perhaps in his ideas, but not in reality.—The Licinian law was indeed carried, but soon transgressed and utterly disregarded. Licinius Stolo himself, who had first "agitated" for the law, was punished because he possessed a larger property in land than was allowed, and the patricians opposed the execution of the law with the greatest obstinacy. We must here call especial attention to the distinction which exists between the Roman, the Greek, and our own circumstances. Our civil society rests on other principles, and in it such measures are not necessary. Spartans and Athenians, who had not arrived at such an abstract idea of the State as was so tenaciously held by the Romans, did not trouble themselves with abstract rights, but simply desired that the citizens should have the means of subsistence; and they required of the state that it should take care that such should be the case.

This is the chief point in the first period of Roman History —that the plebs attained the right of being eligible to the higher political offices, and that by a share which they too managed to obtain in the land and soil, the means of subsistence were assured to the citizens. By this union of the patriciate and the plebs, Rome first attained true internal consistency; and only after this had been realized could the Roman power develop itself externally. A period of satisfied absorption in the common interest ensues, and the citizens are weary of internal struggles. When after civil discords nations direct their energies outward, they appear in their greatest strength; for the previous excitement continues, and no longer having its object within, seeks for it without. This direction given to the Roman energies was able for a moment to conceal the defect of that union; equilibrium was restored, but without an essential centre of unity and support. The contradiction that existed could not but break out again fearfully at a later period; but previously to this time the greatness of Rome had to display itself in war and the conquest of the world. The power, the wealth, the glory derived from these wars, as also the difficulties to which they led, kept the Romans together as regards the internal affairs of the state. Their courage and discipline secured their victory. As compared with the Greek or Macedonian, the Roman art of war has special peculiarities. The strength of the phalanx lay in its mass and in its massive character. The Roman legions also present a close array, but they had at the same time an articulated organization: they united the two extremes of massiveness on the one hand, and of dispersion into light troops on the other hand: they held firmly together, while at the same time they were capable of ready expansion. Archers and slingers preceded the main body of the Roman army when they attacked the enemy—afterwards leaving the decision to the sword.

It would be a wearisome task to pursue the wars of the Romans in Italy; partly because they are in themselves unimportant—even the often empty rhetoric of the generals in Livy cannot very much increase the interest—partly on account of the unintelligent character of the Roman annalists, in whose pages we see the Romans carrying on war only with " enemies " without learning anything further of their individuality—*e.g.* the Etruscans, the Samnites, the Ligurians, with whom they carried on wars during many hundred years.—It is singular in regard to these transactions that the Romans, who have the justification conceded by World-History on their side, should also claim for themselves the minor justification in respect to manifestoes and treaties on occasion of minor infringements of them, and maintain it as it were after the fashion of advocates. But in political complications of this kind, either party may take offence at the conduct of the other, if it pleases, and deems it expedient to be offended.—The Romans had long and severe contests to maintain with the Samnites, the Etruscans, the Gauls, the Marsi, the Umbrians and the Bruttii, before they could make themselves masters of the whole of Italy. Their dominion was extended thence in a southerly direction; they gained a secure footing in Sicily, where the Carthaginians had long carried on war; then they extended their power towards the west: from Sardinia and Corsica they went to Spain. They thus soon came into frequent contact with the Carthaginians, and were obliged to form a naval power in opposition to them. This transition was easier in ancient times than it would perhaps be now, when long practice and superior knowledge are required for maritime service. The mode of warfare at sea was not very different from that on land.

We have thus reached the end of the first epoch of Roman History, in which the Romans by their retail military transactions had become capitalists in a strength proper to themselves, and with which they were to appear on the theatre of the world. The Roman dominion was, on the whole, not yet very greatly extended: only a few colonies had settled on the other side of the Po, and on the south a considerable power confronted that of Rome. It was the Second Punic War, therefore, that gave the impulse to its terrible collision with the most powerful states of the time; through it the Romans came into contact with Macedonia, Asia, Syria, and subsequently also with Egypt. Italy and Rome remained the centre of their great far-stretching empire, but this centre was, as already remarked, not the less an artificial, forced, and compulsory one. This grand period of the contact of Rome with other states, and of the manifold complications thence arising, has been depicted by the noble Achæan, Polybius, whose fate it was to observe the fall of his country through the disgraceful passions of the Greeks and the baseness and inexorable persistency of the Romans.

SECTION II

ROME FROM THE SECOND PUNIC WAR TO THE EMPERORS

THE second period, according to our division, begins with the Second Punic War, that epoch which decided and stamped a character upon Roman dominion. In the first Punic War the Romans had shown that they had become a match for the mighty Carthage, which possessed a great part of the coast of Africa and southern Spain, and had gained a firm footing in Sicily and Sardinia. The second Punic War laid the might of Carthage prostrate in the dust. The proper element of that state was the sea; but it had no original territory, formed no nation, had no national army; its hosts were composed of the troops of subjugated and allied peoples. In spite of this, the great Hannibal with such a host, formed from the most diverse nations, brought Rome near to destruction. Without any support he maintained his position in Italy for sixteen years against Roman patience and perseverance; during which time however the Scipios conquered Spain and entered into alliances with the princes of Africa. Hannibal was at last compelled to hasten to the assistance of his hard-pressed country; he lost the battle of Zama in the year 552 A.U.C. and after six and thirty years revisited his paternal city, to which he was now obliged to offer pacific counsels. The second Punic War thus eventually established the undisputed power of Rome over Carthage; it occasioned the hostile collision of the Romans with the king of Macedonia, who was conquered five years later. Now Antiochus, the king of Syria, is involved in the mêlée. He opposed a huge power to the Romans, was beaten at Thermopylæ and Magnesia, and was compelled to surrender to the Romans Asia Minor as far as the Taurus. After the conquest of Macedonia both that country and Greece were declared free by the Romans—a declaration whose mean-

ing we have already investigated, in treating of the preceding
Historical nation. It was not till this time that the Third
Punic War commenced, for Carthage had once more raised its
head and excited the jealousy of the Romans. After long resistance it was taken and laid in ashes. Nor could the Achæan
league now long maintain itself in the face of Roman ambition:
the Romans were eager for war, destroyed Corinth in the same
year as Carthage, and made Greece a province. The fall of
Carthage and the subjugation of Greece were the central points
from which the Romans gave its vast extent to their sovereignty.

Rome seemed now to have attained perfect security; no
external power confronted it: she was the mistress of the
Mediterranean—that is of the *media terra* of all civilization.
In this period of victory, its morally great and fortunate personages, especially the Scipios, attract our attention. They
were morally fortunate—although the greatest of the Scipios
met with an end outwardly unfortunate—because they devoted
their energies to their country during a period when it enjoyed
a sound and unimpaired condition. But after the feeling of
patriotism—the dominant instinct of Rome—had been satisfied,
destruction immediately invades the state regarded *en masse;*
the grandeur of *individual* character becomes stronger in intensity, and more vigorous in the use of means, on account of
contrasting circumstances. We see the internal contradiction
of Rome now beginning to manifest itself in another form;
and the epoch which concludes the second period is also the
second mediation of that contradiction. We observed that contradiction previously in the struggle of the patricians against
the plebeians: now it assumes the form of private interest, contravening patriotic sentiment; and respect for the state no longer holds these opposites in the necessary equipoise. Rather,
we observe now side by side with wars for conquest, plunder
and glory, the fearful spectacle of civil discords in Rome, and
intestine wars. There does not follow, as among the Greeks
after the Median wars, a period of brilliant splendor in culture,
art and science, in which Spirit enjoys inwardly and ideally
that which it had previously achieved in the world of action.
If inward satisfaction was to follow the period of that external
prosperity in war, the principle of Roman life must be more
concrete. But if there were such a concrete life to evolve as

an object of consciousness from the depths of their souls by imagination and thought, what would it have been! Their chief spectacles were triumphs, the treasures gained in war, and captives from all nations, unsparingly subjected to the yoke of abstract sovereignty. The concrete element, which the Romans actually find within themselves, is only this unspiritual unity, and any definite thought or feeling of a non-abstract kind, can lie only in the idiosyncrasy of individuals. The tension of virtue is now relaxed, because the danger is past. At the time of the first Punic War, necessity united the hearts of all for the saving of Rome. In the following wars too, with Macedonia, Syria, and the Gauls in Upper Italy, the existence of the entire state was still concerned. But after the danger from Carthage and Macedon was over, the subsequent wars were more and more the mere consequences of victories, and nothing else was needed than to gather in their fruits. The armies were used for particular expeditions, suggested by policy, or for the advantages of individuals—for acquiring wealth, glory, *sovereignty* in the abstract. The relation to other nations was purely that of force. The national individuality of peoples did not, as early as the time of the Romans, excite respect, as is the case in modern times. The various peoples were not yet recognized as legitimated; the various states had not yet acknowledged each other as real essential existences. Equal right to existence entails a union of states, such as exists in modern Europe, or a condition like that of Greece, in which the states had an equal right to existence under the protection of the Delphic god. The Romans do not enter into such a relation to the other nations, for their god is only the *Jupiter Capitolinus;* neither do they respect the *sacra* of the other nations (any more than the plebeians those of the patricians); but as conquerors in the strict sense of the term, they plunder the Palladia of the nations. Rome kept standing armies in the conquered provinces, and proconsuls and proprætors were sent into them as viceroys. The Equites collected the taxes and tributes, which they farmed under the State. A net of such fiscal farmers (publicani) was thus drawn over the whole Roman world.—Cato used to say, after every deliberation of the senate: " *Ceterum censeo Carthaginem esse delendam:*" and Cato was a thorough Roman. The Roman principle thereby exhibits itself as the cold abstraction of sovereignty and power, as the pure egotism of the will in opposition to others, involving no moral element of determination, but appearing in a concrete form only in the shape of individual interests. Increase in the number of provinces issued in the aggrandizement of individuals within Rome itself, and the corruption thence arising. From Asia, luxury and debauchery were brought to Rome. Riches flowed in after the fashion of spoils in war, and were not the fruit of industry and honest activity; in the same way as the marine had arisen, not from the necessities of commerce, but with a warlike object. The Roman state, drawing its resources from rapine, came to be rent in sunder by quarrels about dividing the spoil. For the first occasion of the breaking out of contention within it, was the legacy of Attalus, King of Pergamus, who had bequeathed his treasures to the Roman State. Tiberius Gracchus came forward with the proposal, to divide it among the Roman citizens; he likewise renewed the Licinian Agrarian laws, which had been entirely set aside during the predominance of individuals in the state. His chief object was to procure property for the free citizens, and to people Italy with citizens instead of slaves. This noble Roman, however, was vanquished by the grasping nobles, for the Roman constitution was no longer in a condition to be saved by the constitution itself. Caius Gracchus,' the brother of Tiberius, prosecuted the same noble aim as his brother, and shared the same fate. Ruin now broke in unchecked, and as there existed no generally recognized and absolutely essential object to which the country's energy could be devoted, individualities and physical force were in the ascendant. The enormous corruption of Rome displays itself in the war with Jugurtha, who had gained the senate by bribery, and so indulged himself in the most atrocious deeds of violence and crime. Rome was pervaded by the excitement of the struggle against the Cimbri and Teutones, who assumed a menacing position towards the State. With great exertions the latter were utterly routed in Provence, near Aix; the others in Lombardy at the Adige by Marius the conqueror of Jugurtha. Then the Italian allies, whose demand of Roman citizenship had been refused, raised a revolt; and while the Romans had to sustain a struggle against a vast power in Italy, they received the news, that at the command of Mithridates, 80,000 Romans had been put to death in Asia Minor. Mithridates was King of Pontus, governed Colchis and the lands of the Black Sea, as far as the Tauric peninsula, and could summon to his standard in his war with Rome the populations of the Caucasus, of Armenia, Mesopotamia, and a part of Syria, through his son-in-law Tigranes. Sulla, who had already led the Roman hosts in the Social War, conquered him. Athens, which had hitherto been spared, was beleaguered and taken, but " for the sake of their fathers "—as Sulla expressed himself —not destroyed. He then returned to Rome, reduced the popular faction, headed by Marius and Cinna, became master of the city, and commenced systematic massacres of Roman citizens of consideration. Forty senators and six hundred knights were sacrificed to his ambition and lust of power.

Mithridates was indeed defeated, but not overcome, and was able to begin the war anew. At the same time, Sertorius, a banished Roman, arose in revolt in Spain, carried on a contest there for eight years, and perished only through treachery. The war against Mithridates was terminated by Pompey ; the King of Pontus killed himself when his resources· were exhausted. The Servile War in Italy is a contemporaneous event. A great number of gladiators and mountaineers had formed a union under Spartacus, but were vanquished by Crassus. To this confusion was added the universal prevalence of piracy, which Pompey rapidly reduced by a large armament.

We thus see the most terrible and dangerous powers arising against Rome ; yet the military force of this state is victorious over all. Great individuals now appear on the stage as during the times of the fall of Greece. The biographies of Plutarch are here also of the deepest interest. It was from the disruption of the state, which had no longer any consistency or firmness in itself, that these colossal individualities arose, instinctively impelled to restore that political unity which was no longer to be found in men's dispositions. It is their misfortune that they cannot maintain a pure morality, for their course of action contravenes things as they are, and is a series of transgressions. Even the noblest—the Gracchi—were not merely the victims of injustice and violence from without, but were themselves involved in the corruption and wrong that universally prevailed. But that which these individuals purpose and accomplish, has on its side the higher sanction of the World-Spirit, and must eventually triumph. The idea of an organization for the vast empire being altogether absent, the senate could not assert the authority of government. The sovereignty was made dependent on the people—that people which was now a mere mob, and was obliged to be supported by corn from the Roman provinces. We should refer to Cicero to see how all affairs of state were decided in riotous fashion, and with arms in hand, by the wealth and power of the grandees on the one side, and by a troop of rabble on the other. The Roman citizens attach themselves to individuals who flatter them, and who then become prominent in factions, in order to make themselves masters of Rome. Thus we see in Pompey and Cæsar the two foci of Rome's splendor coming into hostile opposition: on the one side, Pompey with the Senate, and therefore apparently the defender of the Republic—on the other, Cæsar with his legions and a superiority of genius. This contest between the two most powerful individualities could not be decided at Rome in the Forum. Cæsar made himself master in succession, of Italy, Spain, and Greece, utterly routed his enemy at Pharsalus, forty-eight years before Christ, made himself sure of Asia, and so returned victor to Rome.

In this way the world-wide sovereignty of Rome became the property of a single possessor. This important change must not be regarded as a thing of chance; it was *necessary* —postulated by the circumstances. The democratic constitution could no longer be really maintained in Rome, but only kept up in appearance. Cicero, who had procured himself great respect through his high oratorical talent, and whose learning acquired him considerable influence, always attributes the corrupt state of the republic to individuals and their passions. Plato, whom Cicero professedly followed, had the full consciousness that the Athenian state, as it presented itself to him, could not maintain its existence, and therefore sketched the plan of a perfect constitution accordant with his views. Cicero, on the contrary, does not consider it impossible to preserve the Roman Republic, and only desiderates some temporary assistance for it in its adversity. The nature of the State, and of the Roman State in particular, transcends his comprehension. Cato, too, says of Cæsar: "His virtues be execrated, for they have ruined my country!" But it was not the mere accident of Cæsar's existence that destroyed the Republic—it was *Necessity*. All the tendencies of the Roman principle were to sovereignty and military force: it contained in it no spiritual centre which it could make the object, occupation, and enjoyment of its Spirit. The aim of patriotism—that of preserving the State—ceases when the lust of personal dominion becomes the impelling passion. The citizens were alienated from the state, for they found in it no objective satisfaction; and the interests of individuals did not take the same direction as among the Greeks, who could set against the incipent corruption of the practical world, the noblest works of art in painting, sculpture and poetry, and especially a highly cultivated philosophy. Their works of art were only what they had collected from every part of Greece, and therefore not productions of their own; their riches were not the fruit of industry, as was the case in Athens, but the result of plunder. Elegance—Culture —was foreign to the Romans *per se;* they sought to obtain it from the Greeks, and for this purpose a vast number of Greek slaves were brought to Rome. Delos was the centre of this slave trade, and it is said that sometimes on a single day, ten thousand slaves were purchased there. To the Romans, Greek slaves were their poets, their authors, the superintendents of their manufactories, the instructors of their children.

The Republic could not longer exist in Rome. We see, especially from Cicero's writings, how all public affairs were decided by the private authority of the more eminent citizens— by their power, their wealth; and what tumultuary proceedings marked all political transactions. In the republic, therefore, there was no longer any security; *that* could be looked for only in a single will. Cæsar, who may be adduced as a paragon of Roman adaptation of means to ends—who formed his resolves with the most unerring perspicuity, and executed them with the greatest vigor and practical skill, without any superfluous excitement of mind—Cæsar, judged by the great scope of history, did the Right; since he furnished a mediating element, and that kind of political bond which men's condition required. Cæsar effected two objects: he calmed the internal strife, and at the same time originated a new one outside the limits of the empire. For the conquest of the world had reached hitherto only to the circle of the Alps, but Cæsar opened a new scene of achievement: he founded the theatre which was on the point of becoming the centre of History. He then achieved universal sovereignty by a struggle which was decided not in Rome itself, but by his conquest of the whole Roman World.

His position was indeed hostile to the republic, but, properly speaking, only to its shadow; for all that remained of that republic was entirely powerless. Pompey, and all those who were on the side of the senate, exalted their *dignitas auctoritas* —their individual rule—as the power of the republic; and the mediocrity which needed protection took refuge under this title. Cæsar put an end to the empty formalism of this title, made himself master, and held together the Roman world by force, in opposition to isolated factions. Spite of this we see the noblest men of Rome supposing Cæsar's rule to be a merely adventitious thing, and the entire position of affairs to be dependent on his individuality. So thought Cicero, so Brutus and Cassius. They believed that if this one individual were out of the way, the Republic would be *ipso facto* restored. Possessed by this remarkable hallucination, Brutus, a man of highly noble character, and Cassius, endowed with greater practical energy than Cicero, assassinated the man whose virtues they appreciated. But it became immediately manifest that only a *single* will could guide the Roman State, and now the Romans were compelled to adopt that opinion; since in all periods of the world a political revolution is sanctioned in men's opinions, when it repeats itself. Thus Napoleon was twice defeated, and the Bourbons twice expelled. By repetition that which at first appeared merely a matter of chance and contingency, becomes a real and ratified existence.

SECTION III

Chapter I.—Rome Under the Emperors

DURING this period the Romans come into contact with the people destined to succeed them as a World-Historical nation; and we have to consider that period in two essential aspects, the *secular* and the *spiritual*. In the secular aspect two leading phases must be specially regarded: first, the position of *the Ruler;* and secondly, the conversion of mere individuals into *persons*—the world of legal relations.

The first thing to be remarked respecting the *imperial rule* is that the Roman government was so abstracted from interest, that the great transition to that rule hardly changed anything in the constitution. The popular assemblies alone were unsuited to the new state of things, and disappeared. The emperor was *princeps senatus,* Censor, Consul, Tribune: he united all their nominally continuing offices in himself; and the military power—here the most essentially important—was exclusively in his hands. The constitution was an utterly unsubstantial form, from which all vitality, consequently all might and power, had departed; and the only means of maintaining its existence were the legions which the Emperor constantly kept in the vicinity of Rome. Public business was indeed brought before the senate, and the Emperor appeared simply as one of its members; but the senate was obliged to obey, and whoever ventured to gainsay his will was punished with death, and his property confiscated. Those therefore who had certain death in anticipation, killed themselves, that if they could do nothing more, they might at least preserve their property to their family. Tiberius was the most odious to the Romans on account of his power of dissimulation: he knew very well how to make good use of the baseness of the senate, in extirpating those among them whom he feared. The power of the Emperor rested, as we have said, on the army, and the Pretorian bodyguard which surrounded him. But the legions, and especially the Pretorians, soon became conscious of their importance, and arrogated to themselves the disposal of the imperial throne. At first they continued to show some respect for the family of Cæsar Augustus, but subsequently the legions chose their own generals; such, viz., as had gained their good will and favor, partly by courage and intelligence, partly also by bribes, and indulgence in the administration of military discipline.

The Emperors conducted themselves in the enjoyment of their power with perfect simplicity, and did not surround themselves with pomp and splendor in Oriental fashion. We find in them traits of simplicity which astonish us. Thus, *e.g.*, Augustus writes a letter to Horace, in which he reproaches him for having failed to address any poem to him, and asks him whether he thinks that that would disgrace him with posterity. Sometimes the Senate made an attempt to regain its consequence by nominating the Emperor: but their nominees were either unable to maintain their ground, or could do so only by bribing the Pretorians. The choice of the senators and the constitution of the senate was moreover left entirely to the caprice of the Emperor. The political institutions were united in the person of the Emperor; no moral bond any longer existed; the will of the Emperor was supreme, and before him there was absolute equality. The freedmen who surrounded the Emperor were often the mightiest in the empire; for caprice recognizes no distinction. In the person of the Emperor isolated subjectivity has gained a perfectly unlimited realization. Spirit has renounced its proper nature, inasmuch as Limitation of being and of volition has been constituted an unlimited absolute existence. This arbitrary choice, moreover, has only one limit, the limit of all that is human—*death;* and even death became a theatrical display. Nero, *e.g.*, died a death, which may furnish an example for the noblest hero, as for the most resigned of sufferers. Individual subjectivity thus entirely emancipated from control, has no inward life, no prospective nor retrospective emotions, no repentance, nor hope, nor fear—not even thought; for all these involve fixed conditions and aims, while here every condition is purely contingent. The springs of action are none other than desire, lust, passion, fancy—in short, caprice absolutely unfettered. It finds so little limitation in the will of others, that the relation of will to will may be called that of absolute sovereignty to absolute slavery. In the whole known world, no will is imagined that is not subject to the will of the Emperor. But under the sovereignty of that One, everything is in a condition of *order;* for as it actually *is* [as the Emperor has willed it], it is in due order, and government consists in bringing all into harmony with the sovereign *One.* The concrete element in the character of the Emperors is therefore of itself of no interest, because the concrete is not of essential importance. Thus there were Emperors of noble character and noble nature, and who highly distinguished themselves by mental and moral culture. Titus, Trajan, the Antonines, are known as such characters, rigorously strict in self-government; yet even these produced no change in the state. The proposition was never made during their time, to give the Roman Empire an organization of free social relationship: they were only a kind of happy chance, which passes over without a trace, and leaves the condition of things as it was. For these persons find themselves here in a position in which they cannot be said to act, since no object confronts them in opposition; they have only to will—well or ill—and it *is* so. The praiseworthy emperors Vespasian and Titus were succeeded by that coarsest and most loathsome tyrant, Domitian: yet the Roman historian tells us that the Roman world enjoyed tranquillizing repose under him. Those single points of light, therefore, effected no change; the whole empire was subject to the pressure of taxation and plunder; Italy was depopulated; the most fertile lands remained untilled: and this state of things lay as a fate on the Roman world.

The second point which we have particularly to remark, is the position taken by individuals as *persons.* Individuals were perfectly equal (slavery made only a trifling distinction), and without any political right. As early as the termination of the Social War, the inhabitants of the whole of Italy were put on an equal footing with Roman citizens; and under Caracalla all distinction between the subjects of the entire Roman empire was abolished. Private Right developed and perfected this equality. The right of property had been previously limited by distinctions of various kinds, which were now abrogated. We observed the Romans proceeding from the principle of abstract Subjectivity, which now realizes itself as Personality in the recognition of Private Right. Private Right, viz., is this, that the social unit as such enjoys consideration in the state, in the reality which he gives to himself—viz., in property. The living political body—that Roman feeling which animated it as its soul—is now brought back to the isolation of a lifeless Private Right. As, when the physical body suffers dissolution, each point gains a life of its own, but which is only the miserable life of worms; so the political organism is here dissolved into atoms—viz., private persons. Such a condition is Roman life at this epoch: on the one side, Fate and the abstract universality of sovereignty; on the other, the *individual* abstraction. "Person," which involves the recognition of the independent dignity of the social unit—not on the ground of the display of the life which he possesses—in his complete individuality—but as the abstract *individuum*.

It is the pride of the social units to enjoy absolute importance as private persons; for the Ego is thus enabled to assert unbounded claims; but the substantial interest thus comprehended—the *meum*—is only of a superficial kind, and the development of private right, which this high principle introduced, involved the decay of political life.—The Emperor *domineered* only, and could not be said to *rule;* for the equitable and moral medium between the sovereign and the subjects was wanting—the bond of a constitution and organization of the state, in which a gradation of circles of social life, enjoying independent recognition, exists in communities and provinces, which, devoting their energies to the general interest, exert an influence on the general government. There are indeed Curiæ in the towns, but they are either destitute of weight, or used only as means for oppressing individuals, and for systematic plunder. That, therefore, which was abidingly present to the minds of men was not their country, or such a moral unity as that supplies: the whole state of things urged them to yield themselves to fate, and to strive for a perfect indifference to life—an indifference which they sought either in freedom of thought or in directly sensuous enjoyment. Thus man was either at war with existence, or entirely given up to mere sensuous existence. He either recognized his destiny in the task of acquiring the means of enjoyment through the favor of the Emperor, or through violence, testamentary frauds, and cunning; or he sought repose in philosophy, which alone was still able to supply something firm and independent: for the systems of that time—Stoicism, Epicureanism, and Scepticism—although within their common sphere opposed to each other, had the same general purport, viz., rendering the soul absolutely indifferent to everything which the real world had to offer. These philosophies were therefore widely extended among the cultivated: they produced in man a self-reliant immobility as the result of Thought, *i.e.* of the activity which produces the Universal. But the inward reconciliation by means of philosophy was itself only an abstract one—in the pure principle of personality; for Thought, which, as perfectly refined, made itself its own object, and thus harmonized itself, was entirely destitute of a real object, and the immobility of Scepticism made aimlessness itself the object of the Will. This philosophy knew nothing but the negativity of all that assumed to be real, and was the counsel of despair to a world which no longer possessed anything stable. It could not satisfy the living Spirit, which longed after a higher reconciliation.

Chapter II.—Christianity

It has been remarked that Cæsar inaugurated the Modern World on the side of *reality,* while its spiritual and inward existence was unfolded under Augustus. At the beginning of that empire, whose principle we have recognized as finiteness and particular subjectivity exaggerated to infinitude, the salvation of the World had its birth in the same principle of subjectivity—viz., as a *particular person,* in abstract subjectivity, but in such a way that conversely, finiteness is only the *form* of his appearance, while infinity and absolutely independent existence constitute the essence and substantial being which it embodies. The Roman World, as it has been described—in its desperate condition and the pain of abandonment by God—came to an open rupture with reality, and made prominent the general desire for a satisfaction such as can only be attained in " the inner man," the Soul—thus preparing the ground for a higher Spiritual World. Rome was the Fate that crushed down the gods and all genial life in its hard service, while it was the power that purified the human heart from all speciality. Its entire condition is therefore analogous to a place of birth, and its pain is like the travail-throes of another and higher Spirit, which manifested itself in connection with the *Christian Re-*

ligion. This higher Spirit involves the reconciliation and emancipation of Spirit; while man obtains the consciousness of Spirit in its universality and infinity. The Absolute Object, *Truth,* is Spirit; and as man himself is Spirit, he is present [is mirrored] to himself in that object, and thus in his Absolute Object has found Essential Being and *his own* essential being.* But in order that the objectivity of Essential Being may be done away with, and Spirit be no longer alien to itself—may be *with* itself [self-harmonized]—the Naturalness of Spirit—that in virtue of which man is a special, empirical existence—must be removed; so that the alien element may be destroyed, and the reconciliation of Spirit be accomplished.

God is thus recognized as *Spirit,* only when known as the Triune. This new principle is the axis on which the History of the World turns. This is *the goal* and the *starting point* of History. " When the fulness of the time was come, God sent his Son," is the statement of the Bible. This means nothing else than that *self-consciousness* had reached the phases of development [Momente], whose resultant constitutes the Idea of Spirit, and had come to feel the necessity of comprehending those phases absolutely. This must now be more fully explained. We said of the Greeks, that the law for their Spirit was: " Man, know thyself." The Greek Spirit was a consciousness of Spirit, but under a limited form, having the element of Nature as an essential ingredient. Spirit may have had the upper hand, but the unity of the superior and the subordinate was itself still Natural. Spirit appeared as specialized in the idiosyncrasies of the genius of the several Greek nationalities and of their divinities, and was represented by *Art,* in whose sphere the Sensuous is elevated only to the middle ground of beautiful form and shape, but not to pure Thought. The element of Subjectivity that was wanting to the Greeks, we found among the Romans: but as it was merely formal and in itself indefinite, it took its material from passion and caprice; —even the most shameful degradations could be here connected with a divine dread (*vide* the declaration of Hispala respecting the Bacchanalia, Livy xxxix. 13). This element of subjectivity is afterwards further realized as Personality of Individuals—

* The harsh requirements of an ungenial tyranny call forth man's highest powers of self-sacrifice; he learns his moral capacity; dissatisfaction with anything short of perfection ensues—consciousness of sin; and this sentiment in its greatest intensity, produces union with God.—ED.

a realization which is exactly adequate to the principle, and is equally abstract and formal. As such an Ego [such a personality], I am infinite to myself, and my phenomenal existence consists in the property recognized as mine, and the recognition of my personality. This inner existence goes no further; all the applications of the principle merge in this. Individuals are thereby posited as atoms; but they are at the same time subject to the severe rule of the *One*, which as *monas monadum* is a power over private persons [the connection between the ruler and the ruled is not mediated by the claim of Divine or of Constitutional Right, or any general principle, but is direct and individual, the Emperor being the immediate lord of each subject in the Empire]. That Private Right is therefore, *ipso facto,* a nullity, an ignoring of the personality; and the supposed condition of Right turns out to be an absolute destitution of it. This contradiction is the misery of the Roman World. Each person is, according to the principle of his personality, entitled only to possesion, while the Person of Persons lays claim to the possession of all these individuals, so that the right assumed by the social unit is at once abrogated and robbed of validity. But the misery of this contradiction is the *Discipline of the World*. "Zucht" (discipline) is derived from "Ziehen" (to draw).* This "drawing" must be towards something; there must be some fixed unity in the background in whose direction that drawing takes place, and for which the subject of it is being trained, in order that the standard of attainment may be reached. A renunciation, a disaccustoming, is the means of leading to an absolute basis of existence. That contradiction which afflicts the Roman World is the very state of things which constitutes such a discipline—the discipline of that culture which compels personality to display its nothingness. But it is reserved for us of a later period to regard this as a training; to those who are thus trained [*trainés,* dragged], it seems a blind destiny, to which they submit in the stupor of suffering. The higher condition, in which the soul itself feels pain and longing—in which man is not only "drawn," but feels that the drawing is into himself [into his own inmost nature]— is still absent. What has been reflection on our part must arise in the mind of the subject of this discipline in the form of a consciousness that in himself he is miserable and null. Out-

---

* So the English " train " from French " trainer "—to draw or drag.—ED.

ward suffering must, as already said, be merged in a sorrow of the inner man. He must feel himself as the negation of himself; he must see that his misery is the misery of his nature —that he is in himself a divided and discordant being. This state of mind, this self-chastening, this pain occasioned by our individual nothingness—the wretchedness of our [isolated] self, and the longing to transcend this condition of soul—must be looked for elsewhere than in the properly Roman World. It is this which gives to the *Jewish People* their World-Historical importance and weight; for from this state of mind arose that higher phase in which Spirit came to absolute self-consciousness—passing from that alien form of being which is its discord and pain, and mirroring itself in its own essence. The state of feeling in question we find expressed most purely and beautifully in the Psalms of David, and in the Prophets; the chief burden of whose utterances is the thirst of the soul after God, its profound sorrow for its transgressions, and the desire for righteousness and holiness. Of this Spirit we have the mythical representation at the very beginning of the Jewish canonical books, in the account of the Fall. Man, created in the image of God, lost, it is said, his state of absolute contentment, by eating of the Tree of the Knowledge of Good and Evil. Sin consists here only in Knowledge: this is the sinful element, and by it man is stated to have trifled away his Natural happiness. This is a deep truth, that evil lies in consciousness: for the brutes are neither evil nor good; the merely Natural Man quite as little.* Consciousness occasions the separation of the Ego, in its boundless freedom as arbitrary choice, from the pure essence of the Will—*i.e.* from the Good. Knowledge, as the disannulling of the unity of mere Nature, is the " Fall," which is no casual conception, but the eternal history of Spirit. For the state of innocence, the paradisaical condition, is that of the brute. Paradise is a park, where only brutes, not men, can remain. For the brute is one with God only implicitly [not consciously]. Only Man's Spirit (that is) has a self-cognizant existence. This existence for self, this consciousness, is at the same time separation from the Universal and Divine Spirit. If I hold to **my** abstract Freedom, in contraposition to the Good, I adopt the standpoint of Evil. The Fall is therefore the eternal Mythus of Man—in fact, the

* " I was alive without the law once," etc. Rom. vii. 9.

very transition by which he becomes man. Persistence in this standpoint is, however, Evil, and the feeling of pain at such a condition, and of longing to transcend it, we find in David, when he says: " Lord, create for me a pure heart, a new *steadfast* Spirit." This feeling we observe even in the account of the Fall; though an announcement of Reconciliation is not made there, but rather one of continuance in misery. Yet we have in this narrative the *prediction* of reconciliation in the sentence, " The serpent's head shall be bruised "; but still more profoundly expressed where it is stated that when God saw that Adam had eaten of that tree, he said, " Behold Adam is become as one of us, knowing Good and Evil." God confirms the words of the Serpent. Implicitly and explicitly, then, we have the truth, that man through Spirit—through cognition of the Universal and the Particular—comprehends God Himself. But it is only God that declares this—not man: the latter remains, on the contrary, in a state of internal discord. The joy of reconciliation is still distant from humanity; the absolute and final repose of his whole being is not yet discovered to man. It exists, in the first instance, only for God. As far as the present is concerned, the feeling of pain at his condition is regarded as a final award. The satisfaction which man enjoys at first, consists in the finite and temporal blessings conferred on the Chosen Family and the possession of the Land of Canaan. His repose is not found in God. Sacrifices are, it is true, offered to Him in the Temple, and atonement made by outward offerings and inward penitence. But that mundane satisfaction in the Chosen Family, and its possession of Canaan, was taken from the Jewish people in the chastisement inflicted by the Roman Empire. The Syrian kings did indeed oppress it, but it was left for the Romans to annul its individuality. The Temple of Zion is destroyed; the God-serving nation is scattered to the winds. Here every source of satisfaction is taken away, and the nation is driven back to the standpoint of that primeval mythus—the standpoint of that painful feeling which humanity experiences when thrown upon itself. Opposed to the universal *Fatum* of the Roman World, we have here the consciousness of Evil and the direction of the mind Godwards. All that remains to be done, is that this fundamental idea should be expanded to an objective universal sense, and be taken as the concrete existence of man—as the completion of his nature. Formerly the Land of Canaan and themselves as the people of God had been regarded by the Jews as that concrete and complete existence. But this basis of satisfaction is now lost, and thence arises the sense of misery and failure of hope in God, with whom that happy reality had been essentially connected. Here, then, misery is not the stupid immersion in a blind Fate, but a boundless energy of longing. Stoicism taught only that the Negative *is not*—that pain must not be recognized as a veritable existence; but *Jewish* feeling persists in acknowledging Reality and desires harmony and reconciliation within its sphere; for that feeling is based on the Oriental Unity of Nature—*i.e.*, the unity of Reality, of Subjectivity, with the substance of the One Essential Being. Through the loss of mere outward reality Spirit is driven back within itself; the side of reality is thus refined to Universality, through the reference of it to the One. The Oriental antithesis of Light and Darkness is transferred to Spirit, and the Darkness becomes Sin. For the abnegation of reality there is no compensation but Subjectivity itself—the Human Will as intrinsically universal; and thereby alone does reconciliation become possible. Sin is the discerning of Good and Evil as separation; but this discerning likewise heals the ancient hurt, and is the fountain of infinite reconciliation. The discerning in question brings with it the destruction of that which is external and alien in consciousness, and is consequently the return of Subjectivity into itself. This, then, adopted into the actual self-consciousness of the World is the *Reconciliation* [atonement] *of the World*. From that unrest of infinite sorrow—in which the two sides of the antithesis stand related to each other—is developed the unity of God with Reality (which latter had been posited as negative) *i.e.*, with Subjectivity which had been separated from Him. The infinite loss is counterbalanced only by its infinity, and thereby becomes infinite gain. The recognition of the identity of the Subject and God was introduced into the World when *the fulness of Time was come:* the consciousness of this identity is the recognition of God in his true essence. The material of Truth is *Spirit* itself —inherent vital movement. The nature of God as pure Spirit, is manifested to man *in the Christian Religion*.

But what is Spirit? It is the one immutably homogeneous Infinite—pure Identity—which in its second phase separates itself from itself and makes this second aspect its own polar opposite, viz. as existence for and in self as contrasted with the Universal. But this separation is annulled by the fact that atomistic Subjectivity, as simple relation to itself [as occupied with self alone] is itself the Universal, the Identical with self. If Spirit be defined as absolute reflection within itself in virtue of its absolute duality—Love on the one hand as comprehending the Emotional [Empfindung], Knowledge on the other hand as Spirit [including the penetrative and active faculties, as opposed to the receptive]—it is recognized as *Triune:* the " Father " and the " Son," and that duality which essentially characterizes it as " Spirit." It must further be observed, that *in* this truth, the relation of man *to* this truth is also posited. For Spirit makes itself its own [polar] opposite—and is the return from this opposite into itself. Comprehended in pure ideality, that antithetic form of Spirit is the Son of God; reduced to limited and particular conceptions, it is the World-Nature and Finite Spirit: Finite Spirit itself therefore is posited as a constituent element [Moment] in the Divine Being. Man himself therefore is comprehended in the Idea of God, and this comprehension may be thus expressed—that the unity of Man with God is posited in the Christian Religion. But this unity must not be superficially conceived, as if God were only Man, and Man, without further condition, were God. Man, on the contrary, is God only in so far as he annuls the merely Natural and Limited in his Spirit and elevates himself to God. That is to say, it is obligatory on him who is a partaker of the truth, and knows that he himself is a constituent [Moment] of the Divine Idea, to give up his merely natural being: for the Natural is the Unspiritual. In this Idea of God, then, is to be found also the *Reconciliation* that heals the pain and inward suffering of man. For Suffering itself is henceforth recognized as an instrument necessary for producing the unity of man with God. This implicit unity exists in the first place only for the thinking speculative consciousness; but it must also exist for the sensuous, representative consciousness—it must become an object for the World—it must *appear,* and that in the sensuous form appropriate to Spirit, which is the human. *Christ has appeared* —a Man who is God—God who is Man; and thereby peace and reconciliation have accrued to the World. Our thoughts naturally revert to the Greek anthropomorphism, of which we affirmed that it did not go far enough. For that natural elation of soul which characterized the Greeks did not rise to the Subjective Freedom of the Ego itself—to the inwardness that belongs to the Christian Religion—to the recognition of Spirit as a *definite positive being.*—The appearance of the Christian God involves further its being *unique* in its kind; it can occur only once, for God is realized as Subject, and as manifested Subjectivity is exclusively One Individual. The Lamas are ever and anon chosen anew; because God is known in the East as Substance, whose infinity of form is recognized merely in an unlimited multeity of outward and particular manifestations. But subjectivity as infinite relation to self, has its form *in itself,* and as manifested, must be a unity excluding all others.— Moreover the sensuous existence in which Spirit is embodied is only a transitional phase. Christ dies; only as dead, is he exalted to Heaven and sits at the right hand of God; only thus is he Spirit. He himself says: "When I am no longer with you, the Spirit will guide you into all truth." Not till the Feast of Pentecost were the Apostles filled with the Holy Ghost. To the Apostles, Christ as living, was not that which he was to them subsequently as the Spirit of the Church, in which he became to them for the first time an object for their truly spiritual consciousness. On the same principle, we do not adopt the right point of view in thinking of Christ only as a historical bygone personality. So regarded, the question is asked, What are we to make of his birth, his Father and Mother, his early domestic relations, his miracles, etc.?—*i.e.* What is he *unspiritually* regarded? Considered only in respect of his talents, character and morality—as a Teacher and so forth —we place him in the same category with Socrates and others, though his morality may be ranked higher. But excellence of character, morality, etc.—all this is not the *ne plus ultra* in the requirements of Spirit—does not enable man to gain the speculative idea of Spirit for his conceptive faculty. If Christ is to be looked upon only as an excellent, even impeccable individual, and nothing more, the conception of the Speculative Idea, of Absolute Truth is ignored. But this is the desideratum, the point from which we have to start. Make of Christ what you will, exegetically, critically, historically—demonstrate as you please, how the doctrines of the Church were

established by Councils attained currency as the result of
this or that episcopal interest or passion, or originated in
this or that quarter;—let all such circumstances have been
what they might—the only concerning question is: What is the
Idea or the Truth in and for itself?

Further, the real attestation of the Divinity of Christ is the
witness of one's own Spirit—not Miracles; for only Spirit
recognizes Spirit. The miracles may lead the way to such recognition. A miracle implies that the natural course of things is
interrupted: but it is very much a question of relation what
we call the "natural course"; and the phenomena of the magnet might under cover of this definition, be reckoned miraculous. Nor does the miracle of the Divine Mission of Christ
prove anything; for Socrates likewise introduced a new self-
consciousness on the part of Spirit, diverse from the traditional
tenor of men's conceptions. The main question is not his Divine Mission but the revelation made in Christ and the purport
of his mission. Christ himself blames the Pharisees for desir-
ing miracles of him, and speaks of false prophets who will perform miracles.

We have next to consider how the Christian view resulted
in the formation of the Church. To pursue the rationale of its
development from the Idea of Christianity would lead us too
far, and we have here to indicate only the general phases which
the process assumed. The first phase is the founding of the
Christian religion, in which its principle is expressed with unrestrained energy, but in the first instance abstractly. This
we find in the Gospels, where the infinity of Spirit—its elevation into the spiritual world [as the exclusively true and authorized existence]—is the main theme. With transcendent boldness does Christ stand forth among the Jewish people. "Blessed
are the pure in heart, for they shall see God," he proclaims in
the Sermon on the Mount—a dictum of the noblest simplicity,
and pregnant with an elastic energy of rebound against all the
adventitious appliances with which the human soul can be
burdened. The pure heart is the domain in which God is present to man: he who is imbued with the spirit of this apophthegm
is armed against all alien bonds and superstitions. The other
utterances are of the same tenor: "Blessed are the peacemak-
ers: for they shall be called the children of God;" and,
"Blessed are they which are persecuted for righteousness' sake:

for theirs is the kingdom of heaven;" and, "Be ye perfect, even as your Father which is in heaven is perfect." Christ enforces here a completely unmistakable requirement. The infinite exaltation of Spirit to absolute purity is placed at the beginning as the foundation of all. The form of the instrumentality by which that result is to be accomplished is not yet given, but the result itself is the subject of an absolute command. As regards the relation of this standpoint of Spirit to secular existence, we find that spiritual purity presented as the substantial basis. " Seek ye first the kingdom of God and his righteousness, and all things shall be added unto you;" and, " The sufferings of this present time are not worthy to be compared with that glory." * Here Christ says that outward sufferings, as such, are not to be feared or fled from, for they are nothing as compared with that glory. Further on, this doctrine, as the natural consequence of its appearing in an abstract form, assumes a *polemical* direction. " If thy right eye offend thee, pluck it out and cast it from thee: if thy right hand offend thee, cut it off and cast it from thee. It is better that one of thy members should perish, and not that thy whole body should be cast into hell." Whatever might disturb the purity of the soul, should be destroyed. So in reference to property and worldly gain, it is said: " Care not for your life, what ye shall eat and drink, nor for your body, what ye shall put on. Is not the life more than meat, and the body more than raiment? Behold the fowls of the air: for they sow not, neither do they reap, nor gather into barns; yet your heavenly Father feedeth them. Are ye not much better than they?" Labor for subsistence is thus reprobated: " Wilt thou be perfect, go and sell what thou hast, and give it to the poor, so shalt thou have a treasure in heaven, and come, follow me." Were this precept directly complied with, a social revolution must take place; the poor would become the rich. Of such supreme moment, it is implied, is the doctrine of Christ, that all duties and moral bonds are unimportant as compared with it. To a youth who wishes to delay the duties of discipleship till he has buried his father, Christ says: " Let the dead bury their dead—follow thou me." " He that loveth father or mother more than me is not worthy of me." He said: " Who is my mother? and who are my brethren? and stretched his hand out over his disciples

* The words in the text occur in Rom. viii. 18, but the import of Matt. v. 12, is nearly the same.

and said, Behold my mother and my brethren! For he that doeth the will of my Father in heaven, the same is my brother, and sister and mother." Yes, it is even said: " *Think not that I am come to send peace on the Earth. I am not come to send peace but the sword. For I am come to set a man against his father, and the daughter against her mother, and the mother-in-law against her daughter-in-law.*" Here then is an abstraction from all that belongs to reality, even from moral ties. We may say that nowhere are to be found such revolutionary utterances as in the Gospels; for everything that had been respected, is treated as a matter of indifference—as worthy of no regard.

The next point is the development of this principle; and the whole sequel of History is the history of its development. Its first realization is the formation by the friends of Christ, of a Society—a Church. It has been already remarked that only after the death of Christ could the Spirit come upon his friends; that only then were they able to conceive the true idea of God, viz., that in Christ man is redeemed and reconciled: for in him the idea of eternal truth is recognized, the essence of man acknowledged to be Spirit, and the fact proclaimed that only by stripping himself of his finiteness and surrendering himself to pure self-consciousness, does he attain the truth. Christ—man as man—in whom the unity of God and man has appeared, has in his death, and his history generally, himself presented the eternal history of Spirit—a history which every man has to accomplish in himself, in order to exist as Spirit, or to become a child of God, a citizen of his kingdom. The followers of Christ, who combine on this principle and live in the spiritual life as their aim, form the *Church,* which is the Kingdom of God. " Where two or three are gathered together in my name " (*i.e.* " in the character of partakers in my being ") says Christ, " there am I in the midst of them." The Church is a real present life in the Spirit of Christ.

It is important that the Christian religion be not limited to the teachings of Christ himself: it is in the Apostles that the completed and developed truth is first exhibited. This complex of thought unfolded itself in the Christian community. That community, in its first experiences, found itself sustaining a double relation—first, a relation to the Roman World, and secondly, to the truth whose development was its aim. We will pursue these different relations separately.

The Christian community found itself in the Roman world, and in this world the extension of the Christian religion was to take place. That community must therefore keep itself removed from all activity in the State—constitute itself a separate company, and not react against the decrees, views, and transactions of the state. But as it was secluded from the state, and consequently did not hold the Emperor for its absolute sovereign, it was the object of persecution and hate. Then was. manifested that infinite inward liberty which it enjoyed, in the great steadfastness with which sufferings and sorrows were patiently borne for the sake of the highest truth. It was less the miracles of the Apostles that gave to Christianity its outward extension and inward strength, than the substance, the truth of the doctrine itself. Christ himself says: " Many will say to me at that day: Lord, Lord! have we not prophesied in thy name, have we not cast out devils in thy name, have we not in thy name done many wonderful deeds? Then will I profess unto them: I never knew you, depart from me all ye workers of iniquity."

As regards its other relation, viz., that to the Truth, it is especially important to remark that the *Dogma*—the Theoretical—was already matured within the Roman World, while we find the development of the State from that principle, a much later growth. The Fathers of the Church and the Councils constituted the dogma; but a chief element in this constitution was supplied by the previous development of *philosophy*. Let us examine more closely how the philosophy of the time stood related to religion. It has already been remarked that the Roman inwardness and subjectivity, which presented itself only abstractly, as soulless personality in the exclusive position assumed by the Ego, was refined by the philosophy of Stoicism and Scepticism to the form of Universality. The ground of Thought was thereby reached, and God was known in Thought as the One Infinite. The Universal stands here only as an unimportant predicate—not itself a Subject, but requiring a concrete particular application to make it such. But the One and Universal, the Illimitable conceived by fancy, is essentially Oriental; for measureless conceptions, carrying all limited existence beyond its proper bounds, are indigenous to the East. Presented in the domain of Thought itself, the Oriental *One* is the invisible and non-sensuous God of the Israelitish people,

but whom they also make an object of conception as a person.
This principle became World-Historical with Christianity.—
In the Roman World, the union of the East and West had taken
place in the first instance by means of conquest: it took place
now inwardly, psychologically, also;—the Spirit of the East
spreading over the West. The worship of Isis and that of
Mithra had been extended through the whole Roman World;
Spirit, lost in the outward and in limited aims, yearned after
an Infinite. But the West desired a deeper, purely inward Universality—an Infinite possessed at the same time of positive
qualities. Again, it was in Egypt—in Alexandria, viz., the
centre of communication between the East and the West—that
the problem of the age was proposed for Thought; and the
solution now found was—Spirit. There the two principles
came into scientific contact, and were scientifically worked out.
It is especially remarkable to observe there, learned Jews such
as Philo, connecting abstract forms of the concrete, which they
derived from Plato and Aristotle, with their conception of the
Infinite, and recognizing God according to the more concrete
idea of Spirit, under the definition of the Λόγος. So, also, did
the profound thinkers of Alexandria comprehend the unity of
the Platonic and Aristotelian Philosophy; and their speculative
thinking attained those abstract ideas which are likewise the
fundamental purport of the Christian religion. The application,
by way of postulate, to the pagan religion, of ideas recognized
as true, was a direction which philosophy had already taken
among the heathen. Plato had altogether repudiated the current
mythology, and, with his followers, was accused of Atheism.
The Alexandrians, on the contrary, endeavored to demonstrate
a speculative truth in the Greek conceptions of the gods: and
the Emperor Julian the Apostate resumed the attempt, asserting that the pagan ceremonials had a strict connection with
rationality. The heathen felt, as it were, obliged to give to
their divinities the semblance of something higher than sensuous conceptions; they therefore attempted to spiritualize them.
Thus much is also certain, that the Greek religion contains a
degree of Reason; for the substance of Spirit is Reason, and
its product must be something Rational. It makes a difference,
however, whether Reason is explicitly developed in Religion,
or merely adumbrated by it, as constituting its hidden basis.
And while the Greeks thus spiritualized their sensuous divin-

ities, the Christians also, on their side, sought for a profounder sense in the historical part of their religion. Just as Philo found a deeper import shadowed forth in the Mosaic record, and idealized what he considered the bare shell of the narrative, so also did the Christians treat their records—partly with a polemic view, but still more largely from a free and spontaneous interest in the process. But the instrumentality of philosophy in introducing these dogmas into the Christian Religion, is no sufficient ground for asserting that they were foreign to Christianity and had nothing to do with it. It is a matter of perfect indifference where a thing originated; the only question is: " Is it true in and for itself?" Many think that by pronouncing the doctrine to be Neo-Platonic, they have *ipso facto* banished it from Christianity. Whether a Christian doctrine stands exactly thus or thus in the Bible—the point to which the exegetical scholars of modern times devote all their attention—is not the only question. The Letter kills, the Spirit makes alive: this they say themselves, yet pervert the sentiment by taking the *Understanding* for the *Spirit*. It was the Church that recognized and established the doctrines in question—*i.e.* the Spirit of the Church; and it is itself an Article of Doctrine: " I believe in a Holy Church;" * as Christ himself also said: " The Spirit will guide you into all truth." In the Nicene Council (A.D. 325), was ultimately established a fixed confession of faith, to which we still adhere: this confession had not, indeed, a speculative *form*, but the profoundly speculative is most intimately inwoven with the manifestation of Christ himself. Even in John (ἐν ἀρχῇ ἦν ὁ λόγος καὶ ὁ λόγος ἦν πρὸς τὸν Θεόν, καί Θεὸς ἦν ὁ λόγος) we see the commencement of a profounder comprehension. The profoundest thought is connected with the personality of Christ—with the historical and external; and it is the very grandeur of the Christian religion that, with all this profundity, it is easy of comprehension by our consciousness in its outward aspect, while, at the same time, it summons us to penetrate deeper. It is thus adapted to every grade of culture, and yet satisfies the highest requirements.

Having spoken of the relation of the Christian community to the Roman World on the one side, and to the truth contained in its doctrines on the other side, we come to the third point—

---

* In the Lutheran ritual, " a holy Catholic Church " is substituted for " *the* Holy Catholic Church," in the Belief.

in which both doctrine and the external world are concerned—
the *Church*. The Christian community is the Kingdom of
Christ—its influencing present Spirit being Christ: for this
kingdom has an actual existence, not a merely future one. This
spiritual actuality has, therefore, also a phenomenal existence;
and that, not only as contrasted with heathenism, but with secular existence generally. For the Church, as presenting this
outward existence, is not merely a *religion* as opposed to another religion, but is at the same time a particular form of
secular existence, occupying a place side by side with other
secular existence. The religious existence of the Church is
governed by Christ; the secular side of its government is left
to the free choice of the members themselves. Into this kingdom of God an organization must be introduced. In the first
instance, all the members know themselves filled with the
Spirit; the whole community perceives the truth and gives expression to it; yet, together with this common participation
of spiritual influence, arises the necessity of a presidency of
guidance and teaching—a body distinct from the community
at large. Those are chosen as presidents who are distinguished
for talents, character, fervor of piety, a holy life, learning, and
culture generally. The presidents—those who have a superior
acquaintance with that substantial Life of which all are partakers, and who are instructors in that Life—those who establish what is truth, and those who dispense its enjoyment—are
distinguished from the community at large, as persons endowed with knowledge and governing power are from the governed. To the intelligent presiding body, the Spirit comes in
a fully revealed and *explicit* form; in the mass of the community that Spirit is only *implicit*. While, therefore, in the presiding body, the Spirit exists as self-appreciating and self-
cognizant, it becomes an authority in spiritual as well as in
secular matters—an authority for the truth and for the relation
of each individual to the truth, determining how he should
conduct himself so as to act in accordance with the Truth. This
distinction occasions the rise of an *Ecclesiastical Kingdom* in
the Kingdom of God. Such a distinction is inevitable; but the
existence of an authoritative government for the Spiritual,
when closely examined, shows that human subjectivity in its
proper form has not yet developed itself. In the heart, indeed,
the evil will is surrendered, but the will, as human, is not yet

interpenetrated by the Deity; the human will is emancipated only abstractly—not in its concrete reality—for the whole sequel of History is occupied with the realization of this concrete Freedom. Up to this point, finite Freedom has been only annulled, to make way for infinite Freedom. The latter has not yet penetrated secular existence with its rays. Subjective Freedom has not yet attained validity as such: Insight [speculative conviction] does not yet rest on a basis of its own, but is content to inhere in the spirit of an extrinsic authority. That *Spiritual* [geistig] kingdom has, therefore, assumed the shape of an *Ecclesiastical* [geistlich] one, as the relation of the substantial being and essence of Spirit to human Freedom. Besides the interior organization already mentioned, we find the Christian community assuming also a definite external position, and becoming the possessor of property of its own. As property belonging to the spiritual world, it is presumed to enjoy special protection; and the immediate inference from this is, that the Church has no dues to pay to the state, and that ecclesiastical persons are not amenable to the jurisdiction of the secular courts. This entails the government by the Church itself of ecclesiastical property and ecclesiastical persons. Thus there originates with the Church the contrasted spectacle of a body consisting only of private persons and the power of the Emperor on the secular side;—on the other side, the perfect democracy of the spiritual community, choosing its own president. Priestly consecration, however, soon changes this democracy into aristocracy;—though the further development of the Church does not belong to the period now under consideration, but must be referred to the world of a later date.

It was then through the Christian Religion that the Absolute Idea of God, in its true conception, attained consciousness. Here Man, too, finds himself comprehended in his true nature, given in the specific conception of " the Son." Man, finite when regarded *for himself*, is yet at the same time the Image of God and a fountain of infinity *in himself*. He is the object of his own existence—has in himself an infinite value, an eternal destiny. Consequently he has his true home in a supersensuous world—an infinite subjectivity, gained only by a rupture with mere Natural existence and volition, and by his labor to break their power within him. This is religious self-consciousness. But in order to enter the sphere and display the

active vitality of that religious life, humanity must become
capable of it. This capability is the δύναμις for that ἐνέργεια.
What therefore remains to be considered is, those conditions
of humanity which are the necessary corollary to the consideration that Man is Absolute Self-consciousness—his Spiritual
nature being the starting-point and presupposition. These conditions are themselves not yet of a concrete order, but simply
the first *abstract principles*, which are won by the instrumentality of the Christian Religion for the *secular State*. First,
under Christianity Slavery is impossible; for man is man—
in the abstract essence of his nature—is contemplated in God;
each unit of mankind is an object of the grace of God and of
the Divine purpose: "God will have *all* men to be saved."
Utterly excluding all speciality, therefore, man, in and for himself—in his simple quality of man—has infinite value; and this
infinite value abolishes, *ipso facto,* all particularity attaching to
birth or country. The other, the second principle, regards the
subjectivity of man in its bearing on the Fortuitous—on Chance.
Humanity has this sphere of free Spirituality in and for itself,
and everything else must proceed from it. The place appropriated to the abode and presence of the Divine Spirit—the
sphere in question—is Spiritual Subjectivity, and is constituted the place to which all contingency is amenable. It follows thence, that what we observed among the Greeks as a form
of Customary Morality, cannot maintain its position in the
Christian world. For *that* morality is spontaneous unreflected
Wont; while the Christian principle is independent subjectivity—the soil on which grows the True. Now an unreflected
morality cannot continue to hold its ground against the principle of Subjective Freedom. Greek Freedom was that of
Hap and "Genius"; it was still conditioned by Slaves and
Oracles; but now the principle of absolute Freedom in God
makes its appearance. Man now no longer sustains the relation of Dependence, but of Love—in the consciousness that he
is a partaker in the Divine existence. In regard to particular
aims [such as the Greeks referred to oracular decision], man
now forms his own determinations and recognizes himself as
plenipotentiary in regard to all finite existence. All that is special retreats into the background before that Spiritual sphere
of subjectivity, which takes a secondary position only in presence of the Divine Spirit. The superstition of oracles and

auspices is thereby entirely abrogated: Man is recognized as the absolute authority in crises of decision.

It is the two principles just treated of, that now attach to Spirit in this its self-contained phase. The inner shrine of man is designed, on the one hand, to train the citizen of the religious life to bring himself into harmony with the Spirit of God; on the other hand, this is the *point du départ* for determining secular relations, and its condition is the theme of Christian History. The change which piety effects must not remain concealed in the recesses of the heart, but must become an actual, present world, complying with the conditions prescribed by that Absolute Spirit. Piety of heart does not, *per se,* involve the submission of the subjective will, in its external relations, to that piety. On the contrary we see all passions increasingly rampant in the sphere of reality, because that sphere is looked down upon with contempt, from the lofty position attained by the world of mind, as one destitute of all claim and value. The problem to be solved is therefore the imbuing of the sphere of [ordinary] unreflected Spiritual existence, with the *Idea* of Spirit. A general observation here suggests itself. From time immemorial it has been customary to assume an opposition between Reason and Religion, as also between *Religion and the World;* but on investigation this turns out to be only a *distinction.* Reason in general is the Positive Existence [Wesen] of Spirit, divine as well as human. The distinction between Religion and the World is only this—that Religion as such, is Reason in the soul and heart—that it is a temple in which Truth and Freedom in God are presented to the conceptive faculty: the State, on the other hand, regulated by the selfsame Reason, is a temple of Human Freedom concerned with the perception and volition of a reality, whose purport may itself be called divine. Thus Freedom in the State is preserved and established by Religion, since moral rectitude in the State is only the carrying out of that which constitutes the fundamental principle of Religion. The process displayed in History is only the manifestation of Religion as Human Reason—the production of the religious principle which dwells in the heart of man, under the form of Secular Freedom. Thus the discord between the inner life of the heart and the actual world is removed. To realize this is, however, the vocation of another people—or other peoples—viz., the *German.* In ancient Rome itself, Christianity cannot find a ground on which it may become actual, and develop an empire.

Chapter III.—The Byzantine Empire

With Constantine the Great the Christian religion ascended the throne of the empire. He was followed by a succession of Christian Emperors, interrupted only by Julian—who however, could do but little for the prostrate ancient faith. The Roman Empire embraced the whole civilized earth, from the Western Ocean to the Tigris—from the interior of Africa, to the Danube (Pannonia, Dacia). Christianity soon spread through the length and breadth of this enormous realm. Rome had long ceased to be the exclusive residence of the Emperors. Many of Constantine's predecessors had resided in Milan or other places; and he himself established a second court in the ancient Byzantium, which received the name of Constantinople. From the first its population consisted chiefly of Christians, and Constantine lavished every appliance to render this new abode equal in splendor to the old. The empire still remained in its integrity till Theodosius the Great made permanent a separation that had been only occasional, and divided it between his two sons. The reign of Theodosius displayed the last faint glimmer of that splendor which had glorified the Roman world. Under him the pagan temples were shut, the sacrifices and ceremonies abolished, and paganism itself forbidden: gradually however it entirely vanished of itself. The heathen orators of the time cannot sufficiently express their wonder and astonishment at the monstrous contrast between the days of their forefathers and their own. "Our Temples have become Tombs. The places which were formerly adorned with the holy statues of the Gods are now covered with sacred bones (relics of the Martyrs); men who have suffered a shameful death for their crimes, whose bodies are covered with stripes, and whose heads have been embalmed, are the object of veneration." All that was contemned is exalted; all that was formerly revered, is trodden in the dust. The last of the pagans express this enormous contrast with profound lamentation.

The Roman Empire was divided between the two sons of Theodosius. The elder, Arcadius, received the Eastern Empire:—Ancient Greece, with Thrace, Asia Minor, Syria, Egypt;

the younger, Honorius, the Western:—Italy, Africa, Spain,
Gaul, Britain.   Immediately after the death of Theodosius,
confusion entered, and the Roman provinces were overwhelmed
by alien peoples.   Already, under the Emperor Valens, the Visigoths, pressed by the Huns, had solicited a domicile on the
hither side of the Danube.   This was granted them, on the condition that they should defend the border provinces of the empire.   But maltreatment roused them to revolt.   Valens was
beaten and fell on the field.   The later emperors paid court to
the leader of these Goths.   Alaric, the bold Gothic Chief, turned
his arms against Italy.   Stilicho, the general and minister of
Honorius, stayed his course A.D. 403, by the battle of Pollentia,
as at a later date he also routed Radagaisus, leader of the
Alans, Suevi, and others.   Alaric now attacked Gaul and Spain,
and on the fall of Stilicho returned to Italy.   Rome was stormed
and plundered by him A.D. 410.   Afterwards Attila advanced
on it with the terrible might of the Huns—one of those purely
Oriental phenomena, which, like a mere storm-torrent, rise to
a furious height and bear down everything in their course, but
in a brief space are so completely spent, that nothing is seen of
them but the traces they have left in the ruins which they have
occasioned.   Attila pressed into Gaul, where, A.D. 451, a vigorous resistance was offered him by Ætius, near Chalons on
the Marne.   Victory remained doubtful.   Attila subsequently
marched upon Italy and died in the year 453.   Soon afterwards
however Rome was taken and plundered by the Vandals under
Genseric.   Finally, the dignity of the Western Emperors became a farce, and their empty title was abolished by Odoacer,
King of the Heruli.

The Eastern Empire long survived, and in the West a new
Christian population was formed from the invading barbarian
hordes.   Christianity had at first kept aloof from the state, and
the development which it experienced related to doctrine, internal organization, discipline, etc.   But now it had become
dominant: it was now a political power, a political motive.
We now see Christianity under two forms: on the one side
barbarian nations whose culture was yet to begin, who have
to acquire the very rudiments of science, law, and polity; on
other side civilized peoples in possession of Greek science and
a highly refined Oriental culture.   Municipal legislation among
them was complete—having reached the highest perfection

through the labors of the great Roman jurisconsults; so that the *corpus juris* compiled at the instance of the Emperor Justinian, still excites the admiration of the world. Here the Christian religion is placed in the midst of a developed civilization, which did not proceed from it. There, on the contrary, the process of culture has its very first step still to take, and that within the sphere of Christianity.

These two empires, therefore, present a most remarkable contrast, in which we have before our eyes a grand example of the necessity of a people's having its culture *developed* in the spirit of the Christian religion. The history of the highly civilized Eastern Empire—where as we might suppose, the Spirit of Christianity could be taken up in its truth and purity —exhibits to us a millennial series of uninterrupted crimes, weaknesses, basenesses and want of principle; a most repulsive and consequently a most uninteresting picture. It is evident here, how Christianity may be abstract, and how as such it is powerless, on account of its very purity and intrinsic spirituality. It may even be entirely separated from the World, as *e.g.* in Monasticism—which originated in Egypt. It is a common notion and saying, in reference to the power of Religion, abstractly considered, over the hearts of men, that if Christian love were universal, private and political life would both be perfect, and the state of mankind would be thoroughly righteous and moral. Such representations may be a pious *wish*, but do not possess truth; for religion is something internal, having to do with conscience alone. To it all the passions and desires are opposed, and in order that heart, will, intelligence may become true, they must be *thoroughly educated;* Right must become Custom—Habit; practical activity must be elevated to rational action; the State must have a rational organization, and then at length does the will of individuals become a truly righteous one. Light shining in darkness may perhaps give color, but not a picture animated by Spirit. The Byzantine Empire is a grand example of how the Christian religion may maintain an abstract character among a cultivated people, if the whole organization of the State and of the Laws is not reconstructed in harmony with its principle. At Byzantium Christianity had fallen into the hands of the dregs of the population—the lawless mob. Popular license on the one side and courtly baseness on the other side, take refuge under the sanction of religion, and degrade the latter to a disgusting object. In regard to religion, two interests obtained prominence: first, the settlement of doctrine; and secondly, the appointment to ecclesiastical offices. The settlement of doctrine pertained to the Councils and Church authorities; but the principle of Christianity is Freedom—subjective insight. These matters therefore, were special subjects of contention for the populace; violent civil wars arose, and everywhere might be witnessed scenes of murder, conflagration and pillage, perpetrated in the cause of Christian dogmas. A famous schism *e.g.* occurred in reference to the dogma of the **Τρισάγιον.** The words read: " Holy, Holy, Holy, is the Lord God of Zebaoth." To this, one party, in honor of Christ, added—" who was crucified for us." Another party rejected the addition, and sanguinary struggles ensued. In the contest on the question whether Christ were ὁμοούσιος or ὁμοιούσιος—that is of *the same* or of *similar* nature with God—the one letter ι cost many thousands their lives. Especially notorious are the contentions about Images, in which it often happened, that the Emperor declared for the images and the Patriarch against, or conversely. Streams of blood flowed as the result. Gregory Nazianzen says somewhere: " This city (Constantinople,) is full of handicraftsmen and slaves, who are all profound theologians, and preach in their workshops and in the streets. If you want a man to change a piece of silver, he instructs you in what consists the distinction between the Father and the Son: if you ask the price of a loaf of bread, you receive for answer—that the Son is inferior to the Father; and if you ask, whether the bread is ready, the rejoinder is that the genesis of the Son was from Nothing." The Idea of Spirit contained in this doctrine was thus treated in an utterly unspiritual manner. The appointment to the Patriarchate at Constantinople, Antioch and Alexandria, and the jealousy and ambition of the Patriarchs likewise occasioned many intestine struggles. To all these religious contentions was added the interest in the gladiators and their combats, and in the parties of the blue and green color, which likewise occasioned the bloodiest encounters; a sign of the most fearful degradation, as proving that all feeling for what is serious and elevated is lost, and that the delirium of religious passion is quite consistent with an appetite for gross and barbarous spectacles.

The chief points in the Christian religion were at last, by degrees, established by the Councils. The Christians of the Byzantine Empire remained sunk in the dream of superstition—persisting in blind obedience to the Patriarchs and the priesthood. Image-Worship, to which we alluded above, occasioned the most violent struggles and storms. The brave Emperor Leo the Isaurian in particular, persecuted images with the greatest obstinacy, and in the year 754, Image-Worship was declared by a Council to be an invention of the devil. Nevertheless, in the year 787 the Empress Irene had it restored under the authority of a Nicene Council, and the Empress Theodora definitively established it—proceeding against its enemies with energetic rigor. The iconoclastic Patriarch received two hundred blows, the bishops trembled, the monks exulted, and the memory of this orthodox proceeding was celebrated by an annual ecclesiastical festival. The West, on the contrary, repudiated Image-Worship as late as the year 794, in the Council held at Frankfort; and, though retaining the images, blamed most severely the superstition of the Greeks. Not till the later Middle Ages did Image-Worship meet with universal adoption as the result of quiet and slow advances.

The Byzantine Empire was thus distracted by passions of all kinds *within,* and pressed by the barbarians—to whom the Emperors could offer but feeble resistance—*without.* The realm was in a condition of perpetual insecurity. Its general aspect presents a disgusting picture of imbecility; wretched, nay, insane passions, stifle the growth of all that is noble in thoughts, deeds, and persons. Rebellion on the part of generals, depositions of the Emperors by their means or through the intrigues of the courtiers, assassination or poisoning of the Emperors by their own wives and sons, women surrendering themselves to lusts and abominations of all kinds—such are the scenes which History here brings before us; till at last—about the middle of the fifteenth century (A.D. 1453)—the rotten edifice of the Eastern Empire crumbled in pieces before the might of the vigorous Turks.

PART IV

THE GERMAN WORLD

THE German Spirit is the Spirit of the new World. Its aim is the realization of absolute Truth as the unilimited self-determination of Freedom—*that* Freedom which has its own absolute form itself as its purport.* The destiny of the German peoples is, to be the bearers of the Christian principle. The principle of Spiritual Freedom—of Reconciliation [of the Objective and Subjective], was introduced into the still simple, unformed minds of those peoples; and the part assigned them in the service of the World-Spirit was that of not merely possessing the Idea of Freedom as the substratum of their religious conceptions, but of producing it in free and spontaneous developments from their subjective self-consciousness.

In entering on the task of dividing the German World into its natural periods, we must remark that we have not, as was the case in treating of the Greeks and Romans, a double external relation—backwards to an earlier World-Historical people, and forwards to a later one—to guide us. History shows that the process of development among the peoples now under consideration, was an altogether different one. The Greeks and Romans had reached maturity within, ere they directed their energies outwards. The Germans, on the contrary, began with self-diffusion—deluging the world, and overpowering in their course the inwardly rotten, hollow political fabrics of the civilized nations. Only then did their *development* begin, kindled by a foreign culture, a foreign religion, polity and legislation. The process of culture they underwent consisted in taking up

* That is: The Supreme Law of the Universe is recognized as identical with the dictates of Conscience—becomes a "law of liberty." Morality—that authority which has the incontestable right to determine men's actions, which there-fore is the only absolutely *free* and unlimited power—is no longer a compulsory enactment, but the free choice of human beings. The good man would make Law for himself if he found none made for him.

341

foreign elements and reductively amalgamating them with their own national life. Thus their history presents an introversion—the attraction of alien forms of life and the bringing these to bear upon their own. In the Crusades, indeed, and in the discovery of America, the Western World directed its energies outwards. But it was not thus brought in contact with a World-Historical people that had preceded it; it did not dispossess a principle that had previously governed the world. The relation to an extraneous principle here only *accompanies* [does not *constitute*] the history—does not bring with it essential changes in the nature of those conditions which characterize the peoples in question, but rather wears the aspect of internal evolution.*—The relation to other countries and periods is thus entirely different from that sustained by the Greeks and Romans. For the Christian world is the world of completion; the grand principle of being is realized, consequently the end of days is fully come. The Idea can discover in Christianity no point in the aspirations of Spirit that is not satisfied. For its individual members, the Church is, it is true, a preparation for an eternal state as something future; since the units who compose it, in their isolated and several capacity, occupy a position of particularity: but the Church has also the Spirit of God actually present in it, it forgives the sinner and is a present kingdom of heaven. Thus the Christian World has no absolute existence outside its sphere, but only a relative one which is already implicitly vanquished, and in respect to which its only concern is to make it apparent that this conquest has taken place. Hence it follows that an external reference ceases to be the characteristic element determining the epochs of the modern world. We have therefore to look for another principle of division.

The German World took up the Roman culture and religion in their completed form. There was indeed a German and Northern religion, but it had by no means taken deep root in the soul; Tacitus therefore calls the Germans: " Securi adversus Deos." The Christian Religion which they adopted, had received from Councils and Fathers of the Church, who possessed the whole culture, and in particular, the philosophy of the Greek and Roman World, a perfected dogmatic system;

* The influence of the Crusades and of the discovery of America was simply *reflex*. No other phase of humanity was thereby merged in Christendom.

the Church, too, had a completely developed hierarchy. To the native tongue of the Germans, the Church likewise opposed one perfectly developed—the Latin. In art and philosophy a similar alien influence predominated. What of Alexandrian and of formal Aristotelian philosophy was still preserved in the writings of Boethius and elsewhere, became the fixed basis of speculative thought in the West for many centuries. The same principle holds in regard to the form of the secular sovereignty. Gothic and other chiefs gave themselves the name of Roman Patricians, and at a later date the Roman Empire was restored. Thus the German world appears, superficially, to be only a continuation of the Roman. But there lived in it an entirely *new Spirit,* through which the World was to be regenerated— the free Spirit, viz. which reposes on itself—the absolutely self-determination [Eigensinn] of subjectivity. To this self-involved subjectivity, the corresponding objectivity [Inhalt] stands opposed as absolutely alien. The distinction and antithesis which is evolved from these principles, is that of *Church* and *State.* On the one side, the Church develops itself, as the embodiment of absolute Truth; for it is the consciousness of this truth, and at the same time the agency for rendering the Individual harmonious with it. On the other side stands secular consciousness, which, with its aims, occupies the world of Limitation—the *State,* based on Heart [emotional and thence *social* affections] or mutual confidence and subjectivity generally. European history is the exhibition of the growth of each of these principles severally, in Church and State; then of an antithesis on the part of both—not only of the one to the other, but appearing within the sphere of each of these bodies themselves (since each of them is itself a totality); lastly, of the harmonizing of the antithesis.

The *three periods* of this world will have to be treated accordingly.

The *first* begins with the appearance of the German Nations in the Roman Empire—the incipient development of these peoples, converts to Christianity, and now established in the possession of the West. Their barbarous and simple character prevents this initial period from possessing any great interest. The Christian world then presents itself as " Christendom "— one mass, in which the Spiritual and the Secular form only different aspects. This epoch extends to Charlemagne.

The *second period* develops the two sides of the antithesis to a logically consequential independence and opposition—the Church for itself as a *Theocracy,* and the State for itself as a *Feudal Monarchy.* Charlemagne had formed an alliance with the Holy See against the Lombards and the factions of the nobles in Rome. A union thus arose between the spiritual and the secular power, and a kingdom of heaven on earth promised to follow in the wake of this conciliation. But just at this time, instead of a spiritual kingdom of heaven, the inwardness of the Christian principle wears the appearance of being altogether directed outwards and leaving its proper sphere. Christian Freedom is perverted to its very opposite, both in a religious and secular respect; on the one hand to the severest bondage, on the other hand to the most immoral excess—a barbarous intensity of every passion. In this period two aspects of society are to be especially noticed: the first is the formation of states —superior and inferior suzerainties exhibiting a regulated subordination, so that every relation becomes a firmly-fixed private right, excluding a sense of universality. This regulated subordination appears in the *Feudal System.* The second aspect presents the antithesis of *Church and State.* This antithesis exists solely because the Church, to whose management the Spiritual was committed, itself sinks down into every kiŋd of worldliness—a worldliness which appears only the more detestable, because all passions assume the sanction of religion.

The time of Charles V's reign—*i.e.,* the first half of the sixteenth century—forms the end of the second, and likewise the beginning of the *third period.* Secularity appears now as gaining a consciousness of its intrinsic worth—becomes aware of its having a value of its own in the morality, rectitude, probity and activity of man. The consciousness of independent validity is aroused through the restoration of Christian freedom. The Christian principle has now passed through the terrible discipline of culture, and it first attains truth and reality through the Reformation. This third period of the German World extends from the Reformation to our own times. The principle of Free Spirit is here made the banner of the World, and from this principle are evolved the universal axioms of Reason. Formal Thought—the Understanding—had been already developed; but Thought received its true material first with the Reformation, through the reviviscent concrete con-

sciousness of Free Spirit. From that epoch Thought began
to gain a culture properly its own: principles were derived
from it which were to be the norm for the constitution of the
State. Political life was now to be consciously regulated by
Reason. Customary morality, traditional usage lost its validity; the various claims insisted upon, must prove their legitimacy as based on rational principles. Not till this era is the
Freedom of Spirit realized.

We may distinguish these periods as Kingdoms of the Father,
the Son, and the Spirit.* The Kingdom of the Father is the
consolidated, undistinguished mass, presenting a self-repeating
cycle, mere change—like that sovereignty of Chronos engulfing
his offspring. The Kingdom of the Son is the manifestation
of God merely in a *relation* to secular existence—shining upon
it as upon an alien object. The Kingdom of the Spirit is the
harmonizing of the antithesis.

These epochs may be also compared with the earlier empires. In the German æon, as the realm of Totality, we see the
distinct *repetition of the earlier epochs.* Charlemagne's time
may be compared with the Persian Empire; it is the period of
substantial unity—this unity having its foundation in the inner
man, the Heart, and both in the Spiritual and the Secular still
abiding in its simplicity.

To the Greek world and its merely *ideal* unity, the time preceding Charles V answers; where *real* unity no longer exists,
because all phases of particularity have become fixed in privileges and peculiar rights. As in the interior of the realms themselves, the different estates of the realm, with their several
claims, are isolated, so do the various states in their foreign
aspects occupy a *merely external* relation to each other. A
diplomatic policy arises, which in the interest of a European
balance of power, unites them *with* and *against* each other.
It is the time in which the world becomes clear and manifest
to itself (Discovery of America). So too does consciousness

* The conception of a mystical *regnum Patris, regnum Filii* and *regnum Spiritûs Sancti* is perfectly familiar to metaphysical theologians. The first represents the period in which Deity is not yet manifested—remains *self-involved.* The second is that of manifestation in an individual being, standing *apart from* mankind generally—" the Son." The third is that in which this barrier is broken down, and an intimate mystical communion ensues between God in Christ and the Regenerated, when God is " all in all." This remark may serve to prevent misconception as to the tone of the remainder of the paragraph. The mention of the Greek myth will appear pertinent in the view of those who admit what seems a very reasonable explanation of it—viz., as an adumbration of the *self-involved* character of the prehistorical period.

gain clearness *in* the supersensuous world and *respecting* it.
Substantial objective religion brings itself to sensuous clearness
in the sensuous element (Christian Art in the age of Pope Leo),
and also becomes clear to itself in the element of inmost truth.
We may compare this time with that of Pericles. The introversion of Spirit begins (Socrates—Luther), though Pericles
is wanting in this epoch. Charles V possesses enormous possibilities in point of outward appliances, and appears absolute
in his power; but the inner spirit of Pericles, and therefore the
absolute means of establishing a free sovereignty, are not in him.
This is the epoch when Spirit becomes clear to itself in separa-
tions occurring in the realm of reality; now the distinct elements of the German world manifest their essential nature.

The third epoch may be compared with the Roman World.
The unity of a universal principle is here quite as decidedly
present, yet not as the unity of abstract universal sovereignty,
but as the Hegemony of self-cognizant Thought. The authority of Rational Aim is acknowledged, and privileges and
particularities melt away before the common object of the
State. Peoples will the Right in and for itself; regard is not
had exclusively to particular conventions between nations, but
principles enter into the considerations with which diplomacy
is occupied. As little can Religion maintain itself apart from
Thought, but either advances to the comprehension of the Idea,
or, compelled by thought itself, becomes intensive belief—or
lastly, from despair of finding itself at home in thought, flees
back from it in pious horror, and becomes Superstition.

SECTION I

THE ELEMENTS OF THE CHRISTIAN GERMAN WORLD

Chapter I.—The Barbarian Migrations

RESPECTING this first period, we have on the whole little to say, for it affords us comparatively slight materials for reflection. We will not follow the Germans back into their forests, nor investigate the origin of their migrations. Those forests of theirs have always passed for the abodes of free peoples, and Tacitus sketched his celebrated picture of Germany with a certain love and longing—contrasting it with the corruption and artificiality of that world to which he himself belonged. But we must not on this account regard such a state of barbarism as an exalted one, or fall into some such error as Rousseau's, who represents the condition of the American savages as one in which man is in possession of true freedom. Certainly there is an immense amount of misfortune and sorrow of which the savage knows nothing; but this is a merely negative advantage, while freedom is essential positive. It is only the blessings conferred by affirmative freedom that are regarded as such in the highest grade of consciousness.

Our first acquaintance with the Germans finds each individual enjoying an independent freedom; and yet there is a certain community of feeling and interest, though not yet matured to a political condition. Next we see them inundating the Roman empire. It was partly the fertility of its domains, partly the necessity of seeking other habitations, that furnished the inciting cause. In spite of the wars in which they engage with the Romans, individuals, and even entire clans, enter their service as soldiers. Even so early as the battle of Pharsalia we find German cavalry united with the Roman forces of Cæsar. In military service and intercourse with civilized peoples, they became acquainted with their advantages—advantages tending

347

to the enjoyment and convenience of life, but also, and principally, those of mental cultivation. In the later emigrations,
many nations—some entirely, others partially—remained behind in their original abodes.

Accordingly, a distinction must be made between the German
nations who remained in their ancient habitations and those
who spread themselves over the Roman empire, and mingled
with the conquered peoples. Since in their migratory expeditions the Germans attached themselves to their leaders of their
own free choice, we find a peculiar duplicate condition of the
great Teutonic families (Eastern and Western Goths; Goths
in all parts of the world and in their original country; Scandinavians and Normans in Norway, but also appearing as
knightly adventurers in the wide world). However different
might be the fates of these peoples, they nevertheless had one
aim in common—to procure themselves possessions, and to
develop themselves in the direction of political organization.
This process of growth is equally characteristic of all.. In the
West—in Spain and Portugal—the Suevi and Vandals are the
first settlers, but are subdued and dispossessed by the Visigoths.
A great *Visigothic* kingdom was established, to which Spain,
Portugal, and a part of Southern France belonged. The second
kingdom is that of the *Franks*—a name which, from the end
of the second century, was given in common to the Istævonian
races between the Rhine and the Weser. They established
themselves between the Moselle and the Scheldt, and under
their leader, Clovis, pressed forward into Gaul as far as the
Loire. He afterwards reduced the Franks on the Lower Rhine,
and the Alemanni on the Upper Rhine; his sons subjugated
the Thuringians and Burgundians. The third kingdom is that
of the *Ostrogoths* in Italy, founded by Theodoric, and highly
flourishing beneath his rule. The learned Romans Cassiodorus
and Boëthius filled the highest offices of state under Theodoric.
But this Ostrogothic kingdom did not last long; it was destroyed by the Byzantines under Belisarius and Narses. In
the second half (568) of the sixth century, the *Lombards* invaded Italy and ruled for two centuries, till this kingdom also
was subjected to the Frank sceptre by Charlemagne. At a
later date, the Normans also established themselves in Lower
Italy. Our attention is next claimed by the *Burgundians*, who
were subjugated by the Franks, and whose kingdom forms a

kind of partition wall between France and Germany. The
Angles and *Saxons* entered Britain and reduced it under their
sway. Subsequently, the Normans make their appearance here
also.

These countries—previously a part of the Roman empire—
thus experienced the fate of subjugation by the Barbarians.
In the first instance, a great contrast presented itself between
the already civilized inhabitants of those countries and the vic-
tors; but this contrast terminated in the hybrid character of
the new nations that were now formed. The whole mental
and moral existence of such states exhibits a divided aspect;
in their inmost being we have characteristics that point to an
alien origin. This distinction strikes us even on the surface,
in their *language,* which is an intermixture of the ancient Roman—already united with the vernacular—and the German.
We may class these nations together as *Romanic*—comprehending thereby Italy, Spain, Portugal, and France. Contrasted
with these stand three others, more or less *German-speaking*
nations, which have maintained a consistent tone of uninterrupted fidelity to native character—Germany itself, Scandinavia, and England. The last was, indeed, incorporated in the
Roman empire, but was affected by Roman culture little more
than superficially—like Germany itself—and was again Germanized by Angles and Saxons. *Germany Proper* kept itself
pure from any admixture; only the southern and western border—on the Danube and the Rhine—had been subjugated by
the Romans. The portion between the Rhine and the Elbe
remained thoroughly national. This part of Germany was inhabited by several tribes. Besides the Ripuarian Franks and
those established by Clovis in the districts of the Maine, four
leading tribes—the Alemanni, the Boioarians, the Thuringians,
and the Saxons—must be mentioned. The *Scandinavians* retained in their fatherland a similar purity from intermixture;
and also made themselves celebrated by their expeditions, under
the name of Normans. They extended their chivalric enter-
prises over almost all parts of Europe. Part of them went to
Russia, and there became the founders of the Russian Empire;
part settled in Northern France and Britain; another established principalities in Lower Italy and Sicily. Thus a part
of the Scandinavians founded states in foreign lands, another
maintained its nationality by the ancestral hearth.

We find, moreover, in the East of Europe, the great *Sclavonic* nation, whose settlements extended west of the Elbe to the Danube. The Magyars (Hungarians) settled in between them. In Moldavia, Wallachia and northern Greece appear the Bulgarians, Servians, and Albanians, likewise of Asiatic origin— left behind as broken barbarian remains in the shocks and counter-shocks of the advancing hordes. These people did, indeed, found kingdoms and sustain spirited conflicts with the various nations that came across their path. Sometimes, as an advanced guard—an intermediate nationality—they took part in the struggle between Christian Europe and unchristian Asia. The Poles even liberated beleaguered Vienna from the Turks; and the Sclaves have to some extent been drawn within the sphere of Occidental Reason. Yet this entire body of peoples remains excluded from our consideration, because hitherto it has not appeared as an independent element in the series of phases that Reason has assumed in the World. Whether it will do so hereafter, is a question that does not concern us here; for in History we have to do with the Past.

The German Nation was characterized by the sense of Natural Totality—an idiosyncrasy which we may call *Heart* [Gemüth].* "Heart" is that undeveloped, indeterminate totality of Spirit, in reference to the Will, in which satisfaction of soul is attained in a correspondingly general and indeterminate way. *Character* is a particular form of will and interest asserting itself; but the quality in question [Gemüthlichkeit] has no particular aim—riches, honor, or the like; in fact does not concern itself with any *objective* condition [a "position in the world" in virtue of wealth, dignity, etc.] but with the entire condition of the soul—a general sense of enjoyment. Will in the case of such an idiosyncrasy is exclusively *formal* Will †—its purely

* The word "Gemüth" has no exactly corresponding term in English. It is used further on synonymously with "Herz," and the openness to various emotions and impressions which it implies, may perhaps be approximately rendered by "Heart." Yet it is but an awkward substitute.

† Formal Will or Subjective Freedom is inclination or mere casual liking, and is opposed to Substantial or Objective Will—also called Objective Freedom— which denotes the principles that form the basis of society, and that have been spontaneously adopted by particular nations or by mankind generally. The latter as well as the former may lay claim to being a manifestation of Human Will.

For however rigid the restraints which those principles impose on individuals, they are the result of no extraneous compulsion brought to bear on the community at large, and are recognized as rightfully authoritative even by the individuals whose physical comfort or relative affections they most painfully contravene. Unquestioning homage to unreasonable despotism, and the severe rubrics of religious penance, can be traced to no natural necessity or stimulus *ab extra*. The principles in which these originate, may rather be called *the settled and supreme determination* of the community that recognizes them. The term "Objective Will" seems therefore not unfitly used to describe the psycho-

subjective Freedom exhibits itself as self-will. To the disposition thus designated, every particular object of attraction
seems important, for " Heart " surrenders itself entirely to
each; but as, on the other hand, it is not interested in the quality
of such aim in the abstract, it does not become exclusively absorbed in that aim, so as to pursue it with violent and evil passion—does not go the length of abstract vice. In the idiosyncrasy we term " Heart," no such absorption of interest presents
itself; it wears, on the whole, the appearance of " well-mean-
ing." *Character* is its direct opposite.*

This is the abstract principle innate in the German peoples,
and that subjective side which they present to the objective in
Christianity. " Heart " has no particular object; in Christianity
we have the Absolute *Object* [*i.e.* it is concerned with the entire
range of Truth]—all that can engage and occupy human subjectivity. Now it is the desire of satisfaction without further
definition or restriction, that is involved in " Heart "; and it is
exactly that for which we found an appropriate application in
the principle of Christianity. The Indefinite as Substance, in
objectivity, is the purely Universal—God; while the reception
of the individual will to a participation in His favor, is the com-
plementary element in the Christian concrete Unity. The absolutely Universal is that which contains in it all determinations,
and in virtue of this is itself indeterminate. Subject [individual
personality] is the absolutely determinate; and these two are
identical.† This was exhibited above as the material content
[Inhalt] in Christianity; here we find it subjectively as
" Heart." Subject [Personality] must then also gain an objective form, that is, be expanded to an object. It is necessary

logical phenomena in question. The
term " *Substantial* Will " (as opposed to
" Formal Will "), denoting the same
phenomena, needs no defence or explanation. The third term, " Objective
Freedom," used synonymously with the
two preceding, is justified on the ground
of the unlimited dominion exercised by
such principles as those mentioned
above. " Deus solus liber." (See remarks to this effect on page 35 of the Introduction, and elsewhere.)

* An incapacity for conspiracy has been
remarked as a characteristic feature of
the *Teutonic* portion of the inhabitants
of the British Isles, as compared with
their Celtic countrymen. If such a difference can be substantiated, we seem
to have an important illustration and
confirmation of Hegel's view.—ED.

† Pure Self—pure subjectivity or personality—not only excludes all that is

manifestly objective, all that is evidently
Not-Self, but also abstracts from any
peculiar conditions that may temporarily
adhere to it, *e.g.* youth or age, riches or
poverty, a present or a future state.
Thus though it seems, *primâ facie*, a
fixed point or atom, it is absolutely unlimited. By loss or degradation of bodily
and mental faculties, it is possible to conceive one's self degraded to a position
which it would be impossible to distinguish from that which we attribute to
the brutes, or by increase and improvement of those faculties, indefinitely elevated in the scale of being, while yet self
—personal identity—is retained. On the
other hand, Absolute Being in the Christian concrete view, is an Infinite Self.
The Absolutely Limited is thus shown
to be identical with the Absolutely Unlimited.

that for the indefinite susceptibilty which we designate
" Heart," the Absolute also should assume the form of an Object, in order that man on his part may attain a consciousness
of his unity with that object. But this recognition of the Absolute [in Christ] requires the purification of man's subjectivity
—requires it to become a real, concrete self, a sharer in general
interests as a denizen of the world at large, and that it should
act in accordance with large and liberal aims, recognize Law,
and find satisfaction in it.—Thus we find here two principles
corresponding the one with the other, and recognize the adaptation of the German peoples to be, as we stated above, the
bearers of the higher principle of Spirit.

We advance then to the consideration of the German principle in its primary phase of existence, *i.e.* the earliest historical
condition of the German nations. Their quality of " Heart "
is in its first appearance quite abstract, undeveloped and destitute of any particular object; for substantial aims are not involved in " Heart " itself. Where this susceptibilty stands
alone, it appears as a want of character—mere inanity.
" Heart " as purely abstract, is dulness; thus we see in the
original condition of the Germans a barbarian dulness, mental
confusion and vagueness. Of the *Religion* of the Germans
we know little.—The Druids belonged to Gaul and were extirpated by the Romans. There was indeed, a peculiar northern
mythology; but how slight a hold the religion of the Germans
had upon their hearts, has been already remarked, and it is
also evident from the fact that the Germans were easily converted to Christianity. The Saxons, it is true, offered considerable resistance to Charlemagne; but this was directed, not
so much against the religion he brought with him, as against
oppression itself. Their religion had no profundity; and the
same may be said of their *ideas* of *law*. Murder was not regarded and punished as a crime: it was expiated by a pecuniary
fine. This indicates a deficiency in depth of sentiment—that
absence of a power of abstraction and discrimination that marks
their peculiar temperament [Nichtentzweitseyn des Gemüthes]
—a temperament which leads them to regard it only as an injury to the community when one of its members is killed, and
nothing further. The blood-revenge of the Arabs is based on
the feeling that the honor of the Family is injured. Among
the Germans the community had no dominion over the indi-

vidual, for the element of freedom is the first consideration in
their union in a social relationship. The ancient Germans were
famed for their love of freedom; the Romans formed a correct
idea of them in this particular from the first. Freedom has
been the watchword in Germany down to the most recent times,
and even the league of princes under Frederick II had its origin in the love of liberty. This element of freedom, in passing
over to a social relationship, can establish only popular communities; so that these communities constitute the whole state,
and every member of the community, as such, is a free man.
Homicide could be expiated by a pecuniary mulct, because the
individuality of the free man was regarded as sacred—permanently and inviolably—whatever he might have done. The
community or its presiding power, with the assistance of members of the community, delivered judgment in affairs of private
right, with a view to the protection of person and property.
For affairs affecting the body politic at large—for wars and
similar contingencies—the whole community had to be consulted. The second point to be observed is, that social nuclei
were formed by free confederation, and by voluntary attachment to military leaders and princes. The connection in this
case was that of *Fidelity;* for Fidelity is the second watchword
of the Germans, as Freedom was the first. Individuals attach
themselves with free choice to an individual, and without external prompting make this relation an inviolable one. This
we find neither among the Greeks nor the Romans. The relation of Agamemnon and the princes who accompanied him was
not that of feudal suit and service: it was a free association
merely for *a particular purpose*—a Hegemony. But the German confederations have their being not in a relation to a mere
external aim or cause, but in a relation to the spiritual self—
the subjective inmost personality. Heart, disposition, the concrete subjectivity in its integrity, which does not attach itself
to any abstract bearing of an object, but regards the whole of
it as a condition of attachment—making itself dependent on
the person *and* the cause—renders this relation a compound of
fidelity to a person and obedience to a principle.

The union of the two relations—of individual freedom in
the community, and of the bond implied in association—is the
main point in the formation of the State. In this, duties and
rights are no longer left to arbitrary choice, but are determined

as fixed relations;—involving, moreover, the condition that the State be the soul of the entire body, and remain its sovereign—that from it should be derived particular aims and the authorization both of political acts and political agents—the generic character and interests of the community constituting the permanent basis of the whole. But here we have the peculiarity of the German states, that contrary to the view thus presented, social relations do not assume the character of general definitions and laws, but are entirely split up into *private* rights and *private* obligations. They perhaps exhibit a social or communal mould or stamp, but nothing *universal;* the laws are absolutely particular, and the Rights are Privileges. Thus the state was a patchwork of private rights, and a rational political life was the tardy issue of wearisome struggles and convulsions.

We have said, that the Germans were predestined to be the bearers of the Christian principle, and to carry out the Idea as the absolutely Rational aim. In the first instance we have only vague volition, in the background of which lies the True and Infinite. The True is present only as an unsolved problem, for their Soul is not yet purified. A long process is required to complete this purification so as to realize concrete Spirit. Religion comes forward with a challenge to the violence of the passions, and rouses them to madness. The excess of passions is aggravated by evil conscience, and heightened to an insane rage; which perhaps would not have been the case, had that opposition been absent. We behold the terrible spectacle of the most fearful extravagance of passion in all the royal houses of that period. Clovis, the founder of the Frank Monarchy, is stained with the blackest crimes. Barbarous harshness and cruelty characterize all the succeeding Merovingians; the same spectacle is repeated in the Thuringian and other royal houses. The Christian principle is certainly the problem implicit in their souls; but these are primarily still crude. The Will—potentially true—mistakes itself, and separates itself from the true and proper aim by particular, limited aims. Yet it is in this struggle with itself and contrariety to its bias, that it realizes its wishes; it contends against the object which it really desires, and thus accomplishes it; for implicitly, *potentially*, it is *reconciled.* The Spirit of God lives in the Church; it is the inward impelling Spirit. But it is in the World that Spirit is to be realized—in a material not yet brought into harmony with it. Now this material is the Subjective Will, which thus has a contradiction in itself. On the religious side, we often observe a change of this kind: a man who has all his life been fighting and hewing his way—who with all vehemence of character and passion, has struggled and revelled in secular occupations—on a sudden repudiates it all, to betake himself to religious seclusion. But in the World, secular business cannot be thus repudiated; it demands accomplishment, and ultimately the discovery is made, that Spirit finds the goal of its struggle and its harmonization, in that very sphere which it made the object of its resistance—it finds that *secular pursuits are a spiritual occupation.*

We thus observe, that individuals and peoples regard that which is their misfortune, as their greatest happiness, and conversely, struggle against their happiness as their greatest misery. *La vérité, en la repoussant, on l'embrasse.* Europe comes to the truth while, and to the degree in which, she has repulsed it. It is in the agitation thus occasioned, that Providence especially exercises its sovereignty; realizing its absolute aim—its honor—as the result of unhappiness, sorrow, private aims and the unconscious will of the nations of the earth.

While, therefore, in the West this long process in the world's history—necessary to that purification by which Spirit in the concrete is realized—is commencing, the purification requisite for developing *Spirit in the abstract* which we observe carried on contemporaneously in the East, is more quickly accomplished. The latter does not need a long process, and we see it produced rapidly, even suddenly, in the first half of the seventh century, in Mahometanism.

Chapter II.—Mohametanism

On the one hand we see the *European* world forming itself anew—the nations taking firm root there, to produce a world of free reality expanded and developed in every direction. We behold them beginning their work by bringing all social relations under the form of *particularity*—with dull and narrow intelligence splitting that which in its nature is generic and normal, into a multitude of chance contingencies; rendering that which ought to be simple principle and law, a tangled web of convention. In short, while the West began to shelter itself in a political edifice of chance, entanglement and particularity, the very opposite direction necessarily made its appearance in the world, to produce the balance of the totality of spiritual manifestation. This took place in the *Revolution of the East,* which destroyed all particularity and dependence, and perfectly cleared up and purified the soul and disposition; making the abstract One the absolute object of attention and devotion, and to the same extent, pure subjective consciousness—the Knowledge of this One alone—the only aim of reality;—making the *Unconditioned* [das Verhältnisslose] the *condition* [Verhältniss] *of existence.*

We have already become acquainted with the nature of the Oriental principle, and seen that its Highest Being is only negative;—that with it the positive imports an abandonment to mere nature—the enslavement of Spirit to the world of realities. Only among the Jews have we observed the principle of pure Unity elevated to a thought; for only among them was adoration paid to the One, as an object of thought. This unity then remained, when the purification of the mind to the conception of abstract Spirit had been accomplished; but it was freed from the particularity by which the worship of Jehovah had been hampered. Jehovah was only the God of that one people— the God of Abraham, of Isaac and Jacob: only with the Jews had this God made a covenant; only to this people hàd he revealed himself. That speciality of relation was done away with in Mahometanism. In this spiritual universality, in this unlimited and indefinite purity and simplicity of conception, human personality has no other aim than the realization of this universality and simplicity. *Allah* has not the affirmative, limited aim of the Judaic God. The worship of the One is the only final aim of Mahometanism, and subjectivity has this worship for the sole occupation of its activity, combined with the design to subjugate secular existence to the One. This One has indeed, the quality of Spirit; yet because subjectivity suffers itself to be absorbed in the object, this One is deprived of every concrete predicate; so that neither does subjectivity become on its part spiritually free, nor on the other hand is the object of its veneration concrete. But Mahometanism is not the Hindoo, not the Monastic immersion in the Absolute. Subjectivity is here living and unlimited—an energy which enters into secular life with a purely negative purpose, and busies itself and interferes with the world, only in such a way as shall promote the pure adoration of the One. The object of Mahometan worship is purely intellectual; no image, no representation of Allah is tolerated. Mahomet is a prophet but still man—not elevated above human weaknesses. The leading features of Mahometanism involve this—that in actual existence nothing can become fixed, but that everything is destined to expand itself in activity and life in the boundless amplitude of the world, so that the worship of the One remains the only bond by which the whole is capable of uniting. In this expansion, this active energy, all limits, all national and caste distinctions vanish; no particular race, political claim of birth or possession is regarded —only *man* as a *believer*. To adore the One, to believe in him, to fast—to remove the sense of speciality and consequent separation from the Infinite, arising from corporeal limitation—and to give alms—that is, to get rid of particular private possession —these are the essence of Mahometan injunctions; but the highest medit is to die for the Faith. He who perishes for it in battle, is sure of Paradise.

The Mahometan religion originated among the Arabs. Here Spirit exists in its simplest form, and the sense of the Formless has its especial abode; for in their deserts nothing can be brought into a firm consistent shape. The flight of Mahomet from Mecca in the year 622 is the Moslem era. Even during his life, and under his own leadership, but especially by following up his designs after his death under the guidance of his successors, the Arabs achieved their vast conquests. They first came down upon Syria and conquered its capital Damascus in the year 634. They then passed the Euphrates and Tigris and turned their arms against Persia, which soon submitted to them. In the West they conquered Egypt, Northern Africa and Spain, and pressed into Southern France as far as the Loire, where they were defeated by Charles Martel near Tours, A.D. 732. Thus the dominion of the Arabs extended itself in the West. In the East they reduced successively Persia, as already stated, Samarkand, and the Southwestern part of Asia Minor. These conquests, as also the spread of their religion, took place with extraordinary rapidity. Whoever became a convert to Islam, gained a perfect equality of rights with all Mussulmans. Those who rejected it, were, during the earliest period, slaughtered. Subsequently, however, the Arabs behaved more leniently to the conquered; so that if they were unwilling to go over to Islam, they were only required to pay an annual poll-tax. The towns that immediately submitted, were obliged to pay the victor a *tithe* of all their possessions; those which had to be captured, a *fifth*.

Abstraction swayed the minds of the Mahometans. Their object was, to establish an abstract worship, and they struggled for its accomplishment with the greatest enthusiasm. This enthusiasm was *Fanaticism,* that is, an enthusiasm for something abstract—for an abstract thought which sustains a negative position towards the established order of things. It is the essence of fanaticism to bear only a desolating destructive relation to the concrete; but that of Mahometanism was, at the same time, capable of the greatest elevation—an elevation free from all petty interests, and united with all the virtues that appertain to magnanimity and valor. *La religion et la terreur* was the principle in this case, as with Robespierre, *la liberté et la terreur.* But real life is nevertheless concrete, and introduces particular aims; conquest leads to sovereignty and wealth, to the conferring of prerogatives on a dynastic family, and to a union of individuals. But all this is only contingent and built on sand; it is to-day, and to-morrow is not. With all the passionate interest he shows, the Mahometan is really indifferent to this social fabric, and rushes on in the ceaseless whirl of fortune. In its spread Mahometanism founded many kingdoms and dynasties. On this boundless sea there is a continual onward movement; nothing abides firm. Whatever curls up into a form remains all the while transparent, and in that very instant glides away. Those dynasties were destitute of the bond of an organic firmness: the kingdoms, therefore, did nothing but degenerate; the individuals that composed them simply vanished. Where, however, a noble soul makes itself prominent—like a billow in the surging of the sea—it manifests itself in a majesty of freedom, such that nothing more noble, more generous, more valiant, more devoted was ever witnessed. The particular determinate object which the individual embraces is grasped by him entirely—with the whole soul. While Europeans are involved in a multitude of relations, and form, so to speak, " a bundle " of them—in Mahometanism the individual is *one* passion and *that alone;* he is superlatively cruel, cunning, bold, or generous. Where the sentiment of love exists, there is an equal *abandon*—love the most fervid. The ruler who loves the slave, glorifies the object of his love by laying at his feet all his magnificence, power and honor—forgetting sceptre and throne for him; but on the other hand he will sacrifice him just as recklessly. This reckless fervor shows itself also in the glowing warmth of the Arab and Saracen poetry. That glow is the perfect freedom of fancy from every fetter—an absorption in the life of its object and the sentiment it inspires, so that selfishness and egotism are utterly banished.

Never has enthusiasm, as such, performed greater deeds. Individuals may be enthusiastic for what is noble and exalted in various particular forms. The enthusiasm of a people for its independence, has also a definite aim. But abstract and therefore all-comprehensive enthusiasm—restrained by nothing, finding its limits nowhere, and absolutely indifferent to all beside—is that of the Mahometan East.

Proportioned to the rapidity of the Arab conquests, was the speed with which the arts and sciences attained among them their highest bloom. At first we see the conquerors destroying everything connected with art and science. Omar is said to have caused the destruction of the noble Alexandrian library. " These books," said he, " either contain what is in the Koran, or something else: in either case they are superfluous." But soon afterwards the Arabs became zealous in promoting the arts and spreading them everywhere. Their empire reached the summit of its glory under the Caliphs Al-Mansor and Haroun Al-Raschid. Large cities arose in all parts of the empire, where commerce and manufactures flourished, splendid palaces were built, and schools created. The learned men of the empire assembled at the Caliph's court, which not merely shone outwardly with the pomp of the costliest jewels, furniture and palaces, but was resplendent with the glory of poetry and all the sciences. At first the Caliphs still maintained entire that simplicity and plainness which characterized the Arabs of the desert, (the Caliph Abubeker is particularly famous in this respect,) and which acknowledged no distinction of station and culture. The meanest Saracen, the most insignificant old woman approached the Caliph as his equals. Unreflecting naïveté does not stand in need of culture; and in virtue of the freedom of his Spirit, each one sustains a relation of equality to the ruler.

The great empire of the Caliphs did not last long: for on the basis presented by Universality nothing is firm. The great Arabian empire fell about the same time as that of the Franks: thrones were demolished by slaves and by fresh invading hordes —the Seljuks and Mongols—and new kingdoms founded, new dynasties raised to the throne. The Osman race at last succeeded in establishing a firm dominion, by forming for themselves a firm centre in the Janizaries. Fanaticism having cooled down, no moral principle remained in men's souls. In the struggle with the Saracens, European valor had idealized itself to a fair and noble chivalry. Science and knowledge, especially that of philosophy, came from the Arabs into the West. A noble poetry and free imagination were kindled among the Germans by the East—a fact which directed Goethe's attention to the Orient and occasioned the composition of a string of lyric pearls, in his " Divan," which in warmth and felicity of fancy cannot be surpassed. But the East itself, when by degrees enthusiasm had vanished, sank into the grossest vice. The most hideous passions became dominant, and as sensual enjoyment was sanctioned in the first form which Mahometan doctrine assumed, and was exhibited as a reward of the faithful in Paradise, it took the place of fanaticism. At present, driven back into its Asiatic and African quarters, and tolerated only in one corner of Europe through the jealousy of Christian Powers, Islam has long vanished from the stage of history at large, and has retreated into Oriental ease and repose.

Chapter III.—The Empire of Charlemagne

The empire of the Franks, as already stated, was founded by Clovis. After his death, it was divided among his sons. Subsequently, after many struggles and the employment of treachery, assassination and violence, it was again united, and once more divided. Internally the power of the kings was very much increased, by their having become princes in *conquered* lands. These were indeed parcelled out among the Frank freemen; but very considerable permanent revenues accrued to the king, together with what had belonged to the emperors, and the spoils of confiscation. These therefore the king bestowed as personal, *i.e.* not heritable, *beneficia,* on his warriors, who in receiving them entered into a personal obligation to him—became his vassals and formed his feudal array. The very opulent Bishops were united with them in constituting the King's Council, which however did not circumscribe the royal authority. At the head of the feudal array was the *Major Domus.* These *Majores Domus* soon assumed the entire power and threw the royal authority into the shade, while the kings sank into a torpid condition and became mere puppets. From the former sprang the dynasty of the Carlovingians. Pepin *le Bref,* the son of Charles Martel, was in the year 752 raised to the dignity of King of the Franks. Pope Zacharias released the Franks from their oath of allegiance to the still living Cnilderic III— the last of the Merovingians—who received the tonsure, *i.e.* became a monk, and was thus deprived of the royal distinction of long hair. The last of the Merovingians were utter weaklings, who contented themselves with the name of royalty, and gave themselves up almost entirely to luxury—a phenomenon that is quite common in the dynasties of the East, and is also met with again among the last of the Carlovingians. The *Majores Domus,* on the contrary, were in the very vigor of ascendant fortunes, and were in such close alliance with the feudal nobility, that it became easy for them ultimately to secure the throne.

The Popes were most severely pressed by the Lombard kings and sought protection from the Franks. Out of gratitude Pepin undertook to defend Stephen II. He led an army twice across the Alps, and twice defeated the Lombards. His victories gave splendor to his newly established throne, and entailed a considerable heritage on the Chair of St. Peter. In A.D. 800 the son of Pepin—Charlemagne—was crowned Emperor by the Pope, and hence originated the firm union of the Carlovingians with the Papal See. For the Roman Empire continued to enjoy among the barbarians the prestige of a great power, and was ever regarded by them as the centre from which civil dignities, religion, laws and all branches of knowledge— beginning with written characters themselves—flowed to them. Charles Martel, after he had delivered Europe from Saracen domination, was—himself and his successors—dignified with the title of " Patrician " by the people and senate of Rome; but Charlemagne was crowned Emperor, and that by the Pope himself.

There were now, therefore, *two* Empires, and in them the

Christian confession was gradually divided into two Churches, the *Greek* and the *Roman*. The Roman Emperor was the born defender of the Roman Church, and this position of the Emperor towards the Pope seemed to declare that the Frank sovereignty was only a continuation of the Roman Empire.

The Empire of Charlemagne had a very considerable extent. Franconia Proper stretched from the Rhine to the Loire. Aquitania, south of the Loire, was in 768—the year of Pepin's death—entirely subjugated. The Frank Empire also included Burgundy, Alemannia (southern Germany between the Lech, the Maine and the Rhine), Thuringia, which extended to the Saale, and Bavaria. Charlemagne likewise conquered the Saxons, who dwelt between the Rhine and the Weser, and put an end to the Lombard dominion, so that he became master of Upper and Central Italy.

This great empire Charlemagne formed into a systematically organized State, and gave the Frank dominion settled institutions adapted to impart to it strength and consistency. This must however not be understood, as if he first introduced the *Constitution* of his empire in its whole extent, but as implying that institutions partly already in existence, were developed under his guidance, and attained a more decided and unobstructed efficiency. The King stood at the head of the officers of the empire, and the principle of hereditary monarchy was already recognized. The King was likewise master of the armed force, as also the largest landed proprietor, while the supreme judicial power was equally in his hands. The *military constitution* was based on the "Arrière-ban." Every freeman was bound to arm, for the defence of the realm, and had to provide for his support in the field for a certain time. This militia (as it would now be called) was under the command of Counts and Margraves, which latter presided over large districts on the borders of the empire—the "Marches." According to the general partition of the country, it was divided into provinces [or counties] over each of which a Count presided. Over them again, under the later Carlovingians, were Dukes, whose seats were large cities, such as Cologne, Ratisbon, and the like. Their office gave occasion to the division of the country into Duchies: thus there was a Duchy of Alsatia, Lorraine, Frisia, Thuringia, Rhætia. These Dukes were appointed by the Emperor. Peoples that had retained their hereditary princes after their subjugation, lost this privilege and received Dukes, when they revolted; this was the case with Alemannia, Thuringia, Bavaria, and Saxony. But there was also a kind of standing army for readier use. The vassals of the emperor, namely, had the enjoyment of estates on the condition of performing military service, whenever commanded. And with a view to maintain these arrangements, commissioners (Missi) were sent out by the emperor, to observe and report concerning the affairs of the Empire, and to inquire into the state of judicial administration and inspect the royal estates.

Not less remarkable is the management of the *revenues of the state.* There were no direct taxes, and few tolls on rivers and roads, of which several were farmed out to the higher officers of the empire. Into the treasury flowed on the one hand judicial fines, on the other hand the pecuniary satisfactions made for not serving in the army at the emperor's summons. Those who enjoyed *beneficia,* lost them on neglecting this duty. The chief revenue was derived from the crown-lands, of which the emperor had a great number, on which royal palaces [Pfalzen] were erected. It had been long the custom for the kings to make progresses through the chief provinces, and to remain for a time in each palatinate; the due preparations for the maintenance of the court having been already made by Marshals, Chamberlains, etc.

As regards the *administration of justice,* criminal causes and those which concern real property were tried before the communal assemblies under the presidency of a Count. Those of less importance were decided by at least seven free men— an elective bench of magistrates—under the presidency of the Centgraves. The supreme jurisdiction belonged to the royal tribunals, over which the king presided in his palace: to these the feudatories, spiritual and temporal, were amenable. The royal commissioners mentioned above gave especial attention in their inquisitorial visits to the judicial administration, heard all complaints, and punished injustice. A spiritual and a temporal envoy had to go their circuit four times a year.

In Charlemagne's time the ecclesiastical body had already acquired great weight. The bishops presided over great cathedral establishments, with which were also connected seminaries and scholastic institutions. For Charlemagne endeavored to restore science, then almost extinct, by promoting the foundation of schools in towns and villages. Pious souls believed that they were doing a good work and earning salvation by making presents to the church; in this way the most savage and barbarous monarchs sought to atone for their crimes. Private persons most commonly made their offerings in the form of a bequest of their entire estate to religious houses, stipulating for the enjoyment of the usufruct only for life or for a specified time. But it often happened that on the death of a bishop or abbot, the temporal magnates and their retainers invaded the possessions of the clergy, and fed and feasted there till all was consumed; for religion had not yet such an authority over men's minds as to be able to bridle the rapacity of the powerful. The clergy were obliged to appoint stewards and bailiffs to manage their estates; besides this, guardians had charge of all their secular concerns, led their men-at-arms into the field, and gradually obtained from the king territorial jurisdiction, when the ecclesiastics had secured the privilege of being amenable only to their own tribunals, and enjoyed immunity from the authority of the royal officers of justice (the Counts). This involved an important step in the change of political relations, inasmuch as the ecclesiastical domains assumed more and more the aspect of independent provinces enjoying a freedom surpassing anything to which those of secular princes had yet made pretensions. Moreover the clergy contrived subsequently to free themselves from the burdens of the state, and opened the churches and monasteries as asylums—that is, inviolable sanctuaries for all offenders. This institution was on the one hand very beneficial as a protection in cases of violence and oppression; but it was perverted on the other hand into a means of impunity for the grossest crimes. In Charlemagne's time, the law could still demand from conventual authorities the surrender of offenders. The bishops were tried by a judicial bench consisting of bishops; as vassals they were properly subject to the royal tribunal. Afterwards the monastic establishments sought to free themselves from episcopal jurisdiction also: and thus they made themselves independent even of the church. The bishops were chosen by the clergy and the religious communities at large; but as they were also vassals of the sovereign, their feudal dignity had to be conferred by him. The contingency of a contest was avoided by the obligation to choose a person approved of by the king.

The imperial tribunals were held in the palace where the emperór resided. The sovereign himself presided in them, and the magnates of the imperial court constituted with him the supreme judicial body. The deliberations of the imperial council on the affairs of the empire did not take place at appointed times, but as occasions offered—at military reviews in the spring, at ecclesiastical councils and on court-days. It was especially these court-days, to which the feudal nobles were invited—when the king held his court in a particular province, generally on the Rhine, the centre of the Frank empire—that gave occasion to the deliberations in question. Custom required the sovereign to assemble twice a year a select body of the higher temporal and ecclesiastical functionaries, but here also the king had decisive power. These conventions are therefore of a different character from the Imperial Diets of later times, in which the nobles assume a more independent position.

Such was the state of the Frank Empire—that first consolidation of Christianity into a political form proceeding from itself, the Roman empire having been swallowed up by Christianity. The constitution just described looks excellent; it introduced a firm military organization and provided for the administration of justice within the empire. Yet after Charlemagne's death it proved itself utterly powerless—externally defenceless against the invasions of the Normans, Hungarians, and Arabs, and internally inefficient in resisting lawlessness, spoliation, and oppression of every kind. Thus we see, side by side with an excellent constitution, the most deplorable condition of things, and therefore confusion in all directions. Such political edifices need, for the very reason that they originate suddenly, the additional strengthening afforded by negativity evolved within themselves: they need reactions in every form, such as manifest themselves in the following period.

SECTION II

THE MIDDLE AGES

WHILE the *first* period of the German World ends brilliantly with a mighty empire, the *second* is commenced by the reaction resulting from the antithesis occasioned by that infinite falsehood which rules the destinies of the *Middle Ages* and constitutes their life and spirit. This reaction is *first,* that of the particular nationalities against the universal sovereignty of the Frank empire—manifesting itself in the splitting up of that great empire. The *second reaction* is that of individuals against legal authority and the executive power—against subordination, and the military and judicial arrangements of the constitution. This produced the *isolation* and therefore *defencelessness* of individuals. The universality of the power of the state disappeared through this reaction: individuals sought protection with the powerful, and the latter became oppressors. Thus was gradually introduced a condition of universal dependence, and this protecting relation is then systematized into the Feudal System. The *third reaction* is that of the church—the reaction of the spiritual element against the existing order of things. Secular extravagances of passion were repressed and kept in check by the Church, but the latter was itself secularized in the process, and abandoned its proper position. From that moment begins the introversion of the secular principle. These relations and reactions all go to constitute the history of the Middle Ages, and the culminating point of this period is *the Crusades;* for with them arises a universal instability, but one through which the states of Christendom first attain internal and external independence.

Chapter I.—The Feudality and the Hierarchy

The *First Reaction* is that of particular nationality against the universal sovereignty of the Franks. It appears indeed, at first sight, as if the Frank empire was divided by the mere choice of its sovereigns; but another consideration deserves attention, *viz.* that this division was popular, and was accordingly maintained by the peoples. It was, therefore, not a mere dynastic act—which might appear unwise, since the princes thereby weakened their own power—but a restoration of those distinct nationalities which had been held together by a connecting bond of irresistible might and the genius of a great man. Louis the Pious [*le Débonnaire*] son of Charlemagne, divided the empire among his three sons. But subsequently, by a second marriage, another son was born to him—Charles the Bald. As he wished to give him also an inheritance, wars and contentions arose between Louis and his other sons, whose already received portion would have to be diminished by such an arrangement. In the first instance, therefore, a private interest was involved in the contest; but that of the nations which composed the empire made the issue not indifferent to them. The western Franks had already identified themselves with the Gauls, and with them originated a reaction against the German Franks, as also at a later epoch one on the part of Italy against the Germans. By the treaty of Verdun, A.D. 843, a division of the empire among Charlemagne's descendants took place; the whole Frank empire, some provinces excepted, was for a moment again united under Charles the Gross. It was, however, only for a short time that this weak prince was able to hold the vast empire together; it was broken up into many smaller sovereignties, which developed and maintined an independent position. These were the Kingdom of Italy, which was itself divided, the two Burgundian sovereignties—Upper Burgundy, of which the chief centres were Geneva and the convent of St. Maurice in Valaise, and Lower Burgundy between the Jura, the Mediterranean and the Rhone—Lorraine, between the Rhine and the Meuse, Normandy, and Brittany. France Proper was shut in between these sovereignties; and thus limited did Hugh Capet find it when he ascended the throne. Eastern Franconia, Saxony, Thuringia, Bavaria, Swabia, remained parts of the German Empire. Thus did the unity of the Frank monarchy fall to pieces. The internal arrangements of the Frank empire also suffered a gradual but total decay; and the first to disappear was the military organization. Soon after Charlemagne we see the Norsemen from various quarters making inroads into England, France and Germany. In England seven dynasties of

Anglo-Saxon Kings were originally established, but in the year 827 Egbert united these sovereignties into a single kingdom. In the reign of his successor the Danes made very frequent invasions and pillaged the country. In Alfred the Great's time they met with vigorous resistance, but subsequently the Danish King Canute conquered all England. The inroads of the *Normans* into France were contemporaneous with these events. They sailed up the Seine and the Loire in light boats, plundered the towns, pillaged the convents, and went off with their booty. They beleaguered Paris itself, and the Carlovingian Kings were reduced to the base necessity of purchasing a peace. In the same way they devastated the towns lying on the Elbe; and from the Rhine plundered Aix-la-Chapelle and Cologne, and made Lorraine tributary to them. The Diet of Worms, in 882, did indeed issue a general proclamation, summoning all subjects to rise in arms, but they were compelled to put up with a disgraceful composition. These storms came from the north and the west. The Eastern side of the empire suffered from the inroads of the *Magyars*. These barbarian peoples traversed the country in wagons, and laid waste the whole of Southern Germany. Through Bavaria, Swabia, and Switzerland they penetrated into the interior of France and reached Italy. The *Saracens* pressed forward from the South. Sicily had been long in their hands: they thence obtained a firm footing in Italy, menaced Rome—which diverted their attack by a composition—and were the terror of Piedmont and Provence.

Thus these three peoples invaded the empire from all sides in great masses, and in their desolating marches almost came into contact with each other. France was devastated by the Normans as far as the Jura; the Hungarians reached Switzerland, and the Saracens Valaise. Calling to mind that organization of the " Arrière-ban," and considering it in juxtaposition with this miserable state of things, we cannot fail to be struck with the inefficiency of all those far-famed institutions, which at such a juncture ought to have shown themselves most effective. We might be inclined to regard the picture of the noble and rational constitution of the Frank monarchy under Charlemagne—exhibiting itself as strong, comprehensive, and well ordered, internally and externally—as a baseless figment. Yet it actually existed; the entire political system being held together only by the power, the greatness, the regal soul of this

one man—not based on the spirit of the people—not having become a vital element in it. It was superficially induced—an *a
priori* constitution like that which Napoleon gave to Spain, and
which disappeared with the physical power that sustained it.
That, on the contrary, which renders a constitution real, is that
it exists as Objective Freedom—the Substantial form of volition—as duty and obligation acknowledged by the subjects
themselves. But obligation was not yet recognized by the German Spirit, which hitherto showed itself only as " Heart " and
subjective choice; for it there was as yet no subjectivity involving unity, but only a subjectivity conditioned by a careless
superficial self-seeking. Thus that constitution was destitute
of any firm bond; it had no objective support in subjectivity;
for in fact no constitution was as yet possible.

This leads us to the *Second Reaction*—that of individuals
against the authority of law. The capacity of appreciating legal
order and the common weal is altogether absent, has no vital
existence in the peoples themselves. The duties of every free
citizen, the authority of the judge to give judicial decisions, that
of the count of a province to hold his court, and interest in the
laws as such, are no longer regarded as valid now that the
strong hand from above ceases to hold the reins of sovereignty.
The brilliant administration of Charlemagne had vanished
without leaving a trace, and the immediate consequence was
the general defencelessness of individuals. The need of protection is sure to be felt in some degree in every well-organized
state: each citizen knows his rights and also knows that for
the security of possession the social state is absolutely necessary.
Barbarians have not yet attained this sense of need—the want
of protection from others. They look upon it as a limitation of
their freedom if their rights must be guaranteed them by others.
Thus, therefore, the impulse towards a firm organization did
not exist: men must first be placed in a defenceless condition,
before they were sensible of the necessity of the organization of a
State. The political edifice had to be reconstructed from the
very foundations. The commonwealth as then organized had
no vitality or firmness at all either in itself or in the minds of
the people; and its weakness manifested itself in the fact that
it was unable to give protection to its individual members. As
observed above, the idea of duty was not present in the Spirit of
the Germans; it had to be restored. In the first instance voli-

tion could only be arrested in its wayward career in reference to the merely external point of *possession;* and to make it feel the importance of the protection of the State, it had to be violently dislodged from its obtuseness and impelled by necessity to seek union and a social condition. Individuals were therefore obliged to consult for themselves by taking refuge with Individuals, and submitted to the authority of certain powerful persons, who constituted a private possession and personal sovereignty out of that authority which formerly belonged to the Commonwealth. As *officers of the State*, the counts did not meet with obedience from those committed to their charge, and they were as little desirous of it. Only for *themselves* did they covet it. They assumed to themselves the power of the State, and made the authority with which they had been intrusted as a *beneficium*, a heritable possession. As in earlier times the King or other magnates conferred fiefs on their vassals by way of rewards, now, conversely, the weaker and poorer surrendered their possessions to the strong, for the sake of gaining efficient protection. They committed their estates to a Lord, a Convent, an Abbot, a Bishop (*feudum oblatum*), and received them back, encumbered with feudal obligations to these superiors. Instead of freemen they became vassals—feudal dependants—and their possession a *beneficium*. This is the constitution of the Feudal System. "*Feudum*" is connected with "*fides*"; the fidelity implied in this case is a bond established on unjust principles, a relation that does indeed contemplate a legitimate object, but whose import is not a whit the less injustice; for the fidelity of vassals is not an obligation to the Commonwealth, but a private one—*ipso facto* therefore subject to the sway of chance, caprice, and violence. Universal injustice, universal lawlessness is reduced to a system of dependence on and obligation to individuals, so that the mere formal side of the matter, the mere fact of compact constitutes its sole connection with the principle of Right.—Since every man had to protect himself, the martial spirit, which in point of external defence seemed to have most ignominiously vanished, was re-awakened; for torpidity was roused to action partly by extreme ill-usage, partly by the greed and ambition of individuals. The valor that now manifested itself, was displayed not on behalf of the State, but of private interests. In every district arose castles; fortresses were erected, and that for the defence of private property, and with a view to plunder the tyranny. In the way just mentioned, the political totality was ignored at those points where individual authority was established, among which the seats of bishops and archbishops deserve especial mention. The bishoprics had been freed from the jurisdiction of the judicial tribunals, and from the operations of the executive generally. The bishops had stewards on whom at their request the Emperors conferred the jurisdiction which the Counts had formerly exercised. Thus there were detached ecclesiastical domains—ecclesiastical districts which belonged to a saint (Germ. Weichbilder). Similar suzerainties of a secular kind were subsequently constituted. Both occupied the position of the previous Provinces [Gaue] or Counties [Grafschaften]. Only in a few towns where communities of freemen were independently strong enough to secure protection and safety, did relics of the ancient free constitution remain. With these exceptions the free communities entirely disappeared, and became subject to the prelates or to the Counts and Dukes, thenceforth known as seigneurs and princes. The imperial power was extolled in general terms, as something very great and exalted: the Emperor passed for the secular head of entire Christendom: but the more exalted the *ideal* dignity of the emperors, the more limited was it in reality. France derived extraordinary advantage from the fact that it entirely repudiated this baseless assumption, while in Germany the advance of political development was hindered by that pretence of power. The kings and emperors were no longer chiefs of the *state,* but of the *princes,* who were indeed their vassals, but possessed sovereignty and territorial lordships of their own. The whole social condition therefore, being founded on individual sovereignty, it might be supposed that the advance to a State would be possible only through the return of those individual sovereignties to an official relationship. But to accomplish this, a superior power would have been required, such as was not in existence; for the feudal lords themselves determined how far they were still dependent on the general constitution of the state. No authority of Law and Right is valid any longer; nothing but chance power—the crude caprice of particular as opposed to universally valid Right; and this struggles against equality of Rights and Laws. Inequality of political privileges —the allotment being the work of the purest haphazard—is the predominant feature. It is impossible that a Monarchy can arise from such a social condition through the subjugation of the several minor powers under the Chief of the State, as such. Reversely, the former were gradually transformed into Principalities [Fürstenthümer], and became united with the Principality of the Chief; thus enabling the authority of the king and of the state to assert itself. While, therefore, the bond of political unity was still wanting, the several seigneuries attained their development independently.

In France the dynasty of Charlemagne, like that of Clovis, became extinct through the weakness of the sovereigns who represented it. Their dominion was finally limited to the petty sovereignty of Laon; and the last of the Carlovingians, Duke Charles of Lorraine, who laid claim to the crown after the death of Louis V, was defeated and taken prisoner. The powerful Hugh Capet, Duke of France, was proclaimed king. The title of King, however, gave him no real power; his authority was based on his territorial possessions alone. At a later date, through purchase, marriage, and the dying out of families, the kings became possessed of many feudal domains; and their authority was frequently invoked as a protection against the oppressions of the nobles. The royal authority in France became heritable at an early date, because the fiefs were heritable; though at first the kings took the precaution to have their sons crowned during their lifetime. France was divided into many sovereignties: the Duchy of Guienne, the Earldom of Flanders, the Duchy of Gascony, the Earldom of Toulouse, the Duchy of Burgundy, the Earldom of Vermandois; Lorraine too had belonged to France for some time. Normandy had been ceded to the Normans by the kings of France, in order to secure a temporary repose from their incursions. From Normandy Duke William passed over into England and conquered it in the year 1066. Here he introduced a fully developed feudal constitution—a network which, to a great extent, encompasses England even at the present day. And thus the Dukes of Normandy confronted the comparatively feeble Kings of France with a power of no inconsiderable pretensions.—Germany was composed of the great duchies of Saxony, Swabia, Bavaria, Carinthia, Lorraine and Burgundy, the Margraviate of Thuringia, etc. with several bishoprics and archbishoprics. Each of those duchies again was divided into several fiefs, enjoying more or less independence. The emperor seems often to have united several duchies under his immediate sovereignty. The Emperor Henry III was, when he ascended the throne, lord of many large dukedoms; but he weakened his own power by enfeoffing them to others. Germany was radically a free nation, and had not, as France had, any dominant family as a central authority; it continued an elective empire. Its princes refused to surrender the privilege of choosing their sovereign for themselves; and at every new election they introduced new restrictive conditions, so that the imperial power was degraded to an empty shadow.—In Italy we find the same political condition. The German Emperors had pretensions to it: but their authority was valid only so far as they could support it by direct force of arms, and as the Italian cities and nobles deemed their own advantage to be promoted by submission. Italy was, like Germany, divided into many larger and smaller dukedoms, earldoms, bishoprics and seigneuries. The Pope had very little power, either in the North or in the South; which latter was long divided between the Lombards and the Greeks, until both were overcome by the Normans.—Spain maintained a contest with the Saracens, either defensive or victorious, through the whole mediæval period, till the latter finally succumbed to the more matured power of Christian civilization.

Thus all Right vanished before individual Might; for equality of Rights and rational legislation, where the interests of the political Totality, of the State, are kept in view, had no existence.

The *Third Reaction*, noticed above, was that of the element of Universality against the Real World as split up into particularity. This reaction proceeded from below upwards—from that condition of isolated possession itself; and was then promoted chiefly by the church. A sense of the *nothingness* of its condition seized on the world as it were universally. In that condition of utter isolation, where only the unsanctioned might of individuals had any validity [where the State was non-existent,] men could find no repose, and Christendom was, so to speak, agitated by the tremor of an evil conscience. In the eleventh century, the fear of the approaching final judgment and the belief in the speedy dissolution of the world, spread through all Europe. This dismay of soul impelled men to the most irrational proceedings. Some bestowed the whole of their possessions on the Church, and passed their lives in continual penance; the majority dissipated their worldly all in riotous debauchery. The Church alone increased its riches by the hallucinations, through donations and bequests.—About the same time too, terrible famines swept away their victims: human flesh was sold in open market. During this state of things, lawlessness, brutal lust, the most barbarous caprice, deceit and cunning, were the prevailing moral features. Italy, the centre of Christendom, presented the most revolting aspect. Every virtue was alien to the times in question; consequently *virtus* had lost its proper meaning: in common use it denoted only violence and oppression, sometimes even libidinous outrage. This corrupt state of things affected the clergy equally with the laity. Their own advowees had made themselves masters of the ecclesiastical estates intrusted to their keeping, and lived on them quite at their own pleasure, restricting the monks and clergy to a scanty pittance. Monasteries that refused to accept advowees were compelled to do so; the neighboring lords taking the office upon themselves or giving it to their sons. Only bishops and abbots maintained themselves in possession, being able to protect themselves partly by their own power, partly by means of their retainers; since they were, for the most part, of noble families.

The bishoprics being secular fiefs, their occupants were bound to the performance of imperial and feudal service. The investiture of the bishops belonged to the sovereigns, and it was their interest that these ecclesiastics should be attached to them. Whoever desired a bishopric, therefore, had to make application to the king; and thus a regular trade was carried on in bishoprics and abbacies. Usurers who had lent money to the sovereign, received compensation by the bestowal of the dignities in question; the worst of men thus came into possession of spiritual offices. There could be no question that the clergy ought to have been chosen by the religious community, and there were always influential persons who had the right of electing them; but the king compelled them to yield to his orders. Nor did the Papal dignity fare any better. Through a long course of years the Counts of Tusculum near Rome conferred it on members of their own family, or on persons to whom they had sold it for large sums of money. The state of things became at last so intolerable, that laymen as well as ecclesiastics of energetic character opposed its continuance. The Emperor Henry III put an end to the strife of factions, by nominating the Popes himself, and supporting them by his authority in defiance of the opposition of the Roman nobility. Pope Nicholas II decided that the Popes should be chosen by the Cardinals; but as the latter partly belonged to dominant families, similar contests of factions continued to accompany their election. Gregory VII (already famous as Cardinal Hildebrand) sought to secure the independence of the church in this frightful condition of things, by two measures especially. *First,* he enforced the *celibacy of the clergy.* From the earliest times, it must be observed, the opinion had prevailed that it was commendable and desirable for the clergy to remain unmarried. Yet the annalists and chroniclers inform us that this requirement was but indifferently complied with. Nicholas II had indeed pronounced the married clergy to be a new sect; but Gregory VII proceeded to enforce the restriction with extraordinary energy, excommunicating all the married clergy and all laymen who should hear mass when they officiated. In this way the ecclesiastical body was shut up within itself and excluded from the morality of the State.—His *second* measure was directed against *simony, i.e.* the sale of or arbitrary appointment to bishoprics and to the Papal See itself. Ecclesiastical offices were thenceforth to be filled by the clergy, who were capable of administering them; an arrangement which necessarily brought the ecclesiastical body into violent collision with secular seigneurs.

These were the two grand measures by which Gregory purposed to emancipate the Church from its condition of dependence and exposure to secular violence. But Gregory made still further demands on the secular power. The transference of benefices to a new incumbent was to receive validity simply in virtue of his ordination by his ecclesiastical superior, and the Pope was to have exclusive control over the vast property of the ecclesiastical community. The Church as a divinely constituted power, laid claim to supremacy over secular authority —founding that claim on the abstract principle that the Divine is superior to the Secular. The Emperor at his coronation—a ceremony which only the Pope could perform—was obliged to promise upon oath that he would always be obedient to the Pope and the Church. Whole countries and states, such as

Naples, Portugal, England and Ireland came into a formal relation of vassalage to the Papal chair.

Thus the Church attained an independent position: the Bishops convoked synods in the various countries, and in these convocations the clergy found a permanent centre of unity and support. In this way the Church attained the most influential position in secular affairs. It arrogated to itself the award of princely crowns, and assumed the part of mediator between sovereign powers in war and peace. The contingencies which particularly favored such interventions on the part of the Church were the marriages of princes. It frequently happened that princes wished to be divorced from their wives; but for such a step they needed the permission of the Church. The latter did not let slip the opportunity of insisting upon the fulfilment of demands that might have been otherwise urged in vain, and thence advanced till it had obtained universal influence. In the chaotic state of the community generally, the intervention of the authority of the Church was felt as a necessity. By the introduction of the " Truce of God," feuds and private revenge were suspended for at least certain days in the week, or even for entire weeks; and the Church maintained this armistice by the use of all its ghostly appliances of excommunication, interdict and other threats and penalties. The secular possessions of the Church brought it however into a relation to other secular princes and lords, which was alien to its proper nature; it constituted a formidable secular power in contraposition to them, and thus formed in the first instance a centre of opposition against violence and arbitrary wrong. It withstood especially the attacks upon the ecclesiastical foundations —the secular lordships of the Bishops; and on occasion of opposition on the part of vassals to the violence and caprice of princes, the former had the support of the Pope. But in these proceedings the Church brought to bear against opponents only a force and arbitrary resolve of the same kind as their own, and mixed up its secular interest with its interest as an ecclesiastical, *i.e.* a divinely substantial power. Sovereigns and peoples were by no means incapable of discriminating between the two, or of recognizing the worldly aims that were apt to intrude as motives for ecclesiastical intervention. They therefore stood by the Church as far as they deemed it their interest to do so; otherwise they showed no great dread of excommunication or other ghostly terrors. Italy was the country where the authority of the Popes was least respected; and the worst usage they experienced was from the Romans themselves. Thus what the Popes acquired in point of land and wealth and direct sovereignty, they lost in influence and consideration.

We have then to probe to its depths the *spiritual element* in the Church—the form of its power. The essence of the Christian principle has already been unfolded; it is the principle of Mediation. Man realizes his Spiritual essence only when he conquers the Natural that attaches to him. This conquest is possible only on the supposition that the human and the divine nature are essentially one, and that Man, so far as he is Spirit, also possesses the essentiality and substantiality that belong to the idea of Deity. The condition of the mediation in question is the consciousness of this unity; and the intuition of this unity was given to man in Christ. The object to be attained is therefore, that man should lay hold on this consciousness, and that it should be continually excited in him. This was the design of the *Mass:* in the *Host* Christ is set forth as actually present; the piece of bread consecrated by the priest is the present God, subjected to human contemplation and ever and anon offered up. One feature of this representation is correct, inasmuch as the sacrifice of Christ is here regarded as an actual and eternal transaction, Christ being not a mere sensuous and single, but a completely universal, *i.e.* divine *individuum;* but on the other hand it involves the error of isolating the sensuous phase; for the Host is adored even apart from its being partaken of by the faithful, and the presence of Chrust is not exclusively limited mental vision and Spirit. Justly therefore did the Lutheran Reformation make this dogma an especial object of attack. Luther proclaimed the great doctrine that the Host had spiritual value and Christ was received only on the condition of *faith* in him; apart from this, the Host, he affirmed, was a mere external thing, possessed of no greater value than any other thing. But the Catholic falls down before the Host; and thus the merely outward has sanctity ascribed to it. The Holy as a mere thing has the character of externality; thus it is capable of being taken possession of by another to my exclusion: it may come into an alien hand, since the process of appropriating it is not one that takes place in Spirit, but is conditioned by its quality as an external object [Dingheit]. The highest of human blessings is in the hands of others. Here arises *ipso facto* a separation between those who possess this blessing and those who have to receive it from others—between the *Clergy* and the *Laity*. The laity as such are alien to the Divine. This is the absolute schism in which the Church in the Middle Ages was involved: it arose from the recognition of the Holy as something external. The clergy imposed certain conditions, to which the laity must conform if they would be partakers of the Holy. The entire development of *doctrine,* spiritual insight and the knowledge of divine things, belonged exclusively to the Church: it has to ordain, and the laity have simply to believe: obedience is their duty—the obedience of faith, without insight on their part. This position of things rendered faith a matter of external legislation, and resulted in compulsion and the stake.

The generality of men are thus cut off from the Church; and on the same principle they are severed from the Holy in every form. For on the same principle as that by which the clergy are the medium between man on the one hand and God and Christ on the other hand, the layman cannot directly apply to the Divine Being in his prayers, but only through mediators —human beings who conciliate God for him, the Dead, the Perfect—*Saints*. Thus originated the adoration of the Saints, and with it that conglomerate of fables and falsities with which the Saints and their biographies have been invested. In the East the worship of images had early become popular, and after a lengthened struggle had triumphantly established itself:—an image, a picture, though sensuous, still appeals rather to the imagination; but the coarser natures of the West desired something more immediate as the object of their contemplation, and thus arose the worship of relics. The consequence was a formal resurrection of the dead in the mediæval period, every pious Christian wished to be in possession of such sacred earthly remains. Among the Saints the chief object of adoration was the *Virgin Mary*. She is certainly the beautiful concept of pure love—a mother's love; but Spirit and Thought stand higher than even this; and in the worship of this conception that of God in Spirit was lost, and Christ himself was set aside. The element of mediation between God and man was thus apprehended and held as something external. Thus through the perversion of the principle of Freedom, absolute Slavery became the established law. The other aspects and relations of the spiritual life of Europe during this period flow from this principle. Knowledge, comprehension of religious doctrine, is something of which Spirit is judged incapable; it is the exclusive possession of a class, which has to determine the True. For man may not presume to stand in a direct relation to God; so that, as we said before, if he would apply to Him, he needs a mediator—a Saint. This view imports the denial of the essential unity of the Divine and Human; since man, as such, is declared incapable of recognizing the Divine and of approaching thereto. And while humanity is thus separated from the Supreme Good, no change of heart, as such, is insisted upon—for this would suppose that the unity of the Divine and the Human is to be found in man himself—but the terrors of Hell are exhibited to man in the most terrible colors, to induce him to escape from them, not by moral amendment, but in virtue of something external—the " *means of grace.*" These, however, are an *arcanum* to the laity; another—the " Confessor," must furnish him with them. The individual has to confess—is bound to expose all the particulars of his life and conduct to the view of the Confessor—and then is informed what course he has to pursue to attain spiritual safety. Thus the Church took the place of *Conscience:* it put men in leading strings like children, and told them that man could not be freed from the torments which his sins had merited, by any amendment of his own moral condition, but by outward actions, *opera operata*—actions which were not the promptings of his own good-will, but performed by command of the ministers of the church; *e.g.* hearing mass, doing penance, going through a certain number of prayers, undertaking pilgrimages—actions which are unspiritual, stupefy the soul, and which are not only mere external ceremonies, but are such as can be even vicariously performed The supererogatory works ascribed to the saints, could be purchased, and the spiritual advantage which they merited, secured to the purchaser. Thus was produced an utter derangement of all that is recognized as good and moral in the Christian Church: only external requirements are insisted upon, and these can be complied with in a merely external way. A condition the very reverse of Freedom is intruded into the principle of Freedom itself.

With this perversion is connected the absolute separation of the spiritual from the secular principle generally. There are

two Divine Kingdoms—the intellectual in the heart and cogni-
tive faculty, and the socially ethical whose element and sphere is
secular existence. It is science alone that can comprehend the
kingdom of God and the socially Moral world as one Idea, and
that recognizes the fact that the course of Time has witnessed
a process ever tending to the realization of this unity. But
Piety [or Religious Feeling] as such, has nothing to do with
the Secular: it may make its appearance in that sphere on a
mission of mercy, but this stops short of a strict socially ethical
connection with it—does not come up to the idea of Freedom.
Religious Feeling is extraneous to History, and has no History;
for History is rather the Empire of Spirit recognizing itself in
its *Subjective* Freedom, as the economy of social morality
[sittliches Reich] in the State. In the Middle Ages that embodying of the Divine in actual life was wanting; the antithesis
was not harmonized. Social morality was represented as
worthless, and that in its *three* most essential particulars.

One phase of social morality is that connected with Love—
with the emotions called forth in the *marriage relation*. It is
not proper to say that Celibacy is contrary to Nature, but that it
is adverse to Social Morality [Sittlichkeit]. Marriage was indeed reckoned by the Church among the Sacraments; but notwithstanding the position thus assigned it, it was degraded, inasmuch as celibacy was reckoned as the more holy state. A
second point of social morality is presented in *Activity*—the
workman has to perform for his subsistence. His dignity consists in his depending entirely on his diligence, conduct, and
intelligence, for the supply of his wants. In direct contravention of this principle, *Pauperism,* laziness, inactivity, was regarded as nobler: and the Immoral thus received the stamp of
consecration. A *third* point of morality is, that *obedience* be
rendered to the Moral and Rational, as an obedience to laws
which I recognize as just; that it be not that blind and uncon-
ditional compliance which does not know what it is doing, and
whose course of action is a mere groping about without clear
consciousness or intelligence. But it was exactly this latter kind
of obedience that passed for the most pleasing to God; a doctrine that exalts the obedience of Slavery, imposed by the arbitrary will of the Church, above the true obedience of Freedom.
In this way the three vows of Chastity, Poverty, and Obedience turned out the very opposite of what they assumed to be,

and in them all social morality was degraded. The Church was no longer a *spiritual* power, but an *ecclesiastical* one; and the relation which the secular world sustained to it was unspiritual, automatic, and destitute of independent insight and conviction. As the consequence of this, we see everywhere vice, utter absence of respect for conscience, shamelessness, and a distracted state of things, of which the entire history of the period is the picture in detail.

According to the above, the Church of the Middle Ages exhibits itself as a manifold *Self-contradiction*. For Subjective Spirit, although testifying of the Absolute, is at the same time *limited* and definitely existing Spirit, as Intelligence and Will. Its limitation begins in its taking up this distinctive position, and here consentaneously begins its contradictory and self-alienated phase; for that intelligence and will are not imbued with the Truth, which appears in relation to them as something *given* [posited *ab extra*]. This externality of the Absolute Object of comprehension affects the consciousness thus:—that the Absolute Object presents itself as a merely sensuous, external thing—common outward existence—and yet claims to be Absolute: in the mediæval view of things this absolute demand is made upon Spirit. The second form of the contradiction in question has to do with the relation which the Church itself sustains. The true Spirit exists in man—is *his* Spirit; and the individual gives himself the certainty of this identity with the Absolute, in worship—the Church sustaining merely the relation of a teacher and directress of this worship. But here, on the contrary, we have an ecclesiastical body, like the Brahmins in India, in possession of the Truth—not indeed by birth, but in virtue of knowledge, teaching and training— yet with the proviso that this alone is not sufficient, an external form, an unspiritual title being judged essential to actual possession. This outward form is Ordination, whose nature is such that the consecration imparted inheres essentially like a sensuous quality in the individual, whatever be the character of his soul—be he irreligious, immoral, or absolutely ignorant. The third kind of contradiction is the Church itself, in its acquisition as an outward existence, of possessions and an enormous property—a state of things which, since that Church despises or professes to despise riches, is none other than a Lie. And we found the State, during the mediæval period, simi-

larly involved in contradictions. We spoke above of an imperial
rule, recognized as standing by the side of the Church and
constituting its secular arm. But the power thus acknowledged
is invalidated by the fact that the imperial dignity in question
is an empty title, not regarded by the Emperor himself or by
those who wish to make him the instrument of their ambitious
views, as conferring solid authority on its possessor; for passion and physical force assume an independent position, and
own no subjection to that merely abstract conception. But
secondly, the bond of union which holds the Mediæval State
together, and which we call Fidelity, is left to the arbitrary
choice of men's disposition [Gemüth] which recognizes no objective duties. Consequently, this Fidelity is the most *unfaithful* thing possible. German Honor in the Middle Ages has
become a proverb; but examined more closely as History exhibits it we find it a veritable *Punica fides* or *Græca fides;* for
the princes and vassals of the Emperor are true and honorable
only to their selfish aims, individual advantage and passions,
but utterly untrue to the Empire and the Emperor; because in
" Fidelity " in the abstract, their subjective caprice receives a
sanction, and the State is not organized as a moral totality.
A *third* contradiction presents itself in the character of individuals, exhibiting, as they do on the one hand, piety—religious
devotion, the most beautiful in outward aspect, and springing
from the very depths of sincerity—and on the other hand a
barbarous deficiency in point of intelligence and will. We find
an acquaintance with abstract Truth, and yet the most uncult-
ured, the rudest ideas of the Secular and the Spiritual: a trucu-
lent delirium of passion and yet a Christian sanctity which
renounces all that is worldly, and devotes itself entirely to holiness. So self-contradictory, so deceptive is this mediæval period; and the polemical zeal with which its excellence is contended for, is one of the absurdities of our times. Primitive
barbarism, rudeness of manners, and childish fancy are not
revolting; they simply excite our pity. But the highest purity
of soul defiled by the most horrible barbarity; the Truth, of
which a knowledge has been acquired, degraded to a mere tool
by falsehood and self-seeking; that which is most irrational,
coarse and vile, established and strengthened by the religious
sentiment—this is the most disgusting and revolting spectacle
that was ever witnessed, and which only Philosophy can com-

prehend and so justify. For such an antithesis must arise in man's consciousness of the Holy while this consciousness still remains primitive and immediate; and the profounder the truth to which Spirit comes into an *implicit* relation—while it has not yet become aware of its own presence in that profound truth—so much the more alien is it to itself in this its unknown form: but only as the result of this alienation does it attain its true harmonization.

We have then contemplated the Church as the *reaction* of the Spiritual against the secular life of the time; but this reaction is so conditioned, that it only subjects to itself that against which it reacts—does not reform it. While the Spiritual, repudiating its proper sphere of action, has been acquiring secular power, a secular sovereignty has also consolidated itself and attained a systematic development—the *Feudal System*. As through their isolation, men are reduced to a dependence on their individual power and might, every point in the world on which a human being can maintain his ground becomes an *energetic* one. While the Individual still remains destitute of the defence of laws and is protected only by his own exertion, life, activity and excitement everywhere manifest themselves. As men are certain of eternal salvation through the instrumentality of the Church, and to this end are bound to obey it only in its spiritual requirements, their ardor in the pursuit of worldly enjoyment increases, on the other hand, in inverse proportion to their fear of its producing any detriment to their spiritual weal; for the Church bestows *indulgences,* when required, for oppressive, violent and vicious actions of all kinds.

The period from the eleventh to the thirteenth century witnessed the rise of an impulse which developed itself in various forms. The inhabitants of various districts began to build enormous churches—Cathedrals, erected to contain the whole community. Architecture is always the first art, forming the inorganic phase, the domiciliation of the divinity; not till this is accomplished does Art attempt to exhibit to the worshippers the divinity himself—the Objective. Maritime commerce was carried on with vigor by the cities on the Italian, Spanish, and Flemish coasts, and this stimulated the productive industry of their citizens at home. The Sciences began in some degree to revive: the Scholastic Philosophy was in its glory. Schools for the study of law were founded at Bologna and other places, as also for that of medicine. It is on the rise and growing importance of the Towns, that all these creations depend as their main condition; a favorite subject of historical treatment in modern times. And the rise of such communities was greatly desiderated. For the Towns, like the Church, present themselves as reactions against feudal violence—as the earliest legally and regularly constituted power. Mention has already been made of the fact that the possessors of power compelled others to put themselves under their protection. Such centres of safety were castles [Burgen], churches and monasteries, round which were collected those who needed protection. These now became burghers [Bürger], and entered into a cliental relation to the lords of such castles or to monastic bodies. Thus a firmly established community was formed in many places. Many cities and fortified places [Castelle] still existed in Italy, in the South of France, and in Germany on the Rhine, which dated their existence from the ancient Roman times, and which originally possessed municipal rights, but subsequently lost them under the rule of feudal governors [Vögte]. The citizens, like their rural neighbors, had been reduced to vassalage.

The principle of free possession however began to develop itself from the *protective* relation of feudal protection; *i.e.* freedom originated in its direct contrary. The feudal lords or great barons enjoyed, properly speaking, no free or absolute possession, any more than their dependents; they had unlimited power over the latter, but at the same time they also were vassals of princes higher and mightier than themselves, and to whom they were under engagements—which, it must be confessed, they did not fulfil except under compulsion. The ancient Germans had known of none other than free possession; but this principle had been perverted into its complete opposite, and now for the first time we behold the few feeble commencements of a reviving sense of freedom. Individuals brought into closer relation by the soil which they cultivated, formed among themselves a kind of union, confederation, or *conjuratio*. They agreed to be and to perform on their own behalf that which they had previously been and performed in the service of their feudal lord alone. Their first united undertaking was the erection of a tower in which a bell was suspended: the ringing of the bell was a signal for a general rendezvous, and the object of the union thus appointed was the formation of a kind of militia. This is followed by the institution of a municipal government, consisting of magistrates, jurors, consuls, and the establishment of a common treasury, the imposition of taxes, tolls, etc. Trenches are dug and walls built for the common defence, and the citizens are forbidden to erect fortresses for themselves individually. In such a community, handicrafts, as distinguished from agriculture, find their proper home. Artisans necessarily soon attained a superior position to that of the tillers of the ground, for the latter were forcibly driven to work; the former displayed activity really their own, and a corresponding diligence and interest in the result of their labors. Formerly artisans had been obliged to get permission from their liege lords to sell their work, and thus earn something for themselves: they were obliged to pay them a certain sum for this privilege of market, besides contributing a portion of their gains to the baronial exchequer. Those who had houses of their own were obliged to pay a considerable quit-rent for them; on all that was imported and exported, the nobility imposed large tolls, and for the security afforded to travellers they exacted safe-conduct money. When at a later date these communities became stronger, all such feudal rights were purchased from the nobles, or the cession of them compulsorily extorted: by degrees the towns secured an independent jurisdiction and likewise freed themselves from all taxes, tolls and rents. The burden which continued the longest was the obligation the towns were under to make provision for the Emperor and his whole retinue during his stay within their precincts, as also for seigneurs of inferior rank under the same circumstances. The trading class subsequently divided itself into *guilds,* to each of which were attached particular rights and obligations. The factions to which episcopal elections and other contingencies gave rise, very often promoted the attainment by the towns of the rights above-mentioned. As it would not infrequently happen that two rival bishops were elected to the same see, each one sought to draw the citizens into his own interest, by granting them privileges and freeing them from burdens. Subsequently arose many feuds with the clergy, the bishops and abbots. In some towns they maintained their position as lords of the municipality; in others the citizens got the upper hand, and obtained their freedom. Thus, *e.g.* Cologne threw off the yoke of its bishop; Mayence on the other hand remained subject. By degrees

cities grew to be independent republics: first and foremost in
Italy, then in the Netherlands, Germany, and France. They
soon come to occupy a peculiar position with respect to the
nobility. The latter united itself with the corporations of the
towns, and constituted as *e.g.* in Berne, a particular guild. It
soon assumed special powers in the corporations of the towns
and attained a dominant position; but the citizens resisted
the usurpation and secured the government to themselves. The
rich citizens (populus crassus) now excluded the nobility from
power. But in the same way as the party of the nobility was
divided into factions—especially those of Ghibellines and
Guelfs, of which the former favored the Emperor, the latter the
Pope—that of the citizens also was rent in sunder by intestine
strife. The victorious faction was accustomed to exclude its
vanquished opponents from power. The *patrician* nobility
which supplanted the feudal aristocracy, deprived the common
people of all share in the conduct of the state, and thus proved
itself no less oppressive than the original noblesse. The history
of the cities presents us with a continual change of constitutions,
according as one party among the citizens or the other—this
faction or that, got the upper hand. Originally a select body
of citizens chose the magistrates; but as in such elections the
victorious faction always had the greatest influence, no other
means of securing impartial functionaries was left, but the
election of foreigners to the office of judge and *podésta*. It also
frequently happened that the cities chose foreign princes as
supreme seigneurs, and intrusted them with the *signoria*. But
all of these arrangements were only of short continuance; the
princes soon misused their sovereignty to promote their own
ambitious designs and to gratify their passions, and in a few
years were once more deprived of their supremacy.—Thus the
history of these cities presents on the one hand, in individual
characters marked by the most terrible or the most admirable
features, an astonishingly interesting picture; on the other
hand it repels us by assuming, as it unavoidably does, the aspect
of mere chronicles. In contemplating the restless and ever-
varying impulses that agitate the very heart of these cities and
the continual struggles of factions, we are astonished to see
on the other side industry—commerce by land and sea—in the
highest degree prosperous. It is the same principle of lively
vigor, which, nourished by the internal excitement in question,
produces this phenomenon.

We have contemplated the Church, which extended its power over all the sovereignties of the time, and the Cities, where a social organizatiọn on a basis of Right was first resuscitated, as powers reacting against the authority of princes and feudal lords. Against these two rising powers, there followed a reactionary movement of princely authority; the Emperor now enters on a struggle with the Pope and the cities. The Emperor is recognized as the apex of Christian, *i.e.* secular power, the Pope on the other hand as that of Ecclesiastical power, which had now however become as decidedly a secular dominion. In theory, it was not disputed that the Roman Emperor was the Head of Christendom—that he possessed the *dominium mundi*—that since all Christian states belonged to the Roman Empire, their princes owed him allegiance in all reasonable and equitable requirements. However satisfied the emperors themselves might be of the validity of this claim, they had too much good sense to attempt seriously to enforce it · but the empty title of Roman Emperor was a sufficient inducement to them to exert themselves to the utmost to acquire and maintain it in Italy. The Othos especially cherished the idea of the continuation of the old Roman empire, and were ever and anon summoning the German princes to join them in an expedition to Rome with a view to coronation there;—an undertaking in which they were often deserted by them and had to undergo the shame of a retreat. Equal disappointment was experienced by those Italians who hoped for deliverance at the hands of the Emperor from the ochlocracy that domineered over the cities, or from the violence of the feudal nobility in the country at large. The Italian princes who had invoked the presence of the Emperor and had promised him aid in asserting his claims, drew back and left him in the lurch; and those who had previously expected salvation for their country, then broke out into bitter complaints that their beautiful country was devastated by barbarians, their superior civilization trodden under foot, and that right and liberty, deserted by the Emperor, must also perish. Especially touching and deep are the lamentations and reproachès which Dante addresses to the Emperors.

The second complication with Italy was that struggle which contemporaneously with the former was sustained chiefly by the great Swabians—the house of *Hohenstaufen*—and whose object was to bring back the secular power of the Church, which had become independent, to its original dependence on the state. The Papal See was also a secular power and sovereignty, and the Emperor asserted the superior prerogative of choosing the Pope and investing him with his secular sovereignty. It was these rights of the State for which the Emperors contended. But to that secular power which they withstood, they were at the same time subject, in virtue of its spiritual pretensions: thus the contest was an interminable contradiction. Contradictory as the varying phases of the contest, in which reconciliation was ever alternating with renewed hostilities, was also the instrumentality employed in the struggle. For the power with which the Emperors made head against their enemy—the princes, their servants and subjects, were divided in their own minds, inasmuch as they were bound by the strongest ties of allegiance to the Emperor and to his enemy at one and the same time. The chief interest of the princes lay in that very assumption of independence in reference to the State, against which on the part of the Papal See the Emperor was contending; so that they were willing to stand by the Emperor in cases where the empty dignity of the imperial crown was impugned, or on some particular occasions—*e.g.* in a contest with the cities—but abandoned him when he aimed at seriously asserting his authority against the secular power of the clergy, or against other princes.

As, on the one hand, the German emperors sought to realize their title in Italy, so, on the other hand, Italy had its political centre in Germany. The interests of the two countries were thus linked together, and neither could gain political consolidation within itself. In the brilliant period of the *Hohenstaufen* dynasty, individuals of commanding character sustained the dignity of the throne; sovereigns like Frederick Barbarossa, in whom the imperial power manifested itself in its greatest majesty, and who by his personal qualities succeeded in attaching the subject princes to his interests. Yet brilliant as the history of the Hohenstaufen dynasty may appear, and stirring as might have been the contest with the Church, the former presents on the whole nothing more than the tragedy of this house itself, and the latter had no important result in the sphere of Spirit. The cities were indeed compelled to acknowledge the imperial authority, and their deputies swore to observe the decisions of the Roncalian Diet; but they kept their word no longer than they were compelled to do so. Their sense of obligation depended exclusively on the direct consciousness of a superior power ready to enforce it. It is said that when the Emperor Frederick I asked the deputies of the cities whether they had not sworn to the conditions of peace, they answered: " Yes, but not that we would observe them." The result was that Frederick I at the Peace of Constance (1183) was obliged to concede to them a virtual independence; although he appended the stipulation, that in this concession their feudal obligations to the German Empire were understood to be reserved. The contest between the Emperors and the Popes regarding investitures was settled at the close of 1122 by Henry V and Pope Calixtus II on these terms: the Emperor was to invest with the sceptre; the Pope with the ring and crosier; the chapter were to elect the Bishops in the presence of the Emperor or of imperial commissioners; then the Emperor was to invest the Bishop as a secular feudatory with the *temporalia,* while the ecclesiastical investiture was reserved for the Pope. Thus the protracted contest between the secular and spiritual powers was at length set at rest.

Chapter II.—The Crusades

The Church gained the victory in the struggle referred to in the previous chapter; and in this way secured as decided a supremacy in Germany, as she did in the other states of Europe by a calmer process. She made herself mistress of all the relations of life, and of science and art; and she was the permanent repository of spiritual treasures. Yet notwithstanding this full and complete development of ecclesiastical life, we find a deficiency and consequent craving manifesting itself in Christendom, and which drove it out of itself. To understand this want, we must revert to the nature of the Christian religion itself, and particularly to that aspect of it by which it has a footing in the Present in the consciousness of its votaries.

The objective doctrines of Christianity had been already so firmly settled by the Councils of the Church, that neither the mediæval nor any other philosophy could develop them further, except in the way of exalting them intellectually, so that they might be satisfactory as presenting the *form* of Thought. And one essential point in this doctrine was the recognition of the Divine Nature as not in any sense an *other-world* existence [ein

Jenseits], but as in unity with Human Nature in the Present and Actual. But this Presence is at the same time exclusively Spiritual Presence. Christ as a particular human personality has left the world; his *temporal* existence is only a past one— *i.e.,* it exists only in mental conception. And since the Divine existence on earth is essentially of a spiritual character, it cannot appear in the form of a Dalai-Lama. The Pope, however high his position as Head of Christendom and Vicar of Christ, calls himself only the Servant of Servants. How then did the Church realize Christ as a *definite and present existence?* The principal form of this realization was, as remarked above, the Holy Supper, in the form it presented as the Mass: in this the Life, Suffering, and Death of the actual Christ were verily present, as an eternal and daily repeated sacrifice. Christ appears as a definite and present existence in a sensuous form as the *Host,* consecrated by the Priest; so far all is satisfactory: that is to say, it is the Church, the Spirit of Christ, that attains in this ordinance direct and full assurance. But the most prominent feature in this sacrament is, that the process by which Deity is manifested, is conditioned by the limitations of particularity—that the Host, this *Thing,* is set up to be adored as God. The Church then might have been able to content itself with this sensuous presence of Deity; but when it is once granted that God exists in external phenomenal presence, this external manifestation immediately becomes infinitely varied; for the need of this presence is infinite. Thus innumerable instances will occur in the experience of the Church, in which Christ has appeared to one and another, in various places; and still more frequently his divine Mother, who as standing nearer to humanity, is a second mediator between the Mediator and man (the miracle-working images of the Virgin are in their way Hosts, since they supply a benign and gracious presence of God). In all places, therefore, there will occur manifestations of the Heavenly, in specially gracious appearances, the stigmata of Christ's Passion, etc.; and the Divine will be realized in *miracles* as detached and isolated phenomena. In the period in question the Church presents the aspect of a world of miracle; to the community of devout and pious persons natural existence has utterly lost its stability and certainty: rather, absolute certainty has turned against it, and the Divine is not conceived of by Christendom under conditions of univer-

sality as the law and nature of Spirit, but reveals itself in isolated and detached phenomena, in which the rational form of
existence is utterly perverted.

In this complete development of the Church, *we* may find
a deficiency: but what can be felt as a want by *it?* What
compels *it*, in this state of perfect satisfaction and enjoyment,
to wish for something else within the limits of its own principles—without apostatizing from itself? Those miraculous
images, places, and times, are only isolated points, momentary
appearances—are not an embodiment of Deity, not of the highest and absolute kind. The Host, the supreme manifestation,
is to be found indeed in innumerable churches; Christ is therein
transubstantiated to a present and particular existence: but
this itself is of a vague and general character; it is not his actual
and very presence as particularized in *Space.* That presence
has passed away, as regards *time;* but as spatial and as concrete in *space* it has a mundane permanence in this particular
spot, this particular village, etc. It is then this mundane existence [in Palestine] which Christendom desiderates, which
it is resolved on attaining. Pilgrims in crowds had indeed been
able to enjoy it; but the approach to the hallowed localities
is in the hands of the Infidels, and it is a reproach to Christendom that the Holy Places and the Sepulchre of Christ in particular are not in possession of the Church. In this feeling
Christendom was united; consequently the *Crusades* were undertaken, whose object was not the furtherance of any special
interests on the part of the several states that engaged in them,
but simply and solely the conquest of the Holy Land.

The West once more sallied forth in hostile array against
the East. As in the expedition of the Greeks against Troy, so
here, the invading hosts were entirely composed of independent
feudal lords and knights; though they were not united under
a real individuality, as were the Greeks under Agamemnon or
Alexander. Christendom, on the contrary, was engaged in an
undertaking whose object was the securing of the *definite and
present existence* [of Deity]—the real culmination of Individuality. This object impelled the West against the East, and
this is the essential interest of the Crusades.

The first and immediate commencement of the Crusades
was made in the West itself. Many thousands of Jews were
massacred, and their property seized; and after this terrible

prelude Christendom began its march. The monk, Peter the Hermit of Amiens, led the way with an immense troop of rabble. This host passed in the greatest disorder through Hungary, and robbed and plundered as they went; but their numbers dwindled away, and only a few reached Constantinople. For rational considerations were out of the question; the mass of them believed that God would be their immediate guide and protector. The most striking proof that enthusiasm almost robbed the nations of Europe of their senses, is supplied by the fact that at a later time troops of children ran away from their parents, and went to Marseilles, there to take ship for the Holy Land. Few reached it; the rest were sold by the merchants to the Saracens as slaves.

At last, with much trouble and immense loss, more regular armies attained the desired object; they beheld themselves in possession of all the Holy Places of note—Bethlehem, Gethsemane, Golgotha, and even the *Holy Sepulchre*. In the whole expedition—in all the acts of the Christians—appeared that enormous contrast (a feature characteristic of the age)—the transition on the part of the Crusading host from the greatest excesses and outrages to the profoundest contrition and humiliation. Still dripping with the blood of the slaughtered inhabitants of Jerusalem, the Christians fell down on their faces at the tomb of the Redeemer, and directed their fervent supplications to him.

Thus did Christendom come into the possession of its highest good. Jerusalem was made a kingdom, and the entire feudal system was introduced there—a constitution which, in presence of the Saracens, was certainly the worst that could be adopted. Another crusade in the year 1204 resulted in the conquest of Constantinople and the establishment of a Latin Empire there. Christendom, therefore, had appeased its religious craving; it could now veritably walk unobstructed in the footsteps of the Saviour. Whole shiploads of earth were brought from the Holy Land to Europe. Of Christ himself no corporeal relics could be obtained, for he was arisen: the Sacred Handkerchief, the Cross, and lastly the Sepulchre, were the most venerated memorials. But in the Grave is found the real point of retroversion; it is in the grave that all the vanity of the Sensuous perishes. At the Holy Sepulchre the vanity of [the cherished] opinion passes away [the fancies by which the substance of truth has been obscured disappear]; there all is seriousness. In the negation of that *definite and present embodiment—i.e.* of the Sensuous—it is that the turning-point in question is found, and those words have an application: " Thou wouldst not suffer thy Holy One to see corruption." Christendom was not to find its ultimatum of truth in the grave. At this sepulchre the Christian world received a second time the response given to the disciples when they sought the body of the Lord there: " *Why seek ye the living among the dead? He is not here, but is risen.*" You must not look for the principle of your religion in the Sensuous, in the grave among the dead, but in the living Spirit in yourselves. We have seen how the vast idea of the union of the Finite with the Infinite was perverted to such a degree as that men looked for a *definite embodiment* of the Infinite in a mere isolated outward object [the Host]. Christendom found the empty Sepulchre, but not the union of the Secular and the Eternal; and so it lost the Holy Land. It was practically undeceived; and the result which it brought back with it was of a negative kind: viz., that the *definite embodiment* which it was seeking, was to be looked for in *Subjective Consciousness alone,* and in no external object; that the definite form in question, presenting the union of the Secular with the Eternal, is the Spiritual self-cognizant independence of the individual. Thus the world attains the conviction that man must look within himself for that *definite embodiment* of being which is of a divine nature: subjectivity thereby receives absolute authorization, and claims to determine for itself the relation [of all that exists] to the Divine.* This then was the absolute result of the Crusades, and from them we may date the commencement of self-reliance and spontaneous activity. The West bade an eternal farewell to the East at the Holy Sepulchre, and gained a comprehension of its own principle of subjective infinite Freedom. Christendom never appeared again on the scene of history as *one* body.

Crusades of another kind, bearing somewhat the character of wars with a view to mere secular conquest, but which involved a religious interest also, were the contests waged by Spain against the Saracens in the peninsula itself. The Christians had been shut up in a corner by the Arabs; but they

---

* All human actions, projects, institutions, etc., begin to be brought to the bar of " principle "—the sanctum of subjectivity—for absolute decision on their merits, instead of being referred to an extraneous authority.

gained upon their adversaries in strength, because the Saracens in Spain and Africa were engaged in war in various directions, and were divided among themselves. The Spaniards, united with Frank knights, undertook frequent expeditions against the Saracens; and in this collision of the Christians with the chivalry of the East—with its freedom and perfect independence of soul—the former became also partakers in this freedom. Spain gives us the fairest picture of the knighthood of the Middle Ages, and its hero is the Cid. Several Crusades, the records of which excite our unmixed loathing and detestation, were undertaken against the South of France also. There an æsthetic culture had developed itself: the Troubadours had introduced a freedom of manners similar to that which prevailed under the Hohenstaufen Emperors in Germany; but with this difference, that the former had in it something affected, while the latter was of a more genuine kind. But as in Upper Italy, so also in the South of France fanatical ideas of purity had been introduced; * a Crusade was therefore preached against that country by Papal authority. St. Dominic entered it with a vast host of invaders, who, in the most barbarous manner, pillaged and murdered the innocent and the guilty indiscriminately, and utterly laid waste the fair region which they inhabited.

Through the Crusades the Church reached the completion of its authority: it had achieved the perversion of religion and of the divine Spirit; it had distorted the principle of Christian Freedom to a wrongful and immoral slavery of men's souls; and in so doing, far from abolishing lawless caprice and violence and supplanting them by a virtuous rule of its own, it had even enlisted them in the service of ecclesiastical authority. In the Crusades the Pope stood at the head of the secular power: the Emperor appeared only in a subordinate position, like the other princes, and was obliged to commit both the initiative and the executive to the Pope, as the manifest generalissimo of the expedition. We have already seen the noble house of Hohenstaufen presenting the aspect of chivalrous, dignified and cultivated opponents of the Papal power, when Spirit [the moral and intellectual element in Christendom] had given up the contest. We have seen how they were

---

* The term " Cathari " (καθαροί). Purists, was one of the most general designations of the dissident sects in question. The German word " Ketzer " = *heretic* is by some derived from it.

ultimately obliged to yield to the Church; which, elastic enough
to sustain any attack, bore down all opposition and would not
move a step towards conciliation. The fall of the Church was
not to be effected by open violence; it was from within—by the
power of Spirit and by an influence that wrought its way upwards—that ruin threatened it. Respect for the Papacy could
not but be weakened by the very fact that the lofty aim of the
Crusades—the satisfaction expected from the enjoyment of
the sensuous Presence—was not attained. As little did the
Popes succeed in keeping possession of the Holy Land. Zeal
for the holy cause was exhausted among the princes of Europe.
Grieved to the heart by the defeat of the Christians, the Popes
again and again urged them to advance to the rescue; but
lamentations and entreaties were vain, and they could effect
nothing. Spirit, disappointed with regard to its craving for
the highest form of the sensuous presence of Deity, fell back
upon itself. A rupture, the first of its kind and profound as
it was novel, took place. From this time forward we witness
religious and intellectual movements in which Spirit—transcending the repulsive and irrational existence by which it is
surrounded—either finds its sphere of exercise within itself,
and draws upon its own resources for satisfaction, or throws
its energies into an actual world of general and morally justified aims, which are therefore aims consonant with Freedom.
The efforts thus originated are now to be described: they were
the means by which Spirit was to be prepared to comprehend
the grand purpose of its Freedom in a form of greater purity
and moral elevation.

To this class of movements belongs in the first place the
establishment of monastic and chivalric orders, designed to
carry out those rules of life which the Church had distinctly
enjoined upon its members. That renunciation of property,
riches, pleasures, and free will, which the Church had designated as the highest of spiritual attainments, was to be a reality
—not a mere profession. The existing monastic and other institutions that had adopted this vow of renunciation, had been
entirely sunk in the corruption of worldliness. But now Spirit
sought to realize in the sphere of the principle of negativity—
purely in itself—what the Church had demanded. The more
immediate occasion of this movement was the rise of numerous
heresies in the South of France and Italy, whose tendency was

in the direction of enthusiasm; and the unbelief which was now gaining ground, but which the Church justly deemed not so dangerous as those heresies. To counteract these evils, new *monastic orders* were founded, the chief of which was that of the Franciscans, or Mendicant Friars, whose founder, St. Francis of Assisi—a man possessed by an enthusiasm and ecstatic passion that passed all bounds—spent his life in continually striving for the loftiest purity. He gave an impulse of the same kind to his order; the greatest fervor of devotion, the sacrifice of all pleasures in contravention of the prevailing worldliness of the Church, continual penances, the severest poverty (the Franciscans lived on daily alms)—were therefore peculiarly characteristic of it. Contemporaneously with it arose the Dominican order, founded by St. Dominic; its special business was preaching. The mendicant friars were diffused through Christendom to an incredible extent; they were, on the one hand, the standing apostolic army of the Pope, while, on the other hand, they strongly protested against his worldliness. The Franciscans were powerful allies of Louis of Bavaria in his resistance of the Papal assumptions, and they are said to have been the authors of the position, that a General Council was higher authority than the Pope; but subsequently they too sank down into a torpid and unintelligent condition. In the same way the ecclesiastical *Orders of Knighthood* contemplated the attainment of purity of Spirit. We have already called attention to the peculiar chivalric spirit which had been developed in Spain through the struggle with the Saracens: the same spirit was diffused as the result of the Crusades through the whole of Europe. The ferocity and savage valor that characterized the predatory life of the barbarians—pacified and brought to a settled state by possession, and restrained by the presence of equals—was elevated by religion and then kindled to a noble enthusiasm through contemplating the boundless magnanimity of Oriental prowess. For Christianity also contains the element of boundless abstraction and freedom; the Oriental chivalric spirit found therefore in Occidental hearts a response, which paved the way for their attaining a nobler virtue than they had previously known. Ecclesiastical orders of knighthood were instituted on a basis resembling that of the monastic fraternities. The same conventual vow of renunciation was imposed on their members—the giving up of all that was worldly. But at the same time they undertook the defence of the pilgrims: their first duty therefore was knightly bravery; ultimately, they were also pledged to the sustenance and care of the poor and the sick. The Orders of Knighthood were divided into three: that of St. John, that of the Temple, and the Teutonic Order. These associations are essentially distinguished from the self-seeking principle of feudalism. Their members sacrificed themselves with almost suicidal bravery for a common interest. Thus these Orders transcended the circle of their immediate environment, and formed a network of fraternal coalition over the whole of Europe. But their members sank down to the level of vulgar interests, and the Orders became in the sequel a provisional institute for the nobility generally, rather than anything else. The Order of the Temple was even accused of forming a religion of its own, and of having renounced Christ in the creed which, under the influence of the Oriental Spirit, it had adopted.

A second impulsion, having a similar origin, was that in the direction of *Science*. The development of Thought—the abstractly Universal—now had its commencement. Those fraternal associations themselves, having a common object, in whose service their members were enlisted, point to the fact that a general principle was beginning to be recognized, and which gradually became conscious of its power. Thought was first directed to Theology, which now became Philosophy under the name of Scholastic Divinity. For philosophy and theology have the Divine as their common object; and although the theology of the Church was a stereotyped dogma, the impulse now arose to justify this body of doctrine in the view of Thought. " When we have arrived at Faith," says the celebrated scholastic, Anselm, " it is a piece of negligence to stop short of convincing ourselves, by the aid of Thought, of that to which we have given credence." But thus conditioned Thought was not free, for its material was already posited *ab extra;* it was to the proof of this material that philosophy devoted its energies. But Thought suggested a variety of questions, the complete answer to which was not given directly in the symbols of the Church; and since the Church had not decided respecting them, they were legitimate subjects of controversy. Philosophy was indeed called an *ancilla fidei,* for it was in subjection to that material of the Church's creed, which had been already definitely settled; but yet it was impossible for the opposition between Thought and Belief not to manifest itself. As Europe presented the spectacle of chivalric contests generally—passages of arms and tournaments—it was now the theatre for intellectual jousting also. It is incredible to what an extent the abstract forms of Thought were developed, and what dexterity was acquired in the use of them. This intellectual tourneying for the sake of exhibiting skill, and as a diversion (for it was not the doctrines themselves, but only the forms in which they were couched that made the subject of debate), was chiefly prosecuted and brought to perfection in France. France, in fact, began at that time to be regarded as the centre of Christendom: there the scheme of the first Crusades originated, and French armies carried it out: there the Popes took refuge in their struggles with the German emperors and with the Norman princes of Naples and Sicily, and there for a time they made a continuous sojourn.—We also observe in the period subsequent to the Crusades, commencements of Art—of Painting, viz.: even during their continuance a peculiar kind of poetry had made it appearance. Spirit, unable to satisfy its cravings, created for itself by imagination fairer forms and in a calmer and freer manner than the actual world could offer.

Chapter III.—The Transition from Feudalism to Monarchy

The moral phenomena above mentioned, tending in the direction of a general principle, were partly of a subjective, partly of a speculative order. But we must now give particular attention to the practical political movements of the period. The advance which that period witnessed, presents a negative aspect in so far as it involves the termination of the sway of individual caprice and of the isolation of power. Its affirmative aspect is the rise of a supreme authority whose dominion embraces all —a political power properly so called, whose subjects enjoy an equality of rights, and in which the will of the individual is subordinated to that common interest which underlies the whole. This is the advance from Feudalism to *Monarchy*. The principle of feudal sovereignty is the *outward* force of individuals—princes, liege lords; it is a force destitute of *intrinsic* right. The subjects of such a Constitution are vassals of a superior prince or seigneur, to whom they have stipulated

duties to perform: but whether they perform these duties or
not, depends upon the seigneur's being able to induce them so
to do, by force of character or by grant of favors:—conversely,
the recognition of those feudal claims themselves was extorted
by violence in the first instance; and the fulfilment of the corresponding duties could be secured only by the constant exercise
of the power which was the sole basis of the claims in question.
The monarchical principle also implies a supreme authority,
but it is an authority over persons possessing no independent
power to support their individual caprice; where we have no
longer caprice opposed to caprice; for the supremacy implied
in monarchy is essentially a power emanating from a political
body, and is pledged to the furtherance of that equitable purpose on which the constitution of a state is based. Feudal
sovereignty is a polyarchy: we see nothing but Lords and
Serfs; in Monarchy, on the contrary, there is one Lord and
no Serf, for servitude is abrogated by it, and in it Right and
Law are recognized; it is the source of real freedom. Thus in
monarchy the caprice of individuals is kept under, and a common gubernatorial interest established. In the suppression of
those isolated powers, as also in the resistance made to that
suppression, it seems doubtful whether the desire for a lawful
and equitable state of things, or the wish to indulge individual
caprice, is the impelling motive. Resistance to kingly authority
is entitled Liberty, and is lauded as legitimate and noble when
the idea of arbitrary will is associated with that authority. But
by the arbitrary will of an individual exerting itself so as to
subjugate a whole body of men, a community is formed; and
comparing this state of things with that in which every point
is a centre of capricious violence, we find a much smaller number of points exposed to such violence. The great extent of
such a sovereignty necessitates general arrangements for the
purposes of organization, and those who govern in accordance
with those arrangements are at the same time, in virtue of their
office itself, obedient to the state: Vassals become Officers of
State, whose duty it is to execute the laws by which the state
is regulated. But since this monarchy is developed from feudalism, it bears in the first instance the stamp of the system from
which it sprang. Individuals quit their isolated capacity and
become members of Estates [or Orders of the Realm] and Corporations; the vassals are powerful only by combination as an

Order; in contraposition to them the cities constitute Powers in virtue of their communal existence. Thus the authority of the sovereign inevitably ceases to be mere arbitrary sway. The consent of the Estates and Corporations is essential to its maintenance; and if the prince wishes to have that consent, he must will what is just and reasonable.

We now see a Constitution embracing various Orders, while Feudal rule knows no such Orders. We observe the transition from feudalism to monarchy taking place in three ways:

1. Sometimes the lord paramount gains a mastery over his independent vassals, by subjugating their individual power—thus making himself sole ruler.

2. Sometimes the princes free themselves from the feudal relation altogether, and become the territorial lords of certain states; or lastly

3. The lord paramount unites the particular lordships that own him as their superior, with his own particular suzerainty, in a more peaceful way, and thus becomes master of the whole.

These processes do not indeed present themselves in history in that pure and abstract form in which they are exhibited here: often we find more modes than one appearing contemporaneously; but one or the other always predominates. The cardinal consideration is that the basis and essential condition of such a political formation is to be looked for in the *particular nationalities* in which it had its birth. Europe presents particular nations, constituting a unity in their very nature, and having the absolute tendency to form a state. All did not succeed in attaining this political unity: we have now to consider them severally in relation to the change thus introduced.

First, as regards the Roman empire, the connection between *Germany* and *Italy* naturally results from the idea of that empire: the secular dominion united with the spiritual was to constitute one whole; but this state of things was rather the object of constant struggle than one actually attained. In Germany and Italy the transition from the feudal condition to monarchy involved the entire abrogation of the former: the vassals became independent monarchs.

Germany had always embraced a great variety of stocks:—Swabians, Bavarians, Franks, Thuringians, Saxons, Burgundians: to these must be added the Sclaves of Bohemia, Germanized Sclaves in Mecklenburg, in Brandenburg, and in a part of Saxony and Austria; so that no such combination as took place in France was possible. Italy presented a similar state of things. The Lombards had established themselves there, while the Greeks still possessed the Exarchate and Lower Italy: the Normans too established a kingdom of their own in Lower Italy, and the Saracens maintained their ground for a time in Sicily. When the rule of the house of Hohenstaufen was terminated, barbarism got the upper hand throughout Germany; the country being broken up into several sovereignties, in which a forceful despotism prevailed. It was the maxim of the electoral princes to raise only weak princes to the imperial throne; they even sold the imperial dignity to foreigners. Thus the unity of the state was virtually annulled. A number of centres of power were formed; each of which was a predatory state: the legal constitution recognized by feudalism was dissolved, and gave place to undisguised violence and plunder; and powerful princes made themselves lords of the country. After the interregnum the Count of Hapsburg was elected Emperor, and the House of Hapsburg continued to fill the imperial throne with but little interruption. These emperors were obliged to create a force of their own, as the princes would not grant them an adequate power attached to the empire. But that state of absolute anarchy was at last put an end to by associations having general aims in view. In the cities themselves we see associations of a minor order; but now *confederations of cities* were formed with a common interest in the suppression of predatory violence. Of this kind was the *Hanseatic League* in the North, the *Rhenish League* consisting of cities lying along the Rhine, and the *Swabian League*. The aim of all these confederations was resistance to the feudal lords; and even princes united with the cities, with a view to the subversion of the feudal condition and the restoration of a peaceful state of things throughout the country. What the state of society was under feudal sovereignty is evident from the notorious association formed for executing criminal justice: it was a private tribunal, which, under the name of the *Vehmgericht*, held secret sittings; its chief seat was the northwest of Germany. A peculiar *peasant association* was also formed. In Germany the peasants were bondmen; many of them took refuge in the towns, or settled down as freemen in the neighborhood of the towns (*Pfahlbürger*); but in Switzerland a peasant fraternity was established. The peasants of Uri, Schwyz, and Unterwalden were under imperial governors; for the Swiss governments were not the property of private possessors, but were official appointments of the Empire. These the sovereigns of the Hapsburg line wished to secure to their own house. The peasants, with club and iron-studded mace [Morgenstern], returned victorious from a contest with the haughty steel-clad nobles, armed with spear and sword, and practised in the chivalric encounters of the tournament. Another invention also tended to deprive the nobility of the ascendancy which they owed to their accoutrements—that of *gunpowder*. Humanity needed it, and it made its appearance forthwith. It was one of the chief instruments in freeing the world from the dominion of physical force, and placing the various orders of society on a level. With the distinction between the weapons they used, vanished also that between lords and serfs. And before gunpowder fortified places were no longer impregnable, so that strongholds and castles now lose their importance. We may indeed be led to lament the decay or the depreciation of the practical value of personal valor—the bravest, the noblest may be shot down by a cowardly wretch at safe distance in an obscure lurking-place; but, on the other hand, gunpowder has made a rational, considerate bravery—Spiritual valor—the essential to martial success. Only through this instrumentality could that superior order of valor be called forth—that valor in which the heat of personal feeling has no share; for the discharge of firearms is directed against a body of men—an abstract enemy, not individual combatants. The warrior goes to meet deadly peril calmly, sacrificing himself for the common weal; and the valor of cultivated nations is characterized by the very fact, that it does not rely on the strong arm alone, but places its confidence essentially in the intelligence, the generalship, the character of its commanders; and, as was the case among the ancients, in a firm combination and unity of spirit on the part of the forces they command.

In *Italy*, as already noticed, we behold the same spectacle as in Germany—the attainment of an independent position by isolated centres of power. In that country, warfare in the hands of the Condottieri became a regular business. The towns were obliged to attend to their trading concerns, and therefore employed mercenary troops, whose leaders often became feudal lords; Francis Sforza even made himself Duke of Milan. In Florence, the Medici, a family of merchants, rose to power. On the other hand, the larger cities of Italy reduced under their sway several smaller ones and many feudal chiefs. A Papal territory was likewise formed. There, also, a very large number of feudal lords had made themselves independent; by degrees they all became subject to the one sovereignty of the Pope. How thoroughly equitable in the view of social morality such a subjugation was, is evident from Machiavelli's celebrated work " The Prince." This book has often been thrown aside in disgust, as replete with the maxims of the most revolting tyranny; but nothing worse can be urged against it than that the writer, having the profound consciousness of the necessity for the formation of a State, has here exhibited the principles on which alone states could be founded in the circumstances of the times. The chiefs who asserted an isolated independence, and the power they arrogated, must be entirely subdued; and though we cannot reconcile with our idea of Freedom, the means which he proposes as the only efficient ones, and regards as perfectly justifiable—inasmuch as they involve the most reckless violence, all kinds of deception, assassination, and so forth—we must nevertheless confess that the feudal nobility, whose power was to be subdued, were assailable in no other way, since an indomitable contempt for principle, and an utter depravity of morals, were thoroughly engrained in them.

In *France* we find the converse of that which occurred in Germany and Italy. For many centuries the Kings of France possessed only a very small domain, so that many of their vassals were more powerful than themselves: but it was a great advantage to the royal dignity in France, that the principle of hereditary monarchy was firmly established there. The consideration it enjoyed was increased by the circumstance that the corporations and cities had their rights and privileges confirmed by the king, and that the appeals to the supreme feudal tribunal—the Court of Peers, consisting of twelve members enjoying that dignity—became increasingly frequent. The king's influence was extended by his affording that protection which only the throne could give. But that which essentially secured respect for royalty, even among the powerful vassals, was the increasing personal power of the sovereign. In various ways, by inheritance, by marriage, by force of arms, etc., the Kings had come into possession of many Earldoms [Graf-schaften] and several Duchies. The Dukes of Normandy had, however, become Kings of England; and thus a formidable power confronted France, whose interior lay open to it by way of Normandy. Besides this there were powerful Duchies still remaining; nevertheless, the King was not a mere feudal suzerain [Lehnsherr] like the German Emperors, but had become a territorial possessor [Landesherr]: he had a number of barons and cities under him, who were subject to his immediate jurisdiction; and Louis IX succeeded in rendering appeals to the royal tribunal common throughout his kingdom. The towns attained a position of greater importance in the state. For when the king needed money, and all his usual resources—such as taxes and forced contributions of all kinds —were exhausted, he made application to the towns and entered into separate negotiations with them. It was Philip the Fair who, in the year 1302, first convoked the deputies of the towns as a Third Estate in conjunction with the clergy and the barons. All indeed that they were in the first instance concerned with was the authority of the sovereign as the power that had convoked them, and the raising of taxes as the object of their convocation; but the States nevertheless secured an importance and weight in the kingdom, and as the natural result, an influence on legislation also. A fact which is particularly remarkable is the proclamation issued by the kings of France, giving permission to the bondsmen on the crown lands to purchase their freedom at a moderate price. In the way we have indicated the kings of France very soon attained great power; while the flourishing state of the poetic art in the hands of the Troubadours, and the growth of the scholastic theology, whose especial centre was Paris, gave France a culture superior to that of the other European states, and which secured the respect of foreign nations.

England, as we have already had occasion to mention, was subjugated by William the Conqueror, Duke of Normandy. William introduced the feudal system into it, and divided the kingdom into fiefs, which he granted almost exclusively to his Norman followers. He himself retained considerable crown possessions; the vassals were under obligation to perform service in the field, and to aid in administering justice: the

King was the guardian of all vassals under age; they could not marry without his consent. Only by degrees did the barons and the towns attain a position of importance. It was especially in the disputes and struggles for the throne that they acquired considerable weight. When the oppressive rule and fiscal exactions of the Kings became intolerable, contentions and even war ensued: the barons compelled King John to swear to Magna Charta, the basis of English liberty, *i.e.* more particularly of the privileges of the nobility. Among the liberties thus secured, that which concerns the administration of justice was the chief: no Englishman was to be deprived of personal freedom, property, or life without the judicial verdict of his peers. Every one, moreover, was to be entitled to the free disposition of his property. Further, the King was to impose no taxes without the consent of the archbishops, bishops, earls, and barons. The towns, also, favored by the Kings in opposition to the barons, soon elevated themselves into a Third Estate and to representation in the Commons' House of Parliament. Yet the King was always very powerful, if he possessed strength of character: his crown estates procured for him due consideration; in later times, however, these were gradually alienated—given away—so that the King was reduced to apply for subsidies to the parliament.

We shall not pursue the minute and specifically historic details that concern the incorporation of principalities with states, or the dissensions and contests that accompanied such incorporations. We have only to add that the kings, when by weakening the feudal constitution, they had attained a higher degree of power, began to use that power against each other in the undisguised interest of their own dominion. Thus France and England carried on wars with each other for a century. The kings were always endeavoring to make foreign conquests; the towns, which had the largest share of the burdens and expenses of such wars, were opposed to them, and in order to placate them the kings granted them important privileges.

The *Popes* endeavored to make the disturbed state of society to which each of these changes gave rise, an occasion for the intervention of their authority; but the interest of the growth of states was too firmly established to allow them to make their own interest of absolute authority valid against it. Princes

and peoples were indifferent to papal clamor urging them
to new crusades. The Emperor Louis set to work to deduce
from Aristotle, the Bible, and the Roman Law a refutation
of the assumptions of the Papal See; and the electors declared
at the Diet held at Rense in 1338, and afterwards still more
decidedly at the Imperial Diet held at Frankfort, that they
would defend the liberties and hereditary rights of the Empire,
and that to make the choice of a Roman Emperor or King valid,
no papal confirmation was needed. So, at an earlier date,
1302, on occasion of a contest between Pope Boniface and
Philip the Fair, the Assembly of the States convoked by the
latter had offered opposition to the Pope. For states and communities had arrived at the consciousness of independent moral
worth.—Various causes had united to weaken the papal authority: the Great Schism of the Church, which led men to
doubt the Pope's infallibility, gave occasion to the decisions of
the Councils of Constance and Basle, which assumed an authority superior to that of the Pope, and therefore deposed and
appointed Popes. The numerous attempts directed against
the ecclesiastical system confirmed the necessity of a reformation. Arnold of Brescia, Wickliffe, and Huss met with sympathy in contending against the dogma of the papal vicegerency
of Christ, and the gross abuses that disgraced the hierarchy.
These attempts were, however, only partial in their scope.
On the one hand the time was not yet ripe for a more comprehensive onslaught; on the other hand the assailants in question did not strike at the heart of the matter, but (especially
the two latter) attacked the teaching of the Church chiefly
with the weapons of erudition, and consequently failed to excite
a deep interest among the people at large.

But the ecclesiastical principle had a more dangerous foe in
the incipient formation of political organizations, than in the
antagonists above referred to. A common object, an aim intrinsically possessed of perfect moral validity,* presented itself
to secularity in the formation of states; and to this aim of
community the will, the desire, the caprice of the individual
submitted themselves. The hardness characteristic of the self-
seeking quality of " Heart," maintaining its position of isolation
—the knotty heart of oak underlying the national temperament

* That is, not a personal aim, whose
self-seeking character is its condemnation, but a general and liberal, conse
quently a *moral* aim.

of the Germans—was broken down and mellowed by the terrible discipline of the Middle Ages. The two iron rods which were the instruments of this discipline were the Church and serfdom. The Church drove the " Heart " [Gemüth] to desperation— made Spirit pass through the severest bondage, so that the soul was no longer its own; but it did not degrade it to Hindoo torpor, for Christianity is an intrinsically spiritual principle and, as such, has a boundless elasticity. In the same way serfdom, which made a man's body not his own, but the property of an- other, dragged humanity through all the barbarism of slavery and unbridled desire, and the latter was destroyed by its own violence. It was not so much *from* slavery as *through* slavery that humanity was emancipated. For barbarism, lust, injustice constitute evil: man, bound fast in its fetters, is unfit for morality and religiousness; and it is from this intemperate and ungovernable state of volition that the discipline in question emancipated him. The Church fought the battle with the violence of rude sensuality in a temper equally wild and terror- istic with that of its antagonist: it prostrated the latter by dint of the terrors of hell, and held it in perpetual subjection, in order to break down the spirit of barbarism and to tame it into repose. Theology declares that every man has this struggle to pass through, since he is by nature evil, and only by passing through a state of mental laceration arrives at the certainty of Reconciliation. But granting this, it must on the other hand be maintained, that the form of the contest is very much al- tered when the conditions of its commencement are different, and when that reconciliation has had an actual realization. The path of torturous discipline is in that case dispensed with (it does indeed make its appearance at a later date, but in a quite different form), for the waking up of consciousness finds man surrounded by the element of a moral state of society. The phase of negation is, indeed, a necessary element in human development, but it has now assumed the tranquil form of edu- cation, so that all the terrible characteristics of that inward struggle vanish.

Humanity has now attained the consciousness of a real in- ternal harmonization of Spirit, and a good conscience in re- gard to actuality—to secular existence. The Human Spirit has come to stand on its own basis. In the self-consciousness to which man has thus advanced, there is no revolt against the

Divine, but a manifestation of that better subjectivity, which recognizes the Divine in its own being; which is imbued with the Good and True, and which directs its activities to general and liberal objects bearing the stamp of rationality and beauty.

Art and Science as Putting a Period to the Middle Ages

Humanity beholds its spiritual firmament restored to serenity. With that tranquil settling down of the world into political order which we have been contemplating, was conjoined an exaltation of Spirit to a nobler grade of humanity in a sphere involving more comprehensive and concrete interests than that with which political existence is concerned. The Sepulchre—that *caput mortuum* of Spirit—and the Ultramundane cease to absorb human attention. The principle of a specific and definite embodiment of the Infinite—that desideratum which urged the world to the Crusades, now developed itself in a quite different direction, viz. in secular existence asserting an independent ground: Spirit made its embodiment an outward one and found a congenial sphere in the secular life thus originated. The Church, however, maintained its former position, and retained the principle in question in its original form. Yet even in this case, that principle ceased to be limited to a bare outward existence [a sacred *thing*, the Host, *e.g.*]: it was transformed and elevated by *Art*. Art spiritualizes—animates the mere outward and material object of adoration with a form which expresses soul, sentiment, Spirit; so that piety has not a bare sensuous embodiment of the Infinite to contemplate, and does not lavish its devotion on a mere *Thing*, but on the higher element with which the material object is imbued—that expressive form with which *Spirit* has invested it.—It is one thing for the mind to have before it a mere Thing—such as the Host *per se*, a piece of stone or wood, or a wretched daub;—quite another thing for it to contemplate a painting, rich in thought and sentiment, or a beautiful work of sculpture, in looking at which, soul holds converse with soul and Spirit with Spirit. In the former case, Spirit is torn from its proper element, bound down to something utterly alien to it—the Sensuous, the Non-Spiritual. In the latter, on the contrary, the sensuous object is a beautiful one, and the Spiritual Form with which it is endued, gives it a soul and contains truth in itself. But on the one hand, this element of truth as thus exhibited, is manifested only in a sensuous mode, not in its appropriate form; on the other hand, while Religion normally involves independence of that which is essentially a mere outward and material object—a mere thing—that kind of religion which is now under consideration, finds no satisfaction in being brought into connection with the Beautiful: the coarsest, ugliest, poorest representations will suit its purpose *equally well*—perhaps better. Accordingly real masterpieces—*e.g.* Raphael's Madonnas—do not enjoy distinguished veneration, or elicit a multitude of offerings: inferior pictures seem on the contrary to be especial favorites and to be made the object of the warmest devotion and the most generous liberality. Piety passes by the former for this very reason, that were it to linger in their vicinity it would feel an inward stimulus and attraction;—an excitement of a kind which cannot but be felt to be alien, where all that is desiderated is a sense of mental bondage in which self is lost— the stupor of abject dependence.—Thus Art in its very nature transcended the principle of the Church. But as the former manifests itself only under sensuous limitations [and does not present the suspicious aspect of abstract thought], it is at first regarded as a harmless and indifferent matter. The Church, therefore, continued to follow it; but as soon as the free Spirit in which Art originated, advanced to Thought and Science, a separation ensued.

For Art received a further support and experienced an elevating influence as the result of the *study of antiquity* (the name *humaniora* is very expressive, for in those works of antiquity honor is done to the Human and to the development of Humanity): through this study the West became acquainted with the true and eternal element in the activity of man. The outward occasion of this revival of science was the fall of the Byzantine Empire. Large numbers of Greeks took refuge in the West and introduced Greek literature there; and they brought with them not only the knowledge of the Greek language but also the treasures to which that knowledge was the key. Very little of Greek literature had been preserved in the convents, and an acquaintance with the language could scarcely be said to exist at all. With the Roman literature it was otherwise; in regard to that, ancient traditions still lingered: Virgil was thought to be a great magician (in Dante he appears as the guide in Hell and Purgatory). Through the influence of the

Greeks, then, attention was again directed to the ancient Greek literature; the West had become capable of enjoying and appreciating it; quite other ideals and a different order of virtue from that with which mediæval Europe was familiar were here presented; an altogether novel standard for judging of what was to be honored, commended and imitated was set up. The Greeks in their works exhibited quite other moral commands than those with which the West was acquainted; scholastic formalism had to make way for a body of speculative thought of a widely different complexion: Plato became known in the West, and in him a new human world presented itself. These novel ideas met with a principal organ of diffusion in the newly discovered *Art of Printing*, which, like the use of gunpowder, corresponds with modern character, and supplied the desideratum of the age in which it was invented, by tending to enable men to stand in an ideal connection with each other. So far as the study of the ancients manifested an interest in human deeds and virtues, the Church continued to tolerate it, not observing that in those alien works an altogether alien spirit was advancing to confront it,

As a *third* leading feature demanding our notice in determining the character of the period, might be mentioned that urging of Spirit *outwards*—that desire on the part of man to become acquainted with *his* world. The chivalrous spirit of the maritime heroes of Portugal and Spain opened a new way to the East Indies and discovered America. This progressive step also, involved no transgression of the limits of ecclesiastical principles or feeling. The aim of Columbus was by no means a merely secular one: it presented also a distinctly religious aspect; the treasures of those rich Indian lands which awaited his discovery were destined in his intention to be expended in a new Crusade, and the heathen inhabitants of the countries themselves were to be converted to Christianity. The recognition of the spherical figure of the earth led man to perceive that it offered him a definite and limited object, and navigation had been benefited by the new found instrumentality of the magnet, enabling it to be something better than mere coasting: thus technical appliances make their appearance when a need for them is experienced.

These three events—the so-called Revival of Learning, the flourishing of the Fine Arts and the discovery of America and of the passage to India by the Cape—may be compared with that *blush of dawn*, which after long storms first betokens the return of a bright and glorious day. This day is the day of Universality, which breaks upon the world **after** the long, eventful, and terrible night of the Middle Ages—a day which is distinguished by science, art and inventive impulse—that is, by the noblest and highest, and which Humanity, rendered free by Christianity and emancipated through the instrumentality of the Church, exhibits as the eternal and veritable substance of its being.

SECTION III

THE MODERN TIME

W E have now arrived at the third period of the German World, and thus enter upon the period of Spirit conscious that it is free, inasmuch as it wills the True, the Eternal—that which is in and for itself Universal.

In this third period also, three divisions present themselves. First, we have to consider the *Reformation* in itself—the all-enlightening *Sun*, following on that blush of dawn which we observed at the termination of the mediæval period; next, the unfolding of that state of things which succeeded the Reformation; and lastly, the Modern Times, dating from the end of the last century.

Chapter I.—The Reformation

The Reformation resulted from the *corruption of the Church*. That corruption was not an accidental phenomenon; it was not the mere *abuse* of power and dominion. A corrupt state of things is very frequently represented as an " abuse "; it is taken for granted that the foundation was good—the system, the institution itself faultless—but that the passion, the subjective interest, in short the arbitrary volition of men has made use of that which in itself was good to further its own selfish ends, and that all that is required to be done is to remove these adventitious elements. On this showing the institute in question escapes obloquy, and the evil that disfigures it appears something foreign to it. But when accidental abuse of a good thing really occurs, it is limited to particularity. A great and general corruption affecting a body of such large and comprehensive scope as a Church, is quite another thing.—The corruption of the Church was a native growth; the principle of that corruption is to be looked for in the fact that the specific and definite embodiment of Deity which it recognizes, is sensuous—that the external in a coarse material form, is enshrined in its inmost being. (The refining transformation which Art supplied was not sufficient.) The higher Spirit—that of the World —has already expelled the Spiritual from it; it finds nothing to interest it in the Spiritual or in occupation with it; thus it retains that specific and definite embodiment;—*i.e.*, we have the sensuous immediate subjectivity, not refined by it to Spiritual subjectivity.—Henceforth it occupies *a position of inferiority to the World-Spirit*; the latter has already transcended it, for it has become capable of recognizing the Sensuous as sensuous, the merely outward as merely outward; it has learned to occupy itself with the Finite in a finite way, and in this very activity to maintain an independent and confident position as a valid and rightful subjectivity.*

The element in question which is innate in the Ecclesiastical principle only reveals itself as a corrupting one when the Church has no longer any opposition to contend with—when it has become firmly established. Then its elements are free to display their tendencies without let or hindrance. Thus it is that externality in the Church itself which becomes evil and corruption, and develops itself as a negative principle in its own bosom.—The forms which this corruption assumes are coextensive with the relations which the Church itself sustains, into which consequently this vitiating element enters.

The ecclesiastical piety of the period displays the very essence of superstition—the fettering of the mind to a sensuous object, a mere Thing—in the most various forms:—slavish deference to *Authority;* for Spirit, having renounced its proper nature in its most essential quality [having sacrificed its characteristic liberty to a mere sensuous object], has lost its Freedom, and is held in adamantine bondage to what is alien to itself;—a credulity of the most absurd and childish character in regard to *Miracles*, for the Divine is supposed to manifest itself in a perfectly disconnected and limited way, for purely finite and particular purposes;—lastly, lust of power, riotous debauchery, all the forms of barbarous and vulgar corruption, hypocrisy and deception—all this manifests itself in the Church; for in fact the Sensuous in it is not subjugated and trained by the Under-

---

* The Church, in its devotion to mere ceremonial observances, *supposes* itself to be engaged with the Spiritual, while it is really occupied with the Sensuous. The World towards the close of the Mediæval period, is equally devoted to the Sensuous, but labors under no such hallucination as to the character of its activity; and it has ceased to feel compunction at the *merely secular* nature of its aims and actions, such as it might have felt (e.g.) in the eleventh century.

standing; it has become free, but only in a rough and barbarous way.—On the other hand the *virtue* which the Church presents, since it is negative only in opposition to sensual appetite, is but abstractly negative; it does not know how to exercise a moral restraint in the indulgence of the senses; in actual life nothing is left for it but avoidance, renunciation, inactivity.

These contrasts which the Church exhibits—of barbarous vice and lust on the one hand, and an elevation of soul that is ready to renounce all worldly things, on the other hand—became still wider in consequence of the energetic position which man is sensible of occupying in his subjective power over outward and material things in the natural world, in which he feels himself free, and so gains for himself an absolute right.— The Church whose office it is to save souls from perdition, makes this salvation itself a mere external appliance, and is now degraded so far as to perform this office in a merely external fashion. The *remission of sins*—the highest satisfaction which the soul craves, the certainty of its peace with God, that which concerns man's deepest and inmost nature—is offered to man in the most grossly superficial and trivial fashion—*to be purchased for mere money;* while the object of this sale is to procure means for dissolute excess. One of the objects of this sale was indeed the building of St. Peter's, that magnificent chef-d'œuvre of Christian fabrics erected in the metropolis of religion. But, as that paragon of works of art, the Athene and her temple-citadel at Athens, was built with the money of the allies and issued in the loss of both allies and power; so the completion of this Church of St. Peter and Michael Angelo's "Last Judgment" in the Sistine Chapel, were the Doomsday and the ruin of this proud spiritual edifice.

The time-honored and cherished *sincerity of the German people* is destined to effect this revolution out of the honest truth and simplicity of its heart. While the rest of the world are urging their way to India, to America—straining every nerve to gain wealth and to acquire a secular dominion which shall encompass the globe, and on which the sun shall never set—we find a simple *Monk* looking for that specific embodiment of Deity which Christendom had formerly sought in an earthly sepulchre of stone, rather in the deeper abyss of the Absolute Ideality of all that is sensuous and external—in the Spirit and the Heart—the heart, which, wounded unspeakably by the offer of the most trivial and superficial appliances to satisfy the cravings of that which is inmost and deepest, now detects the perversion of the absolute relation of truth in its minutest features, and pursues it to annihilation. Luther's simple doctrine is that the specific embodiment of Deity—infinite subjectivity, that is true spirituality, Christ—is in no way present and actual in an outward form, but as essentially spiritual is obtained only in being reconciled to God—*in faith and spiritual enjoyment.* These two words express everything. That which this doctrine desiderates, is not the recognition of a sensuous object as God, nor even of something merely conceived, and which is not actual and present, but of a Reality that is not sensuous. This abrogation of externality imports the reconstruction of all the doctrines, and the reform of all the superstition into which the Church consistently wandered, and in which its spiritual life was dissipated. This change especially affects the doctrine of works; for works include what may be performed under any mental conditions—not necessarily in faith, in one's own soul, but as mere external observances prescribed by authority. Faith is by no means a bare assurance respecting mere finite things—an assurance which belongs only to limited mind—as *e.g.* the belief that such or such a person existed and said this or that; or that the Children of Israel passed dry-shod through the Red Sea—or that the trumpets before the walls of Jericho produced as powerful an impression as our cannons; for although nothing of all this had been related to us, our knowledge of God would not be the less complete. In fact it is not a belief in something that is absent, past and gone, but the subjective assurance of the Eternal, of Absolute Truth, the Truth of God. Concerning this assurance, the Lutheran Church affirms that the Holy Spirit alone produces it—*i.e.* that it is an assurance which the individual attains, not in virtue of his particular idiosyncrasy, but of his essential being.—The Lutheran doctrine therefore involves the entire substance of Catholicism, with the exception of all that results from the element of externality—as far as the Catholic Church insists upon that externality. Luther therefore could not do otherwise than refuse to yield an iota in regard to that doctrine of the Eucharist in which the whole question is concentrated. Nor could he concede to the Reformed [Calvinistic] Church, that Christ is a mere commemoration, a mere reminiscence: in this respect his view was rather in accordance with that of the Catholic Church, viz. that Christ is an actual presence, though only in faith and in Spirit. He maintained that the Spirit of Christ really fills the human heart—that Christ therefore is not to be regarded as merely a historical person, but that man sustains *an immediate relation to him in Spirit.*

While, then, the individual knows that he is filled with the Divine Spirit, all the relations that sprung from that vitiating element of externality which we examined above, are *ipso facto* abrogated: there is no longer a distinction between priests and laymen; we no longer find one class in possession of the substance of the Truth, as of all the spiritual and temporal treasures of the Church; but the heart—the emotional part of man's Spiritual nature—is recognized as that which can and ought to come into possession of the Truth; and this subjectivity is the common property of *all mankind.* Each has to accomplish the work of reconciliation in his own soul.—Subjective Spirit has to receive the Spirit of Truth into itself, and give it a dwelling place there. Thus that absolute inwardness of soul which pertains to religion itself, and Freedom in the Church are both secured. Subjectivity therefore makes the objective purport of Christianity, *i.e.* the doctrine of the Church, its own. In the Lutheran Church the subjective feeling and the conviction of the individual is regarded as equally necessary with the objective side of Truth. Truth with Lutherans is not a finished and completed thing; the subject himself must be imbued with Truth, surrendering his particular being in exchange for the substantial Truth, and making that Truth his own. Thus subjective Spirit gains emancipation in the Truth, abnegates its particularity and comes to itself in realizing the truth of its being. Thus Christian Freedom is actualized. If Subjectivity be placed in feeling only, without that objective side, we have the stand-point of the merely Natural Will.

In the proclamation of these principles is unfurled the new, the latest standard round which the peoples rally—the banner of *Free Spirit*, independent, though finding its life in the Truth, and enjoying independence only in it. This is the banner under which we serve, and which we bear. Time, since that epoch, has had no other work to do than the formal imbuing of the world with this principle, in bringing the Reconciliation implicit [in Christianity] into objective and explicit realization.

Culture is essentially concerned with Form; the work of Culture is the production of the Form of Universality, which is none other than Thought.* Consequently Law, Property, Social Morality, Government, Constitutions, etc., must be conformed to general principles, in order that they may accord with the idea of Free Will and be Rational. Thus only can the Spirit of Truth manifest itself in Subjective Will—in the particular shapes which the activity of the Will assumes. In virtue of that degree of intensity which Subjective Free Spirit has attained, elevating it to the form of Universality, Objective Spirit attains manifestation. This is the sense in which we must understand the State to be based on Religion. States and Laws are nothing else than Religion manifesting itself in the relations of the actual world.

This is the essence of the Reformation: Man is in his very nature destined to be free.

At its commencement, the Reformation concerned itself only with particular aspects of the Catholic Church: Luther wished to act in union with the whole Catholic world, and expressed a desire that Councils should be convened. His theses found supporters in every country. In answer to the charge brought against Luther and the Protestants, of exaggeration—nay, even of calumnious misrepresentation in their descriptions of the corruption of the Church, we may refer to the statements of Catholics themselves, bearing upon this point, and particularly to those contained in the official documents of Ecclesiastical Councils. But Luther's onslaught, which was at first limited to particular points, was soon extended to the doctrines of the Church; and leaving individuals, he attacked institutions at large—conventual life, the secular lordships of the bishops, etc. His writings now controverted not merely isolated dicta of the Pope and the Councils, but the very principle on which such a mode of deciding points in dispute was based—in fact, *the Authority of the Church.* Luther repudiated that authority, and set up in its stead the *Bible* and the testimony of the Human Spirit. And it is a fact of the weightiest import that the Bible has become the basis of the Christian Church: hence-

---

* The community of principle which *really* links together individuals of the same class, and in virtue of which they are similarly related to other existences, assumes a *form* in human consciousness; and that form is the thought or idea which summarily comprehends the constituents of generic character. The primary meaning of the word *ἰδέα* and of the related terms εἶδος and *species,* is "form." Every "Universal" in Thought has a corresponding generic principle in Reality, to which it gives intellectual expression or *form.*

forth each individual enjoys the right of deriving instruction for himself from it, and of directing his conscience in accordance with it. We see a vast change in the principle by which man's religious life is guided: the whole system of Tradition, the whole fabric of the Church becomes problematical, and its authority is subverted. Luther's translation of the Bible has been of incalculable value to the German people. It has supplied them with a People's Book, such as no nation in the Catholic world can boast; for though the latter have a vast number of minor productions in the shape of prayer-books, they have no generally recognized and classical book for popular instruction. In spite of this it has been made a question in modern times whether it is judicious to place the Bible in the hands of the People. Yet the few disadvantages thus entailed are far more than counterbalanced by the incalculable benefits thence accruing: narratives, which in their external shape might be repellent to the heart and understanding, can be discriminatingly treated by the religious sense, which, holding fast the substantial truth, easily vanquishes any such difficulties. And even if the books which have pretensions to the character of People's Books, were not so superficial as they are, they would certainly fail in securing that respect which a book claiming such a title ought to inspire in *individuals*. But to obviate this difficulty is no easy matter, for even should a book adapted to the purpose in every other respect be produced, every country parson would have some fault to find with it, and think to better it. In France the need of such a book has been very much felt; great premiums have been offered with a view to obtaining one, but, from the reason stated, without success. Moreover, the existence of a People's Book presupposes as its primary condition an ability to read on the part of the People; an ability which in Catholic countries is not very commonly to be met with.

The denial of the Authority of the Church necessarily led to a separation. The *Council of Trent* stereotyped the principles of Catholicism, and made the restoration of concord impossible. Leibnitz at a later time discussed with Bishop Bossuet the question of the union of the Churches; but the Council of Trent remains the insurmountable obstacle. The *Churches* became hostile *parties*, for even in respect to secular arrangements a striking difference manifested itself. In the non-Catholic countries the conventual establishments and episcopal foundations were broken up, and the rights of the then proprietors ignored. Educational arrangements were altered; the fasts and holy days were abolished. Thus there was also a secular reform—a change affecting the state of things outside the sphere of ecclesiastical relations: in many places a rebellion was raised against the temporal authorities. In Münster the Anabaptists expelled the Bishop and established a government of their own; and the peasants rose *en masse* to emancipate themselves from the yoke of serfdom. But the world was not yet ripe for a transformation of its political condition as a consequence of ecclesiastical reformation.—The Catholic Church also was essentially influenced by the Reformation: the reins of discipline were drawn tighter, and the greatest occasions of scandal, the most crying abuses were abated. Much of the intellectual life of the age that lay outside its sphere, but with which it had previously maintained friendly relations, it now repudiated. The Church came to a dead stop—" hitherto and no farther!" It severed itself from advancing Science, from philosophy and humanistic literature; and an occasion was soon offered of declaring its enmity to the scientific pursuits of the period. The celebrated Copernicus had discovered that the earth and the planets revolve round the sun, but the Church declared against this addition to human knowledge. Galileo, who had published a statement in the form of a dialogue of the evidence for and against the Copernican discovery (declaring indeed his own conviction of its truth), was obliged to crave pardon for the offence on his knees. The Greek literature was not made the basis of culture; education was intrusted to the Jesuits. Thus does the Spirit of the Catholic world in general sink behind the Spirit of the Age.

Here an important question solicits investigation :—why the Reformation was limited to certain nations, and why it did not permeate the whole Catholic world. The Reformation originated in Germany, and struck firm root only in the purely German nations; outside of Germany itself it established itself in Scandinavia and England. But the Romanic and Sclavonic nations kept decidedly aloof from it. Even South Germany has only partially adopted the Reformation—a fact which is consistent with the mingling of elements which is the general characteristic of its nationality. In Swabia, Franconia, and the

Rhine countries there were many convents and bishoprics, as also many free imperial towns; and the reception or rejection of the Reformation very much depended on the influences which these ecclesiastical and civil bodies respectively exercised; for we have already noticed that the Reformation was a change influencing the political life of the age as well as its religious and intellectual condition. We must further observe, that authority has much greater weight in determining men's opinions than people are inclined to believe. There are certain fundamental principles which men are in the habit of receiving on the strength of authority; and it was mere authority which in the case of many countries decided for or against the adoption of the Reformation. In Austria, in Bavaria, in Bohemia, the Reformation had already made great progress; and though it is commonly said that when truth has once penetrated men's souls, it cannot be rooted out again, it was indisputably stifled in the countries in question, by force of arms, by stratagem or persuasion. The *Sclavonic nations* were *agricultural*. This condition of life brings with it the relation of lord and serf. In agriculture the agency of nature predominates; human industry and subjective activity are on the whole less brought into play in this department of labor than elsewhere. The Sclavonians therefore did not attain so quickly or readily as other nations the fundamental sense of pure individuality—the consciousness of Universality—that which we designated above as " political power," and could not share the benefits of dawning freedom.—But the *Romanic nations* also—Italy, Spain, Portugal, and in part France—were not imbued with the Reformed doctrines. Physical force perhaps did much to repress them; yet this alone would not be sufficient to explain the fact, for when the Spirit of a Nation craves anything no force can prevent its attaining the desired object: nor can it be said that these nations were deficient in culture; on the contrary, they were in advance of the Germans in this respect. It was rather owing to the fundamental character of these nations, that they did not adopt the Reformation. But what is this peculiarity of character which hindered the attainment of Spiritual Freedom? We answer: the pure inwardness of the German nation was the proper soil for the emancipation of Spirit; the Romanic Nations, on the contrary, have maintained in the very depth of their soul—in their Spiritual Consciousness—the

principle of *Disharmony*:* they are a product of the fusion of
Roman and German blood, and still retain the heterogeneity
thence resulting. The German cannot deny that the French,
the Italians, the Spaniards, possess more determination of
character—that they pursue a settled aim (even though it have
a fixed idea for its object) with perfectly clear consciousness
and the greatest attention—that they carry out a plan with great
circumspection, and exhibit the greatest decision in regard to
specific objects. The French call the Germans *entiers*, " entire "—*i.e.*, stubborn; they are also strangers to the whimsical
originality of the English. The Englishman attaches his idea
of liberty to the special [as opposed to the general]; he does
not trouble himself about the Understanding [logical infer-
ence], but on the contrary feels himself so much the more at
liberty, the more his course of action or his license to act contravenes the Understanding—*i.e.*, runs counter to [logical
inferences or] general principles. On the other hand, among
the Romanic peoples we immediately encounter that internal
schism, that holding fast by an abstract principle, and as the
counterpart of this, an absence of the Totality of Spirit and sentiment which we call " Heart "; there is not that meditative introversion of the soul upon itself;—in their inmost being they
may be said to be alienated from themselves [abstract principles
carry them away]. With them the inner life is a region whose
depth they do not appreciate; for it is given over " bodily " to
particular [absorbing] interests, and the infinity that belongs
to Spirit is not to be looked for there. Their inmost being is
not their own. They leave it as an alien and indifferent matter,
and are glad to have its concerns settled for them by another.
That other to which they leave it is the Church. They have
indeed something to do with it themselves; but since that which
they have to do is not self-originated and self-prescribed, not
their very own, they are content to leave the affair to be settled in a superficial way. " *Eh bien*," said Napoleon, " we shall
go to mass again, and my good fellows will say: ' That is the
word of command!' " This is the leading feature in the character of these nations—the separation of the religious from
the secular interest, *i.e.*, from the special interest of individuali-

* The acknowledgment of an external
power authorized to command the entire
soul of man was not supplanted in their
case by a deference to Conscience and
subjective Principle (*i. e.*, the union of
Objective and Subjective freedom) as
the supreme authority.

ty; and the ground of this separation lies in their inmost soul, which has lost its independent entireness of being, its profoundest unity. Catholicism does not claim the essential direction of the Secular; religion remains an indifferent matter on the one side, while the other side of life is dissociated from it, and occupies a sphere exclusively its own. Cultivated Frenchmen therefore feel an antipathy to Protestantism because it seems to them something pedantic, dull, minutely captious in its morality; since it requires that Spirit and Thought should be directly engaged in religion: in attending mass and other ceremonies, on the contrary, no exertion of thought is required, but an imposing sensuous spectacle is presented to the eye, which does not make such a demand on one's attention as entirely to exclude a little chat, while yet the duties of the occasion are not neglected.

We spoke above of the *relation which the new doctrine sustained to secular life,* and now we have only to exhibit that relation in detail. The development and advance of Spirit from the time of the Reformation onwards consist in this, that Spirit, having now gained the consciousness of its Freedom, through that process of mediation which takes place between man and God—that is, in the full recognition of the objective process as the existence [the positive and definite manifestation] of the Divine essence—now takes it up and follows it out in building up the edifice of secular relations. That harmony [of Objective and Subjective Will] which has resulted from the painful struggles of History, involves the recognition of the Secular as capable of being an embodiment of Truth; whereas it had been formerly regarded as evil only, as incapable of Good—the latter being considered essentially ultramundane. It is now perceived that Morality and Justice in the State are also divine and commanded by God, and that in point of substance there is nothing higher or more sacred. One inference is that *Marriage* is no longer deemed less holy than *Celibacy.* Lu'her took a wife to show that he respected marriage, defying the calumnies to which he exposed himself by such a step. It was his duty to do so, as it was also to eat meat on Fridays; to prove that such things are lawful and right, in opposition to the imagined superiority of abstinence. The Family introduces man to community—to the relation of interdependence in society; and this union is a moral one:

while on the other hand the monks, separated from the sphere of social morality, formed as it were the standing army of the Pope, as the janizaries formed the basis of the Turkish power. The marriage of the priests entails the disappearance of the outward distinction between laity and clergy.—Moreover the repudiation of work no longer earned the reputation of sanctity; it was acknowledged to be more commendable for men to rise from a state of dependence by *activity*, intelligence, and industry, and make themselves independent. It is more consonant with justice that he who has money should spend it even in luxuries, than that he should give it away to idlers and beggars; for he bestows it on an equal number of persons by so doing, and these must at any rate have worked diligently for it. Industry, crafts and trades now have their moral validity recognized, and the obstacles to their prosperity which originated with the Church, have vanished. For the Church had pronounced it a sin to lend money on interest: but the necessity of so doing led to the direct violation of her injunctions. The Lombards (a fact which accounts for the use of the term "lombard" in French to denote a loan-office), and particularly the House of Medici, advanced money to princes in every part of Europe. The third point of sanctity in the Catholic Church—blind *obedience*, was likewise denuded of its false pretensions. Obedience to the laws of the State, as the Rational element in volition and action, was made the principle of human conduct. In this obedience man is free, for all that is demanded is that the Particular should yield to the General. Man himself has a conscience; consequently the subjection required of him is a free allegiance. This involves the possibility of a development of Reason and Freedom, and of their introduction into human relations; and Reason and the Divine commands are now synonymous. The Rational no longer meets with contradiction on the part of the religious conscience; it is permitted to develop itself in its own sphere without disturbance, without being compelled to resort to force in defending itself against an adverse power. But in the Catholic Church, that adverse element is unconditionally sanctioned. Where the Reformed doctrine prevails, princes may still be bad governors, but they are no longer sanctioned and solicited thereto by the promptings of their religious conscience. In the Catholic Church on the contrary, it is nothing singular for the conscience to be found in opposition to the laws

of the State.   Assassinations of sovereigns, conspiracies against
the state, and the like, have often been supported and carried into
execution by the priests.

This harmony between the State and the Church has now attained *immediate* realization.*   We have, as yet, no reconstruction of the State, of the system of jurisprudence, etc., for
thought must first discover the essential principle of Right.
The Laws of Freedom had first to be expanded to a system as
deduced from an absolute principle of Right.   Spirit does not
assume this complete form immediately after the Reformation;
it limits itself at first to direct and simple changes, as *e.g.* the
doing away with conventual establishments and episcopal jurisdiction, etc.   The reconciliation between God and the World was
limited in the first instance to an abstract form; it was not yet
expanded into a system by which the moral world could be regulated.

In the first instance this reconciliation must take place in the
individual soul, must be realized by feeling; the individual must
gain the assurance that the Spirit dwells in him—that, in the
language of the Church, a brokenness of heart has been experienced, and that Divine grace has entered into the heart thus
broken.   By Nature man is not what he ought to be; only
through a transforming process does he arrive at truth.   The
general and speculative aspect of the matter is just this—that
the human heart is not what it should be.   It was then required
of the individual that he should know what he is in himself; that
is, the teaching of the Church insisted upon man's becoming
conscious that he is evil.   But the individual is evil only when
the Natural manifests itself in mere sensual desire—when an unrighteous will presents itself in its untamed, untrained, violent
shape; and yet it is required that such a person should know that
he is depraved, and that the good Spirit dwells in him; in fact
he is required to have a direct consciousness of and to "experience" that which was presented to him as a speculative and implicit truth.   The Reconciliation having, then, assumed this abstract form, men tormented themselves with a view to force upon
their souls the consciousness of their sinfulness and to know
themselves as evil.   The most simple souls, the most innocent
natures were accustomed in painful introspection to observe the

* That is, the harmony in question simply exists; its development and results have not yet manifested themselves.

most secret workings of the heart, with a view to a rigid examination of them. With this duty was conjoined that of an entirely opposite description; it was required that man should attain the consciousness that the good Spirit dwells in him—that Divine Grace has found an entrance into his soul. In fact the important distinction between the knowledge of abstract truth and the knowledge of what has actual existence was left out of sight. Men became the victims of a tormenting uncertainty as to whether the good Spirit has an abode in them, and it was deemed indispensable that the entire process of spiritual transformation should become perceptible to the individual himself. An echo of this self-tormenting process may still be traced in much of the religious poetry of that time; the Psalms of David which exhibit a similar character were then introduced as hymns into the ritual of Protestant Churches. Protestantism took this turn of minute and painful introspection, possessed with the conviction of the importance of the exercise, and was for a long time characterized by a self-tormenting disposition and an aspect of spiritual wretchedness; which in the present day has induced many persons to enter the Catholic pale, that they might exchange this inward uncertainty for a formal broad certainty based on the imposing totality of the Church. A more refined order of reflection upon the character of human actions was introduced into the Catholic Church also. The Jesuits analyzed the first rudiments of volition (*velleitas*) with as painful minuteness as was displayed in the pious exercises of Protestantism; but they had a science of casuistry which enabled them to discover a good reason for everything, and so get rid of the burden of guilt which this rigid investigation seemed to aggravate.

With this was connected another remarkable phenomenon, common to the Catholic with the Protestant World. The human mind was driven into the Inward, the Abstract, and the Religious element was regarded as utterly alien to the secular. That lively consciousness of his subjective life and of the inward origin of his volition that had been awakened in man, brought with it the belief in *Evil*, as a vast power the sphere of whose malign dominion is the Secular. This belief presents a parallelism with the view in which the sale of Indulgences originated: for as eternal salvation could be secured for money, so by paying the price of one's salvation through a compact made with the Devil, the riches of the world and the unlimited gratification of desires and passions could be secured. Thus arose that famous legend of Faust, who in disgust at the unsatisfactory character of speculative science, is said to have plunged into the world and purchased all its glory at the expense of his salvation. Faust, if we may trust the poet, had the enjoyment of all that the world could give, in exchange for his soul's weal; but those poor women who were called *Witches* were reputed to get nothing more by the bargain than the gratification of a petty revenge by making a neighbor's cow go dry or giving a child the measles. But in awarding punishment it was not the magnitude of the injury in the loss of the milk or the sickness of the child that was considered; it was the abstract power of the Evil One in them that was attacked. The belief in this abstract, special power whose dominion is the world—in the Devil and his devices—occasioned an incalculable number of *trials for witchcraft* both in Catholic and Protestant countries. It was impossible to prove the guilt of the accused; they were only suspected: it was therefore only a direct knowledge [one not mediated by proofs] on which this fury against the evil principle professed to be based. It was indeed necessary to have recourse to evidence, but the basis of these judicial processes was simply the belief that certain individuals were possessed by the power of the Evil One. This delusion raged among the nations in the sixteenth century with the fury of a pestilence. The main impulse was suspicion. The principle of suspicion assumes a similarly terrible shape during the sway of the Roman Emperors, and under Robespierre's Reign of Terror; when mere disposition, unaccompanied by any overt act or expression, was made an object of punishment. Among the Catholics, it was the Dominicans to whom (as was the Inquisition in all its branches) the trials for witchcraft were intrusted. Father Spee, a noble Jesuit, wrote a treatise against them (he is also the author of a collection of fine poems bearing the title of *"Trutznachtigall,"*) giving a full exposure of the terrible character of criminal justice in proceedings of this kind. Torture, which was only to be applied once, was continued until a confession was extorted. If the accused fainted under the torture it was averred that the Devil was giving them sleep: if convulsions supervened, it was said that the Devil was laughing in them; if they held out steadfastly, the Devil was supposed to give them power. These persecutions spread like an epidemic sickness through Italy, France, Spain and Germany. The earnest remonstrances of enlightened men, such as Spee and others, already produced a considerable effect. But it was Thomasius, a Professor of Halle, who first opposed this prevalent superstition with very decided success. The entire phenomenon is in itself most remarkable when we reflect that we have not long been quit of this frightful barbarity (even as late as the year 1780 a witch was publicly burned at Glarus in Switzerland). Among the Catholics persecution was directed against heretics as well as against witches: we might say indeed that they were placed in one category; the unbelief of the heretics was regarded as none other than the indwelling principle of Evil—a possession similar to the other.

Leaving this abstract form of Subjectiveness we have now to consider the *secular* side—the constitution of the State and the advance of Universality—the recognition of the universal laws of Freedom. This is the second and the essential point.

Chapter II.—Influence of the Reformation on Political Development

In tracing the course of the political development of the period, we observe in the first place the consolidation of Monarchy, and the Monarch invested with an authority emanating from the State. The incipient stage in the rise of royal power, and the commencement of that unity which the states of Europe attained, belong to a still earlier period. While these changes were going forward, the entire body of private obligations and rights which had been handed down from the Middle Age, still retained validity. Infinitely important is this form of private rights, which the organic constituents of the executive power of the State have assumed. At their apex we find a fixed and positive principle—the exclusive right of one family to the possession of the throne, and the hereditary succession of sovereigns further restricted by the law of primogeniture. This gives the State an immovable centre. The fact that Germany was an elective empire prevented its being consolidated into one state; and for the same reason Poland has vanished from the circle of independent states. The State must have a final decisive will: but if an individual is to be the final deciding power, he must be so in a direct and natural way, not as determined by choice and theoretic views, etc. Even among the free Greeks the oracle was the external power which decided their policy on critical occasions; here *birth* is the oracle—something independent of any arbitrary volition. But the circumstance that the highest station in a monarchy is assigned to a family, seems to indicate that the sovereignty is the private property of that family. As such that sovereignty would seem to be divisible; but since the idea of division of power is opposed to the principle of the state, the rights of the monarch and his family required to be more strictly defined. Sovereign possession is not a peculium of the individual ruler, but is consigned to the dynastic family as a trust; and the *estates of the realm* possess security that that trust shall be faithfully discharged, for they have to guard the unity of the body politic. Thus, then, royal possession no longer denotes a kind of private property, private possession of estates, demesnes, jurisdiction, etc., but has become a State-property—a function pertaining to and involved with the State.

Equally important, and connected with that just noticed, is the change of executive powers, functions, duties and rights, which naturally belong to the State, but which had become private property and private contracts or obligations—into possession conferred by the State. The rights of seigneurs and barons were annulled, and they were obliged to content themselves with official positions in the State. This transformation of the rights of vassals into official functions took place in the several kingdoms in various ways. In *France,* e.g., the great Barons, who were governors of provinces, who could claim such offices as a matter of right, and who like the Turkish Pashas, maintained a body of troops with the revenues thence derived— troops which they might at any moment bring into the field against the King—were reduced to the position of mere landed proprietors or court nobility, and those Pashalics became offices held under the government; or the nobility were employed as officers—generals of the army, an army belonging to the *State.* In this aspect the origination of *standing armies* is so important an event; for they supply the monarchy with an independent force and are as necessary for the security of the central authority against the rebellion of the subject individuals as for the defence of the state against foreign enemies. The fiscal system indeed had not as yet assumed a systematic character—the revenue being derived from customs, taxes and tolls in countless variety, besides the subsidies and contributions paid by the estates of the realm; in return for which the right of presenting a statement of grievances was conceded to them, as is now the case in Hungary.—In *Spain* the spirit of chivalry had assumed a very beautiful and noble form. This chivalric spirit, this knightly dignity, degraded to a mere inactive sentiment of honor, has attained notoriety as the Spanish *grandezza*. The Grandees were no longer allowed to maintain troops of their own, and were also withdrawn from the command of the armies; destitute of power they had to content themselves as private persons with an empty title. But the means by which the royal power in Spain was consolidated, was the *Inquisition*. This, which was established for the persecution of those who secretly adhered to Judaism, and of Moors and heretics, soon assumed a political character, being directed against the enemies of the State. Thus the Inquisition confirmed the despotic power of the King: it claimed supremacy even over bishops and archbishops, and could cite them before its tribunal. The frequent confiscation of property—one of the most customary penalties—tended to enrich the treasury of the State. Moreover, the Inquisition was a tribunal which took cognizance of mere suspicion; and while it consequently exercised a fearful authority over the clergy, it had a peculiar support in the national pride. For every Spaniard wished to be considered Christian by descent, and this species of vanity fell in with the views and tendency of the Inquisition. Particular provinces of the Spanish monarchy, as *e.g.* Aragon, still retained many peculiar rights and privileges; but the Spanish Kings from Philip II downwards proceeded to suppress them altogether.

It would lead us too far to pursue in detail the process of the depression of the aristocracy in the several states of Europe. The main scope of this depressing process was, as already stated, the curtailment of the private rights of the feudal nobility, and the transformation of their seigneurial authority into an official position in connection with the State. This change was in the interest of both the King and the People. The powerful barons seemed to constitute an intermediate body charged with the defence of liberty; but properly speaking, it was only their own privileges which they maintained against the royal power on the one hand and the citizens on the other hand. The barons of England extorted Magna Charta from the King; but the citizens gained nothing by it, on the contrary they remained in their former condition. Polish Liberty too, meant nothing more than the freedom of the barons in contraposition to the King, the nation being reduced to a state of absolute serfdom. When liberty is mentioned, we must always be careful to observe whether it is not really the assertion of private interests which is thereby designated. For although the nobility were deprived of their sovereign power, the people were still oppressed in consequence of their absolute dependence, their serfdom, and subjection to aristocratic jurisdiction; and they were partly declared utterly incapable of possessing property, partly subjected to a condition of bond-service which did not permit of their freely selling the products of their industry. The supreme interest of emancipation from this condition concerned the power of the State as well as the subjects—that emancipation which now gave them as citizens the character of free individuals, and determined that what was to be performed for the Commonwealth should be a matter of just allotment, not of mere chance. The aristocracy of possession maintains that possession against both—viz. against the power of the State at large and against individuals. But the aristocracy have a position assigned them, as the support of the throne, as occupied and active on behalf of the State and the common weal, and at the same time as maintaining the freedom of the citizens. This in fact is the prerogative of that class which forms the link between the Sovereign and the People—to undertake to discern and to give the first impulse to that which is intrinsically Rational and Universal; and this recognition of and occupation with the Universal must take the place of positive personal right. This subjection to the Head of the State of that intermediate power which laid claim to positive authority was now accomplished, but this did not involve the emancipation of the subject class. This took place only at a later date, when the idea of right in and for itself arose in men's minds. Then the sovereigns relying on their respective peoples, vanquished the caste of unrighteousness; but where they united with the barons, or where the latter maintained their freedom against the kings, those positive rights or rather wrongs continued.

We observe also as an essential feature now first presenting itself in the political aspect of the time, a connected *system of*

States and a relation of States to each other. They became involved in various wars: the Kings having enlarged their political authority, now turn their attention to foreign lands, insisting upon claims of all kinds. The aim and real interest of the wars of the period is invariably conquest.

Italy especially had become such an object of desire, and was a prey to the rapacity of the French, the Spaniards, and at a later date, of the Austrians. In fact absolute disintegration and dismemberment has always been an essential feature in the national character of the inhabitants of Italy, in ancient as well as in modern times. Their stubborn individuality was exchanged for a union the result of force, under the Roman dominion; but as soon as this bond was broken, the original character reappeared in full strength. In later times, as if finding in them a bond of union otherwise impossible—after having escaped from a selfishness of the most monstrous order and which displayed its perverse nature in crimes of every description— the Italians attained a taste for the *Fine Arts*· thus their civilization, the mitigation of their selfishness, reached only the Grade of Beauty, not that of Rationality—the higher unity of Thought. Consequently, even in poetry and song the Italian nature is different from ours. Improvisation characterizes the genius of the Italians; they pour out their very souls in Art and the ecstatic enjoyment of it. Enjoying a *naturel* so imbued with Art, the State must be an affair of comparative indifference, a merely casual matter to the Italians. But we have to observe also that the wars in which *Germany* engaged, were not particularly honorable to it: it allowed Burgundy, Lorraine, Alsace, and other parts of the empire to be wrested from it. From these wars between the various political powers there arose common interests, and the object of that community of interest was the maintenance of severalty—the preservation to the several States of their independence—in fact the " *balance of power.*" The motive to this was of a decidedly "practical" kind, viz. the protection of the several States from conquest. The union of the States of Europe as the means of shielding individual States from the violence of the powerful—the preservation of the balance of power, had now taken the place of that general aim of the elder time, the defence of Christendom, whose centre was the Papacy. This new political motive was necessarily accompanied by a diplomatic condition—one in which all the members of the great European system, however distant, felt an interest in that which happened to any one of them. Diplomatic policy had been brought to the greatest refinement in Italy, and was thence transmitted to Europe at large. Several princes in succession seemed to threaten the stability of the balance of power in Europe. When this combination of States was just commencing, *Charles V* was aiming at universal monarchy; for he was Emperor of Germany and King of Spain to boot: the Netherlands and Italy acknowledged his sway, and the whole wealth of America flowed into his coffers. With this enormous power, which, like the contingencies of fortune in the case of private property, had been accumulated by the most felicitous combinations of political dexterity—among other things by marriage,—but which was destitute of an internal and reliable bond, he was nevertheless unable to gain any advantage over France, or even over the German princes; nay he was even compelled to a peace by Maurice of Saxony. His whole life was spent in suppressing disturbances in all parts of his empire and in conducting foreign wars. The balance of power in Europe was similarly threatened by *Louis XIV*. Through that depression of the grandees of his kingdom which Richelieu and after him Mazarin had accomplished, he had become an absolute sovereign. France, too, had the consciousness of its intellectual superiority in a refinement of culture surpassing anything of which the rest of Europe could boast. The pretensions of Louis were founded not on extent of dominion, (as was the case with Charles V) so much as on that culture which distinguished his people, and which at that time made its way everywhere with the language that embodied it, and was the object of universal admiration: they could therefore plead a higher justification than those of the German Emperor. But the very rock on which the vast military resources of Philip II had already foundered—the heroic resistance of the Dutch— proved fatal also to the ambitious schemes of Louis. *Charles XII* also presented a remarkably menacing aspect; but his ambition had a Quixotic tinge and was less sustained by intrinsic vigor. Through all these storms the nations of Europe succeeded in maintaining their individuality and independence.

An external relation in which the States of Europe had an interest in common, was that sustained to *the Turks*—the terrible power which threatened to overwhelm Europe from the

East. The Turks of that day had still a sound and vigorous nationality, whose power was based on conquest, and which was therefore engaged in constant warfare, or at least admitted only a temporary suspension of arms. As was the case among the Franks, the conquered territories were divided among their warriors as personal, not heritable possessions; when in later times the principle of hereditary succession was adopted, the national vigor was shattered. The flower of the Osman force, the Janizaries, were the terror of the Europeans. Their ranks were recruited from a body of Christian boys of handsome and vigorous proportions, brought together chiefly by means of annual conscriptions among the Greek subjects of the Porte, strictly educated in the Moslem faith, and exercised in arms from early youth. Without parents, without brothers or sisters, without wives, they were, like the monks, an altogether isolated and terrible corps. The Eastern European powers were obliged to make common cause against the Turks—viz.: Austria, Hungary, Venice and Poland. The battle of Lepanto saved Italy, and perhaps all Europe, from a barbarian inundation.

An event of special importance following in the train of the Reformation was the *struggle of the Protestant Church* for political existence. The Protestant Church, even in its original aspect, was too intimately connected with secular interests not to occasion secular complications and political contentions respecting political possession. The subjects of Catholic princes become Protestant, have and make claims to ecclesiastical property, change the nature of the tenure, and repudiate or decline the discharge of those ecclesiastical functions to whose due performance the emoluments are attached (*jura stolæ*). Moreover a Catholic government is bound to be the *brachium seculare* of the Church; the Inquisition, *e.g.* never put a man to death, but simply declared him a heretic, as a kind of jury; he was then punished according to civil laws. Again, innumerable occasions of offence and irritation originated with processions and feasts, the carrying of the Host through the streets, withdrawals from convents, etc. Still more excitement would be felt when an Archbishop of Cologne attempted to make his archiepiscopate a secular princedom for himself and his family. Their confessors made it a matter of conscience with Catholic princes to wrest estates that had been the property of the

Church out of the hands of the heretics. In Germany, however, the condition of things was favorable to Protestantism
in as far as the several territories which had been imperial fiefs,
had become independent principalities. But in countries like
Austria, the princes were indifferent to Protestants, or even
hostile to them; and in France they were not safe in the exercise of their religion except as protected by fortresses. War
was the indispensable preliminary to the security of Protestants; for the question was not one of simple conscience, but
involved decisions respecting public and private property which
had been taken possession of in contravention of the rights of
the Church, and whose restitution it demanded. A condition
of absolute mistrust supervened; absolute, because mistrust
bound up with the religious conscience was its root. The Protestant princes and towns formed at that time a feeble union,
and the defensive operations they conducted were much feebler
still. After they had been worsted, Maurice the Elector of
Saxony, by an utterly unexpected and adventurous piece of
daring, extorted a peace, itself of doubtful interpretation, and
which left the real sources of embitterment altogether untouched. It was necessary to fight out the battle from the very
beginning. This took place in the *Thirty Years' War*, in which
first Denmark and then Sweden undertook the cause of freedom. The former was compelled to quit the field, but the latter
under Gustavus Adolphus—that hero of the North of glorious
memory—played a part which was so much the more brilliant
inasmuch as it began to wage war with the vast force of the
Catholics, alone—without the help of the Protestant states of
the Empire. The powers of Europe, with a few exceptions,
precipitate themselves on Germany—flowing back towards it
as to the fountain from which they had originally issued, and
where now the right of inwardness that has come to manifest
itself in the sphere of religion, and that of internal independence
and severalty is to be fought out. The struggle ends without
an Ideal result—without having attained the consciousness of
a principle as an intellectual concept—in the exhaustion of all
parties, in a scene of utter desolation, where all the contending
forces have been wrecked; it issues in letting parties simply
take their course and maintain their existence on the basis of
external power. The issue is in fact exclusively of a *political*
nature.

In *England* also, war was indispensable to the establishment of the Protestant *Church:* the struggle was in this case directed against the sovereigns, who were secretly attached to Catholicism because they found the principle of absolute sway confirmed by its doctrines. The fanaticized people rebelled against the assumption of absolute sovereign power—importing that Kings are responsible to God alone (*i.e.* to the Father Confessor)—and in opposition to Catholic externality, unfurled the banner of extreme subjectivity in Puritanism—a principle which, developing itself in the real world, presents an aspect partly of enthusiastic elevation, partly of ridiculous incongruity. The enthusiasts of England, like those of Münster, were for having the State governed directly by the fear of God; the soldiery sharing the same fanatical views prayed while they fought for the cause they had espoused. But a military leader now has the physical force of the country and consequently the government in his hands: for in the State there must be government, and Cromwell knew what governing is. He, therefore, made himself ruler, and sent that praying parliament about their business. With his death however his right to authority vanished also, and the old dynasty regained possession of the throne. Catholicism, we may observe, is commended to the support of princes as promoting the security of their government—a position supposed to be particularly manifest if the Inquisition be connected with the government; the former constituting the bulwark of the latter. But such a security is based on a slavish religious obedience, and is limited to those grades of human development in which the political constitution and the whole legal system still rest on the basis of actual positive possession; but if the constitution and laws are to be founded on a veritable eternal Right, then security is to be found only in the Protestant religion, in whose principle Rational Subjective Freedom also attains development. The *Dutch* too offered a vigorous opposition to the Catholic principle as bound up with the Spanish sovereignty. Belgium was still attached to the Catholic religion and remained subject to Spain: on the contrary, the northern part of the Netherlands—Holland—stood its ground with heroic valor against its oppressors. The trading class, the guilds and companies of marksmen formed a militia whose heroic courage was more than a match for the then famous Spanish infantry. Just as the Swiss peasants had resisted the chivalry of Austria, so here the trading cities held out against disciplined troops. During this struggle on the Continent itself, the Dutch fitted out fleets and deprived the Spaniards of part of their colonial possessions, from which all their wealth was derived. As independence was secured to Holland in its holding to the Protestant principle, so that of *Poland* was lost through its endeavor to suppress that principle in the case of dissidents.

Through the *Peace of Westphalia* the Protestant Church had been acknowledged as an independent one—to the great confusion and humiliation of Catholicism. This peace has often passed for the palladium of Germany, as having established its political constitution. But this constitution was in fact a confirmation of the particular rights of the countries into which Germany had been broken up. It involves no thought, no conception of the proper aim of a state. We should consult "Hippolytus à lapide" (a book which, written before the conclusion of the peace, had a great influence on the condition of the Empire) if we would become acquainted with the character of that German freedom of which so much is made. In the peace in question the establishment of a complete particularity, the determination of all relations on the principle of private right is the object manifestly contemplated—a *constituted anarchy,* such as the world had never before seen;—*i.e.* the position that an Empire is properly a unity, a totality, a state, while yet all relations are determined so exclusively on the principle of private right that the privilege of all the constituent parts of that Empire to act for themselves contrarily to the interest of the whole, or to neglect that which its interest demands and which is even required by law—is guaranteed and secured by the most inviolable sanctions. Immediately after this settlement, it was shown what the *German Empire* was as a state in relation to other states: it waged ignominious wars with the Turks, for deliverance from whom Vienna was indebted to Poland. Still more ignominious was its relation to France, which took possession in time of peace of free cities, the bulwarks of Germany, and of flourishing provinces, and retained them undisturbed.

This constitution, which completely terminated the career of Germany as an Empire, was chiefly the work of *Richelieu,* by whose assistance—Romish Cardinal though he was—religious freedom in Germany was preserved. Richelieu, with a view to further the interests of the State whose affairs he superintended, adopted the exact opposite of that policy which he promoted in the case of its enemies; for he reduced the latter to political impotence by ratifying the political independence of the several parts of the Empire, while at home he destroyed the independence of the Protestant party. His fate has consequently resembled that of many great statesmen, inasmuch as he has been cursed by his countrymen, while his enemies have looked upon the work by which he ruined them as the most sacred goal of their desires—the consummation of their rights and liberties.

The result of the struggle therefore was the forcibly achieved and now politically ratified coexistence of religious parties, forming political communities whose relations are determined according to prescriptive principles of civil or [rather, for such their true nature was] of private right.

The Protestant Church increased and so perfected the stability of its political existence by the fact that one of the states which had adopted the principles of the Reformation raised itself to the position of an independent European power. This power was destined to start into a new life with Protestantism: *Prussia,* viz., which making its appearance at the end of the seventeenth century, was indebted, if not for origination, yet certainly for the consolidation of its strength, to Frederick the Great; and the Seven Years' War was the struggle by which that consolidation was accomplished. Frederick II demonstrated the independent vigor of his power by resisting that of almost all Europe—the union of its leading states. He appeared as the hero of Protestantism, and that not individually merely, like Gustavus Adolphus, but as the ruler of a state. The Seven Years' War was indeed in itself not a war of religion; but it was so in view of its ultimate issues, and in the disposition of the soldiers as well as of the potentates under whose banner they fought. The Pope consecrated the sword of Field-Marshal Daun, and the chief object which the Allied Powers proposed to themselves, was the crushing of Prussia as the bulwark of the Protestant Church. But Frederick the Great not only made Prussia one of the great powers of Europe as a Protestant power, but was also a philosophical King—an altogether peculiar and unique phenomenon in modern times.

There had been English Kings who were subtle theologians, contending for the principle of absolutism: Frederick on the contrary took up the Protestant principle in its secular aspect; and though he was by no means favorable to religious controversies, and did not side with one party or the other, he had the consciousness of Universality, which is the profoundest depth to which Spirit can attain, and is Thought conscious of its own inherent power.

Chapter III.—The Eclaircissement and Revolution*

Protestantism had introduced the *principle* of Subjectivity, importing religious emancipation and inward harmony, but accompanying this with the *belief* in Subjectivity as Evil, and in a power [adverse to man's highest interests] whose embodiment is " the World." Within the Catholic pale also, the casuistry of the Jesuits brought into vogue interminable investigations, as tedious and wire-drawn as those in which the scholastic theology delighted, respecting the subjective spring of the Will and the motives that affect it. This Dialectic, which unsettles all particular judgments and opinions, transmuting the Evil into Good and Good into Evil, left at last nothing remaining but the mere action of subjectivity itself, the Abstractum of Spirit —*Thought*. Thought contemplates everything under the form of Universality, and is consequently the impulsion towards and production of the Universal. In that elder scholastic theology the real subject-matter of investigation—the doctrine of the Church, remained an ultramundane affair; in the Protestant theology also Spirit still sustained a relation to the Ultramundane; for on the one side we have the will of the individual— the Spirit of Man—I myself, and on the other the Grace of God, the Holy Ghost; and so in the Wicked, the Devil. But in Thought, Self moves within the limits of its own sphere; that with which it is occupied—its objects are as absolutely present to it [as they were distinct and separate in the intellectual grade above mentioned]; for in thinking I must elevate the object

* There is no current term in English denoting that great intellectual movement which dates from the first quarter of the eighteenth century, and which, if not the chief cause, was certainly the guiding genius of the French Revolution. The word " Illuminati " (signifying the members of an imaginary confederacy for propagating the open secret of the day), might suggest " Illumination," as an equivalent for the German " Aufklärung "; but the French " Eclaircissement " conveys a more specific idea. —J. S.

to Universality.* This is utter and absolute Freedom, for the pure Ego, like pure Light, is with itself alone [is not involved with any alien principle] ; thus that which is diverse from itself, sensuous or spiritual, no longer presents an object of dread, for in contemplating such diversity it is inwardly free and can freely confront it. A practical interest makes use of, consumes the objects offered to it: a theoretical interest calmly contemplates them, assured that in themselves they present no alien element.—Consequently, the *ne plus ultra* of Inwardness, of Subjectiveness, is Thought. Man is not free, when he is not thinking; for except when thus engaged he sustains a relation to the world around him as to another, an alien form of being. This comprehension—the penetration of the Ego into and beyond other forms of being with the most profound self-certainty [the identity of subjective and objective Reason being recognized], directly involves the harmonization of Being: for it must be observed that the unity of Thought with its Object is already *implicitly* present [*i.e.* in the fundamental constitution of the Universe], for Reason is the substantial basis of Consciousness as well as of the External and Natural. Thus that which presents itself as the Object of Thought is no longer an absolutely distinct form of existence [ein Jenseits], not of an alien and grossly substantial [as opposed to intelligible] nature.

Thought is the grade to which Spirit has now advanced. It involves the Harmony of Being in its purest essence, challenging the external world to exhibit the same Reason which Subject [the Ego] possesses. Spirit perceives that Nature—the World—must also be an embodiment of Reason, for God created it on principles of Reason. An interest in the contemplation and comprehension of the present world became universal. Nature embodies Universality, inasmuch as it is nothing other than Sorts, Genera, Power, Gravitation, etc., phenomenally presented. Thus *Experimental Science* became the science of the World; for experimental science involves on the one hand the observation of phenomena, on the other hand also the discovery of the Law, the essential being, the hidden force that causes

---

* Abstractions (*pure* thoughts), are, *vi termini*, detached from the material objects which suggested them, and are at least as evidently the product of the thinking mind as of the external world. Hence they are ridiculed by the unintelligent as mere fancies. In proportion as such abstractions involve activity and intensity of thought, the mind may be said to be occupied with itself in contemplating them.—J. S.

those phenomena—thus reducing the data supplied by observa
tion to their simple principles. Intellectual consciousness was
first extricated from that sophistry of thought, which unsettles
everything, by *Descartes*. As it was the purely German nations
among whom the principle of *Spirit* first manifested itself, so
it was by the Romanic nations that the *abstract idea* (to which
the character assigned them above—viz., that of internal schism,
more readily conducted them) was first comprehended. Experimental science therefore very soon made its way among
them (in common with the Protestant English), but especially
among the Italians. It seemed to men as if God had but just
created the moon and stars, plants and animals, as if the laws
of the universe were now established for the first time; for
only then did they feel a real interest in the universe, when they
recognized their own Reason in the Reason which pervades it.
The human eye became *clear,* perception quick, thought active
and interpretative. The discovery of the laws of Nature enabled men to contend against the monstrous superstition of
the time, as also against all notions of mighty alien powers
which magic alone could conquer. The assertion was even
ventured on, and that by Catholics not less than by Protestants,
that the External [and Material], with which the Church insisted upon associating superhuman virtue, was external and
material, and nothing more—that the Host was simply *dough,*
the relics of the Saints mere *bones.* The independent authority
of Subjectivity was maintained against belief founded on authority, and the Laws of Nature were recognized as the only
bond connecting phenomena with phenomena. Thus all miracles were disallowed: for Nature is a system of known and
recognized Laws; Man is at home in it, and that only passes
for truth in which he finds himself at home; he is free through
the acquaintance he has gained with Nature. Nor was thought
less vigorously directed to the Spiritual side of things: Right
and [Social] Morality came to be looked upon as having their
foundation in the actual present Will of man, whereas formerly
it was referred only to the command of God enjoined *ab extra,*
written in the Old and New Testament, or appearing in the
form of particular Right [as opposed to that based on general
principles] in old parchments, as *privilegia,* or in international
compacts. What the nations acknowledge as international
Right was deduced empirically from observation (as in the

work of Grotius); then the source of the existing civil and political law was looked for, after Cicero's fashion, in those instincts of men which Nature has planted in their hearts—*e.g.*, the social instinct; next the principle of security for the person and property of the citizens, and of the advantage of the commonwealth—that which belongs to the class of " reasons of State." On these principles private rights were on the one hand despotically contravened, but on the other hand such contravention was the instrument of carrying out the general objects of the State in opposition to mere positive or prescriptive claims. Frederick II may be mentioned as the ruler who inaugurated the new epoch in the sphere of practical life—that epoch in which practical *political interest* attains Universality [is recognized as an abstract principle], and receives an absolute sanction. Frederick II merits especial notive as having comprehended the general object of the State, and as having been the first sovereign who kept the general interest of the State steadily in view, ceasing to pay any respect to particular interests when they stood in the way of the common weal. His immortal work is a domestic code—the Prussian municipal law. How the head of a household energetically provides and governs with a view to the weal of that household and of his dependents—of this he has given a unique specimen.

These general conceptions, deduced from actual and present consciousness—the Laws of Nature and the substance of what is right and good—have received the name of *Reason.* The recognition of the validity of these laws was designated by the term *Eclaircissement* (Aufklärung). From France it passed over into Germany, and created a new world of ideas. The absolute criterion—taking the place of all authority based on religious belief and positive laws of Right (especially political Right)—is the verdict passed by Spirit itself on the character of that which is to be believed or obeyed. After a free investigation in open day, Luther had secured to mankind Spiritual Freedom and the Reconciliation [of the Objective and Subjective] in the concrete: he triumphantly established the position that man's eternal destiny [his spiritual and moral position] must be wrought out *in himself* [cannot be an *opus operatum*, a work performed *for him*]. But the *import* of that which is to take place in him—what truth is to become vital in him, was taken for granted by Luther as something already given, something revealed by religion. *Now*, the principle was set up that this import must be capable of actual investigation—something of which I [in this modern time] can gain an inward conviction—and that to this basis of inward demonstration every dogma must be referred.

This principle of thought makes its appearance in the first instance in a general and abstract form; and is based on the axiom of Contradiction and Identity.* The results of thought are thus posited as finite, and the eclaircissement utterly banished and extirpated all that was speculative from things human and divine. Although it is of incalculable importance that the multiform complex of things should be reduced to its simplest conditions, and brought into the form of Universality, yet this still abstract principle does not satisfy the living Spirit, the concrete human soul.

This formally absolute principle brings us to *the last stage in History, our world, our own time.*

Secular life is the positive and definite embodiment of the Spiritual Kingdom—the Kingdom of the *Will* manifesting itself in outward existence. Mere impulses are also forms in which the inner life realizes itself; but these are transient and disconnected; they are the ever-changing applications of volition. But that which is just and moral belongs to the essential, independent, intrinsically universal Will; and if we would know what Right really is, we must abstract from inclination, impulse and desire as the particular; *i.e.,* we must know what the Will is in itself. For benevolent, charitable, social impulses are nothing more than impulses—to which others of a different class are opposed. What the Will is in itself can be known only when these specific and contradictory forms of volition have been eliminated. Then Will appears as Will, in its abstract essence. The Will is Free only when it does not will anything alien, extrinsic, foreign to itself (for as long as it does so, it is dependent), but wills itself alone—wills the Will. This is absolute Will—the volition to be free. Will making itself its own object is the basis of all Right and Obligation—consequently of all statutory determinations of Right, categorical

---

* The sensational conclusions of the " materialistic " school of the 18th century are reached by the " axiom of Contradiction and Identity," as applied in this simple dilemma: " In cognition, Man is either active or passive; he is **not** *active* (unless he is grossly deceiving himself), therefore he is *passive*; therefore all knowledge is derived *ab extra.*" What this external objective being is of which this knowledge is the cognition, remains an eternal mystery— *i.e.,* as Hegel says: " The results of thought are posited as finite."—J. S.

imperatives, and enjoined obligations. The Freedom of the Will *per se,* is the principle and substantial basis of all Right—is itself absolute, inherently eternal Right, and the Supreme Right in comparison with other specific Rights; nay, it is even that by which Man becomes Man, and is therefore the fundamental principle of Spirit. But the next question is: How does Will assume a definite form? For in willing itself, it is nothing but an identical reference to itself; but, in point of fact, it wills something specific: there *are,* we know, distinct and special Duties and Rights. A particular application, a definite form of Will, is desiderated; for pure Will is its own object, its own application, which, as far as this showing goes, is no object, no application. In fact, in this form it is nothing more than *formal* Will. But the metaphysical process by which this abstract Will develops itself, so as to attain a definite form of Freedom, and how Rights and Duties are evolved therefrom, this is not the place to discuss.* It may however be remarked that the same principle obtained speculative recognition in Germany, in the *Kantian* Philosophy. According to it the simple unity of Self-consciousness, the Ego, constitutes the absolutely independent Freedom, and is the fountain of all general conceptions—*i.e.* all conceptions elaborated by Thought—Theoretical Reason; and likewise of the highest of all practical determinations [or conceptions]—Practical Reason, as free and pure Will; and Rationality of Will is none other than the maintaining one's self in pure Freedom—willing this and this alone—Right purely for the sake of Right, Duty purely for the sake of Duty. Among the Germans this view assumed no other form than that of tranquil theory; but the French wished to give it practical effect. Two questions, therefore, suggest themselves: Why did this principle of Freedom remain merely formal? † and why did the French alone, and not the Germans, set about realizing it?

* "Freedom of the Will," in Hegel's use of the term, has an intensive signification, and must be distinguished from "Liberty of Will" in its ordinary acceptation. The latter denotes a mere liability to be affected by extrinsic motives: the former is that absolute strength of Will which enables it to defy all seductions that challenge its persistency. Its sole object is self-assertion. In fact it is *Individuality* maintaining itself against all *dividing* or distracting forces. And to maintain individuality is to preserve consistency—to "act on principle "—phrases with which Language, the faithful conservator of metaphysical genealogies, connects virtuous associations. In adopting a code of Duties, and in acknowledging Rights, the Will *recognizes its own Freedom* in this intensive sense, for *in such adoption it declares its own ability* to pursue a certain course of action in spite of all inducements, sensuous or emotional, to deviate from it. These remarks may supply some indications of the process referred to in the text.—J. S.

† "Formal Freedom" is mere liberty to do what one likes. It is called "*formal,*" because, as already indicated, the matter of volition—what it is that is willed—is left entirely undetermined. In

With the formal principle more significant categories were indeed connected: one of the chief of these (for instance) was Society, and that which is advantageous for Society: but the aim of Society is itself political—that of the State (vid. " Droits de l'homme et du citoyen," 1791)—the conservation of *Natural* Rights; but Natural Right is Freedom, and, as further determined, it is *Equality* of Rights before the Law. A direct connection is manifest here, for Equality, *Parity,* is the result of the comparison of many;* the " Many " in question being human beings, whose essential characteristic is the same, viz. Freedom. That principle remains formal, because it originated with abstract Thought—with the Understanding, which is primarily the self-consciousness of Pure Reason, and as direct [unreflected, undeveloped] is abstract. As yet, nothing further is developed from it, for it still maintains an adverse position to Religion, *i.e.* to the concrete absolute substance of the Universe.

As respects the second question—why the French immediately passed over from the theoretical to the practical, while the Germans contented themselves with theoretical abstraction, it might be said: the French are hot-headed [ils ont la tête près du bonnet] ; but this is a superficial solution: the fact is that the formal principle of philosophy in Germany encounters a concrete real World in which Spirit finds inward satisfaction and in which conscience is at rest. For on the one hand it was the *Protestant World* itself which advanced so far in Thought as to realize the absolute culmination of Self-Consciousness; on the other hand, Protestantism enjoys, with respect to the moral and legal relations of the real world, a tranquil confidence in the [Honorable] Disposition of men—a sentiment, which, [in the Protestant World,] constituting one and the same thing with Religion, is the fountain of all the equitable arrangements that prevail with regard to private right and the constitution of the State. In Germany the eclaircissement was conducted in the interest of theology: in France it immediately took up a position of hostility to the Church. In Germany the entire compass of secular relations had already undergone a change for the

the next paragraph the writer goes on to show that some definite object was associated with a sentiment otherwise unmeaning or bestial, " Vive la Liberté!" J. S.

* The radical correspondence of " *Gleichheit* " and " *Vergleichung* " is at-

tempted to be rendered in English by the terms *parity* and com*parison*, and perhaps etymology may justify the expedient. The meaning of the derivative " comparatio " seems to point to the connection of its root " paro " with " par."—J. S.

better; those pernicious ecclesiastical institutes of celibacy, voluntary pauperism, and laziness, had been already done away with; there was no dead weight of enormous wealth attached to the Church, and no constraint put upon Morality—a constraint which is the source and occasion of vices; there was not that unspeakably hurtful form of iniquity which arises from the interference of spiritual power with secular law, nor that other of the Divine Right of Kings, *i.e.* the doctrine that the arbitrary will of princes, in virtue of their being "the Lord's Anointed," is divine and holy: on the contrary their will is regarded as deserving of respect only so far as in association with reason, it wisely contemplates Right, Justice, and the weal of the community. The principle of Thought, therefore, had been so far conciliated already; moreover the Protestant World had a conviction that in the Harmonization which had previously been evolved [in the sphere of Religion] the principle which would result in a further development of equity in the political sphere was already present.

Consciousness that has received an abstract culture, and whose sphere is the Understanding [Verstand] can be indifferent to Religion, but Religion is the general form in which Truth exists for *non-abstract* consciousness. And the Protestant Religion does not admit of two kinds of consciences, while in the Catholic world the Holy stands on the one side and on the other side abstraction opposed to Religion, that is to its superstition and its truth. That formal, individual Will is in virtue of the abstract position just mentioned made the basis of political theories; Right in Society is that which the Law wills, and the Will in question appears as an isolated *individual* will; thus the State, as an aggregate of many individuals, is not an independently substantial Unity, and the truth and essence of Right in and for itself—to which the will of its individual members ought to be conformed in order to be true, free Will; but the volitional atoms [the individual wills of the members of the State] are made the starting point, and each will is represented as absolute.

An *intellectual principle* was thus discovered to serve as a basis for the State—one which does not, like previous principles, belong to the sphere of opinion, such as the social impulse, the desire of security for property, etc. nor owe its origin to the religious sentiment, as does that of the Divine appointment of the governing power—but the principle of Certainty, which is identity with my self-consciousness, stopping short however of that of Truth, which needs to be distinguished from it. This is a vast discovery in regard to the profoundest depths of being and Freedom. The consciousness of the Spiritual is now the essential basis of the political fabric, and *Philosophy* has thereby become dominant. It has been said, that the *French Revolution* resulted from Philosophy, and it is not without reason that Philosophy has been called " Weltweisheit " [World Wisdom;] for it is not only Truth in and for itself, as the pure essence of things, but also Truth in its living form as exhibited in the affairs of the world. We should not, therefore, contradict the assertion that the Revolution received its first impulse from Philosophy. But this philosophy is in the first instance only abstract Thought, not the concrete comprehension of absolute Truth—intellectual positions between which there is an immeasurable chasm.

The principle of the Freedom of the Will, therefore, asserted itself against existing Right. Before the French Revolution, it must be allowed, the power of the grandees had been diminished by Richelieu, and they had been deprived of privileges; but, like the clergy, they retained all the prerogatives which gave them an advantage over the lower class. The political condition of France at that time presents nothing but a confused mass of privileges altogether contravening Thought and Reason —an utterly irrational state of things, and one with which the greatest corruption of morals, of Spirit was associated—an empire characterized by Destitution of Right, and which, when its real state begins to be recognized, becomes shameless destitution of Right. The fearfully heavy burdens that pressed upon the people, the embarrassment of the government to procure for the Court the means of supporting luxury and extravagance, gave the first impulse to discontent. The new Spirit began to agitate men's minds: oppression drove men to investigation. It was perceived that the sums extorted from the people were not expended in furthering the objects of the State, but were lavished in the most unreasonable fashion. The entire political system appeared one mass of injustice. The change was necessarily violent, because the work of transformation was not undertaken by the government. And the reason why the government did not undertake it was that the Court, the Clergy, the

Nobility, the Parliaments themselves, were unwilling to surrender the privileges they possessed, either for the sake of expediency or that of abstract Right; moreover, because the government as the concrete centre of the power of the State, could not adopt as its principle abstract individual wills, and reconstruct the State on this basis; lastly, because it was Catholic, and therefore the Idea of Freedom—Reason embodied in Laws—did not pass for the final absolute obligation, since the Holy and the religious conscience are separated from them. The conception, the idea of Right asserted its authority *all at once,* and the old framework of injustice could offer no resistance to its onslaught. A constitution, therefore, was established in harmony with the conception of Right, and on this foundation all future legislation was to be based. Never since the sun had stood in the firmament and the planets revolved around him had it been perceived that man's existence centres in his head, *i.e.* in Thought, inspired by which he builds up the world of reality. Anaxagoras had been the first to say that νοῦς governs the World; but not until now had man advanced to the recognition of the principle that Thought ought to govern spiritual reality. This was accordingly a glorious mental dawn. All thinking beings shared in the jubilation of this epoch. Emotions of a lofty character stirred men's minds at that time; a spiritual enthusiasm thrilled through the world, as if the reconciliation between the Divine and the Secular was now first accomplished.

The two following points must now occupy our attention: 1st. The course which the Revolution in France took; 2d. How that Revolution became World-Historical.

1. Freedom presents two aspects: the one concerns its substance and purport—its objectivity—the thing itself—[that which is performed as a free act]; the other relates to the Form of Freedom, involving the consciousness of his activity on the part of the individual; for Freedom demands that the individual recognize himself in such acts, that they should be veritably his, it being his interest that the result in question should be attained. The three elements and powers of the State in actual working must be contemplated according to the above analysis, their examination in detail being referred to the Lectures on the Philosophy of Right.

(I.) *Laws* of Rationality—of intrinsic Right—Objective or

Real Freedom: to this category belong Freedom of Property and Freedom of Person. Those relics of that condition of servitude which the feudal relation had introduced are hereby swept away, and all those fiscal ordinances which were the bequest of the feudal law—its tithes and dues, are abrogated. Real [practical] Liberty requires moreover freedom in regard to trades and professions—the permission to every one to use his abilities without restriction—and the free admission to all offices of State. This is a summary of the elements of real Freedom, and which are not based on feeling—for feeling allows of the continuance even of serfdom and slavery—but on the thought and self-consciousness of man recognizing the spiritual character of his existence.

(2.) But the agency which gives the laws practical effect is the *Government* generally. Government is primarily the formal execution of the laws and the maintenance of their authority: in respect to foreign relations it prosecutes the interest of the State; that is, it assists the independence of the nation as an individuality against other nations; lastly, it has to provide for the internal weal of the State and all its classes—what is called administration: for it is not enough that the citizen is allowed to pursue a trade or calling, it must also be a source of gain to him; it is not enough that men are permitted to use their powers, they must also find an opportunity of applying them to purpose. Thus the State involves a body of abstract principles and a practical application of them. This application must be the work of a subjective will, a will which resolves and decides. Legislation itself—the invention and positive enactment of these statutory arrangements, is an application of such general principles. The next step, then, consists in [specific] determination and execution. Here then the question presents itself: what is the decisive will to be? The ultimate decision is the prerogative of the monarch: but if the State is based on Liberty, the many wills of individuals also desire to have a share in political decisions. But the *Many* are *All;* and it seems but a poor expedient, rather a monstrous inconsistency, to allow only a few to take part in those decisions, since each wishes that his volition should have a share in determining what is to be law for him. The Few assume to be the *deputies,* but they are often only the *despoilers* of the Many. Nor is the sway of the Majority over the Minority a less palpable inconsistency.

(3.) This collision of subjective wills leads therefore to the consideration of a third point, that of *Disposition*—an *ex animo* acquiescence in the laws; not the mere customary observance of them, but the cordial recognition of laws and the Constitution as in principle fixed and immutable, and of the supreme obligation of individuals to subject their particular wills to them. There may be various opinions and views respecting laws, constitution and government, but there must be a disposition on the part of the citizens to regard all these opinions as subordinate to the substantial interest of the State, and to insist upon them no further than that interest will allow; moreover nothing must be considered higher and more sacred than good will towards the State; or, if Religion be looked upon as higher and more sacred, it must involve nothing really alien or opposed to the Constitution. It is, indeed, regarded as a maxim of the profoundest wisdom entirely to separate the laws and constitution of the State from Religion, since bigotry and hypocrisy are to be feared as the results of a State Religion. But although the aspects of Religion and the State are different, they are radically *one;* and the laws find their highest confirmation in Religion.

Here it must be frankly stated, that with the Catholic Religion no rational constitution is possible; for Government and People must reciprocate that final guarantee of Disposition, and can have it only in a Religion that is not opposed to a rational political constitution.

Plato in his Republic makes everything depend upon the Government, and makes Disposition the principle of the State; on which account he lays the chief stress on Education. The modern theory is diametrically opposed to this, referring everything to the individual will. But here we have no guarantee that the will in question has that right disposition which is essential to the stability of the State.

In view then of these leading considerations we have to trace the course of the *French Revolution* and the remodelling of the State in accordance with the Idea of Right. In the first instance purely abstract philosophical principles were set up: Disposition and Religion were not taken into account. The first Constitutional form of Government in France was one which recognized Royalty; the monarch was to stand at the head of the State, and on him in conjunction with his Ministers was to devolve the executive power; the legislative body on the other hand were to make the laws. But this constitution involved from the very first an internal contradiction; for the legislature absorbed the whole power of the administration: the budget, affairs of war and peace, and the levying of the armed force were in the hands of the Legislative Chamber. Everything was brought under the head of Law. The budget however is in its nature something diverse from law, for it is annually renewed, and the power to which it properly belongs is that of the Government. With this moreover is connected the indirect nomination of the ministry and officers of state, etc. The government was thus transferred to the Legislative Chamber, as in England to the Parliament. This constitution was also vitiated by the existence of absolute mistrust; the dynasty lay under suspicion, because it had lost the power it formerly enjoyed, and the priests refused the oath. Neither government nor constitution could be maintained on this footing, and the ruin of both was the result. A government of some kind however is always in existence. The question presents itself then, Whence did it emanate? Theoretically, it proceeded from the people; really and truly from the National Convention and its Committees. The forces now dominant are the abstract principles—Freedom, and, as it exists within the limits of the Subjective Will—Virtue. This Virtue has now to conduct the government in opposition to the Many, whom their corruption and attachment to old interests, or a liberty that has degenerated into license, and the violence of their passions, render unfaithful to virtue. Virtue is here a simple abstract principle and distinguishes the citizens into two classes only—those who are favorably disposed and those who are not. But disposition can only be recognized and judged of by disposition. *Suspicion* therefore is in the ascendant; but virtue, as soon as it becomes liable to suspicion, is already condemned. Suspicion attained a terrible power and brought to the scaffold the Monarch, whose subjective will was in fact the religious conscience of a Catholic. Robespierre set up the principle of Virtue as supreme, and it may be said that with this man Virtue was an earnest matter. *Virtue* and *Terror* are the order of the day; for Subjective Virtue, whose sway is based on disposition only, brings with it the most fearful tyranny. It exercises its power without legal formalities, and the punishment it inflicts is equally simple

—*Death*. This tyranny could not last; for all inclinations, all interests, reason itself revolted against this terribly consistent Liberty, which in its concentrated intensity exhibited so fanatical a shape. An organized government is introduced, analogous to the one that had been displaced; only that its chief and monarch is now a mutable Directory of Five, who may form a moral, but have not an individual unity; under them also suspicion was in the ascendant, and the government was in the hands of the legislative assemblies; this constitution therefore experienced the same fate as its predecessor, for it had proved to itself the absolute necessity of a governmental *power*. *Napoleon* restored it as a military power, and followed up this step by establishing himself as an individual will at the head of the State: he knew how to rule, and soon settled the internal affairs of France. The *avocats*, idealogues and abstract-principle men who ventured to show themselves he sent " to the right about," and the sway of mistrust was exchanged for that of respect and fear. He then, with the vast might of his character turned his attention to foreign relations, subjected all Europe, and diffused his liberal institutions in every quarter. Greater victories were never gained, expeditions displaying greater genius were never conducted: but never was the powerlessness of Victory exhibited in a clearer light than then. The disposition of the peoples, *i.e.* their religious disposition and that of their nationality, ultimately precipitated this colossus; and in France constitutional monarchy, with the " Charte " as its basis, was restored. But here again the antithesis of Disposition [good feeling] and Mistrust made its appearance. The French stood in a mendacious position to each other, when they issued addresses full of devotion and love to the monarchy, and loading it with benediction. A fifteen years' farce was played. For although the *Charte* was the standard under which all were enrolled, and though both parties had sworn to it, yet on the one side the ruling disposition was a Catholic one, which regarded it as a matter of conscience to destroy the existing institutions. Another breach, therefore, took place, and the Government was overturned. At length, after forty years of war and confusion indescribable, a weary heart might fain congratulate itself on seeing a termination and tranquillization of all these disturbances. But although one main point is set at rest, there remains on the one hand that rupture which the Catholic principle inevitably occasions, on the other hand that which has to do with men's subjective will. In regard to the latter, the main feature of incompatibility still presents itself, in the requirement that the ideal general will should also be the *empirically* general— *i.e.* that the units of the State, in their individual capacity, should rule, or at any rate take part in the government. Not satisfied with the establishment of rational rights, with freedom of person and property, with the existence of a political organization in which are to be found various circles of civil life each having its own functions to perform, and with that influence over the people which is exercised by the intelligent members of the community, and the confidence that is felt in them, "*Liberalism*" sets up in opposition to all this the atomistic principle, that which insists upon the sway of individual wills; maintaining that all government should emanate from their express power, and have their express sanction. Asserting this formal side of Freedom—this abstraction—the party in question allows no political organization to be firmly established. The particular arrangements of the government are forthwith opposed by the advocates of Liberty as the mandates of a particular will, and branded as displays of arbitrary power. The will of the Many expels the Ministry from power, and those who had formed the Opposition fill the vacant places; but the latter having now become the Government, meet with hostility from the Many, and share the same fate. Thus agitation and unrest are perpetuated. This collision, this nodus, this problem is that with which history is now occupied, and whose solution it has to work out in the future.

2. We have now to consider the French Revolution in its organic connection with the *History of the World;* for in its substantial import that event is World-Historical, and that contest of Formalism which we discussed in the last paragraph must be properly distinguished from its wider bearings. As regards outward diffusion its principle gained access to almost all modern states, either through conquest or by express introduction into their political life. Particularly all the Romanic nations, and the Roman Catholic World in special—*France, Italy, Spain*—were subjected to the dominion of Liberalism. But it became bankrupt everywhere; first, the grand firm in France, then its branches in Spain and Italy; twice, in fact, in the states into which it had been introduced. This was the case

in Spain, where it was first brought in by the Napoleonic Constitution, then by that which the Cortes adopted—in Piedmont, first when it was incorporated with the French Empire, and a second time as the result of internal insurrection; so in Rome and in Naples it was twice set up. Thus Liberalism as an abstraction, emanating from France, traversed the Roman World; but Religious slavery held that world in the fetters of political servitude. For it is a false principle that the fetters which bind Right and Freedom can be broken without the emancipation of conscience—that there can be a Revolution without a Reformation.—These countries, therefore, sank back into their old condition—in Italy with some modifications of the outward political condition. Venice and Genoa, those ancient aristocracies, which could at least boast of legitimacy, vanished as rotten despotisms. Material superiority in power can achieve no enduring results: Napoleon could not coerce Spain into freedom any more than Philip II could force Holland into slavery.

Contrasted with these Romanic nations we observe the other powers of Europe, and especially the Protestant nations. *Austria* and *England* were not drawn within the vortex of internal agitation, and exhibited great, immense proofs of their internal solidity. *Austria* is not a Kingdom, but an Empire, *i.e.* an aggregate of many political organizations. The inhabitants of its chief provinces are not German in origin and character, and have remained unaffected by "ideas." Elevated neither by education nor religion, the lower classes in some districts have remained in a condition of serfdom, and the nobility have been kept down, as in Bohemia; in other quarters, while the former have continued the same, the barons have maintained their despotism, as in Hungary. Austria has surrendered that more intimate connection with Germany which was derived from the imperial dignity, and renounced its numerous possessions and rights in Germany and the Netherlands. It now takes its place in Europe as a distinct power, involved with no other. *England*, with great exertions, maintained itself on its old foundations; the English *Constitution* kept its ground amid the general convulsion, though it seemed so much the more liable to be affected by it, as a public Parliament, that habit of assembling in public meeting which was common to all orders of the state, and a free press, offered singular facilities for introducing the French principles of Liberty and Equality among all classes of the people. Was the English nation too backward in point of culture to apprehend these general principles? Yet in no country has the question of Liberty been more frequently a subject of reflection and public discussion. Or was the English constitution so entirely a Free Constitution—had those principles been already so completely realized in it, that they could no longer excite opposition or even interest? The English nation may be said to have approved of the emancipation of France; but it was proudly reliant on its own constitution and freedom, and instead of imitating the example of the foreigner, it displayed its ancient hostility to its rival, and was soon involved in a popular war with France.

The Constitution of England is a complex of mere *particular Rights* and particular privileges: the Government is essentially administrative—that is, conservative of the interests of all particular orders and classes; and each particular Church, parochial district, county, society, takes care of itself, so that the Government, strictly speaking, has nowhere less to do than in England. This is the leading feature of what Englishmen call their Liberty, and is the very antithesis of such a centralized administration as exists in France, where down to the least village the Maire is named by the Ministry or their agents. Nowhere can people less tolerate free action on the part of others than in France: there the Ministry combines in itself all administrative power, to which, on the other hand, the Chamber of Deputies lays claim. In England, on the contrary, every parish, every subordinate division and association has a part of its own to perform. Thus the common interest is concrete, and particular interests are taken cognizance of and determined in view of that common interest. These arrangements, based on particular interests, render a general system impossible. Consequently, abstract and general principles have no attraction for Englishmen—are addressed in their case to inattentive ears.— The particular interests above referred to have positive rights attached to them, which date from the antique times of Feudal Law, and have been preserved in England more than in any other country. By an inconsistency of the most startling kind, we find them contravening equity most grossly; and of institutions characterized by real freedom there are nowhere fewer than in England. In point of private right and freedom of possession they present an incredible deficiency: sufficient proof of which is afforded in the rights of primogeniture, involving the necessity of purchasing or otherwise providing military or ecclesiastical appointments for the younger sons of the aristocracy.

The *Parliament governs*, although Englishmen are unwilling to allow that such is the case. It is worthy of remark, that what has been always regarded as the period of the corruption of a republican people, presents itself here; viz. election to seats in parliament by means of bribery. But this also they call freedom—the power to sell one's vote, and to purchase a seat in parliament.

But this utterly inconsistent and corrupt state of things has nevertheless one advantage, that it provides for the possibility of a government—that it introduces a majority of men into parliament who are statesmen, who from their very youth have devoted themselves to political business and have worked and lived in it. And the nation has the correct conviction and perception that there must be a government, and is therefore willing to give its confidence to a body of men who have had experience in governing; for a general sense of particularity involves also a recognition of that form of particularity which is a distinguishing feature of one class of the community—that knowledge, experience, and facility acquired by practice, which the aristocracy who devote themselves to such interests exclusively possess. This is quite opposed to the appreciation of principles and abstract views which everyone can understand at once, and which are besides to be found in all Constitutions and Charters. It is a question whether the Reform in Parliament now on the tapis, consistently carried out, will leave the possibility of a Government.

The material existence of England is based on commerce and industry, and the English have undertaken the weighty responsibility of being the missionaries of civilization to the world; for their commercial spirit urges them to traverse every sea and land, to form connections with barbarous peoples, to create wants and stimulate industry, and first and foremost to establish among them the conditions necessary to commerce, viz. the relinquishment of a life of lawless violence, respect for property, and civility to strangers.

Germany was traversed by the victorious French hosts, but German nationality delivered it from this yoke. One of the leading features in the political condition of Germany is that code of Rights which was certainly occasioned by French oppression, since this was the especial means of bringing to light the deficiencies of the old system. The fiction of an Empire has utterly vanished. It is broken up into sovereign states. Feudal obligations are abolished, for freedom of property and of person have been recognized as fundamental principles. Offices of State are open to every citizen, talent and adaptation being of course the necessary conditions. The government rests with the official world, and the personal decision of the monarch constitutes its apex; for a final decision is, as was remarked above, absolutely necessary. Yet with firmly established laws, and a settled organization of the State, what is left to the sole arbitrament of the monarch is, in point of substance, no great matter. It is certainly a very fortunate circumstance for a nation, when a sovereign of noble character falls to its lot; yet in a great state even this is of small moment, since its strength lies in the Reason incorporated in it. Minor states have their existence and tranquillity secured to them more or less by their neighbors: they are therefore, properly speaking, not independent, and have not the fiery trial of war to endure. As has been remarked, a share in the government may be obtained by every one who has a competent knowledge, experience, and a morally regulated will. Those who know ought to govern—οἱ ἄριστοι, not ignorance and the presumptuous conceit of " knowing better." Lastly, as to Disposition, we have already remarked that in the Protestant Church the reconciliation of Religion with Legal Right has taken place. In the Protestant world there is no sacred, no religious conscience in a state of separation from, or perhaps even hostility to Secular Right.

This is the point which consciousness has attained, and these are the principal phases of that form in which the principle of Freedom has realized itself;—for the History of the World is nothing but the development of the Idea of Freedom. But Objective Freedom—the laws of *real* Freedom—demand the subjugation of the mere contingent Will—for this is in its nature formal. If the Objective is in itself Rational, human insight and conviction must correspond with the Reason which it embodies, and then we have the other essential element—Subjective Freedom—also realized.* We have confined ourselves

* That is, the will of the individual goes along with the requirements of reasonable Laws.—J. S.

to the consideration of that progress of the Idea [which has led to this consummation], and have been obliged to forego the pleasure of giving a detailed picture of the prosperity, the periods of glory that have distinguished the career of peoples, the beauty and grandeur of the character of individuals, and the interest attaching to their fate in weal or woe. Philosophy concerns itself only with the glory of the Idea mirroring itself in the History of the World. Philosophy escapes from the weary strife of passions that agitate the surface of society into the calm region of contemplation; that which interests it is the recognition of the process of development which the Idea has passed through in realizing itself—*i.e.* the Idea of Freedom, whose reality is the consciousness of Freedom and nothing short of it.

That the History of the World, with all the changing scenes which its annals present, is this process of development and the realization of Spirit—this is the true *Theodicæa,* the justification of God in History. Only *this* insight can reconcile Spirit with the History of the World—viz., that what has happened, and is happening every day, is not only not " without God," but is essentially His Work.

A CATALOG OF SELECTED

DOVER BOOKS

IN ALL FIELDS OF INTEREST

A CATALOG OF SELECTED DOVER
BOOKS IN ALL FIELDS OF INTEREST

DRAWINGS OF REMBRANDT, edited by Seymour Slive. Updated Lippmann, Hofstede de Groot edition, with definitive scholarly apparatus. All portraits, biblical sketches, landscapes, nudes. Oriental figures, classical studies, together with selection of work by followers. 550 illustrations. Total of 630pp. 9⅛ × 12¼.
21485-0, 21486-9 Pa., Two-vol. set $25.00

GHOST AND HORROR STORIES OF AMBROSE BIERCE, Ambrose Bierce. 24 tales vividly imagined, strangely prophetic, and decades ahead of their time in technical skill: "The Damned Thing," "An Inhabitant of Carcosa," "The Eyes of the Panther," "Moxon's Master," and 20 more. 199pp. 5⅜ × 8½. 20767-6 Pa. $3.95

ETHICAL WRITINGS OF MAIMONIDES, Maimonides. Most significant ethical works of great medieval sage, newly translated for utmost precision, readability. Laws Concerning Character Traits, Eight Chapters, more. 192pp. 5⅜ × 8½.
24522-5 Pa. $4.50

THE EXPLORATION OF THE COLORADO RIVER AND ITS CANYONS, J. W. Powell. Full text of Powell's 1,000-mile expedition down the fabled Colorado in 1869. Superb account of terrain, geology, vegetation, Indians, famine, mutiny, treacherous rapids, mighty canyons, during exploration of last unknown part of continental U.S. 400pp. 5⅜ × 8½. 20094-9 Pa. $6.95

HISTORY OF PHILOSOPHY, Julián Marías. Clearest one-volume history on the market. Every major philosopher and dozens of others, to Existentialism and later. 505pp. 5⅜ × 8½. 21739-6 Pa. $8.50

ALL ABOUT LIGHTNING, Martin A. Uman. Highly readable non-technical survey of nature and causes of lightning, thunderstorms, ball lightning, St. Elmo's Fire, much more. Illustrated. 192pp. 5⅜ × 8½. 25237-X Pa. $5.95

SAILING ALONE AROUND THE WORLD, Captain Joshua Slocum. First man to sail around the world, alone, in small boat. One of great feats of seamanship told in delightful manner. 67 illustrations. 294pp. 5⅜ × 8½. 20326-3 Pa. $4.95

LETTERS AND NOTES ON THE MANNERS, CUSTOMS AND CONDITIONS OF THE NORTH AMERICAN INDIANS, George Catlin. Classic account of life among Plains Indians: ceremonies, hunt, warfare, etc. 312 plates. 572pp. of text. 6⅛ × 9¼. 22118-0, 22119-9 Pa. Two-vol. set $15.90

ALASKA: The Harriman Expedition, 1899, John Burroughs, John Muir, et al. Informative, engrossing accounts of two-month, 9,000-mile expedition. Native peoples, wildlife, forests, geography, salmon industry, glaciers, more. Profusely illustrated. 240 black-and-white line drawings. 124 black-and-white photographs. 3 maps. Index. 576pp. 5⅜ × 8½. 25109-8 Pa. $11.95

THE BOOK OF BEASTS: Being a Translation from a Latin Bestiary of the Twelfth Century, T. H. White. Wonderful catalog real and fanciful beasts: manticore, griffin, phoenix, amphivius, jaculus, many more. White's witty erudite commentary on scientific, historical aspects. Fascinating glimpse of medieval mind. Illustrated. 296pp. 5⅜ × 8¼. (Available in U.S. only) 24609-4 Pa. $5.95

FRANK LLOYD WRIGHT: ARCHITECTURE AND NATURE With 160 Illustrations, Donald Hoffmann. Profusely illustrated study of influence of nature—especially prairie—on Wright's designs for Fallingwater, Robie House, Guggenheim Museum, other masterpieces. 96pp. 9¼ × 10¾. 25098-9 Pa. $7.95

FRANK LLOYD WRIGHT'S FALLINGWATER, Donald Hoffmann. Wright's famous waterfall house: planning and construction of organic idea. History of site, owners, Wright's personal involvement. Photographs of various stages of building. Preface by Edgar Kaufmann, Jr. 100 illustrations. 112pp. 9¼ × 10.
23671-4 Pa. $7.95

YEARS WITH FRANK LLOYD WRIGHT: Apprentice to Genius, Edgar Tafel. Insightful memoir by a former apprentice presents a revealing portrait of Wright the man, the inspired teacher, the greatest American architect. 372 black-and-white illustrations. Preface. Index. vi + 228pp. 8¼ × 11. 24801-1 Pa. $9.95

THE STORY OF KING ARTHUR AND HIS KNIGHTS, Howard Pyle. Enchanting version of King Arthur fable has delighted generations with imaginative narratives of exciting adventures and unforgettable illustrations by the author. 41 illustrations. xviii + 313pp. 6⅛ × 9¼. 21445-1 Pa. $5.95

THE GODS OF THE EGYPTIANS, E. A. Wallis Budge. Thorough coverage of numerous gods of ancient Egypt by foremost Egyptologist. Information on evolution of cults, rites and gods; the cult of Osiris; the Book of the Dead and its rites; the sacred animals and birds; Heaven and Hell; and more. 956pp. 6⅛ × 9¼.
22055-9, 22056-7 Pa., Two-vol. set $21.90

A THEOLOGICO-POLITICAL TREATISE, Benedict Spinoza. Also contains unfinished *Political Treatise*. Great classic on religious liberty, theory of government on common consent. R. Elwes translation. Total of 421pp. 5⅜ × 8½.
20249-6 Pa. $6.95

INCIDENTS OF TRAVEL IN CENTRAL AMERICA, CHIAPAS, AND YU-CATAN, John L. Stephens. Almost single-handed discovery of Maya culture; exploration of ruined cities, monuments, temples; customs of Indians. 115 drawings. 892pp. 5⅜ × 8½. 22404-X, 22405-8 Pa., Two-vol. set $15.90

LOS CAPRICHOS, Francisco Goya. 80 plates of wild, grotesque monsters and caricatures. Prado manuscript included. 183pp. 6⅜ × 9⅜. 22384-1 Pa. $4.95

AUTOBIOGRAPHY: The Story of My Experiments with Truth, Mohandas K. Gandhi. Not hagiography, but Gandhi in his own words. Boyhood, legal studies, purification, the growth of the Satyagraha (nonviolent protest) movement. Critical, inspiring work of the man who freed India. 480pp. 5⅜ × 8½. (Available in U.S. only)
24593-4 Pa. $6.95

ILLUSTRATED DICTIONARY OF HISTORIC ARCHITECTURE, edited by Cyril M. Harris. Extraordinary compendium of clear, concise definitions for over 5,000 important architectural terms complemented by over 2,000 line drawings. Covers full spectrum of architecture from ancient ruins to 20th-century Modernism. Preface. 592pp. 7½ × 9⅝. 24444-X Pa. $14.95

THE NIGHT BEFORE CHRISTMAS, Clement Moore. Full text, and woodcuts from original 1848 book. Also critical, historical material. 19 illustrations. 40pp. 4⅝ × 6. 22797-9 Pa. $2.50

THE LESSON OF JAPANESE ARCHITECTURE: 165 Photographs, Jiro Harada. Memorable gallery of 165 photographs taken in the 1930's of exquisite Japanese homes of the well-to-do and historic buildings. 13 line diagrams. 192pp. 8⅜ × 11¼. 24778-3 Pa. $8.95

THE AUTOBIOGRAPHY OF CHARLES DARWIN AND SELECTED LETTERS, edited by Francis Darwin. The fascinating life of eccentric genius composed of an intimate memoir by Darwin (intended for his children); commentary by his son, Francis; hundreds of fragments from notebooks, journals, papers; and letters to and from Lyell, Hooker, Huxley, Wallace and Henslow. xi + 365pp. 5⅜ × 8. 20479-0 Pa. $5.95

WONDERS OF THE SKY: Observing Rainbows, Comets, Eclipses, the Stars and Other Phenomena, Fred Schaaf. Charming, easy-to-read poetic guide to all manner of celestial events visible to the naked eye. Mock suns, glories, Belt of Venus, more. Illustrated. 299pp. 5¼ × 8¼. 24402-4 Pa. $7.95

BURNHAM'S CELESTIAL HANDBOOK, Robert Burnham, Jr. Thorough guide to the stars beyond our solar system. Exhaustive treatment. Alphabetical by constellation: Andromeda to Cetus in Vol. 1; Chamaeleon to Orion in Vol. 2; and Pavo to Vulpecula in Vol. 3. Hundreds of illustrations. Index in Vol. 3. 2,000pp. 6⅛ × 9¼. 23567-X, 23568-8, 23673-0 Pa., Three-vol. set $37.85

STAR NAMES: Their Lore and Meaning, Richard Hinckley Allen. Fascinating history of names various cultures have given to constellations and literary and folkloristic uses that have been made of stars. Indexes to subjects. Arabic and Greek names. Biblical references. Bibliography. 563pp. 5⅜ × 8½. 21079-0 Pa. $7.95

THIRTY YEARS THAT SHOOK PHYSICS: The Story of Quantum Theory, George Gamow. Lucid, accessible introduction to influential theory of energy and matter. Careful explanations of Dirac's anti-particles, Bohr's model of the atom, much more. 12 plates. Numerous drawings. 240pp. 5⅜ × 8½. 24895-X Pa. $4.95

CHINESE DOMESTIC FURNITURE IN PHOTOGRAPHS AND MEASURED DRAWINGS, Gustav Ecke. A rare volume, now affordably priced for antique collectors, furniture buffs and art historians. Detailed review of styles ranging from early Shang to late Ming. Unabridged republication. 161 black-and-white drawings, photos. Total of 224pp. 8⅜ × 11¼. (Available in U.S. only) 25171-3 Pa. $12.95

VINCENT VAN GOGH: A Biography, Julius Meier-Graefe. Dynamic, penetrating study of artist's life, relationship with brother, Theo, painting techniques, travels, more. Readable, engrossing. 160pp. 5⅜ × 8½. (Available in U.S. only) 25253-1 Pa. $3.95

HOW TO WRITE, Gertrude Stein. Gertrude Stein claimed anyone could understand her unconventional writing—here are clues to help. Fascinating improvisations, language experiments, explanations illuminate Stein's craft and the art of writing. Total of 414pp. 4⅝ × 6¾. 23144-5 Pa. $5.95

ADVENTURES AT SEA IN THE GREAT AGE OF SAIL: Five Firsthand Narratives, edited by Elliot Snow. Rare true accounts of exploration, whaling, shipwreck, fierce natives, trade, shipboard life, more. 33 illustrations. Introduction. 353pp. 5⅜ × 8½. 25177-2 Pa. $7.95

THE HERBAL OR GENERAL HISTORY OF PLANTS, John Gerard. Classic descriptions of about 2,850 plants—with over 2,700 illustrations—includes Latin and English names, physical descriptions, varieties, time and place of growth, more. 2,706 illustrations. xlv + 1,678pp. 8½ × 12¼. 23147-X Cloth. $75.00

DOROTHY AND THE WIZARD IN OZ, L. Frank Baum. Dorothy and the Wizard visit the center of the Earth, where people are vegetables, glass houses grow and Oz characters reappear. Classic sequel to *Wizard of Oz*. 256pp. 5⅜ × 8.
24714-7 Pa. $4.95

SONGS OF EXPERIENCE: Facsimile Reproduction with 26 Plates in Full Color, William Blake. This facsimile of Blake's original "Illuminated Book" reproduces 26 full-color plates from a rare 1826 edition. Includes "The Tyger," "London," "Holy Thursday," and other immortal poems. 26 color plates. Printed text of poems. 48pp. 5¼ × 7. 24636-1 Pa. $3.50

SONGS OF INNOCENCE, William Blake. The first and most popular of Blake's famous "Illuminated Books," in a facsimile edition reproducing all 31 brightly colored plates. Additional printed text of each poem. 64pp. 5¼ × 7.
22764-2 Pa. $3.50

PRECIOUS STONES, Max Bauer. Classic, thorough study of diamonds, rubies, emeralds, garnets, etc.: physical character, occurrence, properties, use, similar topics. 20 plates, 8 in color. 94 figures. 659pp. 6⅛ × 9¼.
21910-0, 21911-9 Pa., Two-vol. set $15.90

ENCYCLOPEDIA OF VICTORIAN NEEDLEWORK, S. F. A. Caulfeild and Blanche Saward. Full, precise descriptions of stitches, techniques for dozens of needlecrafts—most exhaustive reference of its kind. Over 800 figures. Total of 679pp. 8⅛ × 11. Two volumes. Vol. 1 22800-2 Pa. $11.95
Vol. 2 22801-0 Pa. $11.95

THE MARVELOUS LAND OF OZ, L. Frank Baum. Second Oz book, the Scarecrow and Tin Woodman are back with hero named Tip, Oz magic. 136 illustrations. 287pp. 5⅜ × 8½. 20692-0 Pa. $5.95

WILD FOWL DECOYS, Joel Barber. Basic book on the subject, by foremost authority and collector. Reveals history of decoy making and rigging, place in American culture, different kinds of decoys, how to make them, and how to use them. 140 plates. 156pp. 7⅞ × 10¾. 20011-6 Pa. $8.95

HISTORY OF LACE, Mrs. Bury Palliser. Definitive, profusely illustrated chronicle of lace from earliest times to late 19th century. Laces of Italy, Greece, England, France, Belgium, etc. Landmark of needlework scholarship. 266 illustrations. 672pp. 6⅛ × 9¼. 24742-2 Pa. $14.95

ILLUSTRATED GUIDE TO SHAKER FURNITURE, Robert Meader. All furniture and appurtenances, with much on unknown local styles. 235 photos. 146pp. 9 × 12. 22819-3 Pa. $7.95

WHALE SHIPS AND WHALING: A Pictorial Survey, George Francis Dow. Over 200 vintage engravings, drawings, photographs of barks, brigs, cutters, other vessels. Also harpoons, lances, whaling guns, many other artifacts. Comprehensive text by foremost authority. 207 black-and-white illustrations. 288pp. 6 × 9. 24808-9 Pa. $8.95

THE BERTRAMS, Anthony Trollope. Powerful portrayal of blind self-will and thwarted ambition includes one of Trollope's most heartrending love stories. 497pp. 5⅜ × 8½. 25119-5 Pa. $8.95

ADVENTURES WITH A HAND LENS, Richard Headstrom. Clearly written guide to observing and studying flowers and grasses, fish scales, moth and insect wings, egg cases, buds, feathers, seeds, leaf scars, moss, molds, ferns, common crystals, etc.—all with an ordinary, inexpensive magnifying glass. 209 exact line drawings aid in your discoveries. 220pp. 5⅜ × 8½. 23330-8 Pa. $4.50

RODIN ON ART AND ARTISTS, Auguste Rodin. Great sculptor's candid, wide-ranging comments on meaning of art; great artists; relation of sculpture to poetry, painting, music; philosophy of life, more. 76 superb black-and-white illustrations of Rodin's sculpture, drawings and prints. 119pp. 8⅜ × 11¼. 24487-3 Pa. $6.95

FIFTY CLASSIC FRENCH FILMS, 1912–1982: A Pictorial Record, Anthony Slide. Memorable stills from Grand Illusion, Beauty and the Beast, Hiroshima, Mon Amour, many more. Credits, plot synopses, reviews, etc. 160pp. 8¼ × 11. 25256-6 Pa. $11.95

THE PRINCIPLES OF PSYCHOLOGY, William James. Famous long course complete, unabridged. Stream of thought, time perception, memory, experimental methods; great work decades ahead of its time. 94 figures. 1,391pp. 5⅜ × 8½. 20381-6, 20382-4 Pa., Two-vol. set $19.90

BODIES IN A BOOKSHOP, R. T. Campbell. Challenging mystery of blackmail and murder with ingenious plot and superbly drawn characters. In the best tradition of British suspense fiction. 192pp. 5⅜ × 8½. 24720-1 Pa. $3.95

CALLAS: PORTRAIT OF A PRIMA DONNA, George Jellinek. Renowned commentator on the musical scene chronicles incredible career and life of the most controversial, fascinating, influential operatic personality of our time. 64 black-and-white photographs. 416pp. 5⅜ × 8¼. 25047-4 Pa. $7.95

GEOMETRY, RELATIVITY AND THE FOURTH DIMENSION, Rudolph Rucker. Exposition of fourth dimension, concepts of relativity as Flatland characters continue adventures. Popular, easily followed yet accurate, profound. 141 illustrations. 133pp. 5⅜ × 8½. 23400-2 Pa. $3.50

HOUSEHOLD STORIES BY THE BROTHERS GRIMM, with pictures by Walter Crane. 53 classic stories—Rumpelstiltskin, Rapunzel, Hansel and Gretel, the Fisherman and his Wife, Snow White, Tom Thumb, Sleeping Beauty, Cinderella, and so much more—lavishly illustrated with original 19th century drawings. 114 illustrations. x + 269pp. 5⅜ × 8½. 21080-4 Pa. $4.50

SUNDIALS, Albert Waugh. Far and away the best, most thorough coverage of ideas, mathematics concerned, types, construction, adjusting anywhere. Over 100 illustrations. 230pp. 5⅜ × 8½. 22947-5 Pa. $4.50

PICTURE HISTORY OF THE NORMANDIE: With 190 Illustrations, Frank O. Braynard. Full story of legendary French ocean liner: Art Deco interiors, design innovations, furnishings, celebrities, maiden voyage, tragic fire, much more. Extensive text. 144pp. 8⅞ × 11¾. 25257-4 Pa. $9.95

THE FIRST AMERICAN COOKBOOK: A Facsimile of "American Cookery," 1796, Amelia Simmons. Facsimile of the first American-written cookbook published in the United States contains authentic recipes for colonial favorites—pumpkin pudding, winter squash pudding, spruce beer, Indian slapjacks, and more. Introductory Essay and Glossary of colonial cooking terms. 80pp. 5⅜ × 8½. 24710-4 Pa. $3.50

101 PUZZLES IN THOUGHT AND LOGIC, C. R. Wylie, Jr. Solve murders and robberies, find out which fishermen are liars, how a blind man could possibly identify a color—purely by your own reasoning! 107pp. 5⅜ × 8½. 20367-0 Pa. $2.50

THE BOOK OF WORLD-FAMOUS MUSIC—CLASSICAL, POPULAR AND FOLK, James J. Fuld. Revised and enlarged republication of landmark work in musico-bibliography. Full information about nearly 1,000 songs and compositions including first lines of music and lyrics. New supplement. Index. 800pp. 5⅜ × 8¼. 24857-7 Pa. $14.95

ANTHROPOLOGY AND MODERN LIFE, Franz Boas. Great anthropologist's classic treatise on race and culture. Introduction by Ruth Bunzel. Only inexpensive paperback edition. 255pp. 5⅜ × 8½. 25245-0 Pa. $5.95

THE TALE OF PETER RABBIT, Beatrix Potter. The inimitable Peter's terrifying adventure in Mr. McGregor's garden, with all 27 wonderful, full-color Potter illustrations. 55pp. 4¼ × 5½. (Available in U.S. only) 22827-4 Pa. $1.75

THREE PROPHETIC SCIENCE FICTION NOVELS, H. G. Wells. *When the Sleeper Wakes, A Story of the Days to Come* and *The Time Machine* (full version). 335pp. 5⅜ × 8½. (Available in U.S. only) 20605-X Pa. $5.95

APICIUS COOKERY AND DINING IN IMPERIAL ROME, edited and translated by Joseph Dommers Vehling. Oldest known cookbook in existence offers readers a clear picture of what foods Romans ate, how they prepared them, etc. 49 illustrations. 301pp. 6⅛ × 9¼. 23563-7 Pa. $6.50

SHAKESPEARE LEXICON AND QUOTATION DICTIONARY, Alexander Schmidt. Full definitions, locations, shades of meaning of every word in plays and poems. More than 50,000 exact quotations. 1,485pp. 6½ × 9¼. 22726-X, 22727-8 Pa., Two-vol. set $27.90

THE WORLD'S GREAT SPEECHES, edited by Lewis Copeland and Lawrence W. Lamm. Vast collection of 278 speeches from Greeks to 1970. Powerful and effective models; unique look at history. 842pp. 5⅜ × 8½. 20468-5 Pa. $11.95

THE BLUE FAIRY BOOK, Andrew Lang. The first, most famous collection, with many familiar tales: Little Red Riding Hood, Aladdin and the Wonderful Lamp, Puss in Boots, Sleeping Beauty, Hansel and Gretel, Rumpelstiltskin; 37 in all. 138 illustrations. 390pp. 5⅜ × 8½.   21437-0 Pa. $5.95

THE STORY OF THE CHAMPIONS OF THE ROUND TABLE, Howard Pyle. Sir Launcelot, Sir Tristram and Sir Percival in spirited adventures of love and triumph retold in Pyle's inimitable style. 50 drawings, 31 full-page. xviii + 329pp. 6½ × 9¼.   21883-X Pa. $6.95

AUDUBON AND HIS JOURNALS, Maria Audubon. Unmatched two-volume portrait of the great artist, naturalist and author contains his journals, an excellent biography by his granddaughter, expert annotations by the noted ornithologist, Dr. Elliott Coues, and 37 superb illustrations. Total of 1,200pp. 5⅜ × 8.
                                                                            Vol. I 25143-8 Pa. $8.95
                                                                            Vol. II 25144-6 Pa. $8.95

GREAT DINOSAUR HUNTERS AND THEIR DISCOVERIES, Edwin H. Colbert. Fascinating, lavishly illustrated chronicle of dinosaur research, 1820's to 1960. Achievements of Cope, Marsh, Brown, Buckland, Mantell, Huxley, many others. 384pp. 5¼ × 8¼.   24701-5 Pa. $6.95

THE TASTEMAKERS, Russell Lynes. Informal, illustrated social history of American taste 1850's–1950's. First popularized categories Highbrow, Lowbrow, Middlebrow. 129 illustrations. New (1979) afterword. 384pp. 6 × 9.
                                                                                          23993-4 Pa. $6.95

DOUBLE CROSS PURPOSES, Ronald A. Knox. A treasure hunt in the Scottish Highlands, an old map, unidentified corpse, surprise discoveries keep reader guessing in this cleverly intricate tale of financial skullduggery. 2 black-and-white maps. 320pp. 5⅜ × 8½. (Available in U.S. only)   25032-6 Pa. $5.95

AUTHENTIC VICTORIAN DECORATION AND ORNAMENTATION IN FULL COLOR: 46 Plates from "Studies in Design," Christopher Dresser. Superb full-color lithographs reproduced from rare original portfolio of a major Victorian designer. 48pp. 9¼ × 12¼.   25083-0 Pa. $7.95

PRIMITIVE ART, Franz Boas. Remains the best text ever prepared on subject, thoroughly discussing Indian, African, Asian, Australian, and, especially, Northern American primitive art. Over 950 illustrations show ceramics, masks, totem poles, weapons, textiles, paintings, much more. 376pp. 5⅜ × 8.   20025-6 Pa. $6.95

SIDELIGHTS ON RELATIVITY, Albert Einstein. Unabridged republication of two lectures delivered by the great physicist in 1920–21. *Ether and Relativity* and *Geometry and Experience.* Elegant ideas in non-mathematical form, accessible to intelligent layman. vi + 56pp. 5⅜ × 8½.   24511-X Pa. $2.95

THE WIT AND HUMOR OF OSCAR WILDE, edited by Alvin Redman. More than 1,000 ripostes, paradoxes, wisecracks: Work is the curse of the drinking classes, I can resist everything except temptation, etc. 258pp. 5⅜ × 8½.   20602-5 Pa. $4.50

ADVENTURES WITH A MICROSCOPE, Richard Headstrom. 59 adventures with clothing fibers, protozoa, ferns and lichens, roots and leaves, much more. 142 illustrations. 232pp. 5⅜ × 8½.   23471-1 Pa. $3.95

PLANTS OF THE BIBLE, Harold N. Moldenke and Alma L. Moldenke. Standard reference to all 230 plants mentioned in Scriptures. Latin name, biblical reference, uses, modern identity, much more. Unsurpassed encyclopedic resource for scholars, botanists, nature lovers, students of Bible. Bibliography. Indexes. 123 black-and-white illustrations. 384pp. 6 × 9. 25069-5 Pa. $8.95

FAMOUS AMERICAN WOMEN: A Biographical Dictionary from Colonial Times to the Present, Robert McHenry, ed. From Pocahontas to Rosa Parks, 1,035 distinguished American women documented in separate biographical entries. Accurate, up-to-date data, numerous categories, spans 400 years. Indices. 493pp. 6½ × 9¼. 24523-3 Pa. $9.95

THE FABULOUS INTERIORS OF THE GREAT OCEAN LINERS IN HISTORIC PHOTOGRAPHS, William H. Miller, Jr. Some 200 superb photographs capture exquisite interiors of world's great "floating palaces"—1890's to 1980's: *Titanic, Ile de France, Queen Elizabeth, United States, Europa,* more. Approx. 200 black-and-white photographs. Captions. Text. Introduction. 160pp. 8⅞ × 11¾. 24756-2 Pa. $9.95

THE GREAT LUXURY LINERS, 1927-1954: A Photographic Record, William H. Miller, Jr. Nostalgic tribute to heyday of ocean liners. 186 photos of Ile de France, Normandie, Leviathan, Queen Elizabeth, United States, many others. Interior and exterior views. Introduction. Captions. 160pp. 9 × 12. 24056-8 Pa. $9.95

A NATURAL HISTORY OF THE DUCKS, John Charles Phillips. Great landmark of ornithology offers complete detailed coverage of nearly 200 species and subspecies of ducks: gadwall, sheldrake, merganser, pintail, many more. 74 full-color plates, 102 black-and-white. Bibliography. Total of 1,920pp. 8⅝ × 11¼. 25141-1, 25142-X Cloth. Two-vol. set $100.00

THE SEAWEED HANDBOOK: An Illustrated Guide to Seaweeds from North Carolina to Canada, Thomas F. Lee. Concise reference covers 78 species. Scientific and common names, habitat, distribution, more. Finding keys for easy identification. 224pp. 5⅜ × 8½. 25215-9 Pa. $5.95

THE TEN BOOKS OF ARCHITECTURE: The 1755 Leoni Edition, Leon Battista Alberti. Rare classic helped introduce the glories of ancient architecture to the Renaissance. 68 black-and-white plates. 336pp. 8⅜ × 11¼. 25239-6 Pa. $14.95

MISS MACKENZIE, Anthony Trollope. Minor masterpieces by Victorian master unmasks many truths about life in 19th-century England. First inexpensive edition in years. 392pp. 5⅜ × 8½. 25201-9 Pa. $7.95

THE RIME OF THE ANCIENT MARINER, Gustave Doré, Samuel Taylor Coleridge. Dramatic engravings considered by many to be his greatest work. The terrifying space of the open sea, the storms and whirlpools of an unknown ocean, the ice of Antarctica, more—all rendered in a powerful, chilling manner. Full text. 38 plates. 77pp. 9¼ × 12. 22305-1 Pa. $4.95

THE EXPEDITIONS OF ZEBULON MONTGOMERY PIKE, Zebulon Montgomery Pike. Fascinating first-hand accounts (1805-6) of exploration of Mississippi River, Indian wars, capture by Spanish dragoons, much more. 1,088pp. 5⅜ × 8½. 25254-X, 25255-8 Pa. Two-vol. set $23.90

A CONCISE HISTORY OF PHOTOGRAPHY: Third Revised Edition, Helmut Gernsheim. Best one-volume history—camera obscura, photochemistry, daguerreotypes, evolution of cameras, film, more. Also artistic aspects—landscape, portraits, fine art, etc. 281 black-and-white photographs. 26 in color. 176pp. 8⅜ × 11¼.
25128-4 Pa. $12.95

THE DORÉ BIBLE ILLUSTRATIONS, Gustave Doré. 241 detailed plates from the Bible: the Creation scenes, Adam and Eve, Flood, Babylon, battle sequences, life of Jesus, etc. Each plate is accompanied by the verses from the King James version of the Bible. 241pp. 9 × 12.
23004-X Pa. $8.95

HUGGER-MUGGER IN THE LOUVRE, Elliot Paul. Second Homer Evans mystery-comedy. Theft at the Louvre involves sleuth in hilarious, madcap caper. "A knockout."—Books. 336pp. 5⅜ × 8½.
25185-3 Pa. $5.95

FLATLAND, E. A. Abbott. Intriguing and enormously popular science-fiction classic explores the complexities of trying to survive as a two-dimensional being in a three-dimensional world. Amusingly illustrated by the author. 16 illustrations. 103pp. 5⅜ × 8½.
20001-9 Pa. $2.25

THE HISTORY OF THE LEWIS AND CLARK EXPEDITION, Meriwether Lewis and William Clark, edited by Elliott Coues. Classic edition of Lewis and Clark's day-by-day journals that later became the basis for U.S. claims to Oregon and the West. Accurate and invaluable geographical, botanical, biological, meteorological and anthropological material. Total of 1,508pp. 5⅜ × 8½.
21268-8, 21269-6, 21270-X Pa. Three-vol. set $25.50

LANGUAGE, TRUTH AND LOGIC, Alfred J. Ayer. Famous, clear introduction to Vienna, Cambridge schools of Logical Positivism. Role of philosophy, elimination of metaphysics, nature of analysis, etc. 160pp. 5⅜ × 8½. (Available in U.S. and Canada only)
20010-8 Pa. $2.95

MATHEMATICS FOR THE NONMATHEMATICIAN, Morris Kline. Detailed, college-level treatment of mathematics in cultural and historical context, with numerous exercises. For liberal arts students. Preface. Recommended Reading Lists. Tables. Index. Numerous black-and-white figures. xvi + 641pp. 5⅜ × 8½.
24823-2 Pa. $11.95

28 SCIENCE FICTION STORIES, H. G. Wells. Novels, *Star Begotten* and *Men Like Gods*, plus 26 short stories: "Empire of the Ants," "A Story of the Stone Age," "The Stolen Bacillus," "In the Abyss," etc. 915pp. 5⅜ × 8½. (Available in U.S. only)
20265-8 Cloth. $10.95

HANDBOOK OF PICTORIAL SYMBOLS, Rudolph Modley. 3,250 signs and symbols, many systems in full; official or heavy commercial use. Arranged by subject. Most in Pictorial Archive series. 143pp. 8⅜ × 11. 23357-X Pa. $5.95

INCIDENTS OF TRAVEL IN YUCATAN, John L. Stephens. Classic (1843) exploration of jungles of Yucatan, looking for evidences of Maya civilization. Travel adventures, Mexican and Indian culture, etc. Total of 669pp. 5⅜ × 8½.
20926-1, 20927-X Pa., Two-vol. set $9.90

CATALOG OF DOVER BOOKS

DEGAS: An Intimate Portrait, Ambroise Vollard. Charming, anecdotal memoir by famous art dealer of one of the greatest 19th-century French painters. 14 black-and-white illustrations. Introduction by Harold L. Van Doren. 96pp. 5⅜ × 8½.
25131-4 Pa. $3.95

PERSONAL NARRATIVE OF A PILGRIMAGE TO ALMANDINAH AND MECCAH, Richard Burton. Great travel classic by remarkably colorful personality. Burton, disguised as a Moroccan, visited sacred shrines of Islam, narrowly escaping death. 47 illustrations. 959pp. 5⅜ × 8½.   21217-3, 21218-1 Pa., Two-vol. set $17.90

PHRASE AND WORD ORIGINS, A. H. Holt. Entertaining, reliable, modern study of more than 1,200 colorful words, phrases, origins and histories. Much unexpected information. 254pp. 5⅜ × 8½.
20758-7 Pa. $5.95

THE RED THUMB MARK, R. Austin Freeman. In this first Dr. Thorndyke case, the great scientific detective draws fascinating conclusions from the nature of a single fingerprint. Exciting story, authentic science. 320pp. 5⅜ × 8½. (Available in U.S. only)
25210-8 Pa. $5.95

AN EGYPTIAN HIEROGLYPHIC DICTIONARY, E. A. Wallis Budge. Monumental work containing about 25,000 words or terms that occur in texts ranging from 3000 B.C. to 600 A.D. Each entry consists of a transliteration of the word, the word in hieroglyphs, and the meaning in English. 1,314pp. 6⅜ × 10.
23615-3, 23616-1 Pa., Two-vol. set $27.90

THE COMPLEAT STRATEGYST: Being a Primer on the Theory of Games of Strategy, J. D. Williams. Highly entertaining classic describes, with many illustrated examples, how to select best strategies in conflict situations. Prefaces. Appendices. xvi + 268pp. 5⅜ × 8½.
25101-2 Pa. $5.95

THE ROAD TO OZ, L. Frank Baum. Dorothy meets the Shaggy Man, little Button-Bright and the Rainbow's beautiful daughter in this delightful trip to the magical Land of Oz. 272pp. 5⅜ × 8.
25208-6 Pa. $4.95

POINT AND LINE TO PLANE, Wassily Kandinsky. Seminal exposition of role of point, line, other elements in non-objective painting. Essential to understanding 20th-century art. 127 illustrations. 192pp. 6½ × 9¼.
23808-3 Pa. $4.50

LADY ANNA, Anthony Trollope. Moving chronicle of Countess Lovel's bitter struggle to win for herself and daughter Anna their rightful rank and fortune—perhaps at cost of sanity itself. 384pp. 5⅜ × 8½.
24669-8 Pa. $6.95

EGYPTIAN MAGIC, E. A. Wallis Budge. Sums up all that is known about magic in Ancient Egypt: the role of magic in controlling the gods, powerful amulets that warded off evil spirits, scarabs of immortality, use of wax images, formulas and spells, the secret name, much more. 253pp. 5⅜ × 8½.
22681-6 Pa. $4.50

THE DANCE OF SIVA, Ananda Coomaraswamy. Preeminent authority unfolds the vast metaphysic of India: the revelation of her art, conception of the universe, social organization, etc. 27 reproductions of art masterpieces. 192pp. 5⅜ × 8½.
24817-8 Pa. $5.95

CHRISTMAS CUSTOMS AND TRADITIONS, Clement A. Miles. Origin, evolution, significance of religious, secular practices. Caroling, gifts, yule logs, much more. Full, scholarly yet fascinating; non-sectarian. 400pp. 5⅜ × 8½.
23354-5 Pa. $6.50

THE HUMAN FIGURE IN MOTION, Eadweard Muybridge. More than 4,500 stopped-action photos, in action series, showing undraped men, women, children jumping, lying down, throwing, sitting, wrestling, carrying, etc. 390pp. 7⅞ × 10⅝.
20204-6 Cloth. $19.95

THE MAN WHO WAS THURSDAY, Gilbert Keith Chesterton. Witty, fast-paced novel about a club of anarchists in turn-of-the-century London. Brilliant social, religious, philosophical speculations. 128pp. 5⅜ × 8½.
25121-7 Pa. $3.95

A CEZANNE SKETCHBOOK: Figures, Portraits, Landscapes and Still Lifes, Paul Cezanne. Great artist experiments with tonal effects, light, mass, other qualities in over 100 drawings. A revealing view of developing master painter, precursor of Cubism. 102 black-and-white illustrations. 144pp. 8¾ × 6⅝.
24790-2 Pa. $5.95

AN ENCYCLOPEDIA OF BATTLES: Accounts of Over 1,560 Battles from 1479 B.C. to the Present, David Eggenberger. Presents essential details of every major battle in recorded history, from the first battle of Megiddo in 1479 B.C. to Grenada in 1984. List of Battle Maps. New Appendix covering the years 1967–1984. Index. 99 illustrations. 544pp. 6½ × 9¼.
24913-1 Pa. $14.95

AN ETYMOLOGICAL DICTIONARY OF MODERN ENGLISH, Ernest Weekley. Richest, fullest work, by foremost British lexicographer. Detailed word histories. Inexhaustible. Total of 856pp. 6½ × 9¼.
21873-2, 21874-0 Pa., Two-vol. set $17.00

WEBSTER'S AMERICAN MILITARY BIOGRAPHIES, edited by Robert McHenry. Over 1,000 figures who shaped 3 centuries of American military history. Detailed biographies of Nathan Hale, Douglas MacArthur, Mary Hallaren, others. Chronologies of engagements, more. Introduction. Addenda. 1,033 entries in alphabetical order. xi + 548pp. 6½ × 9¼. (Available in U.S. only)
24758-9 Pa. $11.95

LIFE IN ANCIENT EGYPT, Adolf Erman. Detailed older account, with much not in more recent books: domestic life, religion, magic, medicine, commerce, and whatever else needed for complete picture. Many illustrations. 597pp. 5⅜ × 8½.
22632-8 Pa. $8.95

HISTORIC COSTUME IN PICTURES, Braun & Schneider. Over 1,450 costumed figures shown, covering a wide variety of peoples: kings, emperors, nobles, priests, servants, soldiers, scholars, townsfolk, peasants, merchants, courtiers, cavaliers, and more. 256pp. 8⅜ × 11¼.
23150-X Pa. $7.95

THE NOTEBOOKS OF LEONARDO DA VINCI, edited by J. P. Richter. Extracts from manuscripts reveal great genius; on painting, sculpture, anatomy, sciences, geography, etc. Both Italian and English. 186 ms. pages reproduced, plus 500 additional drawings, including studies for *Last Supper, Sforza* monument, etc. 860pp. 7⅞ × 10¾. (Available in U.S. only) 22572-0, 22573-9 Pa., Two-vol. set $25.90

THE ART NOUVEAU STYLE BOOK OF ALPHONSE MUCHA: All 72 Plates from "Documents Decoratifs" in Original Color, Alphonse Mucha. Rare copyright-free design portfolio by high priest of Art Nouveau. Jewelry, wallpaper, stained glass, furniture, figure studies, plant and animal motifs, etc. Only complete one-volume edition. 80pp. 9⅜ × 12¼. 24044-4 Pa. $8.95

ANIMALS: 1,419 COPYRIGHT-FREE ILLUSTRATIONS OF MAMMALS, BIRDS, FISH, INSECTS, ETC., edited by Jim Harter. Clear wood engravings present, in extremely lifelike poses, over 1,000 species of animals. One of the most extensive pictorial sourcebooks of its kind. Captions. Index. 284pp. 9 × 12. 23766-4 Pa. $9.95

OBELISTS FLY HIGH, C. Daly King. Masterpiece of American detective fiction, long out of print, involves murder on a 1935 transcontinental flight—"a very thrilling story"—NY Times. Unabridged and unaltered republication of the edition published by William Collins Sons & Co. Ltd., London, 1935. 288pp. 5⅜ × 8½. (Available in U.S. only) 25036-9 Pa. $4.95

VICTORIAN AND EDWARDIAN FASHION: A Photographic Survey, Alison Gernsheim. First fashion history completely illustrated by contemporary photographs. Full text plus 235 photos, 1840–1914, in which many celebrities appear. 240pp. 6½ × 9¼. 24205-6 Pa. $6.00

THE ART OF THE FRENCH ILLUSTRATED BOOK, 1700–1914, Gordon N. Ray. Over 630 superb book illustrations by Fragonard, Delacroix, Daumier, Doré, Grandville, Manet, Mucha, Steinlen, Toulouse-Lautrec and many others. Preface. Introduction. 633 halftones. Indices of artists, authors & titles, binders and provenances. Appendices. Bibliography. 608pp. 8⅜ × 11¼. 25086-5 Pa. $24.95

THE WONDERFUL WIZARD OF OZ, L. Frank Baum. Facsimile in full color of America's finest children's classic. 143 illustrations by W. W. Denslow. 267pp. 5⅜ × 8½. 20691-2 Pa. $5.95

FRONTIERS OF MODERN PHYSICS: New Perspectives on Cosmology, Relativity, Black Holes and Extraterrestrial Intelligence, Tony Rothman, et al. For the intelligent layman. Subjects include: cosmological models of the universe; black holes; the neutrino; the search for extraterrestrial intelligence. Introduction. 46 black-and-white illustrations. 192pp. 5⅜ × 8½. 24587-X Pa. $6.95

THE FRIENDLY STARS, Martha Evans Martin & Donald Howard Menzel. Classic text marshalls the stars together in an engaging, non-technical survey, presenting them as sources of beauty in night sky. 23 illustrations. Foreword. 2 star charts. Index. 147pp. 5⅜ × 8½. 21099-5 Pa. $3.50

FADS AND FALLACIES IN THE NAME OF SCIENCE, Martin Gardner. Fair, witty appraisal of cranks, quacks, and quackeries of science and pseudoscience: hollow earth, Velikovsky, orgone energy, Dianetics, flying saucers, Bridey Murphy, food and medical fads, etc. Revised, expanded In the Name of Science. "A very able and even-tempered presentation."—The New Yorker. 363pp. 5⅜ × 8. 20394-8 Pa. $6.50

ANCIENT EGYPT: ITS CULTURE AND HISTORY, J. E Manchip White. From pre-dynastics through Ptolemies: society, history, political structure, religion, daily life, literature, cultural heritage. 48 plates. 217pp. 5⅜ × 8½. 22548-8 Pa. $4.95

CATALOG OF DOVER BOOKS

SIR HARRY HOTSPUR OF HUMBLETHWAITE, Anthony Trollope. Incisive, unconventional psychological study of a conflict between a wealthy baronet, his idealistic daughter, and their scapegrace cousin. The 1870 novel in its first inexpensive edition in years. 250pp. 5⅜ × 8½. 24953-0 Pa. $5.95

LASERS AND HOLOGRAPHY, Winston E. Kock. Sound introduction to burgeoning field, expanded (1981) for second edition. Wave patterns, coherence, lasers, diffraction, zone plates, properties of holograms, recent advances. 84 illustrations. 160pp. 5⅜ × 8¼. (Except in United Kingdom) 24041-X Pa. $3.50

INTRODUCTION TO ARTIFICIAL INTELLIGENCE: SECOND, EN-LARGED EDITION, Philip C. Jackson, Jr. Comprehensive survey of artificial intelligence—the study of how machines (computers) can be made to act intelligently. Includes introductory and advanced material. Extensive notes updating the main text. 132 black-and-white illustrations. 512pp. 5⅜ × 8½. 24864-X Pa. $8.95

HISTORY OF INDIAN AND INDONESIAN ART, Ananda K. Coomaraswamy. Over 400 illustrations illuminate classic study of Indian art from earliest Harappa finds to early 20th century. Provides philosophical, religious and social insights. 304pp. 6⅛ × 9⅜. 25005-9 Pa. $8.95

THE GOLEM, Gustav Meyrink. Most famous supernatural novel in modern European literature, set in Ghetto of Old Prague around 1890. Compelling story of mystical experiences, strange transformations, profound terror. 13 black-and-white illustrations. 224pp. 5⅜ × 8½. (Available in U.S. only) 25025-3 Pa. $5.95

ARMADALE, Wilkie Collins. Third great mystery novel by the author of *The Woman in White* and *The Moonstone*. Original magazine version with 40 illustrations. 597pp. 5⅜ × 8½. 23429-0 Pa. $9.95

PICTORIAL ENCYCLOPEDIA OF HISTORIC ARCHITECTURAL PLANS, DETAILS AND ELEMENTS: With 1,880 Line Drawings of Arches, Domes, Doorways, Facades, Gables, Windows, etc., John Theodore Haneman. Sourcebook of inspiration for architects, designers, others. Bibliography. Captions. 141pp. 9 × 12. 24605-1 Pa. $6.95

BENCHLEY LOST AND FOUND, Robert Benchley. Finest humor from early 30's, about pet peeves, child psychologists, post office and others. Mostly unavailable elsewhere. 73 illustrations by Peter Arno and others. 183pp. 5⅜ × 8½. 22410-4 Pa. $3.95

ERTÉ GRAPHICS, Erté. Collection of striking color graphics: *Seasons, Alphabet, Numerals, Aces* and *Precious Stones*. 50 plates, including 4 on covers. 48pp. 9⅜ × 12¼. 23580-7 Pa. $6.95

THE JOURNAL OF HENRY D. THOREAU, edited by Bradford Torrey, F. H. Allen. Complete reprinting of 14 volumes, 1837–61, over two million words; the sourcebooks for *Walden*, etc. Definitive. All original sketches, plus 75 photographs. 1,804pp. 8½ × 12¼. 20312-3, 20313-1 Cloth., Two-vol. set $80.00

CASTLES: THEIR CONSTRUCTION AND HISTORY, Sidney Toy. Traces castle development from ancient roots. Nearly 200 photographs and drawings illustrate moats, keeps, baileys, many other features. Caernarvon, Dover Castles, Hadrian's Wall, Tower of London, dozens more. 256pp. 5⅜ × 8¼. 24898-4 Pa. $5.95

AMERICAN CLIPPER SHIPS: 1833–1858, Octavius T. Howe & Frederick C. Matthews. Fully-illustrated, encyclopedic review of 352 clipper ships from the period of America's greatest maritime supremacy. Introduction. 109 halftones. 5 black-and-white line illustrations. Index. Total of 928pp. 5⅜ × 8½.
25115-2, 25116-0 Pa., Two-vol. set $17.90

TOWARDS A NEW ARCHITECTURE, Le Corbusier. Pioneering manifesto by great architect, near legendary founder of "International School." Technical and aesthetic theories, views on industry, economics, relation of form to function, "mass-production spirit," much more. Profusely illustrated. Unabridged translation of 13th French edition. Introduction by Frederick Etchells. 320pp. 6⅛ × 9¼. (Available in U.S. only)
25023-7 Pa. $8.95

THE BOOK OF KELLS, edited by Blanche Cirker. Inexpensive collection of 32 full-color, full-page plates from the greatest illuminated manuscript of the Middle Ages, painstakingly reproduced from rare facsimile edition. Publisher's Note. Captions. 32pp. 9⅜ × 12¼.
24345-1 Pa. $4.95

BEST SCIENCE FICTION STORIES OF H. G. WELLS, H. G. Wells. Full novel *The Invisible Man*, plus 17 short stories: "The Crystal Egg," "Aepyornis Island," "The Strange Orchid," etc. 303pp. 5⅜ × 8½. (Available in U.S. only)
21531-8 Pa. $4.95

AMERICAN SAILING SHIPS: Their Plans and History, Charles G. Davis. Photos, construction details of schooners, frigates, clippers, other sailcraft of 18th to early 20th centuries—plus entertaining discourse on design, rigging, nautical lore, much more. 137 black-and-white illustrations. 240pp. 6⅛ × 9¼.
24658-2 Pa. $5.95

ENTERTAINING MATHEMATICAL PUZZLES, Martin Gardner. Selection of author's favorite conundrums involving arithmetic, money, speed, etc., with lively commentary. Complete solutions. 112pp. 5⅜ × 8½.
25211-6 Pa. $2.95

THE WILL TO BELIEVE, HUMAN IMMORTALITY, William James. Two books bound together. Effect of irrational on logical, and arguments for human immortality. 402pp. 5⅜ × 8½.
20291-7 Pa. $7.50

THE HAUNTED MONASTERY and THE CHINESE MAZE MURDERS, Robert Van Gulik. 2 full novels by Van Gulik continue adventures of Judge Dee and his companions. An evil Taoist monastery, seemingly supernatural events; overgrown topiary maze that hides strange crimes. Set in 7th-century China. 27 illustrations. 328pp. 5⅜ × 8½.
23502-5 Pa. $5.95

CELEBRATED CASES OF JUDGE DEE (DEE GOONG AN), translated by Robert Van Gulik. Authentic 18th-century Chinese detective novel; Dee and associates solve three interlocked cases. Led to Van Gulik's own stories with same characters. Extensive introduction. 9 illustrations. 237pp. 5⅜ × 8½.
23337-5 Pa. $4.95

Prices subject to change without notice.

Available at your book dealer or write for free catalog to Dept. GI, Dover Publications, Inc., 31 East 2nd St., Mineola, N.Y. 11501. Dover publishes more than 175 books each year on science, elementary and advanced mathematics, biology, music, art, literary history, social sciences and other areas.